NETWORKING HANDBOOK

Networking Handbook

Ed Taylor

McGraw-Hill
New York • San Francisco • Washington, D.C.
Auckland • Bogotá • Caracas • Lisbon • London
Madrid • Mexico City • Milan • Montreal • New Delhi
San Juan • Singapore • Sydney • Tokyo • Toronto

McGraw-Hill

A Division of The **McGraw·Hill** *Companies*

1 2 3 4 5 6 7 8 9 0   AGM/AGM   9 0 4 3 2 1 0 9

P/N 0-07-135450-6
PART OF ISBN 0-07-135451-4

*The sponsoring editor for this book was Steven Elliot and the production
supervisor was Clare Stanley. It was set in Century Schoolbook by D&G Limited, LLC.*

Printed and bound by Quebecor/Martinsburg.

*Throughout this book, trademarked names are used. Rather than put a trademark
symbol after every occurrence of a trademarked name, we use names in an editorial
fashion only, and to the benefit of the trademark owner, with no intention of infringement of the trademark. Where such designations appear in this book, they have been
printed with initial caps.*

This book is printed on recycled, acid-free paper containing a minimum of 50
percent recycled de-inked fiber.

To Jim Delong

(the best drummer I know!)

CONTENTS

Contents

Contents

Contents

Contents

Contents

Contents

Contents

Contents

Contents

PREFACE

The purpose of this book is to provide the reader with reference material. My original intent for writing this book was twofold (yes, I am writing this last). First, to present a broad range of reference information I found helpful during my years of networking. Second, to provide solid information, many times from the actual sources. The result is a combination of my experience and insights to what I have found useful.

The practical information, case studies, baseline reference information, have come from first hand experience. The challenge has been to condense the vast amount of material into what seemed appropriate. Throughout the book I reference material and point you to sources where you can obtain additional or complete information on a given topic.

Included with this book is a CD-ROM of Internet related RFCs ranging from those in the 400 range through those listed in the 2600 range. In short, a "complete" listing of RFCs. This CD has been an excellent reference tool for me and I know it will be of great help to you as well. Also included on the CD-ROM are the following:

- *Appendix A:* Internet modem technology reference
- *Appendix B:* Case study on Firewalls and data communications
- *Appendix C:* Internetworking troubleshooting reference
- Detailed glossary and list of acronyms
- Plus RFCs

A thank you is in order to all the participating sources who provided information that contributed to make this a more useful reference tool. My hopes are that it is a place where you can begin your search for information and help you along the way to finding the information you need.

ACKNOWLEDGMENTS

I would like to thank the following for contributions is various aspects of this book.

MJH

IBM

Perrier

McGraw-Hill:

- New York
- New Jersey
- Ohio
- International Division
- Steven Elliot

Information World, Inc.

Fluke

Tektronix

Liebert

Tripp Lite

Adaptec Corporation

Belkin

General Cable

Pass & Seymour

Thomas & Betts

/SMS Data Products

Chase Research

Cayman Systems

Seattle Labs

Sony Corporation

Hewlett – Packard

Siecor Corporation

3COM

BUD Industries

Microsoft Corporation

Wagner Edstrom

Hubbell

Airborne

United Parcel Service (UPS)

Roadway Package System (RPS)

Emery Airfreight

DHL

United States Postal Service

Federal Express

ABOUT THE AUTHOR

Ed Taylor is founder and chief network architect for Information World, Inc. and former network architect for IBM.

Some of Mr. Taylor's consulting experience includes work for NEC, Orange County, CA, BASF, Chrysler, Hewlett-Packard, Dow Jones, Ore-Ida Foods, Mutual of New York (MONY), and IBM Education.

ABOUT THE REVIEWERS

As the leading publisher of technical books for more than 100 years, McGraw-Hill prides itself on bringing you the most authoritative and up-to-date information available. To ensure that our books meet the highest standards of accuracy, we have asked a number of top professionals and technical experts to review the accuracy of the material you are about to read.

We take great pleasure in thanking the following technical reviewers for their insights:

Marc Abrams is an Associate Professor of Computer Science at Virginia Tech. He is one of the designers of the User Interface Markup Language (uiml.org), which facilitates delivery of clients to network-connected devices of any sort, ranging from desktop computers to mobile wireless devices. He designed the caching and transmission scheduling components of a worldwide system to deliver Web pages and other Internet services globally via satellite. His research group is a core member of the World Wide Web Consortium's Web Characterization Activity.

Tony Heskett is a Systems Administrator with 10 years of Unix and networking experience. He has a B.Sc. in electrical and electronic engineering.

Sastry Kuchimanchi is an engineering graduate specializing in electronics and communications. At the very beginning of her career, she worked for a network integration company in India. Sastry was part of a team providing LAN/WAN solutions, operating system sizing, Microsoft product integration and administration, and Novell NetWare product integration. In addition, she worked on voice and data integration for 4 years. She now specializes in Cisco products, and is currently working on WAN design and access security issues.

Amit Shah has a degree in electrical engineering, as well as CCNA and CCDA certifications. He has over 10 years experience in the networking field and over 7 years experience in the Cisco networking field. Amit has worked on various large-scale projects, such as SNA to IP migration and Token Ring to Fast Ethernet/VLAN migration. He is currently working for RealTech Systems as a Network Engineer.

CHAPTER 1

Internetworking
Fundamentals

If you are new to networking of any type, you'll be interested in this book. In this chapter I am presenting some fundamental information that will assist you in understanding different perspectives from which I explain topics in this book as well as places where you can look to for additional information.

Specifically, in this chapter I am presenting a "social" example of protocols and point out how they parallel technical or network protocols. I also explain why protocols are required along with some examples of a few standard related bodies/organziations. Next I present a practical explanation for understanding the OSI model. In short, this chapter is a spring board for your readings throughout the remainder of this book.

How to Understand Protocols

Protocols are relatively easy to understand. Consider the analogy of social behavior compared to a protocol used in computers and networking devices.

Regardless the culture or location, mankind has always had traditions and mores. Consider the marriage ceremony. Depending upon the culture, people might *do* ceremonies differently but they serve the purpose of acknowledging the marriage.

In some cultures people who attend a marriage ceremony wear nice clothes, sit in predetermined places, bring gifts to those getting married, and so on. For example, a culture may implicitly dictate that nice clothes be worn to a marriage ceremony. How do the attendees *know* to do this? Two ways are possible; both may be used.

The first method of communication is general knowledge. In other words, those attending a marriage ceremony are from the same culture, the same region, and interact with others in the community. The acquisition of knowledge of *what* to wear to a marriage ceremony may be considered general knowledge; in other words, one learns this along life's way.

The second method of communication is explicit or direct communication. Those responsible for the occasion would communicate what should be worn. This could be done by mail, human communication (regardless the medium) and other ways. The point is one entity explicitly communicates to the other the expectations of the other. These are social *protocols*. Many would call this common sense. In fact there is little common about it if one contemplates the different cultural backgrounds that represent the human race.

Like human culture, computers and networks have protocols also. The remainder of this section explores network protocols from a variety of different angles.

Protocol Basics

To understand protocols from a non-technical standpoint, this section provides insight upon protocols.

Why Protocols Are Required

Protocols are required because the idea of no protocols cannot exist. This is simply logic at work. If the idea of no protocol exists, then logically that idea is a protocol itself. Do not be confused. This is a brief lesson in logic! That nothing exists in fact means something exists if nothing other than the idea. Put another way, it is saying that it is a logical impossibility for nothing to exist. Hence, the lack of a protocol is in fact a protocol.

Protocols are required in computers, networks, and internetworking devices of all sorts because their operation depends upon it. In computers and networks each function performed, regardless how small, is a quantifiable entity. The entity may be an abstract function, but it is definable and traceable to some tangible line of definition in software or a piece of hardware.

Computer and network protocols are the contrivance of humans. Computers and networks use protocols to define aspects like physical connections, how data is passed across a link between two or more devices, and other examples. Virtually all aspects of computer network functions can be categorically placed into a protocol category. The question now becomes what category and how are protocols made?

How Standards Are Made

Standards are practically synonymous with a protocol. Some split technical hairs about this matter but if implemented, accepted, and used, it seems that this qualifies it to be called a protocol. Standards come about in different ways and they typically reflect the philosophical approaches to technology.

De facto   We live in a de facto world. Something is done, then defined. It is then recorded into some sort of standard. Finally we proclaim to all those that follow to abide by the standard. Is this not how standards are created?

De Facto Protocol Example

An example of something de facto is the DOS operating system used on personal computers. In earlier days, DOS was the primary operating system of the personal computer market. This was not planned in the sense that foresight envisioned the magnitude of market presence that it eventually obtained. I do not have the space to explain the history behind the developments between Bill Gates and IBM in the early 1980s, but suffice it to say that the success of the IBM PC caught IBM off-guard. In the early 1980s DOS was the dominant operating system for PCs. By the late 1980s there was IBM's OS/2 and Microsoft Windows. It should also be noted that SCO Unix for PCs was also available but necessarily dominant outside the "development" community.

Now, I want to explain something I haven't written before but have been called upon to explain in numerous venues. That is that up to and including Windows 95 a considerable percentage of the operating system was DOS. Let me say this another way: Windows 95, Windows 3.1 and 3.11 not only required DOS to operate, but depending upon which operating system one refers to, actually had part of DOS as part of the operating system. This may surprise you—but stay with me.

For example, I would estimate (my personal opinion) about 25 to 40 percent of the Windows 95 operating system is DOS! How can this be? Well, it is easy. Firmware on the motherboards and other hardware is the API to bridge the gap between the actual hardware and the software itself. Some core functions of DOS like the COPY, DELETE, ATTRIB, and other commands are DOS, not Windows commands. The best way to think about Windows version 1.0, 2.0, 3.1, and even Windows 95 is to think of it as part of DOS wrapped with Windows. Remember, "back when" to run Windows it required DOS be loaded on a PC? Well, what changed? Certain components of DOS were bundled into Windows, and now rather than loading DOS and, then Windows on a system one just loads Windows.

Windows 1.0, 2.0 (for 286 processors), 3.1, and version 3.11 were fundamentally a "windowing" mechanism providing a front-end or user interface to DOS. Consider the original design of Windows version 1.0 when it was released in 1986. This version of Windows was to make the DOS operating system easier to use. The same was true with Windows 2.0, but this version was also intended to make printing and files services easier as well. No, I am not being heretical; I am telling you the truth because I was working in this industry in 1986.

In 1986, and the following couple of years, PCs were really just coming through infancy. Networking PCs did not really take off until the last part of the 1980s. Network protocols and software like NetWare, AppleTalk, and TCP/IP were being refined from rudimentary software offerings towards where they have arrived today.

DOS's success by way of Microsoft offerings and IBM's offerings was not planned in the sense that it was widely understood that DOS would become as widespread as it did. Furthermore, the PC phenomenon caught most people off-guard. Granted, many companies profited from the growth of PCs in the marketplace. DOS is a good example of how a product (with potential) came to market with potential at the right time and a significant number of technical companies were capable to exploit it. Furthermore, a customer base was capable to receive it financially and understood how to use it. DOS was not a planned phenomenon, for if it had been this author believes many things would have ended up differently.

The point is no group or individual *planned* strategically that DOS would have the popularity and marketshare it has. Granted, Bill Gates and company along with IBM, and even Digital Equipment and Novell propelled the growth of DOS. In a very real sense DOS simply *happened* as a result of the user community driving it in to existence.

Users liked it, developers created programs for it, and users liked them. Additional hardware was designed and sold to operate with it, and so the spiral continued. Over time, DOS had rivals like OS/2 and SCO UNIX.

The original design of Windows was to make DOS and thus the PC friendlier to use. Operationally, Windows used a *task-switching* method of functioning instead of the more sophisticated *multi-tasking*.

First, task-switching means just that; a supervisory program switches between multiple tasks and continues to execute their instructions until the tasks are complete. The implication here is that this is not a simultaneous event; hence the name task-switching.

Second, multi-tasking is just that. It means that multiple tasks are executed at the same time. Task switching is best understood by thinking of it as parallel processing; multiple things happenings at once.

Now, take my challenge. Get a PC with Windows 95 or previous and load a database program, word processor, and graphics program. For example, start with a database of say 40,000 entries. Make significant changes, like change the dates of each entry. Take a word processor document, say 1,000 pages. And start a drawing of a multi-dimensional illustration. Now, start a re-compile of the database program. Next, start a print operation of the word processor document, then attempt to perform intensive changes to the illustration. If you do this you will observe that all these functions are not performed at the same time. Why is this? Because part of Windows 95 and previous versions are DOS based and DOS *is not* a multi-tasking operating system. Windows "fools" the user by performing multi-tasking very well and hence the casual observer "thinks" multiple things are being performed at the same time; they are not.

Now those of you with any background or understanding of mainframes or UNIX operating systems know that these type operating systems *are multi-tasking*. In summary, if DOS had been "well planned" and thought through with sufficient funding as well, DOS may well have been designed differently to accommodate things that Windows has today. This is a good example of a de facto standard. The market's acceptance of DOS and Windows created a de facto standard. In other words, there are ways that things become a standard other than a plan on behalf of a corporation or a standard making body.

De jure   De jure standards are primarily a result of group efforts. For example, the following are groups that concentrate on standards:

- Institute of Electrical and Electronic Engineers (IEEE)
- American National Standards Institute (ANSI)
- International Standards Organization (ISO)
- International Society for Optical Engineering (SPIE)

These groups, and others that will be named later in this chapter, focus on standards and protocols. Standards and protocols are different. A general definition from the marketplace is that standards are what should be the case. Working protocols are implemented, and they may or may not be a standard.

The difference between de jure and de facto is that de jure standards are comprised of groups of people from different backgrounds that contribute ideas, resources, and other items to aid in the development of a standard. De jure groups could be considered steering committees. The question is how powerful is the steering, and does a de jure standard reflect what the marketplace wants?

De jure standards are prevalent in the networking arena. Some standards are more prevalent than others. However, the intent of de jure groups seems to be to promote and better a technology.

Proprietary Proprietary standards are typically owned outright by some entity. Most corporations in the networking business today are embracing multiple networking solutions. This indicates that corporations of all sizes and focuses are broadening their focus so it is not perceived as proprietary. Ironically, not too long ago proprietary networking, or computing, was the norm; today most companies shun the use of the term proprietary anything.

Proprietary products are not necessarily more restrictive than that those which are not. In fact, the term *open* has emerged as a word used frequently to describe support for multiple standards or protocols. Actually, some proprietary protocols are more robust than those that have not been refined.

Interpreting which standard or protocol is best should be user driven. In most cases this is true.

Examples of Standard Making Bodies

This part lists and briefly describes the intent behind a variety of groups involved in standard making. Some of the names included in this group may be categorized as forums, consortiums, organizations, and other entities. The list is not exhaustive, but it includes dominant and popular groups.

American National Standards Institute (ANSI) ANSI is the agency that published the *American Standard Code for Information Interchange* (ASCII). This is a method used to represent alphanumeric characters and control keys. The way ANSI coordinates standards parallels other standard making bodies in many respects.

International Telegraph Union (ITU) The *International Telegragh Union* (ITU), formerly known as the International Telegraph & Telephone Consultative Committee (CCITT), has been in existence for multiple decades, like ANSI. The ITU has a number of specifications. Some examples are the X and V series of recommendations. Actually, some recommendations are more extensive; they are protocols with widespread implementation. Two examples of ITU recommendations convey the impact of the organization on the technical community. The X.400 electronic mail system is a product of the ITU as well as V.35. The latter is a specification for duplex data transfer over leased lines.

Corporation for Open Systems (COS) This organization is non-profit and focuses upon the promotion of ISO standards. Specifically it is involved in testing products for ISO compliance. Its thrust is providing information about ISO guidelines and helping corporations meet these guidelines.

European Computer Manufacturers Association (ECMA) This group now has representatives from companies located around the world. The focus of the group is upon the European region of telecommunication and related standards. Companies such as IBM, Digital Equipment, and AT&T are members to name a few.

National Institute for Science and Technology NIST has been known previously as the *National Bureau of Standards* (NBS). It is a U. S. government organization that provided workshops that resulted in implementation agreements. These workshops have become formally organized and internationally known. It is one of the major contributors to the International Standards Profiles as part of the ISO.

Institute of Electrical & Electronic Engineers (IEEE) The IEEE is a professional organization comprised of individuals in multiple professions. This organization is active in standards that will be explored later in this book. For our purposes it is sufficient to understand this organization focuses efforts on lower layer protocols such as the 802 series.

International Standard Organization (ISO) The ISO is a dominant organization with a widespread focus. The work of many standard making organizations is incorporated into ISO standards. One example of an ISO standard is the Open Systems Interconnection model. This model is a seven-layer reference reflecting what should occur at each layer within a network.

X/Open This organization focuses is on specifying product requirements for vendors creating product specifications. These products include a variety of offerings. One example of their focus is with POSIX. Another technology group functioning in similar areas is *Unix International* (UI). UI works with this organization in market specifications for applications.

GOSIP *Government Open Systems Interconnection Profile* (GOSIP) is an organization that specifies standards to be adhered to by suppliers of products to the U. S. government. Specifications included in versions of GOSIP include ITU specifications, OSI, and other standards and protocols.

Its thrust is support for OSI protocols supported in equipment supplied to the U. S. government.

Open Software Foundation (OSF)   OSF is a non-profit organization research and development group consisting of vendors, users, educational institutions, and other entities. It began in 1988 and participates with other standard making groups such as the IEEE, X/Open, ANSI, and others. The focus of OSF is distributed computing, distributed management, and a graphical user interface (Motif). UNIX is considered to be a part of open systems, but not a total solution. It includes representatives from vendors such as Digital Equipment, IBM, Hewlett Packard, Convex Computer, MIT, Stanford, and a few hundred other entities representing a variety of concerns.

Unix International (UI)   This organization focuses upon the AT&T UNIX System V operating system. It has hundreds of members like OSF. However, UI is oriented towards the success of the System V as a standard and its continual refinement. UI itself consists of numerous subgroups within the organization such as a technical advisory group and work group focused on specific functions designated by the board of directors. The steering committee focuses upon the priority of work and oversees work groups. Some members in UI include: AT&T, Mississippi State University, Sony Corporation, Texas A & M University, Swedish Telecom, Convex Computer Corporation, United States Air Force, and hundreds of others.

Asynchronous Transfer Mode (ATM)   This organization began in 1991 and focuses upon the advancement of ATM technology. It is now comprised of hundreds of members that represent a worldwide presence. ATM is cell based method for data transfer and operates asynchronously. It operates at lower layers within a network.

OpenView   OpenView is a technical forum that focuses upon network management. This forum focuses upon interacting with users who actually perform heterogeneous network management. This organization also conveys helpful information to attendees to an annual event. The OpenView product concentrates upon managing TCP/IP, NetWare, and SNA based networks. The OpenView forum includes vendors who work with OpenView directly and indirectly making an information exchange between users and vendors direct and helpful.

Other standards organizations exist; this list includes popular and current organizations.

Network Layers

It is possible to identify what happens at each layer within a given network. The International Standards Organization created a seven-layer reference model called the *Open Systems Interconnection* (OSI) model. It is widely used and been presented many ways. This section explains the functions and components that operate at each layer.

Historical Perspective

The idea of a layered network goes further back in time than the late 1970s when the ISO created the OSI model. In fact, IBM introduced a layered networking model in 1974; it is called *Systems Network Architecture* (SNA). A given network may not correlate to all layers the OSI model specifies, but the OSI model is a good baseline to use for layer evaluation.

Th OSI model appears like Figure 1-1. These layers, their function, and associated components are listed in Table 1-1.

These seven layers constitute the OSI model. Viewed differently, this model can be divided into two parts; that is upper layer protocols and lower layer protocols. Figure 1-2 is an example of upper layer and lower layer protocols. The next two parts of this book are devoted to each part, respectively.

Figure 1-1
OSI model

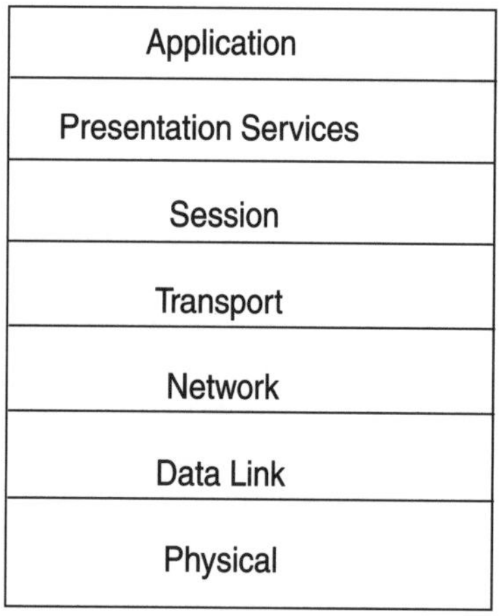

Application
Presentation Services
Session
Transport
Network
Data Link
Physical

Figure 1-2
Upper & lower layer
protocols

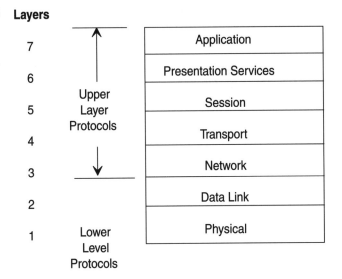

Table 1-1
OSI layer description

Layer	Function	Components
Physical	Generate electrons or photons to be introduced to the medium or removed from the medium	Hardware interface, software in chips on the board
Data Link	Control data flow across a link from one node to another	Firmware, hardware interface board, and software
Network	Routing; and depending upon the protocol, flow control	Usually, software sometimes firmware in certain devices
Transport	Moving data from one node to the other. Performing re-transmissions if required. Providing a reliable or unreliable method for data transfer	Software; however some implementations can implement this in firmware
Session	Providing the logical connection between users and applications or applications if they are peer-to-peer. Addressable end points reside at this layer.	Software; however, in some instances this may be implemented in firmware
Presentation Services	Formats the syntax of data. Data representation is performed here.	Software; but this can be performed by firmware
Application	This layer provides applications for users and depending upon the protocols, it may provide services for applications	Software or firmware

The OSI model shows seven layers when in fact eight layer exist. I call this Ed's layer because at a minimum the function of it must be present. Figure 1-3 depicts this scenario.

The purpose of Figure 1-3 is to highlight that which is the medium. Types of media were presented earlier. And, in all networks a media must exist. Media may be hard or soft—but it must be present.

SUMMARY

Protocols are required in computers and networks to maintain order and communication capabilities. Protocols can be traced to how they originate: de facto, de jure, and proprietary. A considerable number of entities exist today working on refining and developing protocols of different sorts.

A network can be divided into layers of functionality. The OSI model is a good reference point. The OSI reference model can be divided into two categories: upper and lower layer protocols.

Figure 1-3
Ed's model

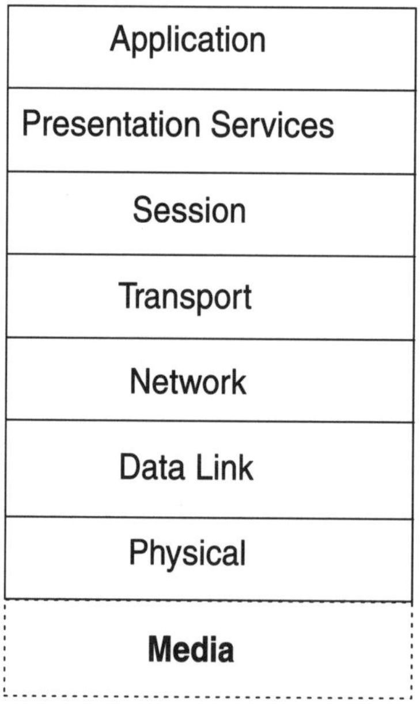

| Application |
| Presentation Services |
| Session |
| Transport |
| Network |
| Data Link |
| Physical |
| **Media** |

Internetworking 101: A Brief Perspective

Network design has evolved over the past twenty years to emerge as an important aspect of the technological arena. When Local Area Networks began to take off in the early 1980s, design and planning was done mostly after the fact. Network design was rudimentary, involving little of what device would be located where. During the mid to late 1980s this began to shift.

Because of rapid invention, creation, manufacturing, consumer awareness and consumption, most technology was deployed without much planning. Certainly this is not true in every case or with large networks, but it does reflect the norm of operation for medium to small environments where technology was utilized. In the time frame of the early to mid-1990s, a shift began to occur in the technical community concerning the planning and design of networks.

By the mid-1990s, sources of all types, such as newspapers, employment agencies, consulting firms, and others, had identified a person with a skill set that reflected the title of Network Architect. Little consensus exists even today around what a Network Architect is able to do. Designing a network involves understanding different disciplines. *Certified Network Engineers* (CNEs) is a group of professionals that have become acknowledged over the past few years. These professionals typically perform a broad range of functions in the technical community including customer support, systems programming, and systems/network integration.

In this chapter, a variety of perspectives are presented for the reader to consider regarding network architecture. The best place to begin is with the basics; and in this case, that means addressing those ideas that need adjustment, removal, or deeper consideration.

Network Emergence

Many different networking technologies were created and/or brought to market during the 1980s and early 1990s. Bringing technology to market has been the order of the day for some time, but anomalies have emerged in some instances of integrated technologies. Think about how much computer and network technology has been created, developed, and brought to market since 1980. In anybody's statistics, it is a profound amount. Because this is true, few people had the ability to work with multiple technologies at the same time simply for the sake of research or to gain pure knowledge.

Generally speaking, prior to the 1980s, most professionals devoted much of their careers to one or another type of network technology. For example, it was normal for one to devote years learning and working with COBOL, Fortran, or another programming language. The same was true for the C programming language.

Similarly, working with technology on a larger scale, one generally spent years working with IBM's *Systems Network Architecture* (SNA), the public domain's *Transmission Control Protocol / Internet Protocol* (TCP/IP), or even Digital Equipment's DECnet architecture. In the mid 1980s, professionals in many locations began to work with multiple network technologies integrating them in various ways. At first this was unusual because previously that was left to groups of researchers in primarily academic settings.

In merely the span of a decade or so, many professionals attempted to master multiple technologies. For example, one would learn TCP/IP and SNA simultaneously. Not too long prior to the mid 1980s, this would most have been laughed upon. Today focus in multiple areas is expected.

The topic of network fundamentals is not new. However, the vast array of topics now included in the arena of network fundamentals is radically different than 20 to 25 years ago. Network fundamentals in the past had traditionally focused on hardware or software. Basically this meant one studied and/or worked with hardware and understood the inner workings of it. Conversely, software designers focused on the design and results programs would yield.

Further delineation could be made by data network fundamentals segmented by vendor. For example, one who studied (SNA) fundamentals would typically not be one who would also study Digital Equipment's *Digital Network Architecture* (DNA). In the mid-1970s, (TCP/IP) was being nurtured, and it was not formally acknowledged in a significant way until 1983 when the U.S. government required supplying vendors be (or become) compliant with TCP/IP. In the 1980s, Apple computer brought AppleTalk to market. Likewise, NetWare was brought to market in the 1980s.

With these facts as a backdrop, consider the following explanation as some common fallacies and misperceptions about network architecture are presented.

Network Types by Architecture

Network architecture did not gain widespread attention until around the early to mid-1990s. This is interesting because the underlying or inner architecture of anything is the infrastructure that supports it. This author is aware that IBM and other vendors had network architects for decades who designed and assisted in the implementation of networks. However, network architecture of LANs, WANs, and the rest of the PC Community has been an emerging phenomenon since the mid 1980s.

A good way to think about network architecture is by way of analogy. For example, everything in your house is built on (directly or indirectly) the architectural design, which was created before any piece of dirt was moved. It is the same with networks, and the larger and more complex the network, the more important it is to design an adequate architecture to support the original design intent of the network's purpose.

Hardware alone does not a network architecture make. Unfortunately, many data networks built in the past have been built around hardware and not architecture. This line of thinking reflects concentration on lower levels of network operation, primarily routing or moving signals from place to place. Some people tend to think hardware alone is the core of a network's architecture. It is not. Hardware is one part of the network. It seems people think this way because hardware is visible and therefore they are able to relate to it. People are more able to relate to things that are tangible than things that are not. So, it stands it to reason that some people tend to relate to the hardware part of a network rather than the operational nature of it, which is abstract. In the final analysis, both physical and logical aspects come together to make a network operational.

Hardware should not be the only consideration of network architecture. Sometimes topologies can be thought of as the entire network architecture. Topologies, such as a BUS, Star, Ring, and other variations, are part of network architecture. Consider Figure 2-1; it shows the logical view of a BUS topology.

This illustration shows multiple devices connected to the network. The illustration depicts a "thick-net" implementation utilizing Ethernet protocol. Granted, this illustration best depicts many networks of the 1980s rather than the 1990s, but it is still valid to show the logical construction of BUS topology. The reason Figure 2-1 is considered *logical* is because, in reality, BUS topologies do not appear this way. Normally cables and other parts of the network are obscured and not as neat as this illustration depicts.

Figure 2-2 is an illustration of a physical implementation of a HUB based network.

This type of topology is a star configuration and generally appears this way in reality. Lower layer protocols might either function as broadcast (not connection oriented at the data link) or some form of token (connection oriented at the data link layer).

Figure 2-1
Logical view of a BUS

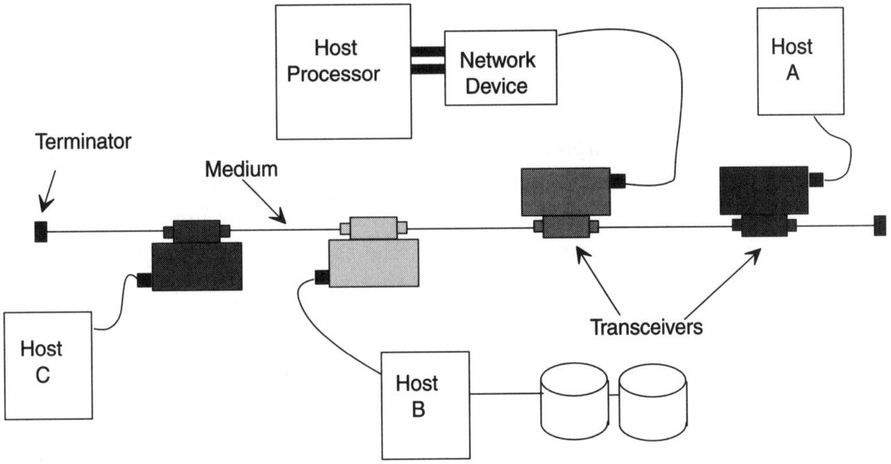

Figure 2-2
Physical implementation of a network

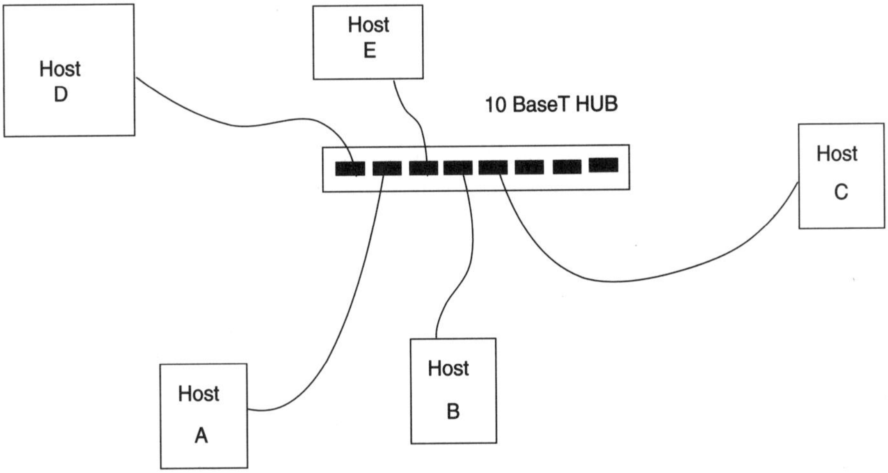

A physical HUB topology can be achieved by a small box or a rack mount device. Figure 2-2 depicts a 10-BASE-T HUB based connection. This example implies Ethernet as a lower layer protocol, hence broadcast technology is used—not a form of token passing.

Figure 2-3 depicts a physical view of a Star implementation. It is rather simplistic. However, the protocols that utilize this technology are not necessarily simple.

Figure 2-4 depicts the operational characteristics of a Star implementation using ring technology.

Figure 2-5 shows another example of a Star topology with a ring implementation.

After hardware components are connected together, the logical operation of data movement becomes a focus. Logical network operation is the result of hardware abilities/inabilities, how hardware is integrated, software characteristics, how software is configured, and any environmental considerations that can affect the network.

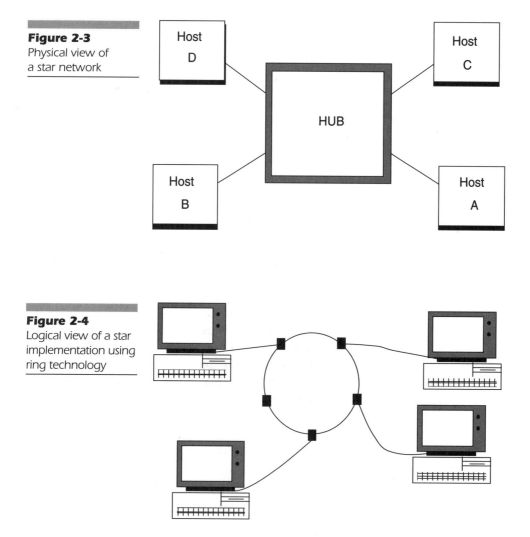

Figure 2-3
Physical view of
a star network

Figure 2-4
Logical view of a star
implementation using
ring technology

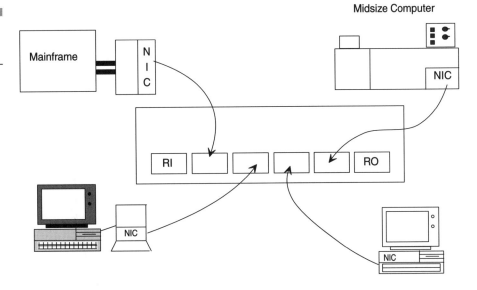

Figure 2-5
Star implementation
ring operation

Software

Both physical and logical (theoretical) architectures exist within networks. After network hardware is in place, software is the part that provides network characteristics, and thus a network actually exhibits behavior. Software determines network aspects such as routing, which applications can be used, and what network functions can be performed. For example, the latter could be software configuration used in a *Systems Network Architecture* (SNA) that permits *Transmission Control Protocol / Internet Protocol* (TCP/IP) routing through SNA.

Software works with hardware to determine capabilities and limitations within networks. Assume an infinite amount of hardware is available in a network and a database software application is used. Unless the software application is able to *address* the amount of physical hardware devices used for storage, this combination of software and hardware does not provide a valid network architecture—at least in this author's opinion. They are contingent on each other to a degree.

Post Hoc Network Design

Many networks created in the past two decades were assembled, and what was created got discussed and drawn on marker boards. In some lucky instances the network got documented. This sounds like a backward way to create a network, and it is. Not all networks designed within the past couple of decades were created this way, but you might be shocked to know how many were. In the past two decades, a tremendous amount of network technology was designed, developed, and brought to market. Fifteen years ago LANs were embryonic. Some network devices that seem to be taken for granted today were developed recently in a technological development time frame. If the reader considers my personal insight, it might shed a different view on technology in use today.

I rarely hear the discussion of technological development put into context using time as a backdrop. Does anyone remember when the first PCs came to market? It was the early 1980s; yes, some existed before then. However, from a practical standpoint it was the mid-1980s when PCs began to take hold and their marketshare began to expand. Think about it. Where were you in 1981? What were you doing? That was the year IBM introduced their first PC.

In 1975 the very idea of PCs was primarily found in places of higher education, think tanks, and in the minds of a few. Let me convey the thoughts about how fast technology has developed another way. Regardless of how long you believe the human race has existed, more technology has been created in the past 50 years than since the beginning of the human race. Lest you desire to argue with me, I have one final comment for you to think about. It has to do with my grandmother.

My grandmother was born in the late 1890s. She witnessed mankind's ability to change travel from horse and carriage to putting the space shuttle into orbit on a regular basis. The amount of technology that has been developed by humans in the past fifty years is unprecedented in the history of mankind.

The point is that much technology was being implemented in the 1980s and early 1990s, yet minimal understanding existed regarding network design. Implications of component integration were just beginning to be explored.

When technology became available to integrate upper layer protocols, it brought an ability to merge networks that had previously been considered incompatible. Reality was a matter of degrees of operational ability, and this was understood about some technology but not all network technology. In many cases, realization of heterogeneous technology integration came after the fact.

A Priori Network Design

By definition, a priori thinking means one goes from a known or assumed case to a deduced conclusion. In network design, this may or may not be the best approach. This view of network design means this thing worked here, it worked there, so it must work *here*! There is a certain degree of truth to this type of reasoning, which is a priori. However, network design should include post hoc thinking as well. Both should be tempered with common sense.

Some of the best approaches to network design include both a priori and post hoc thinking, because the latter represents experience.

Signal Characteristics

Communication between entities is achieved through signals of some sort. This is true with both humans and machines. Humans normally use speech, whereas networks, computers, and internetworking devices use electrical or optic signals. These signals have many characteristics and the signal type, electrical or optic, determines (to a degree) the characteristics of that signal.

This section explores signals and the characteristics related to them. The details presented here are a reference for information needed to work at the fundamental layers within a network.

Signal Types

A signal can be defined or characterized in many ways; however for purposes here the difference between analog and digital signals is explained.

Analog   An analog signal can be described by what it is not. It is neither "on" nor "off," positive nor negative, or some other diametrically opposed position. An example would be a dimmer switch used in electrical lighting. The function of the dimmer switch is to vary light intensity without full intensity or the light being off (unless the latter two states of intensity are desired).

Digital   A digital signal is best defined as being either in an on or off state with no in-between point. In data communications, a digital signal is a binary 1 or 0.

Signaling Methods

Two signaling methods exists: baseband and broadband. Baseband signaling uses digital signal techniques for transmission and broadband signaling uses analog signal techniques for transmission. In general Baseband signaling has a limited bandwidth, whereas broadband signaling has a large bandwidth potential.

Signaling Characteristics

Signals, either analog or digital, are based on fundamental trigonometric functions. As a result, understanding some fundamental principles of trigonometry yields the benefit of being able to evaluate waveforms.

A baseline for evaluating waveforms is rooted in the Cartesian coordinate system. This system of measurement is mathematically unique for defining or locating a point on a line, plane, or in space. Fundamental to this coordinate system are numbered lines that intersect at right angles. See Figure 2-6.

This coordinate system, along with other aspects of trigonometry, is used in signaling. Here the focus is on certain characteristics of signals.

Figure 2-6
Cartesian coordinate system

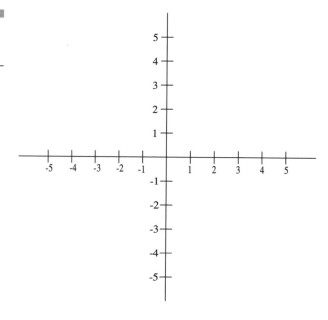

Signals in computers, networking, or data communications can be categorized as being analog or digital. Consequently, the aid of this coordinate system along with other tools makes it possible to explain signals.

Analog and Digital Commonalities

Both analog and digital signals have commonalities. Analog and digital signal commonalities can be evaluated by amplitude, frequency, and phase.

Amplitude   The amplitude of a signal refers to its height with respect to a base line. Height might be a positive or negative voltage. The base line is a zero voltage reference point. This amplitude value is proportional to the movement of the curve about the X-axis of the coordinate system, as shown in Figure 2-7.

Frequency   Frequency is the number of cycles a wave makes per second. Specifically, frequency is measured in Hertz (Hz), which is also known as a unit of frequency. A cycle is a complete signal revolution from zero to the maximum positive voltage past zero to the maximum negative voltage, then back to zero. In the coordinate system, this is a complete revolution from 0 to 360 degrees. Figure 2-7 is an example of signal characteristics, particularly one cycle.

Figure 2-7
Signal characteristics

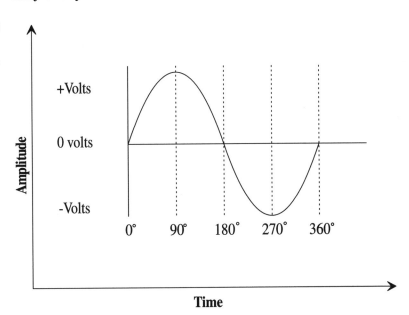

Figure 2-7 shows one cycle of the signal with respect to time and amplitude, as well as frequency.

Phase Phase is normally measured in degrees that represent the location of a waveform. Another way of thinking about phase is that it is the relative time of a signal with respect to another signal. A change of phase without a change of frequency or amplitude results in a scenario depicted by Figure 2-8.

In Figure 2-8, three waveforms are present A, B, and C. In this example, waveform A has a 20-degree phase angle or leads waveform B by 20 degrees. Determination of the leading waveform is derived by visually ascertaining which waveform crosses the X-axis first; in this case, it is waveform A. Waveform C, on the other hand, is lagging waveform A by 40 degrees.

Figure 2-9 is an example of two signal waveforms (better known as sine waves) that have the same frequency but are out of phase with respect to the each other.

In general, signals transmitted over a medium are subject to varying frequencies. Phase can be thought of as the distance a waveform is from its beginning point (which is zero degrees). This is particularly important when examining transmission characteristics of encoded signals. An explanation of encoded signaling characteristics is forthcoming; however, the significance of this information becomes real when one uses different measuring scopes to troubleshoot a line with varying frequencies.

Period A period is best described as the length of a cycle. It is defined as the time required by a signal transmission of a wavelength.

Figure 2-8
Example of a
phase angle

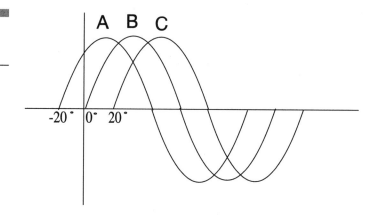

Figure 2-9
Phase differentiation

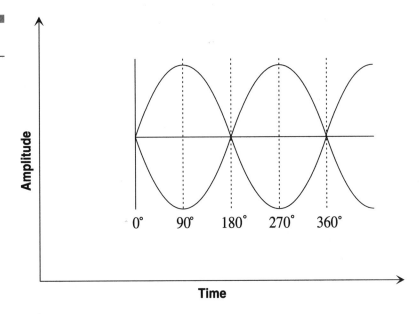

Waveforms

Waveforms come in many forms. Two are discussed here; the sine wave and the square wave.

Sine wave   A sine wave can be defined as a periodic wave. Characteristically, this is a wave's amplitude based upon the sine of its linear quantity of phase or time. See Figure 2-10.

Square wave   A square wave is a wave with a square shape. It too has the same characteristics as the sine wave. Consider Figure 2-11.
   The square wave has similar characteristics to the sine wave, except the *form* of it is square in appearance versus the *wave* appearance of the sine wave.

Data Representation

Before discussing characteristics of transmission, it is important to understand ways data is represented. Two methods of data representation are presented here: binary and hexadecimal.

Figure 2-10
Example of a
sine wave

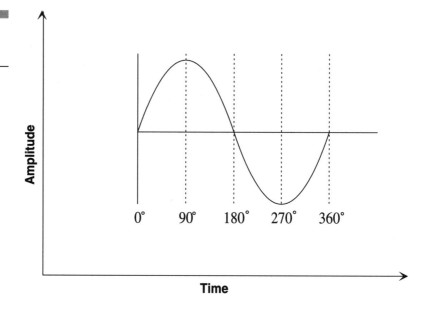

Figure 2-11
Example of a
square wave

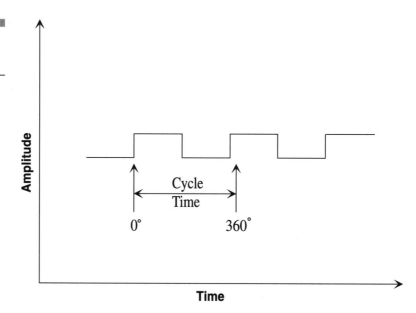

Data Networks

Data networks, as well as voice networks, represent data in a number of
ways. The dominant ones are listed in the remaining part of this chapter.

Binary

Binary data representation uses ones and zeros to represent alphanumeric characters within computer systems. Another way of approaching binary representation is by way of the *American Standard Code for Information Interchange* (ASCII). ASCII is a method of data representation that uses 128 permutations of arrangements of ones and zeros.

This means that with a computer using an ASCII character set, letters, numbers, control codes, and other keyboard symbols have a specific binary relationship. Consider the following examples that show the correlation of a letter or number in the ASCII character set to its binary equivalent (see Table 2-1).

This example means that each time a key is pressed on a keyboard the equivalent binary value is generated (a string of ones and zeros). This value is represented inside the computer as a voltage. That voltage is DC.

Computers for the most part are digital, that is, either a 1 or 0. Hence, converting letters, numbers, or control codes to a numeric value is straightforward. When it comes to how computers work with data representation, consider what I told my friend: "Computers do not negotiate; they are binary, my dear Zac." At the most fundamental place within the representation of data, computers operate in a method similar to being in an "off state" or an "on state."

Table 2-1
ASCII to binary correlation example

Letter or Number	Binary Value
A	01000001
a	01100001
E	01000101
2	00110010
3	00110011
7	00110111
T	01010100
t	01110100
"	00100010
-	00101101

A bit is a single digit, either a one or a zero. A byte is eight bits. Hence, in the previous example, a single letter or number is represented by a combination of ones and zeros. The binary numbering system is based on powers of 2 and is counted from right to left. Consider the following example in Table 2-2.

Powers of Two	Value
2×0	1
2×1	2
2×2	4
2×3	8
2×4	16
2×5	32
2×6	64
2×7	128
2×8	256
2×9	512
2×10	1024
2×11	2048
2×12	4096

Table 2-2

Powers of two

One byte is 2×0, which is eight binary digits (either 1s or 0s).

Hexadecimal

Hex, as the term is so used, refers to a numbering scheme that uses a base 16 for counting. Hex is a shorthand notation for expressing binary values of characters. Consider the following example in Table 2-3.

Table 2-4 correlates a character with a binary representation and hex expression of that value.

	Hexidecimal Value	Decimal Value
Table 2-3 Hexidecimal to decimal value correlation	0	0
	1	1
	2	2
	3	3
	4	4
	5	5
	6	6
	7	7
	8	8
	9	9
	A	10
	B	11
	C	12
	D	13
	E	14
	F	15

As this example indicates, it is easier to represent the letter *z* by hex value 7A than its binary representation.

Other methods of data representation exist. OCTAL which uses base 8 for a numbering system and decimal. Of these, binary and hex are prevalent and understanding this binary representation is helpful with other data communication concepts.

A final word about data representation. IBM uses *Extended Binary Coded Decimal Interchange Code* (EBCDIC) as a prevalent method for representing data, alpha numerics, and control codes. EBCDIC uses an arrangement of 256 ones and zeros to make this possible. And, it should be noted that ASCII and EBCDIC are not one-for-one interchangeable.

Table 2-4

Alpha numeric to
binary & hex
correlation

Letter/Number	Binary	Hex Value
A	01000001	41
a	01100001	61
E	01000101	45
2	00110010	02
3	00110011	03
7	00110111	07
T	01010100	54
k	01101011	6B
m	01101101	6D
z	01111010	7A

SUMMARY

It is helpful to have more than just mere technical information when working with networks. This is the reason I have included more than just technical information in this chapter. You might be familiar with some of the information I presented here, and if so, please bear with those who are learning it for the first time. Regardless of your background, this chapter is helpful by providing some basic information that applies to a wide cross section of networks.

Types of
Networks

Networks based on various forms of technology have been around for decades. Just a short time ago a common definition of "networking" referred to social interaction among humans. Now the term "networking" is generally understood to mean some form of interaction among technological devices. Consider this: It is primarily in the last half of the twentieth century that networks appeared. This chapter focuses on types of networks that can be identified. This delineation is helpful because of the technology available today and the various ways it is merged together. Sometimes a healthy understanding of the pieces makes understanding an entity's characteristics easier.

Perspective on Networks

Computer based networks can be traced back to the 1960s. Some might argue that even a decade or so prior to the 1960s would be valid to include as the era of tangible beginnings for computer networks. Regardless of what starting point one uses for the beginning of computer based networks, it is clear the 1960s was a demarcation of their beginnings.

During the 1960s, the idea of connecting computers together to create a computer network can be identified. For example, groups within IBM were discussing this topic in research facilities and even beginning to deploy rudimentary implementations of what would become known as networks. In addition, the U.S. government had organizations concentrating on this idea.

In the 1970s, IBM launched the beginning of *Systems Network Architecture* (SNA). Since that time, it has undergone significant enhancements and changes. Digital Equipment also brought a network offering to market, and it too has grown in marketshare. However, in all reality, SNA enjoyed a larger marketshare during its "hey day" than DECnet.

The Internet has its origins back to 1957. Most consider the origin dates of the Internet to be the late 1960s, and this is an agreeable time frame to point towards. However, to get to the heart of the matter, the foundations were laid for what would become the Internet in the early 1960s. This author is aware that the technical aspects of the Internet were not available until the late 1960s and even into the early 1970s.

Even though most agree that the Internet was "birthed" in the 1960s, the 1970s saw increased growth in the Internet community. In the 1980s many of the *Request For Comments* (RFCs) became "formal" and the Internet was well on the way towards a more mature network. In 1983 the U.S. government made it official that suppliers of technology to the U.S. government would have to support TCP/IP which was the protocol of the Internet at that time, as well as today.

During the 1980s, in addition to the Internet, other technological developments were underway. In fact, for the first time in the history of the human race, ordinary individuals were beginning to have computers to use and work with on a personal basis.

As the 1980s unfolded, companies, such as IBM, Compaq, Microsoft, Dell, Epson, Novell, the WordPerfect Corporation, Apple Computer, and many, many others, began to bring products to market to support the personal computer. (Dozens of other companies could be included in the list here, and omission of them is not to slight them; my purpose is simply to present a highlight to orient the reader.) When networks are discussed in light of recent history, an entirely different perspective emerges. Ironically, this perspective on networks is slanted toward data-oriented networks. The irony emerges when one understands that most large data networks are based on a voice network infrastructure.

Categories of Networks

Networks can be described by category. Valid network categories include

Data

Voice

Video

Multimedia

Internet

Intranet

Data Networks

At this time data networks are generally referred to by the protocols they use. For the most part the dominant protocols in the marketplace today are

SNA

TCP/IP

NetWare

AppleTalk

Windows Networking

These protocols and others (which are generally called lower layer protocols) comprise the backbone for moving "stuff" through a network. Technically, specific components within each of these network protocols move data and "stuff" through networks. This moving of "stuff" refers to routing. However, data and "stuff" are also moved at a more fundamental level within networks; that level uses data link protocols. Upper and lower layer protocols presented later in this book operate at different levels because their functions differ. Upper layer protocols have some commonalities, such as routings and packaging "stuff" to move through the network.

Voice Networks

Voice networks have been around for some time. Their purpose and operation are different from those of most data networks. Voice networks can be considered analogous to the foundation of a house. Because voice networks are basically the backbone on which data networks are built, a word is in order about voice networks. First of all, what I am calling voice networks is actually nothing more than a telephone infrastructure, such as lines, switching sub-stations, satellites, software and the like. For the most part, voice networks that were in place ten years ago are the same ones in place today. Now consider this: Those networks are used to carry data and other "stuff," because in the world of technology, it is all binary. In the world of communications, multimedia, voice, data, and just about any thing else you can name, everything is digital—a mere one or zero. (Which are you?) With this in mind, it is helpful to have a better grip on a perspective of the voice network that carries most of the "information" traffic today. Consider Figure 3-1.

Differences exist between voice networks. Those in the United States are different from those in Germany, Russia, Japan, China, Brazil, and even Canada. This does not mean any given country has a better network than another; it merely means countries differ as to how their voice networks operate. Because this is true, not all countries with voice network infra-

Figure 3-1
Voice-based network
infrastructure

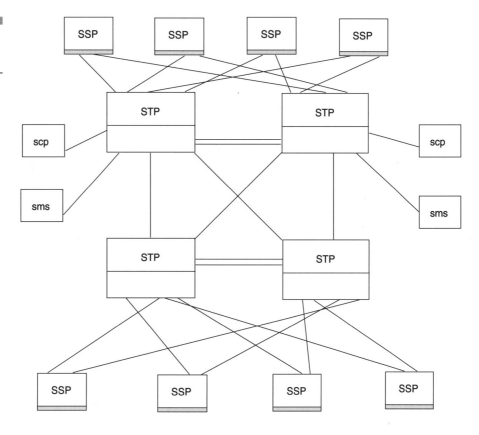

structure speak the same language. To a degree they do; however, at the
most fundamental levels, some voice networks do exist. Even some regions
of the United States have different voice network capabilities. Some of
these differences are due to technological reasons, some to legal reasons,
and some to consumer demand (or the lack thereof).

In the past few decades, technology brought an interesting twist to the
telecommunications industry. The development of wireless technology and
the reliability of it have changed the equation for regions requiring a telecommunication infrastructure. Some countries (and even parts of America)
currently are able to develop telecommunication infrastructures because
through wireless technology they have the option to circumvent many
aspects of a hardwired systems. This development enables them to bypass
the amount of time and money needed to lay such a foundation. Consider
some eastern bloc countries and the continent of Africa. It is possible to use
wireless communications to accommodate an entire region and this has

profound implications. It means that any given region with a telecommunications infrastructure can tap into the global telecommunications infrastructure. Three or four decades make a significant difference.

Voice networks (thought of as those to which telephone and other devices connect) are becoming digitally oriented. They are not completely digital, as some think. This might seem strange, but remember technology did not begin with digital operation; it was analog. Most telephone networks have roots in analog technology. This is significant, because most devices in the world of technology today are digital.

In some cases, modems connect computers to voice networks. Modems modulate and demodulate signals to accommodate digital devices and the analog connection end of the vehicle. Thus analog-to-digital and digital-to-analog signal conversion is accomplished. Not all communication between computers need be converted to analog signals for transmission. This depends on the network that transports data from the origin to the destination and the devices on the ends.

Video Networks

Video networks are interesting. Operation of these networks differs from that of voice or data networks; however, both voice and data might be part of a video network. Consider Figure 3-2.

This illustration depicts a television production location, a remote production location, satellite transmission, transmission via cable, and a typical signal broadcast method. These various mediums used for transmission all carry data, voice, and video. The differences occur in issues such as time delay, positioning of the earth, point-to-point transmission versus broadcast, and other typical data communication matters. One example, seen in Figure 3-2, shows a television network broadcasting a signal from its central location and local receivers picking up the signal. Most television stations have uplink satellite dishes to transport signals to a satellite, as this illustration depicts. Some television networks broadcast their signals via cable or other medium that supports digital signals. Normally, with technology today, a decoder and encoder are required with satellite and cable television transmission and reception. The reason for this is not technical, it is financial and political. One would be amazed at what can be tapped into in the stratosphere.

Video is becoming an increasing proportion of company network traffic. Some companies have dedicated video networks, but at this time most do

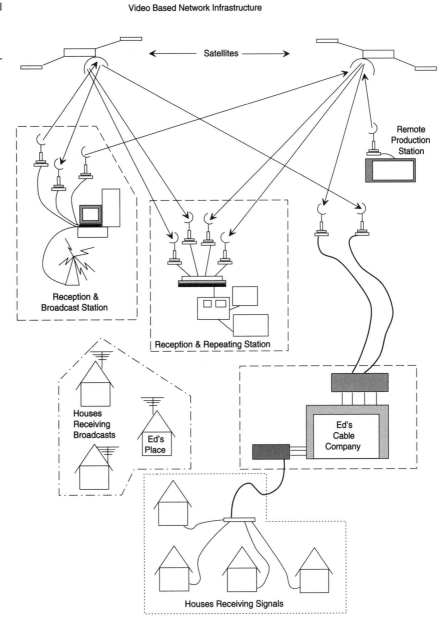

Figure 3-2
Video-based network infrastructure

Video Based Network Infrastructure

not. The current and foreseen trend is movement toward a synthesis of message mediums. This de facto trend is troublesome in many ways. First, it presupposes equipment can accommodate data voice and video.

Many still view video networks as perceived from a consumer viewpoint; that is, many people still think a device is needed for reception, computing, and voice communication. Herein lies the consumer paradox: Many consumers think different devices are needed to support data, voice, and video. Ironically, the system I used to write this documents supports all three; the only caveat is that I had to basically custom order parts and assemble them to make it work. And yes, there were a few additional things to do with the software as well. But the point is that the technology exists today for a single device to support data, voice, and video. Orienting customers to these ideas is currently referred to as multimedia. As I told a friend (who is not computer literate), "Think of my computer as a box with a phone, fax, and TV in a single box."

Multimedia Networks

Multimedia emerged in the 1990s as the new corporate implementation. Ten to fifteen years ago LANs were beginning to emerge. Now, some people actually believe one can move data, voice, video, interactive conferencing video, repository retrieval, and other multimedia functions with the same level/grade of technology one did with LANs moving data only. Technically, it is possible to achieve the former, but the idea of increasing loads on data oriented networks pushes most networks past their limits.

In most cases I have observed, upgrading networks at fundamental levels is required for adequate multimedia implementation in today's marketplace. Because most networks have evolved rather than being planned, this is the order of the day. The consequences are financial—PCs, memory, disk drivers, interface cards, and the connecting medium cause instances where it is cheaper to create a new network with new equipment.

Multimedia networks require more technology than data oriented networks, period. In contrast to multimedia networks which require a variety of technology, data networks require a monitor, input device, processor storage (temporary and possible permanent), and a link between devices. Multimedia networks requires the same components as data networks, but in some cases different viewing input storage, transmission media, and other devices are required. At an application level, this means new applications or in some cases upgrades of previous versions. Figure 3-3 illustrates an example of a multimedia network.

Figure 3-3
Multimedia network
example

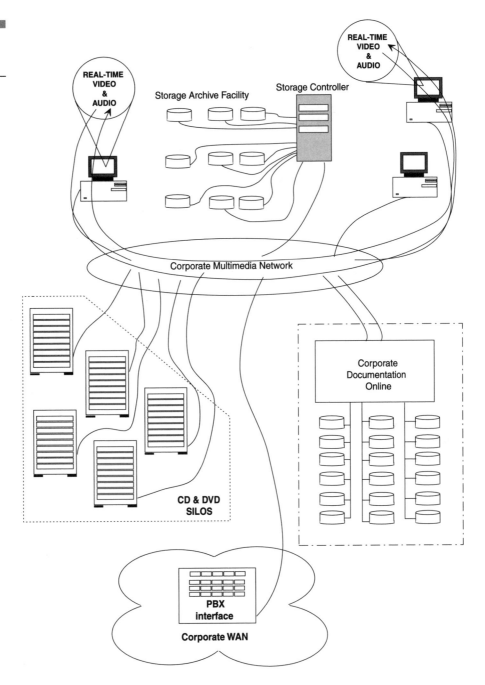

As the illustration shows, a data storage repository is available online where interactive voice documentation between network users and general data network connectivity is shared among users.

Internet

The Internet has gone from basic obscurity in the marketplace to the hottest topic around the country in less than ten years. Ten years ago relatively few people were working with the Internet. Today, practically every form of media outlet has daily remarks concerning aspects of it. A dominant question is "what" or "where" is the Internet? The Internet is a collection of entities around the world. Specifically, in America, these entities include educational institutions, commercial companies, governmental organizations, research facilities, and service providers such as America Online, and others to name a few. Consider Figure 3-4.

Some would argue the accuracy of Figure 3-4, but consider the following. The Internet does have fundamental pieces operating at the very core of it. For example, the Domain Name System is the heart and soul of it. Yes,

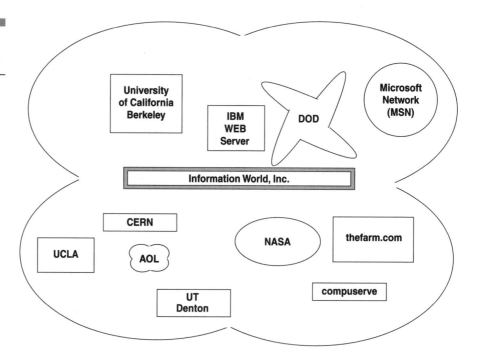

Figure 3-4
Conceptual view of the Internet

there are routers, bridges, gateways, and network-related devices; and to a real degree, the pieces come together and thus the Internet exists. It is more complex than I have room here to explain. Educational institutions, commercial entities, non-profit organizations, governmental entities, and other participating entities are all affected by and contribute to the Internet.

Some say a service provider is merely that; a service provider. However there is a point where the service provider is a part of the Internet itself. America Online is probably a good example of this. Service providers have Internet addresses just like non-service providers that participate in the Internet. Furthermore, what does it mean to be a non-service provider? A lot of service providers provide there own version of magazines, some news, file transfer capabilities, e-mail, and some core functions such as TELNET, FTP, GOPHER, and so forth.

The World Wide Web is part of the Internet; however it is not the Internet. The fact of the matter is that the Web is simply a collection of individual computers that run Web server software. All these individual Web sites make up the Web collectively. Generally, the Web sites on the Internet are little more than a billboard on the freeway. Granted, some Web locations have the ability to listen to audio, watch video, and do other tricks. The bulk of the Internet today is simply a presentation of data in electronic form.

How one uses the Internet is a topic to consider. For example, a user can access the Internet by way of common service providers today. The service provider actually determines the abilities and limitations users have with Internet interaction. Some service providers limit the scope of user functions so that remote logins may not be performed. However, some service providers offer this ability. Prior to service providers today, most access was achieved by an indirect connection through an entity such as a university, organization, or other entity with an address assigned to it.

An example of wide capability of Internet use could be explained by way of a university example. Some major universities have systems that permit users to perform a remote log in to another system on the Internet by way of TELNET. This ability means users connected to the remote host can perform any function they are authorized to do. Another example, is file transfers. The example of a university user access could mean they can execute *File Transfer Protocol* (FTP). This permits users to log into a remote system and perform maintenance functions, file transfer abilities, in binary and text modes, and issue FTP commands against the remote hosts such that changing directories is possible, and other functions. FTP also makes it generally possible wherein one can execute an anonymous FTP. By this mechanism, one can login to a remote host, initiate an execution of a download file transfer, and they do not require advanced support such as security and restrictions to limit virtual sessions to other systems. Another example could be users who can access Web pages at virtually any site where they are supported.

This explanation is made because not all service providers provide the same services or abilities. Rather, they differ in the speeds by which access can be obtained, timelines, and so forth. This is not a negative statement toward any service provider; it is a simple reality in the world of the Internet. Remember, the Internet, to a great degree, was not planned—it just happened.

Intranets

First, there was the Internet; next came intranets. I suppose the extranets will come along shortly. A pressing question still lurks on the intellectual horizon and follows me everywhere I go, that is "What is an intranet?" My standard reply is, "Whoever you ask will most likely have an answer which might not concur with the next person you ask." I like to think simple; to me, an intranet is any network an entity has that supports its purposes. Some vendors are positioning various products and proclaiming this or that is an intranet solution. My purpose is to briefly explain some insights to the topic of intranets. First, consider Figure 3-5.

The notion of the term intranet is rooted in the Internet; at least this author thinks so. One need only think about the Internet and what is available on it and then consider a corporate intranet. Many years ago, and probably still so today, I kept hearing the term intranet and Internet. The former was used by many to refer to their internal network whereas the latter was used to refer to the Internet. Maybe this shows the author's age, but I remember distinctly when one had to clarify the conversation in order to continue with it. Intranets are generally internal with regard to the services they provide, however the scope of the services might geographically cover a large expanse.

The notion of having an intranet is now "old hat." The idea of having an internal network for most companies is as common as having a computer in the company itself. The smallest of companies is moving towards having internal networks installed, even if that is nothing but computers connected through a hub to share files and a printer.

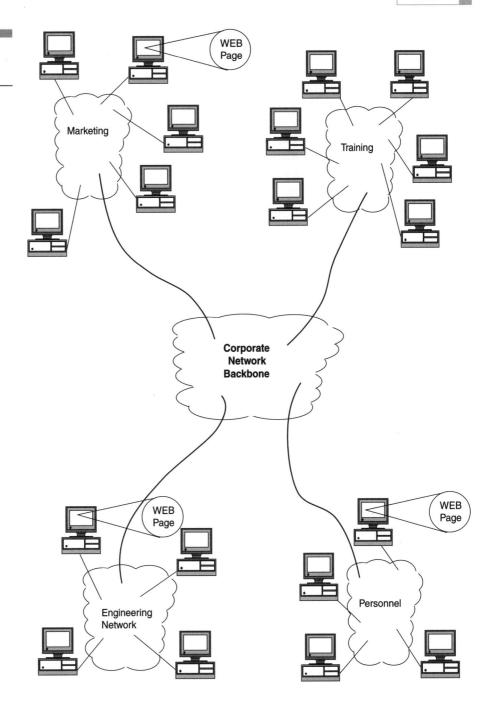

Figure 3-5
Typical corporate intranet

SUMMARY

Network categories generally reflect the type network service provided. The exception is the Internet. It is a class unto itself. The Internet is most unique, because its origins and earlier, even the first twenty or so years, had really no commercial bent. The past ten years has done more to exploit the Internet from a commercial perspective than anything before in the past thirty years.

Commercialization of the Internet will probably continue for many years to come. In fact, I think the Internet will become the commercial exchange medium for not only buying and selling but also communications. The nature of it makes for an attractive tool to use. The Internet itself really consists of multiple types of networks within it. Part of the Internet includes NASA, DoD, America Online, and other service providers.

Considerations for All Networks

Introdution

Networks can be analyzed from many different aspects. Network topics vary from the people required to build them, to the amount of space required to house them. This chapter is an important one for me because I include various topics that need to be thought about depending on what you are doing. I have been a long time reader of networking books. In fact, I started reading the communication series and networking books from McGraw-Hill back when they first started, which was not too long ago. During these years of working with networks, I realized that many good books have been written. Consequently, in this book, I want to include topics that I know can help you.

The remainder of this chapter is a topical presentation of information that has helped me over time. I believe this information will be good reference material for you as well.

Network Planning Considerations

A network's design ultimately needs to include the information in this section. I submit to you that this information should be considered early on if you are one who contributes to a network design. The following questions need to be answered. Consider these questions as soon as you anticipate a new network is to be planned or when additions are to be added to your existing network.

- Who
- What
- Where
- When
- Why
- How
- How Much
- How Long
- The Holistic Approach

It might seem elementary to you, but I have found it is the elementary things to which people generally screw up the most. They are overlooked, I suppose, because so many people take the fundamentals for granted. Let us examine these briefly and see the impact they have on network design.

Who

Who applies across the board. Who plans, installs, maintains, troubleshoots, and works with the network from every angle. It is important to at least pencil in a title for the person to whom the responsibility falls. Who is going to be responsible for seeing the network from marker board to completion? Some person should have this single task assigned to him/her. They might not understand all there is to know about the network, but at least there is a single point of contact. By the way, it should not be the CFO. No offense intended, but finance departments are no more or less important than customer support; that is, they simply serve a required purpose for the entity to operate effectively.

Who is going to be involved in the logical and physical design of the network? Who will be responsible for procurement of all the equipment? Who will be responsible for receiving the equipment? Who will be responsible for maintaining a vendor/resource contact list? Who is responsible for logistics if moving equipment from place to place within an entity is required?

This list of questions is brief but a starter. Your list might include many more "whos." Your list should cover all the bases and might well be in a state of flux during the entire network design and implementation process. In fact, I recommend the "whos" get together and meet regularly to exchange information. You might find things work better this way.

What

The "what" question applies to every feasible part of the network. What are the components to be used? What are the components to do? What are going to be the strategic plans if a certain of piece of equipment does not arrive on time, arrives broken, and so forth? What is the plan to be designed? What are the phases of the network design? What are the phases of network implementation? What are the phases of network maintenance? What are the criteria for milestones of accomplishments in the installation phase of the network? What is the contingency plan? What are the requirements needed to support the number of users on the network? What is the purpose of the network, singularly? Again, your list might include many more "whats" than this, but these certainly should be included.

Where

Location is important. Most real estate agents will tell you the single most important thing about real estate: "location, location, location." It is the same with a network. Where is the network going to be installed? Where is each piece of equipment going to reside? Where are the users? Where is the place for storage after the equipment arrives, prior to installation? Where are all the people located who will participate in the design, implementation, and maintenance of the network? Where will all the equipment come from? Where will network management occur?

As you can see, your list might well include a number of other issues.

When

Timing in anything is very important. Timing in network design, implementation, and maintenance is equally important. Here are some common timing questions that should be answered as soon as possible.

When is the network design phase scheduled to begin? When will update meetings occur to brief concerned parties? When will the milestones for network implementation/installation be reached? When will each phase of network design commence? When will testing occur on each piece of equipment be implemented? When is the scheduled time for completion? When will certain procedures be invoked if initial plans are not met?

This list of "when" is a beginning point for you. Expand on it to embrace your needs and your network.

Why

Why is the network being built to begin with? Why are the people involved with it involved with it? Why are vendors selected the ones selected; that is, what criteria were used to select the vendors? Why is this or that being added to the network? Why is this technology or product being used in this office rather than another office within the company?

Another line of the "why" thought includes some questions such as: Why is the network not including support for the company plans as they are known for the next quarter? Why is the network expansion not inclusive to of all the corporate departments? Why is the network being segmented to include certain departments and yet excluding other departments? Why are the needs of our remote offices not being included into the needs of the entire network redesign?

Your list of "why" could be much longer. It should include the important questions and answers for your environment.

How

This question focuses on logistics primarily. For example, how is the equipment going to be received and stored until the installation phase for the equipment commences? This might seem to be more of a question of where but it is not. How equipment is stored addresses topics such as temperature, humidity, security, and related aspects. The "how" and "where" tend to overlap, but the "how" focuses more upon the step by step plan of action to get certain tasks complete.

Unfortunately, the "how" is not planned for in advance in some instances, and a shipping/receiving department is inundated with incoming equipment to the point where they are paralyzed with regard to daily operations. Another twist on the question "how" is more focused on internal operations. For example, take a company with multiple locations around the world. Assuming a network is being built to connect multiple facilities, the question of how certain pieces of equipment will get from one location to another becomes important. In fact, this could be a show-stopper for some companies. I've seen it happen; that is, equipment is obtained, a network is being built, and equipment arrives in one location but is needed in another. The ultimate question emerges: "How is this going to get there?" When this scenario arises problems usually ensue. Avert this and other problems by addressing this question as soon as possible.

How Much

Costs are important. Unfortunately, in many cases, the costs are not weighed fairly and balanced in proportion. For example, I have seen executives, management at all levels, and even technical people, be what my grandmother used to say, "Penny wise and pound foolish." You might laugh, but it is unfortunately true too many times. I have seen, first hand, educated executives say: "Less is more." If this is true, I suppose it is time to rewrite some of the fundamental laws of the universe. Any reasonable human being knows this is not true in the broadest sense. This type of thinking emerges from numerous premises, one of which is ignorance. I have a proposal for people who think less is more: "If you think less is more, cut your pay in half and send it to me, or just take whatever you consider too much, send it to me, and then we'll see what you really think."

"How much" is a question that should be asked in a threefold context. First, "how much" should examined in light of the overall network with regard to the network's expected life span, products, services offered through the network, scope and capability of the network. Second, "how much" should be asked in light of what is being paid for given products and/or services compared to comparable products and/or services. Third, "how much" should be asked in regard to the estimated payback the network will provide.

Do not underestimate the financial part of your network. Do not expect to get something for nothing. At the same time, "throwing" money at a problem is not wise either. Somewhere along the way during the planning phase of the network, all parties involved should provide reasonable input and be prepared to discuss this in an open civil way for the betterment of the company at large.

How Long

This question of "how long" is broad. It encompasses aspects during the beginning of network design, the implementation phase, and also the length of expected life for the network and its services. "How long" can be directed to the group of people who will perform actual installation of equipment, as well as how long it will take to bring the network into the alpha and beta phases.

This question should be applied to the entire network design and implementation plan. It should also be directed towards backup plans, and unforeseen difficulties that can arise due to people problems or equipment failure. A flip side of the notion "how long" applies to a direct question of survival. How long can certain equipment survive in a worse case scenario?

The "how long" question is general in nature and is supposed to be a principle for you to use to get your thoughts into some sense of order. Work exerted on the front end of network planning can help avert many possible problems later on in the project.

The Holistic Approach

The idea of taking a holistic approach is to provide a comprehensive under-standing of the network. Included in this is everything from the purpose for the network to the method by which equipment will arrive at your facility. The notion of this approach includes understanding the big picture. Once it is in focus, it is much easier to zero in on isolated segments and understand them in context.

I have seen some networks implemented piecemeal. The end result over time is multiple headaches. It is a far better approach to take the compre-hensive view and design your network as best as possible from that per-spective. One thing is sure, if this method is used many problems can be avoided on the front end. I have found this takes a lot of the surprises out of the entire network implementation and use. After all, the fundamental idea behind networks is to provide a common vehicle to access data and to serve people. This thought alone tends to point one towards a comprehen-sive view of a network from the outset of planning.

Network Need Analysis

The best place to start with need analysis is to determine what your com-pany/entity does. There should be some fundamental tenets that your company/entity is based on and hence factor into the driving forces of a network. This being said, other overall needs emerge easily. For example, e-mail, file transfer, data services, and other needs might be reasons for a network in your entity. These comprehensive needs might be departmen-tal and thus reveal additional needs.

For example, say the entity you are working with has a sales, customer service, shipping/receiving, and internal technical support department. Each department can have unique needs. Granted, all of them might need to exchange e-mail and certain files; each department might have inter-departmental needs. Consider the shipping department.

A shipping/receiving department might be quite sizable. Numerous employees might be required to operate it adequately. It might include a large amount of floor space and numerous offices within the department. In this example, a departmental database might be needed to track incoming and outgoing packages. This information may rarely be needed by any other department. Consequently, this example might justify a sub-net or a depart-mental network that is isolated from the rest of the entity.

On the other hand, the shipping/receiving department requires interaction with all the entity's staff. This means access to the corporate network is required. A two-fold need exists. This example illustrates the detailed planning required to anticipate and adequately meet the shipping/receiving department's needs.

This type approach to your entity's size, structure, and requirements should play a large role in the design of your network. A well-designed network will include this level of thought in the preliminary design stages. This aspect of the network planning is based on department needs. It should be part of the overall planning process.

Additional considerations for network planning include evaluation of the following:

- Internal
- External
- Geographical

Internal

A network's primary purpose is to serve the needs inside a company. This being the case, understanding the internal structure of operation is important. This approach includes a detailed examination of internal needs. It also includes a detailed list of current technology in place, its use, and its anticipated use with the addition of a network.

Each company/entity regardless of size has internal needs. Multiple departments, such as shipping/receiving, sales, marketing, operations, support, financial, and personnel services, generally exist. This is not inclusive, but it is a place to begin. This type of examination reveals what departments exist today and those planned for the future.

Internal needs might be subtle, but take time to examine the inner workings of the company. If technology is involved, then engineering, support, and sales may all need access to varying depths of information about the company. What does this mean for a network? At a minimum, it means people in these departments will need to be able to access information and exchange information. The information may include graphics, internal reports, external feedback from potential customers (or existing customers), and possibly a database of information.

Other internal information is likely required for a company to maintain order. On-line calendars are handy. This information is considered public within the company and may well be needed by shipping/receiving. For example, if Ms. Hoover is on vacation this month and receives multiple packages, the receiving department could take advantage of an on-line calendar to know she is out of the office, and whether or not any special instructions are standing regarding her absence.

In addition on-line calendars can help provide a schedule of meetings. Fewer conference rooms will be possible for a company if everyone in the company knows when and where a meeting is scheduled. Parallel to this idea is the needs that exist in the conference room which affect the network. For example, are telephone services needed in the conference room? Are data network services needed in the conference room? If so, how will these services be provided? Will cable outlets exist for those with portable computers to connect? What is the capacity at any given time of connections that can be made in the conference room? These and similar questions factor into the equation of network design. Overlook these points and you may well end up hiring a crew to tear out part of the wall to make something available that should have been available in the first place.

Many other types of information might need to be exchanged within a company. Regardless of what that might be, one should attempt to plan as far into the future as possible when adding this part of the information into the network design equation. No one can plan with 100 percent accuracy five to ten years out, but it is possible to plan for worst and best case scenarios. Do this, and your work with data communication gear will be less painful.

External

Needs external to the company also will affect your network. For example, the way your customers interact with the company is important. If there is a need for them to be able to download files or read certain information made available to the public, then this should be factored into the network design equation.

Beyond awareness of customer interaction with the company is the number of customers (current and planned) that will need this interactive ability. Circumstances may justify an entirely separate network to meet the needs of the customer base. If so, then how this network will or will not interact with the network being designed is an important aspect to investigate.

Geographical

Geographic information is important to include in a category for your network planning. Consider Figure 4-1.

Figure 4-1
Isolated data center

Figure 4-1 shows a single data center network location in one facility in Fort Worth, TX. This type of network is relatively straightforward in regard to network planning. For example, only one location exists, and network users reside in the same physical plant as the network. Now, consider Figure 4-2.

Figure 4-2 shows an entity with a facility in San Francisco and Atlanta. This scenario is more complex to design and install a network in because of differing time zones, long distance service providers, personnel support after installation, logistics of equipment arrival, and coordination of installation. Other matters arise when a network is being installed in multiple locations where two or more time zones are involved.

Still another variation on geographic considerations is illustrated in Figure 4-3.

Figure 4-2
Operations in
multiple locations

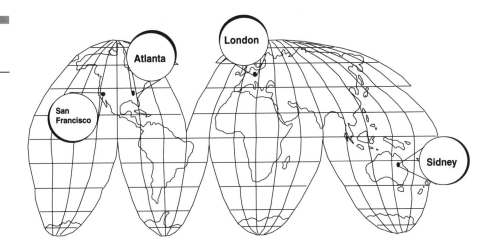

Figure 4-3
Distributed
operations

Figure 4-3 is next in the level of complexity for network planning and installation. It shows a multinational network and poses a myriad of considerations. For example, time zone differences are extreme and make communication a challenge. Each country represented has a different telephone network infrastructure. International laws apply to the integration of all these networks. Even network components procured for implementation must be electrically compatible due to differences in the electrical infrastructure. Network management requires consideration from numerous angles for adequate management to be achieved. Matters such as bandwidth network availability and other considerations are more complex because of the vast geographical distance between each location. These considerations, as well as others, should be taken into account when planning for this type of global network.

Network Physical Aspects

The importance of this section cannot be overstated. When network design commences, hopefully it is done on paper first. I have a philosophy: If I cannot solve a problem or fix something on the marker board (or paper), then I cannot fix the problem in reality. It is easier to work through painstaking areas on marker board than in reality.

Consider the physical part of network design. Before we get to the technical part, we must address fundamentals. Some say I am a master at overstatement; however, in this case enough cannot be said.

Assume you have worked through the needs of the company and customers on paper and you are ready to begin ordering. In this case, assume your physical location is the location where the network will be built. The following should be a minimum checklist you use as a rule of thumb.

1. Is there enough free space so that when equipment begins to arrive it will not impede day-to-day operations?

2. Will any of the equipment arrive on pallets? If multiple pallets of equipment arrive, where will they be put initially when unloaded, and then where will they be stored until the equipment is used?

3. Are stairs used to access the stored equipment? If so, how many?

4. Can a forklift enter the location to unload and load equipment?

5. What is the estimated weight the floor can sustain per square foot?

6. How wide are your doors?

7. Are hand-trucks required for loading and unloading? Are they capable of sustaining the weight of new equipment?

8. Are elevators required to get to a location where the equipment will be stored? How accessible are they? Will using these elevators effect daily operations of your company or another company?

9. Will the storage location be secure until implementation?

10. Does the addition of the new equipment cause any code infringement with fire, police, or any other city, county, state, or federal government entity?

11. If any of the equipment is shipped on pallets or in large boxes, how do you plan to dispose of these items?

12. Is any of the equipment sensitive to any environmental conditions in your location such as heat, cooling, humidity, and so on? Have you verified this with the equipment manufacturer?

13. Do you have a single point of contact with the company shipping equipment to you?

At a minimum, these questions should have clear definable answers before you ever give the OK to receive the first equipment shipment. Your particular location might require additional questions be posed and answered. I encourage you to think through the matter of your physical location. It might even be helpful if you have someone who knows the physical plant well enough to go through this phase with you. Somebody should take responsibility of physical premise evaluation and preparation. If this is not addressed prior to receipt of equipment, one could learn about some matters the hard way and will have to take responsibility like it or not.

Physical Plant Electrical Considerations

It is imperative that you, or the appropriate person, know the electrical capability of your physical location. After you have determined the equipment that is to be deployed, ascertain the specifications about each piece of equipment. When you create the logical network illustration, this information will be critical.

One might think "We have plenty electrical outlets so we will not need additional sources." Here is where the problem begins. Most offices have multiple electrical outlets tied into one circuit breaker. Hence, a given room might have six outlets. Assume that three are being used by a computer, light, and radio. To assume one could add a mid-size photocopier to this room, plug it into an available wall outlet, and run it is at the least misguided. Even the addition of two laser printers could easily overload a single circuit breaker.

My thoughts on network design and electrical considerations begin with determining all pieces of equipment that require electricity. List all the equipment on paper. Next, obtain from the manufacturer the amount of watts, amps, and volts the device will consume upon power-up and in an idle state. You could be in for a surprise.

After you have obtained information about all devices, next determine how power conditioning will be included into the equation. I use both Tipp Lite and Liebert power protection equipment in my network. For power protection equipment to operate properly, one must use it the way the manufacturer designed it.

In the USA, many offices have 20 amp circuit breakers for electrical outlets. Exceptions abound, but this is the general rule. My recommendation is not to exceed 70 to 80 percent of the circuit breaker ability. For example, if you know a given room has four outlets tied into one 20-amp breaker and none of these outlets are currently in use, then you add equipment that will not exceed 15 amps. Why? Odds are when you design your network equipment and install it, 70 to 80 percent of a circuit breaker capacity will not be exceeded. It is possible, however, that someone will come along behind you later and add a few additional items that will use the remaining percentage of the circuit ability.

If no electrical planning went into the location where the network will be installed, you are in for some extra work. Do not assume you can superimpose a network onto an existing site without coping with the electrical factor. If you do not, it will have a plan for you.

Some companies have computer rooms where the bulk of computing/network equipment resides. This room is pre-planned (generally) to handle computing/networking equipment. However, if one does not have such a room or designated area, then you must start from scratch. The best place to begin is to contact the facilities manager. Usually, they will be able to get you in touch with electricians who can answer questions or assist in the planning phase.

Consider my following example. This is a real case scenario in my network.

I have two network printers which are dedicated to the network, and not stand alone in the sense of merely being dedicated to a system. What if I told you these two printers absorb 12.5 to 13.5 amps when powered-up simultaneously? Now assume you have some additional equipment to be added to this outlet. What if you took this equipment and plugged it into the place where you have the network printers connected? Would these additions work without overloading a circuit breaker? This level of detail needs to be obtained and factored into the network design equation.

While plans were formulated for the network, Tektronix test instruments were used to obtain results of existing power supplied to the facility. Consider Figure 4-4.

Figure 4-4 shows a line read using channel one of the Tektronix THS720P scope. (More information about these tools is presented later in this book.) Figure 4-4 reveals a line voltage of 119.7 VAC. This is a *random* line voltage reading. It is a good practice to obtain and maintain preliminary readings prior to installation of any new network equipment. As Figure 4-4 indicates, the frequency is 60 cycles.

Figure 4-5 shows a sine wave reading of the line voltage prior to any network equipment installation. Notice the voltage reading in the upper right hand corner of the graph indicates 122.4 VAC.

Figure 4-4
Initial voltage analysis

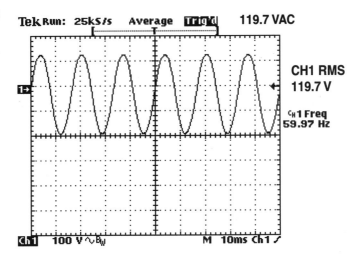

Figure 4-5
Sine wave reading

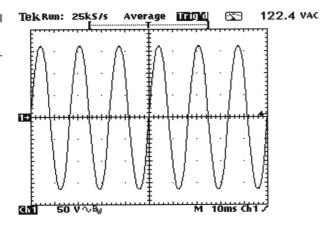

Figure 4-6 is another reading form the same line as the previous readings. This reading is a mathematical analysis of the AC signal. Additional representation is provided later in this book regarding the interpretation of readings like this. For the time being, just realize this information is helpful in the pre-planning stages of the network design implementation.

Figure 4-7 shows additional information obtained about the facilities voltage supply where my network is installed.

Figure 4-7 shows the harmonics from fundamental through the eleventh. Figure 4-8 shows harmonic readings of even harmonics from the second

Figure 4-6

Math calculations of voltage and current

```
Tek AUTO:25kS/s   Average  Trig'd
      RANGE
    Math
 W  =-442.2 w       PF = -0.88
 VA =   501 va      DPF= -0.98
 VAR= 235.5 var     θ  =  169°
```

	Average	Minimum	Maximum
W	-214.1 w	-442.2 w	-25.31 w
VA	243.3 va	55.28 va	501 va
VAR	107.1 var	49.15 var	235.5 var
V	119.7 v	119.5 v	119.9 v
A	2.034 a	461.2 ma	4.193 a

```
Ch1   50 V  Bw Ch2    5 A  Bw M  10ms Ch1
Math       2kW
```

Figure 4-7

Voltage harmonic readings

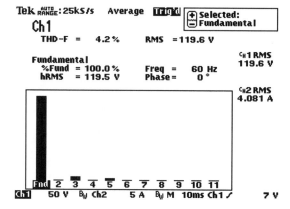

```
Tek AUTO:25kS/s   Average  Trig'd  ⊕ Selected:
      RANGE                        Fundamental
    Ch1
    THD-F =    4.2%      RMS  =119.6 V
                                          Ch1 RMS
    Fundamental                           119.6 V
      %Fund = 100.0%     Freq =   60 Hz
      hRMS  = 119.5 V    Phase=    0°
                                          Ch2 RMS
                                          4.081 A




   Fnd  2  3  4  5  6  7  8  9  10 11
Ch1   50 V  Bw Ch2    5 A  Bw M  10ms Ch1        7 V
```

through the twenty-second. Again, the important thing to understand is this level of information is obtainable by instruments like the Tektronix THS720P oscilloscope and digital multi-meter. Consider Figure 4-9.

Figure 4-9 shows a reading from the input of channel one and channel two. One displays the AC signal, and the other shows the amperage draw on this particular line at this point in time.

Another aspect of electrical consideration has to do with whether or not a raised floor will be used. More information about electrical matters I have experienced are included later in this chapter.

Figure 4-8
Harmonic readings

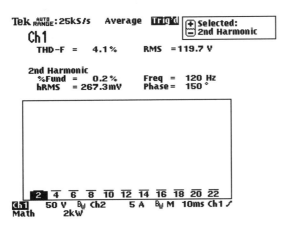

Figure 4-9
Voltage and amperage sample reading

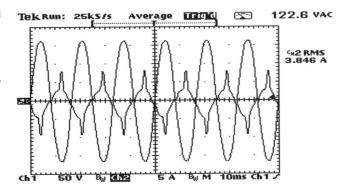

Heating, Ventilation & Air Conditioning (HVAC)

HVAC needs should be included in the design equation. Your location will determine your degree of exploration. For example, if you are building a data center that will have large systems, storage silos, printers and other devices, you may require special HVAC construction.

You might be installing rack cabinets or you might already have rack cabinets installed for your network; if so, consider Figure 4-10.

Figure 4-10 shows a rack cabinet with air blowers in the bottom and nine fans in the fan tray, inside near the top. This level of airflow is required due to the temperatures reached in the cabinet.

Most equipment installed today has circulation requirements. It is a mistake to overlook this aspect when designing your network. For example, the network servers used in my network have stated specifications as to how

Figure 4-10
Air flow within
rack cabinets

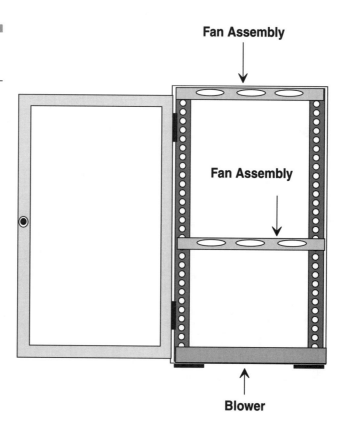

Fan Assembly

Fan Assembly

Blower

much space should be between it and other objects. The same is true for my UPS, printers, monitors, and other devices. One way of obtaining valid temperature readings is through a probe. Figure 4-11 is an example of a temperature reading from within my network lab.

Figure 4-11 shows a temperature of 74.0 degrees Fahrenheit. I recommend obtaining equipment to monitor temperature readings at all times in your facility.

HVAC requirements go beyond what I've mentioned here. I recommend having one person highly skilled in HVAC that can participate in the network design project.

Electrical Terminology

If you are new to electricity, you could be concerned. Don't loose your respect for electricity. If you don't give it respect and become careless, it will take respect. To understand and work with electricity one needs to understand some terminology and concepts. After these terms and concepts are understood; then application of knowledge can be realized. Consider the terminology presented here:

Alternating Current (AC).   Electric current that is continually varying in value and reversing its direction of flow at regular intervals, usually in a sinusoidal manner. Each repetition from zero to a maximum in one direction and then to a maximum in the other direction and back to zero is called a cycle.

Figure 4-11
Sample reading from
the test lab

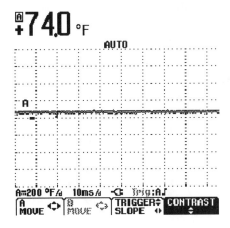

AC Frequency.   This is the speed at which an AC voltage or current waveform repeats itself. Frequency is measured in hertz.

Amperage.   The amount of current in amperes

Ampere.   A practical unit of electrical current. After ampere of current is 6.24 × 10–18 electrons passing one point in 1s., it equals 1C/s. This is the result of 1 Volt across a resistance of 1 ohm.

Apparent Power.   This is the product of current and voltage, and is expressed in kVA. It is the real power (kW) divided by the *power factor* (PF).

Atom.   The smallest particle into which an element can be divided and still retain the chemical properties of that element

Balanced Current.   This refers to a current following in the two conductors of a balanced line so that, at every point along the line, they are equal in magnitude and opposite in direction.

Balanced Line.   This is a transmission line that consist of two conductors which are capable of being operated so that the voltages of the two conductors at any transverse plane are equal in magnitude and opposite in polarity with respect to the ground. The currents in the two conductors are then equal in magnitude and opposite in direction.

Balanced Voltages.   This refers to voltages that are equal in magnitude and opposite in polarity with respect to ground. They are also called push-pull voltages.

Brownout.   Normally a voltage reduction initiated by the utility to counter excessive demand on its electric power generation and distribution system

Conductor.   A material that serves as a conduit for electric current easily because it offers little electrical resistance. Conductors include: tin, metals, salt water, aluminum, copper, gold, nickel, and platinum.

Current.   In electricity, it refers to the flow of electrons, or the movement thereof, through a conductive material. It is the flow of electrons or holes measured in amperes, notated by (A) or in fractions of an ampere such as milliamperes (mA), microamperes (uA), nanoamperes (nA), or picoamperes (pA). Current can be induced by the application of an electric field through a conductor, by changing the electric field through a conductor, or by changing the electric field across a capacitor (which is known as displacement current).

Direct Current (DC). Electric current that flows in one direction

Electric Field. The region around an electrically charged body in which other charged bodies are acted on by an attracting or repelling force

Electricity. A fundamental quantity realized in nature that consists of electrons and protons either at rest or in motion. Electricity at rest (not in motion) has an electric field that possesses potential energy and can exert force. Electricity in motion (not at rest) has the characteristics of an electric and magnetic field that possess potential energy and can exert force.

Electron. An elementary atomic partical that carries the smallest negative electric charge. It is highly mobile and orbits the nucleus of an atom.

Frequency. The number of complete cycles per unit of time for a periodic quantity such as alternating current, sound waves, or radio waves. A frequency of 1 cycle per second is 1 hertz. This is represented by the letter f.

Harmonic. A sinusoidal component of a periodic wave with a frequency that is an integral multiple of the fundamental frequency. The frequency of the second harmonic is twice that of the fundamental frequency of the first harmonic. Also called harmonic component or harmonic frequency

Harmonic Analysis. Any method for identifying and evaluating the harmonics that make up a complex form of voltage, current, or some other varying quantity

Hertz. The SI unit of frequency equal to 1 cycle per second

Impedance. This is the total opposition offered by a component or circuit to the flow of an alternating or varying current. It is represented by the letter Z. Impedance is expressed in ohms and is the combination of resistance R and reactance.

Inductance. This is the property of a circuit or element that opposes a change in current flow. Inductance causes current changes to lag behind voltage changes. Inductance is measured in henrys, millihenrys, and microhenrys. It is represented by the letter L.

kilo. Meaning one thousand

kVA. One thousand volt-amperes. This is a term for rating devices. The number is derived by multiplying the output in amperes by its rate of operating voltage.

Linear. A term used to refer to a relationship in which one function is directly proportional to another function providing a straight sloped line when plotted on a graph.

Magnetic Field. Any space or region that a magnetic force is exerted on moving electric charges. This field can be produced by a current-carrying coil or conductor, by a permanent magnet, or by the earth itself.

Non-Linear. Anything with this characteristic is not directly proportional to its compliment.

Non-Linear Element. This refers to an element in which an increase in applied voltage does not produce a proportional increase in current.

Non-Linear Load. This is a load for which the relationship between voltage and current is not a linear function An example of non-linear loads could be fluorescent lighting or UPS systems. This type of load cause abnormal heating and voltage distortion.

Ohm. This is the SI unit of resistance and impedance. This is electric resistance between two points of a conductor when a constant potential difference of 1 Volt applied to these points produces in the conductor a current of 1 amp; this means the conductor is not the seat of any electromotive force.

Period. The time required for one complete cycle of a regularly repeated series of events

Photon. This is a quantum of electromagnetic radiation equal to Planck's constant multiplied by the frequency in hertz. Electromagnetic radiation can be considered as photons of light, X-rays, gamma rays, or radio rays.

Power. The time rate of doing work or the speed in which work is done. This is represented by the letter P and measured in watts.

Power Factor. The term power factor refers to the extent that the voltage zero differs from the current zero. In AC circuits, inductance and capacitance cause a point where the voltage wave passes through zero to differ from the point where the current wave passes through zero. One complete cycle is 360 degrees; consequently, the difference between zero points (for example voltage and current) can be expressed by an angle. The power factor is the cosine of the angle between zero points and is expressed as a decimal fraction of .8 or 80 percent. The power factor is the ratio of kW and kVA. The kW equals the kVA multiplied by the power factor.

Proton. An elementary particle that has a positive charge equal in magnitude to the negative charge of the electron. The atomic number of an element indicates the number of protons in the nucleus of each atom of that element. The rest mass of a proton is $1.67 \times 10-24g$ or 1836.13 times that of an electron.

Reactance. This is the opposition to the flow of alternating current by pure inductance or capacitance in a circuit expressed in ohms. It is the component of impedance that is not due to resistance.

Resistance. This is the opposition that a device or material offers to the flow of direct current, measured in ohms, kiloohms, or even megaohms. In AC circuits, resistance is the real component of impedance.

Root-Mean-Squared (RMS). This is the square root of the average of the squares of a series of related values. The effective value of an alternating current, corresponding to the DC value that will produce the same heating effect. The RMS value is computed as the square root of the average of the squares of the instantaneous amplitude for one complete cycle. For a sine wave, the RMS value is 0.707 multiplied by the peak value. Unless otherwise specified, alternating quantities are assumed to be the RMS values. Another name used to refer to this is effective value. In simpler terms, this is the effective value of voltage, current, and power when they are expressed with such.

SAG. An AC power line under a voltage condition that lasts more than 1/60 of a second. A condition lasting longer than this is referred to as a brownout.

Sinusoidal. Refers to the varying in proportion to the sine of an angle or time function. An ordinary alternating current is considered sinusoidal.

Spike. A short duration transient whose amplitude considerably exceeds the average amplitude of the associated pulse or signal.

Surge. A long duration over voltage or over current condition

Time. The measure of a duration of an event. The fundamental unit of time is the second.

Transient. A sudden very brief spike of high voltage on a power line caused by lightning, electrostatic discharge, or power-line switching.

Unbalanced Line. This refers to a transmission line that conducts voltage on its two conductors that are not equal with respect to the ground.

Volt. The SI unit of voltage or potential difference. The difference in electrical potential between two points of a conducting wire carrying a constant current of 1 amp when the power dissipated between these points is equal to 1 watt.

Volt-ampere. The unit of apparent power in an AC circuit that contains reactance. Apparent power is equal to the voltage in volts multiplied by the current in amperes, without considering phase.

Watt. The watt is the unit of electric power. It gives rise in one second the energy of one joule. In a AC circuit, the true power is effective volts multiplied by effective amperes, and then multiplied by the circuit power factor.

Wave. This is a propagated disturbance whose intensity at any point in the medium is a function of time, and the intensity at a given instant is a function of the power of the point. A wave can be electric, electromagnetic, acoustic, or mechanical.

Practical Information

If you read many books, you probably realize some of them have little practical value. I am attempting to provide you with practical information in this book. I realize many of you do not have a background in electricity. Thus I am providing basic information here.

Wire

The focus of this section is on electrical wire. Many type of wires exist. Specifically, I want to explain wire sizes and types. Understanding electrical wire is easy. For example, many types of common table lamps have a 14 to 18 guage wire.

Wire is generally referred to by the *Average Wire Gauge* (AWG) number. The smaller the number the larger the wire and hence, the more voltage and current it can accommodate. Consider

26	14	3
24	12	2
22	10	1

20	8	0
18	6	00
16	4	000

A 26-gauge wire is very small, in fact it is smaller than the wire in most telephone cords that connect a handset to the base. Much of the 10BASE-T wire is between 20 and 24 gauge in size. As mentioned previously, many ordinary table lamps are wired with 14 to 18 gauge wire. Some extension cords that can be purchased in stores are 14 to 18 gauge. These are considered *general purpose*.

Most houses are wired with 12-gauge wire; some use 10 gauge. A 12-gauge wire for an extension cord would be considered adequate for many shop type purposes. Many outdoor use extension cords are 12 gauge.

Ten (10) gauge wire is fairly heavy duty. Going up in capability and down in numeric order are 8, 6, 4, 2, and 0 gauge. Wire sizes less than 10 become increasingly large and can carry significant voltage and current. Voltage and current are two different things. Let me illustrate this. Consider Figure 4-12.

As I write this, I am listening to an ordinary AM/FM radio/cassette player. It operates on 120 VAC or batteries. Figure 4-12 shows the voltage, frequency, and the amperage the radio uses. Technically, the voltage and frequency are what is available at the wall outlet. The amperage reading is what the radio is using to operate. Notice the amperage draw as indicated from channel 2 is 191.7 milliamps. This is not very much, and rightfully so —it is simply a desktop radio. You might be thinking this is odd. But wait! Consider Figure 4-13.

Figure 4-13 is the readings I took from a microwave oven! Yes, I took the microwave from the kitchen counter and brought it into the lab. I connected

Figure 4-12
Sample reading #1

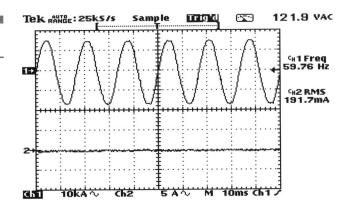

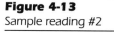

Figure 4-13
Sample reading #2

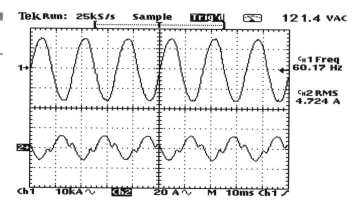

it to the test outlet, and no other device was connected except the Tektronix THS720P power analyzer. Notice the voltage, frequency, and amperage readings. The microwave is drawing 4.724 amps as shown by channel 2, indicated on the lower portion of the figure. This illustration is the snapshot just after initial power-on of the microwave.

Figure 4-13 shows the reading of the microwave oven, and this time the current draw is 7.764 amps. This reading was taken with the microwave in operation, not just after initial power-on. It sustains a significant current draw.

These illustrations are important, because they illustrate the difference in device current requirements. Amperage is how much current a device uses. Yes, this is a loose definition, but stay with me. Current is:

"... the flow of electrons, notated by (A) or in fractions of an ampere such as milliamperes (mA), microamperes (uA), nanoamperes (nA), or picoamperes (pA). Current can be induced by the application of an electric field through a conductor or by changing the electric field through a conductor or by changing the electric field across a capacitor (which is known as displacement current)."

The measure of current (the amperage draw) is technically "how much" electricity a given device uses. For example, the AM/FM radio obviously uses less electricity than the microwave as Figures 4-12 and 4-13 show. How can this be? Don't they both use 120 VAC? The measure of *how much* electricity is used is generally referred to as current. Technically the current draw is referred to in *amperage* (amps). Now, the more current or higher the amperage rating the more electrons are flowing through a wire. The more electrons flowing through a wire the hotter the wire gets. Consequently, the more amps required for a given device to function the larger wire size required to deliver that number of amps.

Most wire sizes have an amperage rating. Ampacity is the word used to refer to the amount of amps a given wire can accommodate. Generally, the smaller the wire size number, such as 6 or 2, the more amps the wire can accommodate. Different tables apply when measuring wire size and amp capacity. Whether or not the wire (also called conductor) is single or multiple, or operating in free air or otherwise factors into the capacity of the wire.

Table 4-1 illustrates the current carrying capacity of 2 or 3 conductors. This chart should be taken as a reference and not literal because length of the cable, heat, and other environmental conditions affect the flow of electrons through the wire; however, this is a good rule-of-thumb chart to have handy. The measurement shown reflects the *Average Wire Gauge* (AWG) in Neoprene jacket. Consider the following as a general reference.

Table 4-1
Rule-of-thumb
amperage capacities

2 or 3 Conductors AWG	Current Capacity
22	6
20	8
18	14
16	18
14	25
12	30
10	40
8	55
6	75
4	95
3	110
2	130
1	150
0	170
00	195
000	225
0000	260

Let me repeat, always factor into the equation the current draw. The longer the wire run, the greater (larger) the wire size needed to deliver multiplied by number of amps. Think about this; it makes sense. Amperage is the movement of electrons. Anytime the length of something is extended, more resistance enters into the equation. Consider the following real world example I encountered in 1986.

In December 1986, the religious group I was affiliated with at the time was going to put on a Christmas special. During the preparation for the musicians, speakers, singers, and so on, we moved considerable electrical equipment to a new location. During setup of the *public address* (PA) equipment, the person directing the show realized we needed an extension cord to provide electricity to the PA equipment. This person proceeded to obtain an extension cord and began connecting everything together. The second day of setup I realized this person had used three 100-foot 14-gauge extension cords to supply electricity to the power amplifier for the PA equipment. I knew from former education and experience that this was not going to work; the voltage drop was too great at that distance. I tried to inform the person of the problem, but he didn't do anything. (I think he thought I was too young to understand.) I finally told him: "Go ahead, the power amps will roll over and go belly-up." He looked at me askance and went on with final touches. This person was also notorious for doing things without trial runs. So, the presentation began and about two minutes into the beginning guess what happened? That's right, the power amps went belly-up. The voltage drop was too great.

Why the personal story? There are a couple of reasons. First, sensitive equipment such as computers, power amplifiers, and the like are very sensitive to voltage drops whether they are the result of a wire that is too long or for other reasons. Second, just because you have access to an extension cord does not mean your equipment will operate correctly. The previous chart of wire size and ampacity indicated a 20-gauge wire could accommodate 8 amps. I doubt this is the case if the 20-gauge wire is 400 feet long! See what I mean?

Still another factor that comes into play with the wire size and ampacity is the number of conductors. For example, some wire has only one conductor, some two, some three, some four, and so on. This factors into the equation as well.

As I mentioned previously, temperature is a factor in the capability of wire. This factors into the equation. Different types of wire shielding work differently according to temperature. Consider Table 4-2.

Table 4-2
Examples of material
& operating
temperatures

Material Type	Operating Temperature Range*
Cross-Linked Polyethylene	−55 to 150
Hermetic	−60 to 125
Hypalon	−30 to 105
EPDM	−60 to 150
Neoprene	−30 to 90
PVC	−35 to 105
Silicone Braided	−75 to 200
Silicone Braidless	−75 to 200
Teflon	−100 to 260

*Temperature Readings are in Celsius.

To convert Celsius into Fahrenheit subtract 32 from the Celsius reading and that is the degrees in Fahrenheit.

The information presented here is from one particular wire vendor; however, other wire vendors refer to wire by type as well and might differ.

Wire used in houses and commercial buildings is typically ROMEX. This is a stiff outside jacket used to wrap the wire. Inside, each conductor is insulated and the earth ground is typically wrapped in a form of heavy gauge paper. In contrast, many ordinary extension cords are a type of SJ cable. This type of jacket is not as stiff as ROMEX and is relatively flexible. Furthermore, another type of jacket called SO and SO-W is more pliable, like rubber. Most of them are oil- and water-resistant. This type of jacketing is used in many commercial grade extension cords.

In summary, the important considerations to remember with wire are

1. Wire size and length determine current capacity.
2. Wire has a voltage rating.
3. The smaller the wire number, the larger the wire.
4. The number of conductors effect the ampacity.
5. The longer the cable length, the more resistance and voltage drop will occur.

Site Wiring

Houses, commercial buildings, and the majority of building facilities in modern cities today are already wired for electricity. Many of them are similar. If you want accuse me of over generalization, consider my explanation here of a highlighted overview of my house used as an example. Consider Figure 4-14.

Figure 4-14 shows a voltage reading of 122.2 VAC. I took this reading inside the load center where the wire connects to a breaker supplying the outlets in my dining room. It is simply a typical reading; most likely the reading of this line taken at a dining room outlet fed by it would yield the same results. Consider Figure 4-15.

Figure 4-15 shows 244.3 volts and a 59.97 cycle reading. I took this voltage measurement at the lines feeding my house load center. Consider Figure 4-16.

Figure 4-14
Load center voltage reading

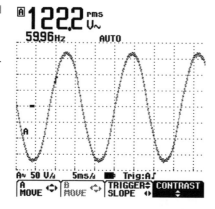

Figure 4-15
Input voltage reading from electric company

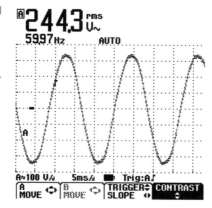

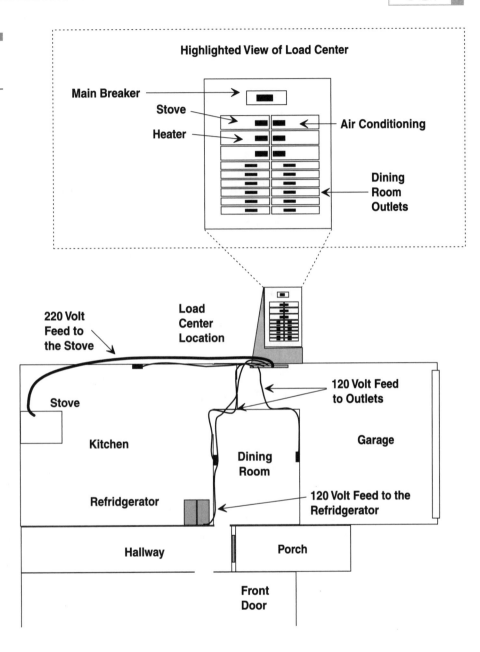

Figure 4-16
Highlighted view of
load center & wiring

Figure 4-16 shows a highlighted view of the load center, the garage,
kitchen, dining room, hallway, porch, front door, and other noted items.
Notice the load center is in the garage. I have illustrated two AC outlets in
the dining room, and this is a fairly accurate representation of where they

are. I show a stove and refrigerator in the kitchen. Notice the stove is wired to the load center and the indication is that it is 220 VAC. The wire size indicated to the stove is larger than to the outlets. The wire size to the stove is a 4 gauge and the size going to the outlets is a 12 gauge. The refrigerator is wired directly to the load center as well and is 120 VAC, using 6-gauge wire. The AC outlets are 120 VAC. The wiring is actually the view as it looks in the attic. A significant point, beside some raw facts, is that many of the outlets in the house are wired in parallel, meaning multiple outlets run from a single breaker. Why is this important? Because, it is similar in the commercial world. Granted in the commercial world more dedicated outlets exist, but the primary reason for this is to save money. Unless you custom build, most builders will install the outlets standard in the industry and to electrical code. Notice also in Figure 4-16 that the stove has a dedicated outlet, along with the heater and air conditioning. Consider Figure 4-17.

Figure 4-17 shows a detailed view of the load center. Notice three leads come in from the electric meter: two 120 VAC feeds and a neutral. Notice the illustration shows the cable going to the dining room outlet, and the hot lead connects to a breaker, whereas the neutral and ground connect to the neutral busbar as shown. Beneath the breakers shown, two busbars carry the voltage and that a single main circuit breaker exists at the top of the load center. This breaker is the single *switch* used to turn on or off the feed to the entire house.

Most load centers are similar to this. They do differ when working with much higher voltage, but commonalities do exist. Consider Figure 4-18.

Figure 4-18 shows the voltage reading at the top of the busbar where the hot feeds come in from the electric meter. Notice I obtained a reading of 243.7 volts at this location. The cable size coming into the load center from the electric meter is 00.

So what is the purpose in this? First, to illustrate some fundamental concepts that you might not normally see as a network or computer educated person. Second, to be aware that electricity is serious business, and if you are not educated about it, always rely on someone who is. Third, these illustrations let you see that not all outlets or even lighting for that matter have a dedicated circuit. Furthermore, most the wiring in my house is 12-gauge, ROMEX wire. A 12-gauge wire is a significant size to use in a house; but considering the various loads that network equipment can generate, one might need a larger wire. Does this matter? Consider what happens if you plug two microwave ovens into the same circuit that is only 20 amps. At 7.764 amps per microwave, as Figure 4-13 shows you, two microwaves would be far beyond a 50 percent utilization of that breaker. Odds are that one more

Figure 4-17
Load center wiring:
detailed view

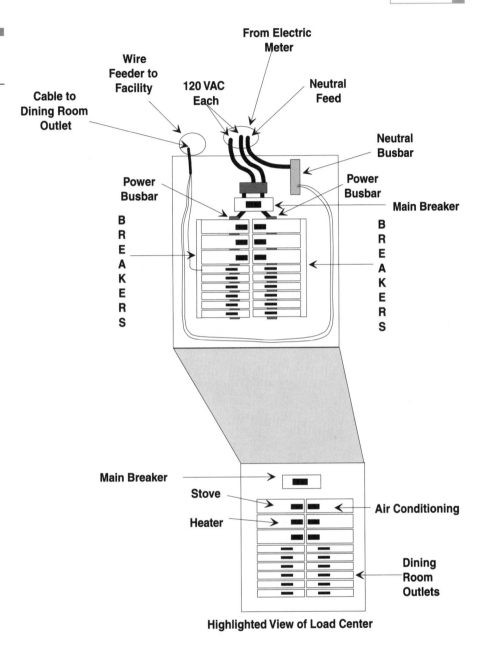

Figure 4-17
Load center wiring:
detailed view

Highlighted View of Load Center

device on that breaker would over load it. Remember this when you begin working with laser or thermal printers. They tend to draw significant current, both at start-up and during the cycles of heating the drum.

Figure 4-18

Voltage feeding the
load center

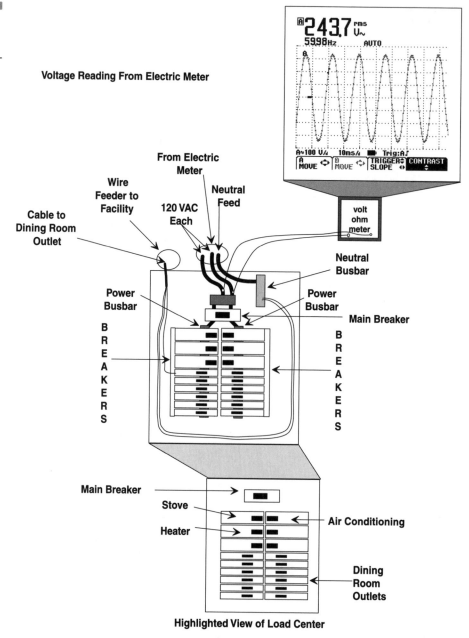

Voltage Reading From Electric Meter

Highlighted View of Load Center

Furthermore, I present this part for you to consider, in light of the
premises where you work. If you think of it with the perspective I give here,
you'll have a healthier view of your environment.

Harmonics

Why harmonics? Harmonic evaluation reveals the quality of power. Depending on your site, this could be very significant; the more sensitive the equipment, the more susceptible it is to harmonic distortion. Remember the definition of harmonics is

> a sinusoidal component of a periodic wave with a frequency that is an integral multiple of the fundamental frequency. The frequency of the second harmonic is twice that of the fundamental frequency or the first harmonic. Also called harmonic component and harmonic frequency.

Remember also that harmonic analysis refers to any method used to identify and evaluate the harmonics (frequencies) that make up a complex form of voltage, current, or some other varying quantity. Consider Figure 4-19.

Figure 4-19 shows channel one and two monitored on the Tektscope. This is a voltage harmonic reading from the fundamental harmonic to the eleventh. Notice the RMS harmonic is 117.9, whereas the RMS voltage is 118 VAC. Now consider Figure 4-20.

Figure 4-20 shows the amperage harmonics when the network printer is at idle after a number of pages have been printed. The RMS amperage reading is 1.038 amps as channel two indicates, whereas the RMS harmonic amperage reading is 835.mA. Notice the scope has also calculated the RMS voltage from channel one and it reads 118.2 VAC. Consider Figure 4-21.

Figure 4-19
1st through 11th harmonics from the base voltage

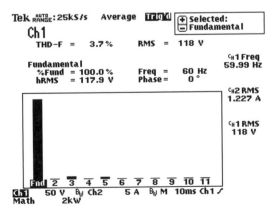

Figure 4-20
Amperage harmonics
example

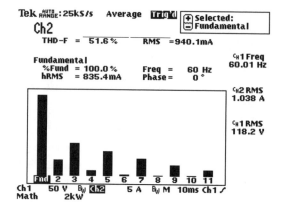

Figure 4-20
Amperage harmonics
example

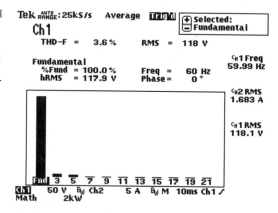

Figure 4-21
Odd harmonics from
fundamental through
21 on voltage

Figure 4-21 shows the odd harmonics of the voltage reading from the fundamental harmonic to the twenty-first. This level of detail is quite helpful for those who need to analyze their power quality. Clean power is important, and ascertaining the harmonic values of various readings is important in the evaluation of the power.

Ground Loops

Ground loops might be a first for you if your background is not in electricity or electronics. Simply put, ground loops occur when multiple grounds exist, and a potential difference exists between them. Be aware that you can incur grounding from network cabling and through your electrical wiring. Hopefully the two don't conflict.

Ground loops can eat away at your bandwidth, because they will inject distortion into a line. Likewise should the ground loop be significant enough, it can cause power quality degradation. Be aware that the potential exists to pick up grounding in equipment wherever it might reside. It is best to check the grounding of you telephone wiring, network cabling, and check for stray wires that could create such an environment.

I encourage you to know early on in your project information such as the electrical requirements you have (what to consider and how to calculate these are in the following section). In addition, you should know the wiring of the existing facility, estimates (if possible) for power quality, and information for planning purposes on the grounding of the facility.

Estimating Power Requirements

I think you would be well advised to consult an electrician if you are planning a network, attempting to make additions to an existing network, or simply thinking about adding components to your office environment. So many times I have seen people who take electricity for granted and end up making mistakes. I am including some additional information here to assist you in you efforts.

Equipment Category & List

If you have not inventoried your network, you should. Here is a practical approach to direct your endeavors. First, it is a good idea to categorize. The categories I derived and worked from are

- Printers
- Computers
- Peripherals
- Required 90 percent of the time
- Required 50 percent of the time
- Required less than 50 percent of the time
- Equipment in multiple locations
- Equipment in one location

- Number of hours afford to lose work
- Amount of money you can afford to lose

This list is where I began categorizing to plan for power requirements. If you do not have an inventory list yet, start one. If you are starting in the middle of an established network, then begin first by inventorying the equipment you currently have. How many computers and monitors do you have? How many printers are networked and how many are stand-alone? Is it feasible for all or some of them to use the same power source? List your peripherals as well. It would be a very good idea to access the original vendor documentation and/or reference the information on the equipment label, and document the electrical and environmental requirements.

Now, list the equipment required 50 percent and 90 percent of the time. In other words, if a PC is used all day everyday in your environment, then list it under the 90 percent column. On the other hand, if you have a system that is used occasionally, then list it appropriately.

It is also wise to list the equipment you have, or will have, by it's installation location. This is important because networks generally span multiple facilities and sometimes multiple locations. You may be required to purchase multiple types of equipment in order to get the coverage you need.

Another important issue is to ask and answer the question how much money can you afford to loose if your equipment is *cooked* by way of a lightning hit. Don't laugh. I know people who lost equipment who did not plan ahead and prepare for this scenario.

Similar to loosing equipment is the number of hours you can loose in lack of productive work. How many man-hours can you afford to loose? If you have 25 people, all using a computer, and you loose an entire day, this equates to 25 man-days.

Calculations

Here I present some information that Liebert helped me with. I selected a 15 kVa UPS from Liebert and use it in my network. First, one question that needs to be asked is whether you have one or three phase equipment. Most of you will have one phase. Be sure you obtain what is considered steady-state operating amperage. This is not the circuit breaker rating, surge current, or inrush current. Use this number in the amperage portion of the equation. If you do not use steady-state current, erroneous conclusions might result. To determine the amount of UPS coverage you need use the following equation:

$$kVA = \frac{V \times A}{1000}$$

The number you arrive at should have about 20 percent to 50 percent added to this. The number you arrive at is the approximate size you need. Now, reflect back to the kVA equation. Load balancing your equipment through the use of a three phase UPS might well be a better solution to your needs than merely sizing a UPS required to sustain the largest load. This topic goes beyond the scope of the purpose here; I recommend contacting a qualified electrician to assist you with these matters.

Types of Power Protection

Many times I have been party to meetings where power protection was the topic for discussion. I have realized that having an adequate understanding of the terminology in a given arena is helpful to understand ideas. Here are some of the basic types of power protection and their purpose.

Surge Protectors

Surge protectors protect against surges. Spikes (sudden voltage increases) are typically inhibited by surge protection devices. This is probably the minimum level of protection you need. Even computer use at home should have this minimum level of protection.

Voltage Regulators

Voltage regulators have the ability to maintain a certain voltage and current level for the device drawing on the electrical source. A voltage regulator is a good device to use with printers, especially laser printers.

Uninterruptible Power Supplies (UPS)

A UPS is a device that is prepared to provide interim power. UPSs are not a solution to power outages; they are an interim solution to bridge the time when power ceases and then is restored. Large UPSs might be able to provide a considerable number of minutes even hours of uptime. However, UPS use pre-supposes power from the electric company will be restored or alternative power supply will be provided from a source such as a generator.

Generators

Generators create or *generate* electricity. They are typically used as alternative power sources in case the main source of power fails. If big enough, a generator can keep generating electric power indefinitely—assuming you can provide the diesel or gasoline to keep it operating. Generators are typically reserved for use in large commercial settings.

Transfer Switch Gear

Transfer switch gear is used to change the source of electric power to a generator. Switch gear does what its name implies; that is, switch.

Parallel Switch Gear

Parallel switch gear is used in settings where multiple generators are used in parallel with the other. This is advanced technology and not for the faint hearted. Generators, transfer switches, and paralleling UPSs are complex. These types of implementations are most always found in complex commercial settings. An example of such could be a hospital complex.

The UPS in my Network

Because of the amount of equipment in my network, I chose a Liebert 15 Kva UPS. Consider Figure 4-22.

Figure 4-22 shows the network equipment used. It also shows the Liebert UPS as the power protection device used to accommodate all the equipment in the network. Consider Figure 4-23.

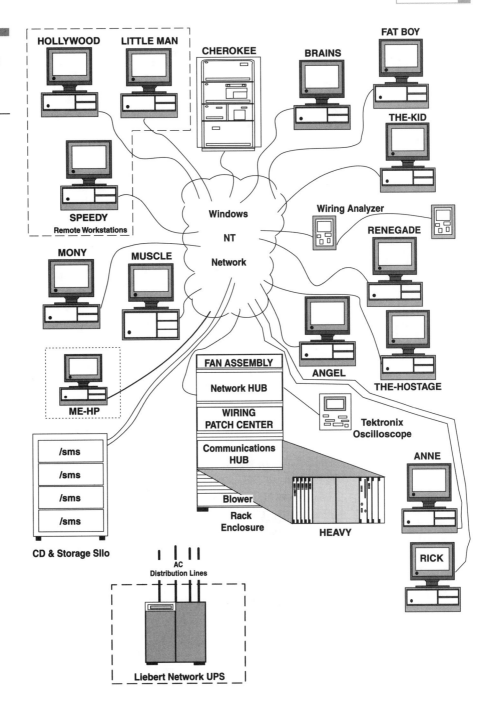

Figure 4-22
Example of amount
of network equip-
ment protected by
UPS

Figure 4-23

Rear view of UPS

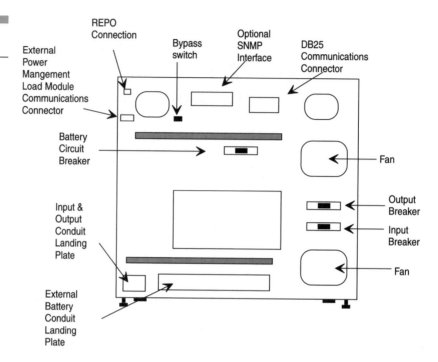

Figure 4-23

Rear view of UPS

Figure 4-23 shows the rear view of the UPS I use in my network. A great advantage of the UPS is the accessibility of the components needing accessibility.

After sizing the UPS, I determined I needed a 15 kVA. It arrived weighing in at over 800 pounds. With the person who made the delivery helping, it only took an hour to get the well-packed UPS in the prepared place I had for it. A couple weeks prior to the UPS arriving, I located the place I wanted to receive it from the shipper. I marked off the locations so enough space would not be obstructed. Doing this level of pre-planning saved a lot of time. It only took about an hour to get the UPS into the place I had prepared to receive it. It then took approximately another hour to get it unpacked and in its final resting place.

Moving an 800 pound UPS is not something I want to do every day of the week. Now that you are reading this, take the time to pre-plan for yourself. If you do, the people who work with you will be all the happier. If you do not, well, you just might have a sizable amount of weight arrive on a pallet and have nowhere to put it.

Another function of the UPS used in my network is its participation in the network through the SNMP interface. The UPS is functional with existing SNMP protocol standards. It supports standard MIB definitions and inter-operates well in the network.

The 15kVA UPS requires wiring into the load center of the facility where it is operating. I recommend you obtain a licensed electrician to assist you in your pre-planning and especially during the installation of the UPS. Working with equipment like this is no trivial task and should not be played with because it can kill you. I don't mean to promote fear, I simply want you to understand that wiring in a UPS the size of the one I have is not for those who are not trained in electricity. Consider Figure 4-24.

Figure 4-24 shows three parts. First, it shows the AC load center that feeds AC to the facility where the network is located. Second, it shows a highlighted view of the UPS wired into the load center. Then, it shows a conceptual view of how some of the equipment is connected to the UPS.

This is the basic overview of how the UPS fits into the network. It is more complex than this because of all the equipment the UPS protects. Since the UPS is capable of protecting the entire network, approximately four output feeds (lines with outlets) were required to accommodate all the components.

This is an overview of the UPS used in this network. Many more details could be included, but the purpose here is to assist you in conceptually understanding the placement and purpose of the UPS. Your situation will vary, however consider how I implemented the UPS here as a reference point for thought.

SUMMARY

Electrical matters must be dealt with before you begin to work with network equipment. You can either deal with them ahead of time or you can wait and let them deal with you! I recommend the former over the latter.

This chapter presented more than just information on electrical matters. I tried to condense a lot of material into what has been helpful to me over a long period of time. The topics I included are both a good reference and planning tool when you need to apply some "how to" with your job. Nevertheless, the remaining chapters in this book cover different topics, but collectively the chapters of this book represent years of experience.

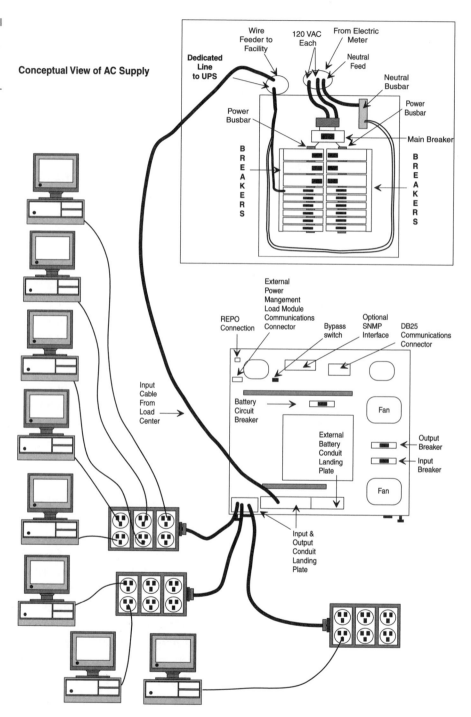

Conceptual View of AC Supply

Voice Over IP

Voice Over Internet Protocol (VOIP) has emerged over the past few years to become more of a topic of conversation. At this point in time, much work is being done behind the scenes so to speak, as well as products being brought to market. My purpose in this chapter is to provide the reader with the following information:

First, I have presented a brief of VOIP related standards and information about them, which you can use to further your study in this topic.

Second, I have included a vendor list with web addresses for the reader to obtain further information if desired.

Third, I have included a VOIP architecture example for your consideration. It is the highlights of a VOIP implementation.

Fourth, I have included a section presenting VOIP Architecture and Future Communications.

Fifth, I have included excerpts from the RFC on Simple Gateway Control Protocol, compliments of The Internet Society. The purpose of including this information is that some of the information in the RFC is used as "foundational" information by numerous vendors. Many developers and those who troubleshoot this technology rely on this information due to the depth provided in it.

VOIP Standards

This section includes basic information on the recommendations that describe IP telephony standards. In addition, there is information here as to how this technology can be implemented on top of existing networks and protocols. The following explanations are "summary" in nature, and consequently I refer you to the original ITU standards for more detailed information.

To send audio across a converged data network, the analog audio waveform has to be encoded into binary bits of data that can be processed by a computer. It is sampled, quantized (assigned discrete bit values), and compressed to take up a minimum amount of bandwidth. When the sound reaches its destination, the process is reversed.

Compression programs (the "co" in codecs) take advantage of pauses between words, periods of silence, and predictable changes in amplitudes to cut the bandwidth requirement for transmitting human speech in half.

The following is a list of some popular *International Telecommunication Union* (ITU) codec standards. Many vendors with VOIP products rely on one or more of these standards and consequently I include their name and location where additional information can be obtained.

These are International Telecommunication Union (ITU) standards:

G.711 3.4 kHz 56K, 64Kbps PCM Simple amplitude compression; Widely deployed in PSTN

G.728 3.4 kHz 16Kbps LD-CELP Same quality as G.711; Low bit rate video conferencing

G.723.1 3.4 kHz 48K, 56K, 64Kbps LP-MLQ Near toll-quality; VOIP Forum base line codec

G.729 and G.729A 3.4 kHz 8Kbps CS-ACELP Lower latency and slightly better quality than G.723.1; Newer IP telephony applications

Recommendation G.711

The ITU standardized *Pulse Code Modulation* (PCM) as G.711. It enables toll-quality audio signal with a bandwidth of 3.4 kHz to be encoded for transmission of data rates of 56 Kbps or 64 Kbps. G.711 uses A-law or Mu-law for simple amplitude compression, and it is the base line requirement for most ITU multimedia communication standards. PCM is the most popular method of encoding analog audio signals and is widely used by the public telephone network. However, PCM does not support bandwidth compression, so other encoding techniques such as *Adaptive Differential PCM* (ADPCM) use estimates based on two consecutive quantized samples to reduce bandwidth.

Recommendation G.728

G.728 encodes toll-quality audio signals with a bandwidth of 3.4 kHz for transmission at a data rate of 16 Kbps. It is commonly used in video conferencing systems that operate at 56 Kbps or 64 Kbps. With a higher computational requirement, G.728 provides the quality of G.711 at one-fourth of the required data rate.

Recommendation G.723.1

G.723.1 defines how an audio signal with a bandwidth of 3.4 kHz can be encoded for transmission at data rates of 5.3 Kbps and 6.4 Kbps. G.723.1 requires a very low transmission rate, while delivering near toll-quality audio. G.723.1 has been selected by the Voice Over IP Forum as the baseline codec for low bit rate IP telephony applications.

Recommendations G.729 and G.729A

Chosen as the official ITU standards in 1996, these recommendations encode near toll-quality audio signals with a bandwidth of 3.4 kHz for transmission at a data rate of 8 Kbps. G.729A requires lower computational power than G.729 and G.723.1. Both G.729 and G.729A have lower latency (the time it takes to convert from analog to digital) than G.723.1. G.729A is expected to have a major impact on compressing voice for transmission over wireless networks.

Recommendation H.323

The *International Telecommunications Union* (ITU) has combined various low-level standards into umbrella standards, including H.323 for multimedia over LANs with No Guaranteed Quality of Service. The H323 standard was approved in October of 1996.

The H.323 standard supports multimedia over Ethernet, Fast Ethernet, FDDI, and Token Ring LANs. In the context of H.323, LANs also include inter-networks composed of multiple LANs interconnected by switches, bridges, and routers. H.323 is a significant specification, because it enables the development of a new generation of LAN-based multimedia applications. The H.323 Version 2 standard was approved in February of 1998. It contributes even more functions in the areas of supplemental services, security, and *registration, admission, and status* (RAS) protocol.

Succinctly, the H.323 standard defines four major components for a LAN-based multimedia conferencing system: terminals, gateways, *multipoint control units* (MCUs), and gatekeepers. Terminals, gateways, and MCUs are considered endpoints, because they can generate and/or terminate H.323 sessions. The gatekeeper is considered a network entity, because it cannot be called, but might be addressed to perform specific functions such as address translation or access control. Each component is presented here in greater detail.

H.323 Terminal

All H.323 implementations are required to have, at a minimum, G.711 audio codec, system controls, and H.224 layer. Note that this recommendation does not include specifications for the LAN interface. H.245 defines the control messages that support end-to-end signaling between two endpoints. H.245 specifies the exact syntax and semantics that implement call control, general commands and indications, the opening and closing of logical channels, round trip delay determination, mode preference requests, flow control messages, and capability exchanges. H.225 provides the multiplex and demultiplex service employed by H.323. It is responsible for packetizing and synchronizing the audio, video, data, and control streams for the transmission across the LAN interface.

H.323 Gateway

As the name suggests, a gateway is a system that provides entry to and exit from a network. Gateways are responsible for translating the system control, audio codec, and transmission protocols between the different ITU standards.

H.323 Over IP Networks

Given the ubiquity of IP networks, the majority of H.323 implementations are based on IP. For example, most IP telephony applications are based on the minimum H.323 configuration, which includes audio codec, system control, and network components.

H.323 requires a reliable end-to-end TCP service for document and control functions. However, it uses unreliable service to transport audio and video information. H.323 relies on the *Real-Time Protocol* (RTP) and the *Real-Time Control Protocol* (RTCP) on top of UDP to deliver audio streams across packet-based networks. Table 5-1 shows the start-up sequence of a typical H.323 session.

Table 5-1

H.323 session information

Action Required	H.323 Protocol	Transport Protocol
1. Endpoint requests permission and bandwidth to begin H.323 session	RAS (Registration, Admission, from gatekeeper and Status)	UDP
2. Endpoints negotiate and establish call setup	Q.931	TCP
3. Endpoints exchange capabilities and set up RTP channels	H.245	TCP
4. Endpoints exchange audio data	H.225	UDP(RTP/RTCP)

The standards and recommendations presented here can be obtained from the *International Telecommunication Union* (ITU) in complete form. The Internet address is: `www.itu.int`.

VOIP Vendor Product List

If you are like me, you like to have lots of reference material! That is the fundamental theme behind this book. Consequently, I am including the following list to provide you with the most current list of vendors and their locations with VOIP product available to the market.

Ascend	`www.ascend.com`
Cisco	`www.cisco.com`
Digi	`www.digi.com`
E–Fusion	`www.efusion.com`
Ericission	`www.ericission.com`
HyperCom	`www.hypercom.com`
Linkon	`www.linkon.com`
Lucent	`www.lucent.com`
Lynk	`www.lynk.com`
Memotec	`www.memotec.com`
Motorola	`www.motorola.com`
Multi-tech	`www.multitech.com`
Netrix	`www.netrix.com`
Netspeak	`www.netspeak.com`
Nokia	`www.nokia.com`
Northern Telecom	`www.northerntelecom.com`
Nuera	`www.nuera.com`
RADvision	`www.radvision.com`
Siemens	`www.siemens.com`
Volcaltec	`www.volcaltec.com`

Architecture Example

VOIP architecture involves different components. To understand VOIP better, I am presenting an illustration later that indicates some of the key components in VOIP implementations. In this section, I present 3Com's 3-tier architecture as an example. It includes gateways, gatekeepers, and back-end servers. This is a simple architecture for the reader to begin to understand some high-level functionality of VOIP, while showing a real technology in the marketplace. Another reason I use this as an example is that it mirrors the C7/SS7 design, enabling seamless integration between the two. Consider Figure 5-1.

Figure 5-1
3 tier architecture
example

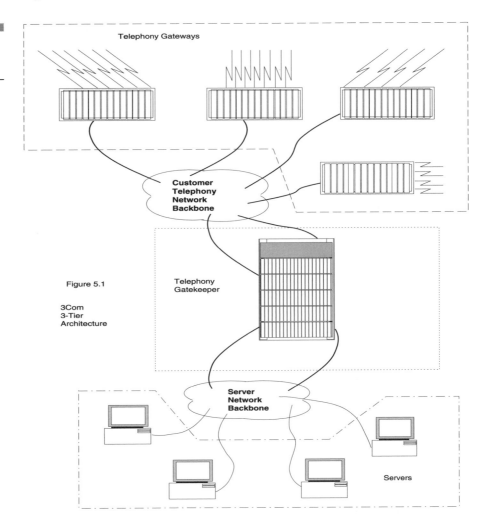

Figure 5.1

3Com
3-Tier
Architecture

Figure 5-1 shows a high level view of a tiered approach to VOIP architecture. In this illustration, telephony gateways, a gatekeeper, and repository of servers are shown.

Implied here is that telephony gateways represent inbound access to a network. This could be a wide spread intranet or the Internet. Regardless of the type or size of the network, the telephony gateways are the vehicle by which all inbound access is made.

The telephony gateway permits a remote access *points-of-presence* (POPS). It can support PC-to-phone and phone-to-phone services over IP networks. In addition the gateway, as shown in Figure 5-1, supports real-time voice communications through IP-based networks. Another function that can be achieved as a result of an implementation of Figure 5-1 is call accounting by collection of *call detail records* (CDRs). This level of detail includes modem connection speed, voice codec type, user name, call duration, and the IP address of gateways.

The telephony gatekeeper is responsible for centralized call control, call routing, zone and resource management, and overall system command and control. The gatekeeper is often referred to as the system "traffic cop." In addition to authorizing network use and routing calls to the appropriate IP address, the gatekeeper logs statistical and event information, and identifies charge rates through the support of back-end database facilities. The gatekeeper also manages port utilization and load on all the gateways within a specified zone. All communication between gateways and back-end servers is managed through a gatekeeper to maximize system availability and reliability.

In Figure 5-1, the gatekeeper operates on a stand-alone platform. In addition each gatekeeper can support at least ten telephony gateways.

Finally, the repository of servers provides customer service and call management functions. In addition, an authentication server functions to verify and authorize legitimate callers on the network. This server also provides fraud detection and prevention features, as well as maintaining each subscriber's account balance and service privileges.

A specific server dedicated as an accounting server maintains *call detail records* (CDRs) and other information used in billing. A record system performs tasks like comprehensive billing capabilities, service level analysis, and management.

Another type of server can maintain directory mapping between the telephone number called and the IP address of the appropriate "hop-off" IP Telephony gateway. This server can also perform dialed number translation and format checking.

From the conceptual perspective, the previous figure shows some basic operation with regard to the operation of a three tiered VIOP architecture. With this in mind, do not forget that, even though not shown, other aspects of the network as shown in Figure 5-1 could be explained. For example, this type network most likely has data, multimedia, and video repositories as well. Hence, a more detailed perspective could reveal a much more intense analysis of traffic through the network, but the focus here is VOIP.

VOIP Technology & Future Communications

The topic of VOIP includes more technologies than one might think of at first glance. This section is a summary of some technologies that might well fit into different platforms and next generation technologies with VOIP.

Asymmetric Digital Subscriber Line (ADSL)

Asymmetric Digital Subscriber Line (ADSL)— a new modem technology— converts existing twisted-pair telephone lines into access paths for multimedia and high-speed data communications. ADSL transmits more than 6 Mbps to a subscriber, and as much as 640 Kbps more in both directions. Such rates expand existing access capacity by a factor of 50 or more without new cabling.

ADSL can literally transform the existing public information network from one limited to voice, text, and low-resolution graphics to a powerful, ubiquitous system capable of delivering multimedia—including full-motion video—to everyone's home in this century.

ADSL will play a crucial role over the next ten or more years as telephone companies enter new markets for delivering information in video and multimedia formats. New broadband cabling will take decades to reach all prospective subscribers, but success of these new services will depend on reaching as many subscribers as possible during the first few years. By bringing movies, television, video catalogs, remote CD-ROMs, corporate LANs, and the Internet into homes and small businesses, ADSL will make these markets viable (and profitable) for telephone companies and application suppliers alike.

ADSL started out as the phone company's way to compete with cable TV by delivering both TV and phone service on your traditional copper phone line. Now it's also a good candidate for high-speed Internet access.

The "A" stands for "Asymmetric," meaning the phone company can send lots of data to you, but you can't send much to them. Originally, only a tiny uplink of 16 or 64kbps was supported; recent flavors of ADSL support up to ten times that much.

ADSL is one member of a continuum of last-mile transport systems called *Digital Subscriber Line* (DSL), which can carry about 1 to 6 megabits/sec over copper lines. It does not include any way to make long-distance data calls, or even local calls. That's another matter entirely—one that is still up in the air.

Public Switched Telephone Network (PSTN)

PSTN is short for *Public Switched Telephone Network*, which refers to the international telephone system based on copper wires carrying analog voice data. This is in contrast to newer telephone networks base on digital technologies, such as ISDN and FDDI.

Telephone service carried by the PSTN is often called *plain old telephone service* (POTS).

Integrated Services Digital Network (ISDN)

ISDN is a high-speed, fully digital telephone service. Just as compact discs have made recorded music digital, ISDN upgrades today's analog telephone network to a digital system.

ISDN can operate at speeds up to 128 kilobits/second, which is five or more times faster than today's analog modems. ISDN can dramatically speed up transfer of information over the Internet or over a remote LAN connection, especially rich media like graphics, audio, video, or applications that normally run at LAN speeds.

ISDN stands for *Integrated Services Digital Network*—the name for digital telephone service that works over existing copper telephone wiring. There are several types of ISDN service, but the most appropriate type for individual computer users, and the type that this site focuses on, is the ISDN *Basic Rate Interface* (BRI).

Basic Rate ISDN divides the telephone line into 3 digital channels: two "B" channels and one "D" channel, each of which can be used simultaneously. The B channels are used to transmit data, at rates of 64k or 56k (depending on your telephone company). The D channel does the administrative work, such as setting up and tearing down the call and communicating with the telephone network. With two B channels, you can make two calls simultaneously.

Most of the world's existing telephone network is already digital. The only part that typically isn't digital is the section that runs from the local exchange to your house or office. ISDN makes that final leg of the network digital.

Frame Relay

Frame Relay is a high-speed communications technology that is used in hundreds of networks worldwide to connect LAN, Internet, and even voice applications. It's a way of sending information over a *wide area network* (WAN) that divides the information into frames or packets. Each frame has an address that the network uses to determine the destination of the frame. The frames travel through a series of switches within the frame relay network and arrive at their destination.

Frame relay employs a simple form of packet switching that is well suited to powerful PCs, workstations, and servers that operate with intelligent protocols, such as TCP/IP.

A frame relay network is not a single physical connection between one endpoint and another. Instead, a logical path, called a virtual circuit, is defined within the network. Bandwidth is allocated to the path until actual data needs to be transmitted, and then bandwidth within the network is allocated on a packet-by-packet basis—hence the name "virtual circuit."

Asynchronous Transfer Mode (ATM)

Asynchronous Transfer Mode (ATM) is the technology adopted for B-ISDN, the broadband network of the future. ATM is potentially capable of efficiently supporting diverse traffic with various service requirements. ATM promises greater integration of capabilities and services, increased and more flexible access to the network, and more efficient and economical service.

ATM carries all traffic on a stream of fixed-size packets called cells, each comprising 5 bytes of header information and a 48-byte information field. Choosing a fixed-size packet ensures that the switching function can be carried out quickly and easily.

ATM is a connection-oriented technology in the sense that before two systems on the network can communicate, they must inform the network of their service requirements during a process called connection establishment. This enables ATM to guarantee a connection's *Quality of Service* (QoS) attributes, such as the Cell Loss Ratio, the Cell Transfer Delay, or the Cell Delay Variation.

Achieving the desired QoS for a variety of traffic types (which might have very different requirements) is much more complex than providing the simple best-effort service, which the networks of today offer.

In an ATM network, each connection is called a *Virtual Circuit* (VL) and is assigned a particular VC Identifier as well as a Virtual Path Identifier. A Virtual Path is something like a "bunch" of VCs. The cells belonging to the connection carry the identifiers on their headers. This allows the capacity of each link to be shared by the connections using that link on a demand basis rather than by fixed allocations.

The remainder of this chapter is the *Simple Gateway Control Protocol* (SGCP) Internet Draft. I have made the document easier to read by dividing into the sections that follow; however, the content of the document is still intact.

Simple Gateway Control Protocol (SGCP)

As a courtesy of The Internet Society, the information presented in this section is a partial representation from RFC ####. The information in this section is helpful for those who work at deeper levels of VOIP. After consideration, I am including a degree of this RFC to assist you your work with VOIP; however, I recommend you obtain the complete RFC from:

`ftp://ftp.ncren.net`

The best place to begin is with that part of the RFC that discusses the application programming interface SGCI and the corresponding protocol SGCP for controlling telephony gateways from external call control elements. A telephony gateway is a network element that provides conversion between the audio signals carried on telephone circuits and data packets carried over the Internet or over other packet networks. Examples of gateways are

■ Trunking gateways, which interface between the telephone network and a Voice Over IP network. Such gateways typically manage a large number of digital circuits.

■ Residential gateways, which provide a traditional analog (RJ11) interface to a Voice Over IP network.

■ Network Access Servers, which can attach a modem to a telephone circuit and provide data access to the Internet. We expect that in the future the same gateways will combine Voice Over IP services and Network Access services.

The SGCP assumes a call control architecture where the call control "intelligence" is outside the gateways and handled by external call control elements. The SGCP assumes that these call control elements, or Call Agents, will synchronize with each other to send coherent commands to the gateways under their control. The SGC defined in this document does not define a mechanism for synchronizing Call Agents.

The SGCP assumes a connection model where the basic constructs are end-points and connections. Endpoints are sources or sinks of data and could be physical or virtual. Examples of physical endpoints are

■ An interface on a gateway that terminates a trunk connected to a PSTN switch (e.g., Class 5, Class 4, and so on). A gateway that terminates trunks is called a trunk gateway.

■ An interface on a gateway that terminates an analog POTS connection to a phone, key system, PBX, and so on. A gateway that terminates residential POTS lines (to phones) is called a residential gateway.

An example of a virtual endpoint is an audio source in an audio-content server. Creation of physical endpoints requires hardware installation, whereas creation of virtual endpoints can be done by software.

Connections may be either point to point or multipoint. A point to point connection is an association between two endpoints with the purpose of transmitting data between these endpoints. After this association is established for both endpoints, data transfer between these endpoints can take place. A multipoint connection is established by connecting the endpoint to a multipoint session.

Correlation to H.323 Standards

The SGCP is designed as an internal protocol within a distributed system that appears to the outside as a single VOIP gateway. This system is composed of a Call Agent, that might or might not be distributed over several computer platforms, and of a set of gateways. In a typical configuration, this distributed gateway system interfaces on one side with one or more telephony (that is, circuit) switches, and on the other side with H.323 conforming systems, as indicated in Table 5-2.

In the SGCP model, the gateways focus on the audio signal translation function, whereas the Call Agent handles the signaling and call processing functions. As a consequence, the Call Agent implements the "signaling" layers of the H.323 standard and presents itself as a "Gatekeeper" to the H.323 systems. Calls are established using the "Gatekeeper Routed" call model.

Table 5-2

H.323 standard interpretation table

Functional Plane	Phone Switch	Terminating Entity	H.323 Conformant Systems
Signaling Plane	Signaling exchanges through SS7/ISUP	Call agent	Signaling exchanges with the call agent through H.225/RAS and H.225/Q.931. Possible negotiation of logical channels and transmission parameters through H.245 with the call agent
		Internal synchronization through SGCP	
Bearer Data Transport Plane	Connection through high speed trunk groups	Telephony gateways	Optional negotiation of logical channels and transmission parameters through H.245 directly with the telephony gateway
			data using RTP, directly between the H.323 station and the gateway.

Correlation to IETF standards

Although H.323 is the recognized standard for VOIP terminals, the IETF has also produced specifications for other types of multi-media applications. These other specifications include

Session Description Protocol (SDP), RFC 2327,

Session Announcement Protocol (SAP),

Session Initiation Protocol (SIP),

Real Time Streaming Protocol (RTSP), RFC 2326.

The latter three specifications are, in fact, alternative signaling standards that allow for the transmission of a session description to an interested party. SAP is used by multicast session managers to distribute a multicast session description to a large group of recipients. SIP is used to invite an individual user to take part in a point-to-point or unicast session. RTSP is used to interface a server that provides real time data. In all three cases, the session description is described according to SDP; when audio is transmitted, it is transmitted through the *Real-time Transport Protocol* (RTP).

The distributed gateway systems and SGCP enable PSTN telephony users to access sessions set up using SAP, SIP, or RTSP. The Call Agent provides for signaling conversion, according to Table 5-3.

Table 5-3

Call agent signal conversion

Functional Plane	Phone Switch	Terminating Entity	IETF Conforming Systems
Signaling Plane	Signaling exchanges through SS7/ISUP	Call agent	Signaling exchanges with the call agent through SAP, SIP or RTSP
			Negotiation of session description parameters through SDP (telephony gateway terminated but passed through the call agent to and from the IETF conforming system)
Bearer Data Transport Plane	Connection through high speed trunk groups	Internal Telephony gateways	Transmission of VOIP data using RTP directly between the remote IP end system and the gateway

The Simple Gateway Control Interface

The interface functions provide for connection control and endpoint control. Both use the same system model and the same naming conventions. The SGCP assumes a connection model where the basic constructs are endpoints and connections. Connections are grouped in calls. One or more connections can belong to one call. Connections and calls are set up at the initiative of one or several Call Agents.

Endpoint names have two components:

Domain name of the gateway that is managing the endpoint

Local name within that gateway

In the case of trunking gateways, endpoints are trunk circuits linking a gateway to a telephone switch. These circuits are typically grouped into a digital multiplex that is connected to the gateway by a physical interface. Such circuits are named in three contexts:

■ In the ISUP protocol, trunks are grouped into trunk groups, identified by the SS7 point codes of the switches that the group connects. Circuits within a trunk group are identified by a circuit number (CIC in ISUP).

■ In the gateway configuration files, physical interfaces are typically identified by the name of the interface, an arbitrary text string. When the interface multiplexes several circuits, individual circuits are typically identified by a circuit number. In SGCP, the endpoints are identified by an endpoint name.

The Call Agents use configuration databases to map ranges of circuit numbers within an ISUP trunk group to corresponding ranges of circuits in a multiplex connected to a gateway through a physical interface. The gateway is identified, in SGCP, by a domain name. The local name is structured to encode both the name of the physical interface, for example X35V3+A4, and the circuit number within the multiplex connected to the interface, for example 13. The circuit number is separated from the name of the interface by a fraction bar, as in

```
X35V31A4/13
```

The circuit number can be omitted if the physical interface only includes one circuit or the Call Agent requests the gateway to choose one available circuit within a multiplex.

Other types of endpoints use different conventions. For example, an endpoint that produces an "all lines busy" announcement could be named:

```
all-lines-busy/loop
```

The exact syntax of such names should be specified in the corresponding server specification.

Names of Calls

Calls are identified by unique identifiers, independent of the underlying platforms or agents. These identifiers are created by the Call Agent. They are treated in SGCP as unstructured octet strings. Call identifiers are expected to be unique within the system. When a Call Agent builds several connections that pertain to the same call, either on the same gateway or in different gateways, these connections are all linked to the same call through the globally unique identifier. This identifier can then be used by accounting or management procedures, which are outside the scope of SGCP.

Names of Connections

Connection identifiers are created by the gateway when it is requested to create a connection. They identify the connection within the context of an endpoint and a call. They are treated in SGCP as unstructured octet strings. The gateway should make sure that a proper waiting period, at least 3 minutes, elapses between the end of a connection that used this identifier and its use in a new connection.

Names of Call Agents and Other Entities

The simple gateway control protocol has been designed to allow the implementation of redundant Call Agents for enhanced network reliability. This means that there is no fixed binding between entities and hardware platforms or network interfaces. Reliability can be improved by the following precautions:

■ Entities such as endpoints or Call Agents are identified by their domain name, not their network addresses. Several addresses can be associated with a domain name. If a command or a response cannot be forwarded to one of the network addresses, implementations should retry the transmission using another address.

■ Entities might move to another platform. The association between a logical name (domain name) and the actual platform are kept in the domain name service. Call Agents and Gateways should keep track of the time-to-live of the record they read from the DNS. They should query the DNS to refresh the information if the time to live has expired.

Digit Maps

The Call Agent can ask the gateway to collect digits dialed by the user. This facility is intended to be used with residential gateways to collect the numbers that a user dials; it might also be used with trunking gateways and access gateways alike, to collect the access codes, credit card numbers, and other numbers requested by call control services. An alternative procedure is for the gateway to notify the Call Agent of the dialed digits, as soon as they are dialed. However, such a procedure generates a large number of interactions. It is preferable to accumulate the dialed numbers in a buffer and to transmit them in a single message.

The problem with this accumulation approach, however, is that it is hard for the gateway to predict how many numbers it needs to accumulate before transmission. For example, using the phone on our desk, we can dial the following numbers:

0	Local operator
00	Long distance operator
xxxx	Local extension number
8xxxxxxx	Local number
#xxxxxxx	Shortcut to local number at other corporate sites
*xx	Star services
91xxxxxxxxxx	Long distance number
9011 + up to 14 digits	International number

The solution to this problem is to load the gateway with a digit map that corresponds to the dial plan. This digital map is expressed using a syntax derived from the UNIX system command, egrep. For example, the dial plan described previously results in the following digit map:

```
(0T     00T    [1-7]xxx8xxxxxxx        axxxxxxx        *xx
91xxxxxxxxxx   9011x.T)
```

The formal syntax of the digit map is described by the following BNF notation:

```
Digit :5 "0"  "1"  "2"  "3"  "4"  "5"  "6"  "7"  "8"  "9"
Timer :5 "T" — matches the detection of a timer
Letter:5 Digit Timer  "a"  "*"  "A"  "B"  "C"  "D"
Range :5 "x"—matches any digit
"[" Letters "]"—matches any of the specified letters
Letters :5 Subrange      Subrange Letters
Subrange :5 Letter—matches the specified letter
Digit "-" Digit—matches any digit between first and — last
Position :5 Letter
Range
StringElement:5 Position—matches an occurrence of
— the position
Position "."—matches an arbitrary number of
— occurrences
— of the position, including 0
String:5 StringElement        StringElement String
StringList:5 String           String "" StringList
DigitMap:5 String             "(" StringList ")"
```

A DigitMap, according to this syntax, is defined either by a "string" or by a list of strings. Each string in the list is an alternative numbering scheme. A gateway that detects digits, letters, or timers will

1. Add the event parameter code as a token to the end of an internal state variable called the "current dial string"

2. Apply the current dial string to the digit map table, attempting a match to each regular expression in the digit map in lexical order.

3. If the result is under-qualified (partially matches at least one entry in the digit map), do nothing further.

If the result matches or is over-qualified (that is, no further digits could possibly produce a match), send the current digit string to the Call Agent. Digit maps are provided to the gateway by the Call Agent whenever the Call Agent instructs the gateway to listen for digits.

Usage of SDP

The Call Agent uses the SGCP to provision the gateways with the description of connection parameters such as IP addresses, UDP port, and RTP profiles. These descriptions follow the conventions delineated in the Session Description Protocol, which is now an IETF proposed standard, documented in RFC 2327. SDP allows for description of multimedia conferences. This version limits SDP usage to the setting of audio circuits and data access circuits. The initial session descriptions contain the description of exactly one media, of type "audio" for audio connections, and "nas" for data access.

Gateway Control Functions

This section describes the commands of the SGCP. The service consists of connection handling and endpoint handling commands. There are five commands in the protocol:

- The Call Agent can issue a NotificationRequest command to a gateway, instructing the gateway to watch for specific events such as hook actions or DTMF tones on a specified endpoint.
- The gateway then uses the Notify command to inform the Call Agent when the requested events occur.
- The Call Agent can use the CreateConnection command to create a connection that terminates in an "endpoint" inside the gateway.
- The Call Agent can use the ModifyConnection command to change the parameters associated to a previously established connection.
- The Call Agent can use the DeleteConnection command to delete an existing connection. The DeleteConnection command might also be used by a gateway to indicate that a connection can no longer be sustained.

These services allow a controller (normally, the Call Agent) to instruct a gateway on the creation of connections that terminate in an endpoint attached to the gateway and be informed about events occurring at the endpoint. An endpoint might be for example:

- A specific trunk circuit, within a trunk group terminating in a gateway
- A specific announcement handled by an announcement server

Connections are grouped into "calls." Several connections might belong to the same call, terminating in the same endpoint. Each connection is qualified by a mode parameter, which can be set to send, receive, send/receive, data, inactive, loopback, or continuity test.

The handling of the audio signals received on these connections is determined by the mode parameters:

- Audio signals received in data packets through connections in receive or send/receive mode are mixed and sent to the endpoint.
- Audio signals originating from the endpoint are transmitted over all the connections whose mode is send or send/receive.

The loopback and continuity test modes are used during maintenance and continuity test operations. There are two flavors of continuity test, one specified by ITU and one used in the U.S. In the first case, the test is a loopback test. The originating switch sends a tone (the go tone) on the bearer circuit and expects the terminating switch to loopback the circuit. If the originating switch sees the same tone returned (the return tone), the COT has passed. If not, the COT has failed. In the second case, the go and return tones are different. The originating switch sends a certain go tone. The terminating switch detects the go tone, it asserts a different return tone in a backward direction. When the originating switch detects the return tone, the COT is passed. If the originating switch never detects the return tone, the COT has failed.

If the mode is set to loopback, the gateway is expected to return the incoming signal from the endpoint back into that same endpoint. This procedure is used typically for testing the continuity of trunk circuits according to the ITU specifications.

If the mode is set to continuity test, the gateway is informed that the other end of the circuit has initiated a continuity test procedure according to the GR specification. The gateway places the circuit in the transponder mode required for dual-tone continuity tests.

NotificationRequest

The NotificationRequest commands are used to request the gateway to send notifications at the occurrence of specified events in an endpoint. For example, a notification might be requested when a gateway detects that an endpoint is receiving tones associated with fax communication. The entity receiving this notification might decide to use a different type of encoding method in the connections bound to this endpoint.

```
NotificationRequest( EndpointId,
NotifiedEntity,
RequestedEvents,
RequestIdentifier,
DigitMap,
SignalRequests)
```

EndpointId is the identifier for the endpoint in the gateway where NotificationRequest executes. NotifiedEntity is an optional parameter that specifies where the notifications should be sent. When this parameter is absent, the notifications should be sent to the originator of the NotificationRequest. RequestIdentifier is used to correlate this request with the notifications that it triggers. RequestedEvents is a list of events that the gateway is requested to detect and report. Such events include, for example

- Fax tones
- Modem tones
- Continuity tone
- Continuity detection (as a result of a continuity test)
- On-hook transition (occurring in classic telephone sets when the user hangs-up the handset)
- Off-hook transition (occurring in classic telephone sets when the user lifts the handset)
- Flash hook (occurring in classic telephone sets when the user briefly presses the hook that holds the handset)
- Wink
- DTMF digits (or pulse digits)

To each event is associated an action, which can be

- Notify the event immediately, together with the accumulated list of observed events
- Swap audio
- Accumulate according to Digit Map
- Ignore the event

Events that are not specified in the list, by default, are ignored.

The Swap Audio action can be used when a gateway handles more than one active connection on an endpoint. This is the case for three-way calling, call waiting, and possibly other feature scenarios. To avoid the round-trip to the Call Agent when just changing which connection is attached to the audio functions of the endpoint, the NotificationRequest can map an event (usually hook flash, but it can be some other event) to a local function swap audio, which selects the "next" connection in a round robin fashion. If there is only one connection, this action is effectively a no-op.

Hook transition events are normally observed only by access gateways. Tone detection can be done by any gateway, including trunking gateways.

The Call Agent can send a NotificationRequest whose RequestedEvent list is empty. It does so, for example, to an access gateway when it does not want to collect any more DTMF digits.

DigitMap is an optional parameter that allows the Call Agent to provision the gateways with a digit map according to which digits are accumulated. This parameter must be present if the RequestedEvent parameters contain a request to "accumulate according to the digit map." The collection of these digits results in a digit string. The digit string is initialized to a null string on reception of the NotificationRequest, so that a subsequent notification only returns the digits that were collected after this request. Signal-Requests is a parameter that contains the set of actions that the gateway is asked to perform on the endpoint, such as, for example

- Ringing
- Distinctive ringing, which can occur in 8 variants numbered 0 to 7
- Ring back tone
- Dial tones
- Intercept tone
- Network Congestion tone
- Busy tone
- Confirm tone
- Answer tone
- Call waiting tone
- Off hook warning tone
- Preemption tone
- Continuity tones
- Continuity test
- Announcement (completed by an announcement name and a parameter)
- ASDI display (and string to be displayed)

The action triggered by the SignalRequests is synchronized with the collection of events specified in the RequestedEvents parameter. For example, if the NotificationRequest mandates "ringing" and the EventRequest asks to look for an off-hook event, the ringing stops as soon as the gateway detects an off hook event. The specific definition of actions that are requested through these SignalRequests, such as the duration of and frequency of a DTMF digit, is outside the scope of SGC. This definition might vary from location to location and hence from gateway to gateway.

The RequestedEvents and SignalRequests refer to the same events. In one case, the gateway is asked to detect the occurrence of the event, and in the other case it is asked to generate it. There are only a few exception to this rule, notably the ASDI display, which can only be signaled but not detected, and the fax and modem tones, which can be detected but can not be signaled. However, we cannot necessarily expect all endpoints to detect all events. For example, a digital trunk interface would normally not detect hook events and might not be able to modulate DTMF digit; signals such as "wink" only make sense in some types of trunks.

Gateways that receive a request to detect an event that they are not equipped to detect or generate a signal that they are not equipped to generate, should refuse the request and return an error code. Similarly, gateways that are equipped to generate announcements but cannot generate the specific announcement that the Call Agent requested should return an appropriate error code. The Call Agent can send a NotificationRequest whose requested signal list is empty. It does so, for example, when tone generation should stop.

Notifications

Notifications are sent through the Notify command and are sent by the gate-way when the observed events occur.

```
Notify( EndpointId,
NotifiedEntity,
RequestIdentifier,
ObservedEvents)
```

EndpointId is the identifier for the endpoint in the gateway that is issuing the Notify command. NotifiedEntity is an optional parameter that identifies the entity to which the notification is sent. This parameter is equal to the NotifiedEntity parameter of the NotificationRequest that triggered this notification. The parameter is absent if there was no such parameter in the triggering request. In this case, the notification is sent to the entity from which the request was received. RequestIdentifier is a parameter that repeats the RequestIdentifier parameter of the NotificationRequest that triggered this notification. It is used to correlate this notification with the request that triggered it. ObservedEvents is a list of events that the gateway detected. A single notification might report a list of events that is reported in the order in which they were detected. The list might only contain the identification of events that were requested in the RequestedEvents parameter of the triggering NotificationRequest. It contains the events that were either accumulated (but not notified) or treated according to digit map (but no match yet), and the final event that triggered the detection or provided a final match in the digit map.

CreateConnection

This command is used to create a connection.

```
ConnectionId,
[SpecificEndPointId,]
[LocalConnectionDescriptor]
<-- CreateConnection(CallId,
EndpointId,
NotifiedEntity,
LocalConnectionOptions,
Mode,
RemoteConnectionDescriptor,
RequestedEvents,
RequestIdentifier,
DigitMap,
SignalRequests)
```

This function creates a connection between two endpoints. A connection is defined by its endpoints. The input parameters in CreateConnection provide the data necessary to build a gateway's "view" of a connection.

CallId is a globally unique parameter that identifies the call (or session) to which this connection belongs. This parameter is unique within the whole network of gateways; connections that belong to the same call share the same call-id. The CallId can be used to identify calls for reporting and accounting purposes.

EndpointId is the identifier for the connection endpoint in the gateway where CreateConnection executes. The EndpointId can be fully-specified by assigning a value to the parameter EndpointId in the function call, or it might be under-specified and the full value is assigned by the gateway and its complete value returned in the SpecificEndPointId parameter of the response.

The NotifiedEntity is an optional parameter that specifies where the Notify or DeleteConnection commands should be sent. If the parameter is absent, the Notify or DeleteConnection commands should be sent to the originator of the CreateConnection command.

LocalConnectionOptions is a structure that describes the characteristics of the data communications from the point of view of the gateway executing

CreateConnection. The fields contained in LocalConnectionOptions are the following

- Encoding method
- Packetization period
- Bandwidth
- Type of Service,
- Usage of echo cancellation

The values of these fields are defined in the SDP standard. For each of the first three fields, the Call Agent has three options:

- It might state exactly one value, which the gateway then uses for the connection.
- It might provide a loose specification, such as a list of allowed encoding methods or a range of packetization periods.
- It might simply provide a bandwidth indication, leaving the choice of encoding method and packetization period to the gateway.

The bandwidth specification shall not contradict the specification of encoding methods and packetization period. If an encoding method is specified, then the gateway is authorized to use it, even if it results in the usage of a larger bandwidth than specified.

The LocalConnectionOptions parameter might be absent in the case of a data call.

The Type of Service specifies the class of service that is used for the connection. When the connection is transmitted over an IP network, the parameter encodes the 8-bit type of service value parameter of the IP header. When the Type of Service is not specified, the gateway shall use a default or configured value.

By default, the telephony gateways always perform echo cancellation. However, it is necessary, for some calls, to turn off these operations. The echo cancellation parameter can have two values, "on" (when the echo cancellation is requested) and "off" (when it is turned off).

RemoteConnectionDescriptor is the connection descriptor for the remote side of a connection, on the other side of the IP network. It includes the same fields as in the LocalConnectionDescriptor, that is, the fields that describe a session according to the SDP standard. This parameter might have a null value when the information for the remote end is not known yet. This occurs because the entity that builds a connection starts by sending a CreateConnection to one of the two gateways involved in it. For the first CreateConnection issued, there is no information available about the other side of the connection. This information might be provided later through a ModifyConnection call. In the case of data connections (mode=data), this parameter describes the characteristics of the data connection.

Mode indicates the mode of operation for this side of the connection. The options are: FullDuplex, ReceiveOnly, SendOnly, Inactive, Loopback, Continuity Test and Data.

- FullDuplex indicates that this side of the connection sends data generated by the associated endpoint and can receive data from the remote end and feed it to the endpoint.

- ReceiveOnly indicates this connection end can only receive data form the remote end and feed it to the associated endpoint.

- SendOnly indicates that this connection end can only send data from its endpoint to the other end of the connection.

- Inactive indicates that this connection end does not send or receive any data. The connection exists but is not active. It has to be explicitly activated by a ModifyConnection command.

- Loopback indicates that the circuit to which the endpoint refers should be placed in loopback mode, so that audio signals received from the phone circuit are sent back on this same circuit.

- Continuity Test indicates that the other end of the circuit has initiated a continuity test procedure according to the GR specification. The gateway places the circuit in the transponder mode required for dual-tone continuity tests.

- Data indicates that the circuit to which the endpoint refers is used for network access (such as Internet access) rather than for Internet telephony.

The gateway returns a ConnectionId, that uniquely identifies the connection within one endpoint, and a LocalConnectionDescriptor, which is a session description that contains information about addresses and RTP ports, as defined in SDP. The LocalConnectionDescriptor is not returned in the case of data connections. The SpecificEndPointId is an optional parameter that identifies the responding endpoint. It can be used when the EndpointId argument referred to a generic endpoint name. When a SpecificEndPointId is returned, the Call Agent should use it as the EndpointId value is successive commands referring to this call.

After receiving a CreateConnection request that did not include a Remote-ConnectionDescriptor parameter, a gateway is in an ambiguous situation.

Because it has exported a LocalConnectionDescriptor parameter, it can potentially receive packets. Because it has not yet received the RemoteConnectionDescriptor parameter of the other gateway, it does not know whether the packets that it receives have been authorized by the Call Agent. It must thus navigate between two risks, that is, clipping some important announcements or listening to insane data. The behavior of the gateway is determined by the value of the Mode parameter:

- If the mode was set to ReceiveOnly, the gateway should accept the voice signals and transmit them through the endpoint.
- If the mode was set to Inactive, Loopback, or Continuity Test, the gateway should refuse the voice signals.

Note that the mode values FullDuplex and SendOnly don't make sense in this situation. They should be treated as ReceiveOnly and Inactive.

The RequestedEvents, RequestIdentifier, DigitMap, and SignalRequests parameters are optional. They can be used by the Call Agent to transmit a NotificationRequest that is executed simultaneously with the creation of the connection. For example, when the Call Agent wants to initiate a call to a residential gateway, it should

- Ask the residential gateway to prepare a connection, to be sure that the user can start speaking as soon as the phone goes off hook
- Ask the residential gateway to start ringing
- Ask the residential gateway to notify the Call Agent when the phone goes off hook

This can be accomplished in a single CreateConnection command, by also transmitting the RequestedEvent parameters for the off hook event, and the SignalRequests parameter for the ringing signal.

When these parameters are present, the creation and the NotificationRequests should be synchronized, which means that both should be accepted, or both refused. In our example, the CreateConnection might be refused if the gateway does not have sufficient resources or cannot get adequate resources from the local network access, and the off-hook Notification-Request can be refused in the glare condition, if the user is already off-hook. In this example, the phone should not ring if the connection cannot be established, and the connection should not be established if the user is already off hook.

ModifyConnection

This command is used to modify the characteristics of a gateway's view of a connection. This view of the call includes both the local connection descriptors as well as the remote connection descriptor.

```
[LocalConnectionDescriptor]
<-- ModifyConnection(CallId,
EndpointId,
ConnectionId,
NotifiedEntity,
LocalConnectionOptions,
Mode,
RemoteConnectionDescriptor,
RequestedEvents,
RequestIdentifier,
DigitMap,
SignalRequests)
```

The parameters used are the same as in the CreateConnection command, with the addition of a ConnectionId that identifies the connection within the call. This parameter is returned by the CreateConnection function, as part of the local connection descriptor. It uniquely identifies the connection within the call.

The ModifyConnection command can be used to affect parameters of a connection in the following ways:

- Provide information on the other end of the connection through the RemoteConnectionDescriptor
- Activate or deactivate the connection, by changing the value of the Mode parameter. This can occur at any time during the connection, with arbitrary parameter values.
- Change the sending parameters of the connection, for example by switching to a different coding scheme, changing the packetization period, or modifying the handling of echo cancellation

Connections can only be activated if the RemoteConnectionDescriptor has been provided to the gateway. The command only returns a Local-ConnectionDescriptor if the local connection parameters, such as RTP ports, were modified. (Usage of this feature is actually for further study.)

The RequestedEvents, RequestIdentifier, DigitMap, and SignalRequests parameters are optional. They can be used by the Call Agent to transmit a

NotificationRequest that is executed simultaneously with the modification of the connection. For example, when a connection is accepted, the calling gateway should be instructed to place the circuit in send-receive mode and to stop providing ringing tones.

This can be accomplished in a single ModifyConnection command, by also transmitting the RequestedEvent parameters, for the on hook event, and an empty SignalRequests parameter, to stop the provision of ringing tones. When these parameters are present, the modification and the NotificationRequests should be synchronized, which means that both should be accepted, or both refused.

DeleteConnection (from the Call Agent)

This command is used to terminate a connection. As a side effect, it collects statistics on the execution of the connection.

```
Connection-parameters < — DeleteConnection(CallId,
EndpointId,
ConnectionId,
NotifiedEntity,
RequestedEvents,
RequestIdentifier,
DigitMap,
SignalRequests)
```

In the general case where a connection has two ends, this command has to be sent to both gateways involved in the connection. Some connections, however, might use IP multicast. In this case, they can be deleted individually. After the connection has been deleted, the endpoint should be placed in inactive mode. Any loopback that has been requested for the connection should be canceled.

In response to the DeleteConnection command, the gateway returns a list of parameters that describe the status of the connection. These parameters are

■ *Number of packets sent* The total number of RTP data packets transmitted by the sender since starting transmission on this connection. The count is not reset if the sender changes its synchronization source identifier (SSRC, as defined in RTP), for example as a result of a Modify command. The value is zero if the connection was set in receive only mode.

■ *Number of octets sent* The total number of payload octets, not including header or padding, transmitted in RTP data packets by the sender since starting transmission on this connection. The count is not reset if the sender changes its SSRC identifier, for example as a result of a ModifyConnection command. The value is zero if the connection was set in receive only mode.

- *Number of packets received* The total number of RTP data packets received by the sender since starting reception on this connection. The count includes packets received from different SSRC, if the sender used several values. The value is zero if the connection was set in send only mode.

- *Number of octets received* The total number of payload octets, not including header or padding, transmitted in RTP data packets by the sender since starting transmission on this connection. The count includes packets received from different SSRC, if the sender used several values. The value is zero if the connection was set in send only mode.

- *Number of packets lost* The total number of RTP data packets that have been lost since the beginning of reception. This number is defined to be the number of packets expected less the number of packets actually received, where the number of packets received includes any which are late or duplicates. The count includes packets received from different SSRC, if the sender used several values. Thus packets that arrive late are not counted as lost, and the loss might be negative if there are duplicates. The count includes packets received from different SSRC, if the sender used several values. The number of packets expected is defined to be the extended last sequence number received, as defined next, less the initial sequence number received. The count includes packets received from different SSRC, if the sender used several values. The value is zero if the connection was set in send only mode. This parameter is omitted if the connection was set in data mode.

- *Interarrival jitter* An estimate of the statistical variance of the RTP data packet's interarrival time measured in milliseconds and expressed as an unsigned integer. The interarrival jitter J is defined to be the mean deviation (smoothed absolute value) of the difference D in packet spacing at the receiver compared to the sender for a pair of packets. Detailed computation algorithms are found in RFC 1889. The count includes packets received from different SSRC, if the sender used several values. The value is zero if the connection was set in send only mode. This parameter is omitted if the connection was set in data mode.

■ *Average transmission delay* An estimate of the network latency expressed in milliseconds. This is the average value of the difference between the NTP timestamp indicated by the senders of the RTCP messages and the NTP timestamp of the receivers, measured when this message is received. The average is obtained by summing all the estimates, and then dividing by the number of RTCP messages that have been received. This parameter is omitted if the connection was set in data mode.

For a detailed definition of these variables, refer to RFC 1889.

The NotifiedEntity, RequestedEvents, RequestIdentifier, DigitMap, and SignalRequests parameters are optional. They can be used by the Call Agent to transmit a NotificationRequest that is executed simultaneously with the deletion of the connection. For example, when a user hangs up is accepted, the gateway should be instructed to delete the connection and to start looking for an off hook event. This can be accomplished in a single DeleteConnection command by also transmitting the RequestedEvent parameters for the off hook event and an empty SignalRequests parameter.

When these parameters are present, the DeleteConnection and the NotificationRequests should be synchronized, which means that both should be accepted, or both refused.

DeleteConnection (from the VOIP Gateway)

In some circumstances, a gateway might have to clear a connection, for example because it has lost the resource associated with the connection, or because it has detected that the endpoint no longer is capable or willing to send or receive voice. The gateway terminates the connection by using a variant of the DeleteConnection command:

```
DeleteConnection( CallId,
EndpointId,
ConnectionId,
Reason-code,
Connection-parameters)
```

In addition to the call, and endpoint and connection identifiers, the gateway also sends the call's parameters that would have been returned to the Call Agent in response to a DeleteConnection command. The reason code indicates the cause of the disconnection.

DeleteConnection (Multiple Connections from the Call Agent)

A variation of the DeleteConnection function can be used by the Call Agent to delete multiple connections at the same time. The command can be used to delete all connections that relate to a Call for an endpoint:

```
DeleteConnection( CallId,
EndpointId)
```

It can also be used to delete all connections that terminate in a given endpoint:

```
DeleteConnection( EndpointId)
```

After the connections have been deleted, the endpoint should be placed in inactive mode. Any loopback that has been requested for the connections should be canceled. This command does not return any individual statistics or call parameters.

Race Conditions

To implement proper call signaling, the Call Agent must keep track of the state of the endpoint. A key element of this state is the position of the hook. A race condition might occur when the user decides to go off-hook before the Call Agent has the time to ask the gateway to notify an off hook event (the "glare" condition well known in telephony), or if the user goes on-hook before the Call Agent has the time to request the event's notification.

To avoid this race condition, the gateway should check the condition of the endpoint before acknowledging a NotificationRequest. It should return an error:

1. If the gateway is requested to notify an off hook transition while the phone is already off hook

2. If the gateway is requested to notify an on hook or flash hook condition while the phone is already on hook

The other state variables of the gateway, such as the list of Requested-Event or list of requested signals, are entirely replaced after each successful NotificationRequest, which prevents any long-term discrepancy between the

Call Agent and the gateway. When a NotificationRequest is unsuccessful, the list of RequestedEvents and requested signals are emptied. They must be reinstated by a new request.

Another race condition might occur when a notification is issued shortly before the reception by the gateway of a NotificationRequest. The Request-Identifier is used to correlate Notify commands with NotificationRequest commands.

Return Codes and Error Codes

All SGCP commands are acknowledged. The acknowledgment carries a return code, which indicates the status of the command. The return code is an integer number, for which three ranges of values have been defined:

- Values between 200 and 299 indicate a successful completion
- Values between 400 and 499 indicate a transient error
- Values between 500 and 599 indicate a permanent error

The values that have been already defined are listed in Table 5-4.

Table 5-4

SGCP codes & meanings

Code	Meaning
200	The requested transaction was executed normally.
250	The connection was deleted.
400	The transaction could not be executed due to a transient error.
401	The phone is already off hook.
402	The phone is already on hook.
500	The transaction could not be executed, because the endpoint is unknown.
501	The transaction could not be executed, because the endpoint is not ready.
502	The transaction could not be executed, because the endpoint does not have sufficient resources.
510	The transaction could not be executed, because a protocol error was detected.
511	The transaction could not be executed, because the command contained an unrecognized extension.

Code	Meaning
512	The transaction could not be executed, because the gateway is not equipped to detect one of the requested events.
513	The transaction could not be executed, because the gateway is not equipped to generate one of the requested signals.
514	The transaction could not be executed, because the gateway cannot send the specified announcement.
515	The transaction refers to an incorrect connection-id (might have been already deleted)

Simple Gateway Control Protocol (SGCP)

The SGCP implements the simple gateway control interface as a set of transactions. The transactions are composed of a command and a mandatory response. There are five types of commands:

- CreateConnection
- ModifyConnection
- DeleteConnection
- NotificationRequest
- Notify

The first four commands are sent by the Call Agent to a gateway. The Notify command is sent by the gateway to the Call Agent. The gateway might also send a DeleteConnection.

General Description

All commands are composed of a Command header, optionally followed by a session description. All responses are composed of a Response header, optionally followed by a session description. Headers and session descriptions are encoded as a set of text lines, separated by a line feed character. The headers are separated from the session description by an empty line.

SGCP uses a transaction identifier to correlate commands and responses. The transaction identifier is encoded as a component of the command header and repeated as a component of the response header.

Transaction identifiers have values between 1 and 999999999. An SGCP entity shall not reuse an identifier sooner than 3 minutes after completion of the previous command in which the identifier was used.

Command Header

The command header is composed of

- A command line, identifying the requested action or verb, the endpoint towards which the action is requested, and the SGC protocol version
- A set of parameter lines, composed of a parameter name followed by a parameter value.

Command Line

The command line is composed of

- The name of the requested verb
- The identification of the transaction
- The name of the endpoint that should execute the command (in notifications, the name of the endpoint that is issuing the notification)
- The protocol version

These four items are encoded as strings of printable ASCII characters separated by white spaces, that is, the ASCII space (0×20) or tabulation (0×09) characters. It is recommended to use exactly one ASCII space separator.

Coding of the Requested Verb

The five verbs that can be requested are encoded as four letter upper or lower case ASCII codes (comparisons should be case insensitive) as defined in Table 5-5.

The transaction identifier is encoded as a string of up to 9 decimal digits. In the command lines, it immediately follows the coding of the verb. New verbs might be defined in further versions of the protocol. It might be necessary, for experimentation purposes, to use new verbs before they are sanctioned in a published version of this protocol. Experimental verbs should be identified by a four-letter code starting with the letter X, such as the example XPER.

Verb	Code
CreateConnection	CRCX
ModifyConnection	MDCX
DeleteConnection	DLCX
NotificationRequest	RQNT
Notify	NTFY

Table 5-5

Verb request codings

Coding of the Endpoint Names

The endpoint names are encoded as e-mail addresses, as defined in RFC 821. In these addresses, the domain name identifies the system where the endpoint is attached, whereas the left side identifies a specific endpoint on that system. Examples of such addresses can be

`1234566gw23.whatever.net`	Circuit number 123456 in gateway 23 of the "Whatever" network
`Call-agent6ca.whatever.net`	Call Agent for the "whatever" network
`Busy-signal6ann12.` `  whatever.net`	The "busy signal" virtual endpoint in the announcementserver number 12

The name of notified entities is expressed with the same syntax with the possible addition of a port number as in:

```
Call-agent5234
```

Coding of the Protocol Version

The protocol version is coded as the key word SGCP followed by a white space and the version number. The version number is composed of a major version, coded by a decimal number, a (.); and a minor version number, coded as a decimal number. The version described in here is version 1.1.

In the initial messages, the version is coded as

```
SGCP 1.1
```

Version 1.1 is a superset of version 1.0. Gateways that implement version 1.1 shall accept commands coded according to version 1.0. They should refrain from using version 1.1.

Parameter Lines

Parameter lines are composed of a parameter name, which in most cases is composed of a single upper case character followed by a colon, a white space, and the parameter value. The parameters that can be present in commands are defined in Table 5-6.

Table 5-6

SGCP coding para-
meter lines

Parameter Name	Code	Parameter Value
CallId	C	Hexadecimal string, at most 32 characters
ConnectionId	I	Hexadecimal string, at most 32 characters
NotifiedEntity	N	An identifier, in RFC 821 format, composed of an arbitrary string and of the domain name of the requestin entity, possibly completed by a port number, as in `Call-agent6ca.whatever.net:5234`
RequestIdentifier	X	Hexadecimal string, at most 32 characters
LocalConnectionOptions	L	See description
Connection Mode	M	See description
RequestedEvents	R	See description
SignalRequests	S	See description
DigitMap	D	A text encoding of a digit map
ObservedEvents	O	See description
ConnectionParameters	P	See description
ReasonCode	E	An arbitrary character string
SpecificEndpointID	Z	An identifier, in RFC 821 format, composed of an arbitrary string, followed by an @ followed by the domain name of the gateway to which this endpoint is attached

The letter M stands for mandatory, O for optional, and F for forbidden.

Table 5-7

Parameter to command correlation

Parameter Name	CRCX	MDCX	DLCX	RQNT	NTFY
CallId	M	M	O	F	F
ConnectionId	F	M	O	F	F
RequestIdentifier	O	O	O	M	M
LocalConnectionOptions	O	O	F	F	F
Connection Mode	M	M	F	F	F
RequestedEvents	O	O	O	O*	F
SignalRequests	O	O	O	O*	F
NotifiedEntity	O	O	O	O	O
ReasonCode	F	F	O	F	F
ObservedEvents	F	F	F	F	M
DigitMap	O	O	O	O	F
Connection parameters	F	F	O	F	F
Specific Endpoint ID	F	F	F	F	F

The parameters are not necessarily present in all commands. Table 5-7 provides the association between parameters and commands.

Note (*) that the RequestedEvents and SignalRequests parameters are optional in the NotificationRequest. If these parameters are omitted, the corresponding lists are considered empty.

If implementers need to experiment with new parameters, for example when developing a new application of SGCP, they should identify these parameters by names that start with the string X-, for example

```
X-FlowerOfTheDay: Daisy
```

The parameters are only recognized by applications that have been upgraded to become part of the experiment. A gateway that receives an extension that it cannot understand should refuse to execute the command. It should respond with an error code 511 (Unrecognized extension).

Local Connection Options

The local connection options describe the operational parameters that the Call Agent suggests to the gateway. These parameters are

- The packetization period in milliseconds, encoded as the keyword p followed by a colon and a decimal number. If the Call Agent specifies a range of values, the range is specified as two decimal numbers separated by a hyphen.
- The preferred type of compression algorithm, encoded as the keyword a followed by a character string. If the Call Agent specifies a list of values, these values are separated by a semicolon.
- The bandwidth in kilobits per second (1000 bits per second), encoded as the keyword b followed by a colon and a decimal number. If the Call Agent specifies a range of values, the range is specified as two decimal numbers separated by a hyphen.
- The echo cancellation parameter, encoded as the keyword e followed by a colon and the value "on" or "off."

Each of the parameters is optional. When several parameters are present, the values are separated by a comma. Examples of connection descriptors are

```
L: p:10, a:G.711
L: p:10, a:G.711;G.726-32
L: p:10-20, b: 64
L: b:32-64, e:off
```

Connection Parameters

Connection parameters are encoded as a string of type and value pairs, where the type is a two-letter identifier of the parameter and the value a decimal integer. Types are separated from value by an (=) sign. Parameters are encoded from each other by a comma.

The connection parameter types are specified in Table 5-8.

An example of connection parameter encoding is

```
P: PS51245, OS562345, PR50, OR50, PL50, JI50, LA548
```

Connection Mode

The connection mode describes the mode of operation of the connection. The possible values are shown in Table 5-9.

Table 5-8

Types of connection parameters

Connection Parameter Name	Code	Connection Parameter Value
Packets sent	PS	The number of packets that were sent on the connection
Octets sent	OS	The number of octets that were sent on the connection
Packets received	PR	The number of packets that were received on the connection
Octets received	OR	The number of octets that were received on the connection
Packets lost	PL	The number of packets that were not received on the connection, as deduced from gaps in the sequence number
Jitter	JI	The average inter-packet arrival jitter, in milliseconds, expressed as an integer number
Latency	LA	Average latency, in milliseconds, expressed as an integer number

Table 5-9

Connection mode operation

Mode	Meaning
M: sendonly	The gateway should only send packets.
M: recvonly	The gateway should only receive packets.
M: sendrecv	The gateway should send and receive packets.
M: inactive	The gateway should neither send nor receive packets.
M: loopback	The gateway should place the circuit in loopback mode.
M: conttest	The gateway should place the circuit in test mode.
M: data	The gateway should use the circuit for network access for data (e.g., PPP, SLIP, etc.).

Coding of Event Names

Event names are mentioned in the RequestedEvents, SignalRequests, and ObservedEvents parameter. Each event is identified by a code, as indicated in the following table. These ASCII encodings are not case sensitive. Values such as "hu," "Hu," "HU," or "hU" should be considered equal. The following codes shown in Table 5-10 are used to identify events:

Table 5-10

Event identifying codes

Code	Event
A string of digits [0–9], hash and star marks [*,#], the letters A, B, C, D and the timer indication T	DTMF tones
ann	Announcement
asdi	ASDI display
aw	Answer tone
bz	Busy tone
cf	Confirm tone
cbk	Call back request
cg	Network Congestion tone
co	Default continuity tone
co1	Continuity tone (single tone)
co2	Continuity test (go tone, in dual tone procedures)
cl	Carrier lost
cv	Continuity verified (response tone, in dual tone procedures)
dl	Dial tone
ft	Fax tones
hd	Off-hook transition
hf	Flash hook
hu	On-hook transition
it	Intercept tone

Code	Event
ld	Long duration connection
mt	Modem tones
ot	Off hook warning tone
pa	Packet arrival
pt	Preemption tone
r0, r1, r2, r3, r4, r5, r6 or r7 (0 ..7)	Distinctive ringing
rg	Ringing
rt	Ring back tone
t	Timer
wk	Wink
wt	Call waiting tone

RequestedEvents

The RequestedEvent parameter provides the list of events that have been requested. The event codes are described in the previous section. In addition to these coded events, the list might also include a parameter specifying digit collection. This parameter could take one of the following forms:

■ Individual digits, pound sign (octothorpe), star sign, or letters A, B, C or D
■ Timer mark T
■ Ranges of digits, enclosed within square brackets, for example "[0–9]" or "[0–9*#T]"

Each event can be qualified by a requested action or by a list of actions. The actions, when specified, are encoded as a list of keywords enclosed in parenthesis and separated by commas. The codes for the various actions are shown in Table 5-11.

Table 5-11

Code-to-action
correlation

Action	Code
Notify immediately	N
Accumulate	A
Treat according to digit map	D
Swap	S
Ignore	I

When no action is specified, the default action is to notify the event. This means that, for example, ft and ft(N) are equivalent. Events that are not listed are ignored. The digit-map action can only be specified for the digits, letters, and timers.

The requested list is encoded on a single line with event/action groups separated by commas. Examples of RequestedEvents encoding are

```
R: hu(N), hf(S,N)
R: hu(N), [0-9aT](D)
```

SignalRequests

The SignalRequests parameter provides the name of the signals that have been requested. Each signal is identified by a code. Two events, announcement, and ASDI display can be qualified by additional parameters:

- The name and parameters of the announcement
- The string that should be displayed

These parameters are enclosed within parenthesis, as in

```
S: asdi(123456 Your friend)
S: ann(no-such-number, 1234567)
```

When several signals are requested, their codes are separated by a comma, as in

```
S: asdi(123456 Your friend), rg
```

ObservedEvent

The ObservedEvent parameters provides the list of events that have been observed. The event codes are the same as those used in the Notification-Request. Events that have been accumulated according to the digit map are grouped in a single string. Examples of observed actions are

```
O: hu
O: 8295555T
O: hf, hf, hu
```

The packet arrival event is used to notify that at least one packet was recently sent to an Internet address that is observed by an endpoint. The event report includes the Internet address, in standard ASCII encoding, between parenthesis:

```
O: pa(192.96.41.1)
```

The call back event is used to notify that a call back has been requested during the initial phase of a data connection. The event report includes the identification of the user that should be called back, between parenthesis:

```
O: cbk(user25)
```

Format of Response Headers

The response header is composed of a response line, optionally followed by headers that encode the response parameters. The response line starts with the response code, which is a three digit numeric value. The code is followed by a white space, the transaction identifier, and an optional commentary.

In the case of a CreateConnection message, the response line is followed by a Connection-Id parameter. It might also be followed a specific Endpoint-Id parameter if the creation request was sent to a generic Endpoint-Id.

In the case of a DeleteConnection message, the response line is followed by a Connection Parameters parameter.

A LocalConnectionDescriptor should be transmitted with a positive response (code 200) to a CreateConnection. It might be transmitted in response to a ModifyConnection command if the modification resulted in a modification of the session parameters. The LocalConnectionDescriptor is encoded as a session description. It is separated from the response header by an empty line.

Encoding of the Session Description

The session description is encoded in conformance with the session description protocol, SDP. SGCP implementations are expected to be fully capable of parsing any conforming SDP message and should send session descriptions that strictly conform to the SDP standard. The usage of SDP actually depends on the type of session that is set, as specified in the mode parameter:

- If the mode is set to data, the session description describes the configuration of a data access service.
- If the mode is set to any other value, the session description is for an audio service.

For an audio service, the gateway considers the information provided in SDP for the audio media. For a data service, the gateway considers the information provided for the network-access media.

Usage of SDP for an Audio Service

In a telephony gateway, we only have to describe sessions that use exactly one media, audio. The parameters of SDP that are relevant for the telephony application are

- *At the session description level*   The IP address of the remote gateway (in commands) or of the local gateway (in responses), or multicast address of the audio conference encoded as an SDP connection data parameter. This parameter specifies the IP address that is used to exchange RTP packets.
- *For the audio media*   Media description field (m) specifying the audio media, the transport port used for receiving RTP packets by the remote gateway (commands) or by the local gateway (responses), the RTP/AVP transport, and the list of formats that the gateway accepts. This list should normally always include the code 0 (reserved for G.711).
- Optionally, RTPMAP attributes that define the encoding of dynamic audio formats
- Optionally, a packetization period (packet time) attribute (Ptime) defining the duration of the packet

■ Optionally, an attribute defining the type of connection (sendonly, recvonly, sendrecv, inactive)

■ The IP address of the remote gateway (in commands) or of the local gateway (in responses) if it is not present at the session level

There is a request, in some environments, to use the SGCP to negotiate connections that use transmission channels other than RTP over UDP and IP. This is detailed in an extension to this document.

Usage of SDP in a Network Access Service

The parameters of SDP that are relevant for a data network access application are

For the data media:

■ *Media description* field (m) specifying the network access media, identified by the code m5nas/xxxx, where xxxx describes the access control method that should be used for parametrixing the network access, specified as follows. The field might also specify the port that should be used for contacting the server, as specified in the SDP syntax.

■ Connection address parameter (c=) specifying the address or the domain name of the server that implemented the access control method. This parameter might also be specified at the session level.

■ Optionally, a bearer type attribute (a=bearer:) describing the type of data connection to be used

■ Optionally, a framing type attribute (a=framing:) describing the type of framing that is used on the channel

■ Optionally, attributes describing the called number (a=dialed:), the number to which the call was delivered (a=called:), and the calling number (a=dialing:)

■ Optionally, attributes describing the range of addresses that could be used by the dial-up client on its LAN (a=subnet:)

■ Optionally, an encryption key encoded as specified in the SDP protocol (k=)

The connection address shall be encoded as specified in the SDP standard. It is used in conjunction with the port specified in the media line to access a server whose type is one of the following shown in Table 5-12.

Table 5-12

Server type
method

Method Name	Method Description
Radius	Authentication according to the Radius protocol
Tacacs	Authentication according to the TACACS+ protocol
Diameter	Authentication according to the Diameter protocol
l2tp	Level 2 tunneling protocol. The address and port are those of the LNS.
Login	Local login. (There is normally no server for that method.)
None	No authentication required. (The call was probably vetted by the Call Agent.)

If needed, the gateway might use the key specified in the announcement to access the service. That key, in particular, might be used for the establishment of an L2TP tunnel. The valid values of the bearer attribute are defined in Table 5-13.

The valid values of the framing attribute are defined in Table 5-14.

The network access authentication parameter provides instructions on the access control that should be exercised for the data call. This optional attribute is encoded as

```
"a5subnet:" <network type> <address type>
<connection address> "/" <prefix length>
```

Table 5-13

Valid bearer
attribute values

Type of Bearer Description	Example of Values
ITU modem standard	V.32, V.34, V.90
ISDN transparent access, 64 kbps	ISDN64
ISDN64 + V.110	ISDN64/V.110
ISDN64 + V.120	ISDN64/V.120
ISDN transparent access, 56 kbps	ISDN56
Informal identification	(Requires coordination between the Call Agent and the gateway)

Table 5-14

Framing
descriptions

Type of Framing Description	Example of Values
PPP, asynchronous framing	ppp-asynch
PPP, HDLC framing	ppp-hdlc
SLIP, asynchronous	slip
Asynchronous, no framing	asynch

where the parameters network type, address type, and connection address are formatted as defined for the connection address parameter (c=) in SDP, and where the prefix length is a decimal representation of the number of bits in the prefix.

Examples of SDP announcement for the network access service could be

```
v50
m5nas/radius
c5IN IP4 radius.example.net
a5bearer:v.34
a5framing:ppp-asynch
a5dialed:18001234567
a5called:12345678901
a5dialing:12340567890
v50
m5nas/none
c5IN IP4 128.96.41.1
a5subnet:IN IP4 123.45.67.64/26
a5bearer:isdn64
a5framing:ppp-sync
a5dialed:18001234567
a5dialing:2345678901
v50
c5IN IP4 access.example.net
m5nas/l2tp
k5clear:some-shared-secret
a5bearer:v.32
a5framing:ppp-asynch
a5dialed:18001234567
a5dialing:2345678901
```

SGCP Transmission over UDP

SGCP messages are transmitted over UDP. Commands are sent to one of the IP addresses defined in the DNS for the specified endpoint. The responses are sent back to the source address of the commands.

When no port is specified for the endpoint, the commands should be sent to the default SGCP port, 2427. SGCP messages, being carried over UDP, might be subject to losses. In the absence of a timely response, commands are repeated. SGCP entities are expected to keep in memory a list of the responses that they sent to recent transactions, that is, a list of all the responses they sent over the last 30 seconds, and a list of the transactions that are currently being executed. The transaction identifiers of incoming commands are compared to the transaction identifiers of the recent responses. If a match is found, the SGCP entity does not execute the transaction, but simply repeats the response. The remaining commands are compared to the list of current transaction. If a match is found, the SGCP entity does not execute the transaction; it is simply ignored.

It is the responsibility of the requesting entity to provide suitable time outs for all outstanding commands and to retry commands when time outs have been exceeded. Furthermore, when repeated commands fail to be acknowledged, it is the responsibility of the requesting entity to seek redundant services and/or clear existing or pending connections.

The specification purposely avoids specifying any value for the retransmission timers. These values are typically network dependent. The retransmission timers should normally estimate the timer by measuring the time spent between the sending of a command and the return of a response. One possibility is to use the algorithm implemented in TCP-IP, which uses the two variables

- The *average acknowledgment delay* (AAD), estimated through an exponentially smoothed average of the observed delays

- The *average deviation* (ADEV), estimated through an exponentially smoothed average of the absolute value of the difference between the observed delay and the current average

The retransmission timer, in TCP, is set to the sum of the average delay plus N times the average deviation. After the any retransmission, the SGCP entity should do the following

- It should double the estimated value of the AAD

- It should compute a random value, uniformly distributed between 0.5 AAD and AAD

- It should set the retransmission timer to the sum of that random value and N times the average deviation.

This procedure has two effects. Because it includes an exponentially increasing component, it automatically slows down the stream of messages in case of congestion. Because it includes a random component, it breaks the potential synchronization between notifications triggered by the same external event.

Security Requirements

If unauthorized entities could use the SGCP, they would be able to set up unauthorized calls or to interfere with authorized calls. We expect that SGCP messages always are carried over secure Internet connections, as defined in the IP security architecture as defined in RFC 1825, using either the IP Authentication Header, defined in RFC 1826, or the IP Encapsulating Security Payload, defined in RFC 1827. The complete SGCP protocol stack would thus include the following layers:

SGCP

UDP

IP security (authentication or encryption)

IP

Transmission media

Adequate protection of the connections is achieved if the gateways and the Call Agents only accept messages for which IP security provided an authentication service. An encryption service can provide additional protection against eavesdropping, thus forbidding third parties from monitoring the connections set up by a given endpoint. The encryption service can also be requested if the session descriptions are used to carry session keys, as defined in SDP.

These procedures do not necessarily protect against denial of service attacks by misbehaving gateways or misbehaving Call Agents. However, they do provide an identification of these misbehaving entities, which should then be deprived of their authorization through maintenance procedures.

Example of Call Flows

To understand the way the SGCP interface is used, we have described here two possible call flows (Table 5-15a & 5-15b) between a TGW, which is a

Table 5-15a

Basic call, RGW to TGW

User	RGW	CA	CDB	ACC	TGW	SS7/ISUP	CO
	<-	Notification Request					
	Ack	->					
Off-hook	Notify	->					
(Dial tone)	<-	Ack					
	<-	Notification Request					
	Ack	->					
Digit	Notify	->					
	<-	Ack					
(pro-	<-	Notification Request					
gress)	Ack	->					
	<-	Create Connection					
	Ack	->					
		Query (E.164 S,D)	->				
		<-	IP				
		Create Connection	—	—	->		
					(cut-in)		
		<-	—	—	Ack		
		IAM	—	—	—	->	
	<-	Modify Connection				IAM	->
	Ack	->				<-	ACM
		<-	—	—	—	ACM	
	<-	Notification Request					
	Ack	->					
						<-	ANM
		<-	—	—	—	ANM	
	<-	Notification Request					
	Ack	->					
	<-	Modify Connection					
	Ack	->					
	(cut-in)	Call start	—	->			

Table 5-15b

Basic call, RGW
to TGW

User	RGW	CA	CDB	ACC	TGW	SS7/ISUP	CO
						<- REL	REL
	<-	<- Delete Connection	—	—	—		
		Delete Connection	—	—	->		
Data	Perf ->						
		<-	—	—	perf data		
On-hook	Notify	Call end ->	—	->			
	<-	Ack					
	<-	Notification Request					
	Ack	->					

trunking gateway that implements SGCP, and an RGW, which is a *residential gateway* that implements SGCP. As well, we describe four call flows describing how SGCP can be used to control a network access service.

The diagrams also show a *Common Database* (CDB) that can be queried for authorization and routing information and an *Accounting Gateway* (ACC) that collects accounting information at the start and the end of calls.

These diagrams are solely meant to exhibit the behavior of the SGCP and to help understanding this protocol. They are not meant as a tutorial on the implementation of a Call Agent. They might very well include miscellaneous errors and imprecisions.

During these exchanges, the SGCP is used by the Call Agent to control both the TGW and the residential gateway. The exchanges occur on two sides.

The first command is a NotificationRequest, sent by the Call Agent to the residential gateway. The request consists of the following lines:

```
RQNT 1201 endpoint21
N: ca5678
X: 0123456789AB
R: hd
```

The gateway, at that point, is instructed to look for an off-hook event, and to report it. It first acknowledges the command, repeating in the acknowledgment message the transaction id that the Call Agent attached to the query.

```
200 1201 OK
```

When the off hook event is noticed, the gateway initiates a Notification-Request to the Call Agent:

```
NTFY 2001 endpoint21
N: ca5678
X: 0123456789AB
O: hd
```

The Call Agent immediately acknowledges that notification.

```
200 2001 OK
```

The Call Agent examines the services associated with an off hook action (it could take special actions in the case of a direct line). In most cases, it sends a NotificationRequest asking for more digits. The current example provides the gateway with a permanent digit map, and requests the gateway to play a dial tone:

```
RQNT 1202 endpoint21
N: ca5678
X: 0123456789AC
R: hu, [0-9a*T](D)
D: (0T 00T [1—7]xxx 8xxxxxxx axxxxxxx *xx 91xxxxxxxxxx 9011x.T)
S:
Dt
```

The gateway immediately acknowledges that command.

```
200 1202 OK
```

The gateway starts accumulating digits according to that digit map. When it has noticed a sufficient set of values, it notifies the observed string to the Call Agent:

```
NTFY 2002 endpoint21
N: ca5678
X: 0123456789AC
O: 912018294266
```

The Call Agent immediately acknowledges that notification.

```
200 2002 OK
```

At this stage, the Call Agent sends a NotificationRequest to stop collecting digits and yet continue watching for an on-hook transition:

```
RQNT 1203 endpoint21
X: 0123456789AD
R: hu
```

The Call Agent immediately acknowledges that command.

```
200 1203 OK
```

The Call Agent then seizes the incoming circuit creating a connection:

```
CRCX 1204 endpoint21
C: A3C47F21456789F0
L: p:10, a:G.711;G.726-32
M: recvonly
```

The gateway immediately acknowledges the creation by sending back the identification of the newly created connection and the session description used to receive audio data:

```
200 1204 OK
I:FDE234C8
v=0
c=IN IP4 128.96.41.1
m=audio 3456 RTP/AVP 0 96
a=rtpmap:96 G72632/8000
```

The SDP announcement, in our example, specifies the address at which the gateway is ready to receive audio data (128.96.41.1), the transport protocol (RTP), the RTP port (3456), and the *audio profile* (AVP). The audio profile refers to RFC 1890, which defines that the payload type 0 has been assigned for G.711 transmission. The gateway is also ready to use ADPCM encoding at 32 Kbps (G.726 4). There is no standard payload type associated to ADPCM, so the gateway mentions its readiness to use a non-standard payload associated to the dynamic type 96. The rtpmap attribute entry associates the payload type 96 to G72632/4.

The Call Agent, having seized the incoming trunk and completed a routing look up to identify the outgoing gateway, must now seize the outgoing trunk. It does so by sending a connection command to the ingress gateway:

```
CRCX 1205 card23/21
C: A3C47F21456789F0
L: p:10, a:G.711;G.726-32
M: sendrecv
```

```
v=0
c=IN IP4 128.96.41.1
m=audio 3456 RTP/AVP 0 96
a=rtpmap:96 G72632/8000
```

The CreateConnection command has the same parameters as the command sent to the ingress gateway, with two differences:

- The EndpointId points towards the outgoing trunk
- The message carries the session description returned by the ingress gateway
- Because the session description is present, the mode parameter is set to send/receive.

We observe that the call identifier is identical for the two connections. This is normal. The two connections belong to the same call, which has a global identifier in our system. The trunking gateway acknowledges the connection command, sending in the session description its own parameters such as address, ports, and RTP profile:

```
200 1205 OK
I:32F345E2
v=0
c=IN IP4 128.96.63.25
m=audio 1297 RTP/AVP 0 96
a=rtpmap:96 G72632/8000
```

The Call Agent relays the information to the ingress gateway using a ModifyConnection command:

```
MDCX 1206 endpoint21
C: A3C47F21456789F0
I:FDE234C8
M: recvonly
v=0
c=IN IP4 128.96.63.25
m=audio 1297 RTP/AVP 0 96
a=rtpmap:96 G72632/8000
```

The residential gateway immediately acknowledges the modification:

```
200 1206 OK
```

At this stage, the Call Agent has established a half-duplex transmission path. The phone attached to the residential gateway is able to receive the signals, such as tones or announcements, that the remote switch might send through the trunking gateway.

When the call progresses, the Call Agent receives progress messages from the remote switch, for example an *address complete message* (ACM). The Call Agent analyzes the message to determine whether signals are transmitted in band. If this is not the case, the Call Agent instructs the RGW to generate ringing tones by sending a NotificationRequest:

```
RQNT 1207 endpoint21
X: 0123456789AE
R: hu
S: rt
```

The gateway immediately acknowledges the command:

```
200 1207 OK
```

After the called user answers the call, the Call Agent receives an *answering message* (ANM) from the CO switch. At that point, it sends a Notification-Request to the residential gateway to stop the ringing tones, and a ModifyConnection command to place the connection in full duplex mode:

```
RQNT 1208 endpoint21
X: 0123456789AF
R: hu
MDCX 1209 endpoint21
C: A3C47F21456789F0
I:FDE234C8
M: sendrecv
```

The residential gateway acknowledges these two commands:

```
200 1208 OK
200 1209 OK
```

At this point, the connection is established.

When the Call Agent receives the REL message from the CO switch, it has to tear down the call. It does so by sending a DeleteConnection command to both gateways:

```
DLCX
1210 endpoint21
C: A3C47F21456789F0
I:FDE234C8
DLCX 1211 card23/21
C: A3C47F21456789F0
I:32F345E2
```

The gateways responds with acknowledgments that should include a call parameters header fields:

```
250 1210 OK
P: PS51245, OS562345, PR5780, OR545123, PL510, JI527,
LA548
250 1211 OK
P: PS5790, OS545700, PR51230, OR561875, PL515, JI527,
LA548
```

At this point, the phone attached to the residential gateway, in our scenario, goes on-hook. This event is notified to the Call Agent according to the policy received in the last NotificationRequest by sending a Notify command:

```
NTFY 2005 endpoint21
X: 0123456789AF
O: hu
```

After this notification, the Call Agent should send an acknowledgment:

```
200 2005 OK
```

It should then issue a new NotificationRequest to be ready to receive the next off-hook detected by the residential gateway:

```
RQNT 1212 endpoint21
X: 0123456789B0
R: hd
```

The gateway acknowledges this message:

```
200 1212 OK
```

Table 5-16a

Basic call, TGW to RGW

CO	SS7/ ISUP	TGW	CA	CDB	ACC	RGW	User
IAM	->						
	IAM	—	->				
			Check	->			
			<-	IP			
		<-	Create				
			Connection				
		Ack	->				
			Create				
			Connection	—	—	->	
			<-	—	—	Ack	
		<-	Modify				
			Connection				

CO	SS7/ISUP	TGW	CA	CDB	ACC	RGW	User
		Ack	-> Notification Request	—	—	->	Ring
			<-	—	—	Ack	
	<-	—	ACM				
<-	ACM						
							Off-hook
			<-	—	—	Notify	
			Ack	—	—	->	
			Notification Request	—	—	->	
			<-	—	—	Ack	
		<-	Modify Connection				
		Ack (cut-in)	-> Call start	—	->		
	<-	—	ANM				
<-	ANM						

Table 5-16b

Basic call, TGW to RGW

CO	SS7/ISUP	TGW	CA	CDB	ACC	RGW	User
							On-hook
			<-	—	—	Notify	
			Ack	—	—	->	
			Delete Connection	—	—	->	
		<-	Delete Connection				
	<-	—	REL				
<-	REL						
		perf data	->				
			<-	—	—	perf data	
			Call end	—	->		
			Notification Request	—	—	->	
			<-	—	—	Ack	

Both gateways, at this point, are ready for the next call as shown in Tables 5-16a and 5-16b.

This diagram shows the various exchanges of messages during a call from a telephone user on the circuit-switched PSTN to a residential user connected to a residential gateway. During these exchanges the Call Agent uses SGCP to control both the TGW and the residential gateway. The exchanges occur on two sides.

On reception of the IAM message, the Call Agent immediately sends a CreateConnection request to the trunking gateway to connect to the incoming trunk creating a connection:

```
CRCX
1237 card23/21
C: A3C47F21456789F0
L: p:10, a:G.711;G.726-32
M: recvonly
```

The trunking gateway immediately acknowledges the creation sending back the identification of the newly created connection and the session description used to receive audio data:

```
200 1237 OK
I: FDE234C8
v=0
c=IN IP4 128.96.41.1
m=audio 3456 RTP/AVP 0 96
a=rtpmap:96 G72632/8000
```

The SDP announcement, in our example, specifies the address at which the gateway is ready to receive audio data (128.96.41.1), the transport protocol (RTP), the RTP port (3456), and the *audio profile* (AVP). The audio profile refers to RFC 1890, which defines that the payload type 0 has been assigned for G.711 transmission. The gateway is also ready to use ADPCM encoding at 32 Kbps (G.726 4). There is no standard payload type associated to ADPCM, so the gateway mentions its readiness to use a non-standard payload associated to the dynamic type 96. The rtpmap attribute entry associates the payload type 96 to G726/4. The Call Agent, having seized the incoming trunk, must now reserve the outgoing circuit. It does so by sending a connection command to the residential gateway:

```
CRCX 1238 endpoint21
C: A3C47F21456789F0
L: p:10, a:G.711;G.726-32
M: sendrecv
v=0
c=IN IP4 128.96.41.1
m=audio 3456 RTP/AVP 0 96
a=rtpmap:96 G72632/8000
```

The CreateConnection command has the same parameters as the command sent to the ingress gateway with two differences:

- The EndpointId points towards the outgoing trunk.
- The message carries the session description returned by the ingress gateway.
- Because the session description is present, the mode parameter is set to send/receive.

We observe that the call identifier is identical for the two connections. This is normal. The two connections belong to the same call, which has a global identifier in our system. The trunking gateway acknowledges the connection command sending in the session description its own parameters such as address, ports, and RTP profile:

```
200 1238 OK
I:32F345E2
v=0
c=IN IP4 128.96.63.25
m=audio 1297 RTP/AVP 0 96
a=rtpmap:96 G72632/8000
```

The Call Agent relays the information to the ingress gateway using a ModifyConnection command:

```
MDCX 1239 card23/21
C: A3C47F21456789F0
I:FDE234C8
M: recvonly
v=0
c=IN IP4 128.96.63.25
m=audio 1297 RTP/AVP 0 96
a=rtpmap:96 G72632/8000
```

The trunking gateway immediately acknowledges the modification:

```
200 1239 OK
```

At this stage, the Call Agent has established a half-duplex transmission path. The Call Agent must now tell the residential gateway to ring the called line. It sends a NotificationRequest consisting of the following lines:

```
RQNT
1240 endpoint21
X: 0123456789B1
R: hd
S: rg
```

The residential gateway, at that point, is instructed to look for an off-hook event and to report it. It first acknowledges the command, repeating in the acknowledgment message the transaction id that the Call Agent attached to the query.

```
200 1240 OK
```

On reception of this message, the Call Agent sends an *address complete message* (ACM) to the calling switch, which generates ringing tones for the calling user. When the gateway notices the off hook event, it sends a Notify command to the Call Agent:

```
NTFY 2001 endpoint21
0123456789B0
O: hd
```

The Call Agent immediately acknowledges that notification.

```
200 2001 OK
```

The Call Agent now asks the residential gateway to send a Notify command on the occurrence of an on-hook event. It does so by sending a NotificationRequest to the residential gateway:

```
RQNT 1241 endpoint21
X: 0123456789B1
R: hu
```

The gateway acknowledges that command:

```
200 1241 OK
```

In parallel, the Call Agent sends a ModifyConnection command to the trunking gateway to place the connection in full duplex mode:

```
MDCX 1242 card23/21
C: A3C47F21456789F0
I:FDE234C8
M: sendrecv
```

The trunking gateway acknowledges that command:

```
200 1242 OK
```

The Call Agent can now send an *answer message* (ANM) to the calling switch. After some time, the Call Agent has to tear down the call. In our example, this is triggered by the residential user who hangs up. The Notify command is sent to the Call Agent:

```
NTFY 2005 endpoint21
X: 0123456789B1
O: hu
```

The Call Agent acknowledges the notification.

```
200 2005 OK
```

It then sends to both gateways a DeleteConnection command:

```
DLCX
1243 endpoint21
C: A3C47F21456789F0
I:FDE234C8
DLCX 1244 card23/21
C: A3C47F21456789F0
I:32F345E2
```

The gateways responds with a message that should include a call parameters header fields:

```
250 1243 OK
P: PS51245, OS562345, PR5780, OR545123, PL510, JI527,
LA548
250 1244 OK
P: PS5790, OS545700, PR51230, OR561875, PL515, JI527,
LA548
```

The Call Agent should now issue a new NotificationRequest to the residential gateway to detect the next off-hook event:

```
RQNT 1245 endpoint21
X: 0123456789B2
R: hd
```

The residential gateway acknowledges this command:

```
200 1245 OK
```

Both gateways, at this point, are ready for the next call.

This diagram shows the exchange of messages during a call from a modem user to an Internet Service Provider, using a trunking gateway that doubles as a Network Access Server. During these exchanges the SGCP is used by the Call Agent to control the trunking gateway. Because there is no "other end" of the call, only the trunk gateway is involved in the call. Tables 5-17a and 5-17b reflect a data call to a TGW.

Table 5-17a

Data call to a TGW

PC	CO	SS7/ISUP	TGW	CA	ACC	Radius
Dials in						
	IAM	->				
		IAM	—	->		
				Check called number		
				Notices data call		
				Call start	->	
		<-		Create Connection (data)		
			Ack	->		
				Connection is completed.		
				Call established	->	
		<-	—	ANM		
	<-	ANM				
Modem	—	—	->			
<-	—	—	Handshake			
PPP	—	—	->			
			Obtain user-id, password			
			Check	—	—	->
			<-	—	—	Ack
<-	—	—	Validates call,			
<-	—	—	procures IP address			
Connected to the Internet						

Table 5-17b

Data call to a TGW

PC	CO	SS7/ISUP	TGW	CA	ACC	Radius
Closes connection						
	REL	->				
		REL	—	->		
			<-	Delete Connection		

PC	CO	SS7/ ISUP	TGW	CA	ACC	Radius
			Perf data			
				->		
		<-	—	RLC		
	<-	RLC				
				Call end	->	

On reception of the IAM message, the Call Agent determines that the call is a data call by bearer capability, the called number, and so on. Using configuration databases, the Call Agent selects the type of modem parameters and authentication parameters that correspond to the called number and to the calling number. It uses this knowledge to send a CreateConnection command to the TGW programming the incoming trunk:

```
CRCX 1237 card23/21
C: A3C47F21456789F0
M: data
X: 0123456789B1
R: cl
v=0
m=nas/radius
c=IN IP4 radius.example.net
a=bearer:v.32
a=framing:ppp-asynch
a=dialed:18001234567
a=dialing:2345678901
```

The trunking gateway checks that it has adequate resources for the call. If the trunking gateway does not have adequate resources, for example if it can not support the requested modem type, it should refuse the creation and send an error response to the Call Agent. If the gateway has sufficient resources, it immediately acknowledges the creation by sending back the identification of the newly created connection. (There is no need to transmit a session description in the case of a data call.)

```
200 1237 OK
I: FDE234C8
```

The Call Agent, knowing that this is a data call, can immediately acknowledge the establishment of the connection by sending an ANM message back to the calling switch.

The trunk gateway connects the incoming trunk to a DSP loaded with the specified modem code. After the call is established, the modem of the calling PC starts a training sequence with the modem associated to the trunk in the trunk gateway. The caller then proceeds to a normal PPP synchronization, which probably implies a PPP logon. The authentication parameters, in our example, are checked using Radius. The Radius server that is used is typically chosen as a function of the called number, which identifies the data service that the calling modem requested. In fact, the number can also be used to identify the specific form of authentication that is requested (but not usually).

In our example, the call is completed when the calling modem hangs up. This triggers an ISUP release message, which is forwarded to the Call Agent. The Call Agent requests the TGW to delete the connection:

```
DLCX 1244 card23/21
C: A3C47F21456789F0
I: FDE234C8
```

The gateways responds with a message that should include a call parameters header fields:

```
250 1244 OK
P: PS51245, OS562345, PR5780, OR545123
```

We should note that because this is a data call, the call parameters only include a count of the packets and octets that were sent and received.

Tables 5-18a and 5-18b show the exchange of messages during a call from an *Internet Service Provider* (ISP) to a modem using a trunking gateway that doubles as a *Network Access Server* (NAS). During these exchanges, the

Table 5-18a

Outgoing data call through a TGW

PC	CO	SS7/ ISUP	TGW	CA	ACC	Router
						Notices packet to PC
			<-	Ack	—	NTFY
					—	->
				Decides to place an outgoing call		
				Call start	->	
		<-		Create Connection		

PC	CO	SS7/ISUP	TGW	CA	ACC	Router
				(data)		
			Ack	->		
		<-	—	IAM		
(Rings)	<-	IAM				
	ACM	->				
		ACM	—	->		
(Answer)	ANM	->				
		ANM	—	->		
				Connection complete Call established	->	
PPP	—	—	->			
<-	—	—	Validates call, announces IP address	—	—	->
Connected to the Internet						

Table 5-18b

Outgoing data call through a TGW

PC	CO	SS7/ISUP	TGW	CA	ACC	Router
Closes connection						
	REL	->				
		REL	—	->		
			<-	Delete Connection		
			Ceases announcing IP address Perf	—	—	->
Data	->					
		<-	—	RLC		
	<-	RLC				
				Call end	->	

SGCP is used by the Call Agent to control both the TGW, and also is used between the Call Agent and a default router of the ISP. In the example configuration, the calls are set on demand when data have to actually be sent from the Internet to the dial-up user. When no connection is established, the local routing is configured to send the packets towards a default router, which might or might not be the same machine as the TGW. In redundant configurations, there can be many default routers. Each default router has been programmed (through a notification request) to send a notification to the Call Agent when it receives a packet on the default route:

```
NTFY 2005 default-route
X:
0123456789AF
O: pa(192.96.41.1)
```

After this notification, the Call Agent should send an acknowledgment:

```
200 2005 OK
```

(We should note here that using SGCP for this function is a stretch. There are other protocols, notably RMON, that already provide an adequate service. These protocols could be used instead of SGCP without affecting the discussion that follows.)

The Call Agent deduces from the notification that a circuit should be established towards the dial-up user or towards the dial-up router. Using configuration databases, the Call Agent selects the number that should be called, and also the type of modem parameters and authentication parameters that correspond to the called number. The Call Agent uses its routing table to select an adequate TGW with an available out going trunk. It uses a create connection command to seize this outgoing trunk:

```
CRCX 1237 card23/21
C: A3C47F21456789F0
M: data
X: 0123456789B1
R: cl
v=0
m=nas/none
c=IN IP4 128.96.41.1
a=subnet:IN IP4 123.45.67.64/26
a=bearer:isdn64
a=framing:ppp-hdlc
a=dialed:18001234567
a=dialing:2345678901
```

The gateway immediately acknowledges the creation by sending back the identification of the newly created connection. (There is no session description in the case of a data call.)

```
200 1237 OK
I: FDE234C8
```

After the trunk has been seized, the Call Agent sends an IAM message to the switch that controls the trunk. The dialed PC "rings" and eventually takes the call, triggering the arrival of progress messages and then an *answer message* (ANM). At that point, the Call Agent knows that the call is established. The DSP associated to the incoming trunk has been loaded with the specified modem code, a simple HDLC framing in our example. After the call is established, the calling PC trains with the modem associated with the trunk. In our example, no authentication is requested. The Call Agent has identified the dialed user through its called number.

After the association is established and the IP service is validated, the gateway announces that it serves the local user. In our example, there is no address configuration performed through PPP: The dialed user has a permanent address, which has been programmed when it subscribed to the service. However, once the circuit is validated, the gateway should start announcing its access to this permanent address in the routing tables.

In our example, the dialed station is in fact an access point to a local network, and the TGW should start announcing accessibility of that local network (123.45.67.64/26) through the local routing procedures (an IGP such as RIP, OSPF, or EIGRP).

Note that the current design makes the hypothesis that the Call Agent "tells" the address of the LAN to the TGW. This is a very debatable design. If a secure IGP is used (for example using embedded keyed MD5 authentication, or using IPSEC) then the routing prefix is naturally exchanged through this IGP. On the other hand, some form of configuration can provide a double check against user errors.

In our example, the call is completed when the called modem hangs up. This triggers an ISUP release message, which is forwarded to the Call Agent. The Call Agent requests the TGW to delete the connection:

```
DLCX 1244 card23/21
C: A3C47F21456789F0
I: FDE234C8
```

The gateways responds with a message that should include a call parameters header fields:

```
250 1244 OK
P: PS51245, OS562345, PR5780, OR545123
```

We should note that because this is a data call, the call parameters only include a count of the packets and octets that were sent and received.

Callback, Using a TGW

There are three classic forms of callback:

1. ANI-based Callback
2. PPP Callback (Microsoft Callback is a variant)
3. Login-based callback

The ANI based callback can be implemented entirely in the Call Agent, as indicated in Table 5-19.

In the PPP callback suppose that the modem first establishes an incoming connection and goes through the authentication exchange. Table 5-20 provides an example of these exchanges.

This diagram shows the exchange of messages during a call from a modem user to an *Internet Service Provider* (ISP), using a trunking gateway that doubles as a *Network Access Server* (NAS). During these exchanges the SGCP is used by the Call Agent to control the TGW.

Table 5-19

Callback using a TGW

PC	CO	SS7/ISUP	TGW	CA	ACC
Dials	IAM	->			
		IAM—	—	->	
				Notices that the called number corresponds to a call back service, and that the calling number has subscribed to that service Terminates the incoming call	
		<-	—	REL	
	<-	REL			
	RLC	->			
Hangup		RLC	—	->	
				Decides to place an outgoing call Call start	->
			<-	Create Connection (data)	
			Ack	->	
		<-	—	ANM	
(Rings)	<-	ANM			

Table 5-20

PPP callback

PC	CO	SS7/ISUP	TGW	CA	ACC
Dials in					
	IAM	->			
		IAM	—	-> Checks called number Notices data call Call start	->
			<-	Create Connection (data)	
			Ack	-> Connection completed Call established	->
		<-	—	ANM	
	<-	ANM			
Modem	—	—	->		
<-	—	—	Handshake		
PPP	—	—	-> Obtain user-id, password check	—	— ->
			<- Reports call back condition	—	— Ack
			NTFY	->	
			<-	ACK Decides to place an outgoing call	
			<-	Delete Connection	
			perf data	->	
		<-	—	REL	
	<-	REL			
	REL	->			
Hangup		REL	—	->	

On reception of the IAM message, the Call Agent notices that the called number corresponds to a data service. Using configuration databases, the

Call Agent selects the type of modem parameters and authentication parameters that correspond to the called number and to the calling number. It uses this knowledge to send a connection command to the TGW, programming the incoming trunk:

```
CRCX 1237 card23/21
C: A3C47F21456789F0
M: data
X: 0123456789B1
R: cl, cbk
v=0
m=nas/radius
c=radius.example.net
a=bearer:v.32
```

Table 5-21

Login based call-back

PC	CO	SS7/ISUP	TGW	CA	ACC
				Call start	->
			<-	Create Connection (data)	
			Ack	->	
		<-	—	IAM	
(Rings)	<-	IAM			
	ACM	->			
		ACM	—	->	
(Answer)	ANM	->			
		ANM	—	->	
				Connection complete Call established	->
PPP	—	—	->		
<-	—	—	Validates call		
Connected to the Internet Closes connection					
	REL	->			
		REL	—	->	
			<-	Delete Connection	
			Perf data	->	
		<-	—	RLC	
	<-	RLC			
				Call end	->

```
a=framing:ppp-asynch
a=dialed:18001234567
a=dialing:2345678901
```

Table 5-21 shows an example of the login based callback.

The gateway immediately acknowledges the creation by sending back the identification of the newly created connection. (There is no session description in the case of a data call.)

```
200 1237 OK
I: FDE234C8
```

The Call Agent, knowing that this is a data call, can immediately acknowledge the establishment of the connection by sending an ANM message back to the calling switch.

The DSP associated to the incoming trunk has been loaded with the specified modem code. After the call is established, the modem of the calling PC is synchronized with the modem associated to the trunk. The caller then proceeds to a normal PPP synchronization, which probably implies a PPP logon. The logon parameters, in our example, are checked using Radius. The Radius server that is used is typically chosen as a function of the called number, which identifies the data service that the calling modem requested. In fact, the number can also be used to identify the specific form of authentication that is requested.

In the call back example, the Radius server indicates that the call cannot be completed as such, and that the user should be called back (for example, using a Callback Framed service type in its access-accept response.) The TGW thus sends a Notify message to the Call Agent indicating that a callback is requested:

```
NTFY 2005 card23/21
X: 0123456789B1
O: cbk(user-id)
```

After this notification, the Call Agent should send an acknowledgment:

```
200 2005 OK
```

The Call Agent checks that the call back request can be followed though. In its databases, it finds the regular address associated with the "user-id," and prepares to set up a call to that address. It first clears the incoming call by sending a DeleteConnection command to the TGW.

In our example, the call is completed when the calling modem hangs up. This triggers an ISUP release message that is forwarded to the Call Agent. The Call Agent requests the TGW to delete the connection and reset the list of observed events:

```
DLCX 1244 card23/21
C: A3C47F21456789F0
I: FDE234C8
X: 0123456789B2
R:
```

The gateways responds with a message that should include a call parameters header fields:

```
250 1244 OK
P: PS52, OS5345, PR51, OR5123
```

We should note that, because this is a data call, the call parameters only include a count of the packets and octets that were sent and received. The Call Agent then proceeds to set up an outgoing data call. This call might be routed through the same TGW that received the incoming call, but can also be routed through an entirely different endpoint, for example if the calling user has moved out of its normal region.

Table 5-22a

Message exchange example

PC	CO	SS7/ ISUP	TGW	CA	ACC	LNS
Dials in						
	IAM	->				
		IAM—	—	->		
				Check called number		
				Notices data call		
				Call start	->	
			<-	Create Connection (data)		
			Ack	->		
				Connection complete		
				Call established	->	
		<-	—	ANM		

PC	CO	SS7/ISUP	TGW	CA	ACC	LNS
	<-	ANM				
Modem	—	—	->			
<-	—	—	Handshake			
PPP	—	—	->			
			Obtain user-id, password Establish Tunnel			
			SCC-REQ	—		—	->
			<-	—	—	SCC-REP
			<-	—	—	SCC-CON
			IC-REQ	—	—	->
			<-	—	—	IC-REP
			<-	—	—	IC-CON
			Spoof PPP/LCP	—	—	->
<-	—	—	Relays PPP	—	—	->
Connected to the Internet						

Table 5-22b

Message exchange example

PC	CO	SS7/ISUP	TGW	CA	ACC	LNS
Closes connection						
	REL	->				
		REL	—	->		
			<-	Delete Connection		
			perf data	->		
		<-	—	RLC		
	<-	RLC				
			CDN	—	—	->
			Stop-CC-N	—	—	->
				Call end	->	

Data Call to a TGW, Using L2TP

Tables 5-22a and 5-22b show the exchange of messages during a call from a modem user to an *Internet Service Provider* (ISP) using a trunking gateway that doubles as a *Network Access Server* (NAS). During these exchanges, the SGCP is used by the Call Agent to control the TGW. The PPP information is relayed to a network server (LNS) using L2TP. On reception of the IAM message, the Call Agent notices that the called number corresponds to a data service. Using configuration databases, the Call Agent selects the type of modem parameters and authentication parameters that correspond to the called number and to the calling number. It uses this knowledge to send a connection command to the TGW, programming the incoming trunk:

```
CRCX 1237 card23/21
C: A3C47F21456789F0
M: data
X: 0123456789B1
R: cl
v=0
c=IN IP4 access.example.net
m=nas/l2tp
k=clear:some-shared-secret
a=bearer:v.32
a=framing:ppp-asynch
a=dialed:18001234567
a=dialing:2345678901
```

The gateway immediately acknowledges the creation by sending back the identification of the newly created connection. (There is no need to transmit a session description in the case of a data call.)

```
200 1237 OK
I: FDE234C8
```

The Call Agent, knowing that this is a data call, can immediately acknowledge the establishment of the connection by sending an ANM message back to the calling switch. The DSP associated to the incoming trunk has been loaded with the specified modem code. After the call is established, the modem of the calling PC is synchronized with the modem associated with the trunk. The caller then proceeds to a normal PPP synchronization, which probably implies a PPP logon.

After PPP has been properly synchronized, the TGW establishes a tunnel towards the LNS. Because L2TP is a two-layer protocol, the TGW must first establish an L2TP control connection between itself and the LNS. This connection might or might not have been established prior to the call set-up.

Tunnel establishment requires a shared secret between the LNS and the TGW; in our example, that secret is passed by the Call Agent, along with the name of the LNS. After the supporting tunnel is installed, the TGW has to establish an L2TP tunnel to relay the incoming call. After the call is established, the PPP packets received on the trunk are relayed over the L2TP tunnel and vice-versa.

In our example, the call is completed when the calling modem hangs up. This triggers an ISUP release message, which is forwarded to the Call Agent. The Call Agent requests the TGW to delete the connection:

```
DLCX 1244 card23/21
C: A3C47F21456789F0
I: FDE234C8
```

The gateways responds with a message that should include a call parameters header fields:

```
250 1244 OK
P: PS51245, OS562345, PR5780, OR545123
```

We should note that, because this is a data call, the call parameters only include a count of the packets and octets that were sent and received.

References

- Atkinson, R. 1995. "Security Architecture for the Internet Protocol." RFC 1825 (August).

- ———. 1995. "IP Authentication Header." RFC 1826 (August).

- ———. 1995. "IP Encapsulating Security Payload (ESP)." RFC 1827 (August).

- ———. "SAP—Session Announcement Protocol." Work in Progress.

- Handley, M, and V. Jacobson. 1998, "SDP: Session Description Protocol." RFC 2327 (April).

■ Handley, M., E. Schooler, and H. Schulzrinne. "Session Initiation Protocol (SIP)." Work in Progress.

■ ITU-T. Recommendation Q.761. "Functional Description of the ISDN User Part of Signalling System No. 7." (Malaga-Torremolinos, 1984; modified at Helsinki, 1993)

■ ———. Recommendation Q.762. "General Function of Messages and Signals of the ISDN User Part of Signalling System No. 7." (Malaga-Torremolinos, 1984; modified at Helsinki, 1993)

■ ———. Recommendation H.323. "Visual Telephone Systems and Equipment for Local Area Networks Which Provide a Non-Guaranteed Quality of Service."

■ ———. Recommendation H.225. "Call Signaling Protocols and Media Stream Packetization for Packet Based Multimedia Communications Systems."

■ ———. Recommendation H.245, "Linr Transmission of Non-Telephone Signals."

■ Schulzrinne, H. 1996. "RTP Profile for Audio and Video Conferences with Minimal Control." RFC 1890 (January).

■ Schulzrinne, H., S. Casner, R. Frederick, and V. Jacobson. 1996. "RTP: A Transport Protocol for Real-Time Applications." RFC 1889 (January).

■ Schulzrinne, H., A. Rao, and R. Lanphier. 1998. "Real Time Streaming Protocol (RTSP)." RFC 2326 (April).

SUMMARY

Voice-Over-IP (VOIP) technology is just beginning compared to technologies that have been in the marketplace for some time. I say this because it is not commonplace in the marketplace at the time of this writing. I have purposely selected a variety of information and presented it here to provide you with the best insight on this topic that I can. By the time this book is in your hands it might well be that other literature is available from numerous sources on the topic. I believe that VOIP is going to gain momentum and grow into the marketplace.

Point-to-Point Protocol (PPP)

Introduction

The PPP topic is one that has been around in the Internet community for some time. It should be no surprise that the Internet community is the best place to get information on this topic. My purpose in this chapter is to provide you with what has helped me and to raise your understanding of the topic. The primary reference (in this author's opinion) for PPP is the RFC 1661. From the standpoint of becoming versed in this topic, I consider this RFC to be quite important. From the standpoint of having the knowledge required to work with PPP at advanced levels, I consider this RFC to be important. On the other hand, how the technology is implemented by vendor varies, and the content of that extends beyond the scope of my purpose here. As a result, based on my experience, RFC 1661 is the best source, and this is my rationale for using a partial rendition of it here. The information here is presented courtesy of The Internet Society and is a partial excerpt from RFC1661. This RFC can be obtained at

`ftp://ftp.ncren.net`

The *Point-to-Point Protocol* (PPP) provides a standard method for transporting multi-protocol datagrams over point-to-point links. PPP consists primarily of three main components:

1. A method for encapsulating multi-protocol datagrams
2. A *Link Control Protocol* (LCP) for establishing, configuring, and testing the data-link connection
3. A family of *Network Control Protocols* (NCPs) for establishing and configuring different network-layer protocols

A Perspective on PPP

The *Point-to-Point Protocol* (PPP) is designed for communication links that transport packets between two peers. These links provide full-duplex operation. It is intended that PPP provide a common solution for easy connection of a wide variety of hosts, bridges, and routers.

PPP encapsulation provides for multiplexing of different network-layer protocols over the same link. The PPP encapsulation has been carefully designed to retain compatibility with most commonly used supporting hardware. Only eight additional octets are necessary to form the encapsulation when used within the default HDLC-like framing. In environments where bandwidth is at a premium, the encapsulation and framing may be shortened to two or four octets.

To support high-speed implementations, the default encapsulation uses only simple fields, and only one of which needs to be examined for demultiplexing. The default header and information fields fall on 32-bit boundaries, and the trailer may be padded to an arbitrary boundary.

To be sufficiently versatile to be portable to a wide variety of environments, PPP provides a *Link Control Protocol* (LCP). The LCP is used to agree automatically on the encapsulation format options, handle varying limits on sizes of packets, detect a looped-back link and other common misconfiguration errors, and terminate the link. Other optional facilities provided are authentication of the identity of its peer on the link and determination of when a link is functioning properly and when it is failing.

Point-to-Point links tend to exacerbate many problems with the current family of network protocols. For instance, assignment and management of IP addresses, which is a problem even in LAN environments, is especially difficult over circuit-switched point-to-point links (such as dial-up modem servers). These problems are handled by a family of *Network Control Protocols* (NCPs), which each manage the specific needs required by their respective network-layer protocols. These NCPs are defined in companion documents.

The original design intent was for PPP links to be easy to configure. By design, the standard defaults handle all common configurations. The implementer can specify improvements to the default configuration, which are automatically communicated to the peer without operator intervention. Finally, the operator may explicitly configure options for the link that enable the link to operate in environments where it would otherwise be impossible.

This self-configuration is implemented through an extensible option negotiation mechanism, where each end of the link describes to the other its capabilities and requirements. Although the option negotiation mechanism described in this document is specified in terms of the *Link Control Protocol* (LCP), the same facilities are designed to be used by other control protocols, especially the family of NCPs.

Because the content here is of RFC origin, the terminology has some particular meaning. To preserve the meaning, I am including the definition of those words that are pertinent throughout the remainder of this document.

MUST   This word, or the adjective "required," means that the definition is an absolute requirement of the specification.

MUST NOT   This phrase means that the definition is an absolute prohibition of the specification.

SHOULD   This word, or the adjective "recommended," means that there may exist valid reasons in particular circumstances to ignore this item, but the full implications must be understood and carefully weighed before choosing a different course.

MAY   This word, or the adjective "optional," means that this item is one of an allowed set of alternatives. An implementation that does not include this option MUST be prepared to interoperate with another implementation that does include the option.

In addition to the definition of these terms, the following terms should be understood in light of their meaning as well.

Datagram   The unit of transmission in the network layer (such as IP). A datagram may be encapsulated in one or more packets passed to the data link layer.

Frame   The unit of transmission at the data link layer. A frame may include a header and/or a trailer, along with some number of units of data.

Packet   The basic unit of encapsulation that is passed across the interface between the network layer and the data link layer. A packet is usually mapped to a frame; the exceptions are when data link layer fragmentation is being performed, or when multiple packets are incorporated into a single frame.

Peer   The other end of the point-to-point link

Silently discard   The implementation discards the packet without further processing. The implementation SHOULD provide the capability of logging the error, including the contents of the silently discarded packet, and SHOULD record the event in a statistics counter.

PPP Encapsulation

The PPP encapsulation is used to disambiguate multi-protocol datagrams. This encapsulation requires framing to indicate the beginning and end of the encapsulation. Methods of providing framing are specified in companion documents. A summary of the PPP encapsulation is shown as follows. The fields are transmitted from left to right.

Protocol	Information	Padding
8/16 bits	*	*

Protocol Field

The Protocol field is one or two octets, and its value identifies the datagram encapsulated in the Information field of the packet. The field is transmitted and received with most significant octet first. The structure of this field is consistent with the ISO 3309 extension mechanism for address fields. All Protocols MUST be odd; the least significant bit of the least significant octet MUST equal "1." Also, all Protocols MUST be assigned such that the least significant bit of the most significant octet equals "0."

Frames received that don't comply with these rules MUST be treated as having an unrecognized Protocol. Protocol field values in the "0***" to "3***" range identify the network-layer protocol of specific packets, and values in the "8***" to "b***" range identify packets belonging to the associated *Network Control Protocols* (NCPs), if any.

Protocol field values in the "4***" to "7***" range are used for protocols with low volume traffic which have no associated NCP. Protocol field values in the "c***" to "f***" range identify packets as link-layer Control Protocols (such as LCP). Table 6-1 contains Protocol Names and their correspnding values.

Developers of new protocols MUST obtain a number from the *Internet Assigned Numbers Authority* (IANA), at IANA@isi.edu.

Table 6-1

Protocol names & values

Value (in hex)	Protocol Name
0001	Padding Protocol
0003 to 001f	Reserved (transparency inefficient)
007d	Reserved (Control Escape)
00cf	Reserved (PPP NLPID)
00ff	Reserved (compression inefficient)
8001 to 801f	Unused
807d	Unused
80cf	Unused
80ff	Unused
c021	Link Control Protocol
c023	Password Authentication Protocol
c025	Link Quality Report
c223	Challenge Handshake Authentication Protocol

Information Field

The Information field is zero or more octets. The Information field contains the datagram for the protocol specified in the protocol field.

The maximum length for the Information field, including Padding but not including the Protocol field, is termed the *Maximum Receive Unit* (MRU), which defaults to 1500 octets. By negotiation, consenting PPP implementations may use other values for the MRU.

Padding

On transmission, the Information field MAY be padded with an arbitrary number of octets up to the MRU. It is the responsibility of each protocol to distinguish padding octets from real information.

PPP Link Operation

To establish communications over a point-to-point link, each end of the PPP link MUST first send LCP packets to configure and test the data link. After the link has been established, the peer MAY be authenticated. Then PPP MUST send NCP packets to choose and configure one or more network-layer protocols. After each of the chosen network-layer protocols has been configured, datagrams from each network-layer protocol can be sent over the link.

The link remains configured for communications until explicit LCP or NCP packets close the link down, or until some external event occurs (an inactivity timer expires or a network administrator intervenes).

Phase Diagram

In the process of configuring, maintaining, and terminating the PPP link, the link goes through several distinct phases, which are specified in the following simplified state diagram:

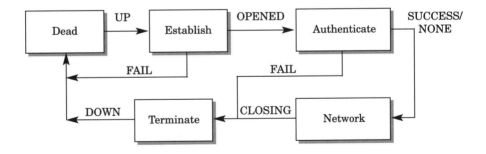

Not all transitions are specified in this diagram. The following semantics MUST be followed.

Link Dead

The link necessarily begins and ends with this phase. When an external event (such as carrier detection or network administrator configuration) indicates that the physical-layer is ready to be used, PPP proceeds to the Link Establishment phase. During this phase, the LCP automaton (described later) is in the Initial or Starting state. The transition to the Link Establishment phase signals an Up event to the LCP automaton.

Typically, a link returns to this phase automatically after the disconnection of a modem. In the case of a hard-wired link, this phase may be extremely short—merely long enough to detect the presence of the device.

Link Establishment Phase

The *Link Control Protocol* (LCP) is used to establish the connection through an exchange of Configure packets. This exchange is complete, and the LCP Opened state entered, after a Configure-Ack packet has been both sent and received. All Configuration Options are assumed to be at default values unless altered by the configuration exchange. It is important to note that only Configuration Options that are independent of particular network-layer protocols are configured by LCP. Configuration of individual network-layer protocols is handled by separate *Network Control Protocols* (NCPs) during the Network-Layer Protocol phase. Any non-LCP packets received during this phase MUST be silently discarded.

The receipt of the LCP Configure-Request causes a return to the Link Establishment phase from the Network-Layer Protocol phase or Authentication phase.

Authentication Phase

On some links, it may be desirable to require a peer to authenticate itself before allowing network-layer protocol packets to be exchanged. By default, authentication is not mandatory. If an implementation desires that the peer authenticate with some specific authentication protocol, then it MUST request the use of that authentication protocol during the Link Establishment phase.

Authentication SHOULD take place as soon as possible after link establishment. However, link quality determination MAY occur concurrently. An implementation MUST NOT allow the exchange of link quality determination packets to delay authentication indefinitely.

Advancement from the Authentication phase to the Network-Layer Protocol phase MUST NOT occur until authentication has completed. If authentication fails, the authenticator SHOULD proceed instead to the Link Termination phase. Only Link Control Protocol, authentication protocol, and link quality monitoring packets are allowed during this phase. All other packets received during this phase MUST be silently discarded. An implementation SHOULD NOT fail authentication simply due to timeout or lack of response. The authentication SHOULD allow some method of retransmission and proceed to the Link Termination phase only after a number of authentication attempts has been exceeded. The implementation responsible for commencing Link Termination phase is the implementation that has refused authentication to its peer.

Network-Layer Protocol Phase

After PPP has finished the previous phases, each network-layer protocol (such as IP, IPX, or AppleTalk) MUST be separately configured by the appropriate *Network Control Protocol* (NCP). Each NCP MAY be Opened and Closed at any time. Because an implementation may initially use a significant amount of time for link quality determination, implementations SHOULD avoid fixed timeouts when waiting for their peers to configure a NCP.

After a NCP has reached the Opened state, PPP carries the corresponding network-layer protocol packets. Any supported network-layer protocol packets received when the corresponding NCP is not in the Opened state MUST be silently discarded. Only protocols that are supported are silently discarded. During this phase, link traffic consists of any possible combination of LCP, NCP, and network-layer protocol packets.

Link Termination Phase

PPP can terminate the link at any time. This might happen because of the loss of carrier, authentication failure, link quality failure, the expiration of an idle-period timer, or the administrative closing of the link.

LCP is used to close the link through an exchange of Terminate packets. After the exchange of Terminate packets, the implementation SHOULD signal the physical-layer to disconnect to enforce the termination of the link, particularly in the case of an authentication failure. The sender of the Terminate-Request SHOULD disconnect after receiving a Terminate-Ack, or after the Restart counter expires. The receiver of a Terminate-Request SHOULD wait for the peer to disconnect and MUST NOT disconnect until at least one Restart time has passed after sending a Terminate-Ack. PPP SHOULD proceed to the Link Dead phase. Any non-LCP packets received during this phase MUST be silently discarded.

The closing of the link by LCP is sufficient. There is no need for each NCP to send a flurry of Terminate packets. Conversely, the fact that one NCP has Closed is not sufficient reason to cause the termination of the PPP link, even if that NCP was the only NCP currently in the Opened state.

The Option Negotiation Automaton

The finite-state automaton is defined by events, actions, and state transitions. Events include reception of external commands such as Open and Close, expiration of the Restart timer, and reception of packets from a peer. Actions include the starting of the Restart timer and the transmission of packets to the peer.

Some types of packets—Configure-Naks and Configure-Rejects, Code-Rejects and Protocol-Rejects, Echo-Requests, Echo-Replies and Discard-Requests—are not differentiated in the automaton descriptions. As described later, these packets do indeed serve different functions. However, they always cause the same transitions, as shown in Table 6-2.

Table 6-2

Packet transition information

Events	Actions
Up = lower layer is Up	tlu = This-Layer-Up
Down = lower layer is Down	tld = This-Layer-Down
Open = administrative Open	tls = This-Layer-Started
Close= administrative Close	tlf = This-Layer-Finished
TO+ = Timeout with counter > 0	irc = Initialize-Restart-Count
TO- = Timeout with counter expired	zrc = Zero-Restart-Count
RCR+ = Receive-Configure-Request (Good)	scr = Send-Configure-Request

Events	Actions
RCR- = Receive-Configure-Request (Bad)	
RCA = Receive-Configure-Ack	sca = Send-Configure-Ack
RCN = Receive-Configure-Nak/Rej	scn = Send-Configure-Nak/Rej
RTR = Receive-Terminate-Request	str = Send-Terminate-Request
RTA = Receive-Terminate-Ack	sta = Send-Terminate-Ack
RUC = Receive-Unknown-Code	scj = Send-Code-Reject
RXJ+ = Receive-Code-Reject (permitted)	
or Receive-Protocol-Reject	
RXJ- = Receive-Code-Reject (catastrophic)	
or Receive-Protocol-Reject	
RXR = Receive-Echo-Request	ser = Send-Echo-Reply
or Receive-Echo-Reply	
or Receive-Discard-Request	

State Transition Table

The complete state transition table follows. States are indicated horizontally, and events are read vertically. State transitions and actions are represented in the form action/new-state. Multiple actions are separated by commas and may continue on succeeding lines as space requires; multiple actions may be implemented in any convenient order. The state may be followed by a letter, which indicates an explanatory footnote. The dash (-) indicates an illegal transition.

The states in which the Restart timer is running are identifiable by the presence of TO events. Only the Send-Configure-Request, Send-Terminate-Request, and Zero-Restart-Count actions start or re-start the Restart timer. The Restart timer is stopped when transitioning from any state where the timer is running to a state where the timer is not running. Table 6-3 is an example.

Table 6-3 State transition table

Events	0 Initial	1 Starting	2 Closed	3 Stopped	4 Closing	5 Stopping	6 Req-Sent	7 Ack-Rcvd	8 Ack-Sent	9 Opened
Up	2	irc,scr/6								
Down		1	0	tls/1		1	1	1	1	tld/1
Open	tls/1	1	irc,scr/6	3r	5r	5r	6	7	8	9r
Close	0	tlf/0	2	2	4	4	irc,str/4	irc,str/4	irc,str/4	tld,irc,str/4
TO+					str/4	str/5	scr/6	scr/6	scr/8	
TO-					tlf/2	tlf/3	tlf/3p	tlf/3p	tlf/3p	
RCR+			sta/2	irc,scr,sca/8	4	5	sca/8	sca,tlu/9	sca/8	tld,scr,sca/8
RCR-			sta/2	irc,scr,scn/6	4	5	scn/6	scn/7	scn/6	tld,scr,scn/6
RCA			sta/2	sta/3	4	5	irc/7	scr/6x	irc,tlu/9	tld,scr/6x
RCN			sta/2	sta/3	4	5	irc,scr/6	scr/6x	irc,scr/8	tld,scr/6x
RTR			sta/2	sta/3	sta/4	sta/5	sta/6	sta/6	sta/6	tld,zrc,sta/5
RTA			2	3	tlf/2	tlf/3	6	6	8	tld,scr/6
RUC			scj/2	scj/3	scj/4	scj/5	scj/6	scj/7	scj/8	scj/9
RXJ+			2	3	4	5	6	6	8	9
RXJ-			tlf/2	tlf/3	tlf/2	tlf/3	tlf/3	tlf/3	tlf/3	tld,irc,str/5
RXR			2	3	4	5	6	7	8	ser/9

The events and actions are defined according to a message passing architecture, rather than a signaling architecture. If an action is desired to control specific signals (such as DTR), additional actions are likely to be required.

[p] Passive option.   See Stopped state discussion

[r] Restart option.   See Open event discussion

[x] Crossed connection.   See RCA event discussion

States

The following is a more detailed description of each automaton state.

Initial   In the Initial state, the lower layer is unavailable (Down), and no Open has occurred. The Restart timer is not running in the Initial state.

Starting   The Starting state is the Open counterpart to the Initial state. An administrative Open has been initiated, but the lower layer is still unavailable (Down). The Restart timer is not running in the Starting state. When the lower layer becomes available (Up), a Configure-Request is sent.

Closed   In the Closed state, the link is available (Up), but no Open has occurred. The Restart timer is not running in the Closed state.

On reception of Configure-Request packets, a Terminate-Ack is sent. Terminate-Acks are silently discarded to avoid creating a loop.

Stopped   The Stopped state is the Open counterpart to the Closed state. It is entered when the automaton is waiting for a Down event after the This-Layer-Finished action or after sending a Terminate-Ack. The Restart timer is not running in the Stopped state. On reception of Configure-Request packets, an appropriate response is sent. On reception of other packets, a Terminate-Ack is sent. Terminate-Acks are silently discarded to avoid creating a loop.

The Stopped state is a junction state for link termination, link configuration failure, and other automaton failure modes. These potentially separate states have been combined. There is a race condition between the Down event response (from the This-Layer-Finished action) and the Receive-Configure-Request event. When a Configure-Request arrives before the Down event, the Down event supersedes by returning the automaton to the Starting state. This prevents attack by repetition.

After the peer fails to respond to Configure-Requests, an implementation MAY wait passively for the peer to send Configure-Requests. In this case, the This-Layer-Finished action is not used for the TO- event in states Req-Sent, Ack-Rcvd, and Ack-Sent.

This option is useful for dedicated circuits, or circuits that have no status signals available, but SHOULD NOT be used for switched circuits.

Closing In the Closing state, an attempt is made to terminate the connection. A Terminate-Request has been sent, and the Restart timer is running, but a Terminate-Ack has not yet been received.

On reception of a Terminate-Ack, the Closed state is entered. On the expiration of the Restart timer, a new Terminate-Request is transmitted, and the Restart timer is restarted. After the Restart timer has expired Max-Terminate times, the Closed state is entered.

Stopping The Stopping state is the Open counterpart to the Closing state. A Terminate-Request has been sent, and the Restart timer is running, but a Terminate-Ack has not yet been received. The Stopping state provides a well-defined opportunity to terminate a link before allowing new traffic. After the link has terminated, a new configuration may occur through the Stopped or Starting states.

Request-Sent In the Request-Sent state an attempt is made to configure the connection. A Configure-Request has been sent, and the Restart timer is running, but a Configure-Ack has not yet been received nor has one been sent.

Ack-Received In the Ack-Received state, a Configure-Request has been sent, and a Configure-Ack has been received. The Restart timer is still running, because a Configure-Ack has not yet been sent.

Ack-Sent In the Ack-Sent state, a Configure-Request and a Configure-Ack have both been sent, but a Configure-Ack has not yet been received. The Restart timer is running, because a Configure-Ack has not yet been received.

Opened In the Opened state, a Configure-Ack has been both sent and received. The Restart timer is not running. When entering the Opened state, the implementation SHOULD signal the upper layers that it is now Up. Conversely when leaving the Opened state, the implementation SHOULD signal the upper layers that it is now Down.

Events

Transitions and actions in the automaton are caused by events.

Up   This event occurs when a lower layer indicates that it is ready to carry packets. Typically, this event is used by a modem handling or calling process, or by some other coupling of the PPP link to the physical media, to signal LCP that the link is entering Link Establishment phase. It also can be used by LCP to signal each NCP that the link is entering Network-Layer Protocol phase. That is, the This-Layer-Up action from LCP triggers the Up event in the NCP.

Down   This event occurs when a lower layer indicates that it is no longer ready to carry packets. Typically, this event is used by a modem handling or calling process, or by some other coupling of the PPP link to the physical media, to signal LCP that the link is entering Link Dead phase. It also can be used by LCP to signal each NCP that the link is leaving Network-Layer Protocol phase. That is, the This-Layer-Down action from LCP triggers the Down event in the NCP.

Open   This event indicates that the link is administratively available for traffic; that is, the network administrator (human or program) has indicated that the link is allowed to be Opened. When this event occurs, and the link is not in the Opened state, the automaton attempts to send configuration packets to the peer. If the automaton is not able to begin configuration (the lower layer is Down, or a previous Close event has not completed), the establishment of the link is automatically delayed.

When a Terminate-Request is received, or other events occur that cause the link to become unavailable, the automaton progresses to a state where the link is ready to re-open. No additional administrative intervention is necessary.

Experience has shown that users execute an additional Open command when they want to renegotiate the link. This might indicate that new values are to be negotiated. Because this is not the meaning of the Open event, it is suggested that when an Open user command is executed in the Opened, Closing, Stopping, or Stopped states, the implementation issue a Down event immediately followed by an Up event. Care must be taken that an intervening Down event does occur from another source.

The Down followed by an Up causes an orderly renegotiation of the link, by progressing through the Starting to the Request-Sent state. This causes the renegotiation of the link without any harmful side effects.

Close   This event indicates that the link is not available for traffic; that is, the network administrator (human or program) has indicated that the link is not allowed to be Opened. When this event occurs, and the link is not in the Closed state, the automaton attempts to terminate the connection. Further attempts to re-configure the link are denied until a new Open event occurs.

When authentication fails, the link SHOULD be terminated to prevent attack by repetition and denial of service to other users. Because the link is administratively available, this can be accomplished by simulating a Close event to the LCP immediately followed by an Open event. Care must be taken that an intervening Close event does occur from another source. The Close followed by an Open causes an orderly termination of the link by progressing through the Closing to the Stopping state, and the This-Layer-Finished action can disconnect the link. The automaton waits in the Stopped or Starting states for the next connection attempt.

Timeout (TO+, TO-)   This event indicates the expiration of the Restart timer. The Restart timer is used to time responses to Configure-Request and Terminate-Request packets. The TO+ event indicates that the Restart counter continues to be greater than zero, which triggers the corresponding Configure-Request or Terminate-Request packet to be retransmitted. The TO- event indicates that the Restart counter is not greater than zero, and no more packets need to be retransmitted.

Receive-Configure-Request (RCR+, RCR-)   This event occurs when a Configure-Request packet is received from the peer. The Configure-Request packet indicates the desire to open a connection and may specify Configuration Options. The RCR+ event indicates that the Configure-Request was acceptable and triggers the transmission of a corresponding Configure-Ack.

The RCR- event indicates that the Configure-Request was unacceptable and triggers the transmission of a corresponding Configure-Nak or Configure-Reject. These events may occur on a connection that is already in the Opened state. The implementation MUST be prepared to immediately renegotiate the Configuration Options.

Receive-Configure-Ack (RCA)   This event occurs when a valid Configure-Ack packet is received from the peer. The Configure-Ack packet is a positive response to a Configure-Request packet. An out of sequence or otherwise invalid packet is silently discarded.

Because the correct packet has already been received before reaching the Ack-Rcvd or Opened states, it is extremely unlikely that another such packet might arrive. As specified, all invalid Ack/Nak/Rej packets are silently discarded, and do not affect the transitions of the automaton. However, it is not impossible that a correctly formed packet arrives through a coincidentally timed cross-connection. It is more likely to be the result of an implementation error. At the very least, this occurrence SHOULD be logged.

Receive-Configure-Nak/Rej (RCN) This event occurs when a valid Configure-Nak or Configure-Reject packet is received from the peer. The Configure-Nak and Configure-Reject packets are negative responses to a Configure-Request packet. An out of sequence or otherwise invalid packet is silently discarded. Although the Configure-Nak and Configure-Reject cause the same state transition in the automaton, these packets have significantly different effects on the Configuration Options sent in the resulting Configure-Request packet.

Receive-Terminate-Request (RTR) This event occurs when a Terminate-Request packet is received. The Terminate-Request packet indicates the desire of the peer to close the connection. This event is not identical to the Close event as seen previously and does not override the Open commands of the local network administrator. The implementation MUST be prepared to receive a new Configure-Request without network administrator intervention.

Receive-Terminate-Ack (RTA) This event occurs when a Terminate-Ack packet is received from the peer. The Terminate-Ack packet is usually a response to a Terminate-Request packet. The Terminate-Ack packet may also indicate that the peer is in a Closed or Stopped state and serves to resynchronize the link configuration.

Receive-Unknown-Code (RUC) This event occurs when an uninterpretable packet is received from the peer. A Code-Reject packet is sent in response. Receive-Code-Reject, Receive-Protocol-Reject (RXJ+,RXJ-) This event occurs when a Code-Reject or a Protocol-Reject packet is received from the peer.

The RXJ+ event arises when the rejected value is acceptable, such as a Code-Reject of an extended code, or a Protocol-Reject of a NCP. These are within the scope of normal operation. The implementation MUST stop sending the offending packet type.

The RXJ- event arises when the rejected value is catastrophic, such as a Code-Reject of Configure-Request, or a Protocol-Reject of LCP! This event communicates an unrecoverable error that terminates the connection. Receive-Echo-Request, Receive-Echo-Reply, Receive-Discard-Request (RXR)

This event occurs when an Echo-Request, Echo-Reply or Discard-Request packet is received from the peer. The Echo-Reply packet is a response to an Echo-Request packet. There is no reply to an Echo-Reply or Discard-Request packet.

Actions

Actions in the automaton are caused by events and typically indicate the transmission of packets and/or the starting or stopping of the Restart timer.

Illegal-Event (-) This indicates an event that cannot occur in a properly implemented automaton. The implementation has an internal error, which should be reported and logged. No transition is taken, and the implementation SHOULD NOT reset or freeze.

This-Layer-Up (tlu) This action indicates to the upper layers that the automaton is entering the Opened state. Typically, this action is used by the LCP to signal the Up event to a NCP, Authentication Protocol, or Link Quality Protocol, or MAY be used by a NCP to indicate that the link is available for its network layer traffic.

This-Layer-Down (tld) This action indicates to the upper layers that the automaton is leaving the Opened state.

Typically, this action is used by the LCP to signal the Down event to a NCP, Authentication Protocol, or Link Quality Protocol, or MAY be used by a NCP to indicate that the link is no longer available for its network layer traffic.This-Layer-Started (tls). This action indicates to the lower layers that the automaton is entering the Starting state and the lower layer is needed for the link. The lower layer SHOULD respond with an Up event when the lower layer is available. The results of this action are highly implementation dependent.

This-Layer-Finished (tlf) This action indicates to the lower layers that the automaton is entering the Initial, Closed, or Stopped states, and the lower layer is no longer needed for the link. The lower layer SHOULD respond with a Down event when the lower layer has terminated.

Typically, this action MAY be used by the LCP to advance to the Link Dead phase, or MAY be used by a NCP to indicate to the LCP that the link may terminate when there are no other NCPs open. The results of this action are highly implementation dependent.

Initialize-Restart-Count (irc)   This action sets the Restart counter to the appropriate value (Max-Terminate or Max-Configure). The counter is decremented for each transmission, including the first. In addition to setting the Restart counter, the implementation MUST set the timeout period to the initial value when Restart timer backoff is used.

Zero-Restart-Count (zrc)   This action sets the Restart counter to zero. This action enables the FSA to pause before proceeding to the desired final state allowing traffic to be processed by the peer. In addition to zeroing the Restart counter, the implementation MUST set the timeout period to an appropriate value.

Send-Configure-Request (scr)   A Configure-Request packet is transmitted. This indicates the desire to open a connection with a specified set of Configuration Options. The Restart timer is started when the Configure-Request packet is transmitted, to guard against packet loss. The Restart counter is decremented each time a Configure-Request is sent.

Send-Configure-Ack (sca)   A Configure-Ack packet is transmitted. This acknowledges the reception of a Configure-Request packet with an acceptable set of Configuration Options.

Send-Configure-Nak (scn)   A Configure-Nak or Configure-Reject packet is transmitted, as appropriate. This negative response reports the reception of a Configure-Request packet with an unacceptable set of Configuration Options. Configure-Nak packets are used to refuse a Configuration Option value and to suggest a new, acceptable value. Configure-Reject packets are used to refuse all negotiation about a Configuration Option, typically because it is not recognized or implemented. The use of Configure-Nak versus Configure-Reject is more fully described in the chapter on LCP Packet Formats.

Send-Terminate-Request (str)   A Terminate-Request packet is transmitted. This indicates the desire to close a connection. The Restart timer is started when the Terminate-Request packet is transmitted to guard against packet loss. The Restart counter is decremented each time a Terminate-Request is sent.

Send-Terminate-Ack (sta)   A Terminate-Ack packet is transmitted. This acknowledges the reception of a Terminate-Request packet or otherwise serves to synchronize the automatons.

Send-Code-Reject (scj)   A Code-Reject packet is transmitted. This indicates the reception of an unknown type of packet.

Send-Echo-Reply (ser)   An Echo-Reply packet is transmitted. This acknowledges the reception of an Echo-Request packet.

Loop Avoidance

The protocol makes a reasonable attempt at avoiding Configuration Option negotiation loops. However, the protocol does NOT guarantee that loops do not happen. As with any negotiation, it is possible to configure two PPP implementations with conflicting policies that never converge. It is also possible to configure policies that do converge, but that take significant time to do so. Implementers should keep this in mind and SHOULD implement loop detection mechanisms or higher level timeouts.

Counters and Timers

Restart Timer   There is one special timer used by the automaton. The Restart timer is used to time transmissions of Configure-Request and Terminate-Request packets. Expiration of the Restart timer causes a timeout event and retransmission of the corresponding Configure-Request or Terminate-Request packet. The Restart timer MUST be configurable, but SHOULD default to three (3) seconds.

The Restart timer SHOULD be based on the speed of the link. The default value is designed for low speed (2,400 to 9,600 bps), high switching latency links (typical telephone lines). Higher speed links or links with low switching latency SHOULD have correspondingly faster retransmission times.

Instead of a constant value, the Restart timer MAY begin at an initial small value and increase to the configured final value. Each successive value less than the final value SHOULD be at least twice the previous value. The initial value SHOULD be large enough to account for the size of the packets, twice the round trip time for transmission at the link speed, and at least an additional 100 milliseconds to allow the peer to process the packets before responding. Some circuits add another 200 milliseconds of satellite delay. Round trip times for modems operating at 14,400 bps have been measured in the range of 160 to more than 600 milliseconds.

Max-Terminate   There is one required restart counter for Terminate-Requests. Max-Terminate indicates the number of Terminate-Request packets sent without receiving a Terminate-Ack before assuming that the peer is unable to respond. Max-Terminate MUST be configurable, but SHOULD default to two (2) transmissions.

Max-Configure   A similar counter is recommended for Configure-Requests. Max-Configure indicates the number of Configure-Request packets sent without receiving a valid Configure-Ack, Configure-Nak, or Configure-Reject before assuming that the peer is unable to respond. Max-Configure MUST be configurable, but SHOULD default to ten (10) transmissions.

Max-Failure   A related counter is recommended for Configure-Nak. Max-Failure indicates the number of Configure-Nak packets sent without sending a Configure-Ack before assuming that configuration is not converging. Any further Configure-Nak packets for peer requested options are converted to Configure-Reject packets, and locally desired options are no longer appended. Max-Failure MUST be configurable, but SHOULD default to five (5) transmissions.

LCP Packet Formats

There are three classes of LCP packets:

1. Link Configuration packets used to establish and configure a link (Configure-Request, Configure-Ack, Configure-Nak and Configure-Reject)

2. Link Termination packets used to terminate a link (Terminate-Request and Terminate-Ack)

3. Link Maintenance packets used to manage and debug a link (Code-Reject, Protocol-Reject, Echo-Request, Echo-Reply, and Discard-Request)

In the interest of simplicity, there is no version field in the LCP packet. A correctly functioning LCP implementation always responds to unknown Protocols and Codes with an easily recognizable LCP packet, thus providing a deterministic fallback mechanism for implementations of other versions.

Regardless of which Configuration Options are enabled, all LCP Link Configuration, Link Termination, and Code-Reject packets (codes 1 through 7) are always sent as if no Configuration Options were negotiated. In particular, each Configuration Option specifies a default value. This ensures that such LCP packets are always recognizable, even when one end of the link mistakenly believes the link to be open. Exactly one LCP packet is encapsulated in the PPP Information field where the PPP Protocol field indicates type hex c021 (Link Control Protocol).

A summary of the Link Control Protocol packet format is shown as follows. The fields are transmitted from left to right.

```
      0                   1                   2                   3
      0 1 2 3 4 5 6 7 8 9 0 1 2 3 4 5 6 7 8 9 0 1 2 3 4 5 6 7 8 9 0 1
     +-----------------+-----------------+---------------------------+
     |     Code        |   Identifier    |          Length           |
     +-----------------+-----------------+---------------------------+
     |     Data...                                                    
     +-----------------
```

Code The Code field is one octet and identifies the kind of LCP packet. When a packet is received with an unknown Code field, a Code-Reject packet is transmitted. Up-to-date values of the LCP Code field are specified in the most recent "Assigned Numbers" RFC [2]. This document concerns the following values:

1. Configure-Request
2. Configure-Ack
3. Configure-Nak
4. Configure-Reject
5. Terminate-Request
6. Terminate-Ack
7. Code-Reject
8. Protocol-Reject
9. Echo-Request
10. Echo-Reply
11. Discard-Request

Identifier The Identifier field is one octet and aids in matching requests and replies. When a packet is received with an invalid Identifier field, the packet is silently discarded without affecting the automaton.

Length The Length field is two octets and indicates the length of the LCP packet, including the Code, Identifier, Length, and Data fields. The Length MUST NOT exceed the MRU of the link. Octets outside the range of the Length field are treated as padding and are ignored on reception. When a packet is received with an invalid Length field, the packet is silently discarded without affecting the automaton.

Data The Data field is zero or more octets, as indicated by the Length field. The format of the Data field is determined by the Code field.

Configure-Request

An implementation wishing to open a connection MUST transmit a Configure-Request. The Options field is filled with any desired changes to the link defaults. Configuration Options SHOULD NOT be included with default values. On reception of a Configure-Request, an appropriate reply MUST be transmitted.

A summary of the Configure-Request packet format is shown as follows. The fields are transmitted from left to right.

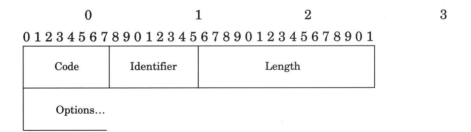

Code 1 for Configure-Request

Identifier The Identifier field MUST be changed whenever the contents of the Options field changes, and whenever a valid reply has been received for a previous request. For retransmissions, the Identifier MAY remain unchanged.

Options   The options field is variable in length and contains the list of zero or more Configuration Options that the sender desires to negotiate. All Configuration Options are always negotiated simultaneously.

Configure-Ack

If every Configuration Option received in a Configure-Request is recognizable and all values are acceptable, then the implementation MUST transmit a Configure-Ack. The acknowledged Configuration Options MUST NOT be reordered or modified in any way. On reception of a Configure-Ack, the Identifier field MUST match that of the last transmitted Configure-Request. Additionally, the Configuration Options in a Configure-Ack MUST exactly match those of the last transmitted Configure-Request. Invalid packets are silently discarded. A summary of the Configure-Ack packet format is shown as follows. The fields are transmitted from left to right.

```
   0                   1                   2                   3
   0 1 2 3 4 5 6 7 8 9 0 1 2 3 4 5 6 7 8 9 0 1 2 3 4 5 6 7 8 9 0 1
  +-------------------+-------------------+---------------------------+
  |      Code         |    Identifier     |          Length           |
  +-------------------+-------------------+---------------------------+
  |   Options...
  +----------------
```

Code   2 for Configure-Ack

Identifier   The Identifier field is a copy of the Identifier field of the Configure-Request that caused this Configure-Ack.

Options   The Options field is variable in length and contains the list of zero or more Configuration Options that the sender is acknowledging. All Configuration Options are always acknowledged simultaneously.

Configure-Nak

If every instance of the received Configuration Options is recognizable, but some values are not acceptable, then the implementation MUST transmit a Configure-Nak. The Options field is filled with only the unacceptable Configuration Options from the Configure-Request. All acceptable Configuration Options are filtered out of the Configure-Nak, but otherwise the Configuration Options from the Configure-Request MUST NOT be reordered. Options that have no value fields (boolean options) MUST use the Configure-Reject reply instead. Each Configuration Option, which is allowed only a single instance, MUST be modified to a value acceptable to the Configure-Nak sender. The default value MAY be used, when this differs from the requested value. When a particular type of Configuration Option can be listed more than once with different values, the Configure-Nak MUST include a list of all values for that option which are acceptable to the Configure-Nak sender. This includes acceptable values that were present in the Configure-Request.

Finally, an implementation may be configured to request the negotiation of a specific Configuration Option. If that option is not listed, then that option MAY be appended to the list of Nak'd Configuration Options, to prompt the peer to include that option in its next Configure-Request packet. Any value fields for the option MUST indicate values acceptable to the Configure-Nak sender. On reception of a Configure-Nak, the Identifier field MUST match that of the last transmitted Configure-Request. Invalid packets are silently discarded.

Reception of a valid Configure-Nak indicates that when a new Configure-Request is sent, the Configuration Options MAY be modified as specified in the Configure-Nak. When multiple instances of a Configuration Option are present, the peer SHOULD select a single value to include in its next Configure-Request packet. Some Configuration Options have a variable length. Because the Nak'd Option has been modified by the peer, the implementation MUST be able to handle an Option length which is different from the original Configure-Request. A summary of the Configure-Nak packet format is shown as follows. The fields are transmitted from left to right.

```
 0                   1                   2                   3
 0 1 2 3 4 5 6 7 8 9 0 1 2 3 4 5 6 7 8 9 0 1 2 3 4 5 6 7 8 9 0 1
+-------+-----------+---------------------+
| Code  | Identifier|        Length       |
+-------+-----------+---------------------+
| Options...
+----------
```

Code   3 for Configure-Nak

Identifier   The Identifier field is a copy of the Identifier field of the Configure-Request that caused this Configure-Nak.

Options   The Options field is variable in length and contains the list of zero or more Configuration Options that the sender is Nak'ing. All Configuration Options are always Nak'd simultaneously.

Configure-Reject

If some Configuration Options received in a Configure-Request are not recognizable or are not acceptable for negotiation (as configured by a network administrator), then the implementation MUST transmit a Configure-Reject. The Options field is filled with only the unacceptable Configuration Options from the Configure-Request. All recognizable and negotiable Configuration Options are filtered out of the Configure-Reject, but otherwise the Configuration Options MUST NOT be reordered or modified in any way. On reception of a Configure-Reject, the Identifier field MUST match that of the last transmitted Configure-Request. Additionally, the Configuration Options in a Configure-Reject MUST be a proper subset of those in the last transmitted Configure-Request. Invalid packets are silently discarded. Reception of a valid Configure-Reject indicates that when a new Configure-Request is sent, it MUST NOT include any of the Configuration Options listed in the Configure-Reject. A summary of the Configure-Reject packet format is shown as follows. The fields are transmitted from left to right.

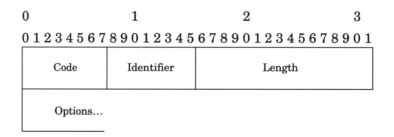

Code   4 for Configure-Reject

Identifier   The Identifier field is a copy of the Identifier field of the Configure-Request that caused this Configure-Reject.

Options   The Options field is variable in length and contains the list of zero or more Configuration Options that the sender is rejecting. All Configuration Options are always rejected simultaneously.

Terminate-Request and Terminate-Ack

LCP includes Terminate-Request and Terminate-Ack codes to provide a mechanism for closing a connection. An implementation wishing to close a connection SHOULD transmit a Terminate-Request. Terminate-Request packets SHOULD continue to be sent until Terminate-Ack is received, the lower layer indicates that it has gone down, or a sufficiently large number have been transmitted such that the peer is down with reasonable certainty. On reception of a Terminate-Request, a Terminate-Ack MUST be transmitted.

Reception of an un-elicited Terminate-Ack indicates that the peer is in the Closed or Stopped states, or is otherwise in need of re-negotiation. A summary of the Terminate-Request and Terminate-Ack packet formats is shown as follows. The fields are transmitted from left to right.

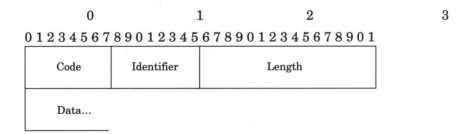

Code   5 for Terminate-Request, 6 for Terminate-Ack

Identifier   On transmission, the Identifier field MUST be changed whenever the content of the Data field changes, and whenever a valid reply has been received for a previous request. For retransmissions, the Identifier MAY remain unchanged. On reception, the Identifier field of the Terminate-Request is copied into the Identifier field of the Terminate-Ack packet.

Data The Data field is zero or more octets, and contains uninterpreted data for use by the sender. The data may consist of any binary value. The end of the field is indicated by the Length.

Code-Reject

Reception of a LCP packet with an unknown Code indicates that the peer is operating with a different version. This MUST be reported back to the sender of the unknown Code by transmitting a Code-Reject. On reception of the Code-Reject of a code that is fundamental to this version of the protocol, the implementation SHOULD report the problem and drop the connection, because it is unlikely that the situation can be rectified automatically. A summary of the Code-Reject packet format is shown as follows. The fields are transmitted from left to right.

```
0                   1                   2                   3
0 1 2 3 4 5 6 7 8 9 0 1 2 3 4 5 6 7 8 9 0 1 2 3 4 5 6 7 8 9 0 1
+---------------+---------------+-------------------------------+
|     Code      |   Identifier  |            Length             |
+---------------+---------------+-------------------------------+
|  Rejected-Packet...
+---------------+
```

Code 7 for Code-Reject

Identifier The Identifier field MUST be changed for each Code-Reject sent.

Rejected-Packet The Rejected-Packet field contains a copy of the LCP packet that is being rejected. It begins with the Information field and does not include any Data Link Layer headers or an FCS. The Rejected-Packet MUST be truncated to comply with the peer's established MRU.

Protocol-Reject

Reception of a PPP packet with an unknown Protocol field indicates that the peer is attempting to use a protocol that is unsupported. This usually occurs when the peer attempts to configure a new protocol. If the LCP automaton is in the Opened state, then this MUST be reported back to the peer by transmitting a Protocol-Reject.

On reception of a Protocol-Reject, the implementation MUST stop sending packets of the indicated protocol at the earliest opportunity. Protocol-Reject packets can only be sent in the LCP Opened state. Protocol-Reject packets received in any state other than the LCP Opened state SHOULD be silently discarded. A summary of the Protocol-Reject packet format is shown as follows. The fields are transmitted from left to right.

```
        0                   1                   2                   3
        0 1 2 3 4 5 6 7 8 9 0 1 2 3 4 5 6 7 8 9 0 1 2 3 4 5 6 7 8 9 0 1
       +---------------+---------------+-------------------------------+
       |     Code      |  Identifier   |            Length             |
       +---------------+---------------+-------------------------------+
       |      Rejected-Protocol...     |      Rejected-Information...   |
       +-------------------------------+-------------------------------+
```

Code   8 for Protocol-Reject

Identifier   The Identifier field MUST be changed for each Protocol-Reject sent.

Rejected-Protocol   The Rejected-Protocol field is two octets and contains the PPP Protocol field of the packet that is being rejected.

Rejected-Information   The Rejected-Information field contains a copy of the packet that is being rejected. It begins with the Information field and does not include any Data Link Layer headers or an FCS. The Rejected-Information MUST be truncated to comply with the peer's established MRU.

Echo-Request and Echo-Reply

LCP includes Echo-Request and Echo-Reply Codes to provide a Data Link Layer loopback mechanism for use in exercising both directions of the link. This is useful as an aid in debugging, link quality determination, performance testing, and for numerous other functions.

On reception of an Echo-Request in the LCP Opened state, an Echo-Reply MUST be transmitted. Echo-Request and Echo-Reply packets MUST only be sent in the LCP Opened state. Echo-Request and Echo-Reply packets received in any state other than the LCP Opened state SHOULD be silently discarded. A summary of the Echo-Request and Echo-Reply packet formats is shown as follows. The fields are transmitted from left to right.

```
 0                   1                   2                   3
 0 1 2 3 4 5 6 7 8 9 0 1 2 3 4 5 6 7 8 9 0 1 2 3 4 5 6 7 8 9 0 1
+---------------+---------------+-------------------------------+
|     Code      |   Identifier  |            Length             |
+---------------+---------------+-------------------------------+
|                         Magic-Number                          |
+---------------------------------------------------------------+
|    Data...
+---------------
```

Code   9 for Echo-Request, 10 for Echo-Reply

Identifier   On transmission, the Identifier field MUST be changed whenever the content of the Data field changes and whenever a valid reply has been received for a previous request. For retransmissions, the Identifier MAY remain unchanged. On reception, the Identifier field of the Echo-Request is copied into the Identifier field of the Echo-Reply packet.

Magic-Number   The Magic-Number field is four octets and aids in detecting links that are in the looped-back condition. Until the Magic-Number Configuration Option has been successfully negotiated, the Magic-Number MUST be transmitted as zero.

Data   The Data field is zero or more octets, and contains uninterpreted data for use by the sender. The data may consist of any binary value. The end of the field is indicated by the Length.

Discard-Request

LCP includes a Discard-Request Code to provide a Data Link Layer sink mechanism for use in exercising the local to remote direction of the link. This is useful as an aid in debugging, performance testing, and for numerous other functions. Discard-Request packets MUST only be sent in the LCP

Opened state. On reception, the receiver MUST silently discard any Discard-Request that it receives. A summary of the Discard-Request packet format is shown as follows. The fields are transmitted from left to right.

```
 0                   1                   2                   3
 0 1 2 3 4 5 6 7 8 9 0 1 2 3 4 5 6 7 8 9 0 1 2 3 4 5 6 7 8 9 0 1
+-------------------------------+---------------+---------------+
|      Code      |   Identifier  |           Length            |
+-------------------------------+-----------------------------+
|                         Magic-Number                         |
+--------------------------------------------------------------+
|  Data...                       
+-------------------            
```

Code   11 for Discard-Request

Identifier   The Identifier field MUST be changed for each Discard-Request sent.

Magic-Number   The Magic-Number field is four octets and aids in detecting links that are in the looped-back condition. Until the Magic-Number Configuration Option has been successfully negotiated, the Magic-Number MUST be transmitted as zero. See the Magic-Number Configuration Option for further explanation.

Data   The Data field is zero or more octets, and contains uninterpreted data for use by the sender. The data may consist of any binary value. The end of the field is indicated by the Length.

LCP Configuration Options

LCP Configuration Options allow negotiation of modifications to the default characteristics of a point-to-point link. If a Configuration Option is not included in a Configure-Request packet, the default value for that Configuration Option is assumed. Some Configuration Options MAY be listed more than once. The effect of this is Configuration Option specific, and is specified by each such Configuration Option description. (None of the Configuration Options in this specification can be listed more than once.) The end of the list of Configuration Options is indicated by the Length field of the LCP packet. Unless otherwise specified, all Configuration Options apply in a half-duplex fashion; typically, in the receive direction of the link from the point of view of the Configure-Request sender.

The options indicate additional capabilities or requirements of the implementation that is requesting the option. An implementation that does not understand any option SHOULD interoperate with one that implements every option. A default is specified for each option that enables the link to correctly function without negotiation of the option, although perhaps with less than optimal performance. Except where explicitly specified, acknowledgment of an option does not require the peer to take any additional action other than the default. It is not necessary to send the default values for the options in a Configure-Request. A summary of the Configuration Option format is shown as follows. The fields are transmitted from left to right.

```
0                       1
0 1 2 3 4 5 6 7 8 9 0 1 2 3 4 5 6 7 8 9
+---------------+---------------+---------------
|     Type      |    Length     |    Data...
+---------------+---------------+---------------
```

Type The Type field is one octet and indicates the type of Configuration Option. Up-to-date values of the LCP Option Type Field are specified in the most recent "Assigned Numbers" RFC [2]. This document concerns the following values:

0	RESERVED
1	Maximum-Receive-Unit
3	Authentication-Protocol
4	Quality-Protocol
5	Magic-Number
7	Protocol-Field-Compression
8	Address-and-Control-Field-Compression

Length   The Length field is one octet and indicates the length of this Configuration Option including the Type, Length, and Data fields. If a negotiable Configuration Option is received in a Configure-Request with an invalid or unrecognized Length, a Configure-Nak SHOULD be transmitted, which includes the desired Configuration Option with an appropriate Length and Data.

Data   The Data field is zero or more octets and contains information specific to the Configuration Option. The format and length of the Data field is determined by the Type and Length fields. When the Data field is indicated by the Length to extend beyond the end of the Information field, the entire packet is silently discarded without affecting the automaton.

Maximum-Receive-Unit (MRU)

This Configuration Option may be sent to inform the peer that the implementation can receive larger packets or to request that the peer send smaller packets. The default value is 1500 octets. If smaller packets are requested, an implementation MUST still be able to receive the full 1500-octet information field in case link synchronization is lost. This option is used to indicate an implementation capability. The peer is not required to maximize the use of the capacity. For example, when a MRU is indicated which is 2048 octets, the peer is not required to send any packet with 2048 octets. The Peer need not Configure-Nak to indicate that it is only sending smaller packets, because the implementation always requires support for at least 1500 octets.

A summary of the Maximum-Receive-Unit Configuration Option format is shown as follows. The fields are transmitted from left to right.

```
 0                   1                   2                   3
 0 1 2 3 4 5 6 7 8 9 0 1 2 3 4 5 6 7 8 9 0 1 2 3 4 5 6 7 8 9 0 1
+-------+-------+-------------------------------+
|  Type |Length |      Maximum-Receive-Unit     |
+-------+-------+-------------------------------+
```

Type 1

Length 4

Maximum-Receive-Unit   The Maximum-Receive-Unit field is two octets and specifies the maximum number of octets in the Information and Padding fields. It does not include the framing, Protocol field, FCS, or any transparency bits or bytes.

Authentication-Protocol

On some links, it may be desirable to require a peer to authenticate itself before allowing network-layer protocol packets to be exchanged. This Configuration Option provides a method to negotiate the use of a specific protocol for authentication. By default, Authentication is not required. An implementation MUST NOT include multiple Authentication-Protocol Configuration Options in its Configure-Request packets. Instead, it SHOULD attempt to configure the most desirable protocol first. If that protocol is Configure-Nak'd, then the implementation SHOULD attempt the next most desirable protocol in the next Configure-Request. The implementation sending the Configure-Request is indicating that it expects authentication from its peer. If an implementation sends a Configure-Ack, then it is agreeing to authenticate with the specified protocol. An implementation receiving a Configure-Ack SHOULD expect the peer to authenticate with the acknowledged protocol. There is no requirement that authentication be full-duplex or that the same protocol be used in both directions. It is perfectly acceptable for different protocols to be used in each direction. This, of course, depends on the specific protocols negotiated. A summary of the Authentication-Protocol Configuration Option format is shown as follows. The fields are transmitted from left to right.

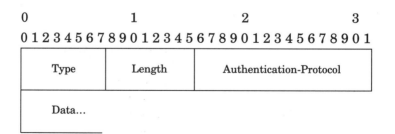

Type   3

Length ≥ 4

Authentication-Protocol The Authentication-Protocol field is two octets and indicates the authentication protocol desired. Values for this field are always the same as the PPP Protocol field values for that same authentication protocol. Up-to-date values of the Authentication-Protocol field are specified in the most recent "Assigned Numbers" RFC [2]. Current values are assigned as follows:

Value (in hex) Protocol

c023 Password Authentication Protocol

c223 Challenge Handshake Authentication Protocol

Data The Data field is zero or more octets, and contains additional data as determined by the particular protocol.

Quality-Protocol

On some links it may be desirable to determine when, and how often, the link is dropping data. This process is called link quality monitoring. This Configuration Option provides a method to negotiate the use of a specific protocol for link quality monitoring. By default, link quality monitoring is disabled. The implementation sending the Configure-Request is indicating that it expects to receive monitoring information from its peer. If an implementation sends a Configure-Ack, then it is agreeing to send the specified protocol. An implementation receiving a Configure-Ack SHOULD expect the peer to send the acknowledged protocol.

There is no requirement that quality monitoring be full-duplex or that the same protocol be used in both directions. It is perfectly acceptable for different protocols to be used in each direction. This, of course, depends on the specific protocols negotiated. A summary of the Quality-Protocol Configuration Option format is shown as follows. The fields are transmitted from left to right.

```
 0                   1                   2                   3
 0 1 2 3 4 5 6 7 8 9 0 1 2 3 4 5 6 7 8 9 0 1 2 3 4 5 6 7 8 9 0 1
+-------+-------+-------------------+
| Type  | Length|  Quality-Protocol |
+-------+-------+-------------------+
| Data...                          |
+------                            
```

Type   4

Length $\geqq 4$

Quality-Protocol   The Quality-Protocol field is two octets and indicates the link quality monitoring protocol desired. Values for this field are always the same as the PPP Protocol field values for that same monitoring protocol. Up-to-date values of the Quality-Protocol field are specified in the most recent "Assigned Numbers" RFC [2]. Current values are assigned as follows:

Value (in hex)	Protocol
c025	Link Quality Report
Data	

The Data field is zero or more octets, and contains additional data as determined by the particular protocol.

Magic-Number

This Configuration Option provides a method to detect looped-back links and other Data Link Layer anomalies. This Configuration Option MAY be required by some other Configuration Options, such as the Quality-Protocol Configuration Option. By default, the Magic-Number is not negotiated, and zero is inserted where a Magic-Number might otherwise be used. Before this Configuration Option is requested, an implementation MUST choose its Magic-Number. It is recommended that the Magic-Number be chosen in the most random manner possible to guarantee with very high probability that an implementation arrives at a unique number. A good way to choose a unique random number is to start with a unique seed. Suggested sources of uniqueness include machine serial numbers, other network hardware addresses, time-of-day clocks, and so on. Particularly good random number seeds are precise measurements of the inter-arrival time of physical events, such as packet reception on other connected networks, server response time, or the typing rate of a human user. It is also suggested that as many sources as possible be used simultaneously.

When a Configure-Request is received with a Magic-Number Configuration Option, the received Magic-Number is compared with the Magic-Number of the last Configure-Request sent to the peer. If the two Magic-Numbers are different, then the link is not looped-back, and the Magic-Number SHOULD be acknowledged. If the two Magic-Numbers are equal, then it is possible, but not certain, that the link is looped-back and that this Configure-Request is actually the one last sent. To determine this, a Configure-Nak MUST be sent specifying a different Magic-Number value. A new Configure-Request SHOULD NOT be sent to the peer until normal processing would cause it to be sent (that is, until a Configure-Nak is received or the Restart timer runs out).

Reception of a Configure-Nak with a Magic-Number different from that of the last Configure-Nak sent to the peer proves that a link is not looped-back, and indicates a unique Magic-Number. If the Magic-Number is equal to the one sent in the last Configure-Nak, the possibility of a looped-back link is increased, and a new Magic-Number MUST be chosen. In either case, a new Configure-Request SHOULD be sent with the new Magic-Number. If the link is indeed looped-back, this sequence (transmit Configure-Request, receive Configure-Request, transmit Configure-Nak, receive Configure-Nak) repeats over and over again. If the link is not looped-back, this sequence might occur a few times, but it is extremely unlikely to occur repeatedly. Most likely, the Magic-Numbers chosen at either end quickly diverge, terminating the sequence. Table 6-4 shows the probability of collisions assuming that both ends of the link select Magic-Numbers with a perfectly uniform distribution.

Good sources of uniqueness or randomness are required for this divergence to occur. If a good source of uniqueness cannot be found, it is recommended that this Configuration Option not be enabled; Configure-Requests with the option SHOULD NOT be transmitted, and any Magic-Number Configuration Options which the peer sends SHOULD be either acknowledged or rejected. In this case, looped-back links cannot be reliably detected by the implementation, although they may still be detectable by the peer.

If an implementation does transmit a Configure-Request with a Magic-Number Configuration Option, then it MUST NOT respond with a Configure-Reject when it receives a Configure-Request with a Magic-Number Configuration Option. That is, if an implementation desires to use Magic-Numbers, then it MUST also allow its peer to do so. If an implementation does receive a Configure-Reject in response to a Configure-Request, it can only

Table 6-4	**Number of Collisions**	**Probability**
Collision probability ratios	1	$1/2**32 = 2.3\,E-10$
	2	$1/2**32**2 = 5.4\,E-20$
	3	$1/2**32**3 = 1.3\,E-29$

mean that the link is not looped-back, and that its peer is not using Magic-Numbers. In this case, an implementation SHOULD act as if the negotiation had been successful (as if it had instead received a Configure-Ack).

The Magic-Number also may be used to detect looped-back links during normal operation, as well as during Configuration Option negotiation. All LCP Echo-Request, Echo-Reply, and Discard-Request packets have a Magic-Number field. If Magic-Number has been successfully negotiated, an implementation MUST transmit these packets with the Magic-Number field set to its negotiated Magic-Number.

The Magic-Number field of these packets SHOULD be inspected on reception. All received Magic-Number fields MUST be equal to either zero or the peer's unique Magic-Number, depending on whether or not the peer negotiated a Magic-Number.

Reception of a Magic-Number field equal to the negotiated local Magic-Number indicates a looped-back link. Reception of a Magic-Number other than the negotiated local Magic-Number, the peer's negotiated Magic-Number, or zero if the peer didn't negotiate one indicates a link that has been misconfigured for communications with a different peer. Procedures for recovery from either case are unspecified, and may vary from implementation to implementation. A somewhat pessimistic procedure is to assume a LCP Down event. A further Open event begins the process of re-establishing the link, which can't complete until the looped-back condition is terminated, and Magic-Numbers are successfully negotiated. A more optimistic procedure (in the case of a looped-back link) is to begin transmitting LCP Echo-Request packets until an appropriate Echo-Reply is received, indicating a termination of the looped-back condition. A summary of the Magic-Number Configuration Option format is shown as follows. The fields are transmitted from left to right.

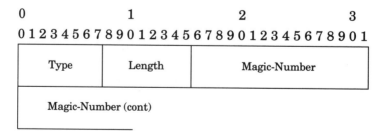

Type   5

Length   6

Magic-Number   The Magic-Number field is four octets and indicates a number that is very likely to be unique to one end of the link. A Magic-Number of zero is illegal and MUST always be Nak'd, if it is not Rejected outright.

Protocol-Field-Compression (PFC)

This Configuration Option provides a method to negotiate the compression of the PPP Protocol field. By default, all implementations MUST transmit packets with two octet PPP Protocol fields. PPP Protocol field numbers are chosen such that some values may be compressed into a single octet form that is clearly distinguishable from the two octet form. This Configuration Option is sent to inform the peer that the implementation can receive such single octet Protocol fields. As previously mentioned, the Protocol field uses an extension mechanism consistent with the ISO 3309 extension mechanism for the Address field; the *Least Significant Bit* (LSB) of each octet is used to indicate extension of the Protocol field. A binary 0 as the LSB indicates that the Protocol field continues with the following octet. The presence of a binary 1 as the LSB marks the last octet of the Protocol field. Notice that any number of 0 octets may be prepended to the field, and yet still indicate the same value (consider the two binary representations for 3, 00000011 and 00000000 00000011).

When using low speed links, it is desirable to conserve bandwidth by sending as little redundant data as possible. The Protocol-Field-Compression Configuration Option enables a trade-off between implementation simplicity and bandwidth efficiency. If successfully negotiated, the ISO 3309 extension mechanism may be used to compress the Protocol field to one octet instead of two. The large majority of packets are compressible, because data protocols are typically assigned with Protocol field values less than 256.

Compressed Protocol fields MUST NOT be transmitted unless this Configuration Option has been negotiated. When negotiated, PPP implementations MUST accept PPP packets with either double-octet or single-octet Protocol fields, and MUST NOT distinguish between them.

The Protocol field is never compressed when sending any LCP packet. This rule guarantees unambiguous recognition of LCP packets. When a Protocol field is compressed, the Data Link Layer FCS field is calculated on the compressed frame, not the original uncompressed frame. A summary of the Protocol-Field-Compression Configuration Option format is shown as follows. The fields are transmitted from left to right.

```
0                    1
0 1 2 3 4 5 6 7 8 9 0 1 2 3 4 5
┌──────────────┬──────────────┐
│     Type     │    Length    │
└──────────────┴──────────────┘
```

Type 7

Length 2

Address-and-Control-Field-Compression (ACFC)

This Configuration Option provides a method to negotiate the compression of the Data Link Layer Address and Control fields. By default, all implementations MUST transmit frames with Address and Control fields appropriate to the link framing. Because these fields usually have constant values for point-to-point links, they are easily compressed. This Configuration Option is sent to inform the peer that the implementation can receive compressed Address and Control fields. If a compressed frame is received when *Address-and-Control-Field-Compression* (ACFC) has not been negotiated, the implementation MAY silently discard the frame. The Address and Control fields MUST NOT be compressed when sending any LCP packet. This rule guarantees unambiguous recognition of LCP packets.

When the Address and Control fields are compressed, the Data Link Layer FCS field is calculated on the compressed frame, not the original uncompressed frame. A summary of the Address-and-Control-Field-Compression Configuration Option format is shown as follows. The fields are transmitted from left to right.

```
0                    1
0 1 2 3 4 5 6 7 8 9 0 1 2 3 4 5
┌──────────────┬──────────────┐
│     Type     │    Length    │
└──────────────┴──────────────┘
```

Type 8

Length 2

REFERENCES

Due to the nature of this topic, I am including the pertinent reference information for you to obtain additional reading. Furthermore, the RFC Index is a good reference for a more exhaustive list of documents related to PPP and *Serial Link Internet Protocol* (SLIP). Also, my research included review of the Microsoft documentation as well; it too is a very good source for information on this topic.

1. Perkins, D.1993. "Requirements for an Internet Standard Point-to-Point Protocol." RFC 1547. Carnegie Mellon University (December).

2. Reynolds, J. and J. Postel.1992. "Assigned Numbers." STD 2. RFC 1340. USC/Information Sciences Institute (July).

Ethernet

Introduction

Ethernet technology is probably the most widely used lower layer network protocol. Ethernet has a proven history and presence among numerous supplying vendors, and it is priced effectively in most market locations. In short, it works and is inexpensive; what better combination can one ask for in a functioning piece of technology.

Origins, Evolution, & Versions

Ethernet can be traced back to Palo Alto, CA in the early 1970s. Specifically, its origins come from the *Palo Alto Research Center* (PARC).

PARC was the outgrowth of a mindset at the Xerox Corporation. The history behind PARC varies depending on the source, but the most substantiated one is the one presented here.

In 1970 Xerox speculated about the future. It was involved in designing, manufacturing, and providing copying machines. Xerox was aware of their products and the surrounding technology. Likewise, they were aware of the possibility that future offices could be populated with computers and terminals, thus fewer needs for copiers would exist. As a result, PARC was launched.

PARC consisted of core of individuals whose focus was turning ideas into products. In 1973 Bob Metcalf worked with a group of individuals whose interest was resolving a fundamental networking problem, that is, the amount of time it took to get data from a computer to a printer. The bottleneck was not the computer or printer, it was getting data from the computer to the printer, which took over ten minutes, even with high-speed links. This was overcome and thus the birth of Ethernet.

The essence of the problem was that if multiple devices were connected to the same media, collisions occurred when two or more devices attempted to communicate. This obstacle of collisions had to be overcome. This problem led to considerations as to how to overcome this obstacle.

A simple analogy explains the crux of the solution. When a professor teaches students, questions inevitably arise. When this happens, some students merely call the professor's name to get his/her attention. This is an effective means of communication when a small amount of students are present; but what happens when the number of students increases? The possibility of more than one student calling the professor's name increases.

As a result the potential *collision* rate increases. When such a scenario exists, those students involved in the collision stop, and one typically proceeds to communication with the professor. This example is called courtesy; another way to say this is that other students "back-off" for a random period of time until communication is finished between the student and professor. Other students continue to listen, and when they sense communication has stopped another attempt to communicate is made by one or more students by calling the professor's name. In short, this is called a back-off algorithm.

The idea of multiple devices listening to a medium to see if communication exists, and then waiting an arbitrary amount of time before attempting to transmit data again is known as Ethernet. The first implementation of Ethernet technology delivered a data rate transfer speed of 2.67-Mb per/sec. This occurred between 1973 and approximately 1975. This version of Ethernet is known as experimental Ethernet. Following this, a paper was co-authored by Robert Metcalf. This paper specified a 3-Mb per/second data rate with approximately 100 nodes attached to the media. Refinement of Ethernet continued for the coming years.

In 1980 a consortium comprised of Digital Equipment, Intel Corporation, and Xerox (also known as DIX) came together with the intent of producing a standard for Ethernet. They did, and it is known as version 1.0, published in 1981. In 1982 DIX produced an Ethernet standard stating the following Ethernet characteristics:

10 Mb/per/sec data rate

Station separation maximum 2.8 kilometers

1024 maximum number of stations

Coaxial cable using baseband signaling

BUS topology

Contention resolution for link procedure

Variable size frames

Theory of Operation

Ethernet operates using broadcast technology. This is best explained by analogy. Consider a seminar held with approximately 150 attendees. Assume someone needs to contact an attendee at the seminar. Assume the one attempting to contact the attendee goes to the room where the seminar is being held, waits for the speaker to stop speaking, and then asks aloud, "Attendee who works for XYZ corporation, are you in here?" Assuming they are normally in there, they would respond. Granted everyone else attending the seminar hears the requests but so does the individual attempting to be reached.

This analogy is similar to how Ethernet operates. This analogy uses a broadcast calling the attendee who works for XYZ Corporation. Equally, hosts participating in an Ethernet network do the same. Consider Figure 7-1.

Figure 7-1 shows a number of hosts connected to an Ethernet based network. Consider this illustration for the explanation of Ethernet communication.

Figure 7-1
Conceptual view of Ethernet communications

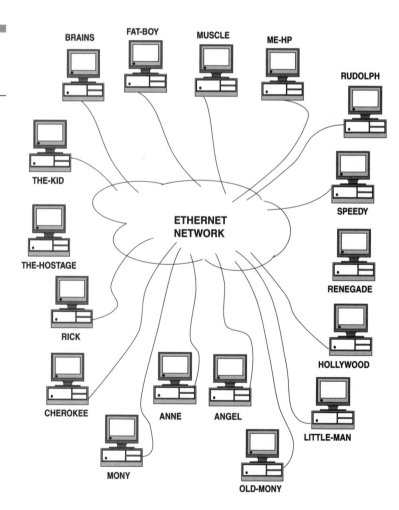

Assume the FATBOY wants to communicate with RENEGADE. In this example, and for our purposes, FATBOY sends a packet of information out onto the network, which basically says, "RENEGADE, are you there"? Assuming RENEGADE is there, he responds: "Yep, I am here and my IP address is thus-n-so." Forgoing a whole bunch of detail here, these are the basics of the initial exchange of information between two hosts during a communication that occurs between two Ethernet *network interface cards* (NICs). This is an example of a broadcast, because all hosts on the medium *hear* the broadcasts, but only the appropriate host responds.

The functional operation of Ethernet is fundamentally different from Token Ring or FDDI technology. Ethernet is a broadcast technology and is not connection oriented at the data link level. Token Ring and FDDI technology are both non-broadcast and connection oriented at the data link level.

Early Days of Ethernet Networking

In earlier days of Ethernet networking, the actual topology and implementation components were different from those of today. For example, consider Figure 7-2. Figure 7-2 shows multiple hosts, the network interface card, cable connecting the card, the transceiver, terminators, and coaxial cable. This type of implementation is still functional today, however it is not as

Figure 7-2
Early Ethernet networking components and configuration

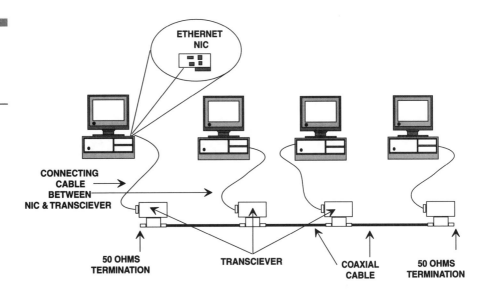

Figure 7-3
Current Ethernet
networking
components and
configuration

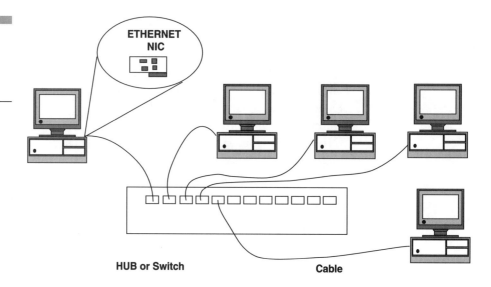

HUB or Switch   **Cable**

popular as it was some ten years ago. Today most networks implement Ethernet as Figure 7-3 shows.

Figure 7-3 show multiple hosts, the network interface card (which actually has a chip installed on it with Ethernet protocol burned into it), cables connecting hosts, and a hub or switch. This implementation is a star topology in contrast to earlier Ethernet implementations, however the technology itself operates in the same manner. Technically speaking, if one could "look inside" the hub, actual communication occurs on a bus inside the hub or switch, yet the same method of operation is used for today's Ethernet as for Ethernet some ten years ago.

Before going onto more topics in this chapter, consider the information here explaining more details of some earlier Ethernet components and Ethernet functionality.

Transceiver Functionality

The transceivers used to connect hosts to the medium perform a specific function. They implement *Carrier Sense Multiple Access with Collision Detection* (CSMA/CD) technology. This means the transceivers themselves are capable of perceiving the carrier on the medium, permitting access for multiple hosts (one per transceiver), and detecting collisions.

Heartbeat

Ethernet functionality requires a technology generally referred to as heartbeat. This is a carrier sense that the transceivers listen for on the network medium and is actually a voltage. This assumes that a bus (namely, coaxial cable) is used for the actual media, and devices called transceivers are used to connect the cable from the network device to the media. In other words, the transceiver is the interface between the actual "cable" and the cable from the network device.

Some receivers require this (heartbeat) for operation; some do not. (Be aware I am explaining this more from a historical perspective of how Ethernet was implemented some years ago rather than how it is today.) The technical term for this is *Signal Quality Error* (SQE). The importance of this is realized when Ethernet is mixed with IEEE 802.3 technology. Delineation between these two is covered later in this chapter. It is important to understand, depending on the vendor and implementation, heartbeat might be required with regard to earlier types of Ethernet implementation technology.

Today Ethernet is primarily implemented with only a hub, an interface board, a cable connecting the two, and some upper layer network protocol that makes network communication possible at higher (user functional) layers. However, be aware that the term heartbeat goes hand in hand with earlier versions of Ethernet.

Collision Detection

The notion of collision detection is important due to the nature of how Ethernet technology functions. Ethernet communication occurs between interface boards or transceivers depending on how implementation is made. Prior to a "logical session" between Ethernet components, an attempt to establish a link between the source and destination occurs. This process includes nodes attached to the medium "listening" for a moment in time where any given node can perform a broadcast. A broadcast is the function where a node's Ethernet component (namely an Ethernet board) asks if the destination node in which communication is desired is present. If so, communication between the source and destination node occurs.

During this process, it is easy to see that the more nodes on a given network potentially increase the amount of communication on the medium.

Consequently, each Ethernet interface board or transceiver listens for collisions; that is, a clash between two or more nodes desiring to talk at the same time. This listening is technically called: collision detection. The collision detection components within an Ethernet interface board have the intelligence required to know when other nodes are talking and/or when collisions occur.

Specifically, when a given node attempts to communicate with another node and a collision occurs, another function of the Ethernet board operates; that function is called the back-off algorithm. After a collision is detected by the Ethernet interface, a random amount of time (in microseconds) elapses before another attempt is made to establishment communication between Ethernet interfaces.

Ethernet Frame Components

Ethernet frames are between 46 and 1500 bytes. Frames less than 60 bytes in the data field are called *runt* frames. Figure 7-4 is an example of an Ethernet frame.

This frame has six fields. The following explains a frame's six fields, and each field's length and function.

Preamble

This is a sequence of 64 encoded bits that the physical layer uses for clock synchronization between circuits attached to the medium.

Destination Address

This is a 48-bit hardware address called the Ethernet address. The first three bytes are assigned by the IEEE and are vendor specific. The last three bytes are assigned by the vendor. Each Ethernet interface board has a 48-bit address; sometimes this address is referred to as the "hard" address, because it reflects the hardware.

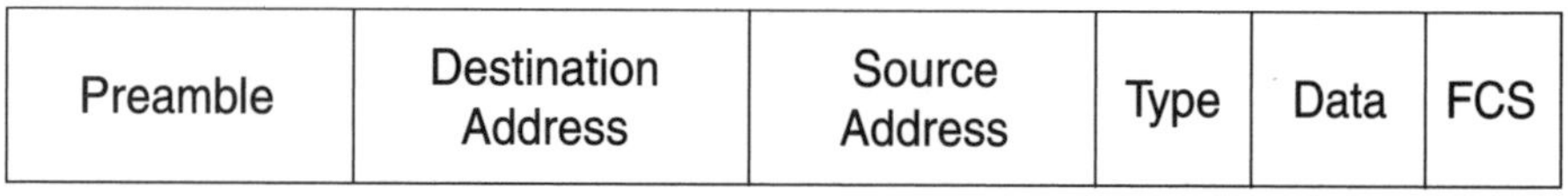

Figure 7-4
Ethernet frame

Preamble	Destination Address	Source Address	Type	Data	FCS

Source Address	This is the 48-bit hardware address of the sending (broadcasting station). It is the Ethernet address and also referred to as a hardware address.
Type	This is a 2-byte field used to indicate the protocol type if multiple upper layer protocols occupy the same physical media.
Data	This field may contain between 46 to 1500 bytes of data.
Frame Check Sequence	This is a 32-bit field used to perform *cyclic redundancy checking* (CRC) on all fields of the frame except the FCS field itself.

The Ethernet frame includes the data being passed from one station to another. It is what traverses the medium from source to destination.

Interestingly the destination and source fields are relative. Any given host might serve as the source in one phase of communication, and then the destination in another phase. The point here is that any given host might be the source or destination depending on which host originates the communications.

802.3 Frame Components

IEEE 802.3 frames are similar to, but not the same as, Ethernet frames. Figure 7.5 depicts an IEEE 802.3 frame.

This frame is similar to the Ethernet frame. Each field performs a specific function and is a specific size. The following explains this frame's fields and each field's length and function.

| Preamble | (7 Bytes) This is a sequence of 7 bytes encoded bits that the physical layer uses for clock synchronization between circuits attached to the medium. |

Figure 7-5
IEEE 802.3 frame

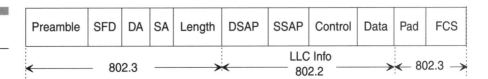

SFD	(1 Byte) Start Frame Delimiter field is binary 10101011. It indicates the start of the frame so the receiver can locate the first bit in the frame.
Destination Address	(6 Bytes) This is a 48-bit hardware address. It is sometimes referred to as the "hard" address, because it reflects the hardware interface board address.
Source Address	(6 Bytes) This is the 48-bit hardware address of the sending broadcasting station. It is also referred to as a hard address.
Length	(2 Bytes) This specifies the amount of LLC bytes to follow.
DSAP	(1 Byte) This is the destination service access point on the destination host.
SSAP	(1 Byte) This is the source service access point on the originating host.
Control	(1 or 2 Bytes) This specifies connectionless unacknowledged service, a type of LLC frame.
Data	(< 1496 Bytes) This field might correlate the data field on the LLC protocol data unit and contains the data.
Pad	This field is variable, but has sufficient room for *padding* to occur so proper collision detection can occur.
Frame Check Sequence	(4 Bytes) This is a 32-bit field used to perform cyclic redundancy checking on all fields of the frame except the FCS field itself.

802.3 theory of operation is the same as Ethernet with the exception of the function of the different field; that being the LENGTH field, which specifies the LLC protocol data unit information to follow. Broadcast technology is used as in Ethernet. It also calls for 10 MB per/sec baseband signaling on coaxial cable or unshielded twisted pair cabling, or broadband signaling at 10-Mb per/sec.

Addressing Schemes

Three basic types of addressing schemes are used with Ethernet. This section explores them.

Singlecast

A singlecast address is the simple implementation where one host communicates with another host. In this case, a destination and source address are used.

Multicast

A multicast address is the usual 6 bytes. It differs however from the single cast address, because it is a special address that particular hosts understand, and they receive it as if the frame were addressed to them with a single cast address. Hosts that are not concerned with this address do not recognize it, therefore performance is basically a non-issue. This type of address is used in special cases where loading different hosts on a network must occur, and other hosts on the network do not need this information.

Broadcast Address

The broadcast address can be used to perform isolated broadcast on networks where multiple subnets are implemented. This type of address is frequently used when the upper layer protocol is TCP/IP.

A broadcast address can be used literally to mask off those networks where the host is not located and therefore no broadcast needs to occur. Figure 7-6 is an example of how a broadcast address might be used.

Figure 7-6 depicts a segmented network backbone where hosts A, B, and C reside. This segmented network is connected through bridges and consequently appears as a single network to the users. This network is logically divided into what are called subnets. Consider the following explanation of communication at a data link and network layer among the hosts residents on the network.

Figure 7-6
Conceptual view of
a broadcast address
used with
subnetworks

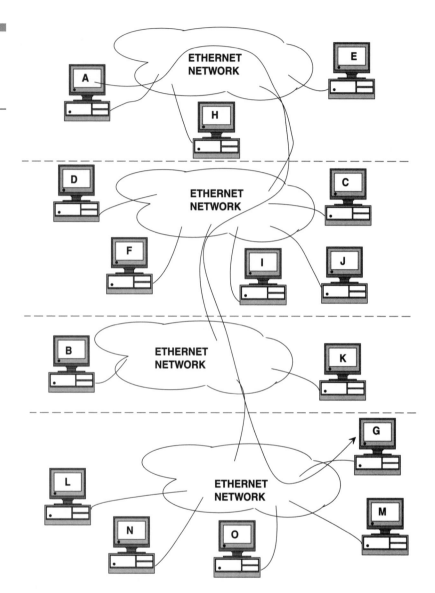

Assume host A needs to communicate with host G. The most efficient method of performing this is *not* to broadcast this frame on the major network backbone or any other subnets, except the one where host G is located. This function is performed well using what is termed a broadcast address.

Another use for the broadcast address is to use it to broadcast a frame to all networks and subnetworks, and *all* hosts on these networks can read the frame. Consequently the use of this address type is generally restricted to use when it is the most efficient method of communicating with all hosts.

An Implementation Example

Ethernet is a good lower layer protocol to use in many environments. Ethernet technology has been refined, is cost effective, can be purchased easily, is understood by many individuals, and is reliable.

The following example is of the Taylor Corporation. It is located in Dallas, Texas. It has multiple floors and separate departments on each floor. This corporation needed departmental LANs while implementing a corporate solution and the ability to segment some departments as necessary. Ethernet was selected to meet the needs of the lower layer protocol because of segmentation capabilities and provisions for a main backbone. Another reason for choosing this type lower layer protocol is so that departments could function independently while maintaining the capability to function in the cooperation with other departments. Figure 7-7 represents the Ethernet implementation at the Taylor Corporation.

Figure 7-7 shows departments located on each floor and each department with a network. It also shows the total solution with all departments together.

Ethernet Via 10BaseT

A popular implementation of Ethernet today is with twisted pair cabling and a hub. When ETHERNET is implemented this way, it is generally referred to as 10BaseT, meaning 10-Mb per/second using baseband signaling over twisted pair cabling.

Whether Ethernet is implemented with 10-BASE-T or some other type of cabling, the functional nature of Ethernet remains the same. It is a broadcast technology and will remain so, because changing this fundamental characteristic of Ethernet technology would be to change the technology itself, thus making it something other than what was created.

Figure 7-7
Ethernet
implementation
example

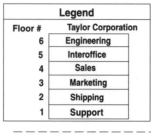

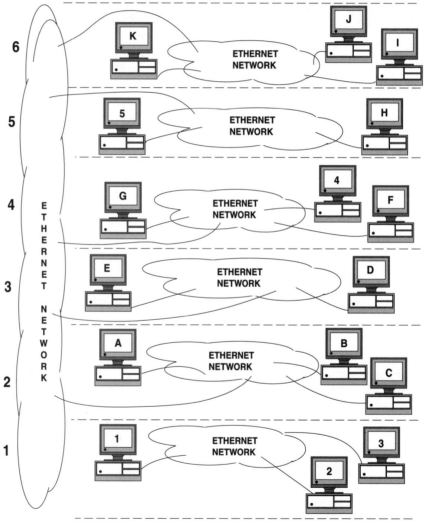

Figure 7-7
Ethernet
implementation
example

SUMMARY

Ethernet technology has been around approximately two decades. It is a cost-effective solution, a proven technology, and understood by many. Ethernet and the IEEE 802.3 solution are similar but not identical. Both can operate together; however Ethernet has its roots with Xerox, Intel, and Digital Equipment. The 802.3 solution has its origins in the IEEE organization and consists of 802.2 and Ethernet together.

Ethernet is primarily implemented today through 10BASET. The speed of Ethernet technology has increased and today 10, 100, and 1000 bits/sec are prevalent in the marketplace. Subsequent chapters cover the faster speeds of Ethernet.

Gigabit Ethernet

Introduction

Ethernet began back in the 1970s. As the previous chapter explained some of Ethernet's origins and technological aspects, so this chapter focuses on the evolution of Ethernet today. Before I begin, let me advise you to consider obtaining the book: *Gigabit Ethernet Handbook* by Stephen Saunders. I am presenting very helpful information here to get you jump started in your work with gigabit Ethernet, and you might want to obtain the gigabit Ethernet handbook for more advanced studies.

In this chapter my purpose is to present a high level perspective of gigabit Ethernet; that is a basic history of gigabit Ethernet, some details of its operation and frame structure, and information for further reading.

Perspective

The question of what is gigabit Ethernet arises even in technical circles. Gigabit Ethernet is the follow-on to Ethernet as it was originally known in its 10 Mbps state. Following 10 Mbps came the 100 Mbps IEEE 802.3 Ethernet standards as they are defined and promoted by the IEEE. Gigabit Ethernet is the movement of data at a data link level at 1000 Mbps. Figure 8-1 illustrates gigabit Ethernet layers.

Even though Figure 8-1 appears to be different from the original Ethernet, backward-functional compatibility exists between the original Ethernet and fast Ethernet.

For years, the IEEE has played an integral part in the technical community, and it still does today. Gigabit Ethernet is known in IEEE parlance as 802.3z, which is a name that refers to the working group of this specification.

Figure 8-1
Gigabit Ethernet layers

Media Access Control	
Gigabit Media Independent Interface	
8B - 10B Encoding/Decoding	Copper Physical Layer Encoder/decoder

In 1996 the IEEE 802.3 working group created the 802.3z Gigabit Ethernet task force. Like the other working groups and other groups within the 802 series of the IEEE, the primary purpose of the 802.3z task force is the development of a gigabit Ethernet standard.

To get you oriented to the differences of gigabit Ethernet as compared to the 10 or 100 MbPs, gigabit Ethernet does permit half and full duplex functionality while running at 1000 Mbps. The same 802.3 frame format is used but with some difference with regard to the distances specified for length. Other differences exist. Later in this chapter, I present more details about them.

Historical Brief

In contrast to the history of original Ethernet going back to the mid to early 1970s, gigabit Ethernet has a different history. Gigabit Ethernet has basically built on the foundation of Ethernet technology and acceptance in the marketplace. Once I was asked why Ethernet was so prevalent in the marketplace, and I responded: "That's easy—it is inexpensive and it works". The growth of gigabit Ethernet in the marketplace is somewhat natural given that it has already had a forerunner. In other words, it is not like ATM or FDDI which had no predecessors.

The past three or four years have had some significant dates related to gigabit Ethernet; some of those are

Year	Significance
1995	The 802.3 group started the high speed group.
1996	The 802.3z task force was created.
1997	The IEEE approved proposals for Gigabit Ethernet.
1997	An alliance of businesses formed a group known as The Gigabit Ethernet Alliance.
1997	Interop showcases gigabit Ethernet network.
1997	The 802.3ab task force is created.
1998	Multiple vendors begin to "emphasize" gigabit products.

Other important dates have no less come and gone with regards to companies, individuals, and entities. The dates just mentioned are some recognizable by many. Another significant occurrence with regard to gigabit Ethernet is the alliance of companies that are working with and promoting this technology. Some of the companies that I am aware who are a part of the alliance include

3Com Corp

Bay Networks

Cisco Systems

Compaq Computer

Granite Systems Inc.

Intel Corporation

LSI Logic

Packet Engines

Sun Microsystems

UB Networks

VLSI Technology

Outlook for Growth

Gigabit Ethernet has the potential to pick up in speed where its predecessors left off. In the early phase of gigabit Ethernet, which includes the present, the protocol seems to be focused on backbone type implementations such as campus type environments. However, if the technology continues to enjoy the successes it has the past couple years, it might well turn into a desktop technology in a couple years. The primary factor today in seemingly withholding gigabit Ethernet is its price.

In the previous two years, a task force known as 802.3z has been working on fiber-optic and shielded jumper cable assembly ("short-haul copper") solutions for gigabit Ethernet. In the spring of 1997, a new task force was formed to work on a "long-haul copper" solution based on four pairs of Category 5 cable wiring. Consequently, this changes the notion of Ethernet implementations. The 802.3ab task force is working to standardize a gigabit Ethernet link on four pairs of Category 5 UTP cabling, with a maximum of a hundred meters in length.

Specification Details

The gigabit Ethernet standards define an interface called the *gigabit media independent interface* (GMII). These standards include

- Access to the Ethernet Media Access Control (MAC) layer
- Management
- Repeater operations
- Topology rules
- Physical layer signaling systems:
  - 1000BASE-SX (short wavelength fiber)
  - 1000BASE-LX (long wavelength fiber)
  - 1000BASE-CX (short run copper)
  - 1000BASE-T (100-meter, four-pair Category 5 UTP)

An aspect of gigabit Ethernet that makes it attractive is the simple migration and support offered by Ethernet. Combined with the scalability and flexibility to handle new applications and data types gigabit Ethernet is the strategic choice for high-speed, high-bandwidth networking.

Conceptually, Figure 8-2 illustrates the correlation of gigabit Ethernet layers to various media with which it can be used.

Figure 8-2 shows gigabit Ethernet can be used with two types of coaxial cable, two different types of fiber optic cabling, and also unshielded twisted pair cabling.

Additionally, the gigabit Ethernet standards also includes

Half and full duplex operation at speeds of 1000 Mbps

Uses 802.3 Ethernet frame format

Implements CSMA/CD with support for one repeater per collision domain

Addresses backward compatibility with 10BASE-T and 100BASE-T

The 802 working task force identified three specific objectives for link distances:

1. Multimode fiber-optic link with a maximum length of 550 meters
2. Single-mode fiber-optic link with a maximum length of 3 kilometers
3. Copper based link with a maximum length of at least 25 meters

Figure 8-2
Gigabit Ethernet
layer to media
correlation

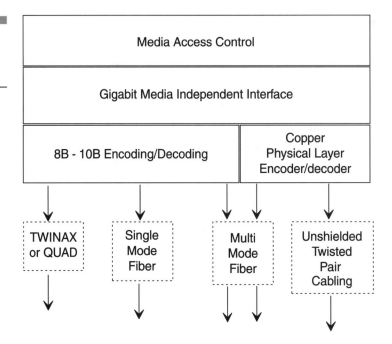

Still another way to view gigabit Ethernet in greater detail is to consider the Figure 8-3.

Figure 8-3 shows the MAC–PHY layers, media type identifications, the 802.3z focus, and the 802.3ab focus. A considerable part of the 802.3z task force is concentrating on the definition and refinement of PHY standards for gigabit Ethernet. Gigabit Ethernet implements functional aspects that adhere to a physical layer standard. Generally speaking, the *physical layer* (PHL) is responsible for defining the mechanical, electrical, and procedural characteristics for establishing, maintaining, and deactivating the physical link between network devices. For gigabit Ethernet communications, several physical layer standards are emerging from the IEEE 802.3z effort.

Two PHYs provide gigabit transmission over fiber-optic cabling as well as standard copper cabling. The 1000BASE-SX is targeted towards lower cost multi-mode fiber runs in backbone applications. On the other hand, the 1000BASE-LX is focused to the longer multi-mode building fiber backbones and also the single-mode campus type backbones. The specifications for multi-mode fiber, defining gigabit transmission over fiber, reflect distances of 300 and 550 meters.

Two standards efforts have been and are in operation for gigabit Ethernet transmission over copper cabling. The first copper standard is being defined by 802.3z and is referred to as 1000BASE-CX. It supports equip-

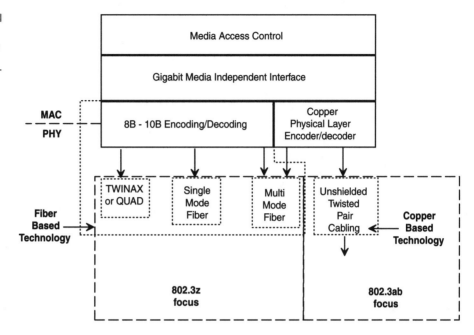

ment cluster connections whereby the physical interface is short-haul copper. It also supports short distances as well, those of 25 meter distances. This standard uses the Fiber Channel-based 8B/10B coding at a rate of 1.25 Gbps. The specifications call for 150-ohm balanced and shielded specialty cabling assemblies known as twinax cable. This copper physical layer standard is relatively inexpensive.

Another copper standard is the 1000BASE-T physical layer standard providing 1 Gbps Ethernet signal transmission over four pairs of category 5 UTP cable. The specification calls for an ability to distance of up to 100 meters.

Gigabit Ethernet Products Brief

Most of the products needed to support gigabit Ethernet are the same as those products required for 10 and 100 Mbps Ethernet. For example, those products/components that gigabit Ethernet shares in common with its predecessors include

Switches/hubs

Uplink/downlink products

Network Interface Cards (NIC)

Routers

Bridges

In addition to these devices, gigabit Ethernet also uses a buffered distributor.

A buffered distributor is a full-duplex device that connects two or more 802.3 links operating at 1 Gbps or faster. It is a non-address-filtering device. For example, a buffered distributor forwards incoming packets to all connected links except the originating link. The consequence is that this provides a shared bandwidth scenario like the 802.3 collision domain. Some groups call the buffered distributor a "CSMA/CD device in a box." Functionally, a buffered distributor buffers one or more incoming frames on each link before forwarding them.

Ethernet Frames

At the heart of Ethernet technology is the Ethernet frame. The IEEE 802.3 group defined this frame and is widely known in the industry by those who work with it. I am presenting the Ethernet frame here for your consideration to review. Consider Figure 8-4.

Figure 8-4 shows the Ethernet frame with the components of it. Notice the first field is the destination address field, the second field is the source address field, the third field is the type or length field and the fifth is where the data and "stuff" from the third layer in the OSI model network is "stuffed." The last field is the frame check sequence field. As the highlighted areas show, the destination field and the source address field can be broken down into two 24-bit sub-fields. As this illustration shows, this is the standard Ethernet frame.

Now before more in-depth information is shown, some explaining of necessary preliminary information is in order. Because the purpose of this section is to present highlights and not be exhaustive, consider this to help you along your way. First, there is a difference between a packet and a frame. A packet is generally a generic term; however it references the control information as well as the data being transmitted over a given link. In Ethernet lingo, a frame and the "controlling" information, indicating the beginning and end, is a packet. A frame, on the other hand, is a collection of information, including the payload that is moved from one place to another in a network. Consider Figure 8-5.

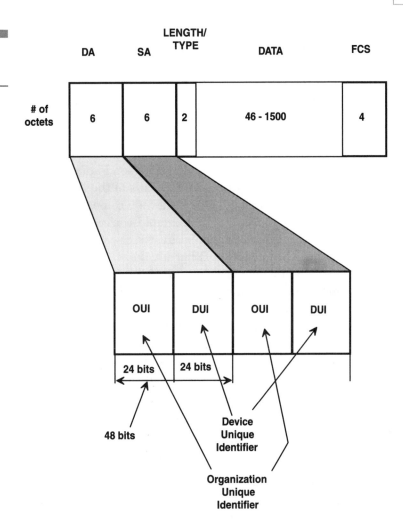

Figure 8-4
Standard ethernet
frame components

The focus of Figure 8-5 is all the information surrounding that which is different from the illustration shown in Figure 8.4. For example, the IPG field is known as the interpacket gap, which is between packets transmitted over a link. The *Start Packet Delimiter* (SPD) is added to the frame by

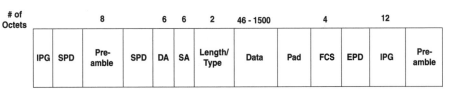

Figure 8-5
Ethernet packet

the transmitter. The *Start Frame Delimiter* (SFD) is added by the transmitter and indicates the start-of-frame. The *Destination Address* (DA) and *Source Address* (SA) are the same functional components as those in the 10 and 100 Mbps Ethernet. The same is true with the length/type field, data, and fcs field. In this figure, I showed the part of the frame known as the pad, which basically serves the purpose of "filling" necessary space for frame transmission. The *End Packet Delimiter* (EPD) is the identifying mark of the packet put on by the transmitter and removed by the receiver.

Now given the similarities between Figure 8-4 and 8-5, the purpose here is to get you oriented to the details of the Ethernet frame and packet. The differences with gigabit Ethernet come into play when examining the encoder and decoder. For example, the coding process of gigabit Ethernet is similar to fiber channel because it is a 8B/10B coding scheme. This is part of the heart of gigabit Ethernet; that is, the conversion of 8-bit parallel data transfer to memory from a 10 bit parallel conversion. This conversion method is part of the beauty of gigabit Ethernet. The peripheral ramifications of this coding scheme include the preclusion of baseline wander. I better stop here, lest I get to deep into this subject.

I do recommend again that you check into the book: *The Gigabit Ethernet Handbook* by Stephen Saunders, also published by McGraw-Hill. It is the best book on the market today of which I am aware.

SUMMARY

Gigabit Ethernet is a topic that numerous books have been written about. It is becoming the "replacement" for ordinary Ethernet. My purpose in this chapter is to introduce you to the topic, present some highlights, and point you towards further reading if your work lends you in that direction.

Asynchronous Transfer Mode

Introduction

Asynchonous Transfer Mode (ATM) has not been on the market for a long time in comparison to other technologies. However, credit is due to researchers at Bell Laboratories for their work in this area long before it came to the forefront of the media attention in the late 1980s to early 1990s. ATM actually began to take shape in the late 1980s and the driving force behind its development was a need for a fast switching technology that supported data, voice, video, and multimedia in general. At the time of this writing (1998), ATM is a technology that can be implemented in a variety of environments supporting multiple types of networks such as data, multimedia, voice, and even hybrid networks. Different angles of presentation have been presented in various books on ATM. Here I am providing some information that is fundamental to ATM. Some aspects of ATM technology are still emerging and changing in standards groups. Many vendors are implementing the technology in different ways.

The remainder of this chapter presents basic ATM technology and some blueprints of possible ATM implementations to use as a guide when planning and designing networks where ATM technology is used.

ATM Architecture & Concepts

Asynchonous Transfer Mode (ATM) is a cell switching technology. Specifically, it uses a 53-byte cell. It consists of a header with routing and other network related information, and an information field for data, images, voice, and/or video. An advantage of ATM is its capability to support multimedia and integrate these services with data over a single type transmission method. ATM makes attaining transmission of multiple types of payloads possible and is capable of resolving timing problems along with other significant issues that accompany different payload traffic in heterogeneous networks. Figure 9-1 is an example of a video production center in San Jose, California connected to another site in Dallas, Texas where there are video servers. These two locations are connected through an ATM connection provided by a long distance service provider.

ATM can be implemented at the enterprise level (privately), in public networks, or both. In reality, the enterprise level is the way it is implemented. Realization of ATM throughout a dispersed network environment is twofold. First, it is implemented at the local level, as in a given organization

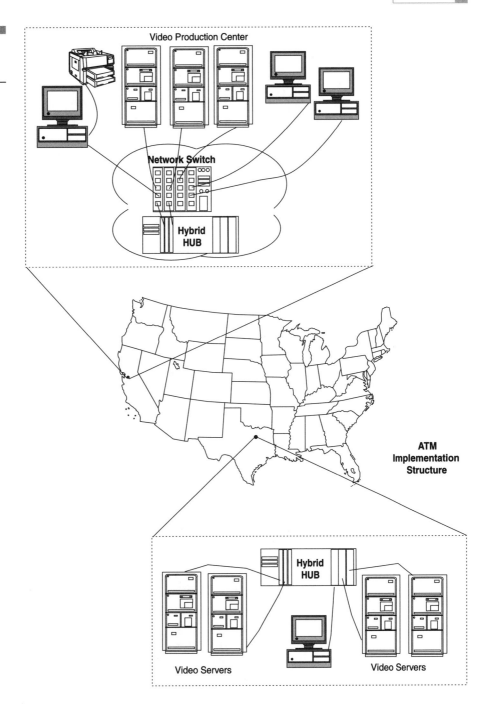

Figure 9-1
ATM implementation structure

or corporation. Second, it is implemented at the public level (or service provider). ATM usage capabilities are customized to meet a given environment's needs, and it is application transparent; therefore integration of multimedia and data does not cause problems.

ATM has been around now for some time. However, it is not as widespread as Ethernet, to use an example. ATM is still considered a fairly high-speed more advanced networking protocol than some other lower level network protocols. ATM growth has been relatively steady in the past few years. It is a protocol that seems to be preferred more to wide area networks as opposed to local area networks.

Implementation Structure

Before examining ATM in greater detail, the following are some core/fundamental concepts of ATM.

- *ADAPTATION* In certain parts of networks, frames of data are divided into cells. This occurs at lower layers in networks whether the data is out-bound or in-bound. Data streams that are continuous, such as video, voice, and assembled, pose an interesting technical challenge for ATM because of the conversion of data frames into cells. In the sending part of the network frames, video or voice, for example, are divided into cells, and then transported to the destination network. The receiving part of the network takes these cells and reconstructs them into data frames that make them usable to the end user. This function is called adaptation. The adaptation function operates at a higher level in a network (technology) than the transport (movement) of cells.

- *CELLS* A cell is a 48 data byte and 5-byte header that all data, voice, video, images, and so on are stored into for transport through ATM devices and ATM networks.

- *CONGESTION CONTROL* This is a form of management in ATM networks. When links or nodes in ATM networks become congested, ATM cells are discarded until the congestion is stopped. ATM cells carry a priority, and hence some lower priority cells can be marked as first to be discarded in a congestion situation. When cells are discarded during congestion, endpoints within ATM networks are not notified. The recovery, and hence the detection, of cell loss is the responsibility of the adaptation function of higher layer protocols at work in the network.

- *ERROR CONTROL*   ATM switching networks check cell headers for errors and discards those with errors. ATM adaptation functions are external to the ATM switching network, and it depends on traffic type; but normally in data traffic, the adaptation layer checks for errors and if found, the entire frame is discarded. ATM networks do not perform retransmission in an attempt to recover from errors that result in loss. Retransmission of any type of traffic in ATM networks is contingent on the end user devices used and the type of traffic moved throughout the network.

- *FLOW CONTROL*   In the inception and early phase of ATM design, flow control was not included as a part of the internal function of ATM. Today, much change has occurred and different guidelines and implementations exist on this topic.

- *HARDWARE BASED SWITCHING*   This idea is that switching techniques are built into hardware, thus providing very high-speed switching. This type of switching might be employed at individual nodes to perform this function.

- *ROUTING*   Moving data from one place to another in an ATM network is achieved by way of paths called virtual channels. A series of virtual channels compose ATM networks and therefore make routing possible. A cell header contains routing information for that cell. Any given group of cells transverse a network using the same virtual channel and are received at the destination location in the same order in which they were received through the ATM network.

ATM Standards

Many network protocols are compared and contrasted against the OSI model. ATM does not fit the structure of the OSI model except for at the physical layer.

ATM Layers

Figure 9-2 depicts ATM structure as a layered approach.

Figure 9-2

Conceptual view of
ATM layers

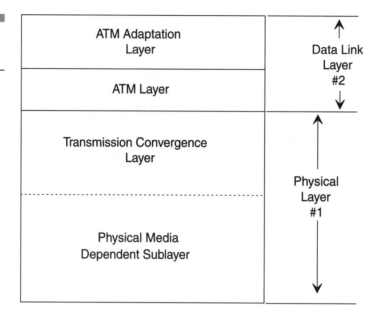

ATM Layers Defined

The physical layer of the ATM layered model can be divided into two sub-layers: the *physical media dependent* (PMD) sub-layer and the transmission convergence sub-layer. The physical media dependent performs two primary functions: bit timing and line coding. The function of the transmission convergence sub-layer is contingent on the interface used beneath it. Some interfaces supported include: *Synchronous Optical Network* (SONET) at 155.52 Mb per/sec, DS3 at 44.736 Mb per/sec, Multimode fiber at 100 Mb per/sec, "pure cells" at 155 Mb per/sec, and others.

Functions at the transmission convergence sub-layer are contingent on the interface used. Some of the functions at this sub-layer include: performing *Header Error Correction* (HEC), which covers the entire cell header (this includes generation and verification); multiplexing; frame generation and recovery; mapping of the ATM cells onto DS3 facilities, if used, by the *physical layer convergence protocol* (PLCP). In addition, PLCP framing and delineation is performed—if DS3 is used. In addition to these functions, others are performed relative to the interface in use.

ATM layer functions include switching, multiplexing, routing, and congestion management. Above this layer is the *ATM Adaptation Layer* (AAL). Here different categories of functions are identifiable. Figure 9-3 is showing

Figure 9-3
ATM adaptation
components
& ATM layer

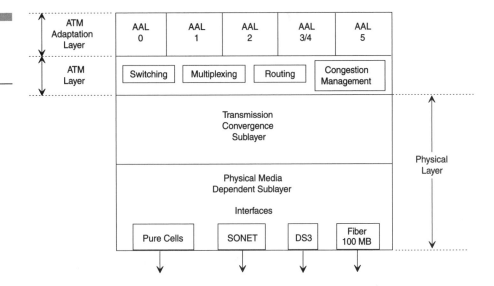

the components at the physical media dependent sub-layer and interface supported, the transmission convergence sub-layer, the ATM layer functional components, and the AAL.

Figure 9-3 shows functions that occur at the ATM layer, and it also shows categories of functions that occur at the AAL. Details of the AAL functions are explained in later on, but the ATM layer is the focus here.

The ATM layer also defines two virtual connections: A *Virtual Channel Connection* (VCC) between two ATM VCC endpoints. This might be either point-to-point or point-to-multipoint. Second, multiple virtual channel connections are carried through *Virtual Path Connection* (VPC) endpoints. This connection is either point-to-point or point-to-multipoint.

This layer also translates the *Virtual Path Indicators* (VPIs) and the *Virtual Channel Indicators* (VCI). It is responsible for cell multiplexing and demultiplexing.

The AAL is responsible for mapping data from higher layers within a network into cell fields and vice versa. This layer operates on functions that are end-to-end functions.

The connection oriented or connectionless conversion protocol incorporates the broadband data service and includes the B-ISDN, *Integrated Switching Data Network* (ISDN) standard. This B-ISDN support includes interactive services including: conversational such as video, voice, and sounds, as well as document messaging for electronic mail and multimedia. It also specifies the way text, data, sound, pictures, and video are transmitted and received.

The *ATM Adaptation Layer* (AAL) layer has been explained as the protocol layer that maps upper layer protocols onto ATM. Devices that use this terminate signals. This layer provides functional support for different types of traffic (signals) that come from upper layer protocols. Consequently, the following categories of functions are explained:

AAL type 0

AAL type 1

AAL type 2

AAL type 3/4

AAL type 5

AAL Type 0

AAL type 0 is considered a placeholder when *Customer Premises Equipment* (CPE) perform required functions at this layer. In a sense, it is a pass through capability for cell-oriented service. Figure 9-4 is a detailed view at the *ATM Adaptation Layer* (AAL).

AAL Type 1

AAL type 1 functions to provide constant bit rate services. This is also known as unstructured circuit transport between points. This type of function is connection-oriented. The *CS* component in AAL 1 in Figure 9-3 is called the convergence sub-layer. It modulates differences that might occur in the different physical interfaces. The *SAR* function performs segmentation and reassembly on data as it moves through AAL 1.

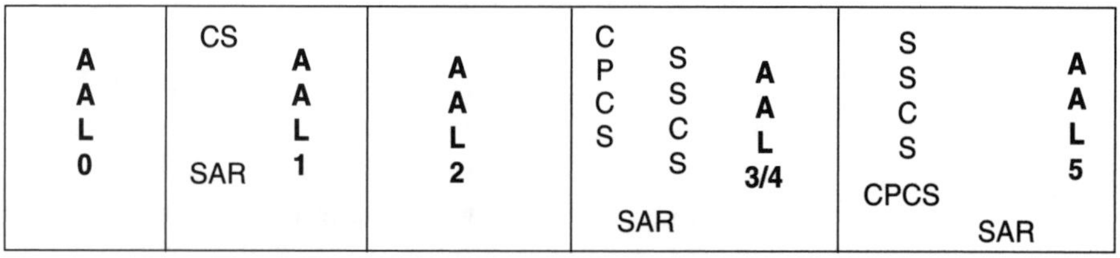

Figure 9-4

Conceptual view of functions at the ATM adaptation layer

AAL Type 2

This service specifies support for isochronous service with varying bit rates. A user of this function is, for example, compressed or packetized video.

AAL Type 3/4

AAL type 3/4 function supports *Local Area Network* (LAN) traffic. It supports a variable bit rate. Both connection-oriented and connectionless-oriented connections are supported. The SSCS is the *Service Specific Convergence Sub-layer*. One of its functions is data translation. It also maps upper layer services to the ATM layer. CPCS is the *Common Part Convergence Sub-layer*. This part works in conjunction with switched multi-megabit data service. SAR is the component that performs segmentation and reassembly of a segment.

AAL Type 5

Type 5 is designed for variable bit rate services. It is similar to type 3/4 , but it differs in that it is easier to implement. Most ATM local area network devices support this type.

The components of an ATM cell, as it appears at the *User Network Interface* (UNI), are shown by Figure 9-5.

ATM Cell Structure

The cell structure shown in Figure 9-5 contains 5 bytes of header information and 48 bytes of user information. The contents of the cell are defined in the following text.

Figure 9-5
ATM cell structure
at the UNI

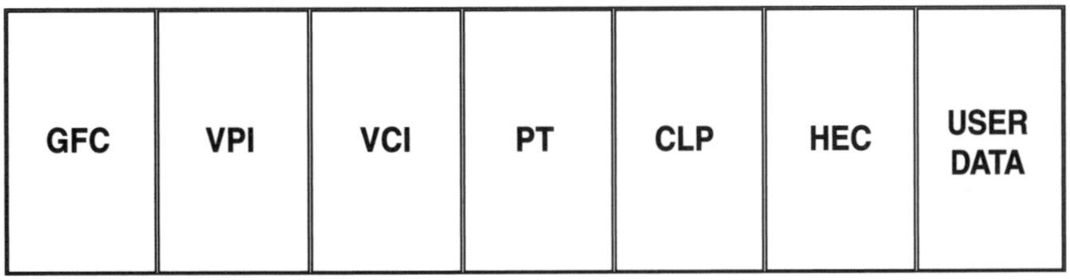

GFC	VPI	VCI	PT	CLP	HEC	USER DATA

ATM Cell Components

The *Generic Flow Control* (GFC) controls data traffic locally and can be used to customize a local implementation. The bit value in this field is not moved from end-to-end. After the cell is in the network, ATM switches to overwrite the fields.

The next two fields are the virtual path identifier and the virtual channel identifier bits. Information stored in these fields performs routing functions. The number of bits here varies, because the bits used for virtual channel identifiers for user-to-user virtual paths are negotiated between the users of that virtual path. These two fields constitute the way nodes communicate.

The *payload type* (PT) indicates if the data being carried is user data or management related information. This field is also used to indicate network congestion.

The *cell loss priority* (CLP) is used to explicitly indicate the cell priority. In short, it indicates whether or not the cell is a candidate for discarding if network congestion occurs.

The header error control field is used by the physical layer. This field is used to detect errors in the header and correct bit errors within the header as well.

The user data field contains the user data from upper layers within the network. This is a 48-byte field. This field does not have error checking performed on it.

The other cell type, known as the *Network Node Interface* (NNI), is similar to Figure 9-5 with the exception of a difference indicated in the header portion of the cell.

ATM Interface Types & Speeds

As indicated in the previous section, two types of nodes are recognized. The *User Network Interface* (UNI) can be divided into two groups:

Private

Public

Private

Private UNIs can best be described by function. They are typically used to connect an ATM user with an ATM switch in which both are considered local and part of the site. The switch itself might be referred to as private and considered to be *Customer Premises Equipment* (CPE). CPE is that ATM equipment located on a customer site and not in the public arena. An ATM user might be a device such as a router or workstation. The ATM switch is a private ATM switch. This ATM switch is what connects the private user to the public interface.

Public

The public *User Network Interface* (UNI) is the interface used to connect an ATM user to an ATM switch in the domain of the public service provider. Figure 9-6 depicts these concepts.

Figure 9-6
Conceptual view of the user network interface

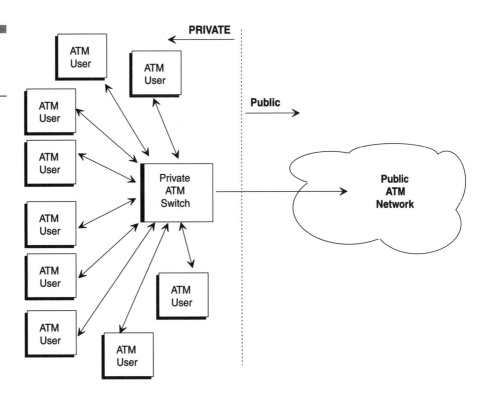

Figure 9-6 shows private customer premise equipment and the public ATM switch. The functionality of the ATM switches (both private and public) utilize the same functionality at the physical layer. However, different media can be implemented.

The network node interface refers to the ATM switches in the public service provider network that communicate with one another to achieve routing and thus end-to-end service. Figure 9-7 is an example of this concept.

Figure 9-7 shows the network nodes implemented in a public ATM network, ATM users, an ATM switch, and implicitly the boundaries between the public ATM network and the private ATM switch.

ATM Transmission Concepts

Three concepts are used with ATM. These include

Transmission Path

Virtual Path

Virtual Circuit

These three concepts are generally found together, because they are part of ATM operation.

Transmission Path

The transmission path is a physical connection between ATM supported devices. These paths might have different characteristics, but they nevertheless exist. The physical transmission path between entities is the virtual concepts and the usage to which they are mapped.

Virtual Path

The idea of a virtual path is derived from having a transmission path on which it can be mapped. The virtual is mapped to the physical. In this case, Figure 9-8 is an example of this concept.

Figure 9-7
Public ATM network

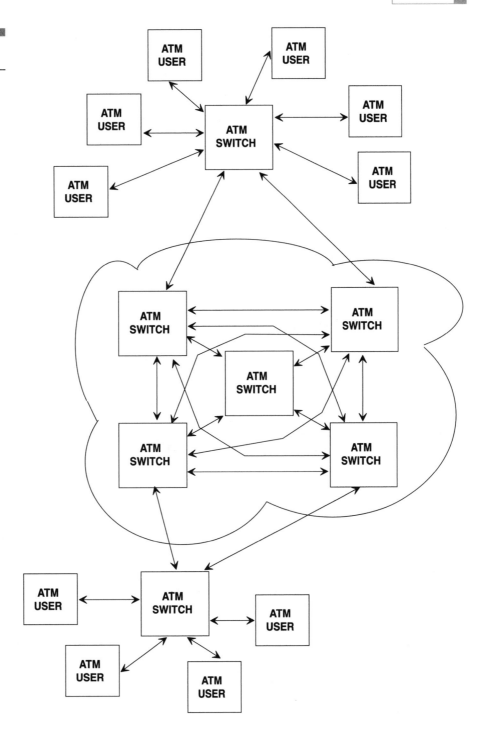

Figure 9-8
Conceptual view of
paths and circuits

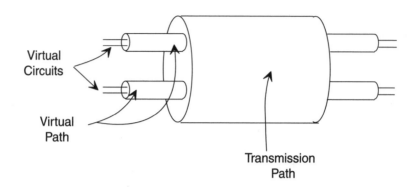

Figure 9-8
Conceptual view of
paths and circuits

Virtual Circuit

The notion of a virtual circuit exists. The virtual circuit (some refer to this as a virtual channel) is mapped to both a virtual path and a transmission path (physical path).

The concepts of transmission path, virtual path, and virtual circuit are implemented at the physical layer in the ATM model. This is merely another method of multiplexing. This structure is a part of the intricate nature of the ATM physical layer and is a part of the robust nature of ATM.

ATM LAN Based Implementations

Where and how is ATM implemented are valid questions. Because its support is versatile and it can accommodate high speeds, multiple possibilities exist as to *how* and *where* it is implemented. This section explores four distinct instances of *how* and *where* ATM is implemented. These include

Local Router & ATM Backbone

ATM Based LANs

ATM Backbone Nodes

ATM LANs & ATM Backbone

Local Router & ATM Backbone

This type of implementation uses routers that support ATM in a local geographical area. Here a LAN exists with other lower layer protocols and network devices; but a router with an ATM interface is used to connect the LAN into the ATM backbone that serves a much larger geographical area. Figure 9-9 portrays this idea.

Figure 9-9 is a practical example of an ATM implementation. It illustrates a router with an ATM interface in a local implementation along with devices attached to it directly or indirectly. It also indicates the local router

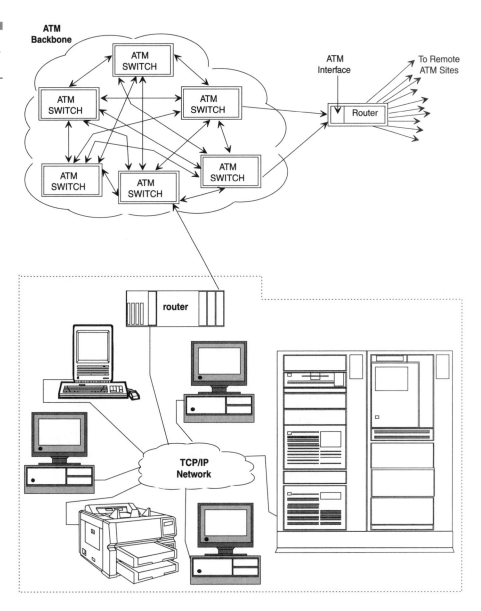

Figure 9-9
Local ATM hub/router & ATM backbone

with an ATM interface connected to an ATM backbone by which other sites connect. The ATM backbone consists of ATM devices. This is one of the simplest examples of those discussed in this section.

ATM Backbone LANs

The notion of ATM backbone LANs is as its name implies; the LAN is built around ATM equipment. Figure 9-10 is an illustration of this idea.

In Figure 9-10, two separate LANs are shown in addition to the network connected through the router with an ATM interface. Two local implementations are shown and one has two ATM based LANs. Each local implementation accesses the ATM network backbone, which consists of all ATM equipment.

ATM Backbone Nodes

ATM backbone nodes are typically implemented in public environments (in contrast to a private enterprise). Many ATM nodes working together constitute an ATM backbone. Figure 9-11 shows multiple ATM nodes creating a wide area network backbone.

Figure 9-11 includes a network attached to the ATM node in Denver. The Denver network enters the ATM network through a router. A similar scenario like this could be repeated in other sites shown in Figure 9-10.

ATM LANs & ATM Backbone

The notion of ATM LANs and an ATM backbone is example of complete ATM implementation. Figure 9-12 depicts this.

Figure 9-12 shows ATM nodes comprising the backbone of the ATM network and the focal point of the networks in Boise and Syracuse. This example shows maximum utilization of ATM locally and in a WAN sense as well.

Variations of the last four figures are possible. These are representative of likely implementations. Other *hybrid* ways of implementing ATM are possible and depend heavily on the particular site.

Figure 9-10
Local GIGABIT
ETHERNET LAN &
local ATM LAN
connected to a public
ATM switch

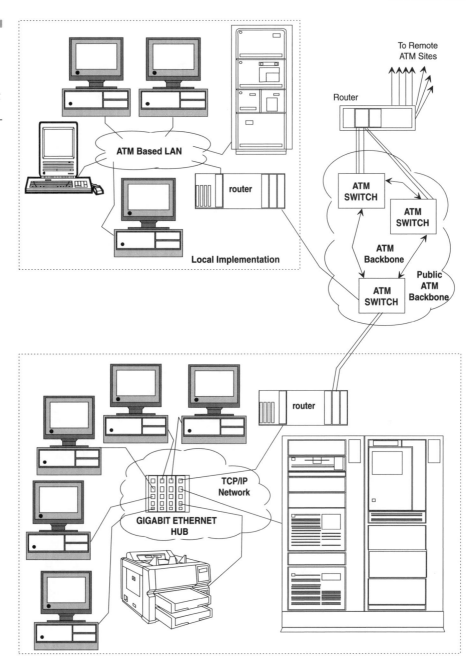

Figure 9-11
Conceptual view of
an ATM backbone

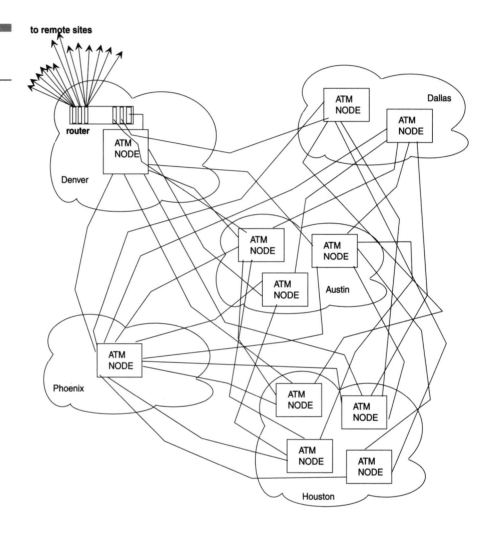

Figure 9-12
Complete ATM
implementation

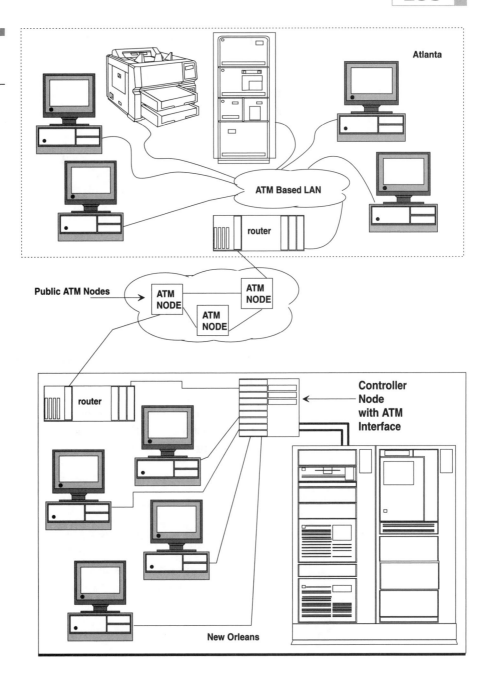

ATM Physical Layer Architecture

Figure 9-3 illustrates details of supported interfaces by the physical media dependent sub-layer. Some of those are presented here:

SONET

DS3

Fiber 100Mb

The interfaces and technical characteristics of the previous list is explained here.

SONET

Synchronous Optical Network (SONET) is one of the supported interfaces indicated by Figure 9-3. Its data rate transfer can accommodate speeds up to 155.52 MB per/sec. SONET frame structure is such that it can easily accommodate ATM. SONET support for ATM is achieved by mapping ATM cells, aligned by row, that correlate to the structure of every SONET byte structure. Figure 9-13 is an example of how SONET, ATM, and other technology can merge together.

Figure 9-13 shows an ATM device connecting into a SONET interface. In turn, an ATM LAN is attached to the ATM device. This implementation utilizes speeds through the SONET interface.

DS3

DS3 can be used as an interface to carry ATM cells. The data rate of DS3 is 44.7 MB per/sec. If this is used, a *Physical Layer Convergence Protocol* (PLCP) must be defined. After this is complete, ATM cells are merely mapped to DS3 PLCP frame. Figure 9-14 shows an example.

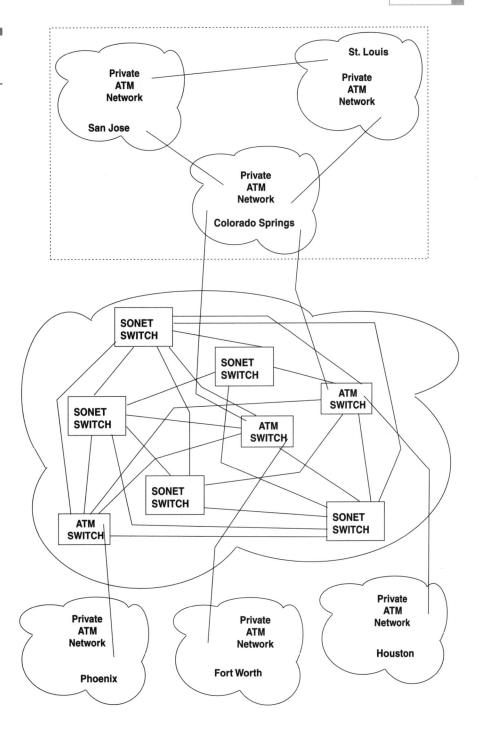

Figure 9-13
Perspective of SONET
& ATM

Figure 9-14
Perspective of DS3 &
ATM

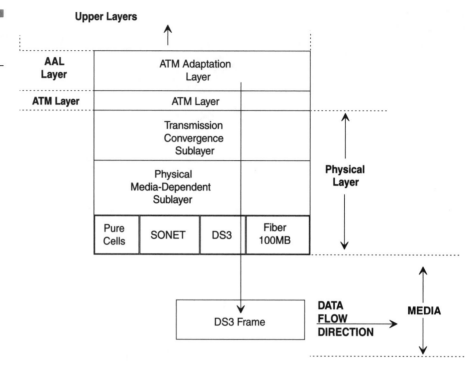

Figure 9-14
Perspective of DS3 &
ATM

Fiber 100 MB

This interface supports up to 100 MB per/sec. The physical link is between the equipment at a given site and a private ATM switch. This specification calls for the current FDDI implementation. Figure 9-15 shows an example.

Other interfaces are supported in the ATM environment; these are good illustrations of how ATM works with other protocols.

Figure 9-15
ATM & FDDI
implementation

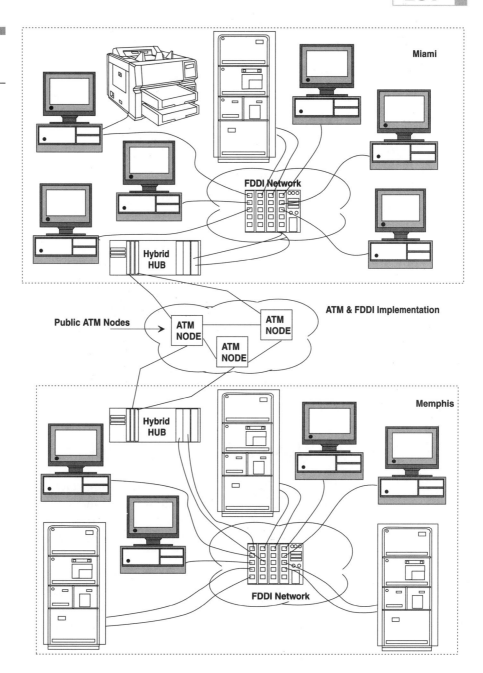

ATM Applications

Some ask when or what applications should be used with ATM technology. These are good questions to address during the planning or migration stage of your network. The following are some reasons I have encountered why ATM is used:

Bandwidth

Isochronous Traffic Support

Capacity per person/per use

Expandable

Bandwidth

One argued reason for using ATM is the bandwidth it offers. One reason for the high bandwidth capacity is the speed at which ATM operates. Earlier in this chapter in Figure 9-3, some physical level implementations of ATM were shown. Notice in this figure, 100 Mbps fiber, DS3, and SONET are possible physical implementations. The capacity of each is much higher than other types of physical layer implementations.

Isochronous Traffic Support

ATM is a strong contender for multimedia, voice, data, and video networks. These technologies require timing-dependent transfer methods. ATM can accommodate all these various forms of user applications. Any given network could be any combination of technologies and ATM is sufficient to carry the payload.

Timing dependent transfer is becoming more and more of a concern today. Many applications that were once segmented fairly obviously as data, voice, video, or multimedia are becoming blurred in today's marketplace. For example, a simple word processor today can include a mixed array of information presentation in other than a text only format. However, some fifteen or so years ago word processors were only that, a word processor. Believe it or not, not too long ago word processors were evaluated on their respective ability to do things like move a block of text (cut and paste) and other things considered rudimentary today. Many word processors today have the ability not only to import graphics but manipulate them. Some can even accommodate multimedia presentations.

Capacity Per Person/Per Use

Another reason for the use of ATM is the ability to accommodate a wide variety of implementations. For example, an ATM backbone could be the right fit for a company where heavy video and multimedia traffic occurs. In this type of environment, some users probably need only minimal network support such as printing and e-mail.

For network users who need only network printing and e-mail, use of ATM is overkill. But, on the flip side, users in a network where heavy video traffic is used might consume large capacities of bandwidth. Hence, utilization of the network can be measured on a per person, per use basis. It might initially seem to cost too much to implement ATM for a complete enterprise wide network, but analyzing it from another perspective could easily tell a different story. For example, the requirements for 70 percent of the network to function adequately might require ATM technology. The remaining 30 percent might not come near this in requirement. The bottom line is this: If ATM is implemented enterprise wide, all users benefit. Hence, in accommodating all user's averages the price per person per use goes down rather than up. The net effect is a well designed ATM network implementation that yields room to grow while accommodating immediate needs as well.

Expandability

Another strong reason for ATM use is the expandability is provides. If designed appropriately, ATM can be scaled upward to accommodate the growth needs of any organization.

ATM Terminology

ATM has a highly specialized vocabulary. Some ATM terms are presented here to serve as a specific ATM reference source.

- *AAL Connection*   The establishment of an association between *ATM Adaptation Layer* (AAL) and higher entities

- *ATM*   A fast packet switched, cell-based method of moving voice, data, video, and other data and telecommunication oriented information from one location to another. The ATM cell is 53 bytes in length: 5 bytes of header information and 48 bytes of user information.

- *ATM Layer Link*   A connection between two ATM layers

- *ATM Link*   A virtual path or a virtual circuit (channel) connection

- *ATM PEER-to-PEER Connection*   This refers to a virtual channel connection or a virtual path connection.

- *ATM Traffic Descriptor*   This is a list of generic traffic parameters. They can be used to obtain traffic characteristics of a given ATM connection.

- *Cell*   A cell is an ATM protocol data unit.

- *Connection Admission Control*   The method used to determine if an ATM link request can be accepted, which is based on the origin and destination's attributes.

- *Connection Endpoint*   A layer connection SAP termination

- *Connection Endpoint Identifier*   The characteristic of an endpoint used to identify a *Service Access Point* (SAP).

- *End System*   The place where an ATM connection is terminated.

- *Header*   The control information that precedes the user information in an ATM cell.

- *Fairness*   The meeting of all specified quality of service requirements through control of active connections across an ATM link

- *Metasignaling*   A way of managing virtual circuits and different types of signals

- *Network Node Interface*   The ATM interface as it relates to the network node

- *Segment*   An ATM link, or group of links, that compose an ATM connection

- *Service Access Point (SAP)*   An addressable end point at a given layer within a network

- *Sub-layer*   The division of a layer logically

- *Switched Connection*   A connection established through a signaling method

- *Symmetric Connection*   A connection where both directions have the same bandwidth

- *Virtual Channel*   Also called a virtual circuit. That which an ATM cell can traverse
- *Virtual Circuit*   Also called a virtual channel. That which an ATM cell can traverse
- *Virtual Path*   The logical association of virtual circuits
- *Virtual Path Connection*   This is a one way joining of virtual path links.
- *Virtual Path Link*   The connection between points where a virtual path identifier is assigned.
- *Virtual Path Terminator*   The system that processes the virtual circuits (channels) after they are de-multiplexed

ATM Example Implementations

Multiple ways to implement ATM technology exist. Figure 9-16 is an example of ATM implemented to provide a network backbone for high-speed data traffic.

Figure 9-16 shows two physical locations implementing ATM and an ATM WAN backbone used to connect the two physical locations. Notice the New York location has multiple users connected to both an FDDI hub and a host as well. The host itself has a printer attached and is attached to a hybrid hub. The hub is attached to an ATM concentrator. It, in turn, is connected to the ATM interface.

The Chicago location has three major hosts connected to an ATM concentrator. This location is primarily a data network with large repositories. This particular blueprint is based on not only an ATM backbone in the public carrier network, but also on the respective locations as well.

This example is a basic implementation for ATM. One aspect not shown is the requirement for ATM interface boards in those devices connected to ATM devices such as a concentrator or hub.

Notice also this blueprint shows a variety of other technologies, as well as ATM. For example, in the New York location a FDDI hub is installed and used to connect personal computers and a host system. A hybrid hub is also installed which could support other lower layer technologies beside ATM and FDDI.

A typical implementation where this scenario would be a good fit is where the need exists for data to be available in real time. ATM can accommodate

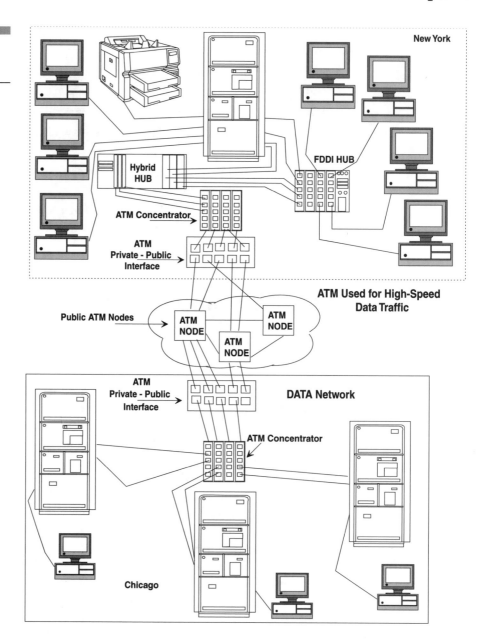

high speeds over great distances. ATM is also a good technology to build an infrastructure with inside a company or other entity.

Another example of ATM implementation is more complex. Consider Figure 9-17.

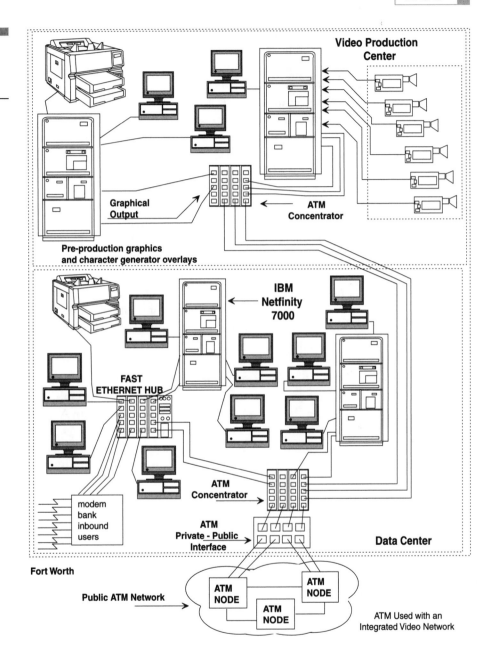

Figure 9-17
ATM used with an integrated video network

Notice two locations are shown in this figure: one in Fort Worth and the other in Dallas. These locations are connected through an ATM backbone network.

The Fort Worth location has a pre-production graphics group and remote video cameras that send live feeds back to the host connected to the ATM concentrator. The pre-production group has a host where graphics are stored and character-generator overlays are produced. The pre-production group requires large amounts of disk storage. Size of stored files used in this group is generally large because of their graphical nature. Because the size of the files are large and require large amounts of storage, other factors come into consideration besides pure speed of data transfer from one location to another. Speed of data transfer on CDs, disk drives, tape drives, and other methods of storage are important. Processor speed is equally important. Bandwidth and other factors need to be considered when designing a network or implementing a blueprint similar to this. The remote video network has different concerns even though they are a part of the same Fort Worth office.

Like the pre-production graphics department, the remote video network needs large amounts of storage as well as. The remote video network is different in that it requires large amounts of bandwidth to move images from the cameras to the system in which they are stored. This unique need reveals requirements for high bandwidth between the intake source and the place of storage. In some instances, the intake (video cameras) direct their input to a specialized device that feeds it directly to the production. Use of images from the cameras requires large capacities for throughput.

The Dallas location in Figure 9-16 shows an ATM interface and ATM concentrator. Other hosts and computers are connected in the network as well. The Dallas location in this example is the broadcast location for the production. This facility requires maximum throughput internally and externally.

Additional Information

Additional ATM information can be obtained from CCITT specifications. Some of these include

I.113

I.121

I.150

I.211

I.311

I.321

I.327

I.361

I.362

I.363

I.413

I.432

I.610

G.707

G.708

G.709

SUMMARY

ATM is a cell based, fast-packet switching technology. It can be implemented privately or publicly. Many public service providers are opting for ATM installations. ATM technology has gained considerable attention since its entry into the technical arena in the late 1980s.

ATM conceptual structure does not correlate one-for-one with the OSI model. ATM layers begin with a physical layer that has two sub-layers. The lowest sub-layer is called Physical Media Dependent Sub-layer, and above it is the Transmission Convergence Sub-layer. Next is the ATM layer that includes four functions as explained previously. The ATM Adaptation Layer is above the ATM layer. Part of the ATM layer and the ATM Adaptation Layer make up layer two. The ATM Adaptation Layer includes five types of functions.

ATM cells are unique because they are small and can handle voice, data, video, and other multimedia information. The ATM adaptation layer protocols are an interface between ATM and upper layer protocols.

ATM utilizes a transmission path, virtual path, and virtual call as part of its implementation and method of passing information. Virtual paths and virtual calls are mapped to a transmission path.

The CCITT has a list of ATM specifications; some of which are directly related and some indirectly.

10

Integrated Services Digital Network (ISDN)

This chapter answers typical questions that arise when ISDN is mentioned. ISDN is a very comprehensive topic that includes vast amount of standards, protocols, and information contributed by a number of standards making bodies. The purpose of this chapter is to orient the reader to ISDN. It begins by clarifying what it is, presents some fundamental standards it is based on, explains some ISDN basic terms and concepts, and briefly explains SS7. Interfaces used with ISDN and their function are presented, in addition to some examples of practical services as a result of ISDN implementations.

What is ISDN?

You might have asked this question to yourself or possibly others if your background is not related to this technology. The technology is not new in that it was just invented a few years ago, but rather the implementation and use of it generally keep it one step removed from most except those who work directly with it.

Working Definition

ISDN is the acronym for *Integrated Services Digital Network*. Practically speaking it has more to do with functionality from the perspective of regional telephone companies and service providers implementations than with an isolated implementation. In fact ISDN *users* realize its benefits and typically are not involved in the "implementation" of it. Clarification on this point is forthcoming.

For example, many telephone companies (in the United States and other countries) have implemented the ISDN technology in central offices, private digital systems, and *private branch exchanges* (PBXs). This is significant, because the technology is based on digital signals, not analog. Digital signals are fundamental to ISDN foundations. They also enable ISDN to support voice, data, video, electronic mail, and numerous other services integrated together to make it a powerful technology to build on. The result is potential services offered through the telephone network that was not possible. Figure 10-1 is a conceptual view of the idea behind ISDN implementations.

Figure 10-1
Conceptual view
of an ISDN
implementation

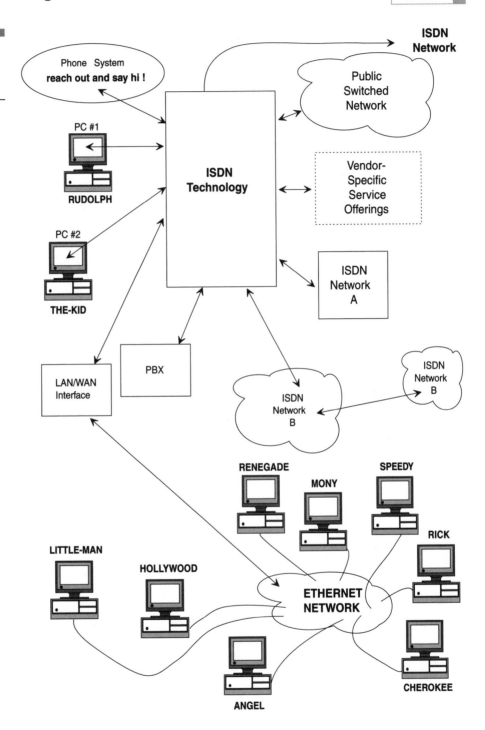

ISDN realization requires more than the telephone system implementation. In fact, ISDN requires that the calling party, the network, and the destination party implement ISDN technology. If these three conditions are not met, some ISDN capabilities are not possible. Further exploration into what this means from a practical standpoint is presented later.

CCITT Recommendations

ISDN is a protocol. Its operation, standards, and recommendations have been defined by the CCITT. The *I* series of CCITT recommendations covers a broad range of ISDN technology. The I series is divided into groups of 100. Table 10-1 categorically describes the CCITT recommendations.

These recommendations, along with many others, detail ISDN according to the CCITT. The source of this series of recommendations is from my reference library, which includes all CCITT recommendations through March 1994. Any of these recommendations can be obtained from sources that provide standards and recommendations from entities such as the CCITT.

Table 10-1
CCITT Numbers-to-Function correlation

CCITT Number	Function
I.100	Contains general information such as terminology used, the structure of the I series of recommendations and basic capabilities of ISDN
I.200	This group of recommendations specifies ISDN service capabilities such as circuit, packet, and a variety of digital services.
I.300	This group of recommendations includes the principles, protocols, and architecture of ISDN.
I.400	The 400 series of recommendations includes specifications of user interfaces and network layer functions.
I.500	The 500 series of recommendations includes interface standards, principles for internetworking ISDN networks, and related topics.
I.600	This series includes ISDN maintenance recommendations including subscriber access, basic access, and primary rate access.

ISDN Channels

ISDN has basic concepts that are applicable in the majority of implementations. The question is "What is used in a given ISDN implementation?" This section explains terms and concepts that ISDN is built on.

Channels

The term channel is used frequently in ISDN to convey the meaning of service provided. Channels are an integral part of ISN technology, and as this section explains different type channels exists.

Channels in general are an entity physical or logical that data, voice, video, or other *information* travels through. This is important, because in ISDN, different type of channels are defined. A definable characteristic of channels is they can be identified as being digital or analog. Either way they carry signals from one entity to another.

The remainder of this section explains the different types of channels available with ISDN.

The D Channel

In ISDN the D channel is used to convey user-signaling messages. This type channel uses out-of-band signaling. This means that network related signals are carried on a separate channel than user data. The signals transmitted over the D channel convey the characteristics of the service on behalf of the user. The name out-of-band arose, because the network signal is out-of-band with the user signal.

The protocol used on the D-channel defines a logical connection between what is called the *Terminal Equipment* (TE) and the *Local Exchange* (LE) through Local Loop Termination Equipment. To use this arrangement *Customer Premise Equipment* (CPE) that performs switching functions is required. Figure 10-2 is a conceptual view of this idea.

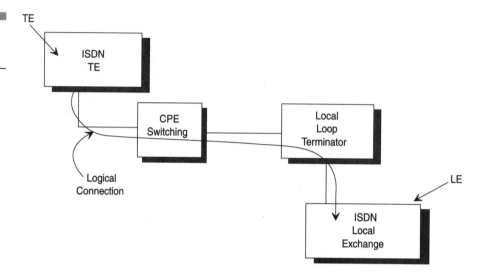

Figure 10-2
Conceptual view of
TE & LE Equipment

The essence of understanding the D channel is to know it uses out-of-band signaling but carries user data. It operates at approximately 16 or 64 Kbytes per/sec and is used by user equipment to transmit requests and messages within the network. In summary the D channel provides signaling service between a user and the network, and provides packet mode data transfer.

The B Channel

The B channel carries voice, data, video, and data. This channel functions at a constant 64 Kbytes per/sec. This channel can be used for packet and circuit switching applications. The difference between the two is that packet switching applications utilize a logical connection through a network and no dedicated facilities exist. This is generally referred to as a store and forward method of data transfer. Circuit switching differs because its switching technology is based on devices that are connected through some resource for the extent of the call (or communication instance).

B and D channels work in harmony. The D channel is used to transfer request for services that are delivered on a B channel. Figure 10-3 is an example of the B and D channels operation.

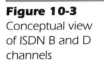

Figure 10-3
Conceptual view
of ISDN B and D
channels

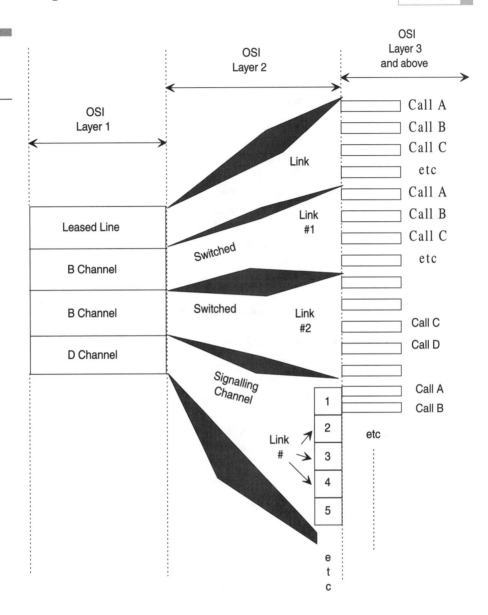

H Channel

Multiple H channels exist. The basic differences between them are the services they offer. As a general rule, H channels have a considerably higher transfer rate than B channels. These channels effectively meet the needs of real-time video conferencing, Digital quality audio, and other services requiring a much higher bandwidth.

The basic H channel known as H0 is comprised of one channel that can provide rates of 384 Kbytes per/sec. H11 channel can support throughput rates of approximately 1536 Mbytes per/sec and the H12 channel sustains rates of up to approximately 1920 Mbytes per/sec. This type channel is most suitable for a trunk where subdivision can be implemented to maximize the effective bandwidth.

Signaling System 7 (SS7)

SS7 is a standard being implemented by regional and long distance telephone companies today. Its relationship to ISDN is important. Without SS7 implementation in the telephone systems, ISDN is somewhat inhibited. They are interrelated in many ways.

The fundamental reason for this is that SS7 is digital by design and link capacity outstrips SS6.

SS7 is a protocol and method for networks of switching entities to communicate with one another. Although ISDN can be implemented without SS7, ISDN with the implementation of SS7 ISDN can be more comprehensive in scope.

Characteristics

SS7 is a complex standard. The CCITT has a series of recommended standards about the signaling system. Some highlights of SS7 characteristics include

- It can accommodate digital communications in networks using digital channels.
- It can also operate with analog communication channels.
- It can be used domestically in the United States or internationally.
- It is a layered architecture.

- Speeds are 56 and 64 Kbits per/sec.
- In regards to information transfer, it is considered reliable, because it ensures sequential movement of signals through a network and provides a mechanism to prevent loss or duplicate signals.
- It can operate in point-to-point network implementations and can be used with satellite communications.
- Its method of handling routing and delivery of control messages is also considered reliable.
- It has built into it management capabilities, maintenance, and also a method for call control.

SS7 CCITT recommendations define packet switched network functions but do not restrict implementation to specific hardware. According to CCITT recommendations, two signaling points are defined: a signaling point and a signaling transfer point. The signaling point is defined as a point in the network capable of handling control information. A signaling transfer point is identified as an entity where routing of messages can be achieved.

Protocol Components

SS7 protocol can be categorized into three groups:

Signaling Connection Control Part (SCCP)

Application

Message Transfer Part (MTP)

The SCCP protocol specifies five classes of network service. These five include

1. Unsequenced connectionless
2. Sequenced connectionless
3. Connection-oriented
4. Flow control connection-oriented
5. Flow control connection-oriented with error recovery

The SCCP supports OSI addressing capabilities and in a sense, functions to deliver messages intended for a specific user, after the message reaches the destination signaling point. The SCCP works with the MTP to achieve OSI network layer support.

The MTP protocol has multiple layers of signaling. The first level corresponds to the physical layer of the OSI model. It functions as the signaling data link. The second level of the protocol operates at the data link layer of the OSI model. It is, by design, a bit oriented protocol, consequently it is robust in its capabilities. The third level corresponds roughly to the network layer of the OSI model. It is concerned with routing and link management.

SS7 application protocol correlates to upper layers in the OSI model. The structure at this layer is divided into a telephone user part, which focuses on signaling processes required for voice communications. The data user part is related to requirements for circuit oriented networks and has been usurped by the ISDN user part.

Additional Information

The CCITT and ANSI standards for SS7 are comprehensive in scope. The following list is only a partial one, but provides an excellent starting point for those who need additional information. Standard source suppliers who maintain lists of standards making bodies, such as the ANSI and the CCITT, can obtain a more complete list.

ANSI T1.110   SS7 Overview

ANSI T1.111   Overview of the Message Transfer Part

ANSI T1.113   ISDN User Part

CCITT Q.700   SS7 Overview

CCITT Q.701   Message Transfer Part

CCITT Q.702   Signaling Data Link

CCITT Q.711—Q.716   Signaling Connection Control Part

CCITT Q.730   ISDN Supplementary Services

CCITT Q.761—Q.766   ISDN User Part

ISDN Interfaces and How They Are Used

Two ISDN user interfaces are explained in this section. They are Basic Rate Interface and the Primary Rate Interface.

Basic Rate Interface

This is a way to access ISDN. It consists of two B channels and one D channel according to CCITT recommendation number I.430. Hence, it is sometimes referred to as the 2B+D interface.

No protocol specification restrictions are applicable here. This interface utilizes circuit switched transparent "pipes" to make a connection between two end users by way of the ISDN network. Examples of where this interface is implemented would be PBXs, individual terminals, videoconference units, personal computers, and workstations.

Primary Rate Interface

This is also a way to access ISDN. This interface calls for one of the following implementations:

23 B channels and 1 D channel

24 B channels and 1 D channel

30 B channels and 1 D channel

These originate from the CCITT I.431 recommendation. In some ways this is basically the bandwidth equivalent to T21s used in the United States. This interface calls for point-to-point, serial, and synchronous communications. A fundamental difference between the primary rate interface and the basic rate interface is the primary rate interface can support H channels as well as B channels. As a result bandwidth is greatly enhanced.

How Interfaces Are Used

These two interfaces are used by a business, personal user, or otherwise to connect them directly to the local telephone company's central office. In large scenarios, the basic rate interface is used to connect individual users to the organizations PBX, and in turn the PBX is connected to the local telephone central office. However, this can be achieved by connecting this latter scenario to an interchange carrier through a broadband interface. The connection is made through an ISDN interface board, ISDN controller, or an external terminal adapter, and the connection is physically established.

Practical Uses with ISDN

Like many technologies used in networks that might not reside inside a user's workplace environment, ISDN is somewhat abstract. ISDN uses can be understood easier than the internal operations, for those who are not technically adept. This section hones in on practical services that are based directly or indirectly on ISDN technology.

Automatic Number Identification (ANI)

ANI is a service that provides the individual being called with the telephone number of the caller, prior to the party answering the call. This service is beneficial for a company who prides itself on customer service.

Simply the telephone number and a well designed and implemented database can be a powerful tool for a company to better serve their customers. The following examples are base on the ANI service and an updated database. Consider the implications.

- Identification of the customer: name, address, phone number(s), and other information pertinent to serving the customer

- Identification of the customer's language preference. Our diverse culture today is a blend of individuals who speak different languages. This is important information for companies who have international customers who do not speak English. With a good database and ANI, a non-English speaking caller can be routed immediately to a service representative who can speak their language. This in itself communicates to the customer the company cares enough about its customers to have individuals who can communicate in a variety of languages.

- Ascertaining caller's telephone numbers who terminate a call before a representative can respond because they have been on hold for an inordinate amount of time. Consequently, a representative can return the customer's call.

- Identifying callers through their number and their files in the database in a particular category. For example, assume a customer purchases large quantities of *widgets* and has been a long-standing account of a particular sales representative, because the representative understands the needs of the caller. In this case, a caller and his/her files can be directed to the appropriate representative.

■ A customer's preferred method of payment can be determined based on their prior payment history and therefore repeating the same numbers and information again can be avoided except to verify appropriate information.

These ANI based services are available today for large system computing to personal computer systems. Regardless of the implementation, the results of such a service generally makes a positive impression on a customer.

Electronic Library Interconnections

With the help of ISDN and supporting technology today, it is possible for libraries in geographically remote parts of the United States to electronically exchange information that would have been impractical a decade ago.

Electronic Manual Access

Many companies such as Philips, Apple Computer, Microsoft, and other companies are beginning to put manuals in electronic media and distribute them to databases through ISDN networks. These manuals span topics such as hardware maintenance, software changes, and a variety of other topics.

Image Retrieval

A major advantage to ISDN and supporting systems is the ability to transmit images, full motion video, text, graphics, data, and pre-recorded video information. This is particularly significant in the realm of medicine. Now CAT scans can be moved in entirety to participating ISDN customers in the medical community.

Other practical everyday uses of ISDN are not generally presented in technical form and explanation to the recipients who utilize the capabilities it offers. Suffice it to say that ISDN is growing in vendor products, telephone system implementations, and even coming close to in home implementation.

Companies such as AT&T, Sprint, and MCI are implementing ISDN and variations thereof. The end result is services provided through networks that a widespread customer base in time can access.

SUMMARY

Actual ISDN technology is removed from most users. The services of ISDN are the result of the implementation. ISDN services provide capabilities for moving voice, data, live video, text, imaging, and variations of multimedia technology from one location to another in real time.

The CCITT and ANSI have numerous recommendations and proposed standards related to ISDN and the support of peripheral equipment. These standards are lengthy; my references on the topic consume many linear feet of bookshelf space. A list of CCITT and ANSI specifications was provided for the reader who needs additional information on the topic.

The B, D, and H ISDN channels were explained in light of their features and differences. SS7 characteristics and protocol components were also presented; and references for additional information was also provided.

ISDN basic rate interface and primary rate interfaces were explained. A brief explanation pertaining to how interfaces are used was presented also.

A section on the practical uses of ISDN was presented to help the reader understand some of the services that are based in ISDN technology, directly or indirectly.

Frame Relay

Frame relay provides real-time communication between end users. This is possible, because frame relay serves as an interface into public and/or private networks. Frame relay networks pass frames from origin to destination without intermediate nodes performing packet assembly and disassembly. Frame relay is also considered a protocol. A frame relay control protocol is also defined explaining how users make service requests in the network.

Frame relay is designed to support data in bursts and provide high speeds. It is not a store-n-forward based technology, but rather a bi-directional conversational method of communication. Most frame relay standards are concentrated at layers one and two, however standards do define the mechanism for upper layer protocols to "hook" into frame relay.

For example, consider the Figure 11-1.

The scenario in Figure 11-1 shows multiple sites using frame relay as an interface into a dispersed frame relay network. Additionally, each site has other protocols implemented in both the upper and lower layers. However, the commonality among all these locations is the frame relay connection over the wide area.

Principles of Frame Relay

Frame relay operates on multiple principles. Some included in this section are virtual links, permanent virtual connections, and the data link connection identifier.

The Virtual Link

A basic frame relay principle is a virtual connection. The concept alone is interesting because the *virtual connection* might differ in respect to the time it exists. Practically the connection is permanent in the sense that it *remains* as long as necessary. Figure 11-2 shows a basic frame relay example.

Figure 11-2 shows three hosts connected to a frame relay node, physical links connecting each host to the node, memory inside the frame relay device, and a connection-mapping table within the frame relay node. Host number 1's physical link supports two *permanent virtual connections* (PVCs). However, host 2 and 3's physical links support one PVC each.

The connection-mapping table is at the heart of frame relay operations within the frame relay node shown in Figure 11-2. The connections made are dynamic and based on requests from the incoming data stream. The connection-

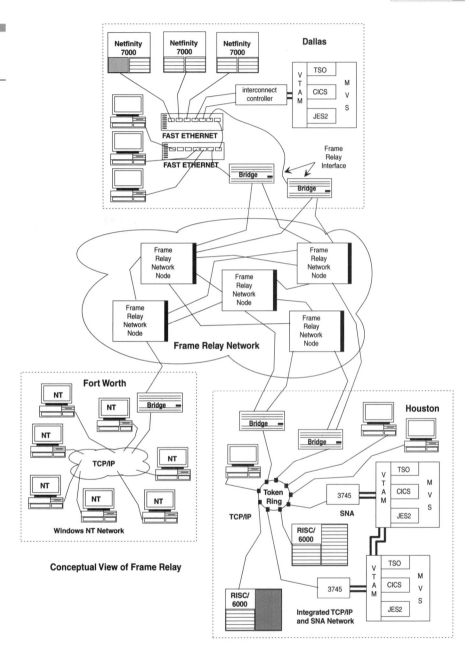

Figure 11-1
Conceptual view of frame relay

mapping table is responsible for matching the request of the source to the destination; this constitutes a route, or in frame relay lingo, a virtual connection.

Figure 11-3 is similar to Figure 11-2, but it shows the frames and a high-lighted view of the mapping table.

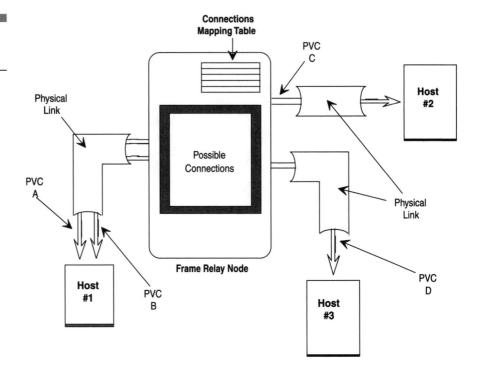

Figure 11-2
Enhanced view of a frame relay node

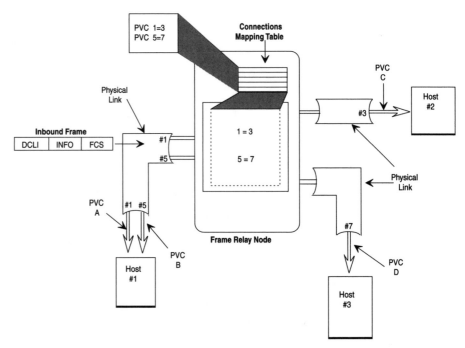

Figure 11-3
Highlighted view of the maping table

Notice Figure 11-3 shows PVC A #1 and PVC B #5 originating at host #1. Figure 11-3 also shows these connecting to PVC C #3 and PVC D #7, respectively. To be more precise, mapping between A #1 and C #3, and B #5 and D #7 is performed inside the frame relay node.

Data Link Connection Identifier (DCLI)

The inbound frame from host #1 through PVC A #1 contains a *Data Link Connection Identifier* (DCLI). The DCLI is the local address in frame relay. The DCLI address is relevant in reference to the particular link. It identifies the frame and its type. This means that the same DCLI value could be used at both ends of the frame relay network where each host connects through a particular link. Differentiating the DCLI is the physical link the frame traverses and the host. Hence, more than one identifying factor is used for frame identification.

In the connection-mapping table, each entry includes the following information:

Node id

Link id

DCLI

Frame Relay Costs

Aside from the hardware and software required to implemented a frame relay connection, additional fees are incurred, for example, the *Commitment Information Rate* (CIR) which is the bandwidth available from one end to another. Another factor is called the port access rate. This refers to access into the frame relay network, and what is considered a network access charge that reflects the costs of the line connecting a given site to the access point in the frame relay network.

Understanding these aspects of frame relay is important. For example, if data is transmitted in bursts, one must know what the burst data rate is. Another factor to understand that relates to this is the normal or average throughput required on a daily basis.

Frame Relay Frame Components

Frame relay frame components are shown in Figure 11-4. Maximum frame size is 8,250 bytes, and the minimum is generally considered 262 bytes.

Figure 11-4 is based on the CCITT I.441 recommendation. Variations of this structure exist, and are primarily those with different methods of implementing addressing. A significant point to note about frame relay is that it utilizes the same standards as those of ISDN.

■ The flag field indicates the beginning of the frame.

■ The address field typically consists of the components in Figure 11-5.

In Figure 11-5, the DLCI fields identify a logical channel connection in a physical channel or port, thus identifying a pre-determined destination (Simply put it identifies the connection). The CR field contains a bit indicating a command response. The EAB field contains a bit set at either 1 or 0, and indicates extended addressing. The FN field is sometimes referred to as the *forward explicit congestion notification* (FECN). The bit in this field indicates whether or not congestion was encountered during the transfer from origin to destination. The BN field indicates congestion was encountered on the return path. The DE field is the discard eligibility field. This field indicates whether or not the frame can be disposed of during transfer if congestion is encountered. A bit setting of 1 means has discard eligibility, whereas a bit setting of 0 indicates a higher setting for the frame and it should not be discarded.

Figure 11-4
CCITT I.411 frame relay frame format

Flag	Address Field	Control	Information	FCS	Flag

Figure 11-5
Highlighted view of the address field

DLCI	CR	EAB	DLCI	FN	BN	DE	EAB

Virtual Circuits

Different frame types of virtual circuits have been defined for use with frame relay. In a sense, these circuits represent different definable services. They include

Switched Virtual Circuit (SVC)

Permanent Virtual Circuit (PVC)

Multicast Virtual Circuit (MVC)

Switched Virtual Circuit (SVC)

This type of circuit is similar to telephone usage. When the circuit is needed, a request is made. When the circuit is not needed, the circuit is not used. Information is passed from origin to destination to set-up the call and to bring it down. Some information provided in the call set-up phase inlcudes bandwidth allocation parameters, quality of service parameters, and virtual channel identifiers, to name a few.

Permanent Virtual Circuit (PVC)

This type of connection is considered point-to-point. It could be though of as a leased line, in that it is dedicated. This type circuit is used for long periods of time. Commands are still used to set-up the call and to bring it down. The difference between the PVC and a SVC is duration.

Multicast Virtual Circuit (MVC)

MVCs are best described as being a connection between groups of users through which individual users can use SVC connections as well as PVC connections. Technically, this type connection is considered permanent. To date, this type connection is generally considered a *Local Management Interface* (LMI) extension.

Access Devices

Different devices can be used to connect devices into a frame relay environment. Some of those are examined here.

Switches

Frame relay networks can be accessed through different types of devices. For example, switches similar to those accommodating X.25 provide a way to access frame relay networks. However, these switches are typically implemented in the sense of creating a backbone. Figure 11-6 is an example of this type device implemented in three environments.

Figure 11-6 shows a network backbone made-up of three components; they are switches in Dallas, Denver, and Bakersfield.

Network Device

A more focused view of Bakersfield could be represented by Figure 11-7.

Figure 11-7 shows a network device (specifically a bridge) connecting a token ring and Ethernet network into the frame relay environment. It also depicts the lines to Dallas and Denver.

FRAD

A *Frame Relay Access Device* (FRAD) is a particular piece of equipment that typically connotes capabilities, including packet assembly/disassembly, speeds of DS0, T1, or fractional T1. Most FRADs can handle multiple protocols and focus network traffic into a centralized managed facility such as Figure 11-8 shows.

FRADs can be the best component to concentrate multiple devices into a single unit. Vendors such as Wellfleet and Cisco Systems provide these types of devices.

Other devices might be used in connecting a variety of resources into a frame relay network. Many vendors offer frame relay support as an additional function. One such example is IBM and their *Network Control Program* (NCP), which operates on a *Front End Controller* (FEP).

Frame Relay

Figure 11-6
Conceptual view of a frame relay network

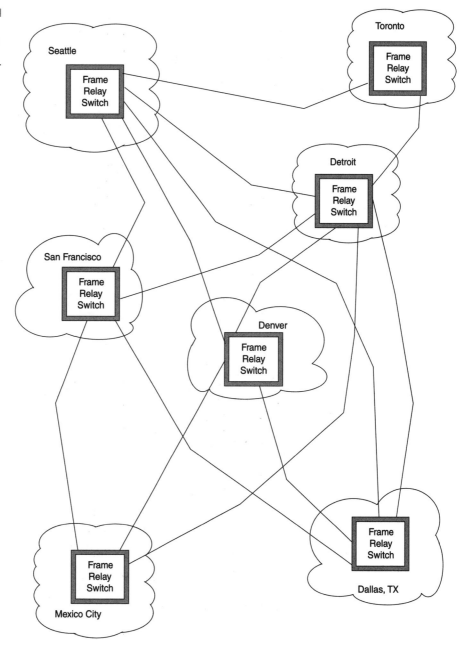

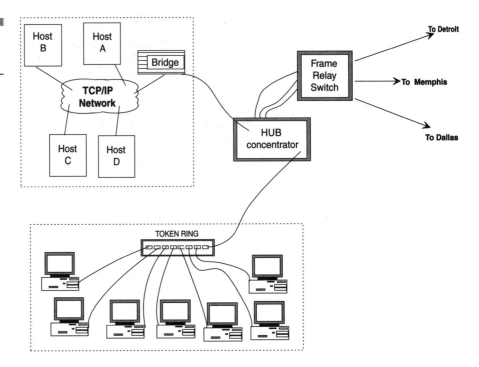

Figure 11-7
Highlighted view of
Denver equipment

Frame Relay with TCP/IP and SNA

Frame relay is a lower layer network protocol. Protocols that operate above it can be integrated into it. For example, TCP/IP can use frame relay as its data link oriented protocol. Consider Figure 11-9.

Figure 11-9 shows the frame relay frame format and a conceptual view of how TCP and UDP would operate with it. Notice TCP and UDP are shown as either. The reason for this is that TCP/IP applications operate on top of TCP or UDP. TELNET, HTTP, FTP are all TCP applications. On the other hand, TFTP, RPC, and others use UDP for a transport layer protocol.

Figure 11-10 illustrates frame relay and SNA.

This illustration shows where an SNA frame would fit into a frame relay frame. Included in this illustration are implied SNA applications such as CICS, TSO, DB/2, and others. Frame relay is not a native SNA protocol, but it is now supported by IBM and hence compatible with native SNA.

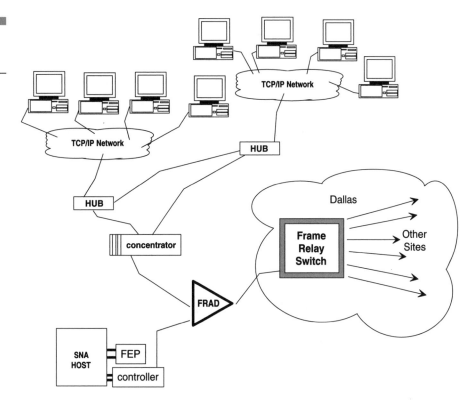

Figure 11-8
Highlighted view
of a FRAD

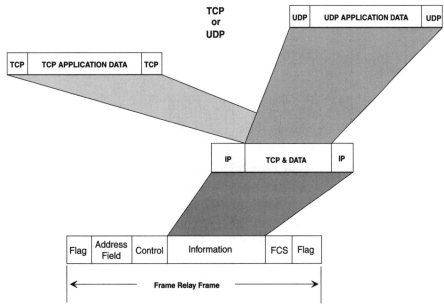

Figure 11-9
Frame relay format
with TCP/IP

Figure 11-10
Frame relay format
with SNA

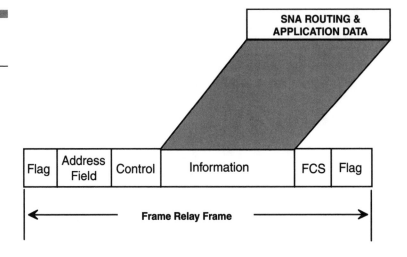

Frame Relay Blueprint #1

Frame relay can be a complex technology to implement. However, some conceptual understanding of how it operates in different implementations makes it easier to plan and design for network operation. Consider Figure 11-11.

This figure shows three network segments connected to a backbone segment. This particular blueprint shows an internal token ring network backbone on the customer premises. This blueprint shows the internal network connected to a frame relay network connecting it to multiple remote sites.

Frame Relay Implementation with TCP/IP

A more complex implementation of frame relay is shown in Figure 11-12.

This illustration shows three sites in different geographic locations connected by a frame relay network. This TCP/IP implementation is an example of implementing networks in diverse locations. It reflects an idea in implementation that is common used in many locations today. For example, this shows multiple servers located in two locations and a concentration of workstations in a third location. Any variation of this could be a valid implementation

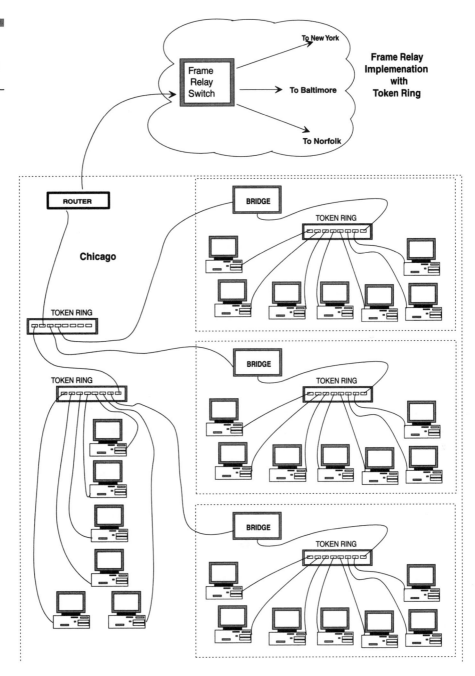

Figure 11-11
Frame relay
implementation with
token ring

Frame Relay
Implemenation
with
Token Ring

Figure 11-12
Frame relay
implementation
with TCP/IP

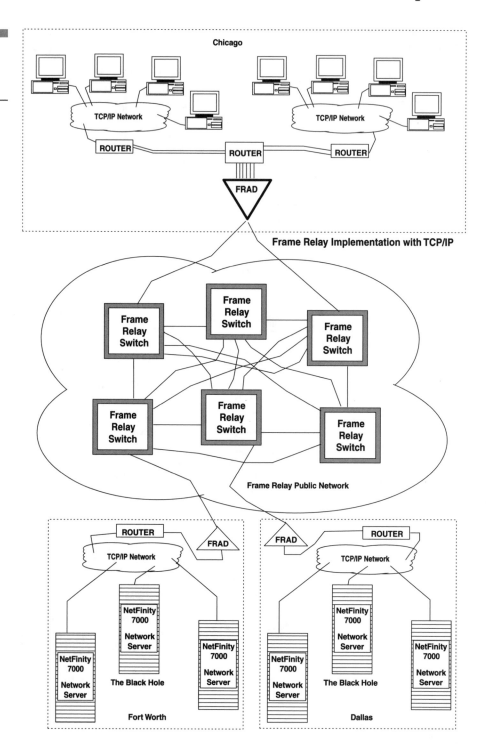

Frame Relay Implementation with TCP/IP

Private Frame Relay Network

Another example of a frame relay is shown in Figure 11-13.

This type frame relay network is viable in many situations where a need exists to distribute information with a large number of users in a single location. One example of this type of private frame relay implementation could be a university campus type setting.

In this example a marketing, data bank, pre-sales support, and product support department are shown as example departments in the hypothetical implementation. Such an internal network is robust enough to sustain large amounts of data traffic and a high number of users. This is well suited for a private (closed) network. A side benefit to this blueprint is that it lends itself easily to incorporation into a public frame relay network, thus connecting it to other locations.

Consumer Tips

During my work and research with frame relay, I encountered some information that is handy— tips for the consumer purchasing frame relay equipment. Some of these tips are included in this section.

TIPS

1. Frame Relay standards are still being defined and implemented by vendors differently.

2. When considering a frame relay device ascertain what it does, specifically.

3. Determine if a frame relay device supports: DCLI support, header bits support, and FCS, FECN, BECN, and DE bits within the frame. Also determine if congestion control is performed to standards and if so, which one(s)? Determine if multiple protocols are supported.

4. Find out in what way a given device supports FECN, BECN, and DE bits. How do they function in respect to congestion management? For example, one might say DE is supported, but what does this mean? Does it mean the bit is read or it can be set? The latter is important.

5. Is link management supported, and if so, what type?

6. Does the device support transparent mode?

Figure 11-13
Private frame relay
network

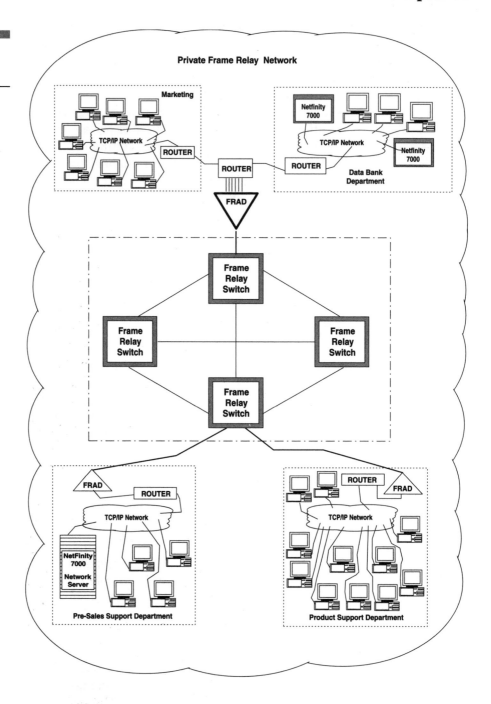

7. Is the device switch oriented or primarily an access device used to provide access into a frame relay network?

This is only a beginning list meant to help those beginning with frame relay.

Additional Information

Listed here are sources that contain considerably more detail then has been the purpose here. The sources are divided by categories:

ANSI:

T1.601 Basic Access Interface

T1.602 ISDN Data Link layer Signaling Specifications

T1S1/90–75 Frame Relay Bearer Service, Architectural Framework Description

T1S1/90–214 Core Aspects of Frame Protocol for Use with Frame Relay Bearer Service

T1S1/90–213 Signaling Specification for Frame Relay Bearer Service

T1.606 ISDN Architectural Framework

T1.607 Digital Subscriber Signaling Service

T1.617 Standards Concerning Customer Interface

T1.618 Standards Concerning Customer Interface

T1S1 /90–051R2 Carrier to Customer Interface

CCITT

I.122	Q.920	1.320	X.25
I.233	Q.921	1.320	X.31
I.130	Q.922	1.430	X.134
I.441	Q.930	1.431	X.213
I.450	Q.931	1.462	X.300
I.451			

SUMMARY

Frame relay principles were explained, including the concept of virtual links, the data link connection identifier, and the associated costs of frame relay beyond supporting hardware and software. Frame relay frame components were presented and the fields that comprise a frame briefly explained.

The concept of virtual circuits was explained. The *Switched Virtual Circuit* (SVC) is similar to a telephone; a *Permanent Virtual Circuit* (PVC) is similar to a leased line arrangement; and a *Multicast Virtual Circuit* (MVC) is where a group of users can be reached through one multicast.

Access devices used in frame relay networks were discussed. The basic function of a switch, a network-related device, and a frame relay access device were explained. Different implementations might use one or more of access devices, consumer tips, and a brief list of reference material.

xDSL Technology & Related Information

Introduction

Most likely, xDSL technology will emerge as a world standard in the coming years. As a result, this author believes this topic is very important and recognizes that numerous books have been written about it. I wanted to present to you what I felt is pertinent information for this handbook and had to make a choice of what to cover. In this author's opinion, the ADSL Forum is the most credible resource on ADSL technology. Consequently, the information provided freely through this forum is very valuable; so much so, I thought it best to relay it onto you, courtesy of the Asymmetric Digital Subscriber Line Forum.

You can obtain additional information at the ADSL Forum web site www.adsl.com.

Networking Technology and ADSL

The ADSL Forum develops technical guidelines for architectures, interfaces, and protocols for telecommunications networks incorporating ADSL transceivers. The following overall network diagram describes the network elements incorporated in multimedia communications, shows the scope of the Forum's work, and suggests a group of transport configurations ADSL can encounter as networks migrate from *Synchronous Transfer Mode* (STM) to *Asynchronous Transfer Mode* (ATM). Consider Figure 12-1.

The following is a legend to use with Figure 12-1.

ADSL   Asymmetric Digital Subscriber Line

STM   Synchronous Transfer Mode

ATM   Asynchronous Transfer Mode

TE   Terminal Equipment

OS   Operations System

SM   Service Module

PDN   Premises Distribution Network reference point definitions

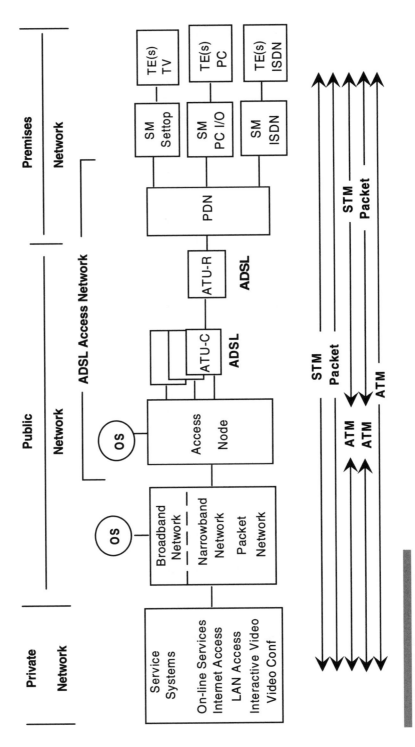

Figure 12-1 Transport modes

301

xDSL Model & Terminology

Figure 12-2 presents an ADSL system reference model.

The following terms should be used for the interpretation of Figure 12-2.

ATU-C   ADSL Transmission Unit at the network end. The ATU-C might be integrated within an Access Node.

ATU-R   ADSL transmission Unit at the customer premises end. The ATU-R might be integrated within a SM.

Access Node   Concentration point for Broadband and Narrowband data. The Access Node might be located at a Central Office or a remote site. Also, a remote Access Node might subtend from a central access node.

B   Auxiliary data input (such as a satellite feed) to Service Module (such as a Set Top Box)

Broadcast   Broadband data input in simplex mode (typically broadcast video)

Broadband Network   Switching system for data rates above 1.5/2.0 Mbps

Loop   Twisted-pair copper telephone line. Loops might differ in distance, diameter, age, and transmission characteristics, depending on network.

Narrowband Network   Switching system for data rates at or below 1.5/2.0 Mbps

POTS   Plain Old Telephone Service

POTS-C   Interface between PSTN and POTS splitter at network end

POTS-R   Interface between phones and POTS splitter at premises end

PDN Premises Distribution Network   System for connecting ATU-R to Service modules. Might be point-to-point or multi-point; might be passive wiring or an active network. Multi-point might be a bus or star.

PSTN   Public Switched Telephone Network

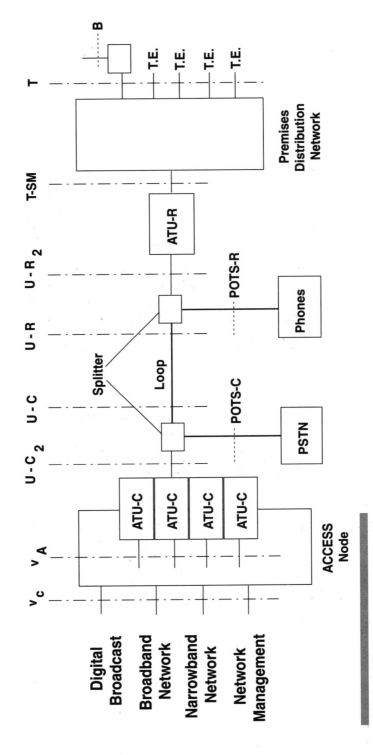

Figure 12-2 System reference model

303

SM   Service Module; Performs terminal adaptation functions. Examples are set top boxes, PC interfaces, or LAN routers.

Splitter   Filters which separate high frequency (ADSL) and low frequency (POTS) signals at network end and premises end. The splitter might be integrated into the ATU, physically separated from the ATU, or divided between high pass and low pass, with the low pass function physically separated from the ATU. The provision of POTS splitters and POTS —related function is optional.

T-SM   Interface between ATU-R and Premises Distribution Network. Might be same as T when network is point-to-point passive wiring. An ATU-R might have more than one type of T-SM interface implemented (for example, a T1/E1 connection and an Ethernet connection). The T-SM interface might be integrated within a Service Module.

T   Interface between Premises Distribution Network and Service Modules. Might be same as T-SM when network is point-to-point passive wiring. Note that T interface might disappear at the physical level when ATU-R is integrated within a Service Module.

U-C   Interface between Loop and POTS Splitter on the network side. Defining both ends of the Loop interface separately arises because of the asymmetry of the signals on the line.

U-C2   Interface between POTS splitter and ATU-C. Note that at present ANSI T1.413 does not define such an interface and separating the POTS splitter from the ATU-C presents some technical difficulties in standardizing this interface.

U-R   Interface between Loop and POTS Splitter on the premises side

U-R2   Interface between POTS splitter and ATU-R. Note that at present ANSI T1.413 does not define such an interface and separating the POTS splitter from the ATU-R presents some technical difficulties in standardizing the interface.

VA   Logical interface between ATU-C and Access Node. As this interface is often within circuits on a common board, the ADSL Forum does not consider physical V$_A$ interfaces. The V interface might contain STM, ATM, or both transfer modes. In the primitive case of point-to-point connection between a switch port and an ATU-C (that is, a case without concentration or multiplexing), the V_A and V_c Interfaces become identical (alternatively, the V_A interface disappears).

Vc Interface between Access Node and network. Might have multiple physical connections (as shown) although might also carry all signals across a single physical connection. A digital carrier facility (for example, a SONET or SDH extension) might be interposed at the V_c interface when the access node and ATU-Cs are located at a remote site. Interface to the PSTN might be a universal tip-ring interface or a multiplexed telephony interface such as specified in Bellcore TR—08, TR—303, ITU-T G.964, or ETSI 300 324. The broadband segment of the V_c interface might be STM switching, ATM switching, or private line type connections.

ATM Over ADSL Recommendation

This section presents the technical report that addresses implementation aspects specific to the transport of ATM over Access Networks based on *Asymmetric Digital Subscriber Line* (ADSL) technology. At the end of this section, a list of reference material is included that correlates to the reference numbers throughout the text in this section. The scope for the first issue of the report is to provide a specification for the transport of ATM over ADSL that is consistent with the ANSI T1.413 standard 1995 [2]. Future issues of this technical report will seek to preserve backward compatibility with this document. The report aims to provide comprehensive guidelines for the selection of bearer channels for the transport of ATM and to provide clear interpretations of the pertinent sections of the ANSI T1.413 standard [2]. Future issues of this specification will address the generic (line code independent) requirements on the ATM-TC to ATM layer interface. As the ADSL Forum is line code neutral, TC variations required for other specific line codes will be addressed in future versions of this document.

This specification provides a detailed *Transmission Convergence* (TC) sub-layer specification that can be used with the ANSI T1.413 standard 1995 [2] and provides outline descriptions of the Access Node and *Network-Termination* (NT) functions. In later issues, effort will be made to provide more detailed functional descriptions. This report concentrates on ATM network layer protocols up to the ATM layer; higher layers are considered to be transported transparently by the ADSL based access network. Interfaces toward both the Local Exchange and Premises Distribution Network are covered. All configurable parameters and a means for managing their configuration are defined.

This report intends to describe the functional blocks of the ADSL based access network from the V_c interface to the T (or other) interface, and not to specify the physical level of the interfaces. Figure 12-3 should be used as a reference to that end. Specifically, Figure 12-3 is a specific reference model for ATM mode.

Although the previous figure shows two paths (Fast and Interleaved), it is only mandatory to implement a single path. Dual latency is strictly optional. The functional groups Broadband NT1, B-NT, B-NT+TA and B-NT+TE and the reference points T, S and R are defined in ITU-T recommendation I.413, B-ISDN User-Network Interface [9].

Functional Block Definitions

Access Node An Access Node performs the adaptation between the ATM Core Network and the Access Network. In the downstream direction, it may perform routing/de-multiplexing, whereas in the upstream direction it may perform multiplexing/concentration.

B-NT1, B-NT, B-NT1TA or B-NT1TE This functional block performs the functions of terminating the ADSL signal entering the users premises through the twisted pair cable and providing either the T, S, or R interface towards the terminal equipment. Such an interface might be absent in the case of integration of the functional block with the Terminal Equipment. Its functions are terminating/originating the transmission line, and handling the transmission interfacing and OAM functions. In addition, it might optionally include routing/multiplexing of the Fast and Interleaved flows.

ATM Layer Functions

In the Access Node, this function performs in the downstream direction routing/de-multiplexing on a VPI and/or VCI basis, and in the upstream direction multiplexing/concentration, again on a VPI and/or VCI basis. If implemented in the B-NT1, B-NT, B-NT+TA or B-NT+TE, this function performs cell routing/(de)multiplexing to the Fast or Interleaved channel in the upstream direction and routing/(de)multiplexing of the two flows into a single ATM stream per T interface instantiation in the downstream direction.

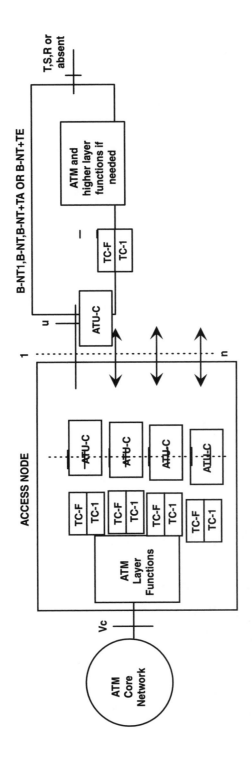

Figure 12-3 ATM mode reference model

307

TC   ATM Transmission Convergence sub-layer functional block

ATU-C   ADSL Transceiver Unit at the Central Office end

ATU-R   ADSL transceiver Unit at the remote terminal end

Transport of ATM over ADSL

Transport classes and bearer channel rates based on multiples of 1.536 Mbps are considered to be inappropriate for the transport of ATM. Reference to the ANSI T1.413 standard [2] is superseded by the information in this section. For the transport of ATM on modems compliant with ANSI T1.413 standard, channels shall be independently set to any bit rate that is an integer multiple of 32 Kbps, up to a maximum aggregate capacity determined by the start-up process. In addition, for each channel the bit rates for the upstream and downstream directions may be set independently from each other.

Channelization

For ATM systems the channelization of different payloads is embedded within the ATM data stream using different Virtual Paths and/or Virtual Channels. Hence, the basic requirements for ATM are for at least one ADSL channel downstream and at least one ADSL upstream channel.

The ANSI T1.413 standard [2] gives the possibility to use both the Interleaved and Fast paths for services with requirements for either high error performance or low latency, respectively. The real need for this dual nature of ATM services depends on the service/application profile and is yet to be confirmed. Consequently, different configurations of the ADSL access could be considered. More specifically, possibly three latency classes could be envisaged:

1. Single latency, not necessarily the same for each direction of transmission

2. Dual latency downstream, single latency upstream

3. Dual latency both upstream and downstream

For the transport of only ATM over ADSL, all modems shall use the AS0 channel downstream and the LS0 channel upstream for the single latency class. Channels AS1 and LS1 are reserved for dual latency.

A hybrid implementation of one or more Bit Synchronous (Plesiochronous) channels together with the ATM channels is not precluded by the preceding information. The bandwidth occupied by the Bit Synchronous channel must first be reserved before allocating the remaining bandwidth to the ATM channel.

In accordance with the previous channel allocation, it is mandatory for compliance with these recommendations to implement at least one single path, either through the fast buffer or the interleaved buffer.

Protocols

With respect to the protocol reference model for B-ISDN [5], only the *Physical Medium Dependent* (PMD) and *Transmission Convergence* (TC) sublayers of the physical layer and the ATM layer are relevant to this report. Figure 12-4 shows the protocol layers for the specific reference model given in Figure 12-3. In Figure 12-4, T interface supports ATM. Non-ATM interfaces are also possible, but not discussed in this report.

Quality of Service (QOS)

Data Rates   Modems compliant to the ANSI T1.413 standard can be programmed to provide bearer channel data rates that are multiples of 32 Kbps. This facility might be exploited for the transport of ATM.

Channel data rates can be set on a semi-permanent basis depending on the loop characteristics for the particular user. Complete flexibility is therefore given to the Network Operator.

Figure 12-4
Protocol layers

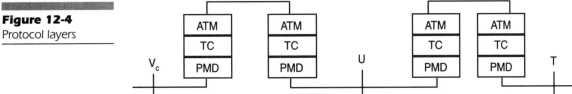

Bit Error Rate (BER)

ANSI T1.413 standard [2] specifies a BER of 10–7 with a 6-dB margin. The Network Operator might decide on a BER/ Latency/ Range combination that meets the required service quality for the network. The effect of ADSL performance impairments on ATM performance requires further study.

Description of Functional Blocks

Access Node ATM Layer Functions   In the downstream direction this block performs cell routing on a VPI and/or VCI basis to the appropriate ADSL modem and optionally to the Fast or Interleaved TC sub-layer of that modem.

In the upstream direction the cell streams are combined/concentrated to form a single ATM cell stream.

Transmission Convergence (TC)

Access Node TC   The ATM Transmission Convergence sub-layer is based on ITU-T recommendation I.432 [3]. There is no specific relationship between the beginning of an ATM cell and the ADSL frame. The transmitter can transmit the cell octets aligned to any bit in the ADSL octets. The receiver shall assume no alignment between ATM cell octets and the ADSL octets. The functions are described in the following sub-sections. The transmission order of the bits is as shown in I.432 [3] for SDH; that is, the *Most Significant Bit* (MSB) of each byte is sent first.

Header Error Control Functions   The *Header Error Control* (HEC) covers the entire cell header. The code used for this function is capable of either

1. Single bit error correction
2. Multiple bit error detection

Error detection shall be implemented as defined in ITU-T recommendation I.432 [3] with the exception that any HEC error might be considered as a multiple bit error, and therefore HEC error correction shall not be performed.

Header Error Control Sequence Generation The HEC byte shall be generated as described in ITU-T recommendation I.432 [3] including the recommended modulo 2 addition (XOR) of the pattern 01010101 to the HEC bits.

The generator polynomial coefficient set used and the HEC sequence generation procedure shall be in accordance with ITU-T Recommendation I.432 [3].

Idle Cells

Idle cells shall be inserted and discarded for cell rate decoupling. Idle cells are identified by the standardized pattern for the cell header given in ITU-T Recommendation I.432 [3].

The ATM layer might also perform cell rate decoupling by inserting and discarding unassigned cells. All implementations shall therefore be capable of receiving and discarding both idle cells (in the physical layer) and unassigned cells (in the ATM layer).

Cell Delineation

The cell delineation function permits the identification of cell boundaries in the payload. It uses the *Header Error Control* (HEC) field in the cell header.

Cell delineation shall be performed using the HEC based algorithm described in ITU-T recommendation I.432 [3].

With reference to I.432 [3], the ADSL Forum makes no recommendation for the values of a and d as the choice of these values is not considered to affect interoperability. However, it should be noted that the use of the values suggested in I.432 could be inappropriate due to the particular transmission characteristics of ADSL.

Cell Payload Scrambling

Scrambling of the cell payload field shall be used to improve the security and robustness of the HEC cell delineation mechanism. In addition, it randomizes the data in the information field, for possible improvement of the transmission performance. The self-synchronizing scrambler polynomial $X^{43}+1$ and procedures defined in ITU-T recommendation I.432 [3] shall be implemented.

[B-NT1, B-NT, B-NT+TA or B-NT+TE] TC   The functions of the TC block will be as those described in the previous information about Access Nodes.

ATM & Higher Layer Functions Block [B-NT1, B-NT+TA or B-NT+TE]

If implemented in the downstream direction, this block combines the cell streams from the Fast and Interleaved buffers into a single ATM cell stream. In the upstream direction, cell routing is performed on a VPI and/or VCI basis to the Fast or Interleaved TC sub-layers.

Management

Non ATM specific OAM issues require further study.

Network Management Across the V Interface

This requires further study.

Operation, Administration and Maintenance (OAM)

Physical Layer OAM functions   Modems compliant with ANSI T1.413 standard shall perform all OAM functions described in that standard.

Further OAM functions specific to ATM (described in ITU-T recommendations I.432 [3] and I.610 [4]) will be performed. LCD indication is derived from a HEC based cell delineation function. In particular, at the ATU-R, the downstream *Loss of Cell Delineation* (LCD) defect (for the interleaved and fast path separately) shall be detected and backward reported to the ATU-C through the indicator bits 14 and 15 in modems compliant to ANSI T1.413 standard, as in Figure 12-5.

The LCD-i (interleaved path) and LCD-ni (fast path) defects are mapped into the reserved indicator bits according to the information as presented in Figure 12-5.

Figure 12-5
Defect Mapping and
indicator bits

Bit 14	Bit 15	Interpretation
1	1	notLCD-i and notLCD-ni
1	0	notLCD-i and LCD-ni
0	1	LCD-i and notLCD-ni
0	0	LCD-i and LCD-ni

Related References to ATM over ADSL Recommendations

1. ADSL Forum Reference model, Figure 12-1
2. ANS, Network and Customer Installation Interfaces—*Asymmetric Digital Subscriber Line* (ADSL) Metallic interface , T1.413–1995
3. ITU-T Recommendation I.432—B-ISDN UNI Physical layer specification
4. ITU-T Recommendation I.610—B-ISDN Operation and Maintenance principles and functions
5. ITU-T Recommendation I.321—B-ISDN Protocol Reference Model and its application
6. ITU-T Recommendation I.361—B-ISDN ATM Layer specification
7. ETSI Technical Report, ETR 328 Transmission and Multiplexing— ADSL Requirements and Performance
8. ITU-T Recommendation I.432.5—B-ISDN User—Network Interface Physical layer for 25600 KBIT/S
9. ITU-T Recommendation I.413—B-ISDN User-Network Interface

Terms Used in ATM over ADSL Recommendation

Access Node   Performs adaptation between the core network and the access network

ADSL   Asymmetric Digital Subscriber Line

ANSI   American National Standard Institution

AS0–3   Downstream simplex sub-channel designators

ATM   Asynchronous Transfer Mode

ATU-C   ADSL Transceiver Unit, central office end

ATU-R   ADSL Transceiver Unit, remote terminal end

BER   Bit Error Ratio

B-ISDN   Broadband ISDN (Broadband Integrated Services Digital Network)

DAVIC   Digital Audio-Visual Council

ETSI   European Telecommunications Standards Institute

FTTC   Fiber to the Curb

FTTH   Fiber to the Home

HAN   Home ATM Network

HEC   ATM cell Header Error Control

HFC   Hybrid Fiber Coaxial

ISDN   Integrated Services Digital Network

ITU-T   International Telecommunications Union-Telecommunications

LCD   Loss of Cell Delineation

LS0–3   Duplex sub-channel designators

NT   Network Termination

B-NT1   B-ISDN Network Termination Type 1

OAM   Operation, Administration and Maintenance

PC   Personal Computer

PDN   Premises Distribution Network. System for connecting the B-NT1 to the Service Modules

PHY   ATM Physical layer function

PMD   ATM Physical Medium Dependent sub-layer

QoS   Quality of Service

RBB   (ATM Forum) Residential Broadband (Working Group)

SM   Service Module; performs terminal adaptation functions

STB   Set-Top-Box

TA   Terminal Adapter

TC   ATM Transmission Convergence sub-layer

TE   Terminal Equipment

UNI   User-Network Interface

VA   Logical interface between ATU-C and Access Node

Vc   Interface between Access Node and network

VDSL   Very high speed Digital Subscriber Line

VPI   Virtual Path Identifier. Identification number for the (logical) connection hierarchy path (virtual path) in B-ISDN networks

VCI   Virtual Channel Identifier. Identification number for the (logical) connection hierarchy channel (virtual channel) in B-ISDN networks

ATM/ADSL Recommendation in Relationship to Reference Models

ATM Forum   The ATM Forum *Residential Broadband* (RBB) Group is defining a complete end to end ATM system both to and from the home and within the home, to a variety of devices, for example, STB, PC, and other home devices. The ATM Forum RBB group has produced a baseline text.

ADSL, together with other technologies such as HFC, FTTC, FTTH, and VDSL, has been accepted as one of the methods to connect an ATM access network to the *Home ATM Network* (HAN).

DAVIC

The pertinent parts of the DAVIC 1.0 specification [7] are the following:

Part 2   System reference models and scenarios
Part 4   Delivery system architectures and APIs
Part 8   Lower layer protocols and physical interfaces

Part 4 of the DAVIC 1.0 specification [7] gives two options for the placement of the ADSL modem at the customer premises: inside the NT, resulting in an access network architecture with an Active NT or located in the Set-Top Box, resulting in an Access network architecture with a Passive NT. These two architectures are shown in Figure 12-6 and Figure 12-7.

Figure 12-6 illustrates a DAVIC ADSL Access Network with active NT.

Figure 12-7 is a different example of DAVIC ADSL.

Notice the difference between Figure 12-6 and 12-7. Figure 12-7 shows DAVIC ADSL Access Network with passive NT.

DAVIC is not concerned with the specification of the A2 and A3 interfaces, therefore for the case of an access network with active NT, the ADSL

Figure 12-6
Access Network with
active NT

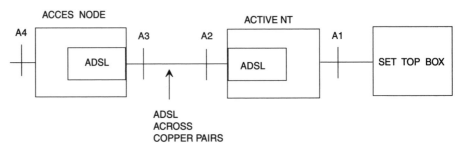

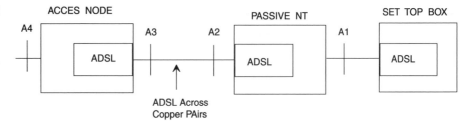

Figure 12-7
Access Network with passive NT

signals are not specified. However in the case of a passive NT, the medium and the protocols at reference points A1, A2, and A3 are equal. In this scenario ADSL signals are specified as they cross the A1 reference point.

Relevant Standards and Known Work in Other Standards Groups or Forums

ANSI T1.413 1995, ETSI TM6   The ETSI Technical Report, ETR 328 Transmission and Multiplexing—ADSL Requirements and Performance, primarily covers performance issues related to particular European specific reference loops, noise models, and transport rate options. This document supersedes sections of ETR 328 with regard to transport rates and bearer channel allocations.

ATM Forum   Most of the work of ATM Forum concerning ADSL is done by the RBB Group. In the ATM Forum, ADSL is seen as one of the possible physical interfaces between the ATM access network and HAN. System aspects of ATM over ADSL are being addressed.

DAVIC   It is DAVIC's belief that "it would be very beneficial to both DAVIC and ADSL Forum to exchange information and views about matters of common interest, to seek consensus and possibly to coordinate respective actions" (quoted from a recent letter from DAVIC's President to ADSL Forum's President).

DAVIC's present status related to ADSL is: DAVIC 1.2 Part 8 contains a section on LONG RANGE BASEBAND ASYMMETRICAL PHY ON COPPER, pointing to the ADSL Forum WT–006-R7. This pointer was included after finalizing the Cell Specific TC sub-layer specification through an intense liaison with the ADSL Forum. DAVIC requested to be informed of further releases and/or updates of the ATM over ADSL Working text.

ADSL Framing & Encapsulation Standards: Packet Mode

This section presents the technical report describing the framing and encapsulation standards for variable length frames transported over ADSL technology. Herein is a method for transferring variable length Layer 2 frames and/or Layer 3 packets over an ADSL link. This section describes the framing mechanisms and protocol encapsulation capabilities required to provide a transmission facility over ADSL links regardless of transmission layer line code. This is one document in a series of ADSL Forum technical reports that addresses transferring variable length frames over an ADSL link. Future documents in this specification series will describe implementation specifics for different physical layers signaling management requirements of other features required to insure multi-vendor interoperability for these ADSL links. This specification makes no recommendations or requirements for the wide area network interface between the ATU-C and the Network Service Provider.

The specification here relies heavily on existing standards, defined by the ISO, ITU-T, ATM Forum, and IETF standards bodies, and applying them with only minimal modification to the transport of data link layer frames over ADSL links. In particular, it defines two allowable operating modes:

PPP in HDLC-like frames (RFC 1662 mode)

ATM Frame UNI (FUNI) frames (FUNI mode)

For this specification, the ADSL physical layer is viewed as simply a point-to-point bit stream provider. The ADSL Forum Reference Model, a Reference Diagram for this specification, and some critical terminology is presented as follows.

ADSL Forum Reference Model

Several topics presented later in this section describe features of this specification by referring to the ADSL Forum's Reference Model. Figure 12-8 is the ADSL Reference Model.

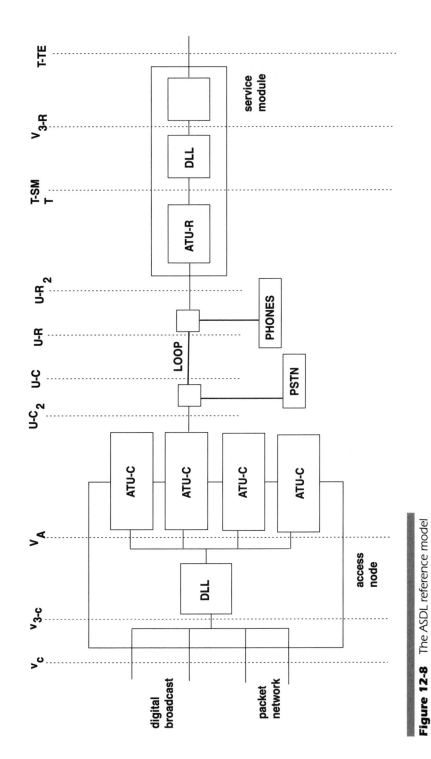

Figure 12-8 The ASDL reference model

319

Packet Mode Reference Diagram

This document uses some additional terms to describe the service points and administrative domains that play a role in this specification. In particular, the document separates the concept of network access from network service. A *Network Access Provider* (NAP) is the administrative entity that terminates the central office end of an ADSL line. The *Network Service Provider* (NSP) is the administrative entity that provides access to higher-level network services. Examples of Network Service Providers are Internet Service Providers or corporate offices providing network services to a remote office or telecommuter. Note that the NAP and NSP might be in the same administrative domain, but need not be. For example, an operator could provide both ADSL service and Internet Access. The NAP and NSP are defined separately in this document to clarify the roles that each play in an end-to-end service scenario. Figure 12-9 shows these entities.

Figure 12-9 shows the ADSL Packet Mode Reference Diagram used in this section and in the recommendation.

Terminology of Requirements

In this document, several words are used to signify the requirements of the specification. These words are often capitalized.

MUST   This word, or the adjective "required," means that the definition is an absolute requirement of the specification.

MUST NOT   This phrase means that the definition is an absolute prohibition of the specification.

SHOULD   This word, or the adjective "recommended," means that there might exist valid reasons in particular circumstances to ignore this item, but the full implications must be understood and carefully weighted before choosing a different course.

MAY   This word, or the adjective "optional," means that this item is one of an allowed set of alternatives. An implementation that does not include this option MUST be prepared to inter-operate with another implementation that does include this option.

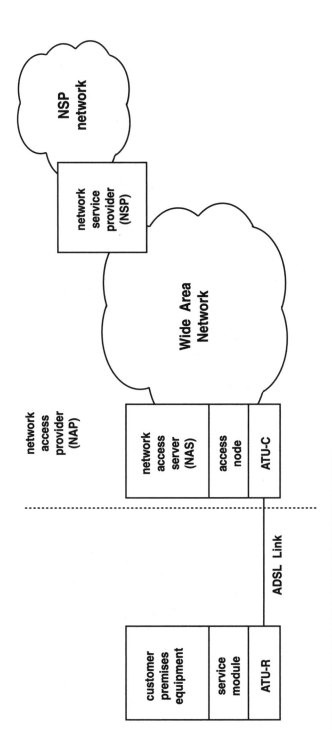

Figure 12-9 ADSL packet made reference diagram

321

ATM Adaptation Layer 5 Terms & Acronyms

Access Node   Concentration point for Broadband and Narrowband data

ADSL   Asymmetric Digital Subscriber Line

ANSI   American National Standards Institute

ATM   Asynchronous Transfer Mode

ATU-C   ADSL Terminal Unit-Central Office

ATU-R   ADSL Terminal Unit-Remote

CLP   Cell Loss Priority

CN   Congestion Notification

CPE   Customer Premise Equipment

CRC   Cyclical Redundancy Check

FCS   Frame Check Sequence

Frames   Layer 2 (data link layer) information bundles

FUNI   Frame User Network Interface (ATM Forum Specification)

HDLC   High-Level Data Link Control

IETF   Internet Engineering Task Force

ILMI   Integrated Local Management Interface

IPCP   Internet Protocol Control Protocol

ISO   International Organization for Standardization

ITU-T   International Telecommunications Union-Telecommunications Standardization Section (formerly CCITT)

LAN   Local Area Network

LAPD   Link Access Protocol D (HDLC derivative for ISDN)

LLC   Logical Link Control

NAP   Network Access Provider (administrative entity for ATU-C equipment)

NSP   Network Services Provider (not necessarily Internet, could be other protocols or other IP-based networks)

OAM   Operation, Administration and Maintenance

OUI/PID   Organizationally Unique Identifier/Protocol Identifier

Packets   Layer 3 (network layer) information bundles

PDU   Protocol Data Unit

POP   Point of Presence

PPP   Point-to-Point Protocol

PSTN   Public Switched Telephone Network

PTT   Postal Telephone and Telegraph

PVC   Permanent Virtual Circuit

PUC   Public Utilities Commission

RBOC   Regional Bell Operating Company (Baby Bell)

RFC   Request For Comments

SDU   Service Data Unit

SNAP   Subnetwork Access Point

SVC   Switched Virtual Circuit

UNI   User to Network Interface

VPI/VCI   Virtual Path Identifier/Virtual Connection Identifier

RFC 1662 MODE

The information here describes one of two operating modes allowed under this standard for transporting variable length frames between an ATU-R and ATU-C over the ADSL link (across the U interface in the ADSL Forum reference diagram; that is Figure 12-9). This operating mode leverages existing implementations of the *Point-to-Point Protocol* (PPP) by following, exactly, the *Internet Engineering Task Force Request for Comments* (IETF RFC) document RFC 1662 PPP in HDLC-like Framing.

PPP in HDLC-like Framing

Implementations operating in this mode MUST conform to RFC 1662, specifically following the recommendations for bit-synchronous links and ignoring specifications for asynchronous and octet-synchronous links. There are several references in RFC 1662 to ISO 3309, the standard for HDLC frame structure. Implementers might refer to that ISO document for clarification, but where there are differences, implementations over the ADSL facility MUST follow RFC1662. Figure 12-10 shows the format of packets transported using this operating mode.

PPP Encapsulation

Data encapsulation within RFC1662 framing is described in many other RFCs that provide a rich system for transporting multi-protocol data over PPP links. In particular, implementers are referred to the following RFCs as examples of the supporting IETF standards documents:

RFC 1661   The Point-to-Point Protocol

RFC 1332   The PPP *Internet Protocol Control Protocol* (IPCP)

Additional RFCs extend PPP for other protocols, bridging, encryption, compression, and authentication. All such implementations that are valid over RFC 1662 are valid over an ADSL facility implementing this PPP

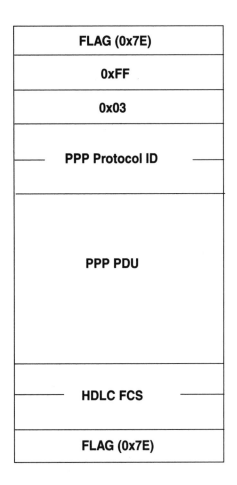

Figure 12-10
RFC 1661 frame PPP
format

FLAG (0x7E)

0xFF

0x03

PPP Protocol ID

PPP PDU

HDLC FCS

FLAG (0x7E)

operating mode with the following exception. Later in this section, a compliant implementation is explained that enables a switch between operation in RFC 1662 mode and FUNI mode operation.

Frame User Network Interface (FUNI) Mode

The second allowed operating mode for standard-compliant implementations is based on the FUNI specifications from the ATM Forum. In particular, ADSL end points transmitting variable length frames or packets across the U interface MUST implement the FUNI variant described in this specification when operating in this FUNI mode. Currently, the only FUNI features specified by this document are basic frame structure and encapsulation methods. Other features such as ILMI and OAM support are under study for future technical reports in this series.

FUNI Framing ATM Frame UNI (currently under revision to version 2, defined in ATM Forum document `strsaa-funi_01.01`) is a derivative of ATM Data Exchange Interface (ATM DXI, ATM Forum `af-dxi-20014_000.doc`). Like the PPP operating mode, the framing is a member of the HDLC family of data link control protocols and, in this implementation, uses the same number of header bytes. It uses standard HDLC start and stop flag bytes to guarantee flag recognition and bit-stuffing to achieve data transparency. The ATM FUNI frame header contains address and control fields. The address field encodes the *Service Data Units* (SDU) virtual connection *Virtual Path Identifier* (VPI) and *Virtual Connection Identifier* (VCI). The multiplexing of multiple network layer protocols on a single FUNI virtual connection using RFC1483 LLC or PPP is discussed forthwith, entitled Protocol Encapsulation.

Consider Figure 12-11, which shows ATM Frame UNI Format Frame Structure.

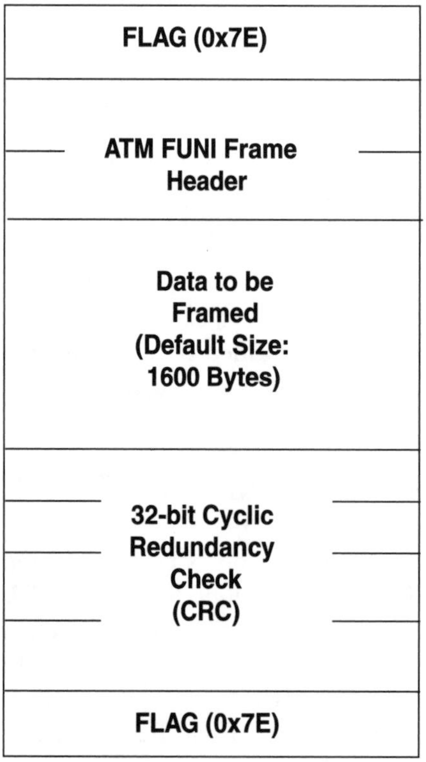

Figure 12-11
AIM frame UNI
format frame
structure

FLAG (0x7E)
—— **ATM FUNI Frame** —— **Header**
Data to be Framed (Default Size: 1600 Bytes)
—— **32-bit Cyclic** —— **Redundancy** —— **Check** —— **(CRC)** ——
FLAG (0x7E)

Implementations of this specification operating in FUNI mode MUST frame data using the ATM FUNI derivative of HDLC framing as described in ATM Forum `str-saa-funi201.01` with specific restrictions as outlined as follows. This framing MUST include a two-byte frame header and four-byte CRC. Implementations SHOULD support the *Congestion Notification* (CN) and *Cell Loss Priority* (CLP) bits as described in ATM Forum `str-saa-funi201.01`. At initialization, the default maximum size of the data framed between the FUNI header and the CRC MUST be 1600 bytes to allow interoperation with most foreseeable encapsulations of 1500 byte Ethernet frames. Implementations MAY negotiate other maximum size frames through mechanisms that are outside the scope of this document.

Address Assignment

Specific VPI/VCI addresses for ADSL physical layer management vendor-specific channel and default user data channel will be defined in future technical reports in this series.

Protocol Encapsulation A conforming FUNI mode implementation at the ADSL U interface MUST support the protocol multiplexing techniques defined in RFC 1483 Multi-Protocol Encapsulation Over ATM AAL5. The specifics of applying RFC 1483 to FUNI mode implementations are described in this section. RFC 1483 describes two multiplexing techniques: LLC encapsulation and Virtual circuit based multiplexing. If an implementation supports this FUNI mode, it MUST support one of these RFC 1483 multiplexing modes over the Frame UNI and SHOULD support the PPP over FUNI virtual circuit based encapsulation.

LLC Encapsulation One encapsulation technique specified in RFC1483 uses a multi-protocol IEEE 802.1 LAN *Logical Link Control* (LLC) header to encapsulate the payload. FUNI mode implementations might use this technique for all FUNI payloads, with one important exception for PPP. PPP PDUs over ADSL FUNI circuits MUST be transported using Virtual circuit based multiplexing.

Virtual Circuit Based Multiplexing

RFC 1483 also allows alternate encapsulations by using virtual circuit based multiplexing. Any payload might be transported in a FUNI frame without any additional encapsulation; there is no in-band LLC based protocol type discriminator at the beginning of the frame's information field. In this scenario, the end systems create a distinct parallel virtual circuit connection for each payload protocol type. The lack of any protocol type discriminator means that there MUST be some other (out-of-band) method for the endpoints to agree on the interpretation of the payload that immediately follows the FUNI header. See RFC 1483 for further explanation of this multiplexing mode. This ADSL Forum standard defines a special case for PPP payloads inside FUNI frames. A compliant implementation that chooses to carry *Point-to-Point Protocol* (PPP) PDUs inside a FUNI frame (PPP over FUNI) MUST carry the PPP PDUs directly over FUNI using Virtual circuit based multiplexing. PPP MUST NOT be encapsulated within an LLC header when framed by a FUNI header across the ADSL U interface.

Implementation Requirements

RFC 1662 mode and FUNI mode define two methods for framing and encapsulating packet data over the U interface. Consider the procedural aspects as they pertain to the ATU-R and the ATU-C.

1. *ATU-C Attributes*   The ATU-C MUST support the following: RFC 1662 mode FUNI mode

2. *ATU-R Attributes*   The ATU-R MUST support AT LEAST ONE of the following: RFC 1662 mode or FUNI mode

3. *General Attributes*   Both the ATU-C and the ATU-R MAY support the following:

Vendor-specific channel for FUNI framing that is an OPTIONAL vendor-specific channel is defined only for FUNI mode. This standard assigns a dedicated PVC channel for this connection. A well-known (TBD) VPI/VCI pair identifies the vendor-specific channel. For payloads that are outside the scope described previously, the vendor-specific virtual connection MUST be implemented and used. Examples of such uses might include Negotiation of or indication of private extension, Flash ROM updates, Proprietary debugging, and other vendor-specific actions.

All packets exchanged over the vendor specific channel MUST use RFC 1483 LLC encapsulation. Those packets containing vendor specific information MUST use a SNAP header having the IEEE assigned *Organizationally Unique Identifier* (OUI) value of the implementing vendor. Packets containing unrecognized OUI values MUST be silently discarded. Compliant devices MUST be able to interoperate without using this vendor-specific channel.

The Vendor Specific Channel may be used to negotiate extensions outside the standard. If both peers indicate agreement to such extensions (in some vendor-specific manner), then those extensions are not restricted in any way by this standard, including use of non-vendor-specific VPI/VCI pairs.

Packet Formats

RFC 1662 Mode Packets are as presented here for PPP-based framing. Figure 12-12 shows an HDLC-like-framed PPP PDU.

Figure 12-12
An HDCC-like framed PPP PDU

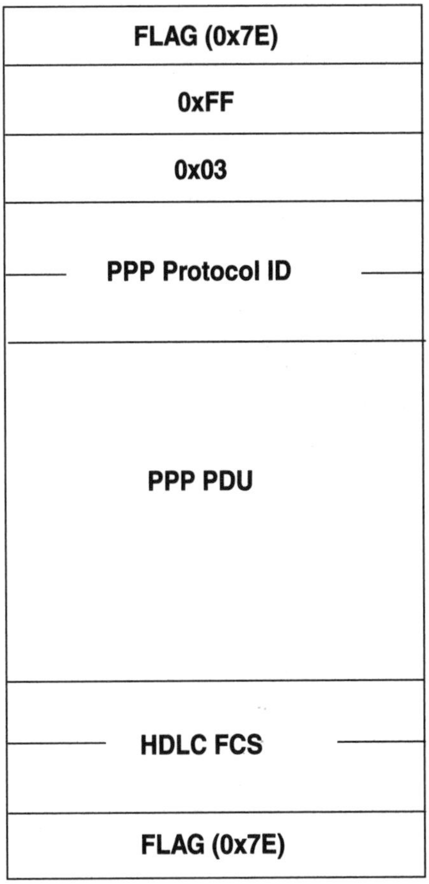

FLAG (0x7E)
0xFF
0x03
PPP Protocol ID
PPP PDU
HDLC FCS
FLAG (0x7E)

FUNI mode Packets

For FUNI implementations, packets (and frames) in the data plane are multiplexed and encapsulated per RFC 1483, using either LLC encapsulation or V_c based multiplexing. PPP frames, if transmitted, MUST be virtual circuit-multiplexed. Because, with V_c-multiplexing, the carried network interconnect protocol is identified implicitly by the corresponding virtual connection, there is no need to include explicit multiplexing information. Therefore, the LLC multiplexing field is not included, and the PPP frame starts at the first byte of the FUNI Service Data Unit field.

The Vendor-specific channel, if implemented, MUST be LLC-encapsulated. The packet formats for FUNI-based framing are illustrated in figures 12.13, 12-14, 12-15, 12-16, and 12-17.

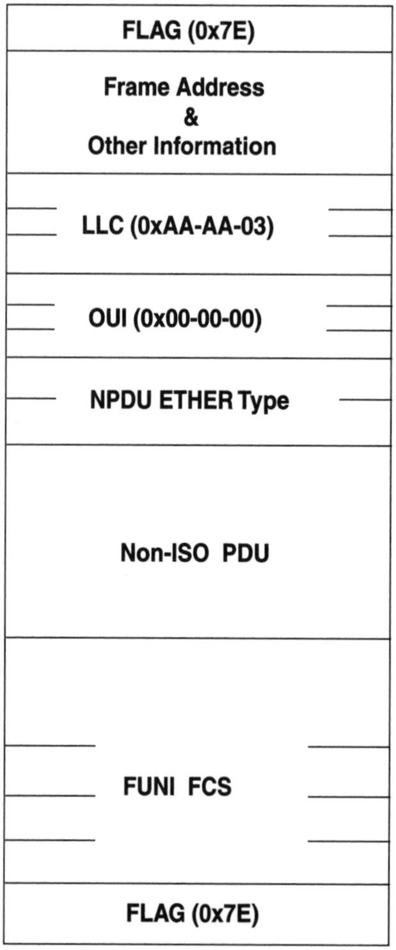

Figure 12-13
FUNI-based LLC-encapsulated non-ISO PDU

FLAG (0x7E)
Frame Address & Other Information
LLC (0xAA-AA-03)
OUI (0x00-00-00)
NPDU ETHER Type
Non-ISO PDU
FUNI FCS
FLAG (0x7E)

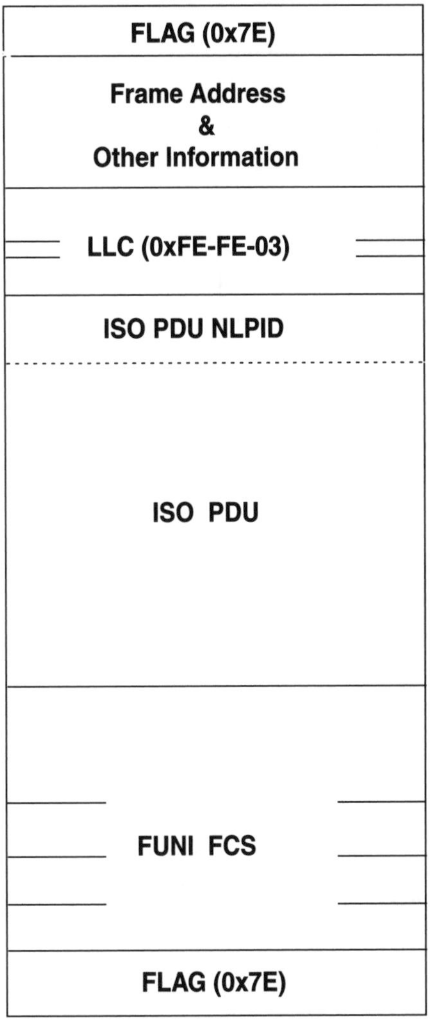

Figure 12-14
FUNI-based LLC-
encapsulated ISO
PDU

FLAG (0x7E)
Frame Address **&** **Other Information**
LLC (0xFE-FE-03)
ISO PDU NLPID
ISO PDU
FUNI FCS
FLAG (0x7E)

Figure 12-15
FUNI-based LLC-
encapsulated MAC
PDU

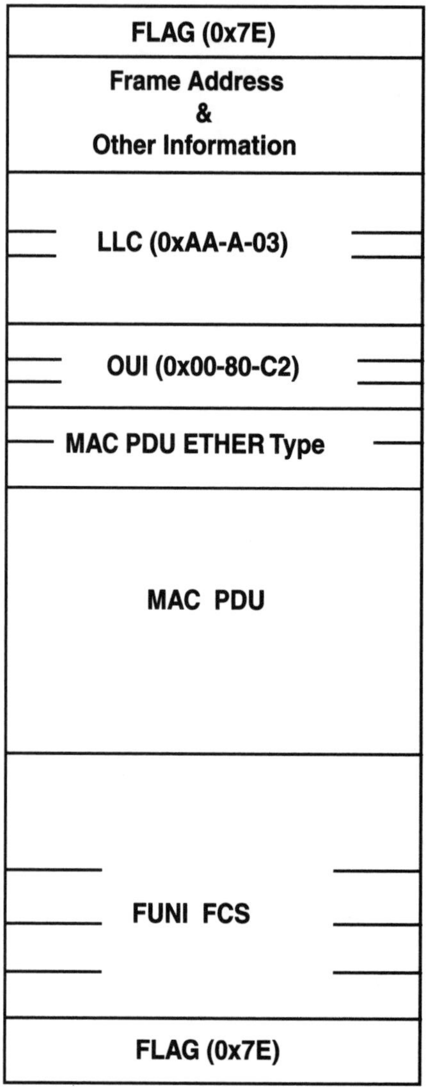

| FLAG (0x7E) |
| Frame Address
&
Other Information |
| LLC (0xAA-A-03) |
| OUI (0x00-80-C2) |
| MAC PDU ETHER Type |
| MAC PDU |
| FUNI FCS |
| FLAG (0x7E) |

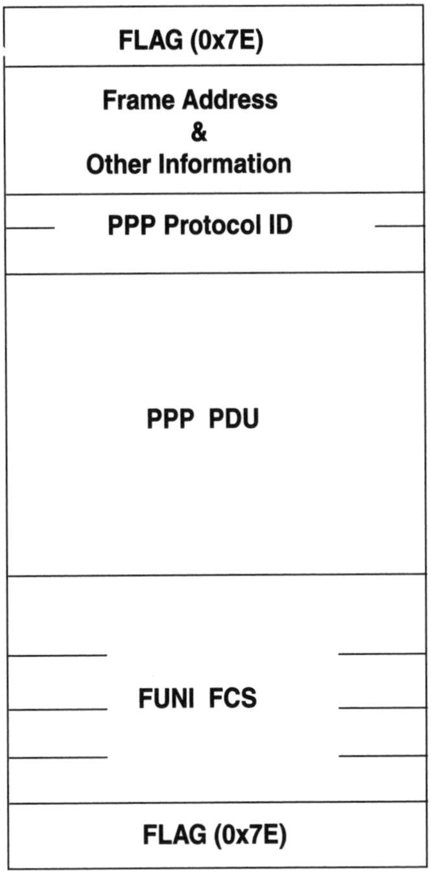

Figure 12-16
FUNI-based VC-
multiplexed PPPPDU

FLAG (0x7E)
Frame Address & Other Information
PPP Protocol ID
PPP PDU
FUNI FCS
FLAG (0x7E)

Figure 12-17
FUNI-based VC-
multiplexed PDU
(requires pair-wise
agreement of ADSL
endpoints)

```
┌─────────────────────────┐
│      FLAG (0x7E)         │
├─────────────────────────┤
│     Frame Address        │
│          &               │
│   Other Information      │
├─────────────────────────┤
│                          │
│                          │
│        ANY  PDU          │
│                          │
│                          │
├─────────────────────────┤
│                          │
│       FUNI  FCS          │
│                          │
├─────────────────────────┤
│      FLAG (0x7E)         │
└─────────────────────────┘
```

References

RFC 1483   Multi-protocol Encapsulation over ATM Adaptation Layer 5

RFC 1661   The *Point-to-Point Protocol* (PPP)

RFC 1662   PPP in HDLC-like Framing

RFC 1663   PPP Reliable Transmission

ISO/IEC 3309   Information Technology—Telecommunications and Information Exchange between systems—*High-level data link control* (HDLC) procedures—Frame Structure

ISO/IEC 8022–2   Information Technology—Telecommunications and information exchange between systems—Local and metropolitan area networks—Specific requirements—Part 2: Logical Link Control

STR-SAA-

FUNI201.01   ATM Forum: Frame based User-to-Network Interface (FUNI) Specification v2

AF-DXI-

0014.000   ATM Forum: ATM Data eXchange Interface (DXI) Specification

Interfaces and System Configurations for ADSL: Customer Premises

This section covers interfaces and system configurations for the ADSL customer premises. It covers electrical interfaces, connectorization, and wiring topologies with emphasis on POTS splitter issues, customer interfaces, and Premises Distribution Networks. Where possible, technical information will be obtained by reference to existing specifications, and by liaison to technical standards groups.

Introduction

Covering of the topic in this section includes efforts to define electrical interfaces, connectorization, and wiring topology for ADSL customer premises installations. Where possible, technical information will be obtained by reference to existing specifications, and by liaison to technical standards groups. The work on this project is limited to addressing the interfaces necessary to support existing single user connections methods, as well as multiuser connection methods utilizing Premises Distribution Networks (passive and active) for Bit Synchronous data, ATM data, and Packet data. Future work might be undertaken that addresses the use of emerging Premises Distribution Networks and the interfaces required to support them.

Acronyms Related ADSL Customer Premises

AC   Alternating Current

ADSL   Asymmetric Digital Subscriber Line

AMI Alternate Mark Inversion

ANSI American National Standards Institute

ATM Asynchronous Transfer Mode

ATU-C ADSL Transmission Unit at the Central Office End

ATU-R ADSL Transmission Unit at the CPE End

CD Compact Disk

CPE Customer Premises Equipment

CEBus Consumer Electronics Bus

CSMA/CD Carrier Sense Multiple Access Collision Detect

DVCR Digital Videocassette Recorder

ETSI European Telecommunications Standards Institute

HPF High Pass Filter

HDB3 High Density Bipolar Three

IEEE Institute of Electrical and Electronics Engineers

I/O Input Output

ISA Industry Standard Architecture (A PC bus standard)

ISDN Integrated Services Digital Network

ITU International Telecommunications Union

ITU G.703 Physical/Electrical Characteristics of Hierarchical Digital Interfaces

ITU G.704 Synchronous Frame Structures Used at Primary and Secondary Hierarchy Levels

LPF   Low Pass Filter

MDSL   Moderate speed Digital Subscriber Line

NID   Network Interface Device

P1394   An IEEE Serial Bus Standard

PC   Personal Computer

PCI   Peripheral Component Interconnect

PCMCIA   Personal Computer Memory Card International Association

POTS   Plain Old Telephony Service

PSTN   Public Switched Telephone Network

RJ45   10BASE-T Connector Standard for Connecting UTP Cabling

TIA422   A Medium Range (typically up to 300m or more) Serial Data Transmission Standard

SONET   Synchronous Optical Network

T1   A Telecommunications Standard Committee

T1.403   Carrier to Customer Installation DS1 Metallic Interface

T1.413–1995   ANSI Standard for ADSL modems

T1E1.4   An ANSI committee for Interfaces, Network Power & Protection Digital Subscriber Loop Access

TBD   To be determined

T.E.   Terminal Equipment

TPA   P1394 signal link

TPB   P1394 signal link

TR41   User Premises Telecom Requirements Committee

TV   Television

UTP   Unshielded Twisted Pair

WT   Working Text

WT2003   Bit Synchronous Mode Working Text

Consider Figure 12-18; it is a view of Customer Premises Specific Reference Model.

This project utilizes the Customer Premises specific Reference Model as shown in Figure 12-18. The interfaces identified in this model are logical interfaces and not necessarily physical implementations. Physical topology and implementation is covered in later sections.

The premises end of a DSL link starts with the access line (twisted-pair telephone line) delineated in the preceding figure by the U-R interface. It ends with one or more *Terminal Equipments* (T.E.) (including but not limited to a personal computer or a television) delineated in the preceding figure by the T interface. The telephone line might or might not be used for *Plain Old Telephone Service* (POTS) as well as ADSL. If it is used for POTS, then the customer premises installation must include a POTS splitter that provides the POTS-R interface as well as the U-R2 interface.

The ATU-R terminates the access line and provides digital signals at the T-SM interface. A *Service Module* (SM) may be installed to convert the received digital signals into signals suitable for a particular Premises Distribution Network or Terminal Equipment at the T-PDN interface. The ATU-R and SM functionality may be integrated in a common device, obviating the need for the T-SM interface.

The U-R, POTS-R, U-R2, T-SM, and T-PDN interfaces will be specified in this document.

Relevant Work in Other Standard Groups or Forums

T1E1.4   ANSI committee T1E1.4 has approved, and ANSI has published, T1.413—1995, an Issue11 standard for ADSL. T1.413—1995 does address POTS splitters (although not completely) but does not address premises wiring. Applicable work is incorporated by reference herein.

Service Available	Target Network Scenarios	Timeframe of Scenario	Priority
1. Internet access via voiceband modem	Internet access via ADSL	NOW	high
2. 2nd line OPTS via DAML	ADSL delivered service	NOW	medium
3. ADSL from CO	ADSL from DLC	future	high
4. ISDN for internet access	ADSL for internet access	NOW	high
5. Internet only via ATM ADSL (DSLAM with 10BT presented to customer	"Full service" set via ATM ADSL (DSLAM with ATM presented to customer)	future	high
6. Internet only via "IP" ADSL (Router plus ETHERNET switch)	"Full service" set via ATM ADSL (DSLAM with ATM approach)	future	high
7. Internet only via "IP" ADSL (Router plus ETHERNET switch)	"Full service" via "IP-Only" ADSL (10BT presented to customer)	future	high
8. ADSL service delivery	VDSL service delivery	future	high
9. Next generation DLC with ADSL (RAM)	ONU with VDSL or ADSL (FTTK)	future	medium
10. VDSL for residential access	VDSL for business services	future	low
11. ADSL for business services	ADSL for residential services	future	low
12. ADSL & POTS	ADSL & 2nd line (2xPOTS)	future	low
13. FTT Node & long range VDSL	FTTK & short range VDSL	future	low
14. FTT Node & VDSL	FTTH	future	low
15. HDSL for Internet access	ADSL for Internet Acccess	NOW	medium
16. IDSL for Internet access	ADSL for Internet Acccess	NOW	medium

TR41   TR41 might be pursuing work related to a Reference Architecture, Residential Wiring, and a Residential Gateway. No specific information is available for the current issue of this document.

ATM Forum   The ATM Forum *Residential Broadband* (RBB) Group is working on a specification that includes a definition of an ATM based customer premises distribution network.

Target Applications and System Implications

The primary applications supported by ADSL will be POTS, data communications, and video on demand. These applications require the transport of packet data, ATM data, or bit synchronous data. The T-SM interface depends on the application being supported.

In some cases, POTS might not be used, in which case the POTS splitter and POTS-R interface might not be needed. Serving these applications likely involves connecting more than one *Terminal Equipment* (T.E.) within a premises, with the second, third, or more terminal connected at some time after the installation of the ADSL modem itself. Furthermore, the installation and use of the ADSL modem should be as simple as possible, with the most reuse of existing wiring as possible, and with the least amount of trouble in migrating from one T.E. to another, as possible.

ATU-R/Splitter Installation

Conceptually, in the most common case to be considered, the installation of an ADSL modem requires breaking an existing telephone line with active POTS service and attached telephones, inserting a POTS splitter, and then reattaching the premises side POTS wiring back to the POTS splitter. (See Figure 12-2, which depicts both logical and physical attributes.) In the US, a *Network Interface Device* (NID, usually comprising surge protectors) establishes the physical demarcation between network and customer premises. The ability to install the POTS Splitter prior to the ATU-R has particular appeal when the ATU-R is owned and installed by the user and not the network provider.

This project will only consider examples of installing the POTS splitter on the CPE side of the primary protection. Country specific installations of POTS splitters might need to address additional safety regulations. Consider Figure 12-19.

Figure 12-19 is a Conceptual ADSL ATU-R/Splitter installation.

POTS Splitter

The POTS splitter, for the purposes of this project, is considered to be the device that splits the POTS signals from the ADSL signals, thus preventing the ADSL signals from reaching the telephone devices.

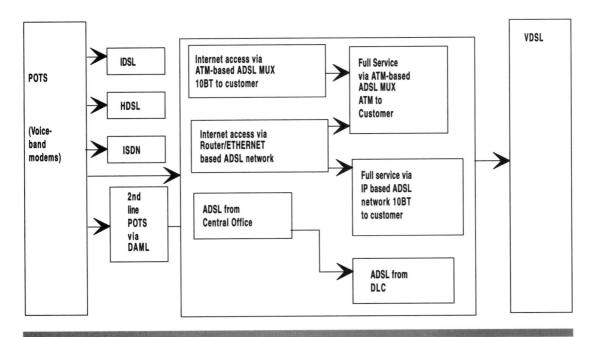

Figure 12-19 Conceptual ADSL ATU-R/Splitter installation

The POTS Splitter might be

- Active or passive, comprise the LPF section and the HPF section or comprise the LPF section only
- Adjacent to the NID or housed within the NID
- Adjacent to each telephone device, adjacent to the ATU—R, or integrated within the ATU-R

The *Low Pass Filter* (LPF) section contains circuitry that passes POTS frequencies (approx. 0 to 4 kHz 1) to and from the telephone equipment and blocks the ADSL signal. The POTS Splitter (LPF only variation) might allow for the complete spectrum, including the ADSL signals (above approx. 20 kHz) to pass to the ATU-R.

In the case that a *High Pass Filter* (HPF) section is needed to prevent low frequency, high level POTS signals from entering the ATU-R front end components, the circuitry might be included in and be considered part of the ATU-R or the circuitry might be included as part of POTS Splitter (along with the LPF).

The ATU-R manufacturer should not assume that the HPF has been implemented external to his equipment. It is recommended that all manufactures of ATU-R equipment plan on explicitly implementing the appropriate HPF.

POTS Splitter Characteristics POTS Splitter characteristics will not be specified in this text. Instead the POTS Splitter is used as an existing system component and is shown along with the other system components, such as ATU-R and wiring, to comprise the configurations detailed in sections to follow.

The ANSI standard T1.413-1995 specifies the loop conditions under which the splitter and ADSL must be able to operate without causing significant degradation to the POTS signal and these characteristics will be incorporated in this document by reference.

Work applicable to the POTS Splitters that is completed in other groups, such as ETSI or ITU, will be addressed when specifics are available.

ATU-R/Splitter Configurations

Various ATU-R/Splitter configurations are discussed forthwith:

- ATU-R adjacent to T.E. with Separate POTS Splitter

- ATU-R adjacent to T.E. and Split POTS Splitter
- ATU-R adjacent to T.E. and Distributed POTS Splitter
- ATU-R with integral POTS splitter adjacent to NID
- ATU-R with integral POTS splitter adjacent to T.E.

A brief introduction for each configuration is presented along with a figure depicting both logical and physical attributes (topology and implementation).

This is followed by a list of advantages and disadvantages for each configuration. These advantages and disadvantages can be utilized to choose the configuration that best suits the needs of any particular deployment.

A suggested list of criteria is provided as follows that when used in conjunction with specific priorities or importance values (as determined by the provider) would allow a selection of the best configuration to be made for any particular ADSL system deployment.

- Criteria
- Type of Splitter—active or passive
- Equipment ownership—customer or network owned splitter, ATU-R Network demarcation point
- Failure effects of splitter, ATU-R
- Installation complexity
- Testing and maintenance—splitter, ATU-R
- ATU-R adjacent to T.E. with separate POTS splitter

Figure 12-20 shows a configuration with the POTS splitter separate from the ATU-R.

The POTS splitter mounts near the NID, whereas the ATU-R is located at a more convenient installation location, perhaps next to the T.E. Wiring to the ATU-R may be existing or new, depending on the quality of the existing wire and the desired location of the ATU-R.

Figure 12-21 shows an ATU-R adjacent to T.E. and Separate POTS Splitter {LPF & HPF}.

Some of the following advantages are achieved as shown in Figure 12-21.

- Putting the ATU-R adjacent to or within T.E. ensures proximity to power
- T-sm interface cabling will be short or non-existent (integral to the T.E.).
- *Accessibility* Additional T.E. might be connected easily to the ATU-R

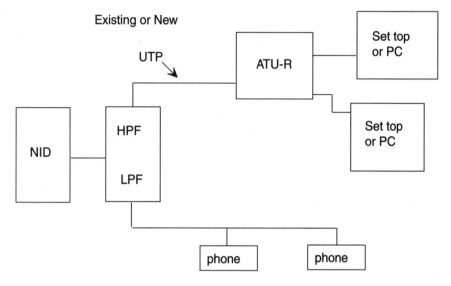

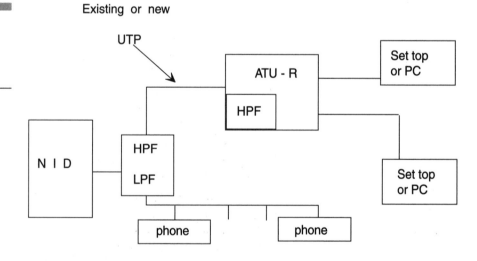

■ The POTS splitter can be installed at some time before the ATU-R.

■ Isolates the ADSL signal path wiring from the CP POTS wiring imperfections (that is, bridged lines, nonstandard wiring gauges, and so on) and allows for the reduction of cross-coupled noise.

The following are its disadvantages:

■ In countries that require an active POTS splitter, the ATU-R might have to power the splitter over the line or another supply provided.

■ Currently, POTS splitter from one manufacturer won't necessarily work with the ADSL modem of another manufacturer. This is primarily due to the required characteristics of the HPF located in the ADSL signal path.

A variant on the POTS splitter is a system where the low pass filter portion of the splitter is physically separate from the high pass filter. Two logical configurations are shown in Figure 12-22 and Figure 12-23.

Figure 12-23 shows the configuration with the LPF located at the physical split in signal paths. This configuration is as efficient in isolating the premises POTS wiring from the ADSL signal path as the explicit integrated splitter; however, it offers an advantage because now each manufacture of ATU-R equipment has control of the HPF characteristics. (It is assumed that the LPF requirements are basically the same regardless of a manufacturer's ADSL implementation).

This split POTS Splitter configuration is the most prevalent configuration currently planned to be deployed.

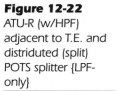

Figure 12-22
ATU-R (w/HPF)
adjacent to T.E. and
distriduted (split)
POTS splitter {LPF-
only}

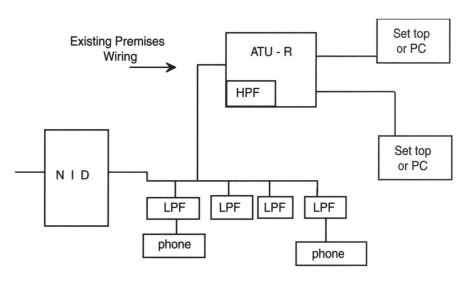

Figure 12-23
ATU-R with integral
POTS splitter (LPF)
adjacent to NID

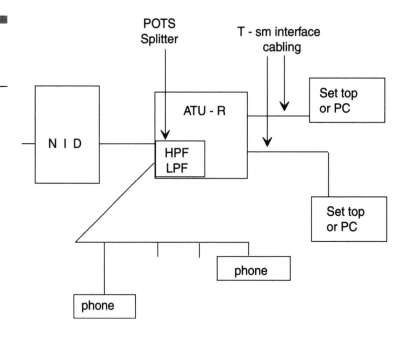

The advantages of Figure 12-23 include:

■ Putting the ATU-R adjacent to or within T.E. ensures proximity to power

■ T-sm interface cabling will be short or non-existent (integral to the T.E.).

■ *Accessibility*   Additional T.E. might be connected easily to the ATU-R

■ The POTS splitter can be installed at some time before the ATU-R.

■ Isolates the ADSL signal path wiring from the premises POTS wiring imperfections (that is, bridged lines, nonstandard wiring gauges, and so on) and allows for the reduction of cross-coupled noise

■ Increases the probability of compatibility between different manufactures of ATU-R equipment and LPF hardware

The disadvantages of Figure 12-23 are

■ In countries that require an active POTS splitter, the ATU-R might have to power the splitter over the line or another supply be provided.

Figure 12-24 shows a variant in which the high pass filter is implemented within the ATU-R and low pass filters are installed in front of each telephone (distributed).

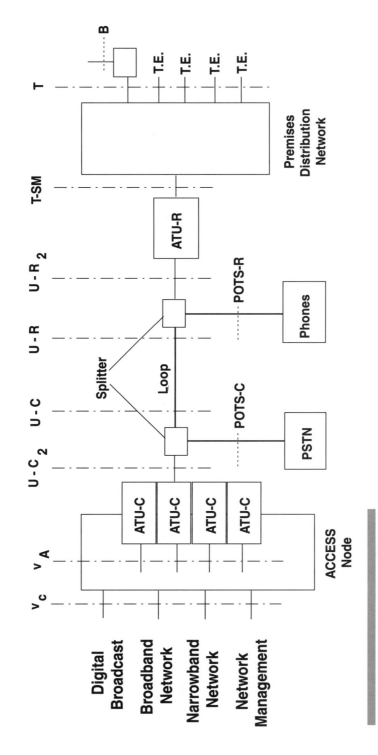

Figure 12-24 System reference model

347

Advantages of Figure 12-24 are

- Putting the ATU-R adjacent to or within T.E. ensures proximity to power

- T-sm interface cabling will be short or non-existent (integral to the T.E.).

- *Accessibility*   Additional T.E. might be connected easily to the ATU-R.

- The POTS splitter(s) can be installed at some time before the ATU-R.

- Increases the probability of compatibility between different manufacturers of ATU-R equipment and LPF hardware

- Obviates reconfiguration of customer premises wiring entirely

The disadvantages of Figure 12-24 are

- In countries that require an active POTS splitters, the ATU-R might have to power the splitter over the line or another supply be provided.

- Customer premises wiring becomes a potential bridging network that can cause frequency response discontinuities and is a factor in determining ATU-R performance. The exact nature of the network frequency response is dependent on the installation wiring each individual CP.

- Improper installation of the LPF at each phone, or the omission of the LPF, can cause significant termination problems on the network, which in turn can have an impact on ATU-R performance.

- Use of unbalanced line within the CP POTS wiring network can result in additional noise ingress into the ATU-R signal spectrum.

- Increased mechanical installation complexities are involved (that is, wall phones).

Figure 12-25 shows the installation with the ATU-R adjacent to or close to (within 5 meters) the NID.

Except for short stubs to connector blocks, this configuration requires no new telephone wiring at the U interface, but will usually require some longer cabling for the T-sm interface.

The advantages of Figure 12-25 are

- ADSL signals pass over virtually no pre-existing premises telephone wiring thus minimizing potential premises wiring related problems.

The disadvantages of Figure 12-25 are

- NIDs and entrance telephone wiring are usually not favorably located for access to power.

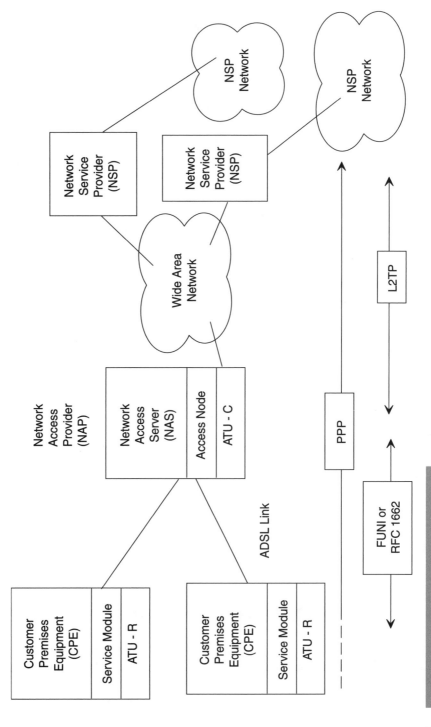

Figure 12-25 Network reference diagram

- ATU-Rs placed in attics, basements, garages, or outside premises might be subject to environmental extremes.

- The installation complexity and length of the T-sm interface wiring to the T.E. (This potentially limits the use of some of the Premises Distribution Networks currently in use.)

Figure 12-26 shows a configuration with the ATU-R adjacent to one T.E. and therefore likely removed from the NID by as much as 100 feet.

This installation requires cutting the telephone line just after the NID, connecting it to the ATU-R over new or existing premises telephone wiring, and then reconnecting the POTS output to the premises telephone system originally serviced by the wire from the NID. In addition, any telephone connected at the ATU-R location must be reconnected on the POTS side.

Advantages of Figure 12-26 are

- Putting the ATU-R adjacent to or within T.E. ensures proximity to power

- T-sm interface cabling will be short or non-existent (integral to the T.E.)

- *Accessibility*   Additional T.E. might be connected easily to the ATU-R.

- This configuration enables a self-contained ADSL NIC for PCs or Set Top boxes (POTS is supported through integral POTS Splitter)

- Good topology for customer owned (and powered) POTS Splitter (Active)

Disadvantages of Figure 12-26 are

- The premises telephone service now connects through the ATU-R, which could accidentally be disconnected from the line, severing POTS service.

- This configuration might require diverse routing of two wire pairs to reduce cross-talk.

- Not good topology for network owned (and powered) POTS Splitter (Active)

ATU-R Deployed without POTS Service

In cases where there is no requirement to support existing or new POTS service in addition to deployment of ADSL, installation becomes less complex. Following the example of the preferred configuration, the ATU-R should be located as close as practical to the CPE. In some cases new wiring

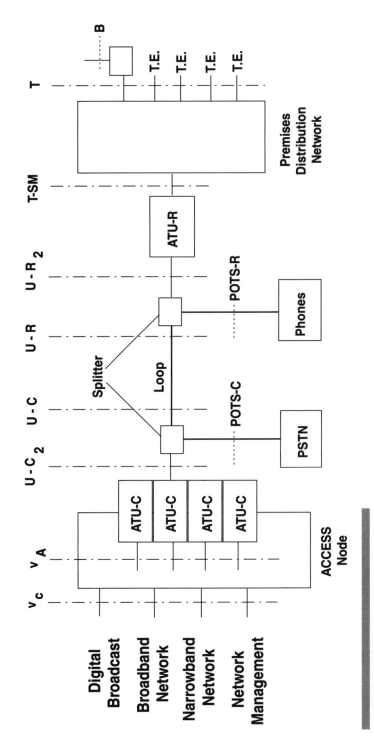

Figure 12-26 System reference model

351

might need to be installed from the telephone line at the NID or other demarcation to the location where the ATU-R is to be connected.

U-R, POTS-R, U-R2 Interfaces

Wiring Recent telephone company experience suggests that the quality of in-home wiring varies so much, and that so much of it falls below a level suitable for ADSL transmission that new wiring of some form or another will be the rule rather than the exception.

New Wiring If new wiring is pulled, it should be UTP Category 5 as specified in EIA/TIA 570. A wall plate shall be installed to terminate the new wiring for DSL.

Interference and the Use of Existing Wiring The running of ADSL signals and POTS signals together through a single two-pair cable cross-couples POTS noises generated by ringing, trip ringing, pulse dialing, and hook switch signaling into the low level ADSL receive signals. Studies have shown that just a few feet of adjacent wiring causes cross-coupling of sufficient magnitude to cause errors in received data. This problem could be reduced by the high pass filtering in the ATU-R. This liability is also mitigated by error control protocols and by interleaving (the noise appears as impulses), but must be recognized as having potential effects on quality of service. However, there is also concern that there might be detrimental effects (unacceptable noise in the telephone user's ear) from cross-coupling of ADSL signals into the post splitter POTS lines. This potential for crosstalk might affect voice band usage that extends near 4000 Hz such as with V.pcm or other high-speed voice band modems.

U-R Screw terminals or RJ11 jack/plug as required by specific configuration wired to center pair (pins 3 and 4).

POTS-R Screw terminals or RJ11 jack/plug as required by specific configuration wired to center pair (pins 3 and 4).

Connections for the ATU-R

External POTS Splitter The U-R2 connector at the wall jack shall be RJ14 (sometimes known as RJ11, 4-wire) with ADSL wired to pins 2 and

5. POTS (optional) will be wired to pins 3 and 4. This wiring precludes the use of a POTS second line on a wire pair connected to pins 2 and 5 for this particular wall jack.

In cases where wiring other than UTP Category 5 is being used, the ADSL signal path from the POTS Splitter to the U-R2 connector at the wall jack must be isolated in a separate sheath. This might require a new cable run.

Internal POTS Splitter   The U-R2 connector at the wall jack shall be as specified in the physical characteristics section of ANSI T1.413—1995.

T-SM Interface

If the ATU-R is merely implementing the basic functions of a bit pump, an external T-sm interface will be necessary to interconnect the ATU-R to a separate Service Module. This interface will have to carry those data, timing, and control signals necessary to permit operation of a variety of services, which might be carried on the ADSL link.

The minimum signal set will be one downstream data circuit plus its clock and one upstream data circuit plus its clock. A number of optional signals may be supported for particular applications:

1. *Secondary data channels*   These may be simplex or duplex channels and will always have an associated clock. Some duplex channels might have a common clock.

2. *Auxiliary data timing signals*   Some channels might require an out-of-band frame or byte start signal, which is extracted from the ADSL framing structure.

3. *Network Timing Reference*   Some service modules might require the 8kHz timing reference when this is carried by the ADSL link.

4. *Control and Status circuits*   The ATU-R and SM might each be required to control the other and/or to receive status indications. These might be global signals or be channel associated.

A basic interface providing the minimum signal set on an RJ45 connector is specified here, where this is sufficient. It is recommended that interfaces that provide additional signals use one of the existing ISO data communications interfaces. The data rate of ADSL equipment requires that only those interfaces using balanced circuits should be used. Suitable interfaces are ISO.4903 (X.21), ISO.2110-Amd1 (TIA.530), or ISO.2593 (V.35). The use of such interfaces will allow existing data communications equipment to connect to an ATU-R without modification. Guidance is given as follows as to the mapping of the T-sm signals onto these interfaces.

Signal Specifications

Each simplex data channel consists of one data circuit (DD or DU) and one clock circuit (CD or CU). The clocks are normally generated by the ATU-R, but in some instances the upstream clock (CU) may be generated by the SM. These clocks should have a nominal 50 percent duty cycle at the maximum data rate. Extended OFF periods may be inserted when burst clocking is being used. The downstream data is generated by the ATU-R and the upstream data by the SM. The data is NRZ encoded with the OFF and ON states representing logic 1 and 0, respectively. Data changes state at OFF to ON clock transitions with the receiver strobing the data at ON to OFF clock transitions.

In addition to the clock and data signals, each channel or group of channels might have other signals associated with them. ATU-R and SM equipment not generating these signals shall leave these circuits unconnected, and equipment receiving these signals shall provide pullups/pulldowns so as to force an ON state in the event an undriven input.

The channel-associated signals might include

1. *Data Qualifier* (QD or QU)   A signal driven by the data source to indicate valid data on its transmitter. This signal may be used in place of, or in addition to, burst clocking.

2. *Channel Control* (CC)   A signal generated by the SM to enable channel(s)

3. *Channel Indication* (CI)   A signal generated by the ATU-R to indicate that channel(s) are in a data-forwarding state

4. *Byte Sync* (BS)   A signal generated by the ATU-R to provide a data alignment signal for byte-structured channels such as G.711 PCM. This signal shall transition from OFF to ON at the byte boundary and might transition from ON to OFF at any other bit boundary.

5. *Frame Sync* (FS)   A signal generated by the ATU-R to provide data alignment for frame-structured channels that do not have an embedded frame delimiter. This signal shall transition from OFF to ON at the frame boundary and may transition from ON to OFF at any other bit boundary.

6. *Network Timing Reference* (NR)   This is a signal with a frequency of 8 kHz, which might be carried by some ADSL links.

Global control and indication signals might be used which relate to the entire ADSL link:

1. *Equipment Status* (SD or SU)   A signal generated by either equipment to indicate that it is operational and to qualify all other signals.

2. *Link Control* (LC)   A signal generated by the SM to enable the ADSL link

3. *Link Indication* (LI)   A signal generated by the ATU-R to indicate that the ADSL link is operational

These notes are applicable to the previous items.

1. In both the preceding lists, item 1 is an alternative to 2 plus 3. This equates to the alternative definitions of circuit 108 in ITU-T V.24 as either Data Terminal Ready or Connect Data Set to Line.

2. Where only one pair of channels is supported, Channel Control/Indication and Link Control/Indication are essentially the same signals.

3. No signals relating to flow control or SM-sourced clocks are specified. It cannot be assumed that an ATU-R is capable of either flow control or speed buffering and therefore all data flow must be slaved to the ATU-R clocks. Where SM equipment needs such facilities, they should be provided internally by the SM.

ISO Interfaces and Connectors

All these interfaces provide one downstream and one upstream channel plus clocks and control signals. The ISO.4903 (X.21) interface uses a 15 pole D connector and supports two control circuits and two timing circuits. The ISO.2110-Amd1 (TIA.530) interface uses either a 25 pole D connector or a 26 pole miniature connector and supports more control circuits. The ISO.2593 (V.35) is an obsolete interface but one that is still commonly used. It uses 34 pole connector and supports the same signal set as ISO.2110.

Where ATU-R and SM have different interfaces, inter-working by means of an adapter cable will be possible on circuits where both transmitter and receiver are balanced (which is true for data and clocks on all these interfaces)

or where a satisfactory unbalanced to balanced conversion can be made. The ISO and ITU-T standards documents address this issue in more detail.

In the ADSL context, the ATU-R is the DCE and will have female connectors, and the SM is the DTE with male connectors. The mapping of T-sm signals to the V.24 and X.24 signals is suggested in Table 12-1.

Here are some related notes:

1. For this application, the X signal is driven by the DCE towards the DTE.

2. The CTS circuit does not have its usual function as these are timing signals. It was chosen because it is a balanced signal on the ISO.2110-Amd1 interface. When the B, F, or X circuit is used to carry these signals, it can only be on either a simplex channel or a full duplex channel pair with identical data rate, as circuit S will need to be a common clock.

3. Where CU is generated by the ATU-R, the X signal is driven by the DCE toward the DTE.

Table 12-1
T-SM V.24-to-X.24 mapping

T-SM	V.24			X.24	NOTES
DD	104 (RXD)			R	
DU	103 (TXD)			T	
CD	115 (RXC)			S	
CU	113 or 114 (TXC)	X		3	
QD	109 (DCD)			C	
QU	105 (RTS)			I	
CC	109 (DCD)			C	
CI	105 (RTS)			I	
SD	107 (DSR)			C	
SU	108/2 (DTR)		I		
LC	108/1 (DTR)		C		
LI	107 (DSR)			I	
BS	106 (CTS)			B	2
FS	106 (CTS)			F	2
NR	106 (CTS)			X	1,2

Basic RJ45 Interface

A data and clock's only interface, providing one downstream channel plus one upstream channel, can be implemented using an RJ45 plug. The drivers and receivers should conform to ITU-T V.11 (TIA−422) and be connected as shown:

CDa	-	Pin #1
CDb	-	Pin #2
DUa	-	Pin #3
CUa	-	Pin #4
CUb	-	Pin #5
DUb	-	Pin #6
DDa	-	Pin #7
DDb	-	Pin #8

The previous correlates the RJ45 Plug for the T-SM Interface.

It might be necessary to use screened RJ45 jacks, plugs, and cables to meet radiated emissions requirements.

T-PDN Interfaces—Existing Premises Distribution Networks

With the addition of a Service Module, the T-SM interface may be converted to a more commonly available interface. When the ATU-R and SM functions are integrated into one device, the T-SM interface disappears at the physical level and the applicable interface then becomes the T-PDN.

The *Premises Distribution Networks* (PDNs) included in the body of this issue will be some of the commonly available PDNs in use for Bit Synchronous (serial interface data communications) Mode, Packet Mode, and ATM Mode of operation. Evolving Premises Distribution Networks are presented in Annex B for reference only.

Bit Synchronous Interfaces

Terminal Equipment such as routers or Set Top boxes may support some of the more common serial interface data communications connections (DTE interfaces) at the T-PDN interface. The Terminal Equipment expects the device attached at the T-PDN interface to act as *Data Communications Equipment* (DCE).

The following specifications are incorporated in this document by reference and will not be further detailed herein:

- TIA—530 or v.35 (ISO 2593) for high-speed serial DTE interface
- T1—1.544 Mbps ANSI T1.403
- E1—2.048 Mbps ITU G.703/G.704

Ethernet 10BaseT interface

The following specifications are incorporated in this document by reference and will not be further detailed herein:

- 10BaseT on a RJ—45 connector
- Ethernet Version 2.0: A CSMA/CD Local Area Network Specification
- ANSI/IEEE 802.3, CSMA/CD Access Method and Physical Layer Specifications

ATM25 Interface

The following specification is incorporated in this document by reference and will not be further detailed herein:

- The ATM Forum Technical Committee, Physical Interface Specification for 25.6 Mb/s over Twisted Pair Cable af-phy—0040.000, November 1995 on a Media Interface Connector specified in ISO/IEC 603–7 (commonly referred to as RJ—45)

Consider Figure 12-27.

Figure 12-28 presents the ADSL Forum System Reference Model for ADSL network systems. The following terms are used in Figure 12-28.

ATU-C   ADSL Transmission Unit at the Central Office end. The ATU-C may be integrated within an Access Node.

ATU-R   ADSL transmission Unit at the customer premises end

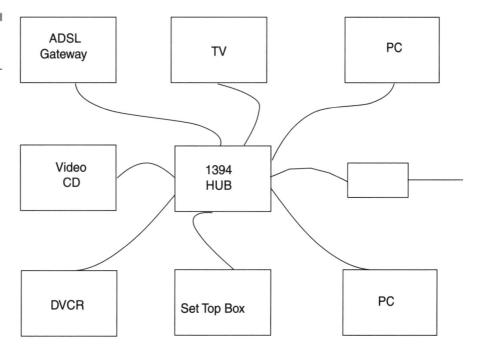

Figure 12-27
1394-based premises distribution network

Access Node   Concentration point for Broadband and Narrowband data. The Access Node may be located at a Central Office or a remote site. Also, a remote Access Node may subtend from a central access node.

B   Auxiliary data input (such as a satellite feed) to Service Module (such as a Set Top Box)

Broadcast   Broadband data input in simplex mode (typically broadcast video)

Broadband Network   Switching system for data rates above 1.5/2.0 Mbps

Loop   Twisted-pair copper telephone line

Narrowband Network   Switching system for data rates at or below 1.5/2 .0 Mbps

POTS   Plain Old Telephone Service

Figure 12-28
USB-based PDN
for ADSL

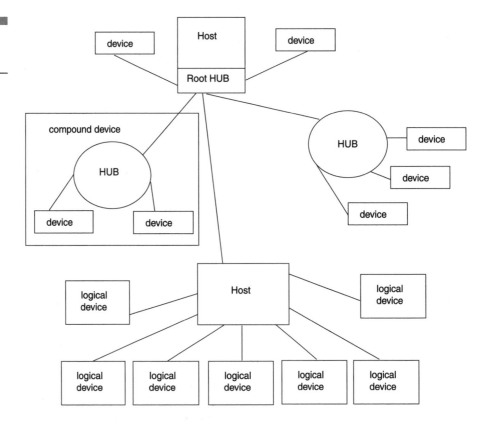

POTS-C   Interface between PSTN and POTS splitter at network end

POTS-R   Interface between phones and POTS splitter at premises end

Premises Distribution Network   System for connecting ATU-R to Service Modules. May be point-point or multi-point; may be passive wiring or an active network. Multi-point may be a bus or star.

PSTN   Public Switched Telephone Network

Service Module (SM)   Performs terminal adaptation functions. Examples are set top boxes, PC interfaces, or LAN router.

Splitter   Filters which separate high frequency (ADSL) and low frequency (POTS) signals at CO end and premises end. The splitter may be integrated into the ATU, physically separated from the ATU, or divided between high pass and low pass, with the low pass function physically separated from the ATU. The provision of POTS splitters and POTS-related functions is optional.

T-SM   Interface between ATU-R and Premises Distribution Network. May be same as T when network is point-to-point passive wiring. An ATU-R may have more than one type of T-SM interface implemented (for example, a T1/E1 connection and an Ethernet connection).

T   Interface between Premises Distribution Network and Service Modules. May be the same as T-SM when network is point-point passive wiring. Note that T interface may disappear at the physical level when ATU-R is integrated within a Service Module.

U-C   Interface between Loop and ATU-C (analog). Defining both ends of the Loop interface separately arises because of the asymmetry of the signals on the line.

U-C2   Interface between POTS splitter and ATU-C. Note that at present ANSI T1.413 does not define such an interface and separating the POTS splitter from the ATU-C presents some technical difficulties in standardizing this interface.

U-R   Interface between Loop and ATU-R (analog)

U-R2   Interface between POTS splitter and ATU-R. Note that at present ANSI T1.413 does not define such an interface and separating the POTS splitter from the ATU-R presents some technical difficulties in standardizing the interface.

VA   Logical interface between ATU-C and Access Node. As this interface will often be within circuits on a common board, the ADSL Forum does not consider physical V_A interfaces. The V interface may contain STM, ATM, or both transfer modes. In the primitive case of point-point connection between a switch port and an ATU-C (that is, a case without concentration or multiplexing), the V_A and V_c interfaces become identical (alternatively, the V_A interface disappears).

Vc   Interface between Access Node and network. May have multiple physical connections (as shown), although it may carry all signals across a single physical connection. A digital carrier facility (for example, a SONET or

SDH extension) may be interposed at the V_c interface when the access node and ATU-Cs are located at a remote site. Interface to the PSTN may be a universal tip-ring interface or a multiplexed telephony interface such as specified in Bellcore TR−08 or TR−303. The broadband segment of the V_c interface may be STM switching, ATM switching, or private line type connections.

Evolving Premises Distribution Networks

The information here is informative and included to provide visibility into the possible use of emerging PDNs for use with ADSL systems. It is not exclusive of other possible PDNs but provides guidance as to how these emerging PDNs may be used in conjunction with ADSL access at the customer premises.

A high-speed digital home network serving the needs of ADSL signal distribution and digital information distribution from other local or network resources can be implemented on a high quality unshielded twisted pair wiring system. This type of infrastructure has been proposed by the *Consumer Electronics Bus* (CEBus) committee, which recommends the installation of Category 5 unshielded twisted pair in a star topology for both voice and data transmission purposes. Category 5 unshielded twisted pair is also the transmission media for 100BaseTX Ethernet and several other systems. Such an infrastructure would be suitable for the ATM based system being proposed by the ATM Forum. Two other possible systems that use different media are described.

IEEE 1394 (FireWire)

The IEEE 1394 is an IEEE serial bus standard originally designed for the inter-connection of computer peripheral devices. The 1394 standard defines a serial interface that can be used to replace traditional PC parallel, serial, or SCSI bus. The 1394 could be very effective at inter-connecting the new generation high capacity and high-speed storage and I/O devices. The 1394 standard is designed to handle both isochronous and asynchronous data transmission. A 1394 based *Premises Distribution Network* (PDN) can be used to distribute ADSL traffic for both data access and video on demand applications, subject to the limitations described as follows.

The current 1394 standard requires the use of a special purpose shielded twisted pair cable. The twisted pair cable consists of two data pairs and one power pair. Each data pair is individually shielded, and three pairs are then all shielded together. Hence, there are two signal links (TPA,TPB) on one physical connection. A typical 1394 twisted pair cable is only about 4.5 meters long. That cable length may be just long enough for connecting a local cluster of equipment together, but might be insufficient to provide interconnection between rooms. There is activity aimed at producing a longer reach version of IEEE 1394, a sub-working group has produced a draft document.

This PDN should have a star topology with a 1394 root device at the center of the star, but daisy chaining of 1394 devices is also permitted. Other data traffic from in-house or other access networks can also be shared on this PDN. A gateway/router is used to connect the ADSL to this PDN, but may require a longer reach technology. Consider Figure 12-29.

The *Universal Serial Bus* (USB) standard was originally designed around the PC architecture for the connection of telephony devices such as telephone/fax/modem adapters, answering machines, scanners as well as PDAs, keyboards, mice, and so on. The standard was specified, and the standard document is available through the USB Forum. Additional assistance is also available through the membership of the Forum. The USB can be used to handle isochronous data transmission. A USB based *Premises Distribution Network* (PDN) might be used to distribute ADSL traffic for both data access and video on demand applications.

Figure 12-29
SNAG domain
reference model

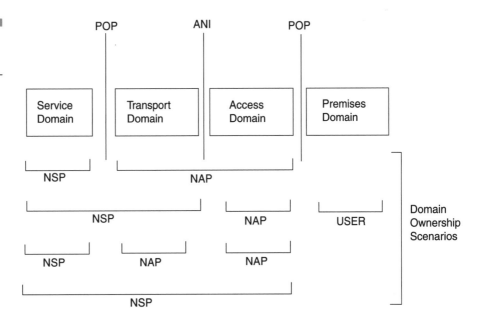

The current USB standard requires the use of a 28 AWG shielded twisted pair cable with a non-twisted power distribution pair of a variable gauge ranging from 20 AWG to 28 AWG. The shielding covers both signal and power distribution pairs. The maximum transmission throughput is 12 Mbps for a maximum cable length of 5 meters. A non-shielded cable can also be used for sub-channel applications, where the transmission rate is 1.5 Mbps.

Data is carried over a USB in packets. The USB employs NRZI data encoding when transmitting packets.

USB Topology

A USB is configured around a host, normally a PC, with devices attached directly or through hubs. A hub can connect a host to multiple devices. All devices are logically connected to the host. There are three layers of communication links between a host and its devices. Shown here are first the physical topology and then the logical topology.

Figure 12-30 illustrates the USB; a dedicated ADSL USB host.

TR41 Residential Gateway

No specific information is available at this time.

1. Out of band signaling tones may need to be passed in some applications (this is outside the scope of this document).

2. Cross-coupled noise would again become a factor if a telephone at the set top or PC uses the same cable for connection back to house telephone wiring.

3. Cross-coupled noise would again become a factor if a telephone at the set top or PC uses the same cable for connection back to house telephone wiring.

4. The frequency response discontinuities manifest themselves as increased insertion loss notches and lower than expected ATU-R line termination impedances. The later can upset the ATU-R hybrid networks by introducing driving impedances that can be 50 percent or more lower than expected.

Figure 12-30
Dedicated ADSL USB
Host

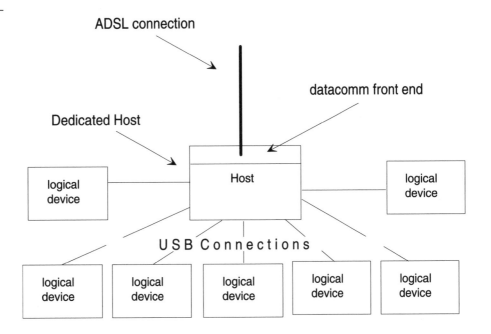

Default VPI/VCI Addresses for FUNI Mode Transport: Packet Mode

This section reflects the information contained in the ADSL Forum reports that specifies the default values for VPI/VCI pairs when used in the ADSL Forum FUNI Mode transport for frames over an ADSL Link.

Introduction

This information defines the default values for VPI/VCI pairs to be used in the absence of any other FUNI address selection mechanism when transporting frames over an ADSL link using FUNI mode[1]. It is intended to complete the required portion in the third report from the ADSL Forum on Address Assignment. This is section reflects just one piece of information in the series topics related by way of the ADSL Forum. Existing documents include:

- Framing and Encapsulations Standards for ADSL: Packet Mode

Future documents in the information presented here are a specification series and will describe

- Packet mode reference model
- Packet mode service model examples
- Address management for FUNI mode transport (this document)
- Channelization for DMT and CAP ADSL line codes (WT−017)
- Signaling for SVC setup
- Management requirements

This series of ADSL documents is required to insure multi-vendor interoperability for ADSL links.

VPI/VCI Assignments

The values defined here should be used for transporting FUNI frames across an ADSL link. Other addresses for end-to-end ATM transport should follow existing ATM Forum standards that reserve and specify certain VPI/VCI values.

Data Transport

In the absence of any data channel address mechanism and for implementations supporting a single data session, an ADSL endpoint operating in FUNI mode MUST transfer user data using the default VPI=1 and VCI=32 values in the FUNI address field. Provisioning may be used to select one or more alternative VPI/VCI values for any user data transport.

Specific Channel

The Vendor Specific Channel MUST be carried in FUNI frames with VPI=1, VCI=33 values in the FUNI address fields. This VPI/VCI pair is reserved and MUST NOT be used for any other purpose when operating in FUNI mode.

Frame Layer Management Channel

Information related to the performance and configuration of the framing (FUNI) layer MUST be carried in FUNI frames with VP=0 as required for OAM cells.

Related ADSL References

ADSL Forum: Framing and Encapsulations Standards for ADSL: Packet Mode

Channelization for DMT & CAP ADSL Line Codes: Packet Mode

This section specifies the use of Physical Media Dependent channelization required to implement Packet Mode data transport over Discrete Multitone and Carrierless AM/PM ADSL systems.

Introduction

Specific uses of the channelization capabilities for two of the common ADSL physical layer implementations as required for transport of frames across an ADSL link. This report describes such channelization for the user data paths only, management and other channels are defined in the relevant PMD standards. This specification refers directly to existing and developing standards defined by the ANSI T1E1 subcommittee. Specifically, it defines channelization standards for systems implemented using the T1.413 DMT standard and systems designed around the CAP line code and being defined by the CAP/QAM RADSL Ad Hoc group.

This information reflects that which is a series of ADSL Forum technical reports that address transferring variable length frames over an ADSL link. Existing documents include

- Framing and Encapsulations Standards for ADSL: Packet Mode

Future documents in this specification series will describe

- Packet mode reference model
- Packet mode service model examples
- Address management for FUNI mode transport (this document)
- Channelization for DMT and CAP ADSL line codes (WT−017)
- Signaling for SVC setup
- Management requirements

The purpose for the documents available from the ADSL Forum is to insure multi-vendor interoperability for ADSL links.

Discrete Multitone (DMT) PMD Specifics

This information proposes a channelization scheme for use in packet mode ADSL equipment using the ANSI T1.413 DMT PMD layer. For packet mode systems, the channelization of different payload formats is handled using the ANSI T1.413 standards simplex and duplex channels. The following channels are defined for packet mode operation:

One required data channel using AS0 downstream and LS0 upstream

One optional data channel using AS1 downstream and LS1 upstream

For the transport of frames over DMT-PMD ADSL, all modems MUST use the AS0 channel downstream and the LS0 channel upstream. Channel AS1 may be used to provide an additional downstream channel and LS1 may be used to provide an additional upstream channel. Any channel may operate over the fast or interleaved paths.

A "hybrid" implementation of one or more Bit Synchronous (Plesiochronous) channels together with the packet mode channels is not precluded by the preceding. The bandwidth occupied by the Bit Synchronous channel must first be reserved before allocating the remaining bandwidth to the packet channel. Simultaneous hybrid operation of Packet Mode and ATM Mode over an ADSL line is precluded by this specification.

Carrierless AM/PM (CAP) PMD Specifics

The CAP-PMD defines a single downstream data channel and a single upstream data channel. All higher layer RFC1662 and FUNI data frames should be mapped to these interfaces. For the transport of data link frames in RFC1662 or FUNI mode, all frames MUST be sent over the asymmetric downstream and upstream channels as currently specified in.

Related References Applicable to this Section

ANSI T1.413-1995, Issue 1; Telecommunications

Network and Customer Installation Interfaces

Asymmetric Digital Subscriber Line (ADSL) Metallic Interface.

Interface Specification Recommendation for Carrierless AM/PM (CAP) Based Rate Adaptive Digital Subscriber Line (RADSL) Circuits-Baseline Text Proposal; ANSI T1E1/97-228.

Requirements & Reference Models for ADSL Access Networks

This section outlines architectural requirements and reference models for ADSL services and service providers. In specific, it defines target applications, various domain ownership, and requirements of different architectures.

Introduction

The *Service Network Architecture Group* (SNAG) was formed in Orlando, meeting on June 18, 1996. The objectives of this group were to compile architecture options, requirements, and reference models for several key ADSL applications, and identify various issues associated with each architecture.

It was not expected that this group could identify the optimal architecture, because it is recognized no architecture would be universally optimal for all carriers. Carriers choose architectures based on not only technical issues but also based on such considerations as business strategy, economics, and regulatory concerns that are outside the expertise of SNAG membership and outside the scope of this document.

In addition, it became increasingly clear as the work of the ADSL Forum continued that there was significant overlap between what the SNAG was attempting to do and the work of the packet and ATM groups. The board of directors thus made a decision to merge the packet and cell based work of the SNAG into the packet and ATM groups, respectively. The requirements and model work, which the SNAG team developed, are presented in this section.

SNAG Terminology

In this document several words are used to signify requirements which are often capitalized.

MUST	This word, or the adjective "required," means that the definition is an absolute requirement of the specification.
MUST NOT	This phrase means that the definition is an absolute prohibition of the specification.
SHOULD	This word, or the adjective "recommended," means that there may exist valid reasons in particular circumstances to ignore this item, but the full implications must be understood and carefully weighted before choosing a different course.
MAY	This word, or the adjective "optional," means that this item is one of an allowed set of alternatives. An implementation that does not include this option, MUST be prepared to inter-operate with another implementation, which does include the option

Revision History

First skeleton draft. 9/1 /96; 0.2
Extended options and limited discussion on issues. 10/1 /96; 0.3
Added text from London meeting. 2/1 /97; 0.4
Very minor edits after the Seattle meeting. 4/21 /97; 0.5
Several rewrites agreed to in Amsterdam. 6/17 /97; 0.6
Agreements from Boston meeting. 9/17 /97; 0.7
Final Agreements from Brussels meeting. 1/26 /98; 0.8

Target Applications

SNAG chose to consider the most likely applications for ADSL services as Internet access and remote LAN access. However, it was decided not to preclude a richer set. Internet access can be for either business customers with multiple PCs or residential customers with one or two PCs. Typically one *Internet Service provider* (ISP) that is selected at the service subscription time services an ADSL subscriber. Dynamic connections to multiple destinations are supported with the regular Internet technology through the ISP. Similar to the Internet access case, remote LAN access may be required by residential subscribers for telecommuting or by a business LAN for corporate private network. Multiple concurrent connection is a requirement for remote LAN access. For instance, three branch offices need to be connected in a mesh topology. Both Internet and remote LAN access may be required simultaneously by ADSL subscribers. In the scenarios described previously, where multiple connections are simultaneously open from one user access point, a potential security issue exists. This is due to the fact that traffic from one service provider access point can be funneled to the other either knowingly or unknowingly by the user's end system. See the section on security for further notes on this topic. To provide a reference perspective within which to specify a set of requirements and describe interactions, a SNAG Logical Reference model was developed by the members of the SNAG group. Consider Figure 12-31.

In this model there are several views of an architecture based on the domain ownership, that is, who owns the components of the architecture outside the user perspective. In this reference model, the ATU-R is located in the premises domain and the ATU-C is located in the access domain. Here, the acronyms used previously are described:

NAP   Network Access Provider

NSP   Network Service Provider

NTP   Network Transport Provider

ANI   Access Network Interface

POP   Point Of Presence

Figure 12-31
SNAG Domain
Reference Model

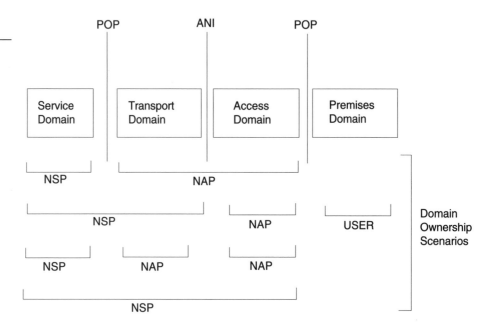

Requirements for ADSL Architectures

This section lists the generic requirements of an end-to-end ADSL network. Each requirements is described and then further broken down in terms of how the requirement specifically affects the User, NAP, NTP, and NSP.

Privacy

Privacy needs to be a key attribute of the access and backbone domains. The existing narrowband world typically defines privacy as that provided by the PSTN through circuit switching and a unique physical connection between the central office and the home.

User Specifics   Traffic directed to one User premise network MUST NOT be present on another User premise network.

NAP Specifics A NAP MUST provide a unique and private connection between a User and an NSP but otherwise be uninvolved in implementing privacy policy. A NAP MUST NOT be prohibited from offering value-added services such as private user groups.

NSP Specifics The NSP needs flexibility in its ability to specify and implement a privacy policy. At a minimum this encompasses interconnect, premise to premise, and NSP to NSP.

Ability to Support Private Address Plans

A User may have business relationships with multiple NSPs. Each NSP may have its own address plan and the User network may also have a private address plan.

User Specifics Users with private local address plans MUST NOT be prohibited from connecting to an NSP with a separately administered address plan. In addition, switching service sessions between separately administered NSP domains MUST be seamless to the user.

NAP Specifics A NAP MUST seamlessly and transparently support sessions between separately administered user and NSP domains.

NSP Specifics An NSP MUST have the ability to serve Users with private address plans. Previous sessions of users with separately administered NSPs MUST not affect a session with a new NSP.

Service Selection

Service selection deals with the User's ability to seamlessly access an NSP.

User Specifics A User MUST have the ability to seamlessly select and connect to multiple NSPs. It should be noted that multiple simultaneous connections to NSPs can expose a potential security risk.

Regulatory Compliance

Access frequently, but not always, occurs across a regulated domain. In this scenario, a mechanism whereby a user can choose a destination must be provided. There is an expectation that the network interface at the ATU-R, including all communication to realize a connection to a service providers point-of-presence, must be able to be disclosed.

User Specifics   A user MUST be able to connect to an NSP in a standard way.

NAP Specifics   A regulated NAP must comply with local regulatory requirements. These are outside the scope of this document.

NSP Specifics   The NSP needs flexibility in its ability to specify and implement a privacy policy, at a minimum. This encompasses interconnect, premise-to-premise, and NSP to NSP.

Session Control

Given that a session between a User and an NSP access may involve the consumption of scarce resources on the NSP's part, and business and billing models may reflect this, the User should have a mechanism to signal intent to the NSP to initiate and terminate a session.

User Specifics   A User MUST have a method of explicitly setting up and tearing down a session. The User SHOULD be notified when a session is terminated by a NAP or NSP. This notification may be generated by mechanisms local to the premise.

NAP Specifics   A NAP MUST be able to detect if a contracted session service between a User and an NSP is being delivered and, where appropriate, perform resource recovery.

NSP Specifics   An NSP MUST know when a user is attempting access and have the ability to accept or reject the connection.

Session Negotiation and Configuration

An end-to-end connection between a user and an NSP may require negotiation and configuration. For example, temporary network addresses and server information may have to be exchanged. Such negotiation and configuration should be supported.

User Specifics   A user MUST have the ability to negotiate and configure session parameters with an NSP. This capability MUST be available on a session by session basis.

NSP Specifics   An NSP MUST be able to negotiate and configure session parameters with a user. This capability MUST be available on a session by session basis.

Simultaneous Access to Multiple NSPs

In some situations, it is expected that multiple users on a premise network will share a single ADSL link. An ADSL network should allow for multiple sessions over the ADSL link to the same or different NSP.

User Specifics   A user on a premise network MUST be able to access an NSP destination through the ADSL link regardless of whether one or more users on the same premise network are simultaneously accessing the same or another NSP destination. A single user MAY be able to access more than one NSP at a time. This is commonly known as multi-homing.

NAP Specifics   The NAP must be able to provide multiple connections to the same user domain.

NSP Specifics   The NSP must be able to terminate more than one connection from the same user.

Minimal Interworking

Maximizing throughput of intermediate systems requires that a minimum of massaging of the data and a minimum of frame/packet hops occur between the home domain and the service domain.

NAP Specifics   It is desirable that the service offered by the NAP be as transparent as possible so as not to be an impediment to services offered by the NSP.

Service Independence

The premise to POP protocol may vary over the different sessions carried by a NAP.

NAP Specifics The NAP MUST be transparent to the actual network protocol supported by the User and the NSP.

Service Tiering

The NAP, NTP, and NSP require the ability to differentiate the transport and access services they provide to the user. This would be in the form of bandwidth and transit guarantees within the backbone and access domains. Ideally this could be dynamically administered to provide different grades of service on a per-service or flow basis.

User Specifics The user SHOULD be able to administer their service quality.

NAP Specifics The NAP SHOULD be able to provide differentiated services.

NSP Specifics The NSP SHOULD be able to provide differentiated services.

Authentication

The mechanisms must be provided whereby the user, NAP, and NSP can both have a high degree of confidence in whom they are dealing. The existing narrowband world supports mutual authentication through the users accessing an NSP through a well-known network identifier (telephone number) which uniquely identifies the service accessed.

User Specifics A user SHOULD connect to an NSP through a well-known, unique network identifier.

NAP Specifics A NAP might or might not want to do authentication. Authentication in the NAP MUST NOT be artificially prohibited.

NSP Specifics An NSP MUST be provided with a mechanism to identify and authenticate a user. For session oriented access, this is typically done through a user name and password for always on authentication the authentication is coupled to the physical or logical connectivity (for example PVC versus copper).

NAP and NSP Accounting Needs

Flexible billing options are necessary at both the NAP and NSP. Both parties should be able to extract appropriate information to authoritatively bill their end-users with a minimum of customer service issues.

NAP Specifics A NAP MUST have the ability to bill a user or NSP for usage. The type of billing should be flexible (time billing, throughput billing, and so on).

NSP Specifics An NSP MUST have the ability to bill a user for usage. The type of billing should be flexible (time billing, throughput billing, and so on). An NSP SHOULD be able to reconcile billing from a NAP with the billing of the NSP's subscribers.

Scalability

A public ADSL network MUST have the ability to scale to a large number of end-users and MAY be required to scale to a suitably large number of service providers.

NAP Specifics A public ADSL network NAP MUST be able to support a large number of users and MAY need support a large number of NSPs with possibly multiple POPs.

NSP Specifics A public ADSL NSP point-of-presence MUST have the ability to logically or physically scale to support a large number of users.

Operational Simplicity

Provisioning at both initial service offering and also over the course of the network's lifetime should be minimal. In addition, an ADSL network should be simple to use. End-to-end connections should be able to be made in a straightforward manner. This serves the needs of both users and NSPs.

User Specifics   A user MUST NOT need special training and MUST NOT have to specially configure the end user system, such as the local PC. An end-user system MUST NOT have to be rebooted to connect to an NSP. The user should not have to be aware what that ADSL link protocol is layer 2.

NAP Specifics   The churn of users from one NSP to another MUST NOT require provisioning on the part of the NAP. The addition of new NSPs MUST require minimal provisioning on the part of the NAP.

NSP Specifics   The addition or deletion of users from an NSP's service MUST NOT require significant provisioning on the part of the NSP or significant coordination with the NAP.

Compatibility with Existing Resources

Many resources that will use a ADSL network already exist. The ADSL network should coexist and interoperate with these resources.

User Specifics   Any proposed architecture MUST coexist gracefully with existing PC protocol stacks and no special configurations should be necessary.

NAP Specifics   Any proposed architecture MUST be capable of utilizing existing backbone structures. An example an existing backbone structure is an ATM PVC network.

NSP Specifics   Any proposed architecture MUST coexist gracefully with existing NSP infrastructures, including the authorization, provisioning, network address assignment, and billing methods.

Evolution Path

The service set offering should not be constrained such that the first deployment maxes out capability. Note: The Network Migration group is producing standards documents that apply here.

Security

The Infrastructure of all Domains must be secured against the subversion of its function and unauthorized access to privileged information. Security is affected if the end-user system provides multiple simultaneous connections between NSPs. For example, if a user has an IP connection to an ISP and also an IP connection to a Corporate Network simultaneously, irrespective of the underlying transport protocol being used, there is a potential security breach. This is due to the fact that two different IP links are simultaneously established to the user's end system and there is no fail safe way to prevent the end system from being subverted into routing traffic from one open connection to the other. Although there are situations where multiple simultaneous connections are desirable, these must be weighed against the potential security risks they impose.

Related References

Many of the following references are examples of various ADSL architectures and concepts as presented at the ADSL Forum which served as the inspiration for this information.

- ADSL IP Concentration, GTE Labs contribution ADSL Forum 96–046, June 1996.

- ITU-T Telecommunication Recommendation I.432, B-ISDN User-Network Interface Physical Layer Specification Business Data Services Platform, 1996 DSL Technologies Summit, 27–28th March, 96

- ATM Forum, Packet Mode Report Working Text.

- Minutes of the ADSL Forum—*Services Network Architecture Group* (SNAG), Seattle, December 1996.

SUMMARY

In this author's opinion, the ADSL Forum is the most credible resource on ADSL technology. Consequently, the information provided freely through this forum is very valuable; so much so, I thought it best to relay it onto your courtesy of the Asymmetric Digital Subscriber Line Forum. The following is applicable to all information provided heretofore in this chapter:

CHAPTER 13

Network Devices

Introduction

Network equipment, be those repeaters, bridges, routers, brothers, switches, gateways, or whatever, can be analyzed with respect to the layers wherein they operate. Today many areas of functionality have become blurred because of such levels of high integration. In fact, I don't think I know of a network that is not integrated to some degree.

Not too long ago, about fifteen years prior to the time of this writing, some of the devices presented here did not exist; or if they did, it was in secluded technological implementations. In fact, the decade of the 1980s might well go down in history as the decade of design and development of internetworking devices. One would only need to glance at some of the trade journals and weeklies that began dominating the industry to realize that something was going on; the question is what?

So many specialized devices were designed and brought to market during the 1980s that a naming problem prevailed, and still does to some degree. This part of the book explores and explains the major networking devices that exist today. But before the exploration begins, consider an example.

In the 1970s the term gateway was used to mean what the term routers means today. Unfortunately depending on with whom you speak (or read), the term gateway might have an elusive meaning. Nevertheless, a chapter is devoted to each meaning in this part, and the explanation is clear so discernment of meaning is possible.

The decade of the 1990s might well go down in the record books as the decade of assimilation and then disintegration, respectively. The 1970s were literally individualistic in regard to computer vendors and their products as they were brought to market. The 1980s was the decade for development of integration devices and then the beginning of integration of various sorts of equipment. Early on in the 1990s was assimilation of diverse equipment with hopes of seamless operation of equipment; later in the 1990s many seamless operations became just that—unraveled at the seams! But wait, the next millennium promises the demise of integration intents. It could well be that the first years of the next millennium might reveal to the masses exactly how difficult and complex technology really is; and this author believes it might also reveal to the masses just how "dumb" technology is. What I mean here is this: Every computer, software program, or whatever is no greater than its maker is. It is fundamental ignorance to believe that artificial intelligence will surpass mans'. Computers and networks merely do things faster than man does, not in a superior way; they are the created, and the created is never greater than the creator is. Consider the remainder of this chapter to be the basis from which you begin to distill your thoughts about how to integrate this information into your environment, and hence troubleshoot your own network.

Device Perspective

Assimilation of disjointed facts into a meaningful level of knowledge is the beginning of intelligence. Here, information about different network devices and functionality with regard to transmission and processing is the focus. Consider Figure 13-1.

Figure 13-1
Transmission
methods and layers

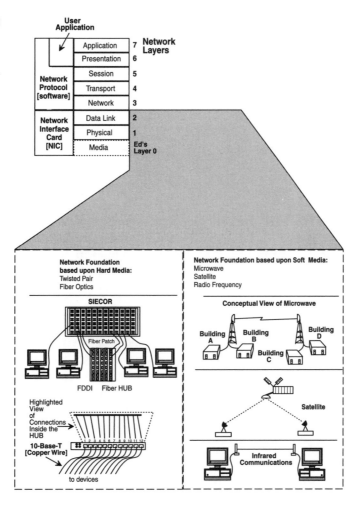

Figure 13-1 shows transmission methods and layers. Notice that hard and soft media methods are presented. Actually, the fiber, copper wire, satellite, microwave, and infrared transmission methods use the media and the physical layer. Technically, some operational function to the methods of transmission extends to the data link layer. This is an overview of these transmission methods; but more focus needs attention here, namely network devices that work at these layers.

Equipment Perspective

Different types of equipment are used in network integration. Most networks have the devices listed in this section and additional information is presented later in this chapter.

Repeaters

Repeaters are devices that operate at the physical layer based on the OSI model. They are generally considered the simplest network devices. They perform one basic function: They repeat a signal. The signal may be electrical or optical.

The basic purpose of a repeater is to extend the distance of something. It might be a network, devices connected together, or even processors—however the word repeater is seldom used to refer to the latter implementation.

Bridges

Bridges operate at layers one and two based on the OSI model. A bridge might be described in numerous ways. For example, some bridges operate with *like* lower layer protocols, whereas other can work with *unlike* lower layer protocols. They might also be described by their operations. Some bridges can only operate in a single physical environment, whereas others can operate in remote environments over switched or leased lines. Other ways of characterizing bridges can be how they perform their bridge functions. Some might perform source routing, whereas others might be capable of what is called *learning*.

Router

Almost no definition is needed here, but for the sake of clarity one is given. Routers route! This is the most profound statement in the book, but it is true. Routers can be characterized as to what and how they route.

First, it is best to note that routers operate at layer three based on the OSI model. This is significant when multi-protocol routers are explained. Routers route data from one location to another. This might be on another floor in a high rise office building, or it might be halfway across the United States.

One way of examining routers is by asking which upper layer protocol does it support? This is what routers do: They route upper layer network protocols. On the other hand, multi-protocol routers *route* multiple upper layer protocols. This does not mean they perform any protocol conversion; it merely means they route multiple protocols to the target location.

Brouter

The brouter is a hybrid device. It can perform bridge and routing functions. Many times the functionality of a brouter is vendor specific. Depending on the device, some can perform bridging and routing functions at the same time.

Servers

Many types of specialized servers are available today. Interestingly, I have had numerous conversations with individuals who referred to a router as a server. I suppose they have a point, in the broadest sense of the word; that is, routers do *serve*, the question is what?

Servers today come in many varieties. For example, there are file, print, terminal, and communication servers, to name a few. And to be honest, there are probably others on the market I am not aware of that fit a niche outside those listed here.

Generally, servers are devices that concentrate on performing a single function. For example, the file server is probably the easiest to understand at first glance. Most file servers perform the function of maintaining files and making them available for requesting parties on an as needed basis. The importance behind this idea is that it removes the redundancy of each participating individual having their own hard disk. It also serves another function of making files accessible to others that might need access to them if authority is granted.

Gateways

Gateways are the most complex devices in the network device category. Gateways perform protocol translation and operate at layer three and above based on the OSI model. Gateways can operate at all layers in a network, meaning they perform protocol conversion at all seven layers.

The basic purpose of gateways is to interconnect heterogeneous networks. They are required to do this or the functionality thereof. Networks that are not architecturally the same, or architecturally compatible, require protocol conversion at all or some layers. The only question remaining is, "Where is this going to be performed?"

Protocol Specific Devices

Some vendors who have proprietary standards require a specific device from themselves or a licensed manufacturer copy. For example, consider IBM's ESCON lower layer protocol. It is fiber based and uses highly specialized equipment. IBM sells repeaters for ESCON, and other reputable companies that IBM has agreed to license the technology to create such devices to do the same.

The same is true with devices that operate with upper layer protocols. For example, some gateways can be implemented that operate at layers three and above in a network. If so, this is done through software. Again, this depends on the vendor contingencies that might exist. One thing is for sure, at the time of this writing, many network devices are not plug-n-play.

What Functions Repeaters Perform

Repeaters are the simplest of networking devices. Their primary purpose is simply to regenerate a signal received from input and correct the signal to its original state for output. In short, they provide signal amplification and also re-timing required to connect the connected segments.

How Repeaters Are Implemented

LANs utilizing Ethernet as a lower layer protocol can use a variety of cabling types, for example, copper stranded twisted pair cabling, thicknet coaxial cable, thinnet coaxial cable, and even fiber optic cabling. By definition, thicknet coaxial cable is 75 ohm and generally RG−50, RG−58, or RG−59. Thinnet cable is 75 ohm and typically RG−6, RG6a, or RG−225. Many Ethernet implementations use what is considered thicknet coaxial cable for a network backbone.

Single Port Repeater

A single port repeater operates with actually two segments; one type has a signal taken from it to boost and pass to the next segment and the other type is a multi-port repeater. Figure 13-2 is an example of a physical plant with three departments: orders, parts, and shipping. Notice three repeaters are used to connect the different Ethernet based LANs in each department.

In Figure 13-2, the configuration is such that all hosts in any department can communicate with one another, because logically one network exists, rather than three physical networks. This type of repeater implementation is straightforward and connects one cable segment to another cable segment. However, a different type of repeater exists.

Figure 13-2
Repeater
implementation

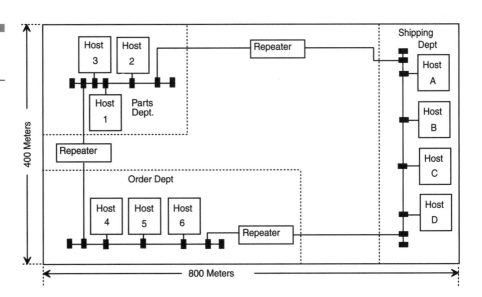

Multi-port Repeater

A multi-port repeater is as its name implies. It has one input and multiple outputs. Consider Figure 13-3.

Figure 13-3 is a good example of how a multi-port repeater can be implemented using two different methods of utilizing Ethernet technology. This is especially beneficial using multiple point-to-point connections. Figure 13-3 shows a 10-BASE-T connection to it through a media access unit. In turn this makes multiple connections to it possible through 10-BASE−2 (10 Mbps using baseband signaling with a maximum segment length of 200 meters).

Smart Repeaters

Smart repeaters can perform packet filtering. In reality, this is a hybrid type of device and is very similar to a bridge in functionality. This device operates by capturing packet(s) destined for another segment and then waiting to transmit the packet(s) until the network is not congested. Ironically, this type of repeater can have an inverse effect with the connecting segments by creating a higher level of collisions.

Optical Repeaters

Repeaters that *repeat* optic signals do the same as those that operate with electronic signals; they repeat the signal. IBM has a fiber-optic channel-extender link referred to as the model 3044. According to the system selection guide, it is used in environments to extend the distances of the traditional non-fiber media to a distance that fiber media can obtain.

Other vendors have repeaters that repeat optic signals over long distances; however, in the traditional sense copper stranded cabling fiber can operate without a repeater in many instances.

Conclusions

Repeaters are the simplest of all networking devices. They perform signal amplification and re-timing for the segments connected. Repeaters can be used with electrical and optical signals; however, they are more popular with electrical signals due to the nature of electrical signals.

Figure 13-3
Multi-port repeater

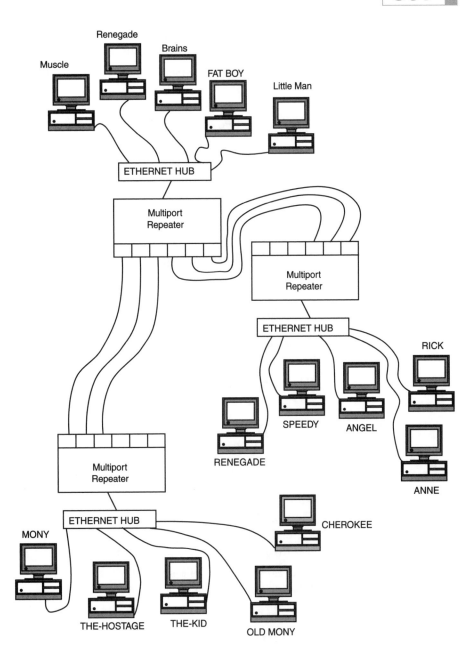

Single and multi-port repeaters are available. Single repeaters are used to connect two segments of cabling. Multi-port repeaters take a single segment and provide the ability for multiple segments to connect.

Smart repeaters are really hybrid devices and are not considered a repeater in the classical sense; unlike regular repeaters, they fit into devices known as bridges.

Bridge Details

Bridges operate at layers one and two based on the OSI model. They work with lower layer protocols. Bridges are more complex than repeaters in that they function with two layers of protocols.

Network Operation

Bridges can serve multiple functions in a network environment. Some functions bridges perform are vendor specific; however companies that sell bridges typically offer products that perform most basic functions. However, because of the diversity in what a bridge can do, vendors differ in their offerings. This almost sounds like a circular conversation, but there is hope! The point is all bridges I have worked with have certain commonalties, but some are capable of performing specialized functions.

Bridge Operation

As mentioned previously, bridges operate at the physical and data link layer. Figure 13-4 is an example of where this occurs.

Figure 13-4 is an example of two hosts and bridges connecting them together. Figure 13-5 is a detailed view of bridge functions.

Figure 13-5 shows two physical interfaces, one for host A and the other for host B. Notice one data link layer, because that is where bridging is performed.

Functional Advantages

Many real world scenarios have multiple LANs throughout an entity, be that a corporation, government agency, or otherwise. When this is the case, it is not uncommon for multiple higher level protocols to be implemented at higher levels in the networks. Because some upper layer protocols have

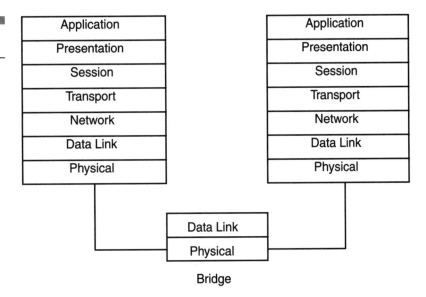

Figure 13-4
Bridge functionality

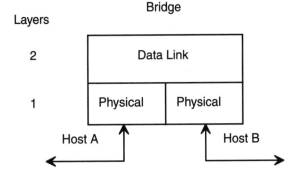

Figure 13-5
Detailed view of
bridge functions

limited capability with others, a bridge can be advantageous to use to connect multiple networks assuming they use the same lower layer protocol. Another advantage of bridges is, in certain situations, they might be a better choice than a router. Bridges are also relatively cheaper and easier to install. Other advantages of bridges include

■ Many bridges can connect networks of different speeds.

■ They are easily managed.

■ Many can be adapted to an environment as it grows.

In fairness bridges have some disadvantages. Common ones include

■ Bridges can be installed in such a way physically that, in reality, the net result is one logical network; consequently, sometimes troubleshooting can be difficult when problems arise.

■ In some implementations, like a cascaded topology, a problem can occur with fast protocols because of delay factors.

■ Bridges are transparent to end systems. By this fact and potential delays encountered relative to the number of bridges, the actual limit could be indirectly imposed on the number of bridges utilized.

■ The potential exists that bridges could impede use of some applications over the Internet. An example of this scenario could be multiple copies of an application operating and unfortunately using the same naming or addressing scheme.

Practically speaking, bridges are good network devices when used for the right need.

Bridge Operation

The three basic functions of bridges are the focus of this section. Bridges can perform forwarding, filtering, and learning functions. Forwarding is passing a frame towards its ultimate destination. Filtering operates by discarding frames where their destination is not. Learning is the function a bridge performs when it does not receive a positive response in return for comparing a frame to its host's table. The following figures explain these functions.

Forwarding

Forwarding is best explained by examining Figure 13-6.

Here are two LANs: A and B. LAN A has SPEEDY, LITTLEMAN, THE-KID, MONY, and HOLLYWOOD connected. They are known on the LAN as A1, A2, A3, and so forth. A bridge connects both LANs. LAN B has multiple systems connected to it; two of which are B4 and B5. Notice the highlighted table next to the bridge used to *know* which hosts are located on which LAN. In the bridge's table, host 5 is shown to be on LAN B. The bridge intercepts the frame, because it knows its target is on LAN B. The packet is still broadcast on LAN A as well, but it is *spent* time wise in a matter of fractions of a second, therefore it does not stay on LAN A.

Figure 13-6
Forwarding frames
and bridges

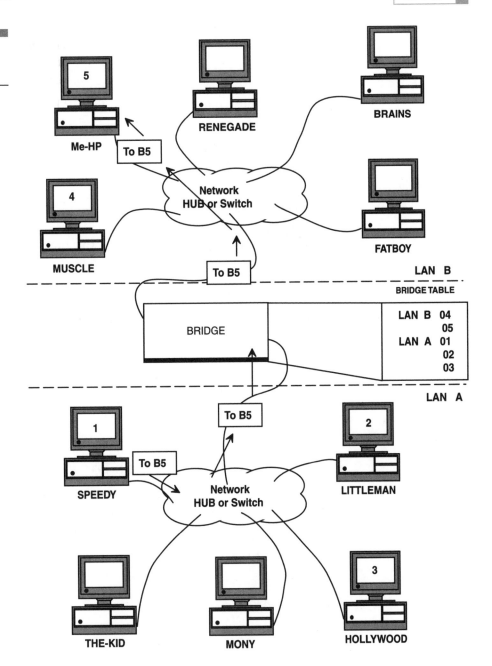

Filtering

Figure 13-7 consist of two LANs and a bridge connecting them.

Figure 13-7 is an example of the filtering function of a bridge. Notice the frame-leaving host 1 destined for host 3 on LAN A. The frame is captured by the bridge and compared against the bridge's table. After the bridge performs its compare function, it discards the frame. Host 3 receives the frame destined for it.

Learning

Bridges are said to learn about a host (be that a computer or another device) when a frame is received by a bridge and the bridge does not have the address of that device in its table. When this happens, the bridge dynamically updates its table and then *knows* about this device; therefore the bridge is considered to have learned of a device. Consider Figure 13-8.

In Figure 13-8, there are two LANs and a bridge connecting them together. Assume host 3 has recently been added to the LAN. Now assume host 3 wants to communicate with host 5 on the other LAN. The bridge knew the location of host 5 and now knows the location of host 3, because it *learned* both its host and network address. Now, any of the hosts on LAN 2 can communicate with any Hosts LAN 1.

Examination of Bridges by Protocol

Bridges can also be characterized by protocol. This is sensible, because they work with lower layer protocols. The simplest approach to understanding how bridges work with different protocols is focusing on the ways a bridge operates with these protocols.

Like Protocols

Different vendors support varying protocols with their bridges. Some of the popular ones include Ethernet and Token Ring.

Ethernet   ETHERNET is a popular lower layer protocol and is widely used throughout the marketplace. It is common for LANs to be created in departments, and then over time realization of multiple disparate LANs is

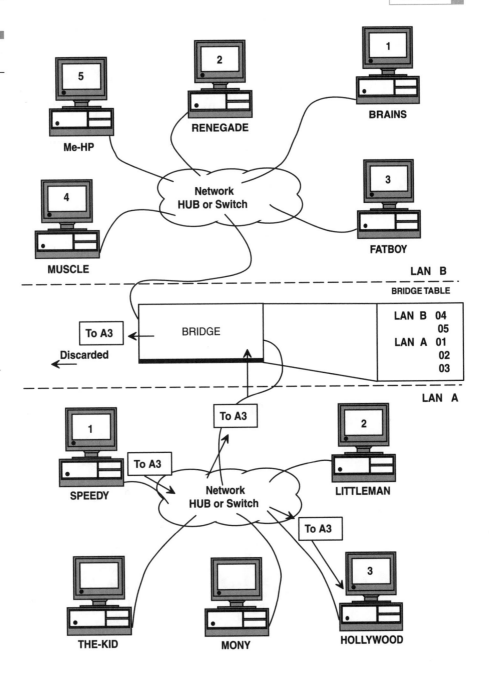

apparent. Multiple LANs can be connected together by bridges thereby creating one logical network, while still permitting independence of departments. Consider Figure 13-9.

Figure 13-8
Bridge leaning

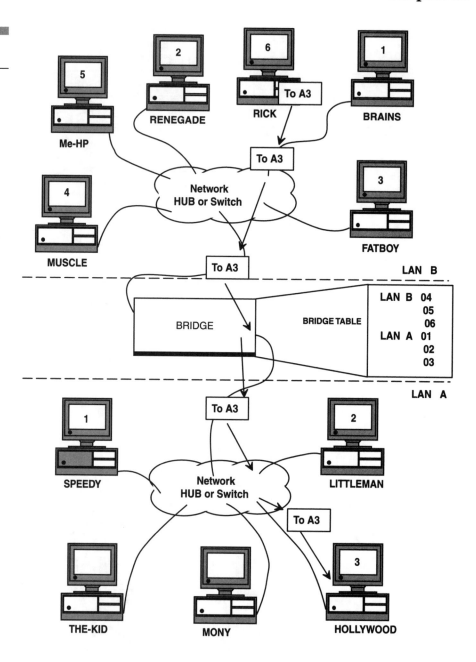

Figure 13-9 shows three departments that perform distinctly different functions. But, these departments need to share files for purposes of creating documents, informing potential customers of products soon to be released, and general communication.

Figure 13-9
ETHERNET bridge

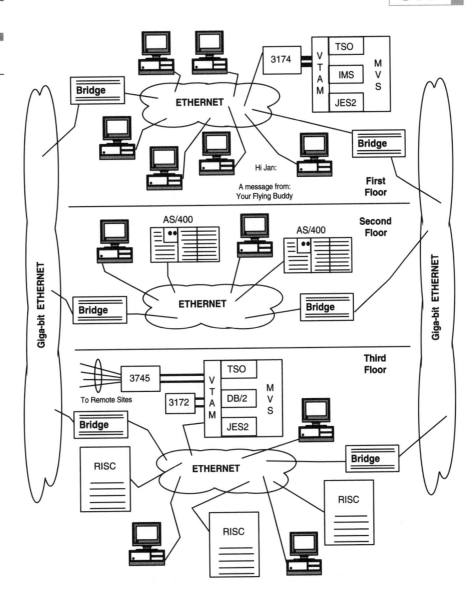

Token Ring   Token ring is another popular lower layer protocol. Like Ethernet multiple upper layer protocols can operate atop of it. Figure 13-10 is an example of how multiple token rings can be connected, thus making a single logical network.

Notice in Figure 13-10 that both 4 and 16 Mbps token ring speeds are used. Many popular bridge vendors offer solutions that fit such a scenario.

Figure 13-10
Token ring bridging

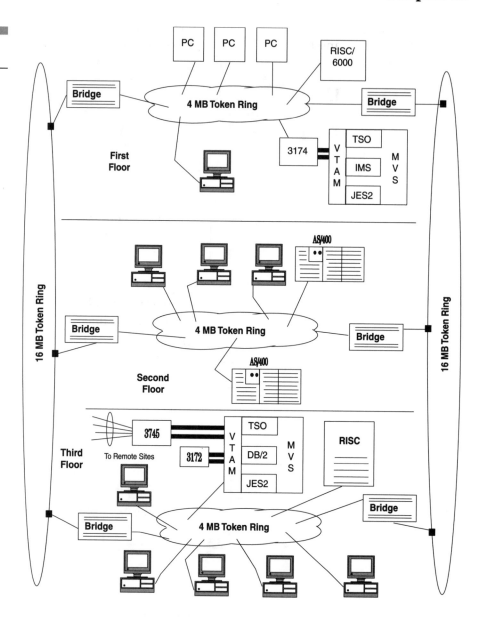

Figure 13-10
Token ring bridging

Figure 13-10 shows three floors of a corporation. Each floor is a different department. The first floor is the collections department, the second is the billing department, and the third is the central data center for this corporation. Each floor has considerable flexibility. Token ring is considered a self-healing technology, and therefore hosts can be inserted and removed from the network at will. Likewise any given floor can be removed from the

16 Mb per/sec corporate backbones. This scenario provides independence and flexibility and characteristically is very dynamic.

Unlike Protocols

Bridges can also perform lower layer protocol conversion. Many reputable vendors have such devices. In fact, these devices have become a commodity in a comparatively short amount of time.

Ethernet-to-Token Ring   An Ethernet to token ring bridge operates bi-directionally. Users on an Ethernet network can communicate with users on a token ring network and vice versa. Figure 13-11 is an example of such an environment.

Figure 13-11 shows three Ethernet based LANs, a 16 Mb token ring backbone, a 4 Mb token ring LAN with multiple hosts, and two large SNA environments connected to another 16 Mb token ring. This configuration makes it possible for interoperability among all hosts. With the exception that some additional components such as software and possible configuration changes might be required.

Some bridges support protocols beyond those shown here. However, most bridge vendors support these protocols. These sample implementations are examples of real installations.

Analysis of Bridge Location

Another way bridges can be examined is with respect to their support for local and remote operations. Some examples of various bridge implementations are presented here.

Local Bridging

Bridges are good devices to use in this type of environment as a general rule. They permit segmentation and connectivity of LANs at the same time. Consider Figure 13-12.

Figure 13-12 shows engineering, marketing, and documentation departments. They each have a LAN and each is connected through a bridge: one between engineering and marketing and the other between marketing and documentation. A two-fold benefit is realized.

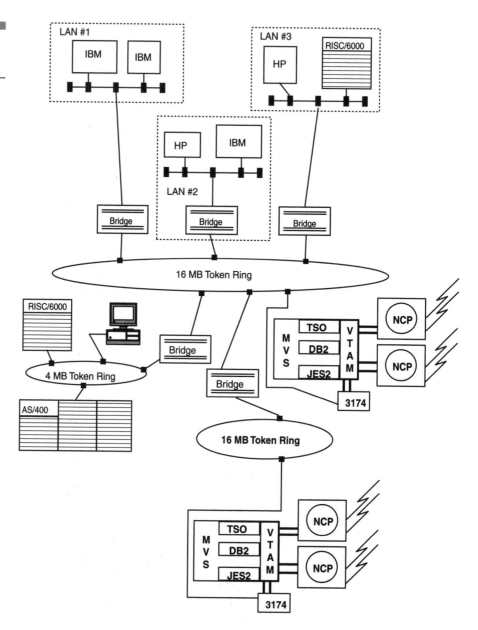

First, all three departments can communicate with any hosts in any of the other departments, thus enterprise wide connectivity is achieved. Second, isolation of departmental computing can be maintained on each network LAN because of the way bridges operate. (This aspect of bridges is explained shortly.) Third, a degree of load balancing can be realized as a result of this scenario.

Figure 13-12
Local bridging

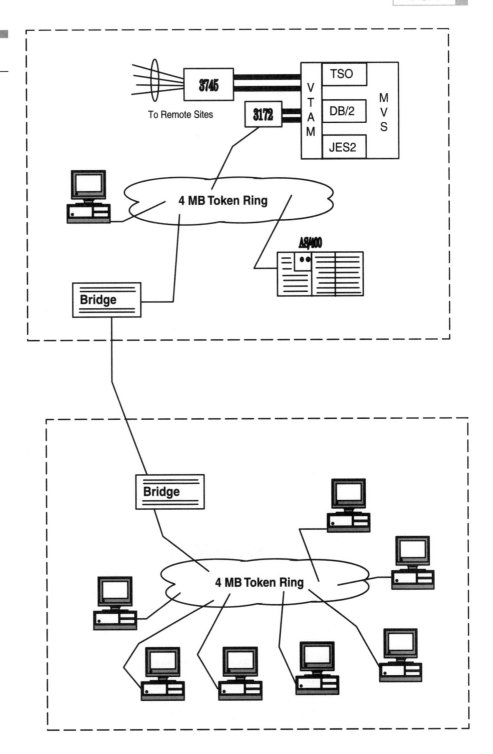

Remote Bridging

Remote bridging does as its name implies; that is, it bridges geographically remote networks. Consider Figure 13-13.

Figure 13-13 shows a site where a remote bridge implementation occurs. The need exists for both LANs to communicate. Now with the advent of remote Ethernet bridging, these LANs can communicate. The connectivity between the two sites could be a switched or a leased line with speeds of generally 56 Kbytes per/sec or higher. However, if a switched line is used, this implies bandwidth on demand and consequently some requirements for bridging this type of environment exist. The result is that users on both networks view all hosts as located on one LAN.

Both local and remote bridging can be performed with token ring networks. Bridges supporting the respective protocols are required. Depending on the vendor offering, other network protocols might be supported as well.

Some vendors offer redundant line support for remote bridges. Others offer data compression on the fly; depending on the vendor, some algorithms can achieve approximately a 4:1 ratio. This is effective utilization of bandwidth. Some vendors also offer network management support for their devices. These and other aspects of a bridge should be discussed with a vendor whose forte is bridges.

Author's Comment

Remote bridging is similar to other aspects of internetworking technology. One question always remains: "Where is the bottleneck?" I am not implying that remote Ethernet, token ring, or other protocol bridging will result in a bottleneck; however, I do intend to raise the question because in data communications a bottleneck always exists. The question is where and to what degree. It might or might not have anything to do with bridging, routing, or gateways; but it, nevertheless, is present.

Source Routing & Transparent Bridges

Attention is required to the way bridges obtain routing information. This is a misnomer in a sense. Bridges do not route in the sense a router does, but they do have to pass frames from a source towards their destination point, wherever that might be. Source routing needs explanation.

Figure 13-13
Remote bridging

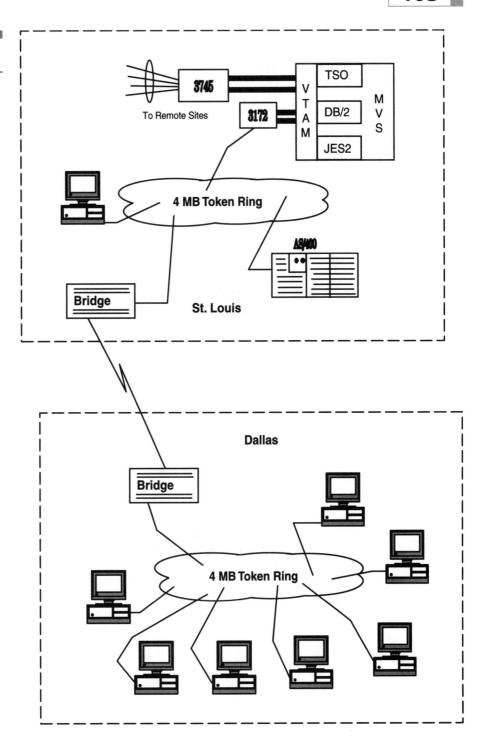

Source Routing   Source routing is an IBM function. It is a method whereby the route to the destination is determined before data leaves the originating point. Sometimes this function is called SRB, short for *Source Route Bridging*. This type of routing is dominant among IBM token ring networks.

Frame Contents   Understanding source routing is easily achieved by understanding the contents of the IBM token ring frame contents.

Figure 13-14 shows the structure and contents of the MAC frame.

Figure 13-14 shows the IBM token ring frame, the highlights of the routing control field, and the highlights at bit level of the routing control field.

This frame itself differs from the IEEE 802.5 frame, in that the token ring frame has a routing information field. Here we explore that field and its contents.

Segment Numbers

The first component in the routing information field is the routing control subfield. It contains information that is used in the routing function and is explained in greater detail shortly. Segment number subfields follow the routing control subfield.

Each segment number reflects two pieces of information. Segment numbers are comprised of a ring number and a bridge number. Each ring is a LAN, and each LAN has a number associated with each ring. Each bridge used is assigned a number. The combination of the ring and bridge number creates a segment number. If multiple rings are connected through bridges, then multiple segment subfields exists as shown in Figure 13-14.

Figure 13-14
IBM token ring frame

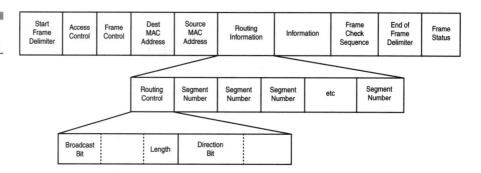

Routing Control Subfield

The routing control subfield has two significant pieces of information: the broadcast bit and the direction bit. The broadcast bit indicates what type of frame it is; that is, a broadcast or non-broadcast frame. The direction bit indicates which way the frame is going. It is either en route from original source to destination or vice versa. This is important because the setting of this bit dictates how the segment number bits are interpreted.

Transparent Bridges

The working definition of transparent bridges is they learn those hosts reachable according to data link, by observing frames as they pass. Another helpful term for this type of bridge is that it is considered a spanning tree bridge.

This type of bridge forwards frames as discussed previously in this chapter. It also maintains and updates a table of MAC addresses of the hosts, which are reachable across the link used to attach multiple rings. Another name sometimes given to this type of bridge is a learning bridge.

A transparent bridge implementation has already been used in an earlier figure, but for convenience of the reader it is also here in Figure 13-15.

Source Routing Theory of Operation

Now that the previous information has been covered, an explanation about how IBM source routing operates is provided. Two types of frames can exist in an IBM token ring network: non-broadcast and broadcast.

Non-broadcast Frame

The term non-broadcast is virtually the same as multicast. If there is a difference, it is minimal. What is important to know is how non-broadcast frames are handled in a multi-ring environment. Consider Figure 13-16.

A non-broadcast frame reveals the significance of the segment numbers previously discussed. Assume host A on ring 1 is the source host and the

Figure 13-15
Conceptual view of a
transparent bridge

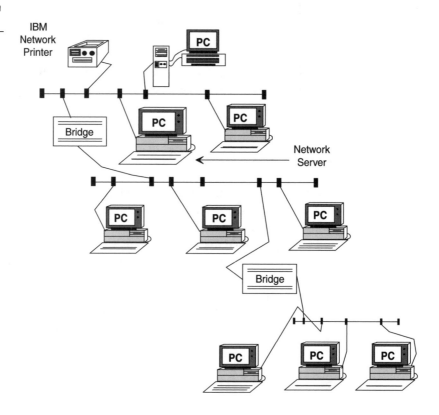

destination host is host G on ring 2. Notice bridge X connects ring 1 and 2 directly. In this case, bridge X recognizes its bridge number and ring number. The bridge simply copies the frame from ring 1 onto ring 2. At the same time, bridge Z receives the same frame. It examines its bridge number and its ring number; no match is made, so the frame is discarded.

Figure 13-16
Non-broadcast
operation

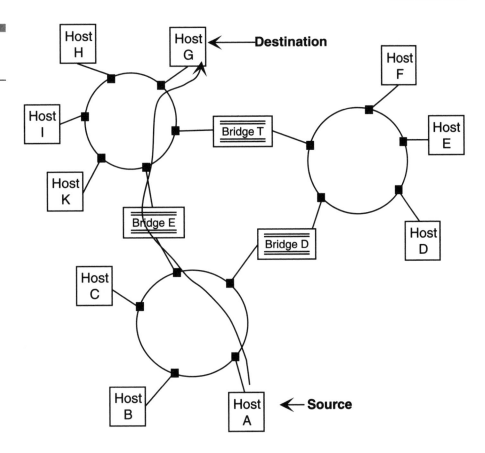

Broadcast Frames

Source routing is implemented by two types of MAC addresses through broadcast frames, according to IBM. One type of MAC frame contains a certain value that is received by all hosts on the ring on which that host exists. This frame is a frame containing a special Hex value. Figure 13-17 illustrates this concept.

Figure 13-17 illustrates the frame with the box with H6 inside as received by all hosts on the ring where it originated. The H6 indicates its destination. However, notice two rings exist connected by a bridge. Notice the H6 frame is not repeated onto ring #2.

The other type of MAC frame contains an address that is considered a broadcast address. It has a different Hex value than the example shown in Figure 13-14. The broadcast frame is sent to all hosts, all rings, and hence all bridges connecting them. Figure 13-18 shows this environment.

Figure 13-17

Conceptual view of a frame contained on one ring

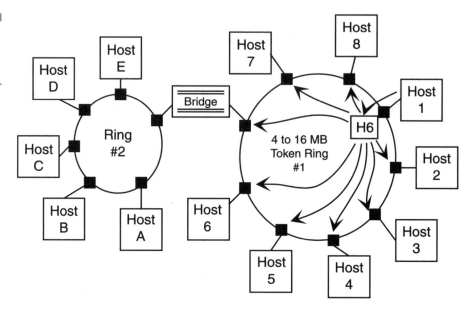

Assume host 8 on ring B sends a broadcast frame. All hosts, each ring, and consequently each bridge receive it. Operationally it works like this: Host 8 sends the frame. Bridge D copies the frame, and adds its bridge number and the number associated with ring C. At the same time the frame reaches bridge T. Bridge T copies the frame, and adds its bridge number along with the number for ring A. The frame then passes to bridge E where bridge E copies it, and adds its bridge number and ring C's number. The process is complete, but one question remains: "Why do this?"

When many hosts exists, isolation of networks needs to be achieved, but total connectivity between LANs is required. Figure 13-18 is an example of how to do this. It provides multiple paths to any given ring; and, the more rings the more reason to have redundancies in paths.

Discovering Routes

The process of discovering routes is twofold. First, assume a source wants to communicate with a destination host. On the first attempt, the source host attempts to send a frame on the ring it (the source host) is located on. If no positive response is encountered then another process is used.

A source host sends a route discovery frame to a destination host to which the source knows its address; the question is, how to get it there. Assume

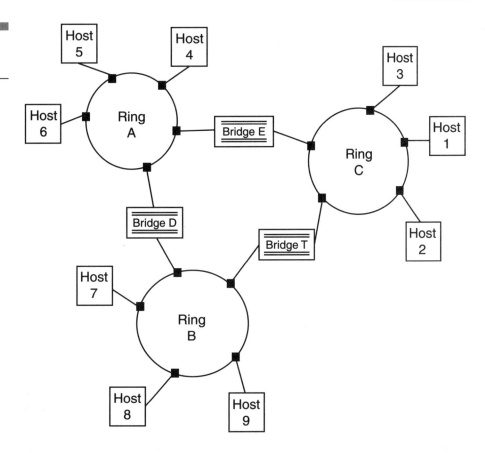

multiple rings are attached to the ring where the source host is located. Each bridge attaching these rings copies the frame from the source, inserts its segment information, and then passes the frame on. After the frames have reached all connected rings and bridges, they begin returning to the source host. If the destination host is located, the bridge inserts routing information into the original route discovery frame and sends it back to the source. Multiple frames might return to the source. When this happens, the source determines the route for additional frames to be sent to the destination host.

Concluding Thoughts on Bridges

Bridges operate at the lower two layers based on the OSI model. They can serve a variety of functions. For example, bridges can be used to merge multiple LANs into one *virtual* network. Another strength of bridges is that they can perform protocol conversion on LANs at the lower two layers. Bridges can convert Ethernet to token ring and vice versa. Some vendors offer bridges that support FDDI bridging.

Transparent bridges perform three basic functions: forwarding, filtering, and learning. This simply means that a transparent bridge forwards frames it receives. It filters out those frames that are not destined for another ring to which it is attached. It learns of hosts throughout its network(s) and stores this information in tables that it in turn uses for routing purposes.

Source routing is a function of another type of bridge. IBM uses source routing and in the MAC frame, a field exists for insertion of routing information. This type of bridge operates by including the destination and the source addresses into the frame. Other functions that source routing bridges perform are different types of frame broadcasting.

Bridges can be used to effectively manage sites where multiple token ring networks exist and where the need for redundancy also exists. Because token ring technology is considered self healing, it is easy to remove and add hosts and devices to these networks.

Bridges also offer advantages to Ethernet based LANs, particularly where multiple Ethernet LANs are geographically dispersed. Remote bridges can create a virtual LAN environment where users *think* they are all attached to the same network in the same physical location.

Implementing bridges remotely should be tempered and evaluated in light of the load in respective sites, the bandwidth available through the link, and other operational considerations.

Many well known vendors have good products to achieve a desired result.

Router Technology

Routers operate at layer three based on the OSI model. Routers route upper layer protocols. They do not perform protocol conversion, assuming they are routers in the classical sense. Routers, like bridges can be examined from different angles. This chapter explores those angles.

Routers

An explanation is in order concerning the term router. This is especially true for those who might be new to networking devices. Sometimes different groups and individuals use terms in loose ways and confusion can be the result.

The routing function can be defined as getting data from point A to point B, wherever that might be. This concept can be traced back to the 1970s when networking began to sprout. Those working in the Internet community were involved with networks that were sometimes in different cities. At any rate, multiple networks existed, and the desire arose to connect to other networks and connect networks together.

As an outgrowth of this desire, devices began to be used to perform this function. At the time, they were generally referred to as gateways. Yes, gateways. An obvious question is why? According to the American Heritage Dictionary, a gateway is defined as: "1. An opening, as in a wall or fence, that might be closed by a gate. 2. A means of access." I believe the informal consensus at the time probably meant the latter part of the definition provided here.

Taking a number of points into consideration, it is understandable why devices that performed a routing function were called gateways. And, unfortunately, the confusion of this terminology still exists today. Taking the definition of gateway as a means of access to explain the function of a device that permitted connectivity of networks *was* reasonable. They did in fact provide such a function. And beyond this, these devices routed information to various networks and locations. With this in mind, coupled with the mindset of the day during the 1970s, it is plausible for the term gateway to be used, but technology changes.

Today an entire industry exists around network devices. In fact a part of this book is devoted to explaining some of these devices. I do not believe that in the 1970s most technically oriented individuals could have envisioned the explosive technological growth of the 1980s of such specialized devices. It might have been conceivable, but not to a detailed level that hindsight provides today. Hence, the dilemma exists.

The term routers and gateways are constantly used in various mediums, and at best the meaning is skewed. For the record, routers route; period. They might perform other peripheral function, but the focus of routers is to simply route data. Gateways, on the hand, perform protocol conversion between heterogeneous networks at layer three and above at a minimum, and can perform protocol conversion at all seven layers, between two networks. Gateways perform protocol conversion, routers do not. Interestingly, some gateways can perform routing functions because of their architectural nature, but they do not necessarily have to. In fact this is a vendor specific offering.

Discussion of internetworking topics with different people can result in confusion if clarification of terms is not agreed on. Many who have worked for years with TCP/IP, UNIX, and Internet related issues still use the term gateway to convey the function of a router. I have often wondered what term they use to name that device used to integrate heterogeneous networks. It would seem a catch−22 exists.

Another comment about routers and terminology is valuable. Different types of routers exist and are explained in this chapter, and not all routers perform the same functions. Many functions are vendor specific. There are a number of prominent router vendors on the market today that sell good equipment. The point is to understand your needs and obtain the appropriate fit so those needs are met.

How Routers Work

Multiple types of routers exist and perform different functions. Some of the names given to router functions tend to overlap in some instances to other identified functions. Routers can be explained by geographic distance they support, that is, local or remote. They can also be explained by the upper layer protocols supported and by their interface support.

Routers operate based on tables of possible networks and routes. These tables are utilized to indicate the path to a given network. Router tables do not locate device addresses such as some types of bridges do. Functionally, routers exploit the information available to them to determine the most expedient route. Another unique aspect of routers is that they receive data addressed to them by hosts or other routers. Route determination is somewhat contingent on the upper layer protocol. For example, TCP/IP uses routing algorithms that differ from SNA based networks. In this respect, routers are protocol dependent. Some routers are simple and function with one protocol, however other types of routers can manipulate multiple protocols, hence their name, multi-protocol routers.

The remainder of this chapter explores various aspects of routers and the specifics of how they operate in certain environments. And similar to bridges, routers have become a basic commodity in internetworking technology.

Dependency of Routers

Routers are protocol dependent. They operate at network layer three based on the OSI model. Consider Figure 13-19.

Figure 13-19 is an example of two hosts shown by layers and where a router operates between them.

As the figure shows, the physical and data link layers are also part of the router, and therefore these aspects must be taken into consideration.

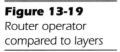
Figure 13-19
Router operator
compared to layers

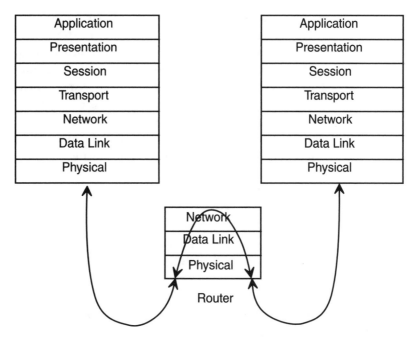

Some large routers (in the sense of what they support) offer a wider variety of physical layer interface support. More than a few reputable router vendors offer fine products that support such interfaces as the following:

RS−232	V.35
AUI	X.21
HISSI	RS−449
Parallel	

Additionally, lower layer protocols must be supported as well. These too are contingent on the vendor and the router. Some examples of popular protocols supported include

ETHERNET	Token ring
SONET	xDSL
ATM	X.25

The network layer is where routing occurs. If you have read other chapters in this book, particularly those in the latter half, you are aware that upper layer network protocols operate differently. For example, the way TCP/IP performs routing is different from the way SNA or APPN performs routing. Consequently, these upper layer protocols drive the router decision to a certain degree. This is because multi-protocol routers exists and support routing to multiple upper layer protocols.

When routing is implemented it brings together two or more networks. The consequence of this from the user standpoint is that it is transparent except for possible time zone inconveniences, but those issues are easily overcome. In essence, the use of routers provide an end-to-end solution. The remainder of the chapter focuses on some examples of different upper layer protocol routing and also aspects of routing in general.

How Routers Work

Routers can be implemented locally or used in an environment where multiple networks exist in different geographic locations and need the ability to exchange data.

Local Implementation   Figure 13-20 is an example of a scenario where routers are used within the same physical facility.

Figure 13-20 shows a single physical site with three distinct Ethernet LANs. Notice a router is the common denominator of them. The result of this configuration is that any of the LANs can communicate directly with any hosts shown through the Internet protocol. Notice all LAN hosts have TCP/IP as their upper layer protocol. By removing the router, connectivity between all three LANs could not be achieved or other means would have to be implemented to achieve the same results.

This particular implementation is straightforward, flexible, and relatively inexpensive. Additionally, the router fits in to the management method that is common among TCP/IP networks.

This example can take on many variations because of the flexibility with routers. In a sense, they can be customized to meet site specific needs fairly easily. The primary reason for this is because routers maintain routing tables within them that can be customized to be a diversity of situations.

Metropolitan Implementation

The notion of a metropolitan implementation might not be popular, but it is frequently a solution that meets many needs. Consider Figure 13-21.

Figure 13-20
Local router
implementation

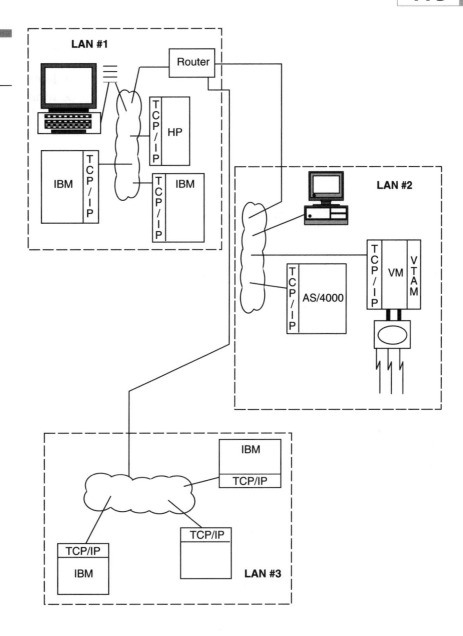

Figure 13-21 shows headquarters in Dallas where master files, statements, accounts receivable, and other operational functions are performed. However, because the agency prospered, it has three satellite offices. Each satellite office is within 35 miles from the headquarters in Dallas.

Figure 13-21
Metropolitan
implementation

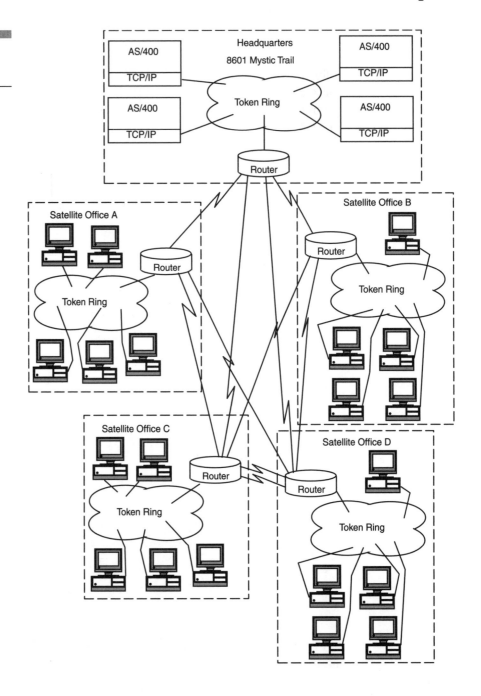

Because data needs to be sent to and from the satellite offices and headquarters, this router solution meets the needs. In fact, the router in the Dallas office can route data from Tulsa to the Fort Worth office, if configured appropriately.

Like the example of a local implementation of a router, this metropolitan implementation of a router is popular, because the link between all sites is not considered long distance and therefore a significant saving is the result.

Remote Continental U.S. Routing

Remote routing is a popular solution for many corporations that are geographically dispersed and in different time zones. Figure 13-22 is an example of this idea.

Figure 13-22 shows facilities in Chicago, Memphis, Dallas, and San Francisco. Each site differs in function and to some degree in equipment type. But through the use of routers, the site in San Francisco can send data to Memphis or any of the sites connected in this virtual network through the router solution.

International Routing

International routing is similar, in theory, to routing multiple sites in the United States. However, time considerations need attention, and understanding the type of work to be done between all connected sites. It is also important to know the peak traffic times in all locations and correlate them; this helps in performance tuning. Consider Figure 13-23.

The significance of the international scenario versus the scenario in the local, metropolitan, or even the continental United States is the issue of time zone differences. Merely coordinating a meeting time for staff representing each site is difficult because of the time difference.

Another reason for routing is a business reason. If a company performs significant amounts of processing, the best place to do this is where it is most cost effective while still achieving the original goals. With distributed processing and exploitation of network devices such as routers, this can be accomplished.

Figure 13-22
Conceptual view of
remote routing

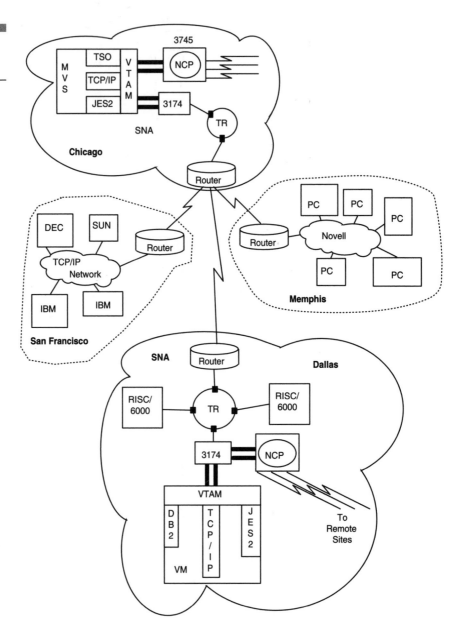

Routing Types

Multiple methods are used in routing. Technically, routing schemes can be
categorically defined. Different vendor network protocols tend to route differently, but some common threads among the different protocols remain.

Figure 13-23
International routing

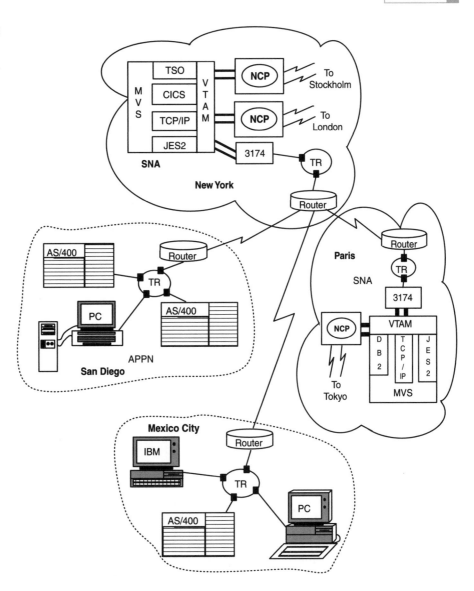

Central Routing

Central based routing is a scenario where a central repository of routing information is maintained. Conceptually, this appears as shown in Figure 13-24.

Figure 13-24
Conceptual view of a
centralized routing
node

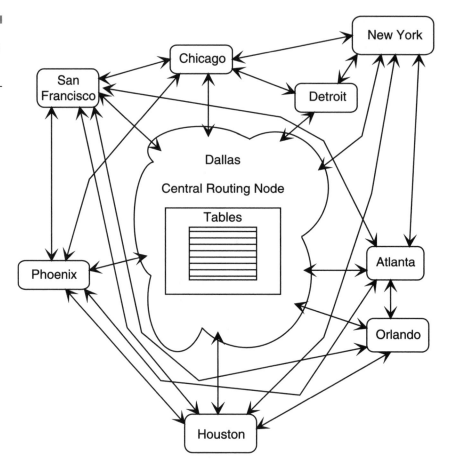

Figure 13-24 shows multiple locations connected in a myriad of combinations. Moving data from one location to another can be accomplished through multiple routes. However, the centralized routing node in Dallas maintains the routing tables.

Here each router informs the centralized node of the potential routing of a local environment. This information is arranged into tables and distributed to each router participating within the network, and the central routing node determines the route capabilities.

Non-centralized Routing

Non-centralized routing is as its name implies. The routing algorithm is not located in a central routing node. Figure 13-25 is a conceptual view of this.

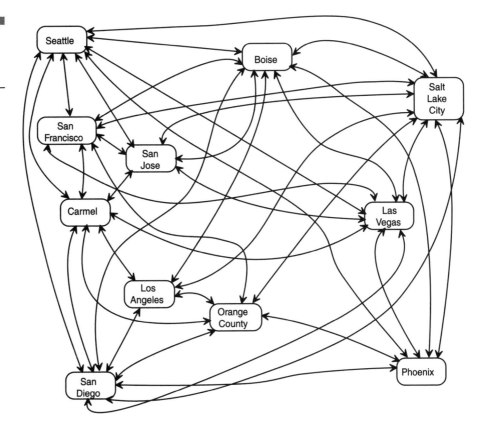

Figure 13-25 is interesting to say the least! However, it does convey the notion of non-centralized routing. In this environment, each router informs its *neighbor* of valid routes. The significant point of the figure is that each router determines the route as the packet arrives. Also, this type of implementation is constantly dynamic as changes are made to individual routes. Each time a change is made updates occur.

Static

This type of routing is where tables and routes are made through network management functions. By definition this means it must be performed when the network is non-operational from a user perspective. A simple way to explain this is that no changes are performed while the network is operational. This means that the routes are therefore *fixed*. Consider Figure 13-26.

Figure 13-26
Conceptual view of
static routing

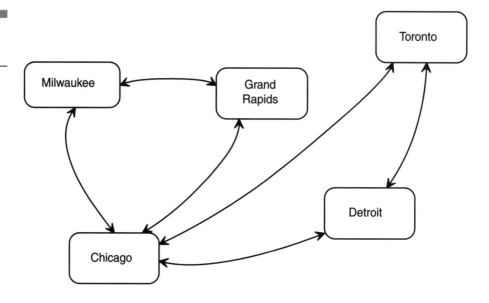

Interpretation of the notion of static routing is easy when considering Figure 13-26. As the lines draw between the cities indicate, a routing path is available. Notice paths *not* available. It is not possible to route directly to Toronto from Grand Rapids without going through Chicago, and this implies that that a routing table for this configuration is predetermined. Also, routing from Detroit to Grand Rapids is not possible without going through Chicago.

This example can be changed after the network is taken offline, but while the network is operational, no changes can be made. Hence, it derives its name, static routing.

These are examples of routing technology. Other methods of routing are possible. Some of these ways are protocol dependent. To provide an example, two different protocols are shown in light of their routing schemes.

SNA Routing

To a considerable degree, routing in SNA is performed on the Front End (the communications controller). The *Network Control Program* (NCP) inside has the routes defined and utilizes this software to exploit the hardware and gear involved in the routing process. Consider Figure 13-27.

Figure 13-27 is an example of pre-defined routes. Each city, Boise, Orange County, Chicago, and Houston have their hosts configured to route data through the indicated connections. For example, notice no direct con-

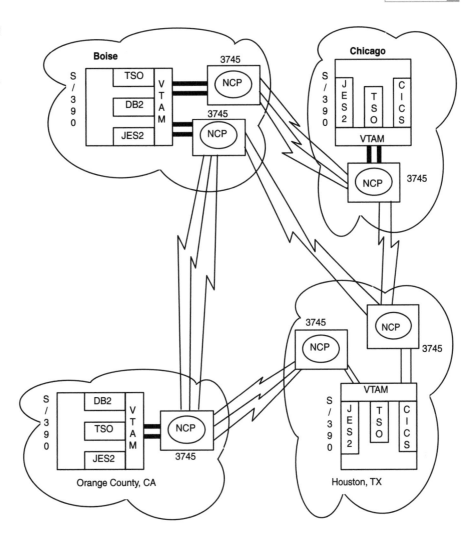

Figure 13-27
Conceptual view of
SNA routing

nection exist between Chicago and Orange County. Does this mean they cannot pass data? Not necessarily, because Boise and Houston are connected to both Chicago and Orange County, they could be configured to route data between those to destinations as well as the ones to which they are physically attached.

In this example, line speed, data compression, type of line (dedicated or switched) and other data communication issues are relatively unimportant. The point in this example is that even though a physical connection might or might not exist directly between two entities does not mean routing to them cannot be achieved. This is a matter of software and obviously some physical route must exist, but beyond this it is a matter of configuration.

TCP/IP Routing

Routing in TCP/IP is performed by IP as was explained in the chapter dedicated to TCP/IP protocol. Figure 13-28 is an example of TCP/IP networks and routers connecting them.

Figure 13-28 show TCP/IP networks in Columbus, Pittsburgh, Norfolk, and Nashville. These locations are connected through routers. Notice all routers have a physical link with one another. Notice also that each LAN host has the same name and could be given the same address. What differentiates them is the fact that they are located on different networks, therefore no naming or addressing conflicts.

In this example, it is the *Internet Protocol* (IP) software in conjunction with one of the routing protocols that makes routing possible. The routing

Figure 13-28

Conceptual view of TCP/IP routing

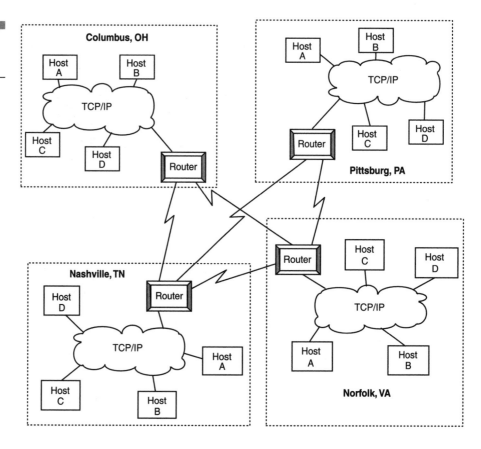

protocols could be either *Router Information Protocol* (RIP), *Open Shortest Path First* (OSPF), or others. Obviously, a routing type of device is required, but nevertheless it is the combination of IP and the routing protocol that makes this process happen.

Maintaining routing tables is a separate issue here. This could be done through the /etc/networks and /etc/hosts files or the *Domain Name System* (DNS). Most likely it is the latter because of the power behind how it operates.

These examples of how different network protocols perform routing is enough to show that in a heterogeneous networking environment routing is not a simple matter. Consider the routing issues involved in the Internet!

Demand Routing

This topic has moved into the forefront of routing in the past few years. The idea of bandwidth on demand routing is as its name implies; in plain English that means the router uses the line when it needs it and does not keep it *dedicated*. Consider the following examples showing the three phases of this routing.

Figure 13-29 shows two multi-vendor networks; one in Monterey and the other in Birmingham with multiple hosts attached to each. It also indicates that no link is established between the two locations. This is important because it means no dedicated line exists and that means some degree of money is involved—typically savings.

Figure 13-30 on the other hand shows a different scenario. It shows the same environment as the previous figure, but this time a link is established between the routers. Also, it indicates that host A in Monterey is communicating with host C in Birmingham.

Figure 13-31 is how the environment appears after communication is complete.

This example of a bandwidth on demand router might well fit the needs of many situations. More than one or two vendors have such devices available today. A consideration for this device is weighing the consequences of purchasing such a device versus having a router with a dedicated line. Determining the amount of usage should dictate which would be the better solution; and my philosophy is the *customer* should make the decision.

Figure 13-29
Bandwidth on
demand routing

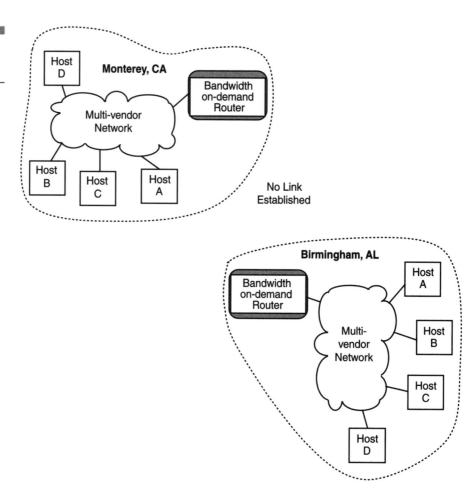

Router Benefits

Routers provide a variety of capabilities that are advantageous to networking of different types. With the influx of growth of LANs in the past decade, routers are sometimes the best solution to meet needs of a given situation.

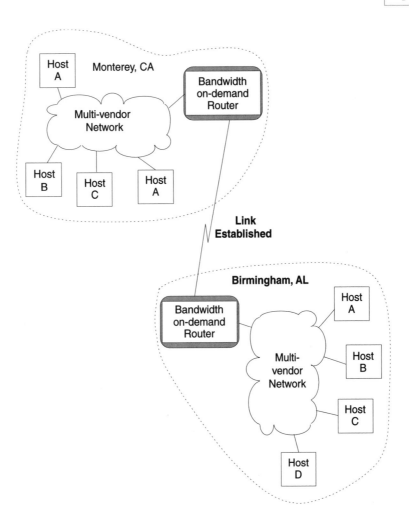

Figure 13-30
Bandwidth-on-demand routing

Segment Isolation

A major advantage routers provide is the ability to split a large network into smaller, more easily manageable ones. This is important, because both the number of LANs is increasing, as is the number of specialized devices attached to them. Figure 13-32 is an example of how routers can be used to create a more manageable LAN environment.

Figure 13-31
Bandwidth on-
demand routing

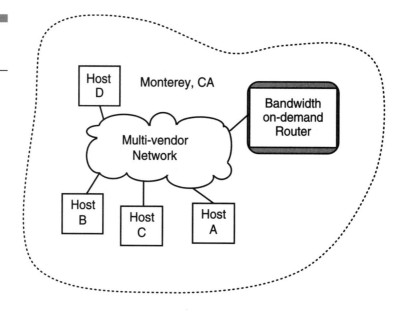

**No Link
Established**

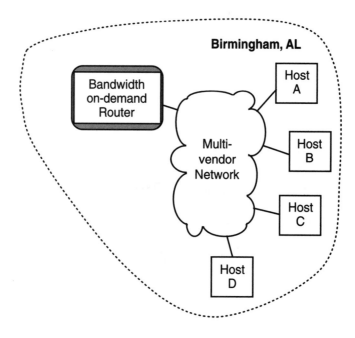

Figure 13-32
Single backbone LAN

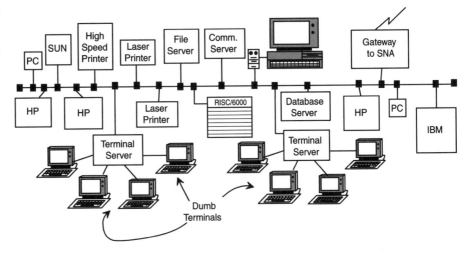

Figure 13-32 portrays a single backbone LAN. It is apparent that it is crowded and difficult to manage. Many different types of traffic are all passed across a single backbone. This puts a load on the network and consequently causes performance degradation.

Figure 13-33 is an example of the same equipment implemented differently.

In Figure 13-33, multiple LAN segments have been created, and a real sense of load balancing is the result. Notice the three routers that tie the segments together. They are able to control the passing of packets to the correct segment or keep packets on a given segment and thus not impede performance. Another advantage is the ability this configuration provides. With this arrangement, a given segment can be removed from other segments if changes need to be made or other management related functions that would effect other LAN segments need to be performed.

Multi-Protocol Support

Many vendors who sell routers have routers that support multiple lower layer protocols quite effectively. Because the IEEE 802.X protocols call for delineation of the data link layer, it is possible to mix and match a variety of lower layer protocols. Consider Figure 13-34.

Figure 13-34 demonstrates different networks with unlike lower layer protocols and interface connections. However, because of the versatility of routers, they came be merged into the router as shown in this figure.

Figure 13-33
Multsegment
network

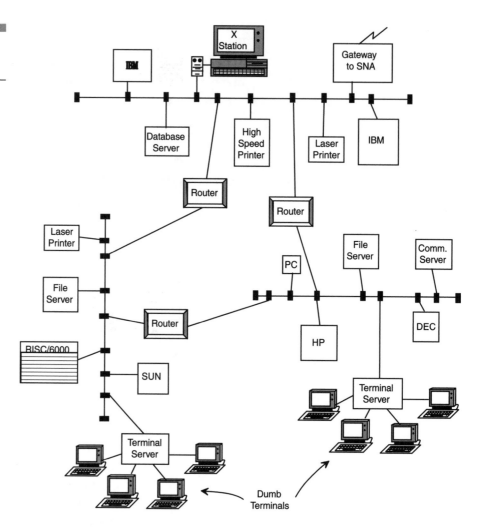

Scaleable Architecture

Another feature offered by some router vendors is a scaleable architecture. For example, some routers can provide basic needs for say one protocol, while being capable of being upgraded to support other types of lower layer protocols. Network topologies are a factor in routers. Some router vendors offer routers that have the flexibility to change and expand to intemperate with topologies that change over time.

Figure 13-34
Mixed protocol
support

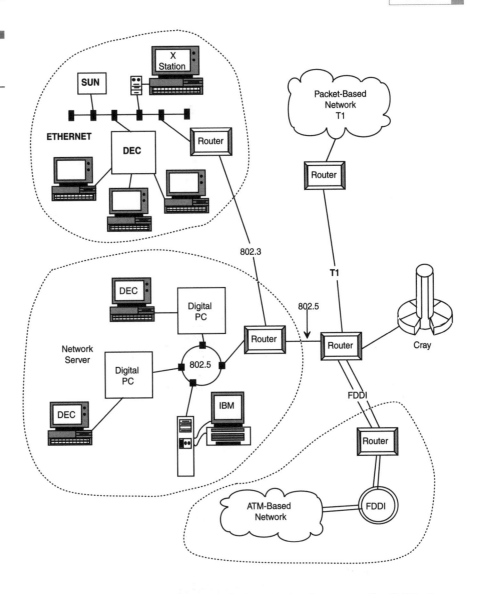

Other advantages of routers include price/performance, flexibility to support local and/or remote sites simultaneously, and be manageable by network management technologies such as *Simple Network Management Protocol* (SNMP). Routers also provide what is considered an intelligent link between networks. They can also protect against network failures by their ability to isolate networks. These and other features offered by router vendors make routers an attractive solution for internetworking requirements.

Multi-Protocol Routers

Much attention has been given to multi-protocol routers in the past few years. Many vendors have brought such devices to the market. A multi-protocol router supports multiple upper and lower layer protocols. By definition this is complex for one device to do. Also, regardless who the vendor is that supplies a multi-protocol router, it must be a *robust* device to function when multiple protocols are being routed at the same time. These are technical facts, not opinion. Think of it. One device that can route IP, IPX, SNA, DECent, and AppleTalk must be a powerful machine and work well.

Various multi-protocol routers support some of the following protocols. After reading the list, it is reasonably conclusive that multi-protocol routers must be robust.

Physical Layer Protocols

RS−232	RS−422	RS−449
V.24	V.35	V.36
X.21		

Physical layers specified by IEEE 802.X

Data Link Protocols

SDLC by IBM
ETHERNET V.2 by DIX
X.25 by CCITT
PPP as in RFC 1171 and 1172
MAC and LLC IEEE protocols
Frame Relay by CCITT and ANSI

Upper Layer Protocols

SNA	TCP/IP	AppleTalk
NetWare	Windows	DECent
XNS	NetBIOS	OSI

Routing Layer Protocol Specific

Internet Protocol (IP)—TCP/IP
Internetwork Datagram Protocol (IDP)—XNS
Datagram Delivery Protocol (DDP)—AppleTalk
Connectionless Network Protocol (CNLP)—OSI
SNA
DECent

Conceptual Examples

Based on the preceding information, some examples showing multi-protocol routing follow. Consider Figure 13-35.

Figure 13-35 is an example of three multi-protocol routers, three networks, and the backbone frame relay network. Because the multi-protocol routers support data layer protocol, connectivity among networks 1, 2, and 3 is possible.

Figure 13-36 is a different example of a multi-protocol router implementation. In this figure, mixed lower layer protocol multi-protocol routers support networks, thus making data exchange among them possible.

Figure 13-35
Multiprotocol routers and mixed protocols

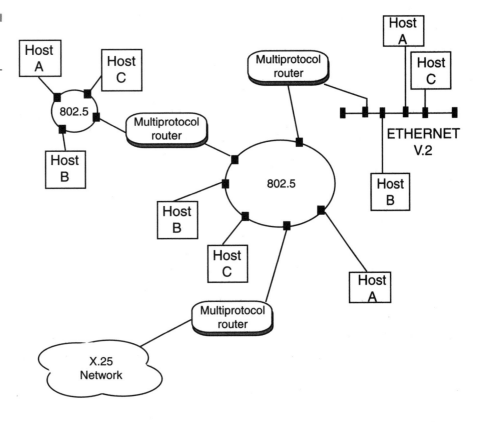

Figure 13-36

Multiprotocol routers, DECnet, and TCP/IP

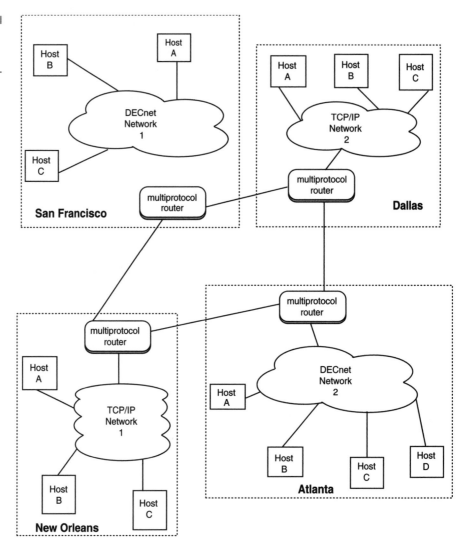

Figure 13-37 is an example of two NetWare and TCP/IP networks integrated using a multi-protocol router. In this figure, the routers are interconnected together thus making the NetWare and TCP/IP networks physically and logically connected. Because NetWare supports TCP/IP, a degree of interoperability can be achieved through this arrangement.

A variety of implementations can be achieved with multi-protocol routers. The number of permutations that can be obtained with multi-protocol routers is considerably large.

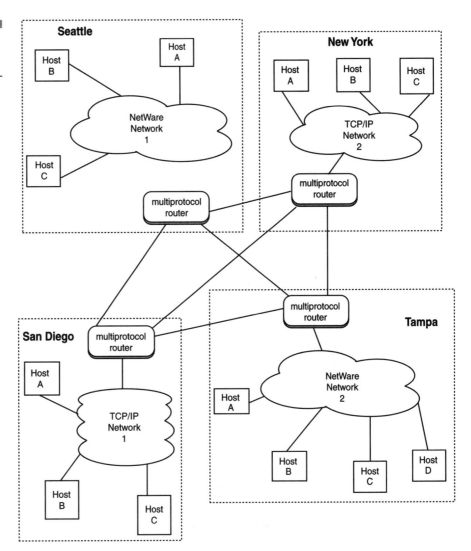

Figure 13-37
Netware, TCP/IP and
multiprotocol routers

IBM, Bay Networks, Cisco, and a variety of other vendors offer multi-protocol routers to the marketplace today.

Router Conclusions

Routers are complex devices and in some form or other have been around for at least two decades. In the late 1960s and 1970s, the device that performed router functions was called a gateway, and to this day some still use this term to refer to a router. In the networking community today, legitimate devices that perform router functions exists, and they are named such. Likewise devices called gateways exist; they too perform a specific function, and generally this is not routing.

Multiple types of routers exists. Some support different upper layer protocols and are protocol specific in their implementation. Others support different lower layer protocols and are specific to that end. Any given router generally supports multiple physical layer interfaces as well as multiple data link layer protocols.

Multiple reasons for routers exists. From a geographical perspective, routers can be used to solve internetworking needs. Some routers are focused on what is considered a metropolitan implementation where a major facility exists and satellite offices exist within a reasonable proximity. Remote routers can be used to solve integration issues of geographically dispersed networks. The same holds true for what is considered internal routing.

Different types of routing are possible. Centralized routing focuses the routing tables within a centralized processing device. Non-centralized routing implements a strategy where routers exchange information about those routers with which they operate. Static routing is where routing tables are predetermined. In other words, the tables and paths for routing are determined and configured when the network is non-operational from a user perspective.

Two examples of different approaches to routing were presented. SNA routes data primarily through its front end processor by way of the network control program, but this appears to be changing. This seems to be the case, because of announcements of products that are now capable of performing functions that not too long ago were considered a front processor type of function. Additionally, with the SNA networking blueprint many areas are in a state of flux.

TCP/IP was used as an example of how routing is achieved. Explanation was provided about the software components that are involved in this process. The versatility of the TCP/IP protocol stack makes it possible for multiple possibilities to be considered for implementation.

A type of router has arrived on the market in the past few years that differentiates itself from some of its predecessors. The bandwidth on demand router was explained, and it offers alternatives to a dedicated line for two geographically distant sites that need a router for intermittent connectivity, that is, on demand.

Multiple advantages are realized for those sites where they are implemented. For example, segment isolation is possible with the implementation of a router. This is significant, because troubleshooting and maintenance are easier with a segmented network than with a single backbone network where crowding exits. Those routers that offer multi-protocol support at the upper and lower layers offer greater flexibility for growing environments. Some routers on the market today are scaleable. For example, immediate needs can be met with the ability to expand and increase support through the router.

A multi-protocol router has a tall order to achieve many functions at the same time. As the example was presented, a router that supports so many different protocols at the physical interface, data link, and upper layer protocol layers must be vigorous in its processing capabilities.

Routers might be a part of an integration equation when multiple protocols are used, but they might not meet all the needs possible. As was said early on in this chapter, routers route.

Gateways

Gateways are the focus of this section. Explanation of the function of this network device is the central purpose. Clarification of the term, implementation of a gateway in different networks, and other topics are covered.

The Internet community has used the term in more of a general sense than a particular one. The term has been used to convey a device that performed functions of what is called a router today. Generally, a gateway conveyed the latter meaning as indicated by the American Heritage Dictionary.

Inadvertently ambiguity in the meaning began to arise from the use of the term in the 1980s. This is most probably due to the fact that in the 1980s, numerous types of networking devices were developed and brought to market. As a result, the terms router and gateway became definable by the functions they performed. A clear distinction was identifiable between devices that performed router functions and gateway functions. The result was, and is, about the meaning of the term gateway.

Gateway Operation

By definition gateways operate at network layer three and above, at a minimum. However, a gateway can operate at all seven layers if necessary. Examine Figure 13-38.

Figure 13-38
Gateway operation
correlated to layers

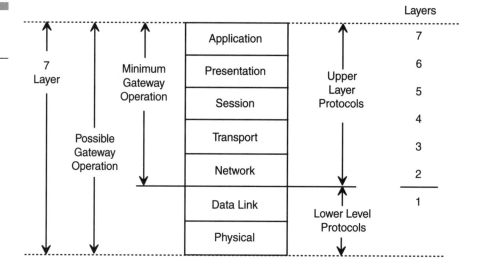

A gateway performs protocol conversion between unlike networks. The question is, which layers require protocol conversion for integration to be achieved and where is the protocol conversion process performed. Integration of heterogeneous networks is the purpose of a gateway. This is its sole purpose, but it can perform other functions.

Currently many good reference sources exists to find information about networking devices. Many of these sources are non-biased; meaning they conduct research about products and make this available to the public through different avenues. The multiple sources I use list devices such as gateways, routers, bridges and the like by category. The result format of such typically lists the vendor and their product name and function. In many cases, those products listed under gateways are not in fact gateways. To be fair, after examining some of the products I am referring to, it seems the validity of listing the product under the gateway category is achieved by referring to the product function as performing that role defined as a number in the American Heritage Dictionary.

A clear example of this is how a device that permits networks into a X.25 network is categorized as a gateway. X.25 is considered a lower layer protocol, even though it operates at part of layer three when compared to the OSI model functions. The point is, classifying a device that permits networks into a X.25 based network as a gateway is a hairsplitter in meaning. On the one hand it could be correct.

For example, consider a token ring based network with TCP/IP used as the upper layer protocols. And, contemplate the X.25 network using something other than TCP/IP as an upper layer network protocol. If this is the case, the reference to the device that performs this function is in fact a gateway. On the other hand, if the device does not perform such function, what is the device called?

Technical Details of Gateways

Gateways operate with protocols; the question is with which ones and at what layers based on the OSI model. This section describes gateways and different protocol environments.

Internet Gateways   The Internet is comprised of numerous individual networks connected together that collectively make-up the Internet. Figure 13-39 is an example of three networks in three different cities that portray this idea.

Figure 13-39 shows each of the networks connected through a router. Traditionally, these routers would have been considered gateways. Indeed, in 1983 the Department of Defense announced that anyone desiring to connect to the Internet must use TCP/IP as the protocol. This drew a line in the ground, so to speak, and since that time connecting to the Internet has been a direct TCP/IP to TCP/IP connection or some variation thereof requiring gateway functionality between the connecting entity and the Internet.

A typical way to connect to a service provider that offers connectivity to the Internet is through a multi-home host. Figure 13-40 is an enhanced view of the Dallas site as shown in Figure 13-39.

Figure 13-39 showed the Dallas site so that it appeared all hosts were connected to the router and were able to connect to the Internet. Figure 13-40 shows reality. All networks and hosts are connected to an Ethernet network, which has a multi-homed host. One side of the host attaches to the Local Ethernet and the other to the router, which in turn connects to the San Francisco and Chicago networks.

Figure 13-39
Conceptual view of
the Internet

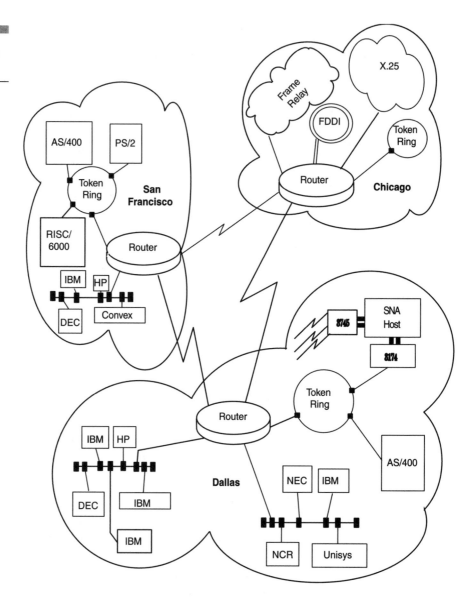

SNA Gateways   SNA gateways function so that connectivity can be achieved between SNA and a different environment. Consider Figure 13-41.

Figure 13-41 shows a DECNET network connected to a SNA network through SNA/DECent gateway. This example shows SNA protocols used in the SNA environment and DECNET protocols used in the DEC environ-

Figure 13-40
Multi-homed host
and the Internet

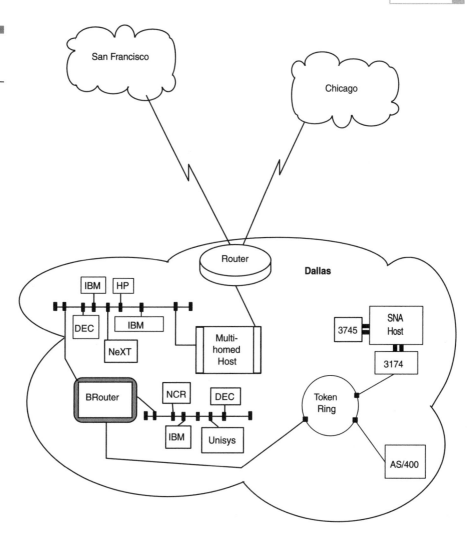

ment. In this case both, upper and lower layer protocols have to be converted. In the DECent, Ethernet is used as a lower layer protocol. The upper layers are DECent oriented. In the SNA environment, SDLC is the lower layer protocol used on the FEP and SNA is the upper layer protocol.

OSI Gateways OSI defines all seven layers. As a protocol, it provides different options at various layers. A chapter was devoted to OSI previously in this book. However, many OSI gateways provide access into an OSI oriented environment where one or more applications are used. Figure 13-42 is an example of an OSI gateway.

Figure 13-41
SNA/DECnet
gateway

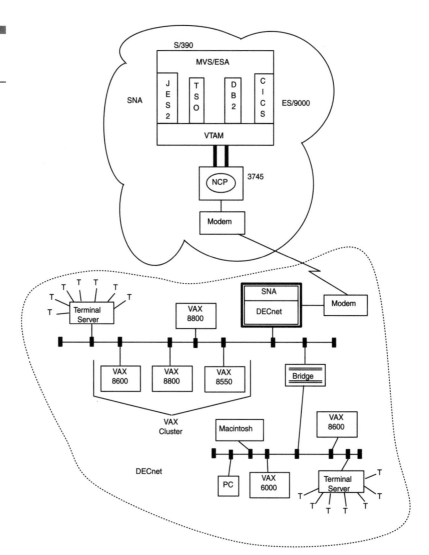

Figure 13-42
OSI based gateway

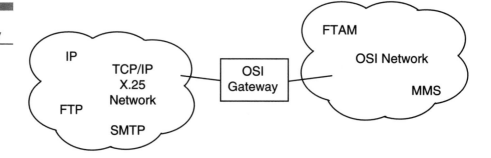

Interestingly the way OSI gateways are portrayed is oriented at applications. In this figure, a TCP/IP network is using X.25, and has FTP and SMTP as standard applications. On the other hand, the OSI network has a complete OSI protocol stack implemented and FTM along with MHS is available.

This scenario implies the exchange between mail systems (SMTP and MHS) and file transfers between (FTP and FTAM). These applications are distinctly different and require conversion between them.

DECent Gateway A DECent gateway is a device that takes networks or devices that are using non-DECent protocols and converts them into DECent requirements. Figure 13-43 is an example of such a scenario.

Figure 13-43 is an example of a sizable DECent environment and also an APPN network comprised of AS/400 hosts that uses a 5250 data stream. This is significant, because the DECent network utilizes an ASCII data stream. In this particular instance, both the protocol and the data stream must be converted in both directions for successful work to be achieved.

Figure 13-43
DECnet gateway

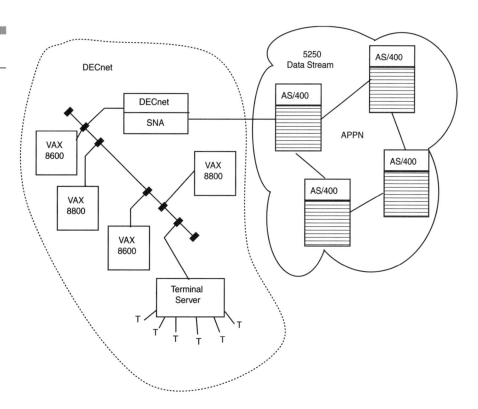

Figure 13-44
AppleTalk gateway

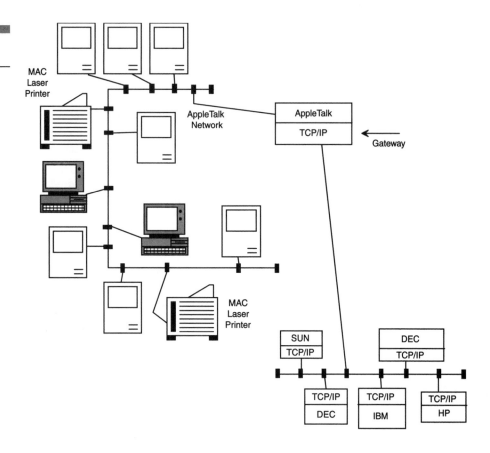

AppleTalk Gateways AppleTalk based networks use the this protocol for the upper layers in the network. Figure 13-44 shows a conceptual example.

Figure 13-44 is an example of a gateway between an AppleTalk and a TCP/IP based network. Multiple devices exist on the AppleTalk based network, and they have interoperability with the hosts on the TCP/IP based network. The gateway is required because of the difference in upper layer protocols.

Bi-directional Functionality Gateways operate between heterogeneous networks. Some exceptions might apply, but most gateways provide bi-directional communication between networks. The degree to which this is possible is vendor dependent. Because some *gateways* perform specific functions, it is difficult to explain the many variations of this concept without performing a vendor analysis, and that is not the purpose of this chapter or book.

Gateway in Light of Previous Information   Other types of gateways exist. Some provide peer-level communication and are highly specialized. Observation of industry magazines provides multiple examples of how the term gateway is used.

The term gateway has been used to convey communication capabilities with UNIX, X.25, SNA, DECent, and other terms. Consideration of the term usage should be given with respect for parallelism when any term has multiple interpretations. Some vendors use the term gateway to define products that give their environment or products the ability to operate with environments such as UNIX, X.25, SNA, or DECent.

The point here is UNIX and SNA are not parallel. UNIX is an operating system. SNA is a network protocol. X.25 is considered a data link layer protocol, but in reality it operates at part of layer three, the network layer. If the term gateway is used to describe products, or their ability to communicate with a different environment, then a comparative analysis should be equal. To use a familiar phrase, comparing apples to apples should be the order of the day. To explain functionality of a device that provides interoperability between devices or networks should be in context.

For example, to call a device that connects heterogeneous networks a gateway and then to use that same term to refer to a device that connects devices or environments to a particular operating system or lower layer protocol is incongruent usage of the term. Fact is, it does not matter what operating system is used in many network protocol implementations. What matters is the networking protocols used. This is entirely different from an operating system. For example, with SNA at least three bonafied operating systems exist. In DECent at least two are noted. OSI can operate with multiple operating systems.

An example here is in order. Consider TCP/IP. It can operate under the following operating systems:

UNIX	VMS
OS/2	MS-DOS
MVS/ESA	VM
Apple	OS/400

Additionally, TCP/IP can operate with multiple data link layer protocols. The following items are examples.

ETHERNET	FDDI
X.25	Token ring
802.X series of protocols	

Understanding these issues should indeed be considered prior to the purchase of a gateway. Actually, it would be best to have any vendor you are working with explain explicitly their gateways' functionality in such a way that no ambiguity exist.

SNA—TCP/IP Gateways

A finite number of upper and lower layer protocols exist and have been explained in this book. As a result, it is possible to identify popular networking protocols in light of their percentage in the worldwide marketplace.

SNA is probably the most dominant vendor network protocol in the world. TCP/IP is probably the most dominant non-vendor protocol in the world. However, an incredible number of vendors support TCP/IP or offer it as a network protocol. DECent has a considerable amount of the marketshare as well. The same can be said about NetWare; it is prevalent also. AppleTalk also has a considerable market share.

To estimate a percentage these networking protocols command in terms of marketshare is difficult because the market has been, and is, in such a state of flux. These protocols are dominant. In terms of gateways, SNA based gateways certainly have a considerable market share. Of this type of gateway, TCP/IP and DECent are probably the most significant protocols that are integrated into SNA through gateways.

SNA and TCP/IP have received considerable attention in the past six to eight years. It seems TCP/IP has penetrated many institutions and companies that have traditionally been SNA based. Interestingly, even DEC systems support TCP/IP. This means DEC customers have an option for protocol use; they can use TCP/IP, DECent, or OSI as it is supported in the DEC environment. In this section however, the focus is on SNA and TCP/IP gateways.

Multiple types of SNA-TCP/IP gateway implementations exist. Most possibilities are presented here. From a user perspective, the question is, which best meets their needs.

Hardware gateways   Hardware gateways almost always operate at all seven layers within a SNA-TCP/IP network. Figure 13-45 is an example of this type of gateway.

The illustration shows three locations: Dallas, Hattiesburg, and San Diego. The office in San Diego was recently acquired because of a recommendation from Jan. Cindy however is responsible for all corporate operations including those in Hattiesburg for which Kelly is responsible for daily operations.

Figure 13-45
Hardware gateway
installation

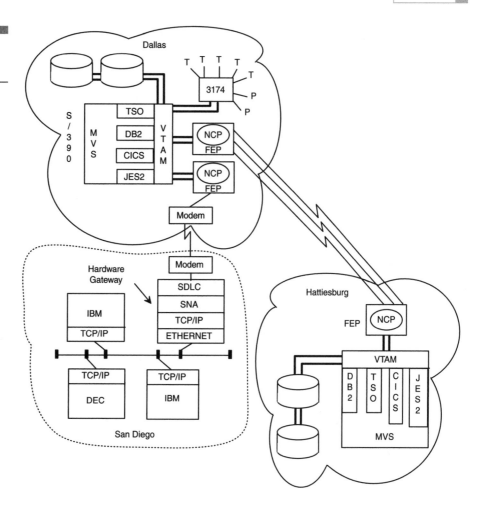

The final result is a hardware gateway in the San Diego office. This provides interoperability between the San Diego office and both the Dallas and Hattiesburg offices. This arrangement provides users in the Hattiesburg office to use files on hosts in the San Diego office.

This type of gateway is required, because the San Diego office has an Ethernet based TCP/IP network. In Dallas and Hattiesburg, SNA is the network protocol and native lower layer protocols are used. Consequently, this means for a gateway to integrate San Diego and the SNA offices, Ethernet and TCP/IP must be converted into SNA and the appropriate lower layer protocol. The most cost effective solution in this case is a hardware based gateway.

In this example, both upper and lower layer protocol conversion is performed on the hardware gateway. Data translation might be performed on the gateway or not. Data translation in this case is contingent on how the vendor implements this type of hardware gateway.

This example of an ETHERNET based TCP/IP network connected to multiple SNA networks is a common scenario in the internetworking community today. A significant number of vendors provide such gateways.

TCP/IP on a SNA Host A different SNA-TCP/IP solution is where TCP/IP is loaded onto an SNA host. When this is the case, TCP/IP is GENned (system generated) as a TCP/IP application. Figure 13-46 is an example of this scenario.

Figure 13-46
TCP/IP as a VTAM application

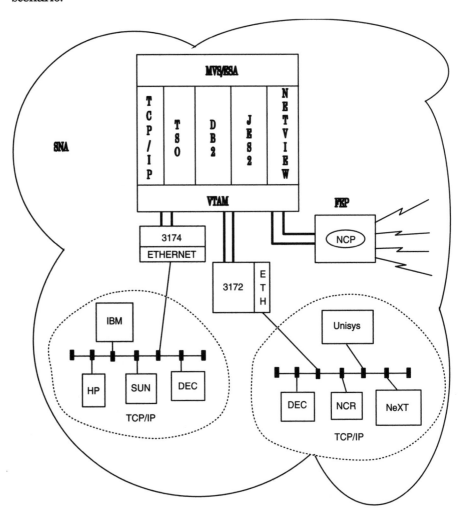

TCP/IP operates as a VTAM application in Figure 13-46. Just because TCP/IP runs as a VTAM application does not mean that it does not perform protocol conversion. In fact when SNA and TCP/IP are integrated, protocol conversion and data translation always takes place; the only question is where. In this example, protocol conversion does in fact have to be performed on the host. Data translation might or might not performed on the host. The location of data translation is contingent on a number of issues. Primarily this is dependent on what type of remote logon and file transfer mechanism is used.

Offload   IBM has what they call an offload option. This is where TCP/IP is loaded on a SNA host, but is offloaded onto a 3172 interconnect controller and then only on the customer desired applications running on the host itself. Figure 13-47 illustrates this offload.

Figure 13-47 shows TCP/IP on the host, on the 3172, and on the disk. So, where is it? TCP and IP have been offloaded onto the 3172 processor. Those applications selected can function where TCP/IP is indicated on the hosts, and the remainder of the TCP/IP suite that is not needed is on hard disk. This type of implementation is versatile. As Figure 13-47 shows, even a remote TCP/IP network (shown as LAN #1) can be integrated into the TCP/IP network, connected to the network, and connected to the 3172 processor through a remote Ethernet bridge.

Software gateway   A software gateway is program code that operates on a workstation. Figure 13-48 is an example of this operation.

In this example, a RISC/6000 implements gateway software. It is used to connect the TCP/IP network in Paris to the SNA network in New York. Notice the TCP/IP network does not indicate a data link, necessarily. The significance of this is that software gateway code can operate on a number of different vendor's hardware. Here, the gateway software is operating on an IBM RISC/6000.

In this type of implementation, the data link layer protocols are left to the host to resolve. In this case, the RISC/6000 supports a very wide variety of data links. In fact the question with this machine is which one does a customer want to use, not which ones can it support. The RISC/6000 host has a robust data link layer protocol support subsystem.

The significance of this example is the software gateway code operates as any other started task in the AIX (IBM's UNIX for the RISC/6000) environment. Therefore, the workstation does not have to be dedicated; however, it could be if so desired. Another interesting fact about this type of solution is that somewhere vendors who supply gateway code can support more than 1,000 LUs. In fact, some software gateway vendors have code that can

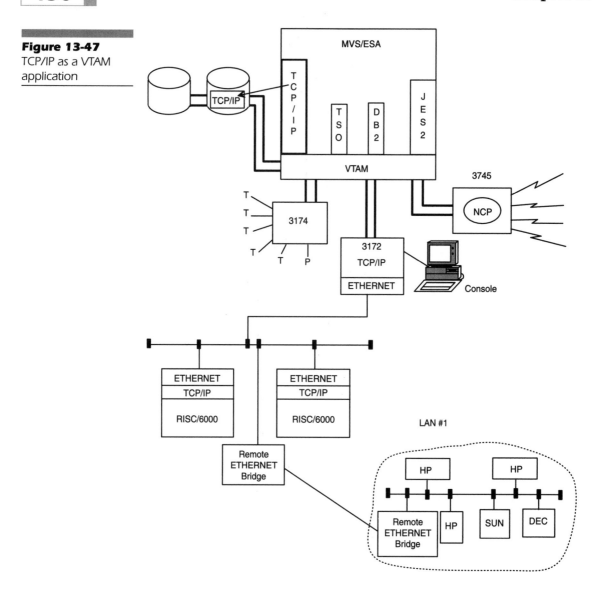

Figure 13-47
TCP/IP as a VTAM
application

operate on considerably smaller workstations. Some software gateway vendors only support certain vendor hardware; so, it is best to determine which vendor hardware is supported by a potential software gateway supplier.

Figure 13-48
Software gateway
implementation

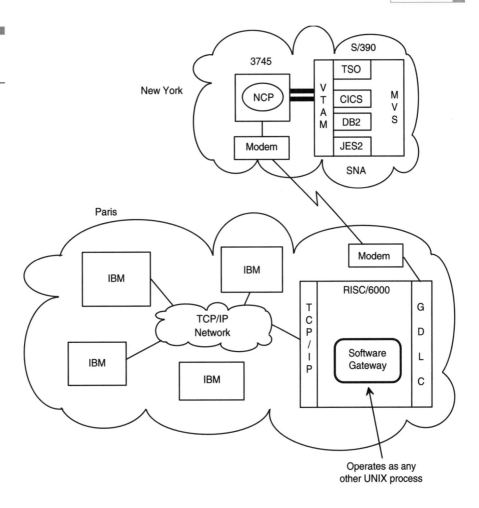

PC Interface Cards and Software

Another way to integrate SNA and TCP/IP is to use interface boards and software with PCs. Consider Figure 13-49.

Figure 13-49 might be the best solution if this type of configuration is similar. However, it is just one of the four previously mentioned. Figure 13-49

Figure 13-49
Interface boards

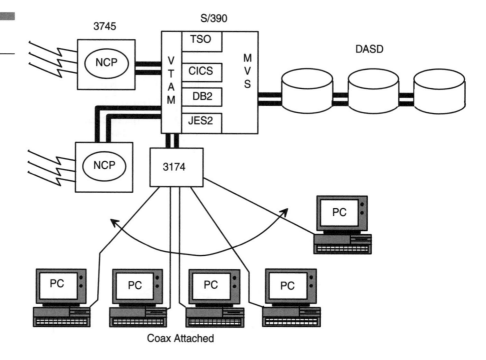

shows multiple PCs exists on site where the S/390 host is located. The PCs have interface boards, software inside, and are coax attached to the 3174 establishment controller.

As the previous five examples have shown, multiple ways are available to integrate SNA and TCP/IP. The last example depicted multiple PCs with interface boards attached to a local 3174. Indeed, multiple ways are currently available to bring together SNA and TCP/IP.

Gateway Usage

To achieve interoperability between SNA and TCP/IP protocol conversion and data translation must be performed. The only question is, where are these functions performed. The previous section provided examples of where protocol conversion was performed; primarily upper layer protocols. However, it did not indicate where data translation occurs or what user oriented functions are supported.

Remote Logon In SNA and TCP/IP, much of the traffic is considered inbound; that is, to the SNA host. Any logon from a TCP/IP based network to a SNA network is considered a remote logon, even if the network is in the same room with the SNA host. When SNA and TCP/IP are integrated through a gateway the issue of data translation is paramount. The SNA arena supports multiple data streams, but the one used interactively is a 3270 data stream. This is significant, because 3270 data streams are based on an EBCDIC character set. Most traditional data streams in TCP/IP networks have been based on the ASCII character set. Multiple ways exist to solve this one issue of data translation. Consider Figure 13-50.

Figure 13-50 shows a SUN user invoking a TELNET client native to the TCP/IP stack on that host. The user executes the client against the TELNET server on the gateway between the network in Salt Lake City and Boise. The

Figure 13-50
Raw TELNET logon

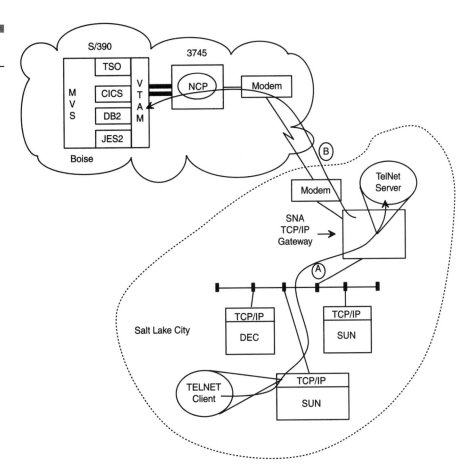

first part of the connection establishes a logical link between the Convex host and the gateway and is labeled (A). The second portion of the connection is labeled (B), and it is established from the gateway to VTAM on the S/390 host. The Convex user *thinks* one logical connection exists between their terminal and VTAM. This type of connection is called a RAW telnet because the telnet client out of the native TCP/IP stack is used to establish a logical connection. In this case, data translation is performed on the gateway; be that a hardware or software gateway.

Figure 13-51 is another example of how a remote logon can be achieved. It shows a TCP/IP based network in New York and a SNA network in Ottawa.

Figure 13-51
TN3270 client and gateway

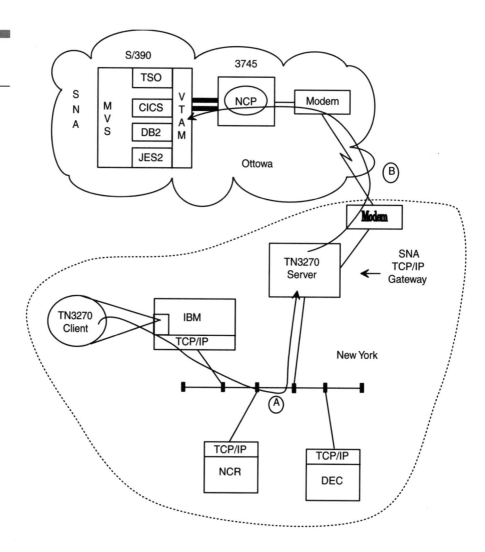

Notice the TN3270 client application shown on the IBM host in the New York network. It indicates, through logical connection (A), that it connects to the TN3270 server on the gateway connecting the two networks. The second part of the connection between New York and Ottawa is shown through connection (B). In this case, data translation occurs on the IBM host.

This is so because TN3270 client applications are designed to output a 3270 data stream. The fact that it is TCP/IP and Ethernet based is insignificant, because data formatting is performed at the presentation layer within a network. By the time any data reaches the physical interface of the host, the data is represented in binary. Hence, what is shipped across the Ethernet are Ethernet frames.

However for a TN3270 application to operate, one of two conditions must be met. Either a TN3270 server must be present as shown on the gateway in Figure 13-51 or the SNA based host must have TCP/IP on it so the TELNET server native to that stack can answer the request of the TN3270 client. Figure 13-52 illustrates this.

Figure 13-52
TN3270 client
and host

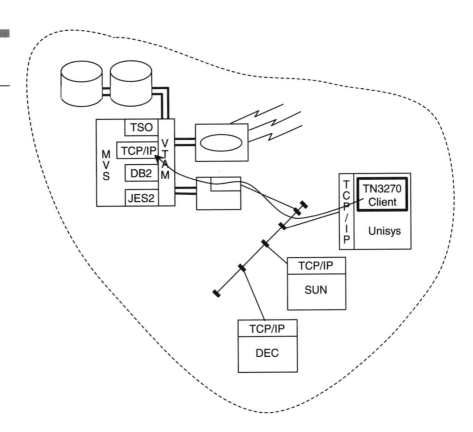

In Figure 13-52, a TN3270 client application is present on the UNISYS host. A user invokes it against the SNA host attached to the TCP/IP based Ethernet network. Notice the TN3270 client application is executed against the TCP/IP stack running as a VTAM application on the SNA based host. Why would this be done? When this type of scenario is implemented, it operates this way because a TELNET server exists by default within the TCP/IP stack running as a VTAM application. Consequently, the data stream inbound to the SNA hosts is 3270 (no conversion needed) and this saves CPU cycles, and CPU cycles costs money.

Other proprietary methods exist that support a remote logon from a TCP/IP based network and a SNA network. Because these are proprietary, they might or might not coexist with industry standards.

File Transfers File transfers can be interactive or programmatic. The former implies human intervention where the latter does not. Both are discussed here.

Interactive Multiple methods exist to perform file transfers between SNA environments and TCP/IP networks. A common way to do this is through FTP. Figure 13-53 is an example.

This example shows a SNA network, TCP/IP network, and gateway connecting them together. Notice the FTP client has been invoked on the SUN host and is executed against the FTP server native to the TCP/IP stack running as a VTAM application. As this figure shows, file XYZ is written from the DASD in the SNA environment to the Sun's disk.

Another method for file transfer between SNA and TCP/IP environments includes support for the IND$FILE program IBM has supported. Figure 13-54 is an example.

Figure 13-54 shows a DEC user invoking a program that supports the IND$FILE program by TSO and CICS under VTAM. As the figure shows file XYZ is moved from DASD on the MVS hosts to a disk connected directly to the DEC host.

Programmatic Files can be transferred programmatically. Multiple reasons exist for this capability. Some companies need to download files at night when little or no operations are being performed within the company. Others need programmatic file transfers due to the nature of the interacting entities. Figure 13-55 best depicts this scenario.

Figure 13-53
FTP client

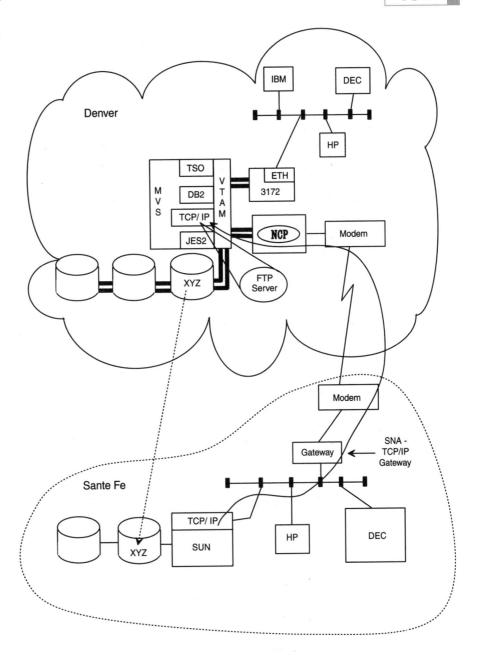

Figure 13-54
INDSFILE file transfer

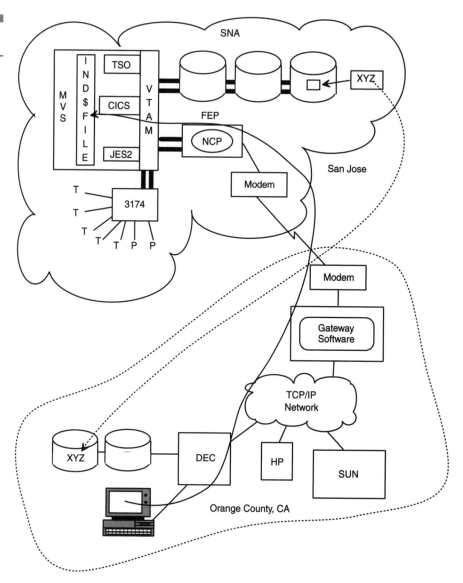

Figure 13-55 is an example where two different types of file transfers are being performed. On the left portion of the drawing is LU6.2 file transfer using hardware gateway with proprietary LU6.2 library support on the gateway itself and the host. On the right side of the figure, socket communication is being performed where socket programming with CICS is communicating with a socket based UDP program on host C in the figure.

Figure 13-55
Problematic file
transfers

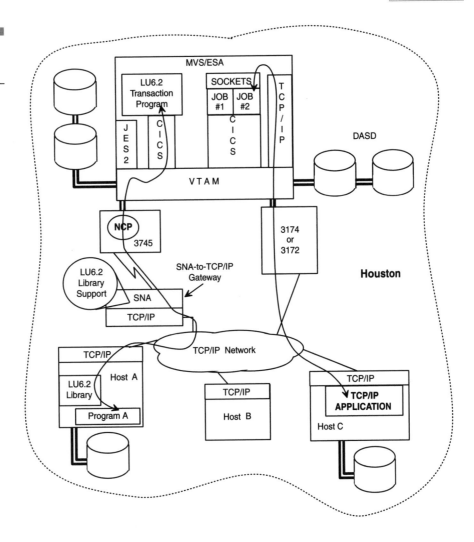

Mail Mail support between SNA and a TCP/IP environment is best depicted by Figure 13-56.

Figure 13-56 is an example of a SNA network in Oak Harbor and a TCP/IP network in Portland. A SNA—TCP/IP gateway is used to connect the two networks. This particular gateway supports SMTP to PROFS mail and vice versa. As a result, those in Oak Harbor can send mail to those users on the network in Portland. Each user in their respective networks can view mail in the format they are accustomed to using. Some vendors have such support for gateways, and some do not.

Management Support The notion of network management is a topic unto itself; however it is important to know if network devices to be integrated into an internetworking arena support the network management

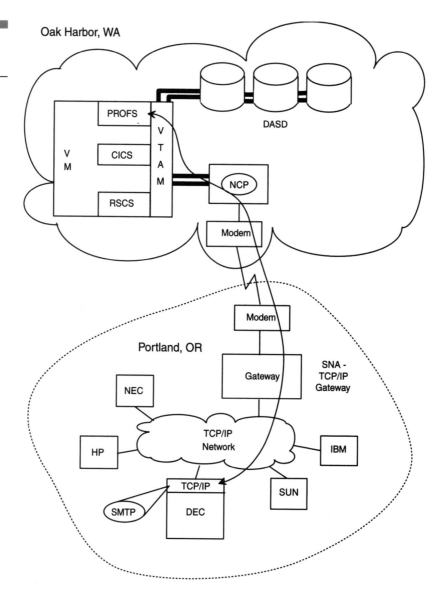

used to manage that network(s). SNA and TCP/IP networks connected together through a gateway means that the gateway should support network management for SNA and TCP/IP. In addition, it should have management capabilities in and of itself; meaning that it should be manageable as an entity unto itself. Figure 13-57 is an example of network management on both sides of the gateway.

Figure 13-57 shows SNMP and TCP/IP network management. It also shows NetView as SNA network management. No particular management is shown for the gateway itself, because this is vendor specific. However, the gateway should have some functional management capabilities that permit a system personnel access information from the gateway if needed.

Working Conclusions about Gateways

The term gateway means different things to different groups of individuals. However, the American Heritage Dictionary does define how the term is used in English. Use of the term in the 1970s with the Internet community took on the meaning of routing. The term did connote an entryway, but technically speaking it was used to convey what the term router means today.

Figure 13-57
Conceptual view of a
file server

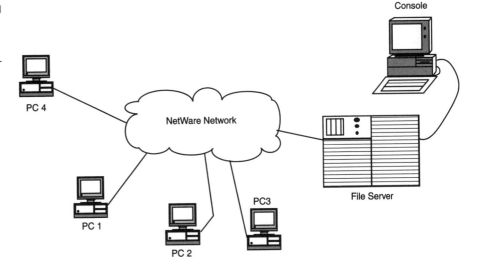

Different types of gateways are marketed today. Gateways to permit connectivity into DECent, TCP/IP, NetWare, SNA, OSI, and AppleTalk can all be purchased. Gateways, by default, perform protocol conversion because this is what makes them a gateway. Gateways can operate at layers three and above based on the OSI model or operate at all layers within a network.

SNA and TCP/IP based gateways are quite popular today. These two environments include a considerable amount of the internetworking community around the world. Other network protocols have market share as well, but even the Digital Equipment Corporation supports TCP/IP for those who want to use it with DEC hosts. DEC also supports OSI.

Multiple types of gateways exist. There are hardware and software based gateways. Regarding TCP/IP and SNA, TCP/IP can be loaded as a VTAM application and operated in this way, or it can be offloaded onto a 3172 interconnect controller. Other possibilities might be available in the near future.

Gateways are used to bring together heterogeneous networks. When this is achieved, multiple user-oriented tasks can be achieved. For example, remote logons, file transfers both interactive and programmatic, exchange of electronic mail, network management, and customized offerings might be provided by some vendors.

Gateways are available in a variety of packaging and support a variety of different end user applications and systems oriented tasks. It is best to check with a specific vendor to determine what is supported by a given gateway.

Server Implementations

A server is a name used in a generic sense many times. But today, many highly specialized types of servers exist. Even so the term is still used loosely to refer to devices such as gateways, routers, and other function specific network devices.

Servers, in the general sense, can be basically any network device. Servers have come of age and are categorized into functions they perform.

Function

Typically, a server provides specific functions to the whole network or at least a significant portion of it. One point of clarification is in order. Some level of confusion still abounds about the notion of *client / server*. Client programs can be invoked manually or programmatically, but either way they always initiate something. Servers, on the other hand, always answer a client's request.

In the context how the term server is used here, it means something different. *Servers*, as network devices, do in a sense provide requests to clients. However, network servers normally provide some functions that separates their function from a *server* program. For example, a file server is a dedicated host with disks dedicated to storing files. These files are used by multiple users throughout the network and therefore centralized storage of common files removes the need for vast amount of disk space for each user. So, in this sense a server takes on a different meaning from the notion of client/server networking, which connotes peer-oriented communication.

The philosophy behind a *server* is that it performs some function in a centralized manner rather than having that function be distributed throughout a network or tied to particular hosts. The growth of servers of all types seems to be the result of networks providing a single commonality among hosts of all types, including PCs. With the proliferation of networks in the 1980s, the notion of delegating functions such as printing to a designated printer seemed to make more sense than each host having a printer.

File Servers

File servers are devices (hardware and software) that function as centralized network disk storage that authorized users on a network can access. These devices can be configured to perform multiple tasks.

One function a file server can perform is file storage. This is advantageous, because one centralized server can be the central repository for all files. Conceptually, the idea of a file server on a network would appear like Figure 13-58.

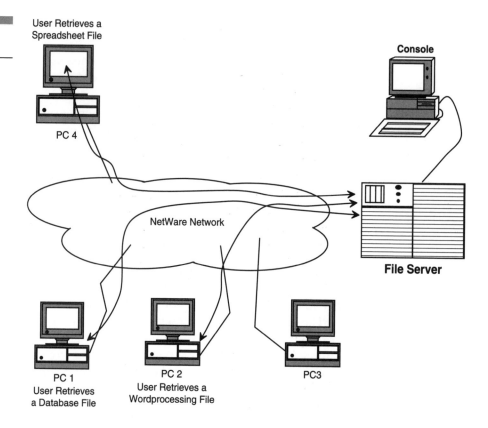

In Figure 13-58, multiple PCs are connected to a NetWare network along with a file server that contains the files required by the PC users. In this type of configuration, any PC can access the server to retrieve a file or store a file onto it.

Figure 13-59 depicts a detailed view of the PC users and their operations with the file server. In this figure, PC users 1, 2, and 4 are accessing the file server. Each is retrieving different files they are working with on their respective PCs. This is possible because of the multitasking capabilities, storage ability, and configuration of the file server. In this example, the file server appears to be a single disk to each user. Each user *thinks* they have their own hard disk. In reality the configuration is such a that a virtual drive is created and each PC is configured to point to this disk (server).

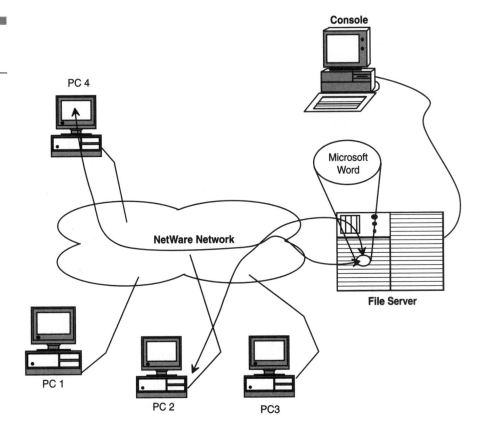

Figure 13-59
File server program
storage

Program Storage

Another function a file server can perform is that of a disk that holds the master copy of software package. For example, the Microsoft Word network edition software package can be purchased and loaded onto a server. Multiple users can utilize it, and immediate savings are realized because multiple packages of the software program do not require purchase. Consider Figure 13-60

In Figure 13-60, PC users 2 and 4 are using the Microsoft Word software package based on the file server. Neither user is aware of the others work because of the nature of the network configuration and how the software package operates. This is a straightforward example of how a network can be utilized to save money. Four users are on this NetWare network and each has access to the Microsoft Word software. One copy of the software was purchased rather than four.

Figure 13-60
Database operations
with a file server

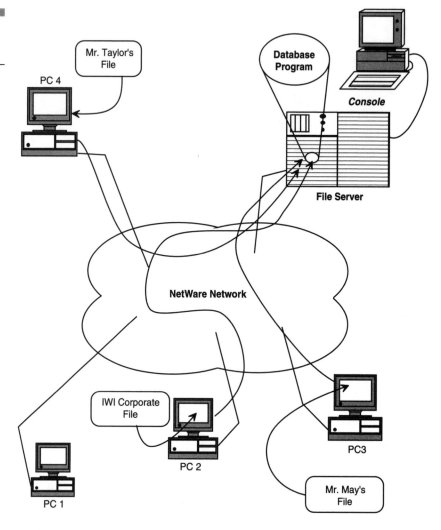

Another example of program storage is exemplified in Figure 13-61. Examine it.

In Figure 13-61, a database is loaded onto the file server, and five users are connected to the network. In this example, the software package happens to be a database package. Notice PC user 3 is working on Mr. Taylor's file, PC user 1 is manipulating the IWI file, and PC user 4 is changing Mr. May's file. These separate functions are happening concurrently. The same file and record locking functions that are standard to most data base programs are also in force in the network edition of this database version.

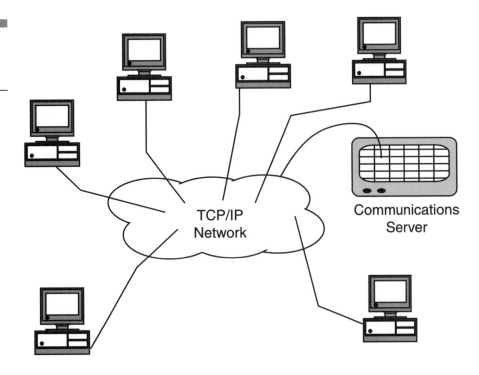

Figure 13-61
Network
communications
server logical view

TCP/IP
Network

Communications
Server

Other functions are possible with a file server such as operating multiple programs simultaneously with multiple users performing different functions. The key issue in such an environment is the file server must be powerful, and depending on the number of users, programs being used, and the size of files, large amounts of disk space is almost a must.

Communication Servers

Communication servers perform basically one role; that is, they provide communication related functions. A variety of these functions exist depending on the communication server.

Modem Pools One function a communication server can perform is to house multiple modems permitting access through various lines and speeds. Consider Figure 13-62.

Figure 13-62 is a logical view of a communication server and the network with a IBM, RISC/6000, and two PCs attached. To the users of these hosts, the communication server logically appears as part of the network—just as another resource.

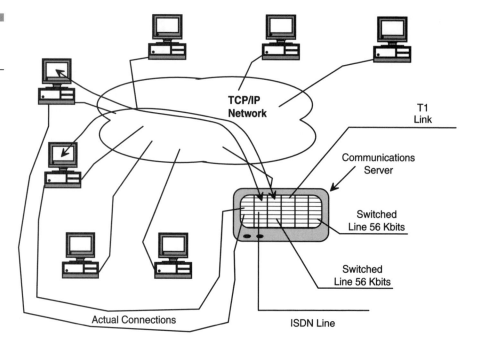

Figure 13-62
Communications
server physical view

Figure 13-63 portrays a physical view of the network showing more detail about the line speeds and connections to the hosts themselves.

Notice in Figure 13-63, the DEC host has a T1 link, the Unisys host a switched 56 Bit per/sec line, the IBM host has a 56 Bit leased line, and the two PCs have access to a dual modem with 56 Bit switched line.

Consumer Tip

Many vendors are listed in charts and magazine listings under the heading of communication servers. The following names and functions are examples.

Multi-protocol Concentrator

X.25 Communications Interface

Video Mux

Multi-protocol Communication Server

Fax Plus

Remote Access Server

Modem Server

Asynchronous LAN Gateway

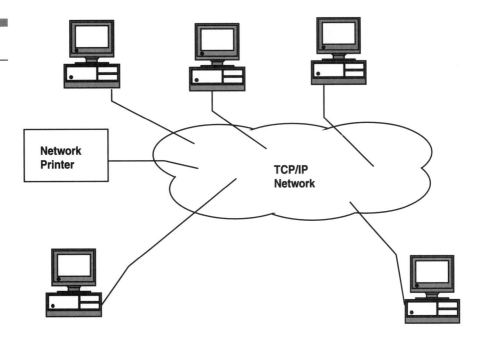

Figure 13-63
Network printer

I believe the point is clear if you read the list. A device that is categorized as a communication server has such broad meanings that research is required to understand what is meant. Some communication servers are highly specialized, so much so that they are vendor specific and the device might only operate with a given vendor's equipment. This is helpful to know when reading about *communication servers*.

Study the following terms and concepts. These are presented here, in this chapter, to better equip you to understand the overall topics in this chapter.

Autobaud

This term is relatively easy to understand, because it does what the name implies. It literally automatically selects the baud rate based on what the destination modem is capable of performing. Generally, the Autobaud process is like bidding. Some modems attempt to move up to the highest speed that either modem will support. But, this is not always the case; this is the reason for Autobaud. If one modem supports a higher baud rate than the other, the higher baud rate modem comes down to the slower speed if the higher speed modem can autobus. This however can differ with vendors, but the term Autobaud is generally agreed on. It is preferable to have an Autobaud modem in most cases because of their versatility.

Line Conditioning

The networks that modems operate on have interference by default in many instances. As the baud rate increases with higher speed modems so does the tendency to incur errors as a result. One problem related to this is amplitude distortion. This is where the signal strength itself varies independent of noise of the line itself. To compensate for this phenomenon, most modems have circuitry built into them to make property adjustments, so the signal is not too disproportional.

The Equalizer

This is an important aspect about modems even though it is not a prevalent topic! Modems operating at baud rates in excess of approximately 2400 baud have an equalizer built into them. The purpose of this equalizer is to serve the function of a filter. This filter is special because its phase characteristics and amplitude are inversely proportional to the lines on which the modem operates. Additionally, equalizers perform a function to correct for propagation delay causing distortions.

Modulation Information

When data is transmitted over a line through a modem, modulation is involved as explained earlier in this book. However, additional details are fitting here in view of the subject. Modulation is simply the conversion of digital signals into analog signals. Conversely, when this signal arrives at the destination, the modem performs reverse modulation if you will; it performs *demodulation*.

Print Server

Reference to a print server might refer to one of two possible entities. One is a general reference to a printer attached to a network where all users with network accessibility can use it. In this instance it is generally referred to as a stand alone printer. Another use of this reference is where a printer is attached to a network host and its print jobs are queued from that host and then sent to the printer. In this instance, the printer appears to be attached to the network directly when in fact it is attached to a network host. This example is loosely referred to as a network printer. Interestingly, little differentiation exists between the phrases, but the implementations differ radically.

Stand Alone Printer   Network printers have existed for some time. The concept is not new, however its presence has been brought to the forefront of many. Figure 13-64 is an example of a network printer.

Figure 13-64 shows multiple hosts attached to a BUS based Ethernet. Any of these hosts can use the network printer, because it is attached to the network and is addressable.

Figure 13-64 shows the highlight of the Ethernet *Network Module* (NM) attached to the side of a Hewlett Packard printer. In this example, the NM makes it possible for the printer to be a stand alone network device. Notice the NM attaches one end to the network transceiver and the other to the parallel port on the printer.

In fact the type of arrangement Figure 13-64 shows makes a printer such that *any* host that can access the network can use this printer to print. This means utilization of communication servers and other devices make remote location computing, but local network printing, possible.

Figure 13-65 is an example of a stand alone printer. In most instances, this scenario implies small quantities of on board memory, and thus printer queue bottlenecks are likely. Generally, they are proportional to the number of users attempting to use it at any given point in time.

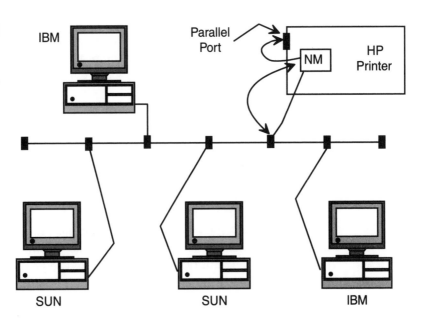

Figure 13-64
Network module
highlight

Figure 13-65
Host queued printing

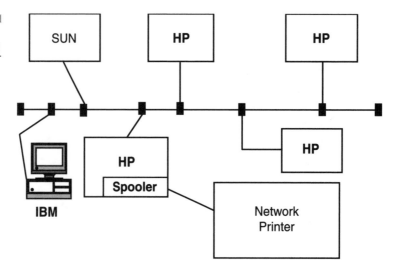

Network Printer

In this example, a printer is attached a host, when it appears to be attached to the network, but its jobs are spooled to it through a host on the network. Consider Figure 13-65.

Notice in Figure 13-65, multiple workstations exist. Even though they do not have a printer attached to their own workstation, they can print on the network printer through the IBM computer to which the printer is physically attached. However as mentioned previously, the printer appears to be attached to the network itself.

Other variations of network printing exist. One such example is Figure 13-66.

Figure 13-66 is an example of printing in an SNA environment. Notice two terminals are connected to the 3174 to which the 3287 printer is attached. These local terminals can print just as those in the New Orleans office and the New York office. But, the printing occurs at the headquarters office on Mystic Trail by the corporate owner himself.

Network printing has a variety of meanings. It is not uncommon for the meaning to be associated with a given vendor network protocol. Regardless, the bottom line is multiple users are using the printer, in contrast to each individual user having a dedicated printer.

Figure 13-66
SNA Printing

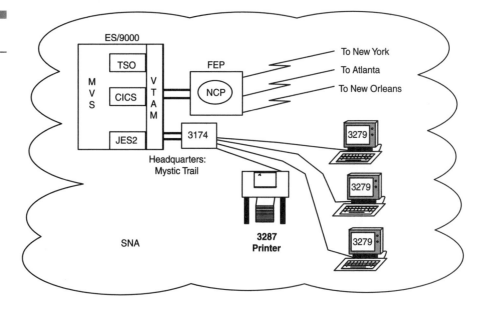

Terminal Server Terminal servers have grown from rare use to commodity items in less than a decade. The fundamental philosophy of terminal servers is the implementation of multiple *dumb* terminals concentrated into one device. Figure 13-67 shows an example.

Figure 13-67 shows multiple hosts, a communications server, a terminal server and six *dumb* terminals. The use of the term *dumb* is defined technically as a device with little intelligence. I suppose this has always been the case, but in networking devices intelligence is measured by levels of degrees.

Figure 13-67 is a TCP/IP based network. The terminal server has a TCP/IP complement inside in PROMS on the motherboard. Hence, the terminal server has a degree of intelligence. Many vendors make terminal servers and most can be configured to accommodate terminals or a modem or two.

The result of a TCP/IP based terminal server is that dumb terminals can be used. The significance behind this is that they cost considerably less than PCs or terminals with a higher level of intelligence. Ironically, what was considered a *dumb* terminal six to eight years is entirely different from what is considered *dumb* at the time of this writing.

Basically two categories of dumb terminals exist. Those which have the basics such as DCE, DTR, DTE, parity, and other fundamental parameters; and those which might have a set of programmable function keys, multiple

Figure 13-67
Terminal server

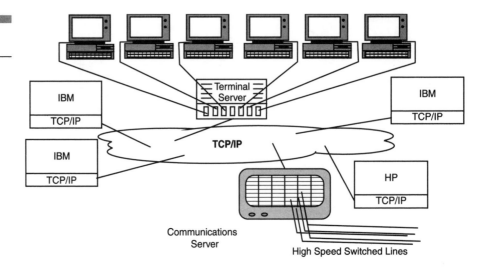

ports, printer capability, and built in calendars, and so on. As one might have concluded, the price differs between these two terminal categories as well.

Interestingly, terminal servers come with a variety of ports. Most terminal servers have anywhere from six to nine ports, and a console port for super user (maintenance) functions. Terminal servers are a very cost effective method of meeting the needs of network users. A *dumb* terminal and terminal server is basically limitless (with the exception of graphic capabilities, and somewhere the ability to perform this function is probably being embarked on). Figure 13-68 depicts what is a minor task.

In Figure 13-68, multiple network devices exist on the TCP/IP based network. In short, the figure includes a terminal server with two terminals attached, a modem attached to the terminal server, an IBM, DEC, RISC/6000, UNISYS, SUN, and IBM hosts. Additionally, the PC is in a remote location to the network. The remote PC user can access the network by dialing the number of the modem indicated in Figure 13-68.

A sequence of five functions are performed by the *dumb* terminal user (no puns or buns intended) #1. These five functions are as listed:

1. Function A is the *dumb* terminal user #1 invoking the TELNET client inside the terminal server against the IBM host. The native TELNET server in the TCP/IP stack on the IBM answers the TELNET client request.

2. User #1 invokes the TELNET client on the IBM against the 3172 attached to the MVS host. The MVS host has TCP/IP running as an offload option, but as default a VTAM application. Hence when user

Figure 13-68
Typical terminal
server operation

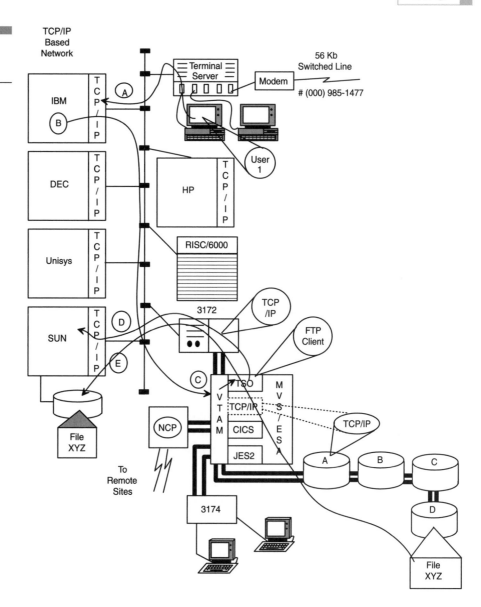

#1 invokes the TELNET client against the TELNET server on the MVS host, user #1 sees the VTAM banner screen.

3. User #1 performs a logon to ISPF editor under the control of TSO. The line mode option is selected and user #1 invokes the FTP client resident on the MVS host.

4. Even though TCP and IP is operating on the 3172, the TELNET and FTP applications are running indirectly as VTAM applications. Hence, user #1 can execute an FTP client against the SUN.

5. Function E is where user #1 moves a file from MVS disk D to the SUN host.

This operation shown in Figure 13-68 is the reality in heterogeneous environments. In fact, I have performed this very operation so many times it is uncountable. The questions that arise as a result of such usage is the terminal server user generally requires some time to accustom to these operations. However, once accustomed to such an environment, the working power within it is unbelievable.

Concluding Thoughts

Server is a generic term used loosely in the marketplace to refer to a specific device. Depending on the context, the meaning differs. After examining three lists in publications listing *servers*, I concluded little continuity exists aside from broad categories such as those mentioned here. Servers have a distinct function and philosophy, ascertaining exactly what this is should be the goal of customers purchasing servers of any kind.

The file server is a specific device that can be used to store files, programs, or both depending on the product—both hardware and software. File servers can be cost efficient if implemented appropriately. File servers can be used interactively or programmatically; using either depends on the need and sophistication of the network environment and the humans.

Communication servers are devices that generally operate with data communication related products. Many operate with modems. Some offer modem pooling exclusively. This term is as vague as the use of other server terms. Some communication servers have the ability to perform multiplexing functions, interfacing into certain network environments.

Many communication servers lend themselves to modem support functions. Modems are complex in their own right. Understanding that, Autobaud means a modem is capable of regulating operating speed relative to the target modem. Line conditioning is factor of communications over telephone lines. Most modems have circuitry built into them to compensate for this phenomenon. Equalizers are special filters used to adjust for phase differentiations.

Modulation is a topic in its own right, but is important when discussing modems and communication with them. Four types of modulation techniques were explained: Amplitude, Frequency Shift Key, Differential Phase Shift Key, and Phase Shift Key are all techniques used. Modems use a specific modulation technique and its impact on modem operation is important.

Print servers are network devices also. In short, this is a printer that *serves* usually the entire network. Two categories of printers are identifiable: the type to which a network interface card is attached is considered a stand-alone printer. This type of print server generally has limited memory, even though this is a relative term. The other category of printer is called a network printer. This printer configuration is such that it is connected to a host and the host generally has a spooling mechanism with enough memory to accommodate the network users. This is obviously the ideal case; in reality differences exist.

Terminal servers are network devices that have come to be used by significantly more users at this point in time than compared to six or eight years ago. Fundamentally, the concept of a terminal server is where multiple *dumb* terminals are connected to a single device that provides network accessibility. *Dumb* terminal is a technical reference to a terminal that has limited software or firmware intelligence. Some *dumb* terminals are more intelligent than others.

Terminal servers differ with network protocols, but in principle they achieve the same function; they provide access to a network. In contrast to a terminal server is a PC or a terminal attached directly to a host. As Figure 13-68 depicted, the power behind a *dumb* terminal and a terminal server is typically only limited by the user behind it.

Troubleshooting Network Devices

Troubleshooting any network device presupposes you understand the operation of the device and its environment. For this reason, the topics were presented in this chapter. Is there any set list of questions one can ask for troubleshooting network devices? Can a chart be made to troubleshoot devices? I have heard these and many similar questions.

First, let me tell you that no reasonable approach to troubleshooting network technology can be a mere list of questions. The best people I know who can troubleshoot technology are those who have a wide experience, are open minded, and think unconventionally. To assume a simple list of questions given to a rookie in the technological community will produce "identified problems" is blissful. It can be done, and I have seen where this approach worked. However, the best rule of thumb is to keep in mind a list of questions and learn to think through technology and scenarios that lend themselves to problem areas. Then you will be better prepared to troubleshoot it.

Consider the following list of questions that will help you in the early phases of troubleshooting technology. The list is broad, and will apply to most situations involving network technology. I am presenting it here for you to consider as a quid; I recommend you make additions to it or remove those questions that do not apply to you situation.

1. What is the geographical area served by the technology?
2. Is the technology serving this area in the same physical location?
3. Does the problem you are working with lend itself to isolation of equipment in a certain geographic location?
4. List all the hardware you are aware of that relates to or with the problem.
5. List all the software related to or with the problem.
6. List the symptoms of the problem.
7. Can the location where the problem area is be isolated from the remainder of the network?
8. Is it possible to segment the network?
9. If the problem is communication related, can you isolate the telecom lines so that each can be tested?
10. If you suspect the problem to be hardware related, do you have a piece of hardware to replace suspect piece?
11. Is it possible to set-up an environment where each piece of equipment duplicating the problem can be tested?
12. How long have the symptoms/problems existed?
13. Have any changes occurred in the past day, two days, three days, week, or month?
14. Do you have testing equipment such as a protocol analyzer, volt/ohm meter, and so forth?
15. Can you obtain any trace information about network traffic where this device has been installed?

Many, many other questions can be added to this list. The purpose of this list here is to get you to thinking. Later in this book, other questions are presented which are more pointed and focused on various topics.

SUMMARY

Networks are complex. The saying goes: The network is the computer. This is true. However, networks today are increasingly difficult to troubleshoot and fix when they break. Technologically speaking, we have come to a point in time where the technology has out-stripped the human ability to keep up with it from a collective sense. It is increasingly difficult to find people who understand the technology well enough to troubleshoot it.

Good troubleshooting practices begin with understanding the technology. Having a checklist is helpful but does little more than produce paper work unless one understands the purpose of it. Consider the information presented in the remainder of the book to assist you in troubleshooting your network.

14

Network Switches: A Case Study in Brief

Introduction

A network switch is a key component in any network. It is equally important to have information about your switch in such a way that you have known good records of its implementation and operation. Many networks have multiple switches, as well as different types of switches. For example, it is not uncommon for more than one switch be part of the backbone configuration of a network. This is particularly true if a network spans multiple physical locations. It is also relatively common to have different types of switches in a network. For example, different vendor switches can interoperate together. For example, in this particular case study, multiple vendor switches are used and connected together in such a way that a single logical network is the result.

Based on experience, I suppose it would be wise to make a comment about the term switch here. The terms hub and switch are similar and many times the terms are used interchangeably. So, what is the difference between a hub and a switch? In some definitions and locations, there is no difference. I have been in places where the term hub and switch were used interchangeably. In my thinking, this can be the case or another scenario can equally be applicable. For example, many consider a hub as a more singular type of device; that is, a device that works with only one protocol such as Ethernet or token ring. Use of the term hub in this case is applicable and works well. On the other hand, the term switch seems to be used today in a manner that conveys the notion of multiple protocol support in a single device. An example of this would be a device where Ethernet, token ring, ATM, FDDI, and possibly other protocols are supported. For purposes of conveying relevant information, the switch highlighted in this brief case study overview supports multiple protocols, and consequently I address the network device "switch" in the broadest of the sense. The information here provides you with real-world insight into my network and some features and the operational nature of the switch I selected to use.

The case study information presented here is a XYLAN switch. The information I present is important to have on hand as a reference point for network files. All information about the network switch is provided courtesy of the XYLAN Corporation; and at the end of this chapter, there is information as to how they can be reached.

Before exploring more details consider the logical view of my network as shown in Figure 14-1. This figure shows a conceptual view of my network and the Omniswitch. The functionality of this switch is such that it carries the entire network payload; consequently, it is a most important network

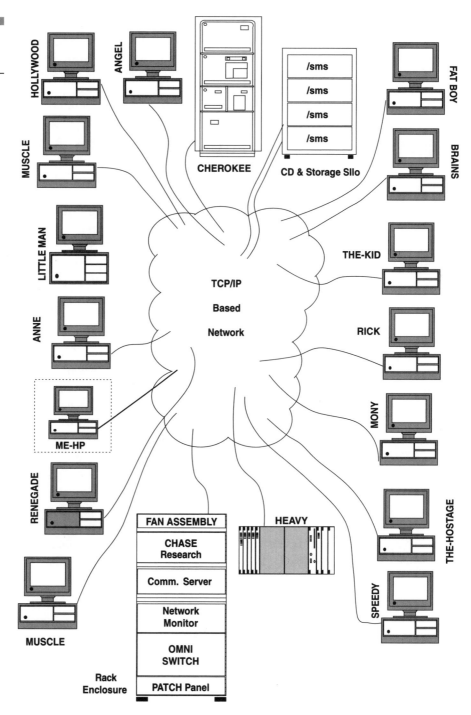

Figure 14-1
Case study network:
a logical view

component. The reason for this is that should the switch become overloaded, it is the single point of failure. However, be aware that this does not have to be the case. When I design networks, I usually do so with redundancy in mind and thus remove the single point of failure problem.

The Network Switch: A Case Study in Brief

My network is probably similar to yours in that numerous types of devices are connected and there is a network backbone "switch" to which these devices connect. This is simply information about my switch. I think you might find it insightful, particularly if you have been reading this entire book.

Cell Switching Modules

The network switch in this case study provides the flexibility to start as a pure LAN switch, gradually migrate to a hybrid LAN/ATM switch, and finally transform into a pure ATM switch capable of supporting multiple Classes of Service and robust traffic management. Making the transition from a LAN switch to an ATM switch requires only a change of interface modules; no backplane upgrade is necessary.

The switch with ATM switching functionality comes in 5-slot and 9-slot versions. Each version supports the same management, frame switching, and cell switching modules. Each version also supports the same bus architecture.

Using a distributed architecture, the switch enables you to increase the switching capacity as you add *Cell Switching Modules* (CSMs). Each CSM provides enough capacity to handle the non-blocking load of its own ports. In this way, the switch scales cost-effectively with the growth requirements of your ATM network.

Virtual Circuits

Console and Network Management software enable you to configure and monitor *Permanent Virtual Circuits* (PVCs) and soft PVCs. *Switched Virtual Circuits* (SVCs) are only monitored. Statistics are provided for all types of virtual circuits. Virtual circuits may be either *Virtual Path Connections* (VPCs) or *Virtual Channel Connections* (VCCs).

A variety of statistics are available at the port and virtual connection levels. These statistics provide information on *Cell Loss Priority* (CLP) cell flows, cell discards, and actions taken as a result of leaky bucket algorithms.

Input Buffering with Output Control

The network switch uses a unique buffer management system that combines the scalability of input buffers and the control of output buffers. Cell buffers are located on input ports, but these buffers are actually controlled by output ports. Each output port sees the traffic destined for it and uses this knowledge to schedule traffic flow across the fabric. To effectively interconnect ATM networks with the "bursty" nature of LANs, the switch uses very large cell buffers that can withstand massive inflows of LAN traffic.

Quality of Service (QoS)

The network-switch buffer management supports six (6) different Class of Service levels that are compatible and expand on ATM Forum QoS specifications. Each QoS level supports a different ATM traffic type (CBR, rt-VBR, nrt-VBR, ABR, or UBR) and supports different *Generic Cell Rate Algorithms* (GCRAs). The levels are organized by priority with additional granularity provided by sixteen (16) different user priority levels assignable at the virtual circuit level.

Partial Packet Discard (PPD) & Random Early Detect (RED)

Partial Packet Discard (PPD) and *Random Early Detect* (RED) are disabled by default for AAL5 traffic (that is, Unspecified Bit Rate and Available Bit Rate). You can enable or disable these features at the virtual circuit level or through `mpm.cmd` file command statements. When these features are enabled, AAL5 frames are discarded during congestion conditions to increase frame-level throughput.

When PPD is enabled, the switch can intelligently discard cells associated with AAL5 PDU during congestion conditions. This feature reduces the bandwidth used along the remaining downstream path. PPD can be enabled for a specific virtual circuit through the cvc command. You can also enable PPD for all new channels by adding the following statement to the switch mpm.cmd file:

```
aal5_dx=1
```

Be sure this statement comes before the cmInit line. When RED is enabled, the switch invokes PPD on logical connections in a round-robin fashion during congestion conditions. This feature smoothes out the waves of congestion retransmits that occur when LAN frames are discarded. You can enable RED by adding the following statement to the switch mpm.cmd file:

```
sp_ccu_enable=1
```

Be sure this statement comes before the cmInit line.

Dual Leaky Buckets

Dual leaky buckets are set up on each virtual circuit and policing algorithms can check for *Peak Cell Rate* (PCR), *Sustained Cell Rate* (SCR), and *Maximum Burst Size* (MBS). Options for enforcement of the traffic contract can be static dropping all cells in excess of the contract regardless of congestion conditions or congestion-based enforcement. Congestion-based enforcement tags or discards cells depending on the level of congestion on the connection and a cell's *Cell Loss Priority* (CLP). The enforcement method is defaulted based on traffic descriptors and is not user-selectable in this release.

Available Bit Rate Traffic

The network switch used in this case study supports Explicit Rate flow control for ABR traffic. *Resource Management* (RM) cells are forwarded along virtual connections. In addition, the *Explicit Forward Congestion Indicator* (EFCI) is supported for all traffic types. Currently SARs do not support ABR resource management. Therefore, ATM End Systems supporting resource management are not available to test at this time, and this feature is not fully operational in this release.

High-Speed Module (HSM)

Many switching modules that operate at speeds in excess of 10 Mbps are actually submodules that attach to a *High-Speed Module* (HSM). Switching modules used in this case study include ATM, FDDI, Token Ring, Frame Relay modules and some 100 Mbps Ethernet modules. The HSM provides the base memory and processing power for these high-throughput switching modules.

The HSM contains RISC processors, RAM for holding software image files, ASICs for performing switching, and *Content Addressable Memory* (CAM) for storing MAC addresses. The HSM comes in three versions: the HSM, HSM2, and HSM3. The option of factory installation of either one or two submodules on an HSM is available. Two submodules double the port count for a particular module. For example, a one-port ATM module contains one submodule attached to an HSM, and a two-port ATM module has two submodules attached to an HSM. The following illustration shows an HSM with an attached submodule. With the HSM and Attached Submodule, you plug the cable directly into a submodule, but it is the HSM module that connects to the switch backplane.

Content Addressable Memory

The switch module within switch used in this network uses *Content Addressable Memory* (CAM). CAM is used to claim frames from the VBUS for forwarding to the ports on that switching module. Modules with 1K of CAM can store 1,024 addresses, modules with 2K of CAM can store 2,048 addresses, and modules with 4K of CAM can store 4,096 addresses.

CAM is located directly on some Ethernet module boards; it is located on the HSM boards for ATM, FDDI, CDDI, Token Ring, and Frame Relay modules. Two CAM sockets are available for all 10 Mbps Ethernet modules and all HSM modules. In a configuration where all switching modules use the standard 1K of CAM, the OmniSwitch can actively manage up to 8,192 MAC addresses in a 9-slot chassis, and up to 4,096 addresses in a 5-slot chassis.

Because the CAM is actually a cache of most recently observed addresses and not all of the addresses in the network, even a 1K CAM can often support networks with many more than 1,024 stations. However, a module with only 1K of CAM can cause problems in networks with large shared media backbones in which more than 1,024 addresses are simultaneously active.

The 2K and 4K CAM options address this limitation by allowing up to 2,048 or 4,096 addresses per switching module. This option provides a larger CAM for address recognition logic, which makes the network switch more robust in networks with large shared media backbones. This option is supported on most switching modules.

This particular network switch software recognizes if more than 1K of CAM is installed on a switching module. The switch can support up 16K of CAM among all switching modules. If you have more than 16K of CAM installed on all switching modules in your chassis, then you can view each module's CAM usage through the camstat command. In such configurations, you might also need to configure each slot's CAM usage through the camcfg command.

If you have 16K CAM or less, then no special configuration is required. The 2K or 4K CAM option is not normally required unless a port on that module is plugged into a backbone in which a large number of addresses are simultaneously active, such as an ATM backbone. Each network is different and the traffic patterns should be observed to best decide when this is used. Another alternative to greatly improve both CAM utilization and network performance is to split the backbone into multiple networks and switch between them.

Source learning and CAM capacity learning of source addresses is affected by the amount of space available in CAM. When CAM capacity is less than 85 percent (870 or fewer entries in a 1K CAM), normal source learning occurs. When CAM capacity is 85 percent or more (870 or more entries in 1K CAM), the source addresses for non-broadcast frames are learned, but broadcast frames are not. At the 95 percent level (972 or more entries in 1K CAM), the CAM does learn the frames destined to a known addresses, but not the source addresses for frames sent to unknown destinations.

Switch Security

Through commands from the Security menu, you can configure system security parameters, such as the password and logout time. The menu also provides a command for rebooting the switch. Enter security at the prompt to enter the Security menu.

An authorized user can press ? and see the following list of commands.

Network Switch Command Security Menu

- *pw* Set a new password for a login account

- ▇ *reboot*   Reboot this system (allowed if the user is admin)
- ▇ *timeout*   Configure Auto Logout Time
- ▇ *Main File Summary*   VLAN Networking
- ▇ *Interface Security*   System Services Help

The pw, reboot, and timeout commands are described in the following sections. The software for authenticated groups displays the following list of commands.

Command Security Menu

- ▇ *pw*   Set a new password for a login account reboot Reboot this system (allowed if the user is admin)
- ▇ *timeout*   Configure Auto Logout Time
- ▇ *avlAddresses*   Define an authentication router port address
- ▇ *avlsAddresses*   Show all of the Authentication router port addresses
- ▇ *avlBanner*   Define the authentication port login banner
- ▇ *avlsBanner*   Display the Authentication port login banner
- ▇ *avlPorts*   Set a port to be a Telnet authenticated port
- ▇ *avlsPorts*   Show ports that are Telnet authenticated ports

Commands with the avl prefix apply to authenticated groups.

Case Study Network Switch: User Interface

The *User Interface* (UI) provides a means of configuring parameters and viewing real-time statistics from a terminal, such as a PC or UNIX workstation, using terminal emulation software. The UI is part of the MPM executable image. When a switch boots up, the boot monitor handles the loading of this executable image and system startup. After the image is loaded and initialized, the UI starts.

Access to the switch itself is made through the *User Interface* (UI). This connection can be made directly through the serial port, through a modem, or over a network through Telnet. You can have up to four simultaneous connections to an OmniSwitch or an OmniStack, and up to three simultaneous connections on a PizzaSwitch or PizzaPort. For Telnet access with the network switch used in this case study, you must first set up an IP address for the switch. After initial login to the network switch, the following main menu displays.

Network Switch Main Menu Command Example

The following is an example of the user interface for the network switch in this case study.

```
*********************************************************************
                        Xylan OmniSwitch
                        All rights reserved.
            OmniSwitch is a trademark of Xylan Corporation
         Registered in the United States Patent and Trademark Office.
*********************************************************************
```

System Name: **IWI-SWITCH**
Primary MPM
Command Main Menu

——-

File	Manager system files
Summary	Display summary info for VLANs, bridge, interfaces, and so on
VLAN	VLAN management
Networking	Configure/view network parameters such as routing, and so on
Interface	Enter the Physical Interface Configuration/Parameter sub-menu
Security	Configure system security parameters
System	View/set system-specific parameters
Services	View/set services parameters
Switch	View/set any to any switching parameters
Help	Help on specific tasks
Diag	Display diagnostic commands
Exit	(Logout) Log out of this session
?	Display contents of current menu

This menu provides a top-level view of all UI menus. The commands are grouped together in the form of sub-menus. Within each sub-menu there is a set of commands and/or another sub-menu.

Network Switch Main Menu Summary

A description of the main menu command functions is provided here.

- *File* Contains options for downloading system software, listing software files, copying, editing, and deleting files

- *Summary* Provides very basic information on the physical switch, such as its name, MACaddress, and resets. It also provides options for viewing the virtual interface and information on the MIB.

- *VLAN* The main menu for configuring Groups, virtual ports, and AutoTracker VLANs. This menu also contains a sub-menu for configuring bridging parameters, such as Spanning Tree and Source Routing.

- *Networking* Contains menu options for managing internetworking protocols, such as SNMP and RMON, IP and IPX, and *Next Hop Resolution Protocol* (NHRP)

- *Interface* The main menu for configuring parameters and viewing statistics for switching modules. This menu has sub-menus for managing ATM, FDDI, Token Ring, Frame Relay, and Fast Ethernet switching modules. In addition it includes a sub-option for configuring SLIP.

- *Security* This menu contains options for changing a password and rebooting the system.

- *System* Contains a wide array of options for configuring and viewing information on a variety of switch functions. Options include displays of switch slot contents, configuring serial ports, and viewing CAM information. Commands used to configure User Interface display options are described in User Interface Display Options. The System menu also includes a sub-menu option that provides additional commands for configuring the MPM module.

- *Services* Provides options for creating, modifying, viewing, and deleting ATM, FDDI, and Frame Relay services. ATM services include PTOP bridging and LAN Emulation. FDDI services include Trunking and 802.10 Trunking. Frame Relay services include bridging, routing, and trunking.

- *Switch* Provides options to precisely define frame translations. A MAC-layer type (Ethernet, Token Ring, and so on) might have more than one type of frame format, such as Ethernet or 802.3. But, by default, each MAC-layer type defaults to certain frame format on translation. This menu enables you to define translations for each frame format. This menu provides textual help on how to use the UI and on each menu or sub-menu. For the item of interest, enter `help <sub-menu name>`.

■ *Diag* This menu, fully available to the diag login account, contains commands to run diagnostic tests.

■ *Exit* Logs you out of the UI. You can also enter `logout` to exit.

■ *?* Displays the options for current menu

Network Switch (Switch-Wide Commands)

The OmniSwitch provides commands to display and configure parameters on a switch-wide basis. These commands are grouped into two menus: the Summary menu and the System menu.

Command Summary Menu

The summary menu consists of commands for displaying summary information about the switch. Enter `summary` at the prompt to enter the Summary menu. Press the question mark (`?`) to see the following commands:

Network Switch Command Summary Menu
ss   Display MIB-II System group variables
sc   OmniSwitch chassis summary
si   Current interface status

Case Study Network Switch System Information

To display basic information on the switch, enter `info` at the system prompt. The following display is an example:

System Make: Xylan OmniSwitch

System Type: 5-slot OmniSwitch

Description: **IWI SWITCH**

Backplane: 5 SLOT Bus Speed: 640

Physical changes to the system since power-up or reset: 2

Logical changes to the system since power-up or reset: 0

Number of Resets to this system: 37

The attached MPM, slot 1, is the Primary

Automatic configuration synchronization is enabled

System base MAC Address: **00:20:da:04:21:f0**

Number of Free Slots: 0

Action on Cold Start: Load & go

Action on Reset: Restart

Script File: /flash/mpm.cmd

Boot File: /flash/mpm.img

Ni Image Suffix: img

The fields displayed by the info command are described as follows.

System Make   The description of the specific type of chassis or device

System Type   The Switch type

Description   A description of the chassis and product. This field is set by the syscfg command.

Backplane   The style of backplane (3-slot, 5-slot, or 9-slot) used in this chassis

Bus Speed   The speed of backplane, in Mbs, used in this chassis. This is 640 Mbs unless you are using an MPM1G or MPM 1GW, in which case it might be 960 Mbs.

Physical changes to the system since power-up or reset   The number of physical changes that has occurred since the last reset or power-on

Logical changes to the system since power-up or reset   The number of logical changes that has occurred since the last reset or power-on

Case Study Network Switch System Menu

The System menu contains commands to view or set system-specific parameters. Enter system at the UI prompt to enter the System menu. If the
system is not set in verbose mode, press a question mark (?), and then press
<Return> and the following commands are shown:

Network Switch Command System Menu

- *info*   Basic info on this system
- *dt*   Set system date and time
- *ser*   View or configure the DTE or DCE port
- *mpm*   Configure a Management Processor Module
- *slot*   View Slot Table information
- *systat*   View system stats related to system, power and environment
- *taskstat*   View task utilization stats
- *memstat*   View memory use statistics
- *fsck*   Perform a file system check on the flash file system
- *newfs*   Erase all file from /flash and create a new file system
- *syscfg*   Configure info related to this system
- *camstat*   View CAM info and usage
- *camcfg*   Configure CAM info and usage
- *ver / ter*   Enables/disables automatic display of menus on entry
- *echo / noecho*   Enable/disable character echo
- *chpr*   Change the prompt for the system
- *Logging*   View system logs

Network Switch Chassis Summary Display

To display chassis summary information, enter sc at the system prompt.
Something similar to the following is displayed.

Type:	Omni-5
Chassis ID:	Xylan

Description:	**CASE-STUDY-**#1-BACKBONE
Backplane:	5 SLOT
Master MPM Serial No.:	00000000
Physical Changes:	7
Logical Changes:	0
Number of Resets:	26
Base MAC Address:	00:20:da:02:04:80
Free Slots:	0
Field Descriptions:	

Type	The description of the specific type of chassis or device
Chassis ID	The chassis ID for this OmniSwitch
Description	The description of this chassis. This field is set by the syscfg command.
Backplane	The style of backplane (3-slot, 5-slot, or 9-slot) used in this chassis
Master MPM Serial No	The serial number for the primary MPM
Physical Changes	The number of physical changes that has occurred since the last reset or power-on
Logical Changes	The number of logical changes that has occurred since the last reset or power-on
Number of Resets	The number of times this switch has been reset since the configuration file (mpm.cnf) was first removed
Base MAC Address	The base MAC address for the primary MPM

Switch Implementation: Highlights & Traffic Flow Trace

The particular case study where the switch is reflected in Figure 14-2. In this example, it serves as the backbone.

Figure 14-2 shows the fiber optic backbone, which every device uses. It also highlights the switch as the single network backbone to move FDDI, Ethernet, ATM, and Token Ring traffic.

To conceptually understand the following material consider Figure 14-3.

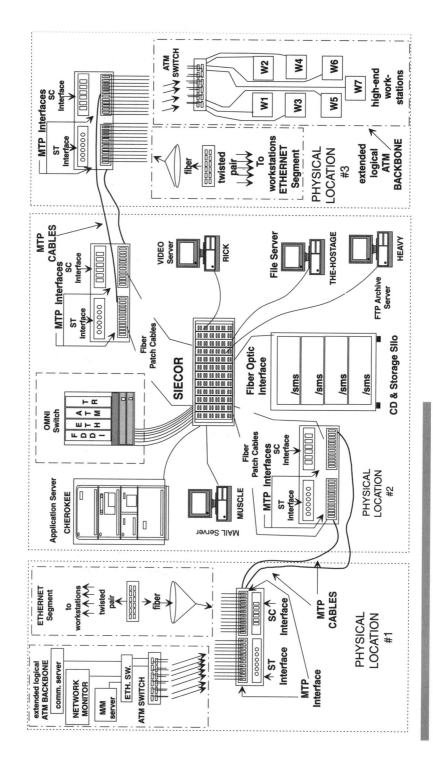

Figure 14-2 Case study network: switch backbone highlights

Figure 14-3
Actual case study
network switch

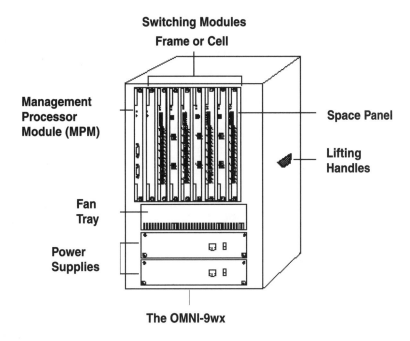

Figure 14-3 depicts the switch used in this case study. I present it in this fashion to provide you with a different perspective of the network and the function of the switch. Consider the following information that I have set aside for beginning baseline information in the switch during this case study.

Case Study: Switch Traffic between Nodes

The following is a trace from the network switch used in this case study. I have selected a "time-slice" of a trace that was run over a period of a couple hours. For purposes here, read through and examine the level of detail. Examine the following information available in the trace:

UDP	NetBIOS
IP	Protocol IDs
LLC	Target IP Addresses
TCP	NBT Session Information
SMB	Session Request Information
Name Queries	Source & Destination Information

```
***************************************************************
Frame Time Src MAC Addr Dst MAC Addr Protocol Description
Src Other Addr Dst Other Addr Type Other Addr
1 50.772 FATBOY WestDg4EB5EC NBIPX Name Recognized INFO
<00> 0.0000C07D73D7 0.0000C04EB5EC IPX/XNS

+ FRAME: Base frame properties
+ ETHERNET: 802.3 Length = 98
+ LLC: UI DSAP=0xE0 SSAP=0xE0 C
+ IPX: NetBIOS Packet-0.0000C07D73D7.455 ->
  0.0000C04EB5EC.455-0 Hops
+ NBIPX: Name Recognized INFO  <00>
00000: 00 00 C0 4E B5 EC 00 00 C0 7D 73 D7 00 54 E0 E0
. . . N . . . . .}s..T..
00010: 03 FF FF 00 50 00 04 00 00 00 00 00 00 C0 4E B5
. . . .P . . . . . . . . . N.
00020: EC 04 55 00 00 00 00 00 00 C0 7D 73 D7 04 55 00 ..U
. . . . . . .}s..U.
00030: 02 00 00 00 00 00 00 00 00 00 00 00 00 00 00 00
. . . . . . . . . . . . . . . .
00040: 00 00 00 00 00 00 00 00 00 00 00 00 00 00 00 C4
. . . . . . . . . . . . . . . .
***************************************************************

Frame Time Src MAC Addr Dst MAC Addr Protocol Description
Src Other Addr Dst Other Addr Type Other Addr 251.312 FAT-
BOY WestDg4EB5EC
NBIPX Name Recognized INFO <00>
0.0000C07D73D7 0.0000C04EB5EC IPX/XNS

+ FRAME: Base frame properties
+ ETHERNET: 802.3 Length = 98
+ LLC: UI DSAP=0xE0 SSAP=0xE0 C
+ IPX:      NetBIOS      Packet — 0.0000C07D73D7.455      ->
  0.0000C04EB5EC.455 — 0 Hops
+ NBIPX: Name Recognized INFO <00>
00000: 00 00 C0 4E B5 EC 00 00 C0 7D 73 D7 00 54 E0 E0
. . . N . . . . .}s..T..
00010: 03 FF FF 00 50 00 04 00 00 00 00 00 00 C0 4E B5
. . . .P . . . . . . . . . N.
00020: EC 04 55 00 00 00 00 00 00 C0 7D 73 D7 04 55 00 ..U
. . . . . . .}s..U.
```

```
00030:  02 00 00 00 00 00 00 00 00 00 00 00 00 00 00 00
. . . . . . . . . . . . . . . .
00040:  00 00 00 00 00 00 00 00 00 00 00 00 00 00 00 C4   . . .
. . . . . . . . . . . . .
```

```
*************************************************************
```

Frame Time Src MAC Addr Dst MAC Addr Protocol Description
Src Other Addr Dst Other Addr Type Other Addr
351.853 **FATBOY WestDg4EB5EC** NBIPX Name Recognized INFO
<00> 0.0000C07D73D7 0.0000C04EB5EC IPX/XNS

+ FRAME: Base frame properties
+ ETHERNET: 802.3 Length = 98
+ LLC: UI DSAP=0xE0 SSAP=0xE0 C
+ IPX: NetBIOS Packet-0.0000C07D73D7.455 ->
  0.0000C04EB5EC.455-0 Hops
+ NBIPX: Name Recognized INFO <00>

```
00000:  00 00 C0 4E B5 EC 00 00 C0 7D 73 D7 00 54 E0 E0   .
. . N . . . . .}s. .T. .
00010:  03 FF FF 00 50 00 04 00 00 00 00 00 00 C0 4E B5
. . . .P . . . . . . . . . N.
00020:  EC 04 55 00 00 00 00 00 00 C0 7D 73 D7 04 55 00   .
.U . . . . . . .}s..U.
00030:  02 00 00 00 00 00 00 00 00 00 00 00 00 00 00 00
. . . . . . . . . . . . . . . .
00040:  00 00 00 00 00 00 00 00 00 00 00 00 00 00 00 C4
. . . . . . . . . . . . .
```

```
*************************************************************
```

Frame Time Src MAC Addr Dst MAC Addr Protocol Description Src Other Addr Dst Other Addr Type Other Addr
4 61.970 FATBOY WestDg4EB5EC NBT
NS: Query req. for BRAINS FATBOY 220.100.100.10 IP

+ FRAME: Base frame properties
+ ETHERNET: ETYPE = 0x0800 : Protocol = IP: DOD Internet
Protocol
+ IP: ID = 0x2D00; Proto = UDP; Len: 78
+ UDP: Src Port: NETBIOS Name Service, (137); Dst Port:
  NETBIOS Name Service (137);
  Length = 58 (0x3A)
+ NBT: NS: Query req. for BRAINS

```
00000: 00 00 C0 4E B5 EC 00 00 C0 7D 73 D7 08 00 45 00
. . . N . . . . . .}s . . . E.
00010: 00 4E 2D 00 00 00 80 11 8C C2 DC 64 64 09 DC 64
.N- . . . . . . . ..dd..d
00020: 64 0A 00 89 00 89 00 3A A8 F5 80 31 01 00 00 01 d
. . . . . . . : . . . 1 . . . .
00030: 00 00 00 00 00 00 20 45 43 46 43 45 42 45 4A 45 .
. . . . ECFCEBEJE
00040: 4F 46 44 43 41 43 41 43 41 43 41 43 41 43 41 43
       OFDCACACACA
       CACAC
```

Frame Time Src MAC Addr Dst MAC Addr Protocol Descrip-
tion Src Other Addr Dst Other Addr Type Other Addr
561.970 FATBOY BRAINS
NETBIOS Name Query (0x0A), FATBOY <00> -> BRAINS
+ FRAME: Base frame properties
+ **ETHERNET: 802.3 Length** = 61
+ LLC: UI DSAP=0xF0 SSAP=0xF0 C
+ **NETBIOS: Name Query (0x0A), FATBOY <00> -> BRAINS**

```
00000: 03 00 00 00 00 01 00 00 C0 7D 73 D7 00 2F F0 F0
. . . . . . . . . }s . . / . .
00010: 03 2C 00 FF EF 0A 00 00 00 00 00 0D 00 42 52 41 .,
. . . . . . . . . . ..BRA
00020: 49 4E 53 20 20 20 20 20 20 20 20 20 20 46 41 54 INS
FAT
00030: 42 4F 59 20 20 20 20 20 20 20 20 20 00 BOY .
```
****
Frame Time Src MAC Addr Dst MAC Addr Protocol Description
Src Other Addr Dst Other Addr Type Other Addr
6 61.970 BRAINS FATBOY NETBIOS Name Recognize (0x0E),
BRAINS -> FATBOY <00>

+ FRAME: Base frame properties
+ ETHERNET: 802.3 Length = 61
+ LLC: UI DSAP=0xF0 SSAP=0xF0 C
+ **NETBIOS: Name Recognize (0x0E), BRAINS -> FATBOY <00>**

```
00000: 00 00 C0 7D 73 D7 00 00 C0 3A B8 EC 00 2F F0 F0 . . .
}s . . . . : . . . /..
```

```
00010: 03 2C 00 FF EF 0E 00 00 00 0D 00 00 00 46 41 54 .,
. . .  . . . . . . . ..FAT
00020: 42 4F 59 20 20 20 20 20 20 20 20 20 00 42 52 41 BOY
.BRA
00030: 49 4E 53 20 20 20 20 20 20 20 20 20 20 INS
*******************************************************
```

Frame Time Src MAC Addr Dst MAC Addr Protocol Description
Src Other Addr Dst Other Addr Type Other Addr
7 61.971 **FATBOY BRAINS NETBIOS Name Query (0x0A), FATBOY
<00> -> BRAINS**

+ FRAME: Base frame properties
+ ETHERNET: 802.3 Length = 61
+ LLC: UI DSAP=0xF0 SSAP=0xF0 C
+ **NETBIOS: Name Query (0x0A), FATBOY <00> -> BRAINS**

```
00000: 00 00 C0 3A B8 EC 00 00 C0 7D 73 D7 00 2F F0 F0
. . . : . . . . . .}s../..
00010: 03 2C 00 FF EF 0A 00 02 00 00 00 0D 00 42 52 41 .,
. . .  . . . . . . . ..BRA
00020: 49 4E 53 20 20 20 20 20 20 20 20 20 20 46 41 54 INS
FAT
00030: 42 4F 59 20 20 20 20 20 20 20 20 20 20 00 BOY .
*******************************************************
```

Frame Time Src MAC Addr Dst MAC Addr Protocol Description
Src Other Addr Dst Other Addr Type Other Addr
8 61.971 **WestDg4EB5EC FATBOY NBT NS: Query (Node Status)
resp. for BRAINS, Success 220.100.100.10 FATBOY IP**

+ FRAME: Base frame properties
+ **ETHERNET: ETYPE** = 0x0800 : Protocol = IP: DOD Internet
Protocol
+ IP: ID = 0x8A04; Proto = UDP; Len: 90
+ **UDP: Src Port: NETBIOS Name Service, (137);
Dst Port: NETBIOS Name Service (137);
Length** = 70 (0x46)
+ **NBT: NS: Query (Node Status) resp. for BRAINS, Success**
```
00000: 00 00 C0 7D 73 D7 00 00 C0 4E B5 EC 08 00 45 00 . . .
}s . . . .N . . . .E.
00010: 00 5A 8A 04 00 00 80 11 2F B2 DC 64 64 0A DC 64 .Z
. . . . . . /..dd..d
```

```
00020: 64 09 00 89 00 89 00 46 83 E5 80 31 85 80 00 00 d
. . . . . F . . . 1 . . . .
00030: 00 01 00 00 00 00 20 45 43 46 43 45 42 45 4A 45 ..
. . . . ECFCEBEJE
00040: 4F 46 44 43 41 43 41 43 41 43 41 43 41 43 41 43 OFD-
        CACACACA
        CACAC
```
****

Frame Time Src MAC Addr Dst MAC Addr Protocol Description
Src Other Addr Dst Other Addr Type Other Addr
9   61.972 **BRAINS FATBOY NETBIOS Name Recognize (0x0E),
BRAINS => FATBOY <00>**

+ FRAME: Base frame properties
+ ETHERNET: 802.3 Length = 61
+ LLC: UI DSAP=0xF0 SSAP=0xF0 C
+ **NETBIOS: Name Recognize (0x0E), BRAINS -> FATBOY** <00>

```
00000: 00 00 C0 7D 73 D7 00 00 C0 3A B8 EC 00 2F F0 F0 . . .
}s . . . . : . . . /..
00010: 03 2C 00 FF EF 0E 00 0C 00 0D 00 00 00 46 41 54 .,
. . . . . . . . . . .FAT
00020: 42 4F 59 20 20 20 20 20 20 20 20 20 00 42 52 41 BOY
.BRA
00030: 49 4E 53 20 20 20 20 20 20 20 20 20 20 INS
```
****

Frame Time Src MAC Addr Dst MAC Addr Protocol Description
Src Other Addr Dst Other Addr Type Other Addr
10   61.972 **FATBOY   FFFFFFFFFFFF ARP_RARP ARP: Request,
Target IP: 220.100.100.12**

+ FRAME: Base frame properties
+ ETHERNET: ETYPE = 0x0806 : Protocol = ARP: Address Res-
  olution Protocol
+ ARP_RARP: **ARP: Request, Target IP: 220.100.100.12**

```
00000: FF FF FF FF FF FF 00 00 C0 7D 73 D7 08 06 00 01 . . .
. . . . . . }s . . . . .
00010: 08 00 06 04 00 01 00 00 C0 7D 73 D7 DC 64 64 09
. . . . . . . . . }s. .dd.
00020: 00 00 00 00 00 00 DC 64 64 0C . . . . . . .dd.
```

```
*************************************************************
Frame Time Src MAC Addr Dst MAC Addr Protocol Description
Src Other Addr Dst Other Addr Type Other Addr
11  61.972 FATBOY BRAINS
LLC SABME
DSAP=0xF0
SSAP50xF0 C POLL

+ FRAME: Base frame properties
+ ETHERNET: 802.3 Length = 17
+ LLC: SABME DSAP=0xF0 SSAP=0xF0 C POLL

00000: 00 00 C0 3A B8 EC 00 00 C0 7D 73 D7 00 03 F0 F0 . . .
:  . . . . ..}s . . . . .
00010: 7F
*************************************************************

Frame Time Src MAC Addr Dst MAC Addr Protocol Description
Src Other Addr Dst Other Addr Type Other Addr
12  61.972 BRAINS FATBOY ARP_RARP ARP: Reply,
Target IP: 220.100.100.9 Target Hdwr Addr: 0000C07D73

+ FRAME: Base frame properties
+ ETHERNET: ETYPE = 0x0806 : Protocol = ARP: Address Resolu-
tion Protocol
+ ARP_RARP: ARP: Reply,
Target IP: 220.100.100.9
Target Hdwr Addr: 0000C07D73D7

00000: 00 00 C0 7D 73 D7 00 00 C0 3A B8 EC 08 06 00 01 . . .
}s . . . . : . . . . . .
00010: 08 00 06 04 00 02 00 00 C0 3A B8 EC DC 64 64 0C . . .
. . . . . . : . . . dd.
00020: 00 00 C0 7D 73 D7 DC 64 64 09 20 20 00 42 52 41
. . . }s..dd. .BRA
00030: 49 4E 53 20 20 20 20 20 20 20 20 20 INS
*************************************************************

Frame Time Src MAC Addr Dst MAC Addr Protocol Description
Src Other Addr Dst Other Addr Type Other Addr
13   61.972  FATBOY  BRAINS  TCP  . . . .S., len:  24,
seq:1144032-1144055, ack:0, win: 8 FATBOY BRAINS IP
```

```
+ FRAME: Base frame properties
+ ETHERNET: ETYPE = 0x0800 : Protocol = IP: DOD Internet
Protocol
+ IP: ID = 0x2E00; Proto = TCP; Len: 64
+ TCP:   . . . .S.,len:24, seq:1144032-1144055, ack:0, win:
8192, src:026 dst:139 (NBT Session)

00000: 00 00 C0 3A B8 EC 00 00 C0 7D 73 D7 08 00 45 00 . . .
: . . . . .}s . . . . E.
00010: 00 40 2E 00 40 00 80 06 4B D9 DC 64 64 09 DC 64
.@..@ . . . K..dd..d
00020: 64 0C 04 02 00 8B 00 11 74 E0 00 00 00 00 B0 02 d
. . . . . . .t . . . . . . .
00030: 20 00 1B A4 00 00 02 04 05 B4 01 03 03 00 01 01
. . . . . . . . . . . . . . .
00040: 08 0A 00 00 00 00 00 00 00 00 01 01 04 02   . . .
. . . . . . . . . . .
************************************************************

Frame Time Src MAC Addr Dst MAC Addr Protocol Description
Src Other Addr Dst Other Addr Type Other Addr
14 61.973 BRAINS FATBOY LLC UA DSAP=0xF0 SSAP=0xF1 R FINAL

+ FRAME: Base frame properties
+ ETHERNET: 802.3 Length = 60
1 LLC: UA DSAP=0xF0 SSAP=0xF1 R FINAL

00000: 00 00 C0 7D 73 D7 00 00 C0 3A B8 EC 00 03 F0 F1 . . .
}s . . . : . . . . . .
00010: 73 00 06 04 00 02 00 00 C0 3A B8 EC DC 64 64 0C s
. . . . . . . . . : . . . dd.
00020: 00 00 C0 7D 73 D7 DC 64 64 09 20 20 00 42 52 41
. . . }s..dd. .BRA
00030: 49 4E 53 20 20 20 20 20 20 20 20 20 INS
************************************************************

Frame Time Src MAC Addr Dst MAC Addr Protocol Description
Src Other Addr Dst Other Addr Type Other Addr
15  61.973 FATBOY BRAINS LLC
RR DSAP=0xF0 SSAP=0xF0 C N(R) = 0x00 POLL

+ FRAME: Base frame properties
+ ETHERNET: 802.3 Length = 18
```

```
+ LLC: RR DSAP=0xF0 SSAP=0xF0 C N(R) = 0x00 POLL

00000: 00 00 C0 3A B8 EC 00 00 C0 7D 73 D7 00 04 F0 F0 . . .
: . . . . .}s . . . . .
00010: 01 01 ..
```

****

```
Frame Time Src MAC Addr Dst MAC Addr Protocol Description
Src Other Addr Dst Other Addr Type Other Addr
16  61.973 BRAINS FATBOY TCP .A..S., len: 4,
seq: 9178662-9178665, ack: 1144033,
win: 8 BRAINS FATBOY IP

+ FRAME: Base frame properties
+ ETHERNET: ETYPE = 0x0800 : Protocol = IP: DOD Internet
Protocol
+ IP: ID = 0xC605; Proto = TCP; Len: 44
+ TCP: .A..S., len: 4, seq: 9178662-9178665,
ack: 1144033, win: 8760,
src: 139 (NBT Session) dst: 1026

00000: 00 00 C0 7D 73 D7 00 00 C0 3A B8 EC 08 00 45 00 . . .
}s . . . . : . . . . .E.
00010: 00 2C C6 05 40 00 80 06 B3 E7 DC 64 64 0C DC 64
.,..@ . . . . . . . dd..d
00020: 64 09 00 8B 04 02 00 8C 0E 26 00 11 74 E1 60 12 d
. . . . . . . .&..t.`.
00030: 22 38 6C CE 00 00 02 04 05 B4 20 20 "8l . . . . . . .
.
```

****

```
Frame Time Src MAC Addr Dst MAC Addr Protocol Description
Src Other Addr Dst Other Addr Type Other Addr
17   61.974  FATBOY   BRAINS   TCP  .A . . . ., len:   0,
seq:1144033-1144033,
ack: 9178663, win: 8 FATBOY BRAINS IP
+ FRAME: Base frame properties
+ ETHERNET: ETYPE = 0x0800 : Protocol = IP: DOD Internet
Protocol
+ IP: ID = 0x2F00; Proto = TCP; Len: 40
+ TCP: .A . . . ., len: 0, seq: 1144033-1144033,
ack: 9178663, win: 8760, src: 1026
dst: 139 (NBT Session)
```

```
00000: 00 00 C0 3A B8 EC 00 00 C0 7D 73 D7 08 00 45 00 . . .
: . . . . .}s . . . E.
00010: 00 28 2F 00 40 00 80 06 4A F1 DC 64 64 09 DC 64
.(/.@ . . . J..dd..d
00020: 64 0C 04 02 00 8B 00 11 74 E1 00 8C 0E 27 50 10 d
. . . . . . .t . . . .'P.
00030: 22 38 84 8B 00 00 "8 . . . .
```
****

Frame Time Src MAC Addr Dst MAC Addr Protocol Description
Src Other Addr Dst Other Addr Type Other Addr
18   61.974 **FATBOY BRAINS NBT SS: Session Request, Dest:
BRAINS,
Source: FATBOY FATBOY BRAINS IP**

+ FRAME: Base frame properties
+ ETHERNET: ETYPE = 0x0800 : Protocol = IP: DOD Internet
Protocol
+ IP: ID = 0x3000; Proto = TCP; Len: 112
+ TCP: .AP . . . , len: 72, seq: 1144033-1144104, ack:
9178663, win: 8760,
src: 1026 dst: 139 (NBT Session)
+ **NBT: SS: Session Request, Dest: BRAINS , Source: FATBOY
<00>, Len: 68**

```
00000: 00 00 C0 3A B8 EC 00 00 C0 7D 73 D7 08 00 45 00 . . .
: . . . . .}s . . . E.
00010: 00 70 30 00 40 00 80 06 49 A9 DC 64 64 09 DC 64
.p0.@ . . . I..dd..d
00020: 64 0C 04 02 00 8B 00 11 74 E1 00 8C 0E 27 50 18 d
. . . . . . .t . . . .'P.
00030: 22 38 56 74 00 00 81 00 00 44 20 45 43 46 43 45 "8Vt
. . . . ..D ECFCE
00040: 42 45 4A 45 4F 46 44 43 41 43 41 43 41 43 41 43
BEJEOFDCACA
CACAC
```
****

Frame Time Src MAC Addr Dst MAC Addr Protocol Description
Src Other Addr Dst Other Addr Type Other Addr
19   61.974 **BRAINS FATBOY LLC
RR DSAP=0xF0 SSAP=0xF1 R N(R) = 0x00 FINAL**

```
+ FRAME: Base frame properties
+ ETHERNET: 802.3 Length = 60
+ LLC: RR DSAP=0xF0 SSAP=0xF1 R N(R) = 0x00 FINAL
00000: 00 00 C0 7D 73 D7 00 00 C0 3A B8 EC 00 04 F0 F1 . . .
}s . . . . : . . . .
00010: 01 01 C6 05 40 00 80 06 B3 E7 DC 64 64 0C DC 64 . . .
.@ . . . . . . dd..d
00020: 64 09 00 8B 04 02 00 8C 0E 26 00 11 74 E1 60 12 d
. . . . . . ..&..t.`.
00030: 22 38 6C CE 00 00 02 04 05 B4 20 20 "8l . . . . . .
.
```

```
************************************************************
```

```
Frame Time Src MAC Addr Dst MAC Addr Protocol Description
Src Other Addr Dst Other Addr Type Other Addr
20  61.974 FATBOY BRAINS
NETBIOS Session Initialize (0x19): LSN = 0x02, RSN = 0x0C
```

```
+ FRAME: Base frame properties
+ ETHERNET: 802.3 Length = 32
+ LLC: I DSAP=0xF0 SSAP=0xF0 C N(S) = 0x00, N(R) = 0x00
POLL
```
+ 1 NETBIOS: Session Initialize (0x19): LSN = 0x02, RSN = 0x0C

```
00000: 00 00 C0 3A B8 EC 00 00 C0 7D 73 D7 00 12 F0 F0 . . .
: . . . . . }s . . . . .
00010: 00 01 0E 00 FF EF 19 8F CA 05 00 00 00 00 0C 02 . . .
. . . . . . . . . . . .
```

```
************************************************************
```

```
Frame Time Src MAC Addr Dst MAC Addr Protocol Description
Src Other Addr Dst Other Addr Type Other Addr
21  61.975 BRAINS FATBOY
```
LLC RR
DSAP=0xF0
SSAP=0xF1 R N(R) = 0x01 FINAL

```
+ FRAME: Base frame properties
+ ETHERNET: 802.3 Length = 60
+ LLC: RR DSAP=0xF0 SSAP=0xF1 R N(R) = 0x01 FINAL
```

```
00000: 00 00 C0 7D 73 D7 00 00 C0 3A B8 EC 00 04 F0 F1 . . .
}s . . . . : . . . . .
```

```
00010: 01 03 C6 05 40 00 80 06 B3 E7 DC 64 64 0C DC 64  . . .
.@ . . . . . . dd..d
00020: 64 09 00 8B 04 02 00 8C 0E 26 00 11 74 E1 60 12  d
. . . . . . . .&..t.`.
00030: 22 38 6C CE 00 00 02 04 05 B4 20 20 "8l . . . . . .
.
```

```
*************************************************************
```

```
Frame Time Src MAC Addr Dst MAC Addr Protocol Description
Src Other Addr Dst Other Addr Type Other Addr
22  61.975 BRAINS FATBOY NETBIOS Session Confirm (0x17):
LSN = 0x0C, RSN = 0x02
```

+ FRAME: Base frame properties
+ ETHERNET: 802.3 Length = 60
+ LLC: I DSAP=0xF0 SSAP=0xF0 C N(S) = 0x00, N(R) = 0x01
POLL
+ NETBIOS: Session Confirm (0x17): LSN = 0x0C, RSN = 0x02

```
00000: 00 00 C0 7D 73 D7 00 00 C0 3A B8 EC 00 12 F0 F0  . . .
}s . . . . : . . . . .
00010: 00 03 0E 00 FF EF 17 81 CA 05 00 00 00 00 02 0C  . . .
. . . . . . . . . . . .  . . .
00020: 64 09 00 8B 04 02 00 8C 0E 26 00 11 74 E1 60 12  d
. . . . . . . .&..t.`.
00030: 22 38 6C CE 00 00 02 04 05 B4 20 20 "8l . . . . . .
.
```

```
*************************************************************
```

```
Frame Time Src MAC Addr Dst MAC Addr Protocol Description
Src Other Addr Dst Other Addr Type Other Addr
23 61.975 FATBOY BRAINS LLC
RR DSAP=0xF0 SSAP=0xF1 R N(R) = 0x01 FINAL
```

+ FRAME: Base frame properties
+ ETHERNET: 802.3 Length = 18
+ LLC: RR DSAP=0xF0 SSAP=0xF1 R N(R) = 0x01 FINAL

```
00000: 00 00 C0 3A B8 EC 00 00 C0 7D 73 D7 00 04 F0 F1  . . .
: . . . . . }s . . . t. ..
00010: 01 03 ..
*************************************************************
```

```
Frame Time Src MAC Addr Dst MAC Addr Protocol Description
Src Other Addr Dst Other Addr Type Other Addr
24 61.975 BRAINS FATBOY
NBT SS: Positive Session Response, Len: 0
BRAINS FATBOY IP
```

+ FRAME: Base frame properties
+ ETHERNET: ETYPE = 0x0800 : Protocol = IP: DOD Internet Protocol
+ IP: ID = 0xC705; Proto = TCP; Len: 44
+ **TCP: .AP . . . , len: 4, seq: 9178663-9178666, ack: 1144105, win: 8688,**
src: 139 (NBT Session) dst: 1026
+ **NBT: SS: Positive Session Response, Len: 0**

```
00000: 00 00 C0 7D 73 D7 00 00 C0 3A B8 EC 08 00 45 00 . . .
}s . . . . : . . . .E.
00010: 00 2C C7 05 40 00 80 06 B2 E7 DC 64 64 0C DC 64
.,..@ . . . . . . dd..d
00020: 64 09 00 8B 04 02 00 8C 0E 27 00 11 75 29 50 18 d
. . . . . . ..'..u)P.
00030: 21 F0 02 7F 00 00 82 00 00 00 20 20 !.. . . . . . .
************************************************************
```

```
Frame Time Src MAC Addr Dst MAC Addr Protocol Descrip-
tion Src Other Addr Dst Other Addr Type Other Addr:
2561.976
FATBOY FFFFFFFFFFFF NBIPX Find Name BRAINS
0.0000C07D73D7 0.FFFFFFFFFFFF IPX/XNS
```

+ FRAME: Base frame properties
+ ETHERNET: 802.3 Length = 98
+ LLC: UI DSAP=0xE0 SSAP=0xE0 C
+ IPX: NetBIOS   Packet-0.0000C07D73D7.455   ->
       0.FFFFFFFFFFFF.455-0 Hops
+ **NBIPX: Find Name BRAINS**

```
00000: FF FF FF FF FF FF 00 00 C0 7D 73 D7 00 54 E0 E0
. . . . . . . . . }s..T..
00010: 03 FF FF 00 50 00 14 00 00 00 00 FF FF FF FF FF . . .
.P . . . . . . . . . ..
```

```
00020: FF 04 55 00 00 00 00 00 00 C0 7D 73 D7 04 55 00  ..U
. . . . . . .}s..U.
00030: 01 00 00 00 00 00 00 00 00 00 00 00 00 00 00 00
. . . . . . . . . . . . . . . .
00040: 00 00 00 00 00 00 00 00 00 00 00 00 00 00 00 00
. . . . . . . . . . . . . . . .
************************************************************
```

Frame Time Src MAC Addr Dst MAC Addr Protocol Description
Src Other Addr Dst Other Addr Type Other Addr
26 61.978
FATBOY BRAINS SMB C negotiate, Dialect = NT LM 0.12
FATBOY BRAINS IP

+ FRAME: Base frame properties
+ ETHERNET: ETYPE = 0x0800 : **Protocol** = IP: DOD Internet
Protocol
+ IP: ID = 0x3100; Proto = TCP; Len: 177
+ **TCP: .AP . . . , len: 137, seq: 1144105-1144241,**
ack: 9178667, win: 8756,
src: 1026 dst: 139 (NBT Session)
+ **NBT: SS: Session Message, Len: 133**
+ **SMB: C negotiate, Dialect = NT LM 0.12**

```
00000: 00 00 C0 3A B8 EC 00 00 C0 7D 73 D7 08 00 45 00  . . .
: . . . ..}s . . . E.
00010: 00 B1 31 00 40 00 80 06 48 68 DC 64 64 09 DC 64
..1.@ . . . Hh.dd..d
00020: 64 0C 04 02 00 8B 00 11 75 29 00 8C 0E 2B 50 18 d
. . . . . . .u) . . . +P.
00030: 22 34 CB 7B 00 00 00 00 00 85 FF 53 4D 42 72 00  "4.{
. . . . . . .SMBr.
00040: 00 00 00 18 43 C8 00 00 00 00 00 00 00 00 00 00
. . . .C . . . . . . . . ..
************************************************************
```

Frame Time Src MAC Addr Dst MAC Addr Protocol Description
Src Other Addr Dst Other Addr Type Other Addr
27 61.978 FATBOY BRAINS NETBIOS Session End (0x18):
LSN = 0x02, RSN = 0x0C

+ FRAME: Base frame properties
+ ETHERNET: 802.3 Length = 32

```
+ LLC: I DSAP=0xF0 SSAP=0xF0 C N(S) = 0x01, N(R) = 0x01
POLL
```
+ **NETBIOS: Session End (0x18): LSN** = 0x02, RSN = 0x0C

```
00000: 00 00 C0 3A B8 EC 00 00 C0 7D 73 D7 00 12 F0 F0 . . .
:  .  .  .  .  .}s  .  .  .  .  ..
00010: 02 03 0E 00 FF EF 18 00 00 00 00 00 00 00 0C 02 . . .
.  .  .  .  .  .  .  .  .  .  .
****************************************************************
```

```
Frame Time Src MAC Addr Dst MAC Addr Protocol Description
Src Other Addr Dst Other Addr Type Other Addr
28 61.979 BRAINS FATBOY LLC
RR DSAP=0xF0 SSAP=0xF1 R N(R) = 0x02 FINAL
```
+ FRAME: Base frame properties
+ ETHERNET: 802.3 Length = 60
+ **LLC: RR DSAP=0xF0 SSAP=0xF1 R N(R) = 0x02 FINAL**

```
00000: 00 00 C0 7D 73 D7 00 00 C0 3A B8 EC 00 04 F0 F1 . . .
}s  .  .  .  .  :  .  .  .  .  .
00010: 01 05 C7 05 40 00 80 06 B2 E7 DC 64 64 0C DC 64 . . .
.@  .  .  .  .  .  dd..d
00020: 64 09 00 8B 04 02 00 8C 0E 27 00 11 75 29 50 18 d
.  .  .  .  .  .  .  ..'..u)P.
00030: 21 F0 02 7F 00 00 82 00 00 00 20 20 !..  .  .  .  .  .  .
****************************************************************
```

```
Frame Time Src MAC Addr Dst MAC Addr Protocol Description
Src Other Addr Dst Other Addr Type Other Addr
29 61.979 FATBOY BRAINS LLC DISC DSAP=0xF0 SSAP=0xF0 C
POLL
```

+ FRAME: Base frame properties
+ ETHERNET: 802.3 Length = 17
+ LLC: DISC DSAP=0xF0 SSAP=0xF0 C POLL

```
00000: 00 00 C0 3A B8 EC 00 00 C0 7D 73 D7 00 03 F0 F0 . . .
:  .  .  .  .  ..}s  .  .  .  .  ..
00010: 53 S
****************************************************************
```

```
Frame Time Src MAC Addr Dst MAC Addr Protocol Description
Src Other Addr Dst Other Addr Type Other Addr
```

```
30 61.979 BRAINS FATBOY SMB R negotiate, Dialect # = 5
BRAINS FATBOY IP
```

+ FRAME: Base frame properties
+ ETHERNET: ETYPE = 0x0800 : **Protocol** = IP: DOD Internet
Protocol
+ IP: ID = 0xC805; **Proto = TCP; Len: 131**
+ **TCP: .AP . . . , len: 91, seq: 9178667-9178757, ack:
1144242,**
win: 8551, src: 139 (NBT Session) dst: 1026
+ **NBT: SS: Session Message, Len: 87**
+ **SMB: R negotiate, Dialect # = 5**

```
00000: 00 00 C0 7D 73 D7 00 00 C0 3A B8 EC 08 00 45 00 . . .
}s . . . . : . . . .E.
00010: 00 83 C8 05 40 00 80 06 B1 90 DC 64 64 0C DC 64 . . .
.@ . . . . . . dd..d
00020: 64 09 00 8B 04 02 00 8C 0E 2B 00 11 75 B2 50 18 d
. . . . . . . ..+..u.P.
00030: 21 67 A6 FA 00 00 00 00 00 57 FF 53 4D 42 72 00 !g
. . . . . . .W.SMBr.
00040: 00 00 00 98 43 C8 00 00 00 00 00 00 00 00 00 00
. . . .C . . . . . . . . . ..
```

****

Frame Time Src MAC Addr Dst MAC Addr Protocol Description
Src Other Addr Dst Other Addr Type Other Addr
31 61.980
BRAINS FATBOY LLC UA DSAP=0xF0 SSAP=0xF1 R FINAL

+ FRAME: Base frame properties
+ ETHERNET: 802.3 Length = 60
+ **LLC: UA DSAP=0xF0 SSAP=0xF1 R FINAL**

```
00000: 00 00 C0 7D 73 D7 00 00 C0 3A B8 EC 00 03 F0 F1 . . .
}s . . . . : . . . . . .
00010: 73 83 C8 05 40 00 80 06 B1 90 DC 64 64 0C DC 64 s
. . . @ . . . . . . dd..d
00020: 64 09 00 8B 04 02 00 8C 0E 2B 00 11 75 B2 50 18 d
. . . . . . . ..+..u.P.
00030: 21 67 A6 FA 00 00 00 00 00 57 FF 53 !g . . . . . .
.W.S
```

****

```
Frame Time Src MAC Addr Dst MAC Addr Protocol Description
Src Other Addr Dst Other Addr Type Other Addr
```
32 62.084 **FATBOY BRAINS**
SMB C session setup & X, Username = , and C tree connect
& X, Share = FATBOY
BRAINS IP

\+ FRAME: Base frame properties
\+ ETHERNET: ETYPE = 0x0800 : Protocol = IP: DOD Internet
Protocol
\+ IP: ID = 0x3200; Proto = TCP; Len: 220
\+ **TCP: .AP . . . , len: 180, seq: 1144242-1144421, ack:**
9178758,
win: 8665, src: 1026 dst: 139 (NBT Session)
\+ **NBT: SS: Session Message, Len: 176**
1 SMB: C session setup & X, Username = , and C tree con-
nect & X, Share = \\BRAINS\IPC$

```
00000: 00 00 C0 3A B8 EC 00 00 C0 7D 73 D7 08 00 45 00 . . .
: . . . . .}s . . . E.
00010: 00 DC 32 00 40 00 80 06 47 3D DC 64 64 09 DC 64 ..2.@
. . . G=.dd..d
00020: 64 0C 04 02 00 8B 00 11 75 B2 00 8C 0E 86 50 18 d
. . . . . . .u . . . . .P.
00030: 21 D9 E2 08 00 00 00 00 00 B0 FF 53 4D 42 73 00 !
. . . . . . . . . .SMBs.
00040: 00 00 00 18 03 C8 00 00 00 00 00 00 00 00 00 00
. . . . . . . . . . . . . . . .
***************************************************************
Frame Time Src MAC Addr Dst MAC Addr Protocol Description
Src Other Addr Dst Other Addr Type Other Addr
```
33 62.086 **BRAINS FATBOY**
SMB R session setup & X, and R tree connect & X,
Type = IPC
BRAINS FATBOY IP

\+ FRAME: Base frame properties
\+ ETHERNET: ETYPE = 0x0800 : Protocol = IP: DOD Internet
Protocol
\+ IP: ID = 0xC905; Proto = TCP; Len: 180
\+ **TCP: .AP . . . , len: 140, seq: 9178758-9178897, ack:**
1144422,

win: 8371, src: 139 (NBT Session) dst: 1026
+ NBT: SS: Session Message, Len: 136
+ SMB: R session setup & X, and R tree connect & X, Type
= IPC

```
00000: 00 00 C0 7D 73 D7 00 00 C0 3A B8 EC 08 00 45 00
. . . }s . . . . .: . . . . .E.
00010: 00 B4 C9 05 40 00 80 06 B0 5F DC 64 64 0C DC 64
. . . .@ . . . . ._.dd..d
00020: 64 09 00 8B 04 02 00 8C 0E 86 00 11 76 66 50 18 d
. . . . . . . . . . ..vfP.
00030: 20 B3 B0 A8 00 00 00 00 00 88 FF 53 4D 42 73 00
. . . . . . . . . .SMBs.
00040: 00 00 00 98 03 C8 00 00 00 00 00 00 00 00 00 00
. . . . . . . . . . . . . . . .
```

****

Frame Time Src MAC Addr Dst MAC Addr Protocol Description
Src Other Addr Dst Other Addr Type Other Addr
34 62.181 **FATBOY FFFFFFFFFFFF SAP**
Nearest Svc Query [Nearest Service Query]
0.0000C07D73D7 0.FFFFFFFFFFFF IPX/XNS

+ FRAME: Base frame properties
+ ETHERNET: 802.3 Length = 52
+ LLC: UI DSAP=0xE0 SSAP=0xE0 C
+   **IPX: SAP   Packet-0.0000C07D73D7.4008   ->**
0.FFFFFFFFFFFF.452-0 Hops
+ SAP: Nearest Svc Query [Nearest Service Query]

```
00000: FF FF FF FF FF FF 00 00 C0 7D 73 D7 00 26 E0 E0 . . .
. . . . . . }s..&..
00010: 03 FF FF 00 22 00 00 00 00 00 00 FF FF FF FF FF . . .
." . . . . . . . . ..
00020: FF 04 52 00 00 00 00 00 00 C0 7D 73 D7 40 08 00 .
.R . . . . . . .}s.@..
00030: 03 00 04 00 . . . .
```

****

Frame Time Src MAC Addr Dst MAC Addr Protocol Description
Src Other Addr Dst Other Addr Type Other Addr
35 62.256 FATBOY BRAINS TCP .A . . . . ., len: 0,

seq: 1144422-1144422, ack: 9178898, win: 8 FATBOY BRAINS IP

+ FRAME: Base frame properties
+ ETHERNET: ETYPE = 0x0800 : Protocol = IP: DOD Internet Protocol
+ IP: ID = 0x3300; Proto = TCP; Len: 40
+ TCP: .A . . . ., len: 0, seq: 1144422-1144422, ack: 9178898,
win: 8525, src: 1026 dst: 139 (NBT Session)

```
00000: 00 00 C0 3A B8 EC 00 00 C0 7D 73 D7 08 00 45 00 . . . 
: . . . ..}s . . . E.
00010: 00 28 33 00 40 00 80 06 46 F1 DC 64 64 09 DC 64 
.(3.@ . . . F..dd..d
00020: 64 0C 04 02 00 8B 00 11 76 66 00 8C 0F 12 50 10 d 
. . . . . . .vf . . . .P.
00030: 21 4D 83 06 00 00 !M . . . .
```
****

Frame Time Src MAC Addr Dst MAC Addr Protocol Description
Src Other Addr Dst Other Addr Type Other Addr
36 62.517 **FATBOY FFFFFFFFFFFF**
**NBIPX Find Name BRAINS 0.0000C07D73D7 0.FFFFFFFFFFFF
IPX/XNS**

+ FRAME: Base frame properties
+ ETHERNET: 802.3 Length = 98
+ LLC: UI DSAP=0xE0 SSAP=0xE0 C
+ **IPX: NetBIOS Packet-0.0000C07D73D7.455 ->
0.FFFFFFFFFFFF.455-0 Hops**
+ NBIPX: Find Name BRAINS

```
00000: FF FF FF FF FF FF 00 00 C0 7D 73 D7 00 54 E0 E0 . . . 
. . . . . . }s..T..
00010: 03 FF FF 00 50 00 14 00 00 00 00 FF FF FF FF FF . . . 
.P . . . . . . . . . ..
00020: FF 04 55 00 00 00 00 00 00 C0 7D 73 D7 04 55 00 ..U 
. . . . . . . .}s..U.
00030: 01 00 00 00 00 00 00 00 00 00 00 00 00 00 00 00 
. . . . . . . . . . . . . .
00040: 00 00 00 00 00 00 00 00 00 00 00 00 00 00 00 00 
. . . . . . . . . . . . . .
```
****

```
Frame Time Src MAC Addr Dst MAC Addr Protocol Description
Src Other Addr Dst Other Addr Type Other Addr
37 62.897 FATBOY FFFFFFFFFFFF SAP
Nearest Svc Query [Nearest Service Query]
0.0000C07D73D7 0.FFFFFFFFFFFF IPX/XNS

+ FRAME: Base frame properties
+ ETHERNET: 802.3 Length = 52
+ LLC: UI DSAP=0xE0 SSAP=0xE0 C
+     IPX:     SAP     Packet-0.0000C07D73D7.4008     ->
0.FFFFFFFFFFFF.452-0 Hops
+ SAP: Nearest Svc Query [Nearest Service Query]

00000: FF FF FF FF FF FF 00 00 C0 7D 73 D7 00 26 E0 E0 . . .
. . . . . }s..&..
00010: 03 FF FF 00 22 00 00 00 00 00 00 FF FF FF FF FF . . .
." . . . . . . . . ..
00020: FF 04 52 00 00 00 00 00 00 C0 7D 73 D7 40 08 00 ..R
. . . . . . }s.@..
00030: 03 00 04 00  . . . .
*************************************************************

Frame Time Src MAC Addr Dst MAC Addr Protocol Description
Src Other Addr Dst Other Addr Type Other Addr
38 63.057 FATBOY FFFFFFFFFFFF NBIPX Find Name BRAINS
0.0000C07D73D7 0.FFFFFFFFFFFF IPX/XNS
+ FRAME: Base frame properties
+ ETHERNET: 802.3 Length = 98
+ LLC: UI DSAP=0xE0 SSAP=0xE0 C
+ IPX: NetBIOS Packet-0.0000C07D73D7.455 ->
0.FFFFFFFFFFFF.455-0 Hops
+ NBIPX: Find Name BRAINS

00000: FF FF FF FF FF FF 00 00 C0 7D 73 D7 00 54 E0 E0
. . . . . . . . }s..T..
00010: 03 FF FF 00 50 00 14 00 00 00 00 FF FF FF FF FF . . .
.P . . . . . . . . . ..
00020: FF 04 55 00 00 00 00 00 00 C0 7D 73 D7 04 55 00 ..U
. . . . . . . }s..U.
00030: 01 00 00 00 00 00 00 00 00 00 00 00 00 00 00 00
. . . . . . . . . . . . . . . .
00040: 00 00 00 00 00 00 00 00 00 00 00 00 00 00 00 00
. . . . . . . . . . . . . . .
```

```
************************************************************
Frame Time Src MAC Addr Dst MAC Addr Protocol Description
Src Other Addr Dst Other Addr Type Other Addr
39  63.618 FATBOY FFFFFFFFFFFF
SAP Nearest Svc Query [Nearest Service Query]
0.0000C07D73D7 0.FFFFFFFFFFFF IPX/XNS
```

+ FRAME: Base frame properties
+ ETHERNET: 802.3 Length = 52
+ LLC: UI DSAP=0xE0 SSAP=0xE0 C
+   **IPX: SAP   Packet-0.0000C07D73D7.4008   ->**
0.FFFFFFFFFFFF.452-0 Hops
+ **SAP: Nearest Svc Query [Nearest Service Query]**

```
00000: FF FF FF FF FF FF 00 00 C0 7D 73 D7 00 26 E0 E0 . . .
. . . . . . }s..&..
00010: 03 FF FF 00 22 00 00 00 00 00 00 FF FF FF FF FF . . .
." . . . . . . . . . ..
00020: FF 04 52 00 00 00 00 00 00 C0 7D 73 D7 40 08 00 ..R
. . . . . . .}s.@..
00030: 03 00 04 00 . . . .
************************************************************
Frame Time Src MAC Addr Dst MAC Addr Protocol Description
Src Other Addr Dst Other Addr Type Other Addr
40  64.339
FATBOY FFFFFFFFFFFF
SAP Nearest Svc Query [Nearest Service Query]
0.0000C07D73D7 0.FFFFFFFFFFFF IPX/XNS
```

+ FRAME: Base frame properties
+ ETHERNET: 802.3 Length = 52
+ LLC: UI DSAP=0xE0 SSAP=0xE0 C
+   **IPX: SAP   Packet-0.0000C07D73D7.4008   ->**
0.FFFFFFFFFFFF.452-0 Hops
+ **SAP: Nearest Svc Query [Nearest Service Query]**

```
00000: FF FF FF FF FF FF 00 00 C0 7D 73 D7 00 26 E0 E0 . . .
. . . . . . }s..&..
00010: 03 FF FF 00 22 00 00 00 00 00 00 FF FF FF FF FF . . .
." . . . . . . . . . ..
00020: FF 04 52 00 00 00 00 00 00 C0 7D 73 D7 40 08 00 ..R
. . . . . . .}s.@..
```

```
00030: 03 00 04 00  . . . .
```
****

Frame Time Src MAC Addr Dst MAC Addr Protocol Description
Src Other Addr Dst Other Addr Type Other Addr
41 65.061
FATBOY FFFFFFFFFFFF SAP
Nearest Svc Query [Nearest Service Query]
0.0000C07D73D7 0.FFFFFFFFFFFF IPX/XNS

+ FRAME: Base frame properties
+ ETHERNET: 802.3 Length = 52
+ LLC: UI DSAP=0xE0 SSAP=0xE0 C
+   **IPX: SAP   Packet-0.0000C07D73D7.4008   ->**
0.FFFFFFFFFFFF.452-0 Hops
+ **SAP: Nearest Svc Query [Nearest Service Query]**

```
00000: FF FF FF FF FF FF 00 00 C0 7D 73 D7 00 26 E0 E0 . . .
 . . . . . . }s..&..
00010: 03 FF FF 00 22 00 00 00 00 00 00 FF FF FF FF FF . . .
 ." . . . . . . . . . ..
00020: FF 04 52 00 00 00 00 00 00 C0 7D 73 D7 40 08 00 ..R
 . . . . . . .}s.@..
00030: 03 00 04 00  . . . .
```
****

Frame Time Src MAC Addr Dst MAC Addr Protocol Description
Src Other Addr Dst Other Addr Type Other Addr
42 65.782 FATBOY FFFFFFFFFFFF SAP
Nearest Svc Query [Nearest Service Query]
0.0000C07D73D7 0.FFFFFFFFFFFF IPX/XNS

+ FRAME: Base frame properties
+ ETHERNET: 802.3 Length = 52
+ LLC: UI DSAP=0xE0 SSAP=0xE0 C
+   **IPX: SAP   Packet-0.0000C07D73D7.4008   ->**
0.FFFFFFFFFFFF.452-0 Hops
+ **SAP: Nearest Svc Query [Nearest Service Query]**

```
00000: FF FF FF FF FF FF 00 00 C0 7D 73 D7 00 26 E0 E0 . . .
 . . . . . . }s..&..
00010: 03 FF FF 00 22 00 00 00 00 00 00 FF FF FF FF FF . . .
 ." . . . . . . . . . ..
```

```
00020: FF 04 52 00 00 00 00 00 00 C0 7D 73 D7 40 08 00 ..R
. . . . . . . }s.
00030: 03 00 04 00 . . . .
*********************************************************
Frame Time Src MAC Addr Dst MAC Addr Protocol Description
Src Other Addr Dst Other Addr Type Other Addr
42  66.503 FATBOY FFFFFFFFFFFF SAP
Nearest Svc Query [Nearest Service Query]
0.0000C07D73D7 0.FFFFFFFFFFFF IPX/XNS

+ FRAME: Base frame properties
+ ETHERNET: 802.3 Length = 52
+ LLC: UI DSAP=0xE0 SSAP=0xE0 C
+    IPX:    SAP    Packet-0.0000C07D73D7.4008    ->
0.FFFFFFFFFFFF.452-0 Hops
+ SAP: Nearest Svc Query [Nearest Service Query]

00000: FF FF FF FF FF FF 00 00 C0 7D 73 D7 00 26 E0 E0 . . .
. . . . . . }s..&..
00010: 03 FF FF 00 22 00 00 00 00 00 00 FF FF FF FF FF . . .
." . . . . . . . . . ..
00020: FF 04 52 00 00 00 00 00 00 C0 7D 73 D7 40 08 00 ..R
. . . . . . . }s.@..
00030: 03 00 04 00 . . . .
*********************************************************

Frame Time Src MAC Addr Dst MAC Addr Protocol Description
Src Other Addr Dst Other Addr Type Other Addr
44  67.224 FATBOY FFFFFFFFFFFF SAP
Nearest Svc Query [Nearest Service Query]
0.0000C07D73D7 0.FFFFFFFFFFFF IPX/XNS

+ FRAME: Base frame properties
+ ETHERNET: 802.3 Length = 52
+ LLC: UI DSAP=0xE0 SSAP=0xE0 C
+    IPX:    SAP    Packet-0.0000C07D73D7.4008    ->
0.FFFFFFFFFFFF.452-0 Hops
+ SAP: Nearest Svc Query [Nearest Service Query]

00000: FF FF FF FF FF FF 00 00 C0 7D 73 D7 00 26 E0 E0 . . .
. . . . . . }s..&..
00010: 03 FF FF 00 22 00 00 00 00 00 00 FF FF FF FF FF . . .
." . . . . . . . . . ..
```

```
00020: FF 04 52 00 00 00 00 00 00 C0 7D 73 D7 40 08 00 ..R
. . . . . . .}s.@..
00030: 03 00 04 00 . . . .
```
****

Frame Time Src MAC Addr Dst MAC Addr Protocol Description
Src Other Addr Dst Other Addr Type Other Addr
45 67.945 **FATBOY FFFFFFFFFFFF SAP**
Nearest Svc Query [Nearest Service Query]
0.0000C07D73D7 0.FFFFFFFFFFFF IPX/XNS

+ FRAME: Base frame properties
+ ETHERNET: 802.3 Length = 52
+ LLC: UI DSAP=0xE0 SSAP=0xE0 C
+   IPX: SAP   Packet−0.0000C07D73D7.4008   −>
0.FFFFFFFFFFFF.452−0 Hops
+ **SAP: Nearest Svc Query [Nearest Service Query]**

```
00000: FF FF FF FF FF FF 00 00 C0 7D 73 D7 00 26 E0 E0 . . .
. . . . . . }s..&..
00010: 03 FF FF 00 22 00 00 00 00 00 00 FF FF FF FF FF . . .
." . . . . . . . . . .
00020: FF 04 52 00 00 00 00 00 00 C0 7D 73 D7 40 08 00 ..R
. . . . . . .}s.@..
00030: 03 00 04 00 . . . .
```
****

Frame Time Src MAC Addr Dst MAC Addr Protocol Description
Src Other Addr Dst Other Addr Type Other Addr
46 68.666 **FATBOY FFFFFFFFFFFF**
SAP Nearest Svc Query [Nearest Service Query]
0.0000C07D73D7 0.FFFFFFFFFFFF IPX/XNS

+ FRAME: Base frame properties
+ ETHERNET: 802.3 Length = 52
+ LLC: UI DSAP=0xE0 SSAP=0xE0 C
+   IPX: SAP   Packet−0.0000C07D73D7.4008   −>
0.FFFFFFFFFFFF.452−0 Hops
+ **SAP: Nearest Svc Query [Nearest Service Query]**

```
00000: FF FF FF FF FF FF 00 00 C0 7D 73 D7 00 26 E0 E0 . . .
. . . . . . }s..&..
00010: 03 FF FF 00 22 00 00 00 00 00 00 FF FF FF FF FF . . .
." . . . . . . . . . .
```

```
00020: FF 04 52 00 00 00 00 00 00 C0 7D 73 D7 40 08 00  ..R
. . . . . . .}s.
00030: 03 00 04 00  . . . .
*************************************************************
```

```
Frame Time Src MAC Addr Dst MAC Addr Protocol Description
Src Other Addr Dst Other Addr Type Other Addr
47  69.387 FATBOY FFFFFFFFFFFF SAP
General Svc Query [General Service Query]
0.0000C07D73D7 0.FFFFFFFFFFFF IPX/XNS
```

```
+ FRAME: Base frame properties
+ ETHERNET: 802.3 Length = 52
+ LLC: UI DSAP=0xE0 SSAP=0xE0 C
+    IPX:    SAP    Packet-0.0000C07D73D7.4008    ->
0.FFFFFFFFFFFF.452-0 Hops
+ SAP: General Svc Query [General Service Query]
```

```
00000: FF FF FF FF FF FF 00 00 C0 7D 73 D7 00 26 E0 E0  . . .
. . . . . . }s..&..
00010: 03 FF FF 00 22 00 00 00 00 00 00 FF FF FF FF FF  . . .
." . . . . . . . . ..
00020: FF 04 52 00 00 00 00 00 00 C0 7D 73 D7 40 08 00  ..R
. . . . . . . .}s.@..
00030: 01 00 04 00  . . . .
*************************************************************
```

```
Frame Time Src MAC Addr Dst MAC Addr Protocol Description
Src Other Addr Dst Other Addr Type Other Addr
48  70.109 FATBOY FFFFFFFFFFFF
SAP General Svc Query [General Service Query]
0.0000C07D73D7 0.FFFFFFFFFFFF IPX/XNS
```

```
+ FRAME: Base frame properties
+ ETHERNET: 802.3 Length = 52
+ LLC: UI DSAP=0xE0 SSAP=0xE0 C
+    IPX:    SAP    Packet-0.0000C07D73D7.4008    ->
0.FFFFFFFFFFFF.452-0 Hops
+ SAP: General Svc Query [General Service Query]
```

```
00000: FF FF FF FF FF FF 00 00 C0 7D 73 D7 00 26 E0 E0  . . .
. . . . . . }s..&..
00010: 03 FF FF 00 22 00 00 00 00 00 00 FF FF FF FF FF  . . .
." . . . . . . . . ..
```

```
00020: FF 04 52 00 00 00 00 00 00 C0 7D 73 D7 40 08 00  ..R
. . . . . . . .}s.@..
00030: 01 00 04 00  . . . .
****************************************************************
```

Frame Time Src MAC Addr Dst MAC Addr Protocol Description
Src Other Addr Dst Other Addr Type Other Addr
49 70.110 **FATBOY BRAINS**
NETBIOS Name Recognize (0x0E), FATBOY -> BRAINS <00>

+ FRAME: Base frame properties
+ ETHERNET: 802.3 Length = 61
+ LLC: UI DSAP=0xF0 SSAP=0xF0 C
+ **NETBIOS: Name Recognize (0x0E), FATBOY-> BRAINS <00>**

```
00000: 00 00 C0 3A B8 EC 00 00 C0 7D 73 D7 00 2F F0 F0
. . . : . . . . .}s../..
00010: 03 2C 00 FF EF 0E 00 00 00 19 00 00 00 42 52 41  .,
. . . . . . . . . .BRA
00020: 49 4E 53 20 20 20 20 20 20 20 20 20 00 46 41 54  INS
.FAT
00030: 42 4F 59 20 20 20 20 20 20 20 20 20 20  BOY
****************************************************************
```

Frame Time Src MAC Addr Dst MAC Addr Protocol Description
Src Other Addr Dst Other Addr Type Other Addr
50 70.110 BRAINS FATBOY
NETBIOS Name Query (0x0A), BRAINS <00> -> FATBOY

+ FRAME: Base frame properties
+ ETHERNET: 802.3 Length = 61
+ LLC: UI DSAP=0xF0 SSAP=0xF0 C
+ NETBIOS: Name Query (0x0A), BRAINS <00> -> FATBOY

```
00000: 00 00 C0 7D 73 D7 00 00 C0 3A B8 EC 00 2F F0 F0  . . .
}s . . . . : . . . /..
00010: 03 2C 00 FF EF 0A 00 0D 00 00 00 19 00 46 41 54  .,
. . . . . . . . . . .FAT
00020: 42 4F 59 20 20 20 20 20 20 20 20 20 20 42 52 41  BOY
BRA
00030: 49 4E 53 20 20 20 20 20 20 20 20 20 00  INS .
****************************************************************
```

```
Frame Time Src MAC Addr Dst MAC Addr Protocol Description
Src Other Addr Dst Other Addr Type Other Addr
51  70.111                           -
```
FATBOY BRAINS
NETBIOS Name Recognize (0x0E), FATBOY -> BRAINS <00>

```
+ FRAME: Base frame properties
+ ETHERNET: 802.3 Length = 61
+ LLC: UI DSAP=0xF0 SSAP=0xF0 C
```
+ **NETBIOS: Name Recognize (0x0E), FATBOY -> BRAINS <00>**

```
00000: 00 00 C0 3A B8 EC 00 00 C0 7D 73 D7 00 2F F0 F0
. . . : . . . . .}s../..
00010: 03 2C 00 FF EF 0E 00 03 00 19 00 00 00 42 52 41 .,
. . . . . . . . . .BRA
00020: 49 4E 53 20 20 20 20 20 20 20 20 20 00 46 41 54 INS
.FAT
00030: 42 4F 59 20 20 20 20 20 20 20 20 20 20 BOY
************************************************************
```

```
Frame Time Src MAC Addr Dst MAC Addr Protocol Description
Src Other Addr Dst Other Addr Type Other Addr
52 70.111 BRAINS FATBOY
```
LLC SABME DSAP=0xF0 SSAP=0xF0 C POLL

```
+ FRAME: Base frame properties
+ ETHERNET: 802.3 Length = 60
+ LLC: SABME DSAP=0xF0 SSAP=0xF0 C POLL
```

```
00000: 00 00 C0 7D 73 D7 00 00 C0 3A B8 EC 00 03 F0 F0 . . .
}s . . . . : . . . . .
00010: 7F 4E CC 05 00 00 80 11 ED B9 DC 64 64 0C DC 64  N
. . . . . . . . . dd..d
00020: 64 0A 00 89 00 89 00 3A 9E 0B 85 18 01 00 00 01 d
. . . . . . . : . . . . . ..
00030: 00 00 00 00 00 00 20 45 47 45 42 46 .. . . . . EGEBF
************************************************************
```

```
Frame Time Src MAC Addr Dst MAC Addr Protocol Description
Src Other Addr Dst Other Addr Type Other Addr
53  70.111 FATBOY BRAINS
```
LLC UA DSAP=0xF0 SSAP=0xF1 R FINAL

```
+ FRAME: Base frame properties
+ ETHERNET: 802.3 Length = 17
+ LLC: UA DSAP=0xF0 SSAP=0xF1 R FINAL

00000: 00 00 C0 3A B8 EC 00 00 C0 7D 73 D7 00 03 F0 F1 . . .
: . . . . .}s . . . . ..
00010: 73 s
***********************************************************
```

Frame Time Src MAC Addr Dst MAC Addr Protocol Description
Src Other Addr Dst Other Addr Type Other Addr
54 70.112 BRAINS FATBOY
LLC RR
DSAP=0xF0
SSAP=0xF0 C N(R) = 0x00 POLL

```
+ FRAME: Base frame properties
+ ETHERNET: 802.3 Length = 60
+ LLC: RR DSAP=0xF0 SSAP=0xF0 C N(R) = 0x00 POLL

00000: 00 00 C0 7D 73 D7 00 00 C0 3A B8 EC 00 04 F0 F0 . . .
}s . . . .: . . . . . .
00010: 01 01 CC 05 00 00 80 11 ED B9 DC 64 64 0C DC 64
. . . . . . . . . ..dd..d
00020: 64 0A 00 89 00 89 00 3A 9E 0B 85 18 01 00 00 01 d
. . . . . : . . . . . . ..
00030: 00 00 00 00 00 00 20 45 47 45 42 46 .. . . . EGEBF
***********************************************************
```

Frame Time Src MAC Addr Dst MAC Addr Protocol Description
Src Other Addr Dst Other Addr Type Other Addr
55 70.112 **FATBOY BRAINS**
LLC RR
DSAP=0xF0
SSAP=0xF1 R N(R) = 0x00 FINAL

```
+ FRAME: Base frame properties
+ ETHERNET: 802.3 Length = 18
+ LLC: RR
DSAP=0xF0
SSAP=0xF1 R N(R) = 0x00 FINAL
00000: 00 00 C0 3A B8 EC 00 00 C0 7D 73 D7 00 04 F0 F1 . . .
: . . . . .}s . . . . ..
00010: 01 01 ..
```

```
************************************************************
Frame Time Src MAC Addr Dst MAC Addr Protocol Description
Src Other Addr Dst Other Addr Type Other Addr
56  70.113 BRAINS FATBOY
NETBIOS Session Initialize (0x19): LSN = 0x0D, RSN = 0x03
```

+ FRAME: Base frame properties
+ ETHERNET: 802.3 Length = 60
+ **LLC: I DSAP**=0xF0 SSAP=0xF0 C N(S) = 0x00, N(R) = 0x00
POLL
+ **NETBIOS: Session Initialize (0x19): LSN = 0x0D, RSN = 0x03**

```
00000: 00 00 C0 7D 73 D7 00 00 C0 3A B8 EC 00 12 F0 F0 . . .
}s . . . .: . . . . . . .
00010: 00 01 0E 00 FF EF 19 8F CA 05 00 00 00 00 03 0D . . .
. . . . . . . . . . . . . .
00020: 64 0A 00 89 00 89 00 3A 9E 0B 85 18 01 00 00 01 d
. . . . . . : . . . . . ..
00030: 00 00 00 00 00 00 20 45 47 45 42 46 .. . . . . EGEBF
************************************************************
Frame Time Src MAC Addr Dst MAC Addr Protocol Description
Src Other Addr Dst Other Addr Type Other Addr
57  70.113 BRAINS FATBOY
```
TCP . . . .S., len: 4, seq: 9187131-9187134,
ack: 0, win: 8 BRAINS FATBOY IP

+ FRAME: Base frame properties
+ ETHERNET: ETYPE = 0x0800 : Protocol = IP: DOD Internet
Protocol
+ IP: ID = 0xCD05; **Proto** = TCP; Len: 44
+ **TCP: . . . .S., len: 4, seq: 9187131-9187134, ack: 0,**
win: 8192, src: 1037 dst: 139 (NBT Session)

```
00000: 00 00 C0 7D 73 D7 00 00 C0 3A B8 EC 08 00 45 00
. . . }s . . . .: . . . .E.
00010: 00 2C CD 05 40 00 80 06 AC E7 DC 64 64 0C DC 64 .,..@
. . . . . . dd..d
00020: 64 09 04 0D 00 8B 00 8C 2F 3B 00 00 00 00 60 02 d
. . . . . . ./; . . . .`.
```

```
00030: 20 00 C2 E8 00 00 02 04 05 B4 42 46    . . . . . . .
. . . BF
```
****

Frame Time Src MAC Addr Dst MAC Addr Protocol Description
Src Other Addr Dst Other Addr Type Other Addr
58 70.113 **FATBOY BRAINS**
LLC RR
DSAP=0xF0
SSAP=0xF1 R N(R) = 0x01 FINAL

+ FRAME: Base frame properties
+ ETHERNET: 802.3 Length = 18
+ **LLC: RR DSAP=0xF0 SSAP=0xF1 R N(R) = 0x01 FINAL**

```
00000: 00 00 C0 3A B8 EC 00 00 C0 7D 73 D7 00 04 F0 F1  . . .
: . . . ..}s . . . . .
00010: 01 03 ..
```
****

Frame Time Src MAC Addr Dst MAC Addr Protocol Description
Src Other Addr Dst Other Addr Type Other Addr
59 70.113 FATBOY BRAINS
NETBIOS Session Confirm (0x17): LSN = 0x03, RSN = 0x0D

+ FRAME: Base frame properties
+ ETHERNET: 802.3 Length = 32
+ LLC: I DSAP=0xF0 SSAP=0xF0 C N(S) = 0x00, N(R) = 0x01
POLL
+ **NETBIOS: Session Confirm (0x17): LSN = 0x03, RSN = 0x0D**

```
00000: 00 00 C0 3A B8 EC 00 00 C0 7D 73 D7 00 12 F0 F0  . . .
: . . . ..}s . . . . .
00010: 00 03 0E 00 FF EF 17 81 CA 05 00 00 00 00 0D 03  . . .
. . . . . . . . . . . .
```
****

Frame Time Src MAC Addr Dst MAC Addr Protocol Description
Src Other Addr Dst Other Addr Type Other Addr
60 70.113
FATBOY BRAINS
TCP .A..S., len: 4, seq: 1151750-1151753,
ack: 9187132, win: 8 FATBOY BRAINS IP

```
+ FRAME: Base frame properties
+ ETHERNET: ETYPE = 0x0800 : Protocol = IP: DOD Internet
Protocol
+ IP: ID = 0x3400; Proto = TCP; Len: 44
+ TCP: .A..S., len: 4, seq: 1151750-1151753,
ack: 9187132, win: 8760, src: 139 (NBT Session) dst: 1037

00000: 00 00 C0 3A B8 EC 00 00 C0 7D 73 D7 08 00 45 00 . . .
: . . . ..}s . . . E.
00010: 00 2C 34 00 40 00 80 06 45 ED DC 64 64 09 DC 64
.,4.@ . . . E..dd..d
00020: 64 0C 00 8B 04 0D 00 11 93 06 00 8C 2F 3C 60 12 d
. . . . . . . . . . ../<`.
00030: 22 38 2D 88 00 00 02 04 05 B4 "8- . . . . . . .
****************************************************************

Frame Time Src MAC Addr Dst MAC Addr Protocol Description
Src Other Addr Dst Other Addr Type Other Addr
61 70.114 BRAINS FATBOY
LLC RR
DSAP=0xF0
SSAP=0xF1 R N(R) = 0x01 FINAL

+ FRAME: Base frame properties
+ ETHERNET: 802.3 Length = 60
+ LLC: RR DSAP=0xF0 SSAP=0xF1 R N(R) = 0x01 FINAL

00000: 00 00 C0 7D 73 D7 00 00 C0 3A B8 EC 00 04 F0 F1 . . .
}s . . . .: . . . . . .
00010: 01 03 CD 05 40 00 80 06 AC E7 DC 64 64 0C DC 64 . . .
.@ . . . . . . dd..d
00020: 64 09 04 0D 00 8B 00 8C 2F 3B 00 00 00 00 60 02 d
. . . . . . ./; . . . . `.
00030: 20 00 C2 E8 00 00 02 04 05 B4 42 46 . . . . . .
. . . BF
****************************************************************

Frame Time Src MAC Addr Dst MAC Addr Protocol Description
Src Other Addr Dst Other Addr Type Other Addr
62 70.114 BRAINS FATBOY TCP .A . . . . .,
len: 0, seq: 9187132-9187132, ack: 1151751,
win: 8 BRAINS FATBOY IP
```

```
+ FRAME: Base frame properties
+ ETHERNET: ETYPE = 0x0800 : Protocol = IP: DOD Internet
Protocol
+ IP: ID = 0xCE05; Proto = TCP; Len: 40
```
+ TCP: .A . . . ., len: 0, seq: 9187132-9187132,
ack: 1151751, win: 8760, src: 1037 dst: 139 (NBT Session)

```
00000: 00 00 C0 7D 73 D7 00 00 C0 3A B8 EC 08 00 45 00
. . . }s . . . . .: . . . .E.
00010: 00 28 CE 05 40 00 80 06 AB EB DC 64 64 0C DC 64 .(..@
. . . . . . dd..d
00020: 64 09 04 0D 00 8B 00 8C 2F 3C 00 11 93 07 50 10 d
. . . . . . ./< . . . .P.
00030: 22 38 45 45 00 00 02 04 05 B4 42 46 "8EE . . . . . .
BF
```
```
************************************************************
```

```
Frame Time Src MAC Addr Dst MAC Addr Protocol Description
Src Other Addr Dst Other Addr Type Other Addr
63 70.115 BRAINS FATBOY
```
NBT SS: Session Request, Dest: FATBOY,
Source: BRAINS BRAINS FATBOY IP

```
+ FRAME: Base frame properties
+ ETHERNET: ETYPE = 0x0800 : Protocol = IP: DOD Internet
Protocol
+ IP: ID = 0xCF05; Proto = TCP; Len: 112
+ TCP: .AP . . . , len: 72, seq: 9187132-9187203,
ack: 1151751, win: 8760, src: 1037 dst: 139 (NBT Session)
+ NBT: SS: Session Request, Dest: FATBOY , Source: BRAINS
<00>, Len: 68
```

```
00000: 00 00 C0 7D 73 D7 00 00 C0 3A B8 EC 08 00 45 00
. . . }s . . . .: . . . .E.
00010: 00 70 CF 05 40 00 80 06 AA A3 DC 64 64 0C DC 64 .p..@
. . . . . . dd..d
00020: 64 09 04 0D 00 8B 00 8C 2F 3C 00 11 93 07 50 18 d
. . . . . . ./< . . . .P.
00030: 22 38 17 2E 00 00 81 00 00 44 20 45 47 45 42 46 "8
. . . . . . .D EGEBF
00040: 45 45 43 45 50 46 4A 43 41 43 41 43 41 43 41 43
       EECEPFJCACA
       CACAC
```

```
*************************************************************
Frame Time Src MAC Addr Dst MAC Addr Protocol Description
Src Other Addr Dst Other Addr Type Other Addr
64 70.115 FATBOY BRAINS
```
NBT SS: Positive Session Response, Len: 0
```
FATBOY BRAINS IP
+ FRAME: Base frame properties
+ ETHERNET: ETYPE = 0x0800 : Protocol = IP: DOD Internet
Protocol
+ IP: ID = 0x3500; Proto = TCP; Len: 44
```
+ TCP: .AP . . . , len: 4, seq: 1151751-1151754,
ack: 9187204, win: 8688, src: 139 (NBT Session)
dst: 1037 + NBT: SS: Positive Session Response, Len: 0

```
00000: 00 00 C0 3A B8 EC 00 00 C0 7D 73 D7 08 00 45 00 . . .
: . . . . .}s . . . E.
00010: 00 2C 35 00 40 00 80 06 44 ED DC 64 64 09 DC 64
.,5.@ . . . D..dd..d
00020: 64 0C 00 8B 04 0D 00 11 93 07 00 8C 2F 84 50 18 d
. . . . . . . . . . ../.P.
00030: 21 F0 C3 38 00 00 82 00 00 00 !..8 . . . . . .
*************************************************************
Frame Time Src MAC Addr Dst MAC Addr Protocol Description
Src Other Addr Dst Other Addr Type Other Addr
65   70.116
```
BRAINS FATBOY
NETBIOS Session End (0x18): LSN = 0x0D, RSN = 0x03

```
+ FRAME: Base frame properties
+ ETHERNET: 802.3 Length = 60
+ LLC: I DSAP=0xF0 SSAP=0xF0 C N(S) = 0x01, N(R) = 0x01
POLL
```
+ NETBIOS: Session End (0x18): LSN = 0x0D, RSN = 0x03

```
00000: 00 00 C0 7D 73 D7 00 00 C0 3A B8 EC 00 12 F0 F0 . . .
}s . . . .: . . . . . .
00010: 02 03 0E 00 FF EF 18 00 00 00 00 00 00 00 03 0D . . .
. . . . . . . . . . .
00020: 64 09 04 0D 00 8B 00 8C 2F 3C 00 11 93 07 50 18 d
. . . . . . ./< . . . .P.
00030: 22 38 17 2E 00 00 81 00 00 44 20 45 "8 . . . . . .
.D E
```

```
************************************************************
Frame Time Src MAC Addr Dst MAC Addr Protocol Description
Src Other Addr Dst Other Addr Type Other Addr
66  70.116 FATBOY BRAINS
LLC RR
DSAP=0xF0
SSAP=0xF1 R N(R) = 0x02 FINAL

+ FRAME: Base frame properties
+ ETHERNET: 802.3 Length = 18
+ LLC: RR DSAP=0xF0 SSAP=0xF1 R N(R) = 0x02 FINAL

00000: 00 00 C0 3A B8 EC 00 00 C0 7D 73 D7 00 04 F0 F1 . . .
:  . . . . ..}s . . . . ..
00010: 01 05 ..
************************************************************
```

The previous information is a snapshot (trace) from the network switch used in this case study. The purpose of presenting it to you is to provide insight to the traffic between nodes that occurs in a network.

In this particular example, traffic occurred between FAT BOY and BRAINS—two computers in the network using the switch to communicate. The depth of information obtained directly from the switch is advantageous to baselining, troubleshooting, and performance analysis. Additional trace information is presented later in this chapter. Use this as an example of what you need to begin to understand traffic that flows through a network switch.

Network Switch ETHERNET Interface

The network switch in this case study uses the Ethernet interface ESM-100C, and it can be configured with four or eight ports that connect to 100Base-Tx devices. Each set of four ports is one collision domain that connects to a fifth internal port. This internal port connects directly to the switch backplane and has a unique MAC address. Each front panel port on the ESM-100C is capable of using the full 100 Mbps of dedicated bandwidth. However, when more than one connection is made to each set of four ports, those connections must share the 100 Mbps of bandwidth. Front panel ports receive data from attached 100BaseTx devices and from the fifth internal port (which connects to the switch backplane). In addition, data received on any front panel port is automatically passed on to the other three ports that share its collision domain and to the internal port.

The internal switch port receives data from the switch backplane and the 100Base-Tx front panel ports. This port passes data destined for the front panel ports (from other switch ports) in one direction, and passes data destined for other switch ports (from the front panel ports) in the other direction. This internal port has its own set of LEDs separate from the front panel port LEDs. Set of 4 100BASE-TX Ports Switch Backplane Internal Port 100BASE-TX Devices ****author . . . text is missing?*****

Network Switch FDDI Interface

The FSM-M FDDI switching module may contain one or two *dual-attachment station* (DAS) connections for support of dual FDDI rings. Each DAS connection is a set of A/B *media interface connectors* (MIC). The FSM-M supports multimode connections. (The FSM-S module supports single mode DAS connections.) In addition each DAS connection has an optical bypass port that may be used to disconnect a port from the FDDI ring, or bypass this DAS connection.

The FSM-M is actually a sub-module, or daughtercard, that attaches to a *High-Speed Module* (HSM). The HSM contains memory and processing power for switching modules that operate at speeds greater than 10 Mbps. You plug your fiber optic cable directly into the FSM-M sub-module, but it is the HSM module that connects to the switch backplane.

Network Switch Token Ring Interface

The network switch in this case study uses a TSM-CD−6 that contains six shielded ports that each may be separately configured as a Station or Lobe port. As a Station port, the TSM-CD−6 port plugs directly into a MAU; as a Lobe port, the port acts as an MAU port and a Token Ring station plugs directly into the module. You configure the ports as Station or Lobe through the `tsc` command. By default, ports are configured as Lobe ports.

Each port can support either *unshielded twisted pair* (UTP) or *shielded twisted pair* (STP) connections. No configuration is necessary to set up a port for UTP or STP. Each port supports a fully switched connection at either 4 or 16 Mbps. Ring Speed is configurable through the `tpcfg` command. By default, ports are configured at 16 Mbps.

Automatic speed detection software used automatically modifies the Ring Speed if there is a discrepancy with the ring to which the port is connected. A TSM-CD−6 port detects this difference in Ring Speed as it is inserted into the ring, and then it resets itself and comes up in the new Ring Speed.

The new Ring Speed, however, is not saved in the system configuration file, `mpm.cfg`. After the port inserts into the ring, automatic Ring Speed detection is disabled (that is, thereafter the port will not change speed automatically). Both Station and Lobe ports handle automatic speed detection this way.

If a TSM-CD−6 port is the first device on the ring, then the Ring Speed is automatically set to the port's configured speed. The port does not reset to match the Ring Speed, its speed becomes the Ring Speed. If the port is not the first device, then it autodetects the ring speed and matches that speed as described in the preceding paragraph.

The TSM-CD−6 is actually a sub-module, or daughtercard, that attaches to a *High-Speed Module* (HSM). The HSM contains memory and processing power for switching modules that operate at speeds greater than 10 Mbps. You plug your cable directly into the TSM-CD−6 sub-module, but it is the HSM module that connects to the switch backplane.

Network Switch ATM Interface

The network switch also has an ATM access switch module, which permits connectivity of devices using ATM protocol. ATM modules support OC−3, DS−3, and E3 interfaces (155, 44.736, and 34.368 Mbps respectively), which can all be used and include the following:

- *ASM-155Fx*   One or two port fiber single mode or multimode OC−3 switching module

- *ASM2–155Fx*   One or two port fiber single mode or multimode OC−3 switching module. This is a higher performance version of the ASM−155Fx.

- *ASM-155C*   One or two port UTP OC−3 switching module

- *ASM2–622F*   One or two port fiber single mode or multimode OC−12 switching module
- *ASM2–622FR*   Two or four port redundant fiber single mode or multimode OC−12 switching module. Each port pair includes a primary and backup port.
- *ASM-DS3*   One or two port DS−3 switching module
- *ASM-E3*   One or two port E3 switching module
- *ASM-CE*   One ATM uplink port (OC−3, DS−3 or E3), two T1/E1 ports, and two serial ports supporting ATM circuit emulation

The OC−3 modules are suited for connecting the switch to an ATM campus backbone or directly to an ATM server. Through the use of Point-to-Point Bridging (RFC 1483), you can extend all LAN traffic over the ATM backbone. Several OmniSwitches can be connected over one or more backbones. In such a configuration, you combine the flexibility of the OmniSwitch any-to-any switching with the power and speed of the ATM backbone without the use of an ATM backbone switch.

If the network switches are connected directly to an ATM server, all non-ATM devices in the LAN can communicate with a high-speed ATM device through the switch. If your network uses an ATM backbone switch, then if the switch has an ATM module, it allows all non-ATM devices in the network to have access to the ATM network through the use of *LAN Emulation* (LANE) or VLAN Clusters. Depending on the network switch, classical IP (RFC 1577) may also be used to extend LAN traffic over ATM through the network switch.

In this network switch, ASM2 modules do not support *point-to-point bridging* (PTOP) private configurations. However they do support PTOP 1483 configurations.

The DS−3 and E3 modules are well suited for connecting the switch to ATM carrier services offered by Telco service providers. Software controls on the switch enable you to control and monitor activity on ATM modules. On each ATM port, you can configure the connection type (SVC or PVC), *Virtual Channel Connections* (VCC), segment sizes, and loopback controls. On each VCC, you can configure *Quality of Service* (QoS), Best Effort, Traffic Descriptor, and Peak Cell Rate variables. In addition, you can configure all ATM bridging and trunking services (Point-to-Point Bridging, LANE, and Classical IP).

Viewing Network Switch System Statistics

The systat command displays statistics related to system, power, and environment. To view these parameters, enter systat at the system prompt. A screen similar to the following is displayed.

```
System Uptime 1 days, 12:09:22.64
MPM Transmit Overruns : 0
MPM Receive Overruns : 22
MPM total memory : 16 MB
MPM free memory : 6522536 bytes
MPM CPU Utilization(5 sec) : 5% ( 0% intr 0% kernel 3% task 95% idle)
MPM CPU Utilization(60 sec) : 5% ( 0% intr 0% kernel 3% task 96%
idle)
Power Supply 1 State : OK
Power Supply 2 State : Not Present
Temperature Sensor : OK-Under Threshold
Temperature Alarm Masking : Disabled
Temperature Alarm Masking Delay : 5 minutes
```

The time since the last boot that the system has been running, displayed in days, hours, minutes, and seconds (to the nearest hundredth).

Statistics Descriptions

- *MPM Transmit Overruns* The number of times a VSE transmit buffer could not be allocated by a task on the MPM

- *MPM Receive Overruns* The number of times packets were dropped because the bus had more packets to deliver than the MPM could handle. This is a receive overrun condition which can happen when a storm occurs or when the switch is first powered up and many unknown MAC frames are being forwarded to the MPM.

- *MPM Total Memory* The amount of total memory installed on the MPM

- *MPM Free Memory* The amount of free, or unused, memory available in the MPM. This data is also displayed by the memstat command.

- *MPM CPU Utilization (5 seconds)* The amount of time, by percent, the MPM processor actually worked during the last 5 seconds

- *MPM CPU Utilization (60 sec)*　The amount of time, by percent, that the MPM processor actually did work during the last minute

- *Power Supply 1 State*　Valid states are OK, Not Present, and Bad. A power supply that has been turned off is in the Bad state. If not installed, it is in the Not Present state.

- *Power Supply 2 State*　Valid states are OK, Not Present, and Bad. A power supply that has been turned off is in the Bad state. If not installed, it is in the Not Present state.

- *Temperature Sensor*　Indicates whether the MPM temperature sensor detects overheating. Valid states are Under Threshold, Over Threshold, and Not Present.

- *Temperature Alarm Masking*　Indicates whether temperature alarm masking is Enabled or Disabled. You enable masking through the `maskta` command.

- *Temperature Alarm Masking Delay*　The amount of time after which the TEMP LED turns off when alarm masking is partially enabled through the `maskta` command. This field only displays if the value is greater than zero.

- *Network Switch System Resets*　The number of times this switch has been reset since the last cold start. The `info` command also displays the number of MPMs, their location in chassis, and which one is the primary and which one is the secondary. In addition, it also displays whether automatic configuration synchronization is enabled.

- *System Base MAC Address*　The base MAC address for the primary MPM in chassis

- *Number of Free Slots*　The number of slots not occupied by a module

- *Action on Cold Start*　The action taken when you switch the power on

- *Action on Reset*　The action taken when you reboot

- *Script File*　The name of the command file (`mpm.cmd` is the default) containing user-configurable commands

- *Boot File*　The boot file (`mpm.img` is the default) used by the switch when it boots up or reboots

- *Ni Image Suffix*　The name of the file extension (`img` is the default) indicating that the file is an executable binary file

Network Switch Traces

In addition to the information presented previously, it is a good idea to obtain information about your network through the switch itself. In this section, I am presenting to you information I obtained by accessing the network through the switch. Consequently, you see a variety of information that reflects different layers in the network itself. I recommend this to you as a reference point to consider for obtaining information on your network.

The following hosts were active through the switch at the time of the traces.

MUSCLE

SPEEDY

THE-HOSTAGE

The following statistical information reflects interaction among these three systems. The first trace I ran shows two hosts and the network switch.

```
*****************************************************************
           HEWLETT-PACKARD NETWORK ADVISOR
                Node Discovery measurement
           Run started on 1–1–00 @ the beginning
           Run stopped on 1–1–00 @ the beginning
                     2 nodes observed
                Display format: Observed Nodes
                  Print: All displayed records
*****************************************************************
```

* New address observed on network

\# Known address observed on network

~ New address-name mapping; no traffic observed

\> Selected record

Address Layer	Type/ID	Comment/Name
> **MUSCLE**		
*> **Kingston**−30-C2–43	Ethernet	
*> **220.100.100.10**	**IP**	
*> 00000001–000000000001	IPX	
*> ADMINISTRATOR	NetBIOS	ADMINISTRATOR
* MUSCLE	NetBIOS	MUSCLE
> **THE-HOSTAGE**		
*> **00–60–08–98–1D**−33	**Ethernet**	

*> **220.100.100.172**	**IP**	
*> THE-HOSTAGE	NetBIOS	THE-HOSTAGE
> *NEW XYLAN-A76640		
*> **XYLAN——A7–66–40**	**ETHERNET**	
> *NEW XYLAN-AC9EB5		
*> **XYLAN——AC–9E-B5**	**ETHERNET**	

Probably the most important trace one can run first is one that identifies which hosts are talking on the network. After this is done, then calculations can be performed to estimate traffic through the switch. After completing this trace, I ran another to show the functional addition of SPEEDY. Consider the following:

```
****************************************************************
```

HEWLETT-PACKARD NETWORK ADVISOR
Node Discovery measurement
Run started on Sep 15, 2000 16:48
Run stopped on Sep 15. 2000 17:18
2 nodes observed
Display format: Observed Nodes
Print: All displayed records

```
****************************************************************
```

* New address observed on network
\# Known address observed on network
~ New address-name mapping; no traffic observed
> Selected record

Address Layer	Type/ID	Comment/Name
> MUSCLE		
*> Kingston−30-C2–43	Ethernet	
*> 220.100.100.10	IP	
*> 00000001–000000000001	IPX	
*> ADMINISTRATOR	NetBIOS	ADMINISTRATOR
* MUSCLE	NetBIOS	MUSCLE
> SPEEDY		
*> WstDigt—CF−08-F3	Ethernet	
*> 220.100.100.111 IP		
*> SPEEDY	NetBIOS	SPEEDY
> THE-HOSTAGE		
*> 00–60–08–98–1D−33	Ethernet	
*> 220.100.100.172 IP		
*> THE-HOSTAGE	NetBIOS	THE-HOSTAGE

```
> *NEW XYLAN-A76640
*> XYLAN——A7–66–40          ETHERNET
> *NEW XYLAN-AC9EB5
*> XYLAN——AC–9E-B5          ETHERNET
```

This trace shows an entry that reflects the switch itself. This might be tedious to you now, but remember when you are troubleshooting, the more information you have the better off you are. With the new node (SPEEDY) working on the network, I took some additional snapshots (traces with the Internet Advisor). My first was a brief network stack decode; and with this, the information can be used in the management and troubleshooting of the network.

Managing Network Switches

Another aspect to consider with network switch is management. I use a HP Internet Advisor to facilitate that function in my network. This network tool makes network switch management easier. Consider the following trace obtained from my network. Notice that part of the trace that I have bolded. This information is very helpful in determining network communication and the precise information exchanged between nodes.

```
****************************************************************
*****         HEWLETT PACKARD NETWORK ADVISOR         *****
*****                                                 *****
*****    Measurement:     Brief Network Stack Decode  *****
*****    Print Type:      All Frames                  *****
*****    Open Views:      Summary                     *****
*****    Display Mode:    Viewing All Frames          *****
*****    Print Date:      00/01 /01                    *****
*****    Print Time:      12:01:01                     *****
****************************************************************

1 20:31.649    HP----21-08-A0     HP----21-08-A0     ARP    R
  PA=[15.6.72.18] HA=0060B02108A0
2 20:34.052 00000000-HP--210  00000000-Broadcast SAP C Find
  general Unkn service
3 20:34.057 00000000-HP--210  00000000-Broadcast SAP C Find
  general Unkn service
4 20:34.057 00000000-Kingst30C 00000000-HP--210 SAP R MUSCLE
5 20:34.061 00000000-HP--210  00000000-Broadcast SAP C Find
  general Unkn service
```

6 20:34.065 00000000-HP--210 00000000-**Broadcast SAP C Find general Unkn service**

7 20:34.104 **220.100.100.111 220.100.100.255 SMB C Transaction name \MAILSLOT\BROWSE**

8 20:34.104 00000000-WstDigCF0 00000000-**Broadcast IPX Type**=20 IPX WAN Broadcast LEN=223

9 20:36.108 WstDigt-CF-08-F3 03-00-00-00-00-01 **SMB C Transaction name \MAILSLOT\BROWSE**

10 21:08.948 00000000-006008981 00000000-**Broadcast SAP C Find nearest file server**

11 21:09.055 **00000000-006008981 00000000-Broadcast SAP C Find general file server**

12 21:09.065 00000000-006008981 00000000-Broadcast SAP C Find general file server

13 21:09.145 00000000-006008981 00000000-Broadcast SAP C Find nearest file server

14 21:09.155 00000000-006008981 00000000-Broadcast SAP C Find nearest file server

15 21:09.164 00000000-006008981 00000000-Broadcast SAP C Find general file server

16 21:09.175 00000000-006008981 00000000-Broadcast SAP C Find general file server

17 21:09.184 00000000-006008981 00000000-Broadcast SAP C Find nearest file server

18 21:09.196 00000000-006008981 00000000-Broadcast IPX NCP Unknown type=0000

19 21:09.197 00000000-006008981 00000000-**Broadcast IPX RIP Request**

20 21:09.648 **220.100.100.10 Broadcast BOOTP Request**

21 21:10.800 00-60-08-98-1D-33 03-00-00-00-00-01 **SMB C Transaction name \MAILSLOT\BROWSE**

22 21:13.301 00000000-Kingst30C 00000000-**Broadcast IPX RIP Response: 1 networks**

23 21:17.064 00000000-006008981 00000000-**Broadcast IPX RIP Request**

24 21:20.022 00000000-006008981 00000000-**Broadcast IPX RIP Request**

25 21:20.333 **220.100.100.10 Broadcast BOOTP Request**

26 21:22.653 00000000-006008981 00000000-**Broadcast SAP C Find general file server**

```
27 21:27.084 00000000-Kingst30C 00000000-Broadcast SAP R MUS-
   CLE
28 21:33.913   HP----21-08-A0   HP----21-08-A0   ARP   R
   PA=[15.6.72.18] HA=0060B02108A0
29 21:34.145 220.100.100.10 Broadcast BOOTP Request
30 21:34.253 220.100.100.111 220.100.100.255 SMB C Transaction
   name \MAILSLOT\BROWSE
31 21:34.880 00000000-HP--210 00000000-Broadcast SAP C Find
   general Unkn service
32 21:34.884 00000000-HP--210 00000000-Broadcast SAP C Find
   general Unkn service
33 21:34.885 00000000-Kingst30C 00000000-HP--210 SAP R MUSCLE
34 21:34.892 00000000-HP--210 00000000-Broadcast SAP C Find
   general Unkn service
35 21:34.899 00000000-HP--210 00000000-Broadcast SAP C Find
   general Unkn service
36 21:36.257 WstDigt-CF-08-F3 03-00-00-00-00-01 SMB C Transac-
   tion name \MAILSLOT\BROWSE
37 21:52.164 220.100.100.10 Broadcast BOOTP Request
38 22:00.163   HP----21-08-A0   HP----21-08-A0   ARP   R
   PA=[15.6.72.18] HA=0060B02108A0
39 22:00.683 00000000-HP--210 00000000-Broadcast SAP C Find
   general Unkn service
40 22:00.687 00000000-HP--210 00000000-Broadcast SAP C Find
   general Unkn service
41 22:00.688 00000000-Kingst30C 00000000-HP--210 SAP R MUSCLE
42 22:00.692 00000000-HP--210 00000000-Broadcast SAP C Find
   general Unkn service
43 22:00.696 00000000-HP--210 00000000-Broadcast SAP C Find
   general Unkn service
44 22:11.623 220.100.100.172 220.100.100.255 SMB C Transaction
   name \MAILSLOT\BROWSE
45 22:13.317 00000000-Kingst30C 00000000-Broadcast IPX RIP
   Response: 1 networks
46 22:22.651 00000000-006008981 00000000-Broadcast SAP C Find
   nearest file server
47 22:27.099 00000000-Kingst30C 00000000-Broadcast SAP R MUS-
   CLE
48 23:13.333 00000000-Kingst30C 00000000-Broadcast IPX RIP
   Response: 1 networks
49 23:14.978 220.100.100.10 Broadcast BOOTP Request
50 23:17.935 00000000-006008981 70001600-840565047 IPX Type=20
   IPX WAN Broadcast LEN=228
```

```
51 23:22.649 00000000-006008981 00000000-Broadcast SAP C Find
   general file server
52 23:24.239 Kingston-30-C2-43 03-00-00-00-00-01 NETB Name query
   SPEEDY
53 23:24.240 00000001-000000000 00000000-Broadcast NETB Find
   Name SPEEDY
54 23:24.244    Kingston-30-C2-43    Broadcast    ARP    C
   PA=[220.100.100.111]
55 23:24.781 00000001-000000000 00000000-Broadcast NETB Find
   Name SPEEDY
56 23:25.132 220.100.100.10 Broadcast BOOTP Request
57 23:25.322 00000001-000000000 00000000-Broadcast NETB Find
   Name SPEEDY
58 23:27.115 00000000-Kingst30C 00000000-Broadcast SAP R MUS-
   CLE
```

Notice the level of detail available in this trace. A request to find a general file server, a SAP broadcast from Muscle, BOOTP request, and browsing mailslots. This is the level detail that is very helpful in managing your switch. This trace shows the communication between SPEEDY and MUSCLE, and it also shows the essence of the communication between the nodes themselves.

Granted this is an isolated example; in a more populated network, it might well be that dozens or hundreds of hosts are monitored as their traffic passes across the backbone of the switch.

ARPA Protocol: Case Study of Switch Traffic

I decided to take another trace of the ARPA stack; however my purpose for doing so was to catch SPEEDY communicating. Examine the following trace data that displays this functionality in the switch.

Read this trace carefully and you can see the SMB protocol exchange as well as IP and other information used between nodes talking on the network.

```
****************************************************************
*****                                                      *****
*****        HEWLETT PACKARD NETWORK ADVISOR               *****
*****                                                      *****
```

```
*****      Measurement:      ARPA Stack Decode        *****
*****      Print Type:       Current frame 22         *****
*****      Open Views:       Detailed                 *****
*****      Display Mode:     Viewing All Frames       *****
*****      Print Date:       09/15 /00                *****
*****      Print Time:       11:19:53                 *****
*****                                                 *****

*************************************************************
```

Frame: 22 Time: Aug 2216:33.5805780 Length: 253

SMB

Identifier	**SMB**	
Command Code	25	Transaction
Name		
Error Class	00	**Success**
Reserved	00	
Error Code	0000	**Success**
Flags	00000000	**Good**
Response Request	0	**Request**
Client Notification	. 0	Flag Not Set
File Lock	. . 0	Flag Not Set
Canonical Form	. . . 0 . . .	Flag Not Set
Case Sensitive	. . . . 0 . . .	Flag Not Set
Reserved	. . . . . 0 . .	
Rcv Buffer Posted	. . . . . . 0 .	Flag Not Set
Subdialect	 0	Flag Not Set
Flags_2	0000	
Reserved (Truncated)	00-00-00-00-00-00-00-	
	00-0	
Authenticated	0000	
Resource ID		
Callers Process ID	0000	
Unauthenticated	0000	
User ID		
Multiplex ID	0000	
Word Count	17	
Parameters	0000	
Parameters	0027	
Parameters	0000	
Parameters	0000	

Parameters (Truncated)	00-02-00-01-00-01-00-03-0	
Buffer Count	56	
ASCII Data	**\MAILSLOT\BROWSE**	
Buffer Type	01	**Server Data**
Block		
ASCII Data	**SPEEDY**	
ASCII Data	**@ SPEEDY**	
NetBIOS		
Service Type :		**Datagram**
Service		
Packet Type :		**Direct_Group**
Datagram		
Msg_Type	11	
Flags	1A	See Bit
Fields Below		
Reserved Bits	0001 . . .	**Warning: Reserved Bit**
Not Zero		
Source End-Node Type	. . . . 1 0 . .	Mixed (M)node
FIRST Flag	. . . . . . 1 .	First
Fragment		
MORE Flag	 0	Last Fragment
DGM ID	6	
Source IP	**220.100.100.111**	**Source IP**
Address		
Source Port	**138**	**Source Port**
Number		
DGM Length	193	
Packet Offset	0	
Name Length	32	
Source Name	**SPEEDY**	**NetBIOS Name**
Name Length	32	
Destination Name	**INFO.COM**	" **NetBIOS Name**
User Data	SMB Data-See SMB Decode	
UDP		
Source port	**138**	**NETBIOS**
Destination port	**138**	**NETBIOS**
Length	215	
Checksum	69-AF	
> **Data size**	**207**	

```
> New address
IP
Version                     4
Internet header length                                5         (32
bit words)
Precedence              000 . - . . .            Routine
Delay                   . . . 0 - . . .          Delay normal
Throughput              . . . . - 0 . . .        Throughput
normal
Reliability             . . . . - . 0 . .        Reliability
normal
Reserved                . . . . - . . 0 0
Total Length            235
Identification          1792
Reserved                00 . . - . . . .
May / Do Not Fragment   . 0 . . . - . . .        Fragmentation
allowed
Last / More Fragments   . . 0 . - . . .          Last fragment
Offset                  0
Time To Live            32
Next Protocol           17 UDP
Checksum                10-CB
Source                  220.100.100.111
Destination 220.100.100.255
> Data size             215
  802.3/Ethernet
Destination address     Broadcast                Broadcast
Source address          WstDigt-CF-08-F3         Individual
global
Type                    08-00 IP
Frame check sequence    89-20-23-99
------------------------------------
```

This is a different level of information from that presented before. For example, notice that the source address, IP version, and other frame level details are provided. With this information, it is possible to isolate a problem down to the interface or the protocol that is operating within the network layer where logical communication occurs.

███████ # Case Study: Traces of Switches and Nodes

The following is a trace of the network stack decode for 39 frames. Notice the switch Ethernet address shows up in the trace data as well as the following indicators:

MUSCLE

THE-HOSTAGE

SPEEDY

IP Version 4

The domain INFO.COM

NETBIOS

RIP

IPX data

This level of detail is very helpful when troubleshooting. This trace takes information from the perspective of the entire protocol stack and decodes it. I suppose it would be well to point out that understanding the network layers and reading HeX would be helpful for you. On a personal note, I recommend you become able to read HeX on the fly to be able to effectively function at deeper level of troubleshooting.

The first step to using information like this is having this level of information on file. I recommend obtaining this level of information and maintaining dated material as such to troubleshoot your network more efficiently. In addition, I realize that some of the readers might not understand all of the trace as presented, but use it as a beginning point to assist you in your learning endeavors.

```
****************************************************************
*****                                                      *****
*****       HEWLETT PACKARD NETWORK ADVISOR                *****
*****                                                      *****
*****     Measurement:    Network Stack Decode             *****
*****     Print Type:     All Frames                       *****
*****     Open Views:     Detailed                         *****
*****     Display Mode:   Viewing All Frames               *****
*****     Print Date:     09/15 /00                        *****
*****     Print Time:     11:27:58                         *****
*****                                                      *****
```

```
**********************************************************
Frame: 1              Time: Aug 2225:32.4611636   Length: 64
   ARP/RARP
Hardware                    1                      Ethernet
Protocol                    08-00                  IP
HW addr length              6
Phys addr length            4
Operation                   2                      ARP Reply
Sender HW addr              00-60-B0-21-08-A0
Sender internet addr        15.6.72.18
Target HW addr              00-00-00-00-00-00
Target internet addr        15.6.72.18
802.3/Ethernet
Destination address         HP-----21-08-A0        Warning:
Duplicate source
   and destination address
Source address              HP-----21-08-A0        Warning:
Duplicate source
   and destination address
Type                        08-06                  ARP
Frame check sequence        F3-11-34-41
> Data size                 46
> Protocol warning
**********************************************************
Frame: 2              Time: Aug 2225:34.1306347   Length: 64
   802.2
Destination SAP             42 Unknown             SAP
Source SAP                  42 Unknown             SAP
Command/Response            . . . . - . . . 0      Command
Type                        03                     Unnumbered
Poll                        . . . 0- . . . .
Modifier                    000. - 00. .           Information
   802.3/Ethernet
Destination address         01-80-C2-00-00-00      Group,
global
Source address              XYLAN--AC-9E-B5        Individual,
global
Length                      38
Padding:
   DC-B1-66-F8-AD-94-E3-36
Frame check sequence        B1-6C-E1-34
```

```
> Data size              38
**************************************************************
Frame: 3 Time: Aug 2225:34.3275052 Length: 244
  IPX
Checksum                FFFF
IPX Length              223
Transport Control       00
Packet Type             20              Experimental
Destination Network     00000000
Destination Node        FFFFFFFFFFFF    Broadcast
Destination Socket      0553
Source Network          00000000
Source Node             0000C0CF08F3
Source Socket           0553
  802.2
Destination SAP         E0              IPX
Source SAP              E0 IPX
Command/Response        . . . .- . . . 0    Command
Type                    03              Unnumbered
Poll                    . . . 0- . . . .
Modifier                000 . -00. .    Information
802.3/Ethernet
Destination address     Broadcast       Broadcast
Source address                          CF-08-F3
Individual,
global
Length                  226
Frame check sequence    0F-D4-C0-72
> Data size             226
**************************************************************
Frame: 4        Time: Aug 2225:34.8463663 Length: 64
  802.2
Destination SAP         42              Unknown SAP
Source SAP              42              Unknown SAP
Command/Response        . . . .- . . . 0    Command
Type                    03              Unnumbered
Poll                    . . . 0- . . . .
Modifier                000.-00.. Information
  802.3/Ethernet
Destination address     01-80-C2-00-00-00    Group,
global
```

| **Source address** | **XYLAN--AC-9E-B5** | Individual, |

global

| Length | 38 |

Padding:
  DC-B1-66-F8-AD-94-E3-36

| Frame check sequence | B1-6C-E1-34 |
| > **Data size** | **38** |

```
************************************************************
```

Frame: 5   Time: Aug 2225:36.8467995 Length: 64
  802.2

Destination SAP	42	Unknown SAP
Source SAP	42	Unknown SAP
Command/Response	. . . .- . . . 0	Command
Type 03	Unnumbered	
Poll	. . . 0-	
Modifier	000 .- 00. .	Information

  802.3/Ethernet

| Destination address | 01-80-C2-00-00-00 | Group, |

global

| **Source address** | **Xylan--AC-9E-B5** | Individual, |

global

| Length | 38 |

Padding:
  DC-B1-66-F8-AD-94-E3-36

| Frame check sequence | B1-6C-E1-34 |
| > Data size | 38 |

```
************************************************************
```

Frame: 6   Time: Aug 2225:38.8471699 Length: 64
  802.2

Destination SAP	**42**	Unknown SAP
Source SAP	42	Unknown SAP
Command/Response	. . . .- . . . 0	Command
Type	03	Unnumbered
Poll	. . . 0-	
Modifier	000.-00. .	Information

  802.3/Ethernet

| Destination address | 01-80-C2-00-00-00 | Group, |

global

| **Source address** | **XYLAN--AC-9E-B5** | Individual, |

global

| Length | 38 |

```
Padding:
   DC-B1-66-F8-AD-94-E3-36
Frame check sequence     B1-6C-E1-34
> Data size              38
*********************************************************
Frame: 7        Time: Aug 2225:40.8477201  Length: 64
   802.2
Destination SAP          42                  Unknown SAP
Source SAP               42                  Unknown SAP
Command/Response         . . . .- . . . 0    Command
Type                     03                  Unnumbered
Poll                     . . . 0- . . . .
Modifier                 000.-00. .          Information
   802.3/Ethernet
Destination address      01-80-C2-00-00-00   Group,
global
Source address           XYLAN--AC-9E-B5     Individual,
global
Length                   38
Padding:
   DC-B1-66-F8-AD-94-E3-36
Frame check sequence     B1-6C-E1-34
> Data size              38
*********************************************************
Frame: 8        Time: Aug 2225:41.4800509  Length: 346
   BOOTP
Operation code           1                   Bootp
Request
Hardware type            1                   Ethernet
Hardware address length                      16
Hop count                0
Transaction ID           961603691
Seconds since boot       5888
Client IP                220.100.100.115
Gateway IP               0.0.0.0
Hardware address (hex)   52-41-53-20-90-42-70-1D-
Host name (first 8 bytes)                    00-00-00-00-
00-00-00-00
Boot file name (hex)     00-00-00-00-00-00-00-00
```

```
Vendor magic cookie IP   99.130.83.99
Host name                MUSCLE
UDP
Source port              68                        BOOTPS
Destination port         67                        BOOTPS
Length                   308
Checksum                 25-A8
    IP
Version                  4
Internet header length   5                         (32        bit
words)
Precedence               000 .- . . . .            Routine
Delay                    . . . 0- . . . .          Delay normal
Throughput               . . . . -0 . . .          Throughput
normal
Reliability              . . . .- . 0 . .          Reliability
normal
Total Length             328
Identification           58402
May / Do Not Fragment    . 0 . . - . . .           Fragmenta-
tion
allowed
Last / More Fragments    . . 0 . - . . .           Last    frag-
ment
Offset                   0
Time To Live             128
Next Protocol            17                        UDP
Checksum                 15-14
Source                   220.100.100.10
Destination              Broadcast
> Data size              308
  802.3/Ethernet
Destination address      Broadcast                 Broadcast
Source address           Kingston-30-C2-43         Individual,
global
Type 08-00 IP
Frame check sequence B5-14-FE-4B
> Data size 328
**************************************************************
Frame: 9        Time: Aug 2225:42.1361021 Length: 64
  Novell SAP
```

```
Service Adv. Protocol    0001                    General
Service Query
Server Type              FFFF
IPX
Checksum                 FFFF
IPX Length               34
Transport Control        00
Packet Type              17                      NCP
Destination Network      00000000
Destination Node FFFFFFFFFFFF Broadcast
Destination Socket       0452                    Service
Advertising Packet
Source Network           00000000
Source Node              0060B02108A0
Source Socket            4001
  SNAP
Organization code        00-00-00
Type                     81-37                   IPX
  802.2
Destination SAP          AA                      SNAP
Source SAP               AA                      SNAP
Command/Response         . . . . - . . . 0       Command
Type                     03                      Unnumbered
Poll                     . . . 0- . . . .
Modifier                 000.- 00 . .            Information
  802.3/Ethernet
Destination address Broadcast Broadcast
Source address           HP----21-08-A0          Individual,
global
Length                   42
Padding:
  00-00-00-00
Frame check sequence     F2-67-62-C1
> Data size              42
**********************************************************
Frame: 10        Time: Aug 2225:42.1403283 Length: 64
  Novell SAP
Service Adv. Protocol    0001                    General
Service Query
Server Type              FFFF
  IPX
```

```
Checksum                  FFFF
IPX Length                34
Transport Control         00
Packet Type               17                    NCP
Destination Network       00000000
Destination Node          FFFFFFFFFFFF          Broadcast
Destination Socket        0452                  Service
Advertising Packet
Source Network            00000000
Source Node               0060B02108A0
Source Socket             4001
  802.2
Destination SAP           E0                    IPX
Source SAP                E0                    IPX
Command/Response          . . . .- . . . 0      Command
Type                      03                    Unnumbered
Poll                      . . . 0- . . . .
Modifier                  000.-00. .            Information
  802.3/Ethernet
Destination address       Broadcast             Broadcast
Source address            HP-----21-08-A0       Individual,
global
Length                    37
Padding:    00-00-00-00-00-00-00-00 00
Frame check sequence      23-51-92-A9
> Data size               37
************************************************************
Frame: 11      Time: Aug 2225:42.1410254  Length: 182
  Novell SAP
Service Adv. Protocol     0002                  General
Service Response
Server Type               0640
Server Name               MUSCLE
SAP Network Address       00000001
SAP Node Address          000000000001
SAP Socket Address        E885
Hops To Server            1
Server Type               064E
Server Name               MUSCLE!!!!!!!!!!A5569B20A
SAP Network Address       00000001
SAP Node Address          000000000001
```

```
SAP Socket Address        4010
Hops To Server            1
IPX
Checksum                  FFFF
IPX Length                160
Transport Control         00
Packet Type               17                      NCP
Destination Network       00000000
Destination Node          0060B02108A0
Destination Socket        4001
Source Network            00000000
Source Node               00C0F030C243
Source Socket             0452                    Service
Advertising Packet
  802.2
Destination SAP           E0                      IPX
Source SAP                E0                      IPX
Command/Response          . . . . - . . . 0       Command
Type                      03                      Unnumbered
Poll                      . . . 0- . . . .
Modifier                  000 .- 00. .            Information
802.3/Ethernet
Destination address       HP----21-08-A0          Individual,
global
Source address            Kingston-30-C2-43       Individual,
global
Length                    164
Frame check sequence      E3-B7-41-28
> Data size               164
**********************************************************
Frame: 12        Time: Aug 2225:42.1448953  Length: 64
Novell SAP
Service Adv. Protocol     0001                    General
Service Query
Server Type               FFFF
  IPX
Checksum                  FFFF
IPX Length                34
Transport Control         00
Packet Type               17                      NCP
Destination Network       00000000
```

```
Destination Node          FFFFFFFFFFFF        Broadcast
Destination Socket        0452                Service
Advertising Packet
Source Network            00000000
Source Node               0060B02108A0
Source Socket             4001
802.3/Ethernet
Destination address       Broadcast           Broadcast
Source address            HP----21-08-A0      Individual,
global
Length                    34                  IPX
Padding:
  00-00-00-00-00-00-00-00  00-00-00-00
Frame check sequence      78-8A-D8-9A
> Data size               34
***********************************************************
Frame: 13       Time: Aug 2225:42.1491827 Length: 64
Novell SAP
Service Adv. Protocol     0001                General
Service Query
Server Type               FFFF
  IPX
Checksum                  FFFF
IPX Length                34
Transport Control         00
Packet Type               17                  NCP
Destination Network       00000000
Destination Node          FFFFFFFFFFFF        Broadcast
Destination Socket        0452                Service
Advertising Packet
Source Network            00000000
Source Node               0060B02108A0
Source Socket             4001
802.3/Ethernet
Destination address       Broadcast           Broadcast
Source address            HP----21-08-A0      Individual,
global
Type                      81-37               IPX
Frame check sequence      93-E9-A4-48
> Data size               46
***********************************************************
```

```
Frame: 14          Time: Aug 2225:42.8481737 Length: 64
   802.2
Destination SAP         42                    Unknown SAP
Source SAP              42                    Unknown SAP
Command/Response        . . . .- . . . 0      Command
Type 03                 Unnumbered
Poll                    . . . 0- . . . .
Modifier                000.-00. .            Information
802.3/Ethernet
Destination address     01-80-C2-00-00-00     Group,
global
Source address          XYLAN--AC-9E-B5       Individual,
global
Length                  38
Padding: DC-B1-66-F8-AD-94-E3-36
Frame check sequence    B1-6C-E1-34
> Data size             38
**********************************************************
Frame: 15 Time: Aug 2225:44.8485252          Length: 64
   802.2
Destination SAP         42                    Unknown SAP
Source SAP              42                    Unknown SAP
Command/Response        . . . .- . . . 0      Command
Type                    03                    Unnumbered
Poll                    . . . 0- . . . .
Modifier                000.-00. .            Information
   802.3/Ethernet
Destination address     01-80-C2-00-00-00     Group,
global
Source address          XYLAN--AC-9E-B5       Individual,
global
Length                  38
Padding:
  DC-B1-66-F8-AD-94-E3-36
Frame check sequence    B1-6C-E1-34
> Data size             38
**********************************************************
Frame: 16               Time: Aug 2225:46.8490595 Length:
64
   802.2
Destination SAP         42                    Unknown SAP
```

Source SAP	42	Unknown SAP
Command/Response	. . . .- . . . 0	Command
Type	03	Unnumbered
Poll	. . . 0-	
Modifier	000 .- 00. .	Information
802.3/Ethernet		
Destination address global	**01-80-C2-00-00-00**	Group,
Source address global	**XYLAN--AC-9E-B5**	Individual,
Length 38		
Padding:		
DC-B1-66-F8-AD-94-E3-36		
Frame check sequence	B1-6C-E1-34	
> Data size	38	

****

Frame: 17   Time: Aug 2225:48.8495315 Length: 64
   802.2

Destination SAP	42	Unknown SAP
Source SAP	42	Unknown SAP
Command/Response	. . . .- . . . 0	Command
Type	03	Unnumbered
Poll	. . . 0-	
Modifier	000 .- 00. .	Information
802.3/Ethernet		
Destination address global	**01-80-C2-00-00-00**	Group,
Source address global	XYLAN--AC-9E-B5	Individual,
Length	38	
Padding:		
DC-B1-66-F8-AD-94-E3-36		
Frame check sequence	B1-6C-E1-34	
> Data size	38	

****

Frame: 18   Time: Aug 2225:50.8498854 Length: 64
   802.2

Destination SAP	42	Unknown SAP
Source SAP	42	Unknown SAP
Command/Response	. . . .- . . . 0	Command
Type	03	Unnumbered

```
Poll                      . . . 0- . . . .
Modifier                  000.- 00 . .          Information
  802.3/Ethernet
Destination address       01-80-C2-00-00-00     Group,
global
Source address            XYLAN--AC-9E-B5       Individual,
global
Length                    38
Padding:
  DC-B1-66-F8-AD-94-E3-36
Frame check sequence      B1-6C-E1-34
> Data size               38
***********************************************************
Frame: 19      Time: Aug 2225:52.8504332 Length: 64
  802.2
Destination SAP           42                    Unknown SAP
Source SAP                42                    Unknown SAP
Command/Response          . . . .- . . . 0      Command
Type                      03                    Unnumbered
Poll                      . . . 0- . . . .
Modifier                  000.-00. .            Information
  802.3/Ethernet
Destination address       01-80-C2-00-00-00     Group,
global
Source address            XYLAN--AC-9E-B5       Individual,
global
Length                    38
Padding:
  DC-B1-66-F8-AD-94-E3-36
Frame check sequence      B1-6C-E1-34
> Data size               38
***********************************************************
Frame: 20      Time: Aug 2225:52.9576613 Length: 64
  ARP/RARP
Hardware                  1                     Ethernet
Protocol                  08-00                 IP
HW addr length            6
Phys addr length          4
Operation                 1                     ARP Request
Sender HW addr            00-C0-F0-30-C2-43
Sender internet addr       220.100.100.10
```

| Target HW addr | 00-00-00-00-00-00 | |
| Target internet addr | 220.100.100.111 | |

802.3/Ethernet

| Destination address | Broadcast | Broadcast |
| **Source address** | **Kingston-30-C2-43** | Individual, |

global

Type	08-06	ARP
Frame check sequence	53-2D-B4-10	
> Data size	46	

```
**********************************************************
```

Frame: 21   Time: Aug 2225:54.3223507 Length: 119

  IPX

Checksum	FFFF	
IPX Length	98	
Transport Control	00	
Packet Type 4 PEP		
Destination Network	00000000	
Destination Node	FFFFFFFFFFFF	Broadcast
Destination Socket	0551	
Source Network	00000000	
Source Node	**0000C0CF08F3**	
Source Socket	**0552**	

  802.2

Destination SAP	E0 I	PX
Source SAP	E0	IPX
Command/Response	. . . .- . . . 0	Command
Type	03	Unnumbered
Poll	. . . 0-	
Modifier	000 .- 00. .	Information

802.3/Ethernet

| Destination address | Broadcast | Broadcast |
| **Source address** | **WstDigt-CF-08-F3** | Individual, |

global

Length	**101**	
Frame check sequence	68-44-52-6C	
> **Data size 101**		

```
**********************************************************
```

Frame: 22   Time: Aug 2225:54.3302484 Length: 64

  ARP/RARP

| Hardware | 1 | Ethernet |
| Protocol | 08-00 | IP |

```
HW addr length             6
Phys addr length           4
Operation                  1                    ARP Request
Sender HW addr             00-00-C0-CF-08-F3
Sender internet addr       220.100.100.111
Target HW addr             00-00-00-00-00-00
Target internet addr       220.100.100.172
  802.3/Ethernet
Destination address        Broadcast            Broadcast
Source address             WstDigt-CF-08-F3     Individual,
global
Type                       08-06                ARP
Frame check sequence       02-18-9C-AA
> Data size                46
***************************************************************
Frame: 23        Time: Aug 2225:54.3346122  Length: 65
  NetBIOS
Header Length              44
Delimiter                  EFFF
Command                    0A                   NAME_QUERY
Optional Data 1            1A                   Warning:
Data
in reserved
  field
    Name Type              11                   Unique name
type
    Session Number         00
Transmit Correlator        0000                 Reserved
field
Response Correlator        0011
Destination Name           THE-HOSTAGE
Source Name                SPEEDY
  802.2
Destination SAP            F0                   NetBios
Source SAP                 F0                   NetBios
Command/Response           . . . .- . . . 0     Command
Type                       03                   Unnumbered
Poll                       . . . 0- . . . .
Modifier                   000.-00. .           Information
  802.3/Ethernet
Destination address        03-00-00-00-00-01    Group, local
```

Source address	WstDigt-CF-08-F3	Individual, global
Length	47	
Frame check sequence	2E-CF-0D-1B	
> Data size	47	

```
**********************************************************
```

Frame: 24   Time: Aug 2226:00.1796446 Length: 346
  BOOTP

Operation code	1	**Bootp Request**
Hardware type	1	**Ethernet**
Hardware address length		**16**
Hop count	0	
Transaction ID	961603691	
Seconds since boot	**10752**	
Client IP	**220.100.100.115**	
Gateway IP	0.0.0.0	
Hardware address (hex)	**52-41-53-20-90-42-70-1D-**	
Host name (first 8 bytes)		00-00-00-00-00-00-00-00
Boot file name (hex)	00-00-00-00-00-00-00-00	
Vendor magic cookie IP	**99.130.83.99**	
Host name	**MUSCLE**	

  UDP

Source port	68	**BOOTPS**
Destination port	67	**BOOTPS**
Length	308	
Checksum	12-A8	

  IP

Version	**4**	
Internet header length words)	5	(32 bit
Precedence	000 .- . . .	Routine
Delay	. . . 0- . . .	Delay normal
Throughput normal	. . . .- 0 . . .	Throughput
Reliability normal	. . . . .- . 0 . .	Reliability
Total Length	328	
Identification	4131	

```
May / Do Not Fragment    . 0 . .- . . .        Fragmenta-
tion
allowed
Last / More Fragments    . . 0.- . . .         Last    frag-
ment
Offset                   0
Time To Live             128
Next Protocol            17                     UDP
Checksum                 E9-13
Source                   220.100.100.10
Destination              Broadcast
> Data size              308
  802.3/Ethernet
Destination address      Broadcast              Broadcast
Source address           Kingston-30-C2-43      Individual,
global
Type                     08-00                  IP
Frame check sequence     15-C7-AE-30
> Data size              328
***********************************************************
Frame: 25        Time: Aug 2226:08.9609173  Length: 65
  NetBIOS
Header Length            44
Delimiter                EFFF
Command                  0A                     NAME_QUERY
Optional Data 1          17                     Warning:
Data
in reserved
  field
    Name Type            0F                     Unique name
type
  Session Number         00
Transmit Correlator      0000 Reserved field
Response Correlator      000F
Destination Name         MUSCLE
Source Name              THE-HOSTAGE
  802.2
Destination SAP          F0                     NetBios
Source SAP               F0                     NetBios
Command/Response         . . . .- . . . 0       Command
Type                     03                     Unnumbered
```

```
Poll                        . . . 0- . . . .
Modifier                    000.-00. .              Information
  802.3/Ethernet
Destination address         03-00-00-00-00-01       Group, local
Source address              00-60-08-98-1D-         33  Individ-
ual,
global
Length                      47
Frame check sequence        84-52-3B-16
> Data size                 47
*********************************************************
Frame: 26      Time: Aug 2226:11.7606845  Length: 195
SMB
Identifier                  SMB
Command Code                25                      Transaction
Name
Error Class                 00                      Success
Reserved                    00
Error Code                  0000                    Success
Flags                       00000000                Good
Response Request            0 . . . . . .           Request
Client Notification         . 0 . . . . .           Flag Not Set
File Lock                   . . 0 . . . .            Flag Not Set
Canonical Form              . . . 0 . . .           Flag Not Set
Case Sensitive              . . . . 0 . . .         Flag Not Set
Reserved                    . . . . . 0 . .
Rcv Buffer Posted           . . . . . . 0.          Flag Not Set
Subdialect                  . . . . . . . 0         Flag Not Set
Flags_2                     0000
Reserved (Truncated)        00-00-00-00-00-00-00-00-
Authenticated Resource ID                           0000
Callers Process ID          0000
Unauthenticated User ID                             0000
Multiplex ID                0000
Word Count                  17
Parameters                  0000
Parameters                  002C
Parameters                  0000
Parameters                  0000
Parameters (Truncated)      00-02-00-01-00-01-00-03-
Buffer Count                61
```

ASCII Data	**\MAILSLOT\BROWSE**	
Buffer Type	01	Server Data
Block		
ASCII Data	**à"_ THE-HOSTAGE**	
ASCII Data	**C __Uª THE-HOSTAGE**	
NetBIOS		
Header Length	44	
Delimiter	EFFF	
Command	08	DATAGRAM
Optional Data 1	00	Reserved
field		
Optional Data 2	0000	Reserved
field		
Transmit Correlator	0000	Reserved
field		
Response Correlator	0000	Reserved
field		
Destination Name	**INFO.COM**	
Source Name	**THE-HOSTAGE**	
802.2		
Destination SAP	F0	NetBios
Source SAP	F0	NetBios
Command/Response	. . . .- . . . 0	Command
Type	03	Unnumbered
Poll	. . . 0-	
Modifier	000 .- 00. .	Information
802.3/Ethernet		
Destination address	**03-00-00-00-00-01**	Group, local
Source address	**00-60-08-98-1D-33**	Individual,
global		
Length	**177**	
Frame check sequence	**DB-89-E3-1F**	
> Data size	**177**	

```
**************************************************************
```

Frame: 27   Time: Aug 2226:13.3800071 Length: 64

Novell RIP

Routing Info. Protocol	**0002**	**Reply**
Network Number	**00000001**	
Number Of Hops	**1**	
Number Of Ticks	**2**	
IPX		

```
Checksum                    FFFF
IPX Length                  40
Transport Control           00
Packet Type                 1                  Routing
Information Packet
Destination Network         00000000
Destination Node            FFFFFFFFFFFF       Broadcast
Destination Socket          0453               Routing
Information Packet
Source Network              00000000
Source Node                 00C0F030C243
Source Socket               0453 Routing
Information Packet
802.2
Destination SAP E0 IPX
Source SAP E0 IPX
Command/Response            . . . . - . . . 0  Command
Type                        03                 Unnumbered
Poll                        . . . 0- . . . .
Modifier                    000 .- 00. .       Information
  802.3/Ethernet
Destination address         Broadcast          Broadcast
Source address              Kingston-30-C2-43  Individual,
global
Length                      44
Padding:
  00-00
Frame check sequence        51-6F-D4-AD
> Data size                 44
*************************************************************
Frame: 28      Time: Aug 2226:22.6438210 Length: 64
  Novell SAP
Service Adv. Protocol       0003               Nearest
Server
Query
Server Type                 0004
  IPX
Checksum                    FFFF
IPX Length                  34
Transport Control           00
Packet Type                 17                 NCP
```

```
Destination Network      00000000
Destination Node         FFFFFFFFFFFF            Broadcast
Destination Socket       0452                    Service
Advertising Packet
Source Network           00000000
Source Node              006008981D33
Source Socket            401C
   802.2
Destination SAP          E0                      IPX
Source SAP               E0                      IPX
Command/Response         . . . .- . . . 0        Command
Type                     03                      Unnumbered
Poll                     . . . 0- . . . .
Modifier                 000.-00. .              Information
   802.3/Ethernet
Destination address      Broadcast               Broadcast
Source address           00-60-08-98-1D-33       Individual,
global
Length 37
Padding:    00-04-00-04-00-04-00-04 00
Frame check sequence     FD-69-6C-C8
> Data size              37
***********************************************************
Frame: 29      Time: Aug 2226:27.1631141  Length: 182
Service Adv. Protocol    0002                    General
Service Response
Server Type              0640
Server Name              MUSCLE
SAP Network Address      00000001
SAP Node Address         000000000001
SAP Socket Address       E885
Hops To Server           1
Server Type              064E
Server Name              MUSCLE!!!!!!!!!A5569B20A
SAP Network Address      00000001
SAP Node Address         000000000001
SAP Socket Address       4010
Hops To Server           1
   IPX
Checksum                 FFFF
IPX Length               160
```

Transport Control	00	
Packet Type	**4 PEP**	
Destination Network	00000000	
Destination Node	FFFFFFFFFFFF	Broadcast
Destination Socket	0452	Service
Advertising Packet		
Source Network	00000000	
Source Node	**00C0F030C243**	
Source Socket	**0452** Service	
Advertising Packet		
802.2		
Destination SAP	E0	IPX
Source SAP	E0	IPX
Command/Response	. . . .- . . . 0	Command
Type	03	Unnumbered
Poll	. . . 0-	
Modifier	000.-00. .	Information
802.3/Ethernet		
Destination address	Broadcast	Broadcast
Source address	**Kingston-30-C2-43**	Individual,
global		
Length	164	
Frame check sequence	CF-BB-1B-19	
> **Data size**	**164**	

```
********************************************************
```

Frame: 30   Time: Aug 2226:34.2421174 Length: 253

SMB

Identifier	**SMB**	
Command Code	**25**	**Transaction**
Name		
Error Class	00	**Success**
Reserved	00	
Error Code	0000	Success
Flags	00000000	**Good**
Response Request	0	Request
Client Notification	. 0	Flag Not Set
File Lock	. . 0	Flag Not Set
Canonical Form	. . . 0 . . .	Flag Not Set
Case Sensitive	. . . .0 . . .	Flag Not Set
Reserved	. . . . . 0 . .	
Rcv Buffer Posted	. . . . . . 0 .	Flag Not Set

```
Subdialect                 . . . . . . . 0        Flag Not Set
Flags_2 0000
Reserved (Truncated)       00-00-00-00-00-00-00-00-
Authenticated Resource     ID 0000
Callers Process ID         0000
Unauthenticated User ID                           0000
Multiplex ID               0000
Word Count                 17
Parameters                 0000
Parameters                 0027
Parameters                 0000
Parameters                 0000
Parameters (Truncated)     00-02-00-01-00-01-00-03-
Buffer Count               56
ASCII Data                 \MAILSLOT\BROWSE
Buffer Type                01                     Server Data
Block
ASCII Data                 _ã"_  SPEEDY
ASCII Data                 A ___Uª SPEEDY
NetBIOS
Service Type :                                    Datagram
Service
Packet Type :                                     Direct_Group
Datagram
Msg_Type                   11
Flags                      1A                     See       Bit
Fields
Below
  Reserved Bits            0001 . . .             Warning:
Reserved Bit Not
  Zero
  Source End-Node Type     . . . . 1 0. .         Mixed      (M)
node
  FIRST Flag               . . . . . . 1 .        First  Frag-
ment
  MORE Flag                . . . . . . . 0        Last   Frag-
ment
DGM ID                     21
Source IP                  220.100.100.111        Source  IP
Address
Source Port                138                    Source Port
```

Number		
DGM Length	193	
Packet Offset	0	
Name Length	32	
Source Name	**SPEEDY**	**NetBIOS Name**
Name Length	32	
Destination Name	**INFO.COM** "	**NetBIOS Name**
User Data		SMB Data—See
SMB Decode		
UDP		
Source port	**138**	NETBIOS
Destination port	138	NETBIOS
Length	215	
Checksum	E4-F4	
IP		
Version	**4**	
Internet header length words)	**5**	**(32 bit**
Precedence	000 . -	Routine
Delay	. . . 0 -	Delay normal
Throughput normal	. . . . - 0 . . .	Throughput
Reliability normal	. . . . - . 0 . .	Reliability
Total Length	235	
Identification	4359	
May / Do Not Fragment tion allowed	. 0 . . - . . .	Fragmenta-
Last / More Fragments ment	. . 0 . - . . .	Last frag-
Offset	0	
Time To Live	32	
Next Protocol	**17**	**UDP**
Checksum	06-C4	
Source	**220.100.100.111**	
Destination	220.100.100.255	
> **Data size**	**215**	
802.3/Ethernet		
Destination address	**Broadcast**	Broadcast
Source address	**WstDigt-CF-08-F3**	Individual,

```
global
Type                          08-00                  IP
Frame check sequence          02-BC-97-FA
> Data size                   235
************************************************************
Frame: 31        Time: Aug 2226:36.2474343 Length: 190
  SMB
Identifier                    SMB
Command Code                  25                     Transaction
Name
Error Class                   00                     Success
Reserved                      00
Error Code                    0000                   Success
Flags                         00000000               Good
Response Request              0 . . . . . .          Request
Client Notification           . 0 . . . . .          Flag Not Set
File Lock                     . . 0 . . . .          Flag Not Set
Canonical Form                . . . 0 . . .          Flag Not Set
Case Sensitive                . . . . 0 . .          Flag Not Set
Reserved                      . . . . . 0 . .
Rcv Buffer Posted             . . . . . . 0 .        Flag Not Set
Subdialect                    . . . . . . . 0        Flag Not Set
Flags_2                       0000
Reserved (Truncated)          00—00—00—00—00—00—00—00-
Authenticated Resource ID                            0000
Callers Process ID            0000
Unauthenticated User ID                              0000
Multiplex ID                  0000
Word Count                    17
Parameters                    0000
Parameters                    027
Parameters                    0000
Parameters                    0000
Parameters (Truncated)        00—02—00—01—00—01—00—03-
Buffer Count                  56
ASCII Data                    \MAILSLOT\BROWSE
Buffer Type                   01                     Server Data
Block
ASCII Data                    _à"_ SPEEDY
ASCII Data                    A __Uª SPEEDY
NetBIOS
```

```
Header Length            44
Delimiter                EFFF
Command                  08                      DATAGRAM
Optional Data 1          00                      Reserved
field
Optional Data 2          0000                    Reserved
field
Transmit Correlator      0000                    Reserved
field
Response Correlator      0000                    Reserved
field
Destination Name         INFO.COM
Source Name              SPEEDY
  802.2
Destination SAP          F0                      NetBios
Source SAP               F0                      NetBios
Command/Response         . . . .- . . . 0        Command
Type                     03                      Unnumbered
Poll                     . . . 0- . . . .
Modifier                 000 .- 00. .            Information
  802.3/Ethernet
Destination address      03—00—00—00—00—01       Group, local
Source address           WstDigt — CF208-F3      Individual,
global
Length                   172
Frame check sequence     F9—8A-A4—55
> Data size              172
*************************************************************
Frame: 32                Time: Aug 2227:00.9503546 Length:
65
NetBIOS
Header Length            44
Delimiter                EFFF
Command                  0A NAME_QUERY
Optional Data 1          1A                      Warning:
Data
in reserved
field
Name Type                12                      Unique name
type
Session Number           00
```

Transmit Correlator field	0000	Reserved
Response Correlator	0012	
Destination Name	THE-HOSTAGE	
Source Name	SPEEDY	

   802.2

Destination SAP	F0	NetBios
Source SAP	F0	NetBios
Command/Response	. . . .- . . . 0	Command
Type	03	Unnumbered
Poll	. . . 0-	
Modifier	000. - 00. .	Information

802.3/Ethernet

Destination address	03-00-00-00-00-01	Group, local
Source address	WstDigt—CF-08-F3	Individual, global
Length	47	
Frame check sequence	13-3C-63-3B	
> Data size	47	

****

Frame: 33   Time: Aug 2227:08.9693520 Length: 64

ARP/RARP

Hardware	**1**	**Ethernet**
Protocol	**08-00**	**IP**
HW addr length 6		
Phys addr length	**4**	
Operation	**1**	**ARP Request**
Sender HW addr	**00-60-08-98-1D-33**	
Sender internet addr	220.100.100.172	
Target HW addr	00-00-00-00-00-00	
Target internet addr	**220.100.100.10**	

   802.3/Ethernet

Destination address	Broadcast	Broadcast
Source address	00-60-08-98-1D-33	Individual, global
Type	**08-06**	**ARP**
Frame check sequence	3D-DF-67-6B	
> Data size	46	

****

Frame: 34 Time: Aug 2227:12.0436369 Length: 258

SMB

Identifier SMB		
Command Code	25	**Transaction**
Name		
Error Class	00	Success
Reserved	00	
Error Code	0000	Success
Flags	00000000	Good
Response Request	0	Request
Client Notification	. 0	Flag Not Set
File Lock	. . 0	Flag Not Set
Canonical Form	. . . 0	Flag Not Set
Case Sensitive	. . . . 0 . . .	Flag Not Set
Reserved	. . . . . 0 . .	
Rcv Buffer Posted	. . . . . . 0.	Flag Not Set
Subdialect	0	Flag Not Set
Flags_2	0000	
Reserved (Truncated)	00-00-00-00-00-00-00-00-	
Authenticated Resource ID		0000
Callers Process ID	0000	
Unauthenticated User ID		0000
Multiplex ID	0000	
Word Count	17	
Parameters	0000	
Parameters	002C	
Parameters	0000	
Parameters	0000	
Parameters (Truncated)	00-02-00-01-00-01-00-03-	
Buffer Count	61	
ASCII Data	**\MAILSLOT\BROWSE**	
Buffer Type	01	Server Data
Block		
ASCII Data	**à"_ THE-HOSTAGE**	
ASCII Data	**C __Uª THE-HOSTAGE**	
NetBIOS		
Service Type :		Datagram
Service		
Packet Type :		Direct_Group
Datagram		
Msg_Type	11	
Flags	02	See Bit
Fields		

```
Below
  Reserved Bits              0000 . . . .
  Source End-Node Type       . . . .00..        Broadcast (B)
node
  FIRST Flag                 . . . . . 1.        First   Frag-
ment
  MORE Flag                  . . . . . .0        Last Fragment
DGM ID                       104
Source IP                    220.100.100.172     Source IP
Address
Source Port                  138                 Source Port
Number
DGM Length                   198
Packet Offset                0
Name Length                  32
Source Name                  THE-HOSTAGE         NetBIOS Name
Name Length                  32
Destination Name             INFO.COM   "        NetBIOS Name
User Data                                        SMB Data—See
SMB Decode
  UDP
Source port                  138                 NETBIOS
Destination port             138                 NETBIOS
Length                       220
Checksum                     F6-2D
  IP
Version                      4
Internet header length       5                   (32      bit
words)
Precedence                   000 .- . . . .      Routine
Delay                        . . . 0- . . . .    Delay normal
Throughput                   . . . . -0 . . .    Throughput
normal
Reliability                  . . . . -. 0 . .    Reliability
normal
Total Length                 240
Identification               28937
May / Do Not Fragment        . 0 . . - . . . .   Fragmenta-
tion
allowed
```

```
Last / More Fragments    . . 0 . - . . . .    Last    frag-
ment
Offset                   0
Time To Live             128
Next Protocol            17                   UDP
Checksum                 46-7F
Source                   220.100.100.172
Destination              220.100.100.255
> Data size              220
802.3/Ethernet
Destination address      Broadcast             Broadcast
Source address           00-60-08-98-1D-33     Individual,
global
Type                     08-00                 IP
Frame check sequence     1E-67-FF-02
> Data size              240
**************************************************************
Frame: 35        Time: Aug 2227:13.3956444  Length: 64
  Novell RIP
Routing Info. Protocol   0002                  Reply
Network Number           00000001
Number Of Hops           1
Number Of Ticks          2
  IPX
Checksum                 FFFF
IPX Length               40
Transport Control        00
Packet Type              1                     Routing
Information Packet
Destination Network      00000000
Destination Node         FFFFFFFFFFFF          Broadcast
Destination Socket       0453                  Routing
Information Packet
Source Network           00000000
Source Node              00C0F030C243
Source Socket            0453                  Routing
Information Packet
  802.2
Destination SAP          E0                    IPX
Source SAP               E0                    IPX
Command/Response         . . . .- . . . 0      Command
```

```
Type                    03              Unnumbered
Poll                    . . . 0- . . . .
Modifier                000.-00..       Information
   802.3/Ethernet
Destination address     Broadcast       Broadcast
Source address          Kingston-30-C2-43    Individual,
global
Length                  44
Padding:
   00-00
Frame check sequence    51-6F-D4-AD
> Data size             44
************************************************************
Frame: 36        Time: Aug 2227:21.4612320  Length: 346
   BOOTP
Operation code          1               Bootp
Request
Hardware type           1               Ethernet
Hardware address length                 16
Hop count               0
Transaction ID          509547022
Seconds since boot      0
Client IP               0.0.0.0
Gateway IP              0.0.0.0
Hardware address (hex)  52-41-53-20-90-42-70-1D-
Host name (first 8 bytes)                    00-00-00-00-
00-00-00-00
Boot file name (hex)    00-00-00-00-00-00-00-00
Vendor magic cookie IP  99.130.83.99
   Host name            MUSCLE
   UDP
Source port             68              BOOTPS
Destination port        67              BOOTPS
Length                  308
Checksum                2D-F7
   IP
Version                 4
Internet header length  5               (32      bit
words)
Precedence              000 . - . . . .  Routine
Delay                   . . . 0 - . . . .  Delay normal
```

Throughput normal	. . . . - 0 . . .	Throughput
Reliability normal	. . . . - . 0 . .	Reliability
Total Length	328	
Identification	54307	
May / Do Not Fragment tion allowed	. 0 . . -	Fragmenta-
Last / More Fragments ment	. . 0 . -	Last frag-
Offset	0	
Time To Live	**128**	
Next Protocol	**17**	**UDP**
Checksum	25-13	
Source	**220.100.100.10**	
Destination	Broadcast	
> Data size 308		
802.3/Ethernet		
Destination address	Broadcast	Broadcast
Source address global	**Kingston-30-C2-43**	Individual,
Type	08-00	IP
Frame check sequence	A7-E1-49-70	
> Data size	328	

****

Frame: 37   Time: Aug 2227:22.6418899 Length: 64

  Novell SAP

Service Adv. Protocol Service Query	**0001**	**General**
Server Type IPX	**0004**	
Checksum	FFFF	
IPX Length	34	
Transport Control	00	
Packet Type	**17**	**NCP**
Destination Network	00000000	
Destination Node	FFFFFFFFFFFF	Broadcast
Destination Socket Advertising Packet	0452	Service
Source Network	00000000	

```
Source Node              006008981D33
Source Socket            401C
  802.2
Destination SAP E0 IPX
Source SAP               E0 IPX
Command/Response         . . . . - . . . 0      Command
Type                     03                     Unnumbered
Poll                     . . . 0- . . . .
Modifier                 000 .- 00. .           Information
  802.3/Ethernet
Destination address      Broadcast              Broadcast
Source address           00-60-08-98-1D-33      Individual,
global
Length                   37
Padding:                 00-04-00-04-00-04-00-04 00
Frame check sequence     62-F7-57-24
> Data size              37
**********************************************************
Frame: 38      Time: Aug 2227:27.1779325  Length: 182
Service Adv. Protocol    0002                   General
Service Response
Server Type              0640
Server Name              MUSCLE
SAP Network Address      00000001
SAP Node Address         000000000001
SAP Socket Address       E885
Hops To Server           1
Server Type              064E
Server Name              MUSCLE!!!!!!!!!!A5569B20A
SAP Network Address      00000001
SAP Node Address         000000000001
SAP Socket Address       4010
Hops To Server           1
  IPX
Checksum                 FFFF
IPX Length               160
Transport Control        00
Packet Type              4                      PEP
Destination Network      00000000
Destination Node         FFFFFFFFFFFF           Broadcast
Destination Socket       0452                   Service
```

```
Advertising Packet
Source Network          00000000
Source Node             00C0F030C243
Source Socket           0452                    Service
Advertising Packet
  802.2
Destination SAP         E0                      IPX
Source SAP              E0                      IPX
Command/Response        . . . . - . . . 0       Command
Type                    03                      Unnumbered
Poll                    . . . 0- . . . .
Modifier                000.- 00 . .            Information
  802.3/Ethernet
Destination address     Broadcast               Broadcast
Source address          Kingston-30-C2-43       Individual,
global
Length                  164
Frame check sequence    CF-BB-1B-19
> Data size             164
*************************************************************
Frame: 39       Time: Aug 2227:31.1044369 Length: 346
  BOOTP
Operation code          1                       Bootp
Request
Hardware type           1                       Ethernet
Hardware address length                         16
Hop count               0
Transaction ID          509547022
Seconds since boot      2560
Client IP               0.0.0.0
Gateway IP              0.0.0.0
Hardware address (hex)  52-41-53-20-90-42-70-1D-
Host name (first 8 bytes)                       00-00-00-00-
00-00-00-00
Boot file name (hex)    00-00-00-00-00-00-00-00
Vendor magic cookie IP  99.130.83.99
  Host name             MUSCLE
  UDP
Source port             68                      BOOTPS
Destination port        67                      BOOTPS
Length                  308
```

```
Checksum                 23-F7
IP
Version 4
Internet header length   5                        (32       bit
words)
Precedence               000.- . . .              Routine
Delay                    . . . 0- . . .           Delay normal
Throughput               . . . .-0 . . .          Throughput
normal
Reliability              . . . .-.0..             Reliability
normal
Total Length             328
Identification           60195
May / Do Not Fragment    .0..- . . .              Fragmentation
allowed
Last / More Fragments    ..0.- . . . .
Last fragment Offset     0
Time To Live             128
Next Protocol            17                        UDP
Checksum                 0E-13
Source                   220.100.100.10
Destination              Broadcast
> Data size              308
  802.3/Ethernet
Destination address      Broadcast                Broadcast
Source address           Kingston-30-C2-43        Individual,
global
Type                     08-00                     IP
Frame check sequence     D3-1F-B1-72
> Data size              328
```

This trace can be used to examine different layers in the network layer model. For example, notice in many of the frames the Ethernet address is presented. Also, indication of the type frame is shown first, for example, bootp, SMB, RIP, ARP, and others. When one troubleshoots a network, he or she generally knows what is the problem; in other words, the problem is typically isolated.

This is an important aspect of troubleshooting; that is, isolating the problem. However, prior to isolating the problem, identification of the problem is the first step. In a recent conversation I had with an individual, it was obvious that he did not understand that the act of troubleshooting

(identification and isolation of a problem) is different from repairing or fix-
ing a problem.

With regard to the network, the previous trace is very helpful in conveying information about network traffic. This includes data flow, upper layer
protocol operation across the network, and routing information as well.

Again, my purpose here is to present information to you based on my
case study of the network switch in hopes that it might better help you
organize your network's information and assist you in determining the
information that should be obtained and maintained about your network
switch.

I took another trace and it shows another view of a brief network stack
decode. Notice similar information is shown here as with the previous network stack decode.

```
*************************************************************
*****                                                   *****
*****       HEWLETT PACKARD NETWORK ADVISOR             *****
*****                                                   *****
*****       Measurement:   Brief Network Stack Decode   *****
*****       Print Type:    All Frames                   *****
*****       Open Views:    Summary                      *****
*****       Display Mode:  Viewing All Frames           *****
*****       Print Date:    08/22 /01                    *****
*****       Print Time:    11:42:31                     *****
*****                                                   *****
*************************************************************
1 40:46.700   HP----21-08-A0   HP----21-08-A0   ARP    R
  PA=[15.6.72.18] HA=0060B02108A0
2 40:50.382  00000000-HP--210   00000000-Broadcast  SAP  C
  Find general Unkn service
3 40:50.386  00000000-HP--210   00000000-Broadcast  SAP  C
  Find general Unkn service
4 40:50.387  00000000-Kingst30C  00000000-HP--210   SAP  R
  MUSCLE
5 40:50.391  00000000-HP--210   00000000-Broadcast  SAP  C
  Find general Unkn service
6 40:50.396  00000000-HP--210   00000000-Broadcast  SAP  C
  Find general Unkn service
7 41:12.811 00-60-08-98-1D-33 03-00-00-00-00-01 SMB C Transac-
  tion name \MAILSLOT\BROWSE
```

8 41:13.614 00000000-Kingst30C 00000000-Broadcast IPX RIP Response: 1 networks

9 41:19.334 Kingston-30-C2-43 03-00-00-00-00-01 SMB C Transaction name \MAILSLOT\BROWSE

10 41:19.343 00000001-000000000 00000000-Broadcast NETB Find Name INFO.COM

11 41:19.884 00000001-000000000 00000000-Broadcast NETB Find Name INFO.COM

12 41:20.425 00000001-000000000 00000000-Broadcast NETB Find Name INFO.COM

13 41:20.967 00000001-000000000 00000000-Broadcast IPX Type=20 IPX WAN Broadcast LEN=217

14 41:20.968 220.100.100.10 220.100.100.255 SMB C Transaction name \MAILSLOT\BROWSE

15 41:22.615 00000000-006008981 00000000-Broadcast SAP C Find general file server

16 41:27.397 00000000-Kingst30C 00000000-Broadcast SAP R MUSCLE1741:47.639 WstDigt—CF-08-F3 Broadcast
 ARP C PA=[220.100.100.172]

18 41:47.640 220.100.100.111 220.100.100.172 SMB C Tree connect

19 41:47.642 220.100.100.111 220.100.100.172 SMB C Transaction name \PIPE\LANMAN

20 41:47.644 WstDigt—CF-08-F3 03-00-00-00-00-01 NETB Name query THE-HOSTAGE

21 41:47.644 WstDigt—CF-08-F3 00-60-08-98-1D-33 LLC C S=F0 D=F0 SABME P

22 41:47.645 WstDigt—CF-08-F3 00-60-08-98-1D-33 LLC C S=F0 D=F0 RR NR=0 P

23 41:47.646 WstDigt—CF-08-F3 00-60-08-98-1D-33 NETB S=13 D=10 Session init

24 41:47.646 WstDigt—CF-08-F3 00-60-08-98-1D-33 LLC R S=F0 D=F0 RR NR=1 F

25 41:47.647 WstDigt—CF-08-F3 00-60-08-98-1D-33 SMB C Negotiate Protocol PC NETWORK PROGRAM 1.0

26 41:47.648 WstDigt—CF-08-F3 00-60-08-98-1D-33 LLC R S=F0 D=F0 RR NR=2

27 41:47.649 WstDigt—CF-08-F3 00-60-08-98-1D-33 SMB C Session setup Len=34

28 41:47.650 WstDigt—CF-08-F3 00-60-08-98-1D-33 LLC R S=F0 D=F0 RR NR=3

```
29 41:47.650  WstDigt—CF-08-F3   00-60-08-98-1D-33   SMB   C
   Transaction name \PIPE\LANMAN
30 41:47.651 WstDigt—CF-08-F3 00-60-08-98-1D-33 LLC R S=F0
   D=F0 RR NR=4
31 41:49.434 220.100.100.10 Broadcast BOOTP Request
32 41:58.797 220.100.100.10 Broadcast BOOTP Request
```

This trace depicts session setup, BOOTP request, and other information passed at the network level across the switch backbone.

The following trace is a baseline of the traffic load on the network as introduced by the Internet Advisor. It shows the performance of the switch itself. This information is helpful to gauge any possible aberrations that could exist in the future. For example, with this traffic load and the hosts connected as presented here, it is easy to reproduce the conditions and actually test the switch itself. Much of troubleshooting network equipment involves being able to duplicate conditions. Consider this level of detail when you begin you baseline your switch.

************ ETHERNET TRAFFIC GENERATOR ***************
Added traffic Load:
   6% utilization
   7829 frames/second
   Inter-frame spacing: 0 ms.
Number of times to send activated frames: Continuous

Msg#	Message Type	Length	Source	Destination	FCS type
1	802.3 Fox Message	76	HP-------21-08-A0	HP-------14-02-01	Good

****

SUMMARY

The network switch is a key component in any network. It is a good idea to be able to obtain a wide variety of information about your switch. The information I presented to you in this chapter is simply snapshot information from the case study of the network switch used. This information has helped me to plan various aspects of my network, and I encourage you to consider this information when working with your network switch and determining what you need to do to make your network better.

I elected to use Ethernet as my example to you; however I do have similar baseline information about the switch in my lab for all network protocols used with it, including FDDI, ATM, and Token Ring. In this case study, a XYLAN switch was used; for further information about their products, you can contact them at:

XYLAN Corporation
26707 West Agoura Road
Calabasas, CA 91302
PH: 818.880.3500
Internet: www.xylan.com

Microsoft
Networking

As I began working with this topic for Chapter 15, I realized something; that is, the very topic of this chapter is a phenomenon! Who would have thought fifteen years ago that in the span of a decade or so an entire chapter would be devoted to networking the Microsoft way? Better yet, who would have thought that bookstores would have rows of books on the topic? Nevertheless, the topic of Microsoft Networking is no trivial task. Consequently, I have been selective about what information I decided to put into this chapter. I have also been selective about the source of information here.

Because of my experience with Microsoft products, I decided to include information provided as a courtesy by the Microsoft Corporation and case study information that I gathered throughout the testing I conducted in preparation for this book. As you read through this chapter, I provide references for further information, as it can be obtained from Microsoft.

The purpose of the information I am presenting is to assist you in your networking efforts with Microsoft products. Because I am aware of the time lapse of implementation and upgrades as they are made in the marketplace, I include information about multiple Microsoft operating systems and components. The remaining part of this chapter includes information on the following:

- Author's perspective
- Windows 2000
- Internet Information Services
- Microsoft TCP in Windows 2000
- Windows 2000: TAPI and NetMeeting
- Windows 2000 Distributed File System
- NT Workstation & Server: Highlights
- Windows Terminology
- NT File Structure Support
- NT Architecture & Conceptual Overview
- NT Administration Concepts
- NT Workstation & Server Commonalities
- Useful Network Commands
- Commands Usage: Brief Networking Case Study
- Networking & Services in Windows
- Windows 2000, NT, and Servers
- Windows Networking Peripherals

■ Windows Administration: Practical Examples
■ Summary

Author's Perspective

As of this writing, I have been personally working with Microsoft products for 13 years. I have a copy of Microsoft Windows version 1.0. Since the time around when that version became available, which was 1986, I have worked intimately with all the versions of MS Windows as well as Windows NT technology. The purpose of telling this story is to lay the foundation, so to speak, for the presentation of the material to follow.

Prior to Windows 2000 was Windows NT version 5.0, both server and workstation in beta form. Late in 1998, NT version 5.0 was renamed to Windows 2000. I believe that Windows 2000 is the convergence of Microsoft Windows technology and Windows NT technology. Heretofore, Windows was focused toward the user environment, whereas Windows NT was focused toward the business community. Moreover, Windows NT version 4.0 was clearly a mix of Microsoft engineers and thinkers and native UNIX oriented thinkers. Hence, Windows version 3.1, Windows 95, and Windows 98 do have inherent operational and visible differences from Windows NT. Because this is the case, coupled with the fact that Windows 2000 is a convergence of prior Microsoft operating systems, it is good to understand the historical perspective and thus have the information in this chapter available to you.

Windows NT is a Microsoft product. Its origins date back to 1988. Some characteristics included with the original design intent were: be compatible among a variety of hardware platforms and operating systems, be easily adaptable to internationalization, be portable, and be a system with high security standards.

Windows 2000

I believe the single best source for information about Microsoft products is Microsoft itself. In my years of experience with them, they almost always have been able to answer my questions. Consequently, I recommend you take advantage of the information Microsoft makes available. You can reach them at

Microsoft Corporation
One Microsoft Way
Redmond, WA 98052–6399
`www.microsoft.com`

The information Microsoft provides to those who desire it is helpful for a couple reasons. First, the information available through the Web is diverse. For example, Microsoft has information focused toward the following groups:

- Developers
- Users
- IT Professionals
- Media
- Educators
- Partners
- Resellers
- Customers
- Home users

Remember the focus of this book is not to provide all the answers or even all of the technology in a single book. My singular purpose is to present what I feel is very helpful information based on my experience.

Internet Information Services

To not include information about Microsoft's product interaction with the Internet is to overlook an extremely important aspect of Microsoft technology today. Internet Information Services (IIS) has gone through many iterations as of this writing. The following information in this section is provided as a courtesy of the Microsoft corporation. Additional information can be obtained through the Internet at

`www.microsoft.com/technet/default.asp`

The Microsoft® Windows® 2000 Server operating system integrates Internet technologies across all services, from File and Print to advanced line-of-business application services. Windows 2000 Server meets the needs of a broad spectrum of users, from corporate intranets to Internet Service Providers hosting Web sites receiving millions of hits per day. Because Internet Information Server 5.0 (IIS) is fully integrated at the operating system level, Windows 2000 Server enables organizations to add Internet capabilities that weave directly into the rest of their computing infrastructure.

Specifically, Windows 2000 Server enables organizations to:

1. Share information more efficiently using the Web. In the past, performing standard file operations on a network file share was much easier than performing similar operations on a remote Web site. Now, Windows 2000 Server technologies, such as Web Distributed Authoring and Versioning (WebDAV), make it as easy to carry out standard file operations on a Web share and create Web-based business applications.

2. Creating Web-based applications that integrate well into traditional business applications can be difficult. Windows 2000 Server overcomes this burden by sharing Internet-aware application development tools with IIS that extends applications to the Web and eliminates awkward bridges between internal and external processes.

3. Bring server operating system functionality to the Web. It extends basic file and print services to the Web, Windows 2000 Server supports applications, media, and communications and networking services from a common server platform. This convergence means that everything a company can do with Windows 2000 Server is automatically supported in a fully integrated Web environment.

4. Support for Web Distributed Authoring and Versioning (WebDAV). WebDAV is an Internet standard that enables multiple people to collaborate on a document using an Internet-based shared file system. It addresses issues such as file access permissions, offline editing, file integrity, and conflict resolution when competing changes are made to a document. WebDAV expands an organization's infrastructure by using the Internet as the central location for storing shared files.

5. Web Folders Support for Web Folders enables users to navigate to a WebDAV-compliant server and view the content as if it were part of the same namespace as the local system. Users can drag and drop files, retrieve or modify file property information, and perform other file system-related tasks. Web Folders let users maintain a

consistent look and feel between navigating the local file system, a networked drive, and an Internet Web site.

6. Support for FrontPage Server Extensions Windows 2000 Server enables administrators to use Microsoft FrontPage® Web authoring and management features to deploy and manage Web sites. With FrontPage Server Extensions, administrators can view and manage a Web site in a graphical interface, so creating Web sites with the FrontPage Web site creation and management tool is as easy as clicking a check box on a property page for the Web site. In addition, authors can create, edit, and post Web pages to IIS remotely.

7. Support for latest Internet standards. Using the integrated Web services in Windows 2000 Server, organizations can take advantage of the latest Internet standards to publish and share information over the Web. Microsoft Internet Information Services (IIS) 5.0 complies with the HTTP 1.1 standard, including features such as PUT and DELETE, the ability to customize HTTP error messages, and support for custom HTTP headers. Support for the latest protocols provides optimum performance for Web server connections.

8. Support for multiple sites with one IP address. With support for host headers, an organization can host multiple Web sites on a single computer running Microsoft Windows 2000 Server with only one Internet Protocol (IP) address. This enables Internet service providers (ISPs) and corporate intranets to host multiple Web sites on a single server while offering separate user domains for each site.

9. News and Mail Administrators can use Simple Mail Transfer Protocol (SMTP) and Network News Transport Protocol (NNTP) Services to set up intranet mail and news services that work in conjunction with IIS. SMTP is a commonly used protocol for sending e-mail messages between servers; NNTP is the protocol used to post, distribute, and retrieve USENET messages.

10. PICS Ratings Administrators can apply Platform for Internet Content Selection (PICS) ratings to sites that contain content for mature audiences. This enables them to host a variety of sites and provide information about suitability for particular audiences.

11. HTTP compression enables faster transmission of pages between the Web server and compression-enabled clients. This is useful in situations where bandwidth is limited.

12. File Transfer Protocol (FTP) and FTP Restart. The File Transfer Protocol (FTP) service, used to publish information to a Web server, is integrated into Windows 2000 Server. FTP Restart provides a

faster, smoother way to download information from the Internet. Now, if an interruption occurs during data transfer from an FTP site, a download can be resumed without having to download the entire file over again.

13. Active Server Pages. Microsoft Active Server Pages (ASP) enables developers to create dynamic content by using server-side scripting and components to create browser-independent dynamic content. ASP provides an easy to use alternative to Common Gateway Interface (CGI) and Internet Server Application Program Interface (ISAPI) by letting content developers embed any scripting language or server component into their HTML pages. ASP pages provide standards-based database connectivity and the ability to customize content for different browsers. ASP also provides error-handling capabilities for Web-based applications.

Performance-enhanced Objects ASP provides performance-enhanced versions of its popular installable components. These objects scale reliably in a wide range of Web application environments.

14. XML Integration. Just as HTML enables developers to describe the format of a Web document, Extensible Markup Language (XML) enables them to describe complex data structures. Developers can share this information across a variety of applications, clients, and servers. Using the new Microsoft XML Parser, developers can create applications that enable their Web server to exchange XML-formatted data with both Microsoft Internet Explorer and any server capable of parsing XML.

15. Windows Script Components. ASP supports the new scripting technology, Windows Script Components. This enables developers to turn business logic script procedures into reusable COM components for Web applications and other COM-compliant programs.

16. Browser Capabilities Component. ASP has a new feature for determining the exact capabilities of a browser. When a browser sends a cookie describing its capabilities (such a cookie can be installed by using a simple client-side script), developers can create an instance of the Browser Capabilities Component that retrieves the browser's properties as returned by the cookie. Developers can use this feature to discover a browser's capabilities and adjust an application accordingly.

17. ASP Self-Tuning. ASP now senses when executing requests are blocked by external resources and automatically provides more threads to simultaneously execute additional requests while

continuing processing. If the CPU becomes overburdened, ASP curtails the number of threads to reduce the constant switching that occurs when too many non-blocking requests are executing simultaneously.

18. **Encoded ASP Scripts.** Traditionally, Web developers have been unable to prevent others from reading their scripting code. ASP now supports a new script encoding utility provided with Microsoft Visual Basic Scripting Edition (VBScript) and Microsoft JScript 5.0. Web developers can apply an encoding scheme to both client and server-side scripts that makes the programmatic logic unreadable. When un-encoded, the logic appears in standard ASCII characters. Encoded scripts are decoded at run time by the script engine, so there's no need for a separate utility. Although this feature is not intended as a secure, encrypted solution, it can prevent most casual users from browsing or copying scripts.

19. **Application Protection.** IIS 5.0 offers improved protection and increased reliability for Web applications. By default, IIS runs all applications in a common or pooled process that is separate from core IIS processes. In addition, administrators can still isolate mission-critical applications that should be run outside of both core IIS and pooled processes.

20. **ADSI 2.0.** Administrators and application developers can add custom objects, properties, and methods to the existing Active Directory Service Interfaces (ADSI) provider, giving administrators more flexibility in configuring sites. ADSI is a COM-based directory service model that enables ADSI-compliant client applications to access a wide variety of distinct directory protocols, including Windows Directory Services and Lightweight Directory Access Protocol (LDAP), while using a single standard set of interfaces. ADSI shields the client application from the implementation and operational details of the underlying data store or protocol.

21. **Multisite Hosting.** Often Web sites for several departments can run on a single server, freeing a company from spending the time and money to set up and manage multiple servers. Windows 2000 Server offers a comprehensive platform for hosting multiple Web sites on a single server. In addition, Windows 2000 Server's multisite hosting capability enables ISPs to host Web sites that can scale from hosting thousands of small sites on a single server to hosting a great number of sites across multiple servers.

22. **Multiple User Domains.** The integration between the Web servers and directory services (the Active Directory) in Windows 2000 Server enables organizations to host multiple Web sites with independent user domains—that is, each Web site on a single server has its own user database.

23. **User Management Delegation.** This enables an IT or ISP administrator who hosts multiple Web sites on a single server to delegate the day to day management of the Web site.

24. **Process Throttling.** This enables administrators to limit the amount of CPU time a Web application or site can use during a predetermined period of time to ensure that processor time is available to other Web sites or to non-Web applications.

25. **Per Web Site Bandwidth Throttling.** This enables administrators to regulate the amount of server bandwidth each site uses. This enables an ISP, for example, to guarantee a predetermined amount of bandwidth to each site.

26. **Integrated Setup & Upgrade Internet Information Server (IIS) 5.0** installs as a networking service of Windows 2000 Server. Customers with any existing version of Windows NT Server 3.51 or 4.0 will automatically be upgraded to the new Web services in Windows 2000 Server and can take advantage of the new features and services of Windows 2000 Server and IIS.

27. **Microsoft Management Console (MMC) Task Pad.** The MMC task pad considerably simplifies the administration of an IIS server. For example, if a user selects a server under the IIS MMC snap-in, the task pad displays wizards for creating new Web and FTP sites. Administrators simply select the task they want to complete, and a wizard walks them through the steps.

28. **Dfs as Filing System for IIS.** You can use Microsoft Dfs as the filing system for IIS by selecting the root for the web site as a Dfs root. Doing so enables you to move resources within the Dfs tree without affecting any HTML links. (Windows Media Services content can also be stored in the Dfs tree.)

29. **Improved Command-line Administration Scripts IIS** ships with scripts that can be executed from the command line to automate the management of common Web server tasks. Administrators can create custom scripts that automate the management of IIS.

30. Reliable IIS Restart. Users can stop and restart all Internet services from within the IIS MMC snap-in, which makes it unnecessary to restart the computer when applications become unavailable.

31. Backing Up and Restoring IIS. Administrators can back up and save metabase settings to make it easy to return to a safe, known state. (A metabase is structure for storing IIS configuration settings; the metabase performs some of the same functions as the system registry, but uses less disk space.)

32. Process Accounting Process Accounting, which is enabled and customized on a per-site basis, enables administrators to monitor and log how Web sites use CPU resources on the server. Both system administrators and application developers can use this feature to determine CPU utilization.

30. Internet service providers (ISPs) can use this information to determine which sites are using disproportionately high CPU resources or that might have malfunctioning scripts or Common Gateway Interface (CGI) processes. IT managers can use this information to charge back the cost of hosting a Web site and/or application to the appropriate division within a company.

31. Improved Custom Error Messages. Administrators can now send informative messages to clients when HTTP or ASP errors occur on their Web sites. They can use the custom errors that IIS 5.0 provides or create their own.

32. Configuration Options Administrators can set permissions for read, write, execute, script, and FrontPage Web operations at the site, directory, or file level.

32. Remote Administration IIS 5.0 has Web-based administration tools that allow remote management of a server from almost any browser on any platform. With IIS 5.0, administrators can set up administration accounts called Operators with limited administration privileges on Web sites to help distribute administrative tasks.

33. Terminal Services. The Terminal Services support in Windows 2000 Server enables administrators to remotely administer IIS by using the Microsoft Management Console (MMC) over a dial-up or PPTP connection. To do this, the Terminal Services client must be installed on client computers.

34. Centralized Administration Administrators can use the MMC snap-in for IIS from a computer running Windows 2000 Professional to

administer a computer on their intranet running Internet Information Services on Windows 2000 Server.

35. Integrated Web Security. The Windows 2000 Server Web services are fully integrated with the Kerberos security infrastructure. The Kerberos Version 5 authentication protocol, which provides fast single logon to Windows 2000 Server, replaces NTLM as the primary security protocol for access to resources within or across Windows 2000 domains. Users can securely authenticate themselves to a Windows 2000 Server Web site and do not have to undergo a separate authentication (logon) to use other resources.

In addition, Windows 2000 Server supports the following standard authentication protocols, which are applicable to Web-based users and ordinary network users alike:

- Digest Authentication is the latest authentication standard of the World Wide Web

- Consortium (W3C) is the organization that sets standards for the Web and HTML.

- Server-Gated Cryptography (SGC) is used by financial institutions to transmit private documents through the Internet.

- Fortezza is the U.S. government security standard.

- Secure Communications Secure Sockets Layer (SSL) 3.0 and Transport Layer Security (TLS) provide a secure way to exchange information between clients and servers. In addition, SSL 3.0 and TLS provide a way for the server to verify whom the client is before the user logs on to the server. In IIS 5.0 programmers can track users through their sites. Also, IIS 5.0 enables administrators to control access to system resources based on the client certificate.

- Digest Authentication Digest Authentication enables secure authentication of users across proxy servers and firewalls. It offers the same features as basic authentication, but improves on it by "hashing" the password traveling over the Internet, instead of transmitting it as clear text.

- For those who choose not to use Digest Authentication, Anonymous, HTTP Basic, and integrated Windows authentication (formerly called Windows NT Challenge/Response authentication) and NT LAN Manager (NTLM) authentication are still available.

- Server-gated Cryptography SGC, an extension of Secure Sockets Layer (SSL), enables financial institutions with export versions of IIS to use strong 128-bit encryption. Although SGC capabilities are built into IIS 5.0, a special SGC certificate is required to use SGC.

■ Security Wizards.   These security wizards simplify server administration tasks. Certificate Wizard simplifies certificate administration tasks, such as creating certificate requests and managing the certificate life cycle. Secure Sockets Layer (SSL) security is an increasingly common requirement for Web sites that provide e-commerce and access to sensitive business information. The new wizard makes it easy to set up SSL-enabled Web sites on a Windows 2000 Server—administrators can easily establish and maintain SSL encryption and client certificate authentication. (A client certificate contains detailed identification information about the user and organization that issued the certificate.)

■ Permission Wizard walks administrators through the tasks of setting up permissions and authenticated access on an IIS Web site, making it much easier to set up and manage a Web site that requires authenticated access to its content.

■ Certificate Trust Lists (CTL) Wizard enables administrators to configure certificate trust lists (CTLs). A CTL is a list of trusted certification authorities (CAs) for a particular directory. CTLs are especially useful for Internet service providers (ISPs) who have several Web sites on their server and who need to have a different list of approved certification authorities for each site. IP and Internet Domain Restrictions Administrators can grant or deny Web access to individual computers, groups of computers, or entire domains.

■ Kerberos Version 5 Authentication Protocol Compliance. IIS is fully integrated with the Kerberos v5 authentication protocol implemented in Microsoft Windows 2000. This means administrators can pass authentication credentials among connected computers running Windows.

■ Certificate Storage. IIS certificate storage is now integrated with the Windows CryptoAPI storage. The Windows Certificate Manager provides a single point of entry that enables administrators to store, back up, and configure server certificates.

■ Fortezza IIS 5.0 supports the U.S. government security standard, commonly called Fortezza. This standard satisfies the Defense Message System security architecture with a cryptographic mechanism that provides message confidentiality, integrity, authentication, and access control to messages, components, and systems. These features can be implemented both with server and browser software and with PCMCIA card hardware.

Microsoft's TCP in Windows 2000

This section includes information courtesy of the Microsoft corporation. It is important because TCP/IP is a recognized standard and defined in the RFCs as maintained by The Internet Society. The following chapter gives details about TCP/IP, which I have been working in for some thirteen years now, from a "market" perspective. However, it is very important to understand some particulars about the TCP protocol as Microsoft implements it. I found this information to be so helpful, I determined that you needed it also. Microsoft has more information at their Web site, and I recommend that you take the time to examine the Web site for all they make available. Their address is:

www.microsoft.com

TCP provides a connection-based, reliable byte-stream service to applications. Microsoft networking relies on the TCP transport for logon, file and print sharing, replication of information between domain controllers, transfer of browse lists, and other common functions. It can only be used for one to one communications.

TCP uses a checksum on both the headers and data of each segment to reduce the chance that network corruption goes undetected. NDIS 5.0 provides support for task offloading, and Windows 2000 TCP takes advantage of this by allowing the NIC to perform the TCP checksum calculations if the NIC driver offers support for this function. Offloading the checksum calculations to hardware can result in performance improvements in very high-throughput environments. Windows 2000 TCP has also been hardened against a variety of attacks that were published over the past couple of years and has been subject to an internal security review intended to reduce susceptibility to future attacks.

TCP Receive Window Size Calculation and Window Scaling

The TCP receive window size is the amount of receive data (in bytes) that can be buffered at one time on a connection. This specification is made in RFC 1323. The sending host can send only that amount of data before waiting for an acknowledgment and window update from the receiving host. The Windows 2000 TCP/IP stack was designed to tune itself in most environments and uses larger default window sizes than earlier versions. Instead of using a hard-coded default receive window size, TCP adjusts to even increments of the maximum segment size (MSS) negotiated during connection setup. Matching the receive window to even increments of the MSS increases the percentage of full-sized TCP segments used during bulk data transmission.

To help you understand this better, consider how the receive window size calculates to the defaults. The first connection request sent to a remote host advertises a receive window size of 16 KB (16,384). On establishing the connection, the receive window size is rounded up to an increment of the maximum TCP segment size (MSS) that was negotiated during connection setup. If that is not at least four times the MSS, it is adjusted to 4 MSS with a maximum size of 64 KB unless a window scaling option (RFC 1323) is in effect.

For Ethernet, the window is normally set to 17,520 bytes (16 KB rounded up to twelve 1460-byte segments.) There are two methods for setting the receive window size to specific values:

- The *TcpWindowSize* registry parameter
- The setsockopt Windows Sockets function (on a per-socket basis)

To improve performance on high-bandwidth, high-delay networks, RFC 1323 support has been introduced in Windows 2000. This RFC details a method for supporting scaleable windows by allowing TCP to negotiate a scaling factor for the window size at connection establishment. This enables for an actual receive window of up to 1 gigabyte (GB).

Consider the following (courtesy of The Internet Society) which is an excerpt from RFC 1383 about this topic.

Window Scale Option

The three-byte Window Scale option may be sent in a SYN segment by a TCP. It has two purposes: (1) indicate that the TCP is prepared to do both send and receive window scaling, and (2) communicate a scale factor to be applied to its receive window. Thus, a TCP that is prepared to scale windows should send the option, even if its own scale factor is 1. The scale factor is limited to a power of two and encoded logarithmically, so it may be implemented by binary shift operations.

TCP Window Scale Option (WSopt):
Kind: 3 Length: 3 bytes

Kind=3	Length=3	shift.cnt

This option is an offer, not a promise; both sides must send Window Scale options in their SYN segments to enable window scaling in either direction. If window scaling is enabled, then the TCP that sent this option right-shifts its true receive-window values by 'shift.cnt' bits for transmission in SEG.WND. The value 'shift.cnt' may be zero (offering to scale, while applying a scale factor of 1 to the receive window).

This option may be sent in an initial <SYN> segment (that is, a segment with the SYN bit on and the ACK bit off). It may also be sent in a <SYN,ACK> segment, but only if a Window Scale option was received in the initial <SYN> segment. A Window Scale option in a segment without a SYN bit should be ignored. The Window field in a SYN (that is, a <SYN> or <SYN,ACK>) segment itself is never scaled.

Windows 2000 uses window scaling automatically if the *TcpWindowSize* is set to a value greater than 64 KB. Window scaling can be disabled with the *Tcp1323Opts* registry parameter.

Delayed Acknowledgments

As specified in RFC 1122, TCP uses delayed acknowledgments (ACKs) to reduce the number of packets sent on the media. The Microsoft stack takes a common approach to implementing delayed ACKs. As data is received by TCP on a connection, it only sends an acknowledgment back if one of the following conditions is met:

No ACK was sent for the previous segment received. A segment is received, but no other segment arrives within 200 milliseconds for that connection. In summary, normally an ACK is sent for every other TCP segment received on a connection, unless the delayed ACK timer (200 milliseconds) expires.

TCP Selective Acknowledgment

Microsoft uses TCP selective acknowledgment in a way the reader should understand. Windows 2000 introduces support for an important performance feature known as *Selective Acknowledgment* (SACK). SACK is especially important for connections using large TCP window sizes. Prior to SACK, a receiver could only acknowledge the latest sequence number of contiguous data that had been received or the left edge of the receive window. With SACK enabled, the receiver continues to use the ACK number to acknowledge the left edge of the receive window, but it can also acknowledge other blocks of received data individually. SACK uses TCP header options, as shown as follows.

To understand Windows 2000 and TCP usage, consider the following information. An excerpt from RFC 2018 is presented here courtesy of The Internet Society.

Sack-Permitted Option

This two-byte option may be sent in a SYN by a TCP that has been extended to receive (and presumably process) the SACK option after the connection has opened. It MUST NOT be sent on non-SYN segments.

TCP Sack-Permitted Option:
Kind: 4

Kind=4	Length=2

Sack Option Format

The SACK option is to be used to convey extended acknowledgment information from the receiver to the sender over an established TCP connection.

TCP SACK Option:
Kind: 5

	Kind=5	Length
Left Edge of 1st Block		
Right Edge of 1st Block		
. . .		
Left Edge of nth Block		
Right Edge of nth Block		

With SACK enabled (the default) a packet or series of packets can be dropped, and the receiver can inform the sender of exactly which data has been received, and where the holes in the data are. The sender can then selectively retransmit the missing data without needing to retransmit blocks of data that have already been received successfully. SACK is controlled by the SackOpts registry parameter. The following trace clip illustrates a host acknowledging all data up to sequence number 54857341, plus the data from sequence number 54858789—54861685.

```
1 FRAME: Base frame properties
1 ETHERNET: ETYPE = 0X0800 : Protocol = IP: DOD Internet Protocol
1 IP: ID = 0X1A0D; Proto 5 TCP; Len: 64
TCP: .A . . . ., len:0, seq:925104-925104, ack:54857341,
win:32722, src:1242 dst:139
TCP: Source Port = 0X04DA
TCP: Destination Port = NETBIOS Session Service
TCP: Sequence Number = 925104 (0xE1DB0)
TCP: Acknowledgment Number = 54857341 (033450E7D)
TCP: Data Offset = 44 (032C)
TCP: Reserved = 0 (0X0000)
1 TCP: Flags = 0310 : .A . . . .
TCP: Window = 32722 (0X7FD2)
TCP: Checksum = 0X4A72
TCP: Urgent Pointer = 0 (0X0)
TCP: Options
TCP: Option Nop = 1 (0X1)
TCP: Option Nop = 1 (0X1)
+ TCP: Timestamps Option
TCP: Option Nop = 1 (0X1)
TCP: Option Nop = 1 (0X1)
TCP: SACK Option
TCP: Option Type = 0X05
TCP: Option Length = 10 (0xA)
TCP: Left Edge of Block = 54858789 (0X3451425)
TCP: Right Edge of Block = 54861685 (0X3451F75)
```

TCP Time Stamps

Another RFC 1323 feature introduced in Windows 2000 is support for TCP time stamps. Like SACK, this is important for connections using large window sizes. Time stamps were conceived to assist TCP in accurately measuring round-trip time (RTT) to adjust retransmission time-outs.

Consider the following TCP (RFC 1323) header option for time stamps. It is presented here courtesy of The Internet Society.

TCP Timestamps Option (TSopt):

Kind: 8

Length: 10 bytes

Kind=8	10	TS Value (TSval)	TS Echo Reply (TSecr)
1	1	4	4

The Timestamps option carries two four-byte timestamp fields. The Timestamp Value field (TSval) contains the current value of the timestamp clock of the TCP sending the option.

The Timestamp Echo Reply field (TSecr) is only valid if the ACK bit is set in the TCP header; if it is valid, it echos a timestamp value that was sent by the remote TCP in the TSval field of a Timestamps option. When TSecr is not valid, its value must be zero. The TSecr value is generally from the most recent Timestamp option that was received; however, there are exceptions that are explained as follows.

A TCP may send the Timestamps option (TSopt) in an initial <SYN> segment (that is, segment containing a SYN bit and no ACK bit), and may send a TSopt in other segments only if it received a TSopt in the initial <SYN> segment for the connection.

The time-stamp option field can be viewed in a Network Monitor trace by expanding the TCP options field, as shown as follows:

```
TCP: Timestamps Option
TCP: Option Type = Timestamps
TCP: Option Length = 10 (0xA)
TCP: Timestamp = 2525186 (0X268802)
TCP: Reply Timestamp = 1823192 (0X1BD1D8)
```

Windows 2000 enables the use of time stamps by default.

PMTU (Path Maximum Transmission Unit) Discovery

PMTU discovery is described in RFC 1191. When a connection is established, the two hosts involved exchange their TCP maximum segment size (MSS) values. The smaller of the two MSS values is used for the connection.

Historically, the MSS for a host has been the MTU at the link layer minus 40 bytes for the IP and TCP headers. However, support for additional TCP options, such as time stamps, has increased the typical TCP+IP header to 52 or more bytes.

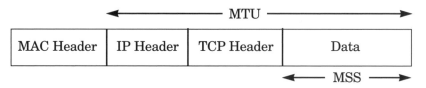

MTU versus MSS

When TCP segments are destined to a non-local network, the "don't fragment" bit is set in the IP header. Any router or media along the path can have an MTU that differs from that of the two hosts. If a media segment has an MTU that is too small for the IP datagram being routed, the router attempts to fragment the datagram accordingly. It then finds that the "don't fragment" bit is set in the IP header. At this point, the router should inform the sending host that the datagram cannot be forwarded further without fragmentation. This is done with an ICMP Destination Unreachable message. Most routers also specify the MTU that is allowed for the next hop by putting the value for it in the low-order 16 bits of the ICMP header field that is labeled unused in the ICMP specification. RFC 1191 describes the format of this message. On receiving this ICMP error message, TCP adjusts its MSS for the connection to the specified MTU minus the TCP and IP header size so that any further packets sent on the connection are no larger than the maximum size that can traverse the path without fragmentation.

The minimum MTU permitted by RFCs is 68 bytes, and Windows 2000 TCP enforces this limit.

Some non-compliant routers might silently drop IP datagrams that cannot be fragmented or might not correctly report their next-hop MTU. If this occurs, it might be necessary to make a configuration change to the PMTU detection algorithm. There are two registry changes that can be made to the TCP/IP stack in Windows 2000 to work around these problematic devices.

EnablePMTUBHDetect adjusts the PMTU discovery algorithm to attempt to detect black hole routers. Black Hole detection is disabled by default.

EnablePMTUDiscovery completely enables or disables the PMTU discovery mechanism. When PMTU discovery is disabled, an MSS of 536 bytes is used for all non-local destination addresses. PMTU discovery is enabled by default.

The PMTU between two hosts can be discovered manually using the *ping* command with the -f (don't fragment) switch, as follows:

```
ping -f -n <number of pings> -l <size> <destination ip address>
```

The following example shows the *size* parameter can be varied until the MTU is found. The *size* parameter used by ping is the size of the data buffer to send, not including headers. The ICMP header consumes 8 bytes, and the IP header would normally be 20 bytes. In the following case (Ethernet), the link layer MTU is the maximum-sized ping buffer plus 28, or 1500 bytes:

```
C:\>ping -f -n 1 -l 1472 10.99.99.10
Pinging 10.99.99.10 with 1472 bytes of data:
Reply from 10.99.99.10: bytes=1472 time<10ms TTL=128
Ping statistics for 10.99.99.10:
Packets: Sent = 1, Received 5 1, Lost 5 0 (0% loss),
Approximate round trip times in milli-seconds:
Minimum = 0ms, Maximum 5 0ms, Average 5 0ms
C:\>ping -f -n 1 -l 1473 10.99.99.10
Pinging 10.99.99.10 with 1473 bytes of data:
Packet needs to be fragmented but DF set.
Ping statistics for 10.99.99.10:
Packets: Sent = 1, Received = 0, Lost = 1 (100% loss),
Approximate round trip times in milli-seconds:
Minimum = 0ms, Maximum = 0ms, Average = 0ms
```

In the example shown previously, the IP layer returned an ICMP error message that ping interpreted. If the router had been a black hole router, ping would simply not be answered after its size exceeded the MTU that the router could handle. Ping can be used in this manner to detect such a router. Consider the following example that is an ICMP destination unreachable error message.

```
Src Addr Dst Addr Protocol Description
10.99.99.10   10.99.99.9   ICMP   Destination   Unreachable:
10.99.99.10
+ FRAME: Base frame properties
+ ETHERNET: ETYPE 5 030800 : Protocol 5 IP: DOD Internet Protocol
+ IP: ID = 0X4401; Proto = ICMP; Len: 56
ICMP: Destination Unreachable: 10.99.99.10 See frame 3
ICMP: Packet Type = Destination Unreachable
ICMP: Unreachable Code = Fragmentation Needed, DF Flag Set
ICMP: Checksum = 0xA05B
```

```
ICMP: Next Hop MTU = 576 (0×240)
ICMP: Data: Number of data bytes remaining = 28 (03001C)
ICMP: Description of original IP frame
ICMP: (IP) Version = 4 (0×4)
ICMP: (IP) Header Length = 20 (0×14)
ICMP: (IP) Service Type = 0 (0×0)
ICMP: Precedence = Routine
ICMP:    . . . 0 . . .  = Normal Delay
ICMP:    . . . .0 . . .  = Normal Throughput
ICMP:    . . . ..0.. = Normal Reliability
ICMP: (IP) Total Length = 1028 (0×404)
ICMP: (IP) Identification = 45825 (0xB301)
ICMP: Flags Summary = 2 (0×2)
ICMP:    . . . . . . .0 = Last fragment in datagram
ICMP:    . . . . . . 1. = Cannot fragment datagram
ICMP: (IP) Fragment Offset = 0 (0×0) bytes
ICMP: (IP) Time to Live = 32 (0×20)
ICMP: (IP) Protocol = ICMP-Internet Control Message
ICMP: (IP) Checksum = 0xC91E
ICMP: (IP) Source Address = 10.99.99.9
ICMP: (IP) Destination Address = 10.99.99.10
ICMP: (IP) Data: Number of data bytes remaining = 8 (0×0008)
ICMP: Description of original ICMP frame
ICMP: Checksum = 0xBC5F
ICMP: Identifier = 256 (0×100)
ICMP: Sequence Number = 38144 (0×9500)
00000: 00 AA 00 4B B1 47 00 AA 00 3E 52 EF 08 00 45 00
. . . K.G . . . >R . . . E.
00010: 00 38 44 01 00 00 80 01 1B EB 0A 63 63 0A 0A 63 .8D
. . . . . . ..cc..c
00020: 63 09 03 04 A0 5B 00 00 02 40 45 00 04 04 B3 01 c
. . . .[ . . . @E . . . . ..
00030: 40 00 20 01 C9 1E 0A 63 63 09 0A 63 63 0A 08 00 @.
. . . .cc..cc . . .
00040: BC 5F 01 00 95 00 ._ . . . .
```

This error was generated by using ping -f –n 1 -l 1000 on an Ethernet-based host to send a large datagram across a router interface that only supports an MTU of 576 bytes. When the router tried to place the large frame onto the network with the smaller MTU, it found that fragmentation was not allowed. Therefore, it returned the error message indicating that the largest datagram that could be forwarded is 0×240, or 576 bytes.

Dead Gateway Detection

Dead gateway detection is used to allow TCP to detect failure of the default gateway and to make an adjustment to the IP routing table to use another default gateway. The Microsoft TCP/IP stack uses the TRIGGERED RESELECTION method described in RFC 816 with some slight modifications based on customer experiences and feedback.

With regards to Windows 2000, understanding routing TCP through routers is also important. An attempt to route a TCP packet through a default gateway to a specific destination a given number of times equal to one-half of the registry value (*TcpMaxDataRetransmissions*) without receiving a response changes the Route Cache Entry (RCE) for that IP address. Thus, it forces the use of the next default gateway in the list. When 25 percent of the TCP connections have moved to the next default gateway, the algorithm advises IP to change the computer's default gateway to the one that the connections are now using.

For example, assume that there are currently TCP connections to 11 different IP addresses that are being routed through the default gateway. Assume the default gateway fails, a second default gateway is configured, and that the value for *TcpMaxDataRetransmissions* is at the default of 5. When the first TCP connection tries to send data, it does not receive any acknowledgments. After the third retransmission, the RCE for that remote IP address is switched to use the next default gateway in the list. At this point, any TCP connections to that one remote IP address have switched over, but the remaining connection still tries to use the original default gateway.

When the second TCP connection tries to send data, the same thing happens. Now, two of the 11 RCEs point to the new gateway. When the third TCP connection tries to send data after the third retransmission, three of the 11 RCEs have been switched to the second default gateway. Because, at this point, over 25 percent of the RCEs have been moved, the default gateway for the whole computer is moved to the new one. Now, the default gateway remains the primary one for the computer until it experiences problems (causing the dead gateway algorithm to try the next one in the list again) or until the computer is restarted. When the search reaches the last default gateway, it returns to the beginning of the list.

TCP Retransmission Behavior

TCP starts a retransmission timer when each outbound segment is handed down to IP. If no acknowledgment has been received for the data in a given segment before the timer expires, the segment is retransmitted. For new connection requests, the retransmission timer is initialized to 3 seconds, and the request (SYN) is resent up to *TcpMaxConnectRetransmissions* times (the default for Windows 2000 is 2 times).

On existing connections, the number of retransmissions is controlled by the *TcpMaxDataRetransmissions* registry parameter (5 by default). RFC 793 applies to the retransmission time-out as it operates in Windows 2000. It is adjusted on the fly to match the characteristics of the connection using Smoothed Round Trip Time (SRTT) calculations. The timer for a given segment is doubled after each retransmission of that segment. Using this algorithm, TCP tunes itself to the normal delay of a connection. TCP connections over high-delay links take much longer to time out than those over low-delay links. Adding to the registry parameter *TcpMaxDataRetransmissions* or *TcpMaxConnectRetransmissions* approximately doubles the total retransmission timeout period. If it is necessary to configure longer timeouts, these parameters should be increased very gradually.

Some circumstances exist under which TCP retransmits data prior to the time that the retransmission timer expires. The most common of these occurs due to a feature known as *fast retransmit*. When a receiver that supports fast retransmit receives data with a sequence number beyond the current expected one, it is likely that some data was dropped. To help make the sender aware of this event, the receiver immediately sends an ACK with the ACK number set to the sequence number that it was expecting. It continues to do this for each additional TCP segment that arrives containing data subsequent to the missing data in the incoming stream. When the sender starts to receive a stream of ACKs that are acknowledging the same sequence number and that sequence number is earlier than the current sequence number being sent, it can infer that a segment (or more) must have been dropped. Senders that support the fast retransmit algorithm immediately resend the segment for which the receiver is expecting to fill in the gap in the data without waiting for the retransmission timer to expire for that segment. This optimization greatly improves performance in a lousy network environment.

By default, Windows 2000 re-sends a segment if it receives three ACKs for the same sequence number and that sequence number lags the current one. This is controllable with the *TcpMaxDupAcks* registry parameter.

TCP Keep-Alive Messages

A TCP keep-alive packet is simply an ACK with the sequence number set to one less than the current sequence number for the connection. A host receiving one of these ACKs responds with an ACK for the current sequence number. Keep-alives can be used to verify that the computer at the remote end of a connection is still available. TCP keep-alives can be sent once every *KeepAliveTime* (defaults to 7,200,000 milliseconds or two hours) if no other data or higher-level keep-alives have been carried over the TCP connection. If there is no response to a keep-alive, it is repeated once every *KeepAliveInterval* seconds. *KeepAliveInterval* defaults to 1 second. NetBT connections, such as those used by many Microsoft networking components, send NetBIOS keep-alives more frequently, so normally no TCP keep-alives are sent on a NetBIOS connection. TCP keep-alives are disabled by default, but Windows Sockets applications can use the **setsockopt** function to enable them.

Slow Start Algorithm and Congestion Avoidance

The Internet Society has RFC1122, which explains this concept in greater detail. Some of the concepts here are presented courtesy of The Internet Society. When a connection is established, TCP starts slowly at first to assess the bandwidth of the connection and to avoid overflowing the receiving host or any other devices or links in the path. The send window is set to two TCP segments, and if that is acknowledged, it is incremented to three segments. Instead of sending one TCP segment when starting out, Windows NT/Windows 2000 TCP starts with two. This avoids the need to wait for the delayed ACK timer to expire on the first send to the target computer, which improves performance for some applications. If those are acknowledged, it is incremented again and so on until the amount of data being sent per burst reaches the size of the receive window on the remote host. At that point, the slow start algorithm is no longer in use, and flow control is governed by the receive window. However, at any time during transmission, congestion could still occur on a connection. If this happens (evidenced by the need to retransmit), a congestion-avoidance algorithm is used to reduce the send window size temporarily and to grow it back towards the receive window size. Slow start and congestion avoidance are discussed further in RFC 1122.

Silly Window Syndrome (SWS)

Silly Window Syndrome is described in RFC 1122. A brief explanation of it is presented here courtesy of The Internet Society. In brief, SWS is caused by the receiver advancing the right window edge whenever it has any new buffer space available to receive data and by the sender using any incremental window, no matter how small, to send more data. The result can be a stable pattern of sending tiny data segments, even though both sender and receiver have a large total buffer space for the connection.

Windows 2000 TCP/IP implements SWS avoidance as specified in RFC 1122, hence, sending more data until there is a sufficient window size advertised by the receiving end to send a full TCP segment. It also implements SWS at the receive end of a connection by not opening the receive window in increments of less than a TCP segment.

The Nagle Algorithm

Windows NT and Windows 2000 TCP/IP implement the Nagle algorithm described in The Internet Society's RFC 896. The purpose of this algorithm is to reduce the number of very small segments sent, especially on high-delay (remote) links. The Nagle algorithm allows only one small segment to be outstanding at a time without acknowledgment. If more small segments are generated while awaiting the ACK for the first one, these segments are coalesced into one larger segment. Any full-sized segment is always transmitted immediately, assuming that there is a sufficient receive window available. The Nagle algorithm is effective in reducing the number of packets sent by interactive applications, such as Telnet, especially over slow links.

TCP TIME-WAIT Delay

When a TCP connection is closed, the socket-pair is placed into a state known as *TIME-WAIT*. The purpose for this is that a new connection does not use the same protocol, source IP address, destination IP address, source port, and destination port until enough time has passed to ensure that any segments that might have been mis-routed or delayed are not delivered unexpectedly. The length of time that the socket-pair should not be reused is specified by in The Internet Society's RFC 793. In this RFC, the specification explains two maximum segment lifetimes or four minutes.

This is the default setting for Windows NT and Windows 2000. However, with this default setting, some network applications that perform many outbound connections in a short time might use up all available ports before the ports can be recycled.

According to Microsoft, Windows NT and Windows 2000 offer two methods of controlling this behavior. First, the *TcpTimedWaitDelay* registry parameter can be used to alter this value. Windows NT and Windows 2000 allow it to be set as low as 30 seconds, which should not cause problems in most environments.

Second, the number of user-accessible ephemeral ports that can be used to source outbound connections is configurable through the *MaxUserPorts* registry parameter. By default, when an application requests any socket from the system to use for an outbound call, a port between the values of 1024 and 5000 is supplied. The *MaxUserPorts* parameter can be used to set the value of the uppermost port that the administrator chooses to be used for outbound connections. For instance, setting this value to 10,000 (decimal) would make approximately 9000 user ports available for outbound connections. You can obtain additional information about this topic from The Internet Society's RFC 793 at

```
ftp://ftp.ncren.net/rfc
```

TCP & Multihomed Hosts

When TCP connections are made *to* a multihomed host, both the WINS client and the Domain Name Resolver (DNR) become involved in the resolution process. An attempt to determine whether any of the destination IP addresses provided by the name server are on the same subnet as any of the interfaces in the local computer. If so, these addresses are sorted to the top of the list so the application can try them prior to trying addresses that are not on the same subnet. If none of the addresses are on a common subnet with the local computer, behavior is different depending on the name space.

In the WINS name space, the client is responsible for randomizing or load balancing between the provided addresses. The WINS server always returns the list of addresses in the same order, and the WINS client randomly picks one of them for each connection.

In the DNS name space, the DNS server is usually configured to provide the addresses in a round robin fashion. The DNR does not attempt to further randomize the addresses. In some situations, it is desirable to connect to a specific interface on a multihomed computer. The best way to accomplish this is to provide the interface with its own DNS entry.

For example, consider a host named ED; and the host ED has two network interface boards and is thus multihomed. It has one DNS entry listing both IP addresses. This means that two separate records exist in the DNS with the same name. Hence, the result is that DNS records for ED are ED#1 and ED#2. Each DNS record is associated with just one of the IP address assigned to ED (the computer).

When TCP connections are made from a multihomed host, things get a bit more complicated. If the connection is a Winsock connection using the DNS name space, after the target IP address for the connection is known, TCP attempts to connect from the best source IP address available. The route table determines the best source IP address. If there is an interface in the local computer that is on the same subnet as the target IP address, its IP address is used as the source in the connection request. If there is no best source IP address to use, the system chooses one randomly.

If a NetBIOS-based connection uses the redirector not much routing information is available at the application level when viewed from a troubleshooting perspective. A NetBIOS interface supports connections over various protocols and has no "knowledge" of IP. Consequently, the result is that the redirector relies on the transports bound to it. If two interfaces are used in a host with one protocol implemented, two transports are available to the redirector.

Functionally, calls are placed on both and the NetBIOS transport submits a connection request to the protocol stack. One IP address from each interface is used and thus it can be the case that both "calls" are successful. If they are successful, then the redirector cancels one of them as determined by the settings in the system registry.

Throughput Considerations

Microsoft has information that explains throughput considerations in great detail. The Windows 2000 Resource Kit is a good reference to obtain additional information on this topic. However, here I want to present some basic information about the topic in light of TCP and Windows 2000.

The Internet Society RFC 1323 explains TCP with regard to throughput. Throughput requires consideration of many different topics. Some of those include:

- Link speed
- Weather
- Propagation delay
- Bandwidth upstream as in a service provider

- TCP Window size
- Internetworking devices such as bridges, routers, and so on
- Network traffic
- Hardware Interface component capacity
- Hosts Bus Capacities
- Other factors

Windows 2000: TAPI & Netmeeting

Microsoft provided me with some insight to this topic, in addition to "standard" documentation. However, the essence of what is presented at the Microsoft Internet site conveys this as well. The information I present to you here is small compared what you can obtain from Microsoft and I suggest you obtain information about this topic from Microsoft if you are working with this topic.

Microsoft's NetMeeting is a conferencing and collaboration tool designed for Internet or intranet use. It provides programming interfaces to add conferencing to applications. It makes possible real-time communications and collaboration with IP telephony and conferencing functionality. NetMeeting can be used by individuals to make communication possible through the Microsoft Internet Locator Server (ILS). This enables users to call each other from a dynamic directory within NetMeeting or from a Web page. While connected to a network users can communicate with both voice and video, work together on virtually any Windows-based application, exchange or mark up graphics on an electronic whiteboard, transfer files, or use the text-based chat program. Microsoft has additional information on this topic, and you can locate it at:

```
http://www.microsoft.com/netmeeting.
```

NetMeeting 2.0 Features

Some applicable standards like H.323 standards, which apply to voice and video conferencing, apply to NetMeeting. Real-time, point-to-point audio conferencing over the Internet or corporate intranet enables a user to make voice calls to associates and organizations around the world. NetMeeting voice conferencing includes support for half-duplex and full-duplex audio support for real-time conversations. Support also exists for automatic microphone sensitivity level setting. Voice conferencing supports network TCP/IP connections.

Support for the H.323 protocol enables interoperability between Net-Meeting 2.0 and other H.323-compatible voice clients. The H.323 protocol supports the ITU G.711 and G.723 audio standards and IETF RTP and RTCP specifications for controlling audio flow to improve voice quality. With MMX-enabled computers, MMX-enabled voice codecs can be used to improve performance with voice compression and decompression algorithms. Hence, the result is lower CPU use and improved voice quality during a call.

NetMeeting 2.0 enables a user to send and receive real-time visual images with another conference participant using any video for Windows-compatible equipment. They can communicate face to face (with a camera). Combined with the video and data capabilities of NetMeeting 2.0, a user can both see and hear the other conference participant. This H.323 stan-dards–based video technology is also compliant with the H.261 and H.263 video codecs.

NetMeeting also supports multipoint data conferencing using T.120. This means that two or more users can communicate as a group in real time. Participants can share applications, exchange information through a shared clipboard, transfer files, collaborate on a shared whiteboard, and use a text-based chat feature. Support for the T.120 data conferencing standard also enables interoperability with other T.120-based products and services.

The following features comprise multipoint data conferencing.

Application sharing Users can share a program running on one computer with other participants in the conference. Participants can review the same data or information and see the actions as the person sharing the application works on the program. For example, content editing or scrolling through information is possible. Users can share Windows-based applications transparently without any special knowledge of the application capabilities.

The person sharing the application can choose to work with other conference participants, and they can take turns editing or controlling the application. Only the person sharing the program needs to have the given application installed on their computer.

Shared Clipboard This enables a user to exchange its contents with other participants in a conference, using familiar cut, copy, and paste operations. For example, a participant can copy information from a local document and paste the contents into a shared application as part of group work.

File Transfer With this a user can send a file in the background to one or all of the conference participants. When one user drags a file into the main window, the file is automatically sent to each person in the conference; they can then accept or decline receipt. This file transfer capability is compliant with the T.127 standard.

Whiteboard Multiple users can simultaneously work with the whiteboard to review, create, and update graphic information. The whiteboard is object-oriented (versus pixel-oriented) enabling participants to manipulate the contents by clicking and dragging with the mouse. In addition, they can use a remote pointer or highlighting tool to point out specific contents or sections of shared pages.

Chat A user can type text messages to share common ideas or topics with participating users or record meeting notes as a result of the meeting process. Conference users can also use the chat function to communicate in the absence of audio support. A whisper feature enables a user to have a separate, private conversation with another person during a group chat session.

NetMeeting Software Development Kit

This SDK enables developers to integrate conferencing functionality directly into their customs applications or Web pages. This open development environment supports international communication and conferencing standards, and enables interoperability with products and services from multiple vendors.

NetMeeting SDK are APIs used to add nonstandard codecs and to access ILS servers through LDAP, as well as an ActiveX™ control to simplify adding conferencing capabilities to Web pages. You can obtain additional information about this topic at:

```
http://www.microsoft.com/netmeeting/sdk.
```

Features of TAPI 3.0 and NetMeeting 2.0

Mircosoft currently has TAPI 3.0 and NetMeeting 2.0, both support core IP telephony capabilities. However, each platform offers unique benefits. First, TAPI 3.0 integrates traditional telephony with IP telephony, providing a COM-based, protocol-independent call-control and a data-streaming infrastructure. Second, NetMeeting 2.0 SDK supports T.120 conferencing and application sharing, in addition to IP Telephony. TAPI 3.0 applications and NetMeeting 2.0 API interoperate using H.323 audio and video conferencing.

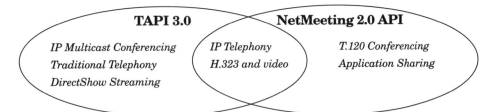

TAPI 3.0 and NetMeeting 2.0 both support core IP telephony capabilities (including support for H.323). Those of you who work with developers and support applications using this technology need to consider the following recommended guidelines when choosing an API for your IP telephony applications by Microsoft. Hence, these have been (at the time of this writing) to some degree a standard.

TAPI 3.0.   This is API is primarily for use with those applications implementing IP telephony. TAPI 3.0 is a good tool in computer telephony integration for combining IP telephony with traditional telephony and for IP multicast of voice and video.

NetMeeting 2.0 API   This API is used for those applications of real-time functions to integrate voice, video, and data conferencing. The NetMeeting API is useful for applications to integrate application sharing, whiteboard functionality, and multipoint file transfer with voice and video sessions.

Windows 2000 Distributed File System

Microsoft made further information available to me as a result of the case study work being done. The information in this section is provide to you courtesy of the Microsoft Corporation. Their web address is:

www.microsoft.com

Another aspect of change to Windows is the distributed file system. Windows 2000 uses this technology, and in fact, some aspects of the technology has been around for some time. The following concepts, terms, and conventions can help orient you to this technology if it is new.

Concepts, Terms, and Conventions

Dfs Root   A Dfs Root is a local share that serves as the starting point and host to other shares. Any shared resource can be published into the Dfs name space.

Accessing a Dfs Volume   A Dfs volume is accessed using a standard UNC name:

```
\\Server_Name\Dfs_Share_Name\Path\File
```

Where the *Server_Name* is the name of the host Dfs computer name, *Dfs_Share_Name* maps to any share that is designated to be the root of your Dfs, and *Path\File* is any valid Win32® path name. You can *net use* a drive to any place in the Dfs. Dfs provides a level of indirection between such a UNC name and the underlying server and share that is actually hosting the file or directory.

Shares participating in a Dfs may be hosted by any server accessible by clients of the Dfs. This includes shares from the local host, shares on any Windows NT server or workstation, or shares accessible to Windows NT through client software.

With the directory service–enabled version of Dfs, a Dfs volume can also be accessed by both its fault-tolerant name and its domain name:

```
\\Fault_Tolerant_Name\Dfs_Share_Name\Path\File
\\Domain_Name\Fault_Tolerant_Name\Path\File
```

This is where the *Fault_Tolerant_Name* is a name that the administrator selects to specify a Dfs volume stored in the DS (this might be a group of computers providing root level fault tolerance), and *Domain_Name\Volume* is the name of a standard volume object in Windows directory services.

Hosting a Dfs Volume

A network can host many individual Dfs volumes, each having a distinct name. Any Windows NT 4.0 or Windows 20000 server can run the Dfs service and host a Dfs volume. For the Windows NT 4.0 release of Dfs, a server can host one and only one Dfs. No architectural limits exist that prevent a Windows NT–based operating system from hosting multiple Dfs volumes in future releases.

A typical Dfs scenario would have a Dfs volume composed of link volumes from multiple servers throughout an organization. For example, consider an organization in the banking industry that has a pool of workers who handle word processing needs. This pool of workers would need access to documents stored in every department and branch throughout the organization. A single Dfs volume hosted locally could tie together only those servers and the specific share points that are typically used to store word processing information. The following table shows a typical Dfs.

Courtesy of the Microsoft Corporation

UNC Name	Maps to	Description
\\Server\Public	\\Server\Public	Root of the organization's Dfs
\\Server\Public\Intranet	\\IIS\Root	Junction to the intranet launching point
\\Server\Public\Intranet\ CorpInfo Corporate_HTML	\\Marketing\Info\	Junction to departmental intranet content
\\Server\Public\Users	\\Server\Public\Users	Collection of home directories
\\Server\Public\Users\ Bob	\\Server\Public\Users	Junction from Users to Bob's directory on the corporate development server
\\Server\Public\Users\ Bob\Java_Apps Java_Apps	\\Bob1\Data\	Junction point from Bob's development directory to one of Bob's personal workstations
\\Server\Public\Users\ Bob\Java_Apps Java_Apps	\\Bob2\Backups\	ALTERNATE Volume: Manually maintained backup of Bob's work
\\Server\Public\Users\ Ray	\\Server\Public\Users	Down-level Volume: junction to a non-SMB volume (such as NetWare or NFS)

Consider the hierarchical diagram of the information in the previous table.

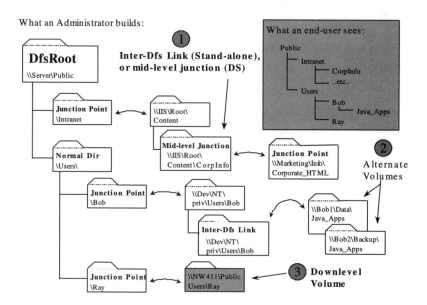

Typical Dfs

In addition to representing the table of previous junctions, the following are also presented:

- Post-junction junctions
- Alternate volumes
- Down-level volumes
- Post-Junction Junctions

This is a junction that has child junctions. There are two methods of setting this up: inter-Dfs links and mid-level junctions.

Inter-Dfs Links

It is possible to join one Dfs volume to another Dfs volume. As an example, individual departments within an organization can choose to set up and administer a logical name space that matches their work needs. The corporate Dfs volume could link together all departmental Dfs volumes. The effect of an Inter-Dfs link is that as you cross the junction, you have changed the server that you reference as your Dfs root. Although this is transparent to the end user, the Dfs client now receives its referrals from the new Dfs root.

Midlevel Junctions

Future releases of Dfs might support unlimited hierarchical junctioning that does not require inter-Dfs links. All referrals can be resolved from the original Dfs root, reducing points of failures and minimizing the number of referrals required to resolve deeply nested paths.

Alternate Volumes

If two (or more) shares in an organization are exact replicas of one share and you want to leverage the volumes, you can mount them at a single point in your Dfs name space. Dfs makes no attempt to ensure that the data stored between the two shares is replicated. Dfs replicas should be considered alternative sources of synchronized or replicated data (replication can be manual or automatic). If content is not replicated, alternate volumes can still be beneficial in a read-only scenario where any data writes are performed through physical naming across all alternates.

Dfs has a limit of 32 alternates for any given junction point; there is no limit to the number of junctions created at any point in your Dfs tree.

Down-Level Volumes

Any volume that is Windows NT Server 4.0 or later can host a Dfs volume and participate as an inter-Dfs link. All other volumes are considered to be *down-level*. Down-level volumes can be published in the Dfs volume, but cannot host Dfs or be joined to other volumes. Down-level volumes include Windows NT Workstation (all versions), Windows 98, Windows 95, Windows for Workgroups, and all non-Microsoft shares for which client redirectors are available. Windows 95 and Windows 98 Dfs-aware clients can take referrals for all up-level volumes and all SMB (Microsoft) down-level volumes, but cannot negotiate non-SMB volumes. Dfs enables special handling of security issues at session setup and with ACLs that are not consistent system-wide.

Session Setups

The process of session setup converges as each junction is crossed and cached for the first time; the Dfs-aware client establishes a session setup with the server on the other side of the junction. The credentials that the user originally supplied to connect with Dfs are used (for example, Net Use * \\Server\Dfs_Share /u:domain\User). If the user did not supply credentials, the credentials cached when the user logged into his or her workstation are used.

ACLs

File ACLs are administered at each individual physical share. There is no mechanism to administrate ACLs system-wide from the Dfs root, nor is there an attempt to keep ACLs consistent between alternate volumes. There are several reasons for this.

A centrally administrated logical ACL database could be bypassed, as users could Net Use directly to the physical resource. The logical Dfs volume can cross between FAT and NTFS volumes, as well as contain leaves from other network operating systems. There is no reasonable way to set an inherited Deny ACL that starts on an NTFS volume, passes to FAT, passes back to NTFS, and concludes on a NetWare volume.

A tool that walks the logical name space, setting ACLs appropriately, would require a complicated message and transactioning engine to ensure that ACLs were queued and updated over loosely connected and/or unreliable networks.

Storage quotas available in Windows 2000 require an additional burden of tallying storage for all possible users across all possible volumes to establish when users have exceeded their storage allotment.

Application Considerations

Consideration for free space, connections, file systems, backup, and restoration for developers writing applications using Dfs exist. Some of these include.

Free Space   When enumerating the available storage space on a volume, GetDiskFreeSpace returns the space available at the root of the Dfs volume. It does not walk the tree summing up the space available across assorted junctions. GetDiskFreeSpaceEX is a new function to return the space available at a specified point within a name space, which enables you to obtain the free space on the other side of a junction. This result depends on whether alternate volumes are mounted and alternates have identical storage devices.

Connections   Dfs permits workstations and servers to participate equally as junction points, a Windows NT workstation only allows only 10 clients to connect to it. This means that a share on a Windows NT workstation published in Dfs cannot be accessed after 10 connections have been established to that workstation (whether or not those connections use the private Dfs). Stand-alone servers do not have this limitation. Only Windows NT Server can host a Dfs root, but any share or volume accessible through the network can participate in the Dfs name space.

File Systems   Dfs is always hosted on Windows NT Server 4.0 or Windows 2000 Server, either in FAT or NTFS format. As junctions are crossed, you can change from one file format to another. With down-level volumes, you can also change from Windows NT to an alternate NOS that is formatted uniquely and has a different security model. Another effect of junction to different physical servers is that the network address can change between logical sub-directories (this is transparent to users and applications).

Backup and Restoration   With Dfs, a volume can be built to encompass all storage on your network. This allows all storage to be backed up through a single name space. Your backup solution must be aware of your Dfs topology. For example, if you want to restore a portion of your logical name space when those physical servers no longer exist, you must be able to identify that fact and determine what to do with the data. In this situation, you could choose to queue the restore operation, on the assumption that the server is temporarily down, move the contents to another location, and automatically reconfigure the logical name space or cancel the operation.

In Windows 2000, Dfs takes advantage of numerous new features. First, directory services for storing existing administrative information. LDAP as the protocol for updating and querying for Dfs information. Directory services store for providing root-level fault tolerance in Dfs. Directory services for keeping all participating computers in any Dfs root synchronized in their perception of the Dfs structure. Directory services site topology for providing intelligent replica selection. Content Replication Service for keeping alternate volumes synchronized with one another.

More information is available from Microsoft. You can get this information at:

`www.microsoft.com`

Windows NT Workstation & Server: Highlights

Windows NT is two products; that is, a workstation and a server. The workstation product is currently marketed and sold as an operating system. The same is true with the server product. Those of you familiar with this product will understand this; those are you who are not will benefit from it.

The operational idea behind Windows NT is the peer operation concept. Another way this can be viewed operationally is considering the workstation as the client and the server as the *server*. Now, both are not required to function. For example, if you are an ordinary user and chose a workstation for an operating system the server product is not required. However, if this workstation user decides to participate in a network wherein NT server is used, then the workstation component required for the NT network operation is already present.

NT server is also sold as a stand alone operating system and can be used as such. It is fully capable of functioning as a single stand alone operating system. Granted, most instances wherein NT server is used it is not functioning merely as a stand-alone operating system. In most instances NT server is used to operate on a system wherein the product enables *server* functionality.

Together workstation and server function in a physically networked environment and no additional software is required to make communication between hosts running the workstation product and the host(s) running the server product function. The reason this is so is because the workstation and server have upper layer protocols included in the product, hence adding upper layer software is not required. A network adapter, drivers for the adapter, cabling, and a network hub/concentrator are required to make the systems running a workstation and server operate in the network. In fact, these components make up the network.

Notice Figure 15-1 shows NT server on the Netfinity and NT workstation on two different systems beneath. One NT workstation is connected to

Figure 15-1
Windows NT
Workstation and
Server

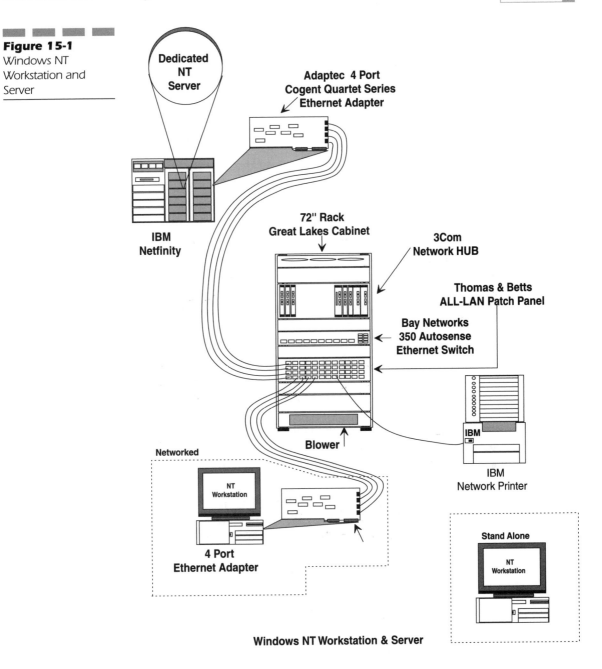

Windows NT Workstation & Server

the network, and the other is considered to be a stand-alone system. The stand-alone workstation could be integrated into the network with a network adapter card, driver, and cabling to the patch panel interface. Notice the Netfinity system has NT server operating on it. It is the network server and also functions as a *workstation*. Administration of the server can be performed locally (a user working on it) or remotely (a user working on another computer on the network—assuming the server is configured for remote administration).

NT is essentially a hybrid operating system. The reason I say this is, because its appearance and operation is a mix between earlier versions of Windows and also UNIX. NT has some functions clearly carried over from previous versions of Windows, while at the same time it has characteristics of UNIX operating systems as well.

Windows Terminology

Account   A method of record keeping that can maintain statistical information about users on a given system or network.

Account Policy   A given set of rules or permissions that explain what a users can and cannot do; for example, reading, writing, and deleting files is defined in a user account policy. The term is used in NT, Unix, and other large computer operating system environments

Application Server   Typically a term used to refer to a system that maintains application software that may be distributed to users throughout a network.

Architecture   A term that is increasingly used in the computer/network industry to refer to the design of something. That something might be a program design, network design, operating system design, or other such structural component of reference. An architect is one who designs various aspects of computers and/or networks. For example, as an architect designs physical houses, building, and so on, so a network architect designs computer networks.

Auditing   A term used to refer to the detection and recording of security related events in the NT operating system.

Authentication   The process used at login time to verify a password and/or user profile.

Backup Domain Controller   A term used in Windows NT workstation and server operating systems that refers to the computer that acts as an alternate computer for the system and that keeps the security policy, the domain's database, and authenticates the network logins.

Boot Loader   The program used in the beginning setup of NT that defines the system startup such as the location for the operating system's file. After the boot loader is created and each time the system is booted, the boot loader file is checked to see if any changes have been made.

Boot Partition   That part of a hard disk, floppy disk, CD-ROM, or other media used in computing that maintains basic system level information required to bridge the system's operation from firmware instructions in BIOS to the actual operating system in the system. The Boot Partition is formatted either in File Allocation Table (FAT), New Technology File System (NTFS), or High Performance File System (HPFS).

Cold Boot   Reference to a system being turned off physically (electrical power removed) and then turned back on. This is in contrast to a system that is *cycled* or *re-booted* by way of pressing a certain key stroke sequence.

Computer Name   A unique name given to a computer or other network device used to identify that computer or device; in NT up to fifteen characters can be used in naming as long as they are unique on a given network part.

Configuration Registry   The program storage that keeps a database of a computer's configuration. In contrast, a computer's autoexec.bat, config.sys, win.ini, and system.ini are similar but used on other operating systems primarily.

Connected User   Reference to a person or program using the resources of a given computer on a network.

Data Link Control (DLC)   A low level (data link; ios layer 2) protocol interface in NT to enable the connectivity between NT and IBM's SNA network equipment.

Default   A term used to refer to a set of conditions or parameters used if no choice is made to make a selection when such option is given. A default printer is one that is used when no other selection is made.

Dial-up Networking   Reference to a computer connected to a network through a telephone line.

Disabled User Account   Reference to an user account that does not permit logons.

Disk Configuration Information   Reference to NT registry information that contains disk configuration information such as the assigned drive letters, stripe sets, mirror sets, volume sets, and also stripes sets with parity.

Domain   In the context of NT, this is a computer, or computers, that share a common database and security policy for a given logical configuration. It is a method of identification as well as control. The term *trust* is used to further explain functional description of a domain.

Domain Controller   That system used in a collection of NT server and workstation based computers that maintains the security policy for those computers and network devices assigned to it, as well as maintains the master database of functional information for those computers and devices. Domain controllers and *servers* can validate a logon; however, a domain controller is required to be contacted to make changes to passwords.

Domain Name   An identifier used to refer to a collection of computers and devices in the network.

Ethernet   A lower layer protocol that operates functionally at layers two and one in the OSI model.

Event   A significant occurrence of something in a NT workstation or server operating system.

Event Log   A file maintained in NT based systems that record significance occurrences and can be viewed.

FAT File System   A file maintained on a media like a hard disk, floppy disk, and so on, which keeps track of the space segments on the storage medium.

Group   A specific account that lists (contains) other accounts called members. The notion of *groups* or *grouping* is a way to make certain common capabilities available to the members in that group. In NT server, groups are managed through the User Manager.

Global Account   The reference to a user's own home domain account.

Global Group   This is a way to identify a collection of users that can access resources in the domain wherein those users reside (identified) and also access resources outside the domain in which they reside.

Hardware Compatibility List   A list of hardware that has been tested and approved by Microsoft to be known to operate with a given operating system such as Windows NT 4.0.

High Performance File System   A file system designed to work with IBM's OS/2 operating system version 1.2.

Kernel   A term used to refer to the inner most part of an operating system, which includes those functions as memory, files, and device management. It also includes the management of overall system resource allocation.

Local Account   A way to identify a user in an non-trusted domain; hence it is considered local in regards to use an functional description of the user's global account.

Local Group   Reference to a collection of users that have rights to access only one NT Workstation. As far as NT Server, this means the identified collection of users can only access the server in their domain.

NetBEUI   A netBIOS Extended User Interface protocol, which is fast but not routable.

NTFS   The file system designed specifically for Windows NT operating systems. It is an object oriented file system that treats fields as objects that have system and user attributes.

Permission   Definition of rules that apply to objects on a per user basis that dictate what functions can be performed with that object, for example the ability to read, write, or delete a file.

Personal Group   The definition of associated program items associated with a given logon id and becomes logically attached to that id after the user is logged on.

Personal User Profile   The characteristics assigned to each user by the administrator that identify the abilities and limitations for each user. As each user signs on and makes changes to settings which can change, an update is made to invoke the next time that user logs onto the system.

Primary Domain Controller   This system performs security policy functions, maintains the master database, and authenticates domain logons for a given domain.

Remote Access Service   That portion of Windows NT software component that enables connectivity between two computers over telephone lines.

Right   The use of this term implies what a user can do to system level actions, in contrast to permissions that are applicable to specific objects.

SAM   Security Accounts Manager

SAM Database   That information maintained including account names, passwords, and security policy settings.

Shared Directory   A directory to which network users can connect.

Shared Resource   Anything on the network considered to be of value and available to more than one user.

Trust Relationship   The notion of this idea is the ability for interaction between multiple domains that have been configured to *trust* one another. This means that certain user accounts can access other domains that are deemed *trusted*. Domains that *trust* acknowledge and approve the logon request of users that are identified in a another (different) domain.

User Account   Information defined to a NT system which includes a user's password, name, groups in which the user can access and thus the rights and privileges of the user.

User Manager   Reference to a NT tool used to administrate accounts, groups, and security policies.

User Rights Policy The management definition of user rights to accounts and groups.

NT File Structure Support

Windows NT supports three types of file systems. They are:

- File Allocation Table (FAT)
- New Technology File System (NTFS)
- High Performance File System (HPFS)
- CD-ROM File System (CDFS)

At this time, NT is unique in its operation and relation to supporting file systems. During the installation phase of NT, either FAT, NTFS, or HPFS must be selected as the default file system support. This further makes NT a powerful operating system due to its file system support selectability. The impact of this is displayed in a positive way where in a single environment, the need top support FAT and NTFS is required.

FAT

Not too long ago the FAT file system was the default file system on personal computers and notebooks. The reason for this was that the Disk Operating System (DOS) was the dominant operating system on these computers, and this operating system used the FAT for file management. In the past twenty years, great evolution and revolution has occurred. Now, multiple operating systems work with personal computers. However, because of the dominance of DOS and MS-Windows applications, continued support for the FAT file system is needed.

The FAT file system is the only file system supported by Windows NT where floppy disk drives are used. Before examining more information about the FAT and other methods of file systems, some terminology needs to be understood.

Contiguous Sector Storage locations on media that are in consecutive locations.

Cluster The basic unit of space allocated on a disk. A cluster may contain one or more sectors.

Directory   A logical, hierarchical form of file organization used on various forms of media.

Fragmented File   This refers to a file that is stored on a disk in noncontiguous sectors.

Sector   This is the smallest logical storage unit used on a physical storage medium.

Track   This identification of storage is comprised of sectors. It is the largest logical unit of storage on physical storage media.

Volume   This is the division, or part, of a physical storage medium. The hard drives in computers are generally referred to by letters such as C, D, E, and so on.

NTFS

The New Technology File System is NT's native file system. However, as stated previously at the installation of NT, the desired file system support can be selected. One aspect of NTFS is the ability of NTFS to be used in overall security procedures of NT environments.

A NTFS has what is referred to as a master file table. This table includes administrative information, a description of the MFT itself, and a mirror record that is used as a back up source in case the first record is lost or corrupted in some manner. The MFT and the backup MFT are not only located in the boot sector but also in the logical center portion of the disk drive as well.

The NTFS MFT also maintains a log file. This file is used primarily for fault tolerance and file recovery if needed. At the core of NTFS is its operational nature, which is object and attribute based. Some basic terms and concepts need to be understood in light of this type file system. Consider these terms.

Attributes   Characteristics ascribed to files that can be categorized as system-defined and user-defined. Attributes include reading, sharing, hidden, archive, and other functions or abilities that can be performed or not performed against a given file.

Boot Sector   This part of a boot drive is read on initial startup. It contains files that are used in the initial startup of a system.

File Attributes This refers to the name, data, and other information ascribed to files or even a given directory. Generally, it refers to all attributes of files and directories.

Log File This type file contains information required to recover a system in the event of a system crash. It also maintains information regarding the state of the file system in use.

Mirror File This file contains the backup copy of a user created file or record and is kept by the operating system. It contains information needed to restore a file or record.

Master File Table (MFT) This is the NTFS primary table for storing NTFS file objects and attributes.

Non-resident Attributes This is information relevant to NTFS files that is not stored in the MFT table.

Object A file in a NTFS.

Resident Attributes Characteristics of a file that can physically fit into the MFT table.

System Files Those files that contain parameters required for the proper start-up and operation of an operating system.

Unicode A standard used to represent characters in NT. It is similar to ASCII character representation. ASCII character representation uses 8 bits to represent characters, which translates into a possible 256 characters. Unicode uses a 16-bit method for character representation, hence 65,536 different characters can be represented. Therefore, Unicode can easily be used to accommodate the needs of a wide range of languages including Japanese, Chinese, and others.

The following are some types of attributes and the content of those attributes that relate to files in the NTFS file system.

Attribute List All attributes for files considered to be large.

Bitmap Reference to those bitmaps in use for the MFT or the directory.

Data   Reference to an actual data file.

Extended Attributes   Characteristics used in reference to OS/2 based file servers that is not used by NT.

Extended Attribute Information   Characteristics used in reference to OS/2 based on file servers that is not used by NT.

Filename   This refers to the long filename that is stored by way of unicode characters as the standard MS-DOS filename.

Index Allocation   This reference to allocation is specific to the type of directory implemented.

Index Root   This component is used to implement directories.

Security Descriptor   This reference to characteristics includes access, ownership, and other characteristics.

The NTFS is particularly advantageous in recovery from system crashes. Granted, not all data may be recovered from a crash due to anomalies such as Input/Output problems, however the NTFS is suited to a high degree of probable recovery if a system crashes. The function of disk mirroring and parity striping on disks also contributes to the ability to recovery from system crashes. Hot-fixing is also a characteristic of NTFS. This is the ability of NTFS to move a disk's sector data and mark the sector on the disk as bad. This hot-fixing is transparent to the user and eliminates the manual intervention required in some systems prior to the offering of this aspect of NT.

High Performance File System (HPFS)

In times past, IBM had an operating system that was considered to be a possible contender for the next generation operating system in the marketplace. That system was OS/2. It is still around today, however it is not prevalent in marketshare when compared to Microsoft's operating systems.

OS/2 used the HPFS file system. The idea behind support for this in earlier versions of NT was upgradeability. Users working with OS/2 would not have any problems using NT. However, now this is not such an issue the further removed in time we become from the onset of IBM's OS/2.

CD-ROM File System

This file system is native to NT. It supports what has traditionally been called *long file names*. Long file name supports enable CDs to be read only, hence making them good candidates for boot media.

NT Architecture & Conceptual Overview

At the most basic level of Windows NT is the division of this software into workstation and server. The workstation software can operate well in a stand alone environment. In fact, the server software can also perform the same way. However, the server software is generally thought of as that software being used with a dedicated system to serve the needs of others in a network. Consider Figure 15-2.

Notice this is a simple network with two segments. Multiple NT workstations are located on each segment. Each workstation can operate independently of the network; however they interact with other network workstations and servers because of the architectural design compatibility between NT workstations and servers. Two NT server systems are also located in this network.

NT workstation does come with the networking component. It can easily be configured to operate in a networked environment. NT Server is software capable of supporting a variety of workstations in a networked environment. Consider Figure 15-3.

In Figure 15-3, the server software is operating on an IBM Netfinity 7000. This illustration is a typical real-world approach to using the NT Server along with multiple workstations. Notice two /SMS network storage silos are located in the network as well. Each workstation participating in the network can access the /SMS storage silos. The workstations can also function well as stand alone workstations. However, because they are illustrated as part of the network, they can interact with all the benefits of the network.

These illustrations and explanations are typical of NT architecture from an implementation perspective.

Figure 15-2
Multi-Segment NT
based network

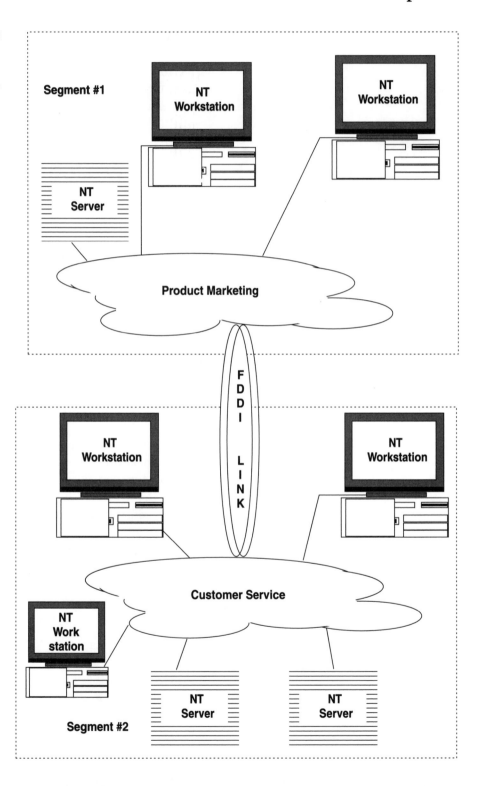

Figure 15-3
NT Server
Environment

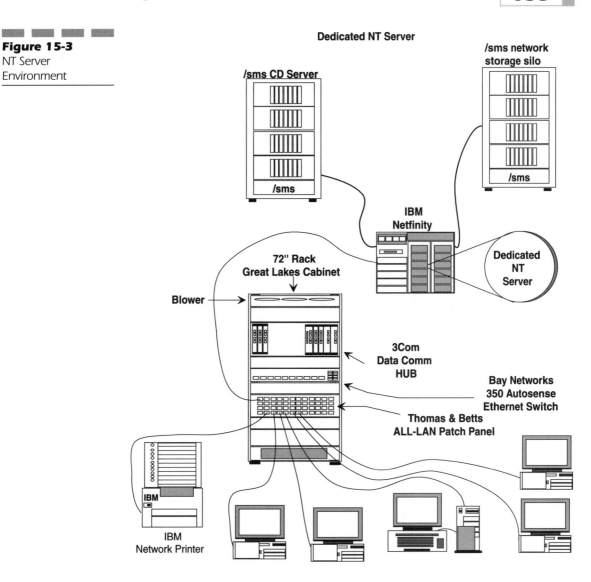

Dedicated NT Server

/sms CD Server

/sms network storage silo

/sms

/sms

IBM Netfinity

72" Rack Great Lakes Cabinet

Dedicated NT Server

Blower

3Com Data Comm HUB

Bay Networks 350 Autosense Ethernet Switch

Thomas & Betts ALL-LAN Patch Panel

IBM Network Printer

NT is capable of supporting a significant amount of resources. The standard server version of NT supports 2 gigabytes of RAM per process address limit. However, the Enterprise Edition supports 3 gigabytes of RAM without any new APIs—thus no additional overhead.

Windows NT architecture is considered modular, because it contains multiple components. Consider the following illustration.

Figure 15-4
NT Component
Architecture

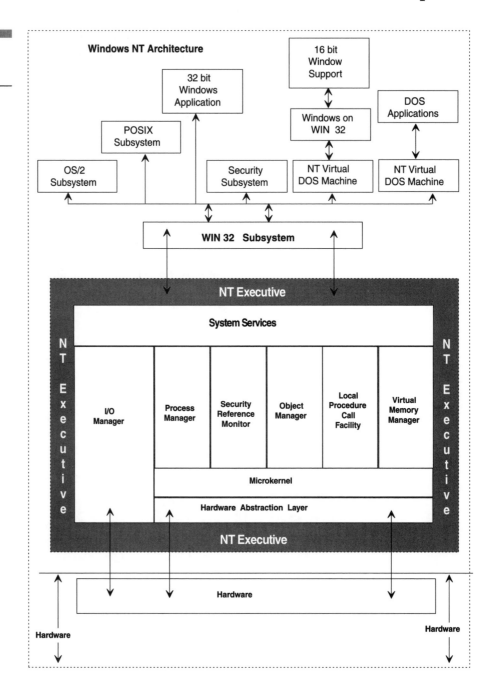

Figure 15-4 shows NT in from a component architecture perspective. The following distinct components can be identified. These components include

- NT Executive Services
- Object manager
- Security reference monitor
- Process manager
- Local procedure call facility
- Virtual memory manager
- I/O manager
- System services
- Kernel
- Hardware Abstraction Layer (HAL)
- WIN32 Subsystem (Application Environment Subsystems)

NT Executive Services

The NT executive is the highest order of control within the operating system. Actually, this component can be further subdivided into these smaller components.

- Object manager
- Security reference monitor
- Process manager
- Local procedure call facility
- Virtual memory manager
- I/O manager

Object Manager   The NT executive uses the object manager to manage objects. The object manager creates, deletes, and modifies objects. Objects are nothing more than abstract data types used as operating system resources. Objects can be ports (physical) or threads (logical). The object manager also works in the system to clean up stray objects that could exist if a program crashes. Another function of the object manager is to keep track of the resources used by each resource. For example, one resource used by objects is memory. The object manager keeps objects in-line with system resources and enables a balanced system to be possible.

Process Manager   The process manager is involved in all processes and threads. General consensus defines a process as that which has an identifiable virtual address space, one or more threads, some system resources, and an executable program code. In NT, when an application is started the object manager is called to create a process that sequentially creates an initial thread.

Security Reference Monitor   The security reference monitor is the core of NT security. A logon process and local security authority process is used in the implementation of security with NT.

Virtual Memory Manager (VMM)   The VMM translates a system's process memory address into actual memory addresses. In short, it manages virtual memory. Virtual memory in personal computers operates on the same principles as large computers. Some aspects might be augmented or enhanced, but the foundation of the idea is the same.

NT's modular design makes it robust. It has a great degree of hardware independence. Some of the hardware platforms NT can operate on include:

- X86 uni-processor computers
- X86 multi-processor computers
- AXP RISC architecture
- AXP RISC multiprocessor computers
- MIPS RISC architecture
- MIPS RISC multiprocessor architecture
- Motorola PowerPC

Another powerful aspect of NT is its use of unicode, rather than ASCII, for a character set. Unicode is based on 16 bits meaning this character set can represent 65, 536 characters. Hence, unicode is more powerful than its ASCII counterpart, which uses 8 bits that yields only 256 characters. The inherent meaning of this is multi-national characters are supported such as Japanese, Chinese, Russian, Swedish, and others.

Kernel

The NT kernel is part of the NT Executive. For practical purposes, the kernel is referred to as the microkernel. However, the microkernel is not the same as *kernel mode*. The kernel is that part of NT code that comprises the most fundamental and core aspects of NT. The term microkernel is a term used to refer that part of NT code that has been reduced to the single most important code that the operating system uses.

Traced back to its origin, the term micro-kernel (within the context of how it's used in the Microsoft camp) has its roots at Carnegie Mellon University in the mid 1980s. A project was underway there called MACH, meaning Micro-Kernel architecture. Granted the name is a little awkward, but consider this. The idea brought with it architecture for an operating system that limited functions of that system to a *micro-kernel*. This is the core feature of NT operating system; that is, it has a very small collection of routines, considered the core, on which all other routines are built. The notion behind this type design was that it would make the operating system relatively portable from different operating environments. Because NT adapted this philosophy, the operating system can support 32-bit windows programs and UNIX or DOS styled programs.

Within NT Interprocess Communication (IPC), functionality is possible. This is simply the ability for any process or program to communicate with another while it is operating along side it. A lot of operating systems do not provide this ability.

From a processor viewpoint, the notion of privileged levels of operation is common. Intel processors have what they call *rings* of processor protection. Consider Figure 15-5.

Notice Figure 15-5 shows four boxes, each inside the other. The centermost box is what is called level 0. This is the centermost part of a processor's operation, and it is the safest—or most protected. This is where the operating system kernel runs. Notice the *rings* go outward, away from the center most part of the processor. Level 1 and 2 are where operating system services are performed. Then the outermost *ring* is where applications run, in respect the internal design of the microprocessor.

Akin to this conversation is something many computer users have encountered and wondered what it meant. Have you ever encountered a message on your computer monitor, *"general protection fault"*? Well, when the processor detects a violation in a level of protection, this is the message generated. This is interesting for a couple reasons. First, the *general*

Figure 15-5
Processor Rings of
Protection

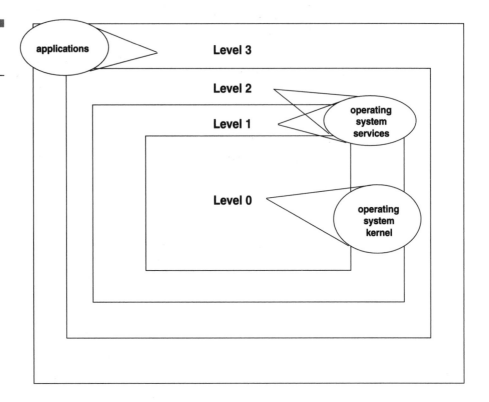

protection fault message is being generated at just about the lowest (or most crucial) level in a computer. Second, this message is an indicator that some combination of programs or functions have merged to create such a low level error. It also indicates when the set of conditions that caused the message to be generated in the first place is in a state wherein the entire system is unstable.

Windows NT has what is called *user mode* and *kernel mode*. Figure 15-6 illustrates this.

These modes, user and kernel, are akin to the privileged and unprivileged mode processors use. These modes define the level or degree to which programs running in the computer have access to resources such as hardware and other programs.

The easiest way to describe the user and kernel mode in NT is this: Only the microkernel, HAL, and the device drivers run in the kernel mode. All other parts of NT run in user mode. The kernel mode applications are kept from incidental mishaps by the inherent design of the microprocessor. On the other hand, user mode applications are kept secure because of the design of the NT operating system.

Figure 15-6
Conceptual view
of NT

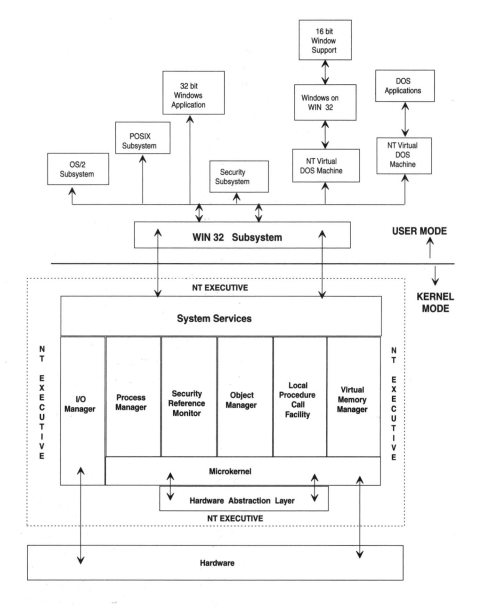

The kernel basically dispatches and schedule threads used in the operating system. Each thread gets a priority number assigned to it ranging from 0 to 31. For those new to the terminology of thread as used in this context, the following definition is adequate: A *thread* is an executable object that belongs to a process. An *object* can be something as "concrete" as a device port or an application. Now, the function of the kernel is to dispatch threads to run on processors based on the priority numbers assigned to them.

The microkernel itself is part of the NT Executive. It operates in kernel mode. The microkernel runs in kernel mode and communicates with the NT Executive through very low level primitives. In a crude way, one could think of the microkernel as that part which controls the entire system. Because NT is based around preemptive multitasking, it controls time slices and manages to pass control to other processes.

In summary, the microkernel runs in kernel mode. This means it operates in a privileged processor mode. In this mode, the microprocessor is responsible for protecting the operating system kernel. The end result is the operating system kernel runs in a safe environment wherein system crashes are not the norm.

Hardware Abstraction Layer (HAL)

The HAL is a Dynamic Load Library (DLL) used between a system's hardware and the operating system software. In short, it is software; specifically, it is that software that serves as the interface between the hardware and the operating system itself.

The purpose of HAL is to keep NT from being concerned with I/O interrupts, and thereby makes NT easily portable. Technically, HAL is the only part of NT that talks directly with hardware. All other NT components talk indirectly to the hardware. For example, the kernel, device drivers, and I/O manager talk to the hardware through HAL. Because of HAL, NT is considered portable between different type operating systems. It also provides support for Symmetrical Multi-Processing (SMP). The result is that NT can be used on Intel, MIPS, Alpha processors and others.

Because of HAL, there is a hardware compatibility list with the NT operating system. For the most part NT is compatible with many vendors' hardware; however, because of HAL the question of compatibility is an issue. I have been using NT version 4.0. During the development of the network, I discovered some hardware components that NT would not (or could not) acknowledge. At first, I thought the author had a problem and then I realized the problem was a fundamental lack of NT to *know* a certain piece of hardware existed. No, I am not telling what the hardware was that NT could not acknowledge for that would serve no purpose. Now, NT and this piece of hardware are compatible.

Application Environmental Subsystem

The Application Environment Subsystem is that part above the *WIN 32 Subsystem*. The WIN 32 Subsystem is the main subsystem for NT. It includes WIN 32 bit Application Program Interfaces (API's). Beyond support for 32 bit programs, the WIN 32 Subsystem supports application programs for other operating environments.

Input/Output (I/O) Manager This part of NT handles input and output processing. The I/O manager coordinates all system I/O. Drivers, installable file systems, network directors, and caching memory management.

Local Procedure Call (LPC) Facility This part of NT functions as an interface between all clients and servers on an NT system. Functionality of LPC is similar to Remote Program Call (RPC) facility. However, LPC and RPC are not equals, because LPC permits exchange of information between two thread processes on a local machine.

Administration Concepts

Administration of NT involves understanding some concepts presented here in this section. Topics for consideration include

- Workgroups
- Domains
- Trust Relationships
- User Attributes

Workgroups

The concept of a workgroup exists in Windows NT. Technically a workgroup is a logical grouping of computers on the network. Multiple workgroups are possible in NT. For example, it is possible to have a workgroup named support and one named sales. Now assume six computers are listed under the workgroup named support. Assume one NT server is in the support work-group. In this example, the support users can access the server in this group.

Assume six users and a server are listed under the sales workgroup. The users in the sales workgroup can access this server. However, a distinction is made between the support and sales workgroups. Security is implemented on each server; so this means for any user to access either the support or sales server, they must have a valid account on that server. Generally, in the confines of a workgroup, those computers that are a part of that workgroup can access the server(s) in that workgroup. Another way to look at this is to remember that for any computer to access a server in a workgroup, the computer must have an account setup for each computer.

Domains

The concept of a domain in NT carries a different twist to it than work-groups. A domain is a collection of computers that share a common *user policy* and *security account database*. For example, say a domain exist with seven workstations and one server. In the context of a domain, all seven workstations share the same user policy—whatever that might be. In this sense, the user policy is a "global" setting applicable to all workstations. The same is true for the security database; that is, all seven workstations share the same one. In a nutshell, a domain could be considered a workgroup with centralized security.

The way these functions are implemented in a domain is through a domain controller. A *domain controller* is identified during the installation phase of NT Server. Functions of a domain controller include managing the security and policy database for all users in the domain. Two type of domain controllers exist; they are: primary and backup. A primary domain controller performs all the functions required to make the domain work effectively. The backup domain controller is like a mirror image of the primary domain controller and exists in case a failure occurs in the primary domain controller. It is a good idea to have a backup domain controller in the domain if a primary domain controller has been defined.

Two primary domain controllers cannot exist in the same domain. If two exist initially, one will win out. Basically, the two go into a contention mode and the workstations in the domain quickly acknowledge one and not the other.

One last note about domain controllers and domains. A domain controller is identified and defined during the installation phase of NT. It cannot be defined at any other time. This is a very important aspect of the setup phase of the network.

Trust Relationships

A *trust* relationship among domains simply means two or more domains *trust* the other. This does not mean that inherent in this relationship all users in one domain have automatic access to resources in the other domain. Further definition of access is required. In addition, the notion of a global domain is required for operation wherein multiple domains exist. One could think of this "loosely" as: *the great global domain in the sky!* The purpose behind it is to facilitate coordination of domains and users within various domains.

Another concept to remember about domains is that trust relationships among them are one way, not two-way. For example, user A in domain A may trust resource B in domain B; this does not however mean that resource B in domain B trusts user A in domain A.

The simplest way to think of trust and domains are these three examples. First, a master domain has domains that have trust relationships with it. Second, where two domains have bi-directional trust relationships. This could be called loosely peer-to-peer. Third, a scenario where three or more domains have multiple trust relationships among more than one domain.

User Attributes

NT users have attributes associated with them. The following list reflects the list generally associated with a user:

- account
- password
- group memberships
- account policy
- user rights
- user profile

This information is used by administrators to customize a wide-variety of user profiles. Some users might have much broader abilities than others due to their work requirements. This degree of information in user profiles enables great control over user access and provides system security.

The account and password for NT users is similar to other operating systems. It is a way to provide a unique identifier to users and a level of security through a password.

NT *group memberships* is a way to assign resources to a collection of users. For example, assume the group "work" exists and has seven users. Now suppose an eighth user is to be added. With the implementation of *groups*, this eighth user would have all the same abilities and limitations as the previous seven members of this group. The use of groups is powerful because multiple groups can be defined in a given domain. It is an administrative way to associate users with other users who need similar privileges. The scope of *how* groups are implemented is determined on a site by site basis by the network administrator. If your network does not have an administrator, like mine, then guess what? You are elected, so it's time to learn more! I recommend obtaining some NT books mentioned later in this chapter that provide excellent information.

Account policy is a feature of NT not always used in implementations, however in implementations wherein security is of greater importance, this feature is generally used. The account policy enables a more complex implementation. For example, the password age, length, history, and any account lockout on failed logon attempts is manipulated.

User rights are basically definitions as to what a user can or cannot do to the operating system. For example, changing the system time, restoring files and directories, shutting down the system, taking ownership of files, forcing a shutdown of a remote system, backing up files and directories, accessing a given computer from the network, managing the audit and security log of systems, and controlling logons (either remotely or locally).

The *user profile* specifies the program groups available. This is where definition whether or not the run command can be executed on the file menu.

Workstation & Server Commonalities

Windows NT is clearly delineated into two distinct parts. This section highlights those aspects/parts the workstation and server have in common.

Both the NT workstation and server use what is considered advanced file systems. NT supports the NT file system (NTFS) and the file allocation table (FAT). NTFS supports long file names, file level compression, file data forking support (required for Macintosh systems), international filenames, software level sector support for fault tolerance, and file level security permissions.

FAT support makes NT backwards compatible with DOS. Floppy drives use FAT and RISC systems using NT use FAT in the boot partition.

Both workstation and server support TCP/IP. NetBIOS is supported also as defined in RFCs 1001 and 1002. This means logical naming at a session level is possible. The NetBIOS interface also supports Dynamic Data Exchange (DDE). DDE enables sharing data embedded within documents.

NT workstation and server also share Dynamic Host Configuration Protocol (DHCP) client. This means an NT station can participate in an environment to obtain DNS addresses, IP addresses, gateway addresses, and netmasks.

NT provides support for SNMP. This makes workstations and servers capable of participating in environments that use management tools such as OpenView, SunNet Manager, and SystemView.

Both support Remote Access Service (RAS). In NT version 4, point-to-point-tunneling-protocol enables a virtual network to be created over a wide distance. NT data encryption makes this part of NT popular.

Both workstation and serve provide support for C2-level security. Protecting data on a system is achieved by Access Control Lists (ACLs). This enables directory and file level security maintenance.

NT workstation and server are administered the same way. Some of the tools by which this is done include:

- DHCP Manager
- Disk Manager
- Event Viewer
- Performance Monitor
- RAS Administrator
- Server Manager
- User Manager
- WINS Manager

The DHCP manager is used to configure the station to obtain required information on startup. In addition to the DHCP manager is the DHCP server service; this permits remote control of DHCP servers.

The disk manager is the tool by which disk partitions are created, mirrored disks, and volume set disk partitioning.

The event viewer enables a user to view events on local and remote systems. Information such as the system log, security log, and application log can be obtained.

The performance monitor provides a method for real-time monitoring. The performance monitor also makes sending administrative alerts to remote systems possible, monitoring performance counters, and maintaining performance logs.

The Remote Access Service administrator is a configuration tool used to designate certain users privileged to gain access to a network node. RAS administrator can also be used to configure remote stations.

The server manager tool is used to create domain systems for workstations (NT), stand-alone servers, and domain controllers. It is also used to determine the status of servers and users logged-on.

The user manager enables the creation and management of user accounts. When used on a domain controller, inter-domain trust relationships are setup by this tool. It is the tool used to setup user rights, system-wide passwords, and auditing functions.

The Windows Internet Name Service (WINS) manager is used to manage the WINS server service. This function of NT can be used to manage a local host or remote host. The basic purpose of WINS is dynamic name resolution.

Useful Networking Commands

I have installed multiple NT networks and found the following commands very helpful in the setup and maintenance of these networks. These are not my commands; in fact, they are Microsoft's commands. All the commands I have listed here can be viewed through the help facility after selecting "my computer" on the "desktop." The information they provide is valuable, especially to administrators and integrators. Following these commands are real samples taken from the case study network used.

Net (command options) Many Windows NT networking commands begin with the word net. These net commands have some common properties:

You can see a list of all available net commands by typing net /?.

You can get syntax help at the command line for a net command by typing net help command. For example, for help with the net accounts command, type net help accounts.

All net commands accept /yes and /no options (can be abbreviated /y and /n). The /y option automatically answers 'yes' to any interactive prompt that the command generates; /n answers 'no.' For example, net stop server usually prompts you to confirm that you want to stop all services that depend on the Server service; net stop server /y automatically answers 'yes' to the prompt and the Server service shuts down.

Net Accounts   Updates the user accounts database and modifies password and logon requirements for all accounts. The Net Logon service must be running on the computer for which you want to change account parameters.

> net accounts [/forcelogoff:{minutes | no}] [
>
> /minpwlen:length] [/maxpwage:{days | unlimited}] [
>
> /minpwage:days] [/uniquepw:number] [/domain]
>
> net accounts [/sync] [/domain]

Parameters   none

Type net accounts without parameters to display the current settings for password, logon limitations, and domain information.

/forcelogoff:{minutes | no}   Sets the number of minutes to wait before ending a user's session with a server when the user account or valid logon time expires. The no option prevents forced logoff. The default is no.

When the /forcelogoff:minutes option is specified, Windows NT sends a warning minutes before it forces the user off of the network. If any files are open, Windows NT warns the user. If minutes is less than two, Windows NT warns the user to log off from the network immediately.

/minpwlen:length   Sets the minimum number of characters for a user-account password. The range is 0–14 characters; the default is 6 characters.

/maxpwage:{days | unlimited}   Sets the maximum number of days that a user account's password is valid. A value of unlimited sets no maximum time. The /maxpwage option must be greater than /minpwage. The range is 1–49,710 days (unlimited); the default is 90 days.

/minpwage:days   Sets the minimum number of days before a user can change a new password. A value of 0 sets no minimum time. The range is 0–49,710 days; the default is 0 days.

/uniquepw:number   Requires that a user not repeat the same password for number password changes. The range is 0–8 password changes; the default is 5 password changes.

/domain   Performs the operation on the primary domain controller of the current domain. Otherwise, the operation is performed on the local computer.
   This parameter applies only to Windows NT Workstation computers that are members of a Windows NT Server domain. By default, Windows NT Server computers perform operations on the primary domain controller.

/sync   When used on the primary domain controller, causes all backup domain controllers in the domain to synchronize. When used on a backup domain controller, causes that backup domain controller only to synchronize with the primary domain controller. This command applies only to computers that are members of a Windows NT Server domain.

Net Computer   Adds or deletes computers from a domain database. This command is available only on computers running Windows NT Server.

   net computer \ \computername {/add | /del}

Parameters

\ \computername   Specifies the computer to add or delete from the domain.

/add   Adds the specified computer to the domain.

/del   Removes the specified computer from the domain.

Net Config   Displays the configurable services that are running, or displays and changes settings for a service.

   net config [service [options]]

Parameters   none
   Type net config without parameters to display a list of configurable services.

service   Is a service (server or workstation) that can be configured with the net config command.

options   Are specific to the service. See net config server or net config workstation for complete syntax.

Net Config Server   Displays or changes settings for the Server service while the service is running.

  net config server [/autodisconnect:time]

  [/srvcomment:"text "] [/hidden:{yes | no}]

Parameters   none
  Type net config server to display the current configuration for the Server service.

/autodisconnect:time   Sets the maximum number of minutes a user's session can be inactive before it is disconnected. You can specify −1 to never disconnect. The range is −1–65535 minutes; the default is 15.

/srvcomment:"text "   Adds a comment for the server that is displayed in Windows NT screens and with the net view command. The comment can have as many as 48 characters. Enclose the text in quotation marks.

/hidden:{yes | no}   Specifies whether the server's computer name appears on display listings of servers. Note that hiding a server does not alter the permissions on that server. The default is no.

Net Config Workstation   Displays or changes settings for the Workstation service while the service is running.

  net config workstation [/charcount:bytes]

  [/chartime:msec] [/charwait:sec]

Parameters   none
  Type net config workstation to display the current configuration for the local computer.

/charcount:bytes   Specifies the amount of data Windows NT collects before sending the data to a communication device. If /chartime:msec is also set, Windows NT acts on whichever option is satisfied first. The range is 0–65535 bytes; the default is 16 bytes.

/chartime:msec   Sets the number of milliseconds Windows NT collects data before sending the data to a communication device. If /charcount:bytes is also set, Windows NT acts on whichever option is satisfied first. The range is 0–65535000 milliseconds; the default is 250 milliseconds.

/charwait:sec   Sets the number of seconds Windows NT waits for a communication device to become available. The range is 0–65535 seconds; the default is 3600 seconds.

Net Continue

Reactivates suspended services.

net continue service

Parameters

service   Services that can be continued are: file server for Macintosh (Windows NT Server only), ftp publishing service, lpdsvc, net logon, network dde, network dde dsdm, nt lm security support provider, remoteboot (Windows NT Server only), remote access server, schedule, server, simple tcp/ip services, and workstation.

Net File   Displays the names of all open shared files on a server and the number of file locks, if any, on each file. This command also closes individual shared files and removes file locks.

net file [id [/close]]

Parameters   none
Type net file without parameters to get a list of the open files on a server.

id   Is the identification number of the file.

/close   Closes an open file and releases locked records. Type this command from the server where the file is shared.

Net Start Computer Browser   Starts the Computer Browser service.

net start "computer browser"

Net Start DHCP Client   Starts the DHCP Client service. This command is available only if the TCP/IP protocol has been installed.

net start "dhcp client"

Net Start Eventlog   Starts the event logging service, which logs events on the local computer. This service must be started prior to using the Event Viewer to view the logged events.

net start eventlog

Net Start File Server for Macintosh   Starts the File Server for Macintosh service, permitting the sharing of files with Macintosh computers. This command is available only on computers running Windows NT Server.

net start "file server for macintosh"

Net Start FTP Publishing Service   Starts the FTP publishing service. This command is available only if Internet Information Server has been installed.

net start "ftp publishing service"

Net Group   Adds, displays, or modifies global groups on Windows NT Server domains. This command is available for use only on Windows NT Server domains.

net group [groupname [/comment:"text"]] [/domain]

net group groupname {/add [/comment:"text"] | /delete} [/domain]

net group groupname username[. . .] {/add | /delete} [/domain]

Parameters   none
Type net group without parameters to display the name of a server and the names of groups on the server.

groupname   Is the name of the group to add, expand, or delete. Supply only a groupname to view a list of users in a group.

/comment:"text"   Adds a comment for a new or existing group. The comment can have as many as 48 characters. Enclose the text in quotation marks.

/domain   Performs the operation on the primary domain controller of the current domain. Otherwise, the operation is performed on the local computer.

This parameter applies only to Windows NT Workstation computers that are members of a Windows NT Server domain. By default, Windows NT Server computers perform operations on the primary domain controller.

username[...]   Lists one or more usernames to add to or remove from a group. Separate multiple username entries with a space.

/add   Adds a group, or adds a username to a group. An account must be established for users added to a group with this command.

/delete   Removes a group, or removes a username from a group.

Net Help   Provides a list of network commands and topics you can get help with, or provides help with a specific command or topic. The available net commands are also listed in the Commands window of this Command Reference under N.

    net help [command]
    net command {/help | /?}

Parameters   none
    Type net help without parameters to display a list of commands and topics for which you can get help.

command   Is the command you need help with. Don't type net as part of command.

/help   Provides an alternate way to display the help text.

/?   Displays the correct syntax for the command.

Net Localgroup   Adds, displays, or modifies local groups.

    net localgroup [groupname [/comment:"text"]] [/domain]
    net localgroup groupname {/add [/comment:"text"] | /delete} [/domain]
    net localgroup groupname name [...] {/add | /delete} [/domain]

Parameters   none
   Type `net localgroup without parameters` to display the name of the server and the names of local groups on the computer.

groupname   Is the name of the local group to add, expand, or delete. Supply only a groupname to view a list of users or global groups in a local group.

/comment:"text"   Adds a comment for a new or existing group. The comment can have as many as 48 characters. Enclose the text in quotation marks.

/domain   Performs the operation on the primary domain controller of the current domain. Otherwise, the operation is performed on the local computer.
   This parameter applies only to Windows NT Workstation computers that are members of a Windows NT Server domain. By default, Windows NT Server computers perform operations on the primary domain controller.

name [...]   Lists one or more usernames or groupnames to add or to remove from a local group. Separate multiple entries with a space. Names may be local users, users on other domains, or global groups, but not other local groups. If a user is from another domain, preface the username with the domain name (for example, SALES\RALPHR).

/add   Adds a global groupname or username to a local group. An account must first be established for users or global groups before it is added to a local group with this command.

/delete   Removes a groupname or username from a local group.

Net Name   Adds or deletes a messaging name (sometimes called an alias), or displays the list of names the computer accepts messages for. The Messenger service must be running to use net name.

   net name [name [/add | /delete]]

Parameters   none
   Type `net name without parameters` to display a list of names currently in use.

name   Specifies the name to receive messages. The name can have as many as 15 characters.

/add   Adds a name to a computer. Typing /add is optional; typing net name name works the same way as typing net name name /add .

/delete   Removes a name from a computer.

Net Pause   Pauses running services.

  net pause service

Parameters

service   Is file server for Macintosh (Windows NT Server only), ftp publishing service, lpdsvc, net logon, network dde, network dde dsdm, nt lm security support provider, remoteboot (Windows NT Server only), remote access server, schedule, server, simple tcp/ip services, or workstation.

Net Print   Displays or controls print jobs and printer queues.

  net print \\computername\sharename
  net print [\\computername] job# [/hold | /release | /delete]

Parameters

computername   Is the name of the computer sharing the printer queue(s).

sharename   Is the name of the printer queue. When including the sharename with the computername, use a backslash (\) to separate the names.

job#   Is the identification number assigned to a print job in a printer queue. A computer with one or more printer queues assigns each print job a unique number. If a job number is being used in one printer queue shared by a computer, that number is not assigned to any other job on that computer, not even to jobs in other printer queues on that computer.

/hold   When used with job#, holds a print job waiting in the printer queue. The print job stays in the printer queue, and other print jobs bypass it until it is released.

/release   Releases a print job that has been held.

/delete   Removes a print job from a printer queue.

Net Send   Sends messages to other users, computers, or messaging names on the network. The Messenger service must be running to receive messages.

   net send {name | * | /domain[:name] | /users} message

Parameters

name   Is the username, computername, or messaging name to send the message to. If the name is a computername that contains blank characters, enclose the alias in quotation marks (" ").

*   Sends the message to all the names in your group.

/domain[:name]   Sends the message to all the names in the computer's domain. If name is specified, the message is sent to all the names in the specified domain or workgroup.

/users   Sends the message to all users connected to the server.

message   Is text to be sent as a message.

Net Session   Lists or disconnects the sessions between a local computer and the clients connected to it.

   net session [\\computername] [/delete]

Parameters   none
   Type net session without parameters to display information about all sessions with the local computer.

\\computername   Identifies the computer for which to list or disconnect sessions.

/delete   Ends the computer's session with \\computername and closes all open files on the computer for the session. If \\computername is omitted, all sessions on the local computer are canceled.

Net Share   Creates, deletes, or displays shared resources.

   net share sharename

   net share sharename=drive:path [/users:number | /unlimited]
      [/remark:"text"]

   net share sharename [/users:number | unlimited] [/remark:"text"]

   net share {sharename | drive:path} /delete

Parameters   none
   Type `net share without parameters` to display information about all resources being shared on the local computer.

sharename   Is the network name of the shared resource. Type `net share with a sharename` only to display information about that share.

drive:path   Specifies the absolute path of the directory to be shared.

/users:number   Sets the maximum number of users who can simultaneously access the shared resource.

/unlimited   Specifies an unlimited number of users who can simultaneously access the shared resource.

/remark:"text"   Adds a descriptive comment about the resource. Enclose the text in quotation marks.

/delete   Stops sharing the resource.

Net Start Alerter   Starts the Alerter service. The Alerter service sends alert messages.

net start alerter

Net Start   Starts a service, or displays a list of started services. Service names of two or more words, such as Net Logon or Computer Browser, must be enclosed in quotation marks (" ").

   net start [service]

Parameters   none

Type net start without parameters to display a list of running services.

service   Includes alerter, client service for Netware, clipbook server, computer browser, dhcp client, directory replicator, eventlog, ftp publishing service, lpdsvc, messenger, net logon, network dde, network dde dsdm, network monitor agent, nt lm security support provider, ole, remote access connection manager, remote access isnsap service, remote access server, remote procedure call (rpc) locator, remote procedure call (rpc) service, schedule, server, simple tcp/ip services, snmp, spooler, tcp/ip netbios helper, ups, and workstation.

These services are available only on Windows NT Server: file server for Macintosh, gateway service for netware, Microsoft dhcp server, print server for Macintosh, remoteboot, and Windows Internet name service.

Netstat   Displays protocol statistics and current TCP/IP network connections. This command is available only if the TCP/IP protocol has been installed.

netstat [-a] [-e] [-n] [-s] [-p protocol] [-r] [interval]

Parameters

-a   Displays all connections and listening ports; server connections are normally not shown.

-e   Displays Ethernet statistics. This may be combined with the -s option.

-n   Displays addresses and port numbers in numerical form (rather than attempting name look-ups).

-s   Displays per-protocol statistics. By default, statistics are shown for TCP, UDP, ICMP, and IP; the -p option may be used to specify a subset of the default.

-p protocol   Shows connections for the protocol specified by proto; proto may be tcp or udp. If used with the -s option to display per-protocol statistics, proto may be tcp, udp, icmp, or ip.

-r Displays the contents of the routing table.

interval Redisplays selected statistics, pausing interval seconds between each display. Press CTRL+C to stop redisplaying statistics. If this parameter is omitted, netstat prints the current configuration information once.

Net Start ClipBook Server Starts the ClipBook Server service. Service names with two words, such as ClipBook Server, must be enclosed in quotation marks (" ").

    net start "clipbook server"

Net Start Client Service for NetWare Starts the Client Service for NetWare service. This command is available only on Windows NT Workstation if Client Service for NetWare has been installed.

    net start "client service for netware"

Net Stop Stops a Windows NT network service.

    net stop service

Parameters

service Includes alerter, client service for netware, clipbook server, computer browser, directory replicator, ftp publishing service, lpdsvc, messenger, net logon, network dde, network dde dsdm, network monitor agent, nt lm security support provider, ole, remote access connection manager, remote access isnsap service, remote access server, remote procedure call (rpc) locator, remote procedure call (rpc) service, schedule, server, simple tcp/ip services, snmp, spooler, tcp/ip netbios helper, ups, and workstation.

These services are available only on Windows NT Server: file server for Macintosh, gateway service for netware, Microsoft dhcp server, print server for Macintosh, Windows Internet name service.

Net Time Synchronizes the computer's clock with that of another computer or domain. Used without the /set option, displays the time for another computer or domain.

    net time [\\computername | /domain[:name]] [/set]

Parameters

\\computername Is the name of a server you want to check or synchronize with.

/domain[:name] Specifies the domain with which to synchronize time.

/set Synchronizes the computer's clock with the time on the specified computer or domain.

Net Use Connects a computer to or disconnects a computer from a shared resource, or displays information about computer connections. The command also controls persistent net connections.

```
net use [devicename | *] [\\computername\
sharename[\volume]] [password | *]] [/user:[
domainname\]username] [[/delete] | [/persistent:{yes | no}]]
net use devicename [/home[password | *]] [/delete:{yes | no}]
net use [/persistent:{yes | no}]
```

Parameters none
Type net use without parameters to get a list of network connections.

devicename Assigns a name to connect to the resource or specifies the device to be disconnected. There are two kinds of devicenames: disk drives (D: through Z:) and printers (LPT1: through LPT3). Type an asterisk instead of a specific devicename to assign the next available devicename.

\\computername\sharename Is the name of the server and the shared resource. If the computername contains blank characters, enclose the double backslash (\\) and the computername in quotation marks (" "). The computername may be from 1 to 15 characters long.

\volume Specifies a NetWare volume on the server. You must have Client Service for NetWare (Windows NT Workstation) or Gateway Service for NetWare (Windows NT Server) installed and running to connect to NetWare servers.

password Is the password needed to access the shared resource.

*   Produces a prompt for the password. The password is not displayed when you type it at the password prompt.

/user   Specifies a different username with which the connection is made.

domainname   Specifies another domain. For example, net use d: \ \
    server\share /user:admin\mariel connects the user mariel as if the connection were made from the admin domain. If domain is omitted, the current logged on domain is used.

username   Specifies the username with which to log on.

/home   Connects a user to their home directory.

/delete   Cancels the specified network connection. If the user specifies the connection with an asterisk, all network connections are canceled.

/persistent   Controls the use of persistent network connections. The default is the setting used last. Deviceless connections are not persistent.

yes   Saves all connections as they are made, and restores them at next logon.

no   Does not save the connection being made or subsequent connections; existing connections are restored at next logon. Use the /delete switch to remove persistent connections.

Net User   Adds or modifies user accounts or displays user-account information.

    net user [username [password | *] [options]] [/domain]
    net user username {password | *} /add [options] [/domain]
    net user username [/delete] [/domain]

Parameters   none
    Type net user without parameters to view a list of the user accounts on the computer.

username   Is the name of the user account to add, delete, modify, or view. The name of the user account can have as many as 20 characters.

password   Assigns or changes a password for the user's account. A password must satisfy the minimum length set with the /minpwlen option of the net accounts command. It can have as many as 14 characters.

*   Produces a prompt for the password. The password is not displayed when you type it at a password prompt.

/domain   Performs the operation on the primary domain controller of the computer's primary domain.
   This parameter applies only to Windows NT Workstation computers that are members of a Windows NT Server domain. By default, Windows NT Server computers perform operations on the primary domain controller.
   NOTE: This action is taken on the primary domain controller of the computer's primary domain. This may not be the logged on domain.

/add   Adds a user account to the user accounts database.

/delete   Removes a user account from the user accounts database.
   options are as follows:

/active:{no | yes}   Enables or disables the user account. If the user account is not active, the user cannot access resources on the computer. The default is yes (active).

/comment:"text"   Provides a descriptive comment about the user's account. This comment can have as many as 48 characters. Enclose the text in quotation marks.

/countrycode:nnn   Uses the operating-system country codes to implement the specified language files for a user's help and error messages. A value of 0 signifies the default country code.

/expires:{date | never}   Causes the user account to expire if date is set; never sets a time limit on the user account. Expiration dates can be in mm/dd/yy, dd/mm/yy, or mmm,dd,yy format, depending on the /countrycode. Note that the account expires at the beginning of the date specified. Months can be a number, spelled out, or abbreviated with three letters. Years can be two or four numbers. Use commas or slashes to separate parts of the date (no spaces). If yy is omitted, the next occurrence of the date (according to your computer's date and time) is assumed. For example, the following date entries are equivalent if entered between Jan. 10, 1994, and Jan. 8, 1995: jan,9 1/9 /95 january,9,1995 1/9

/fullname:"name"   Specifies a user's full name rather than a username. Enclose the name in quotation marks.

/homedir:path   Sets the path for the user's home directory. The path must exist.

/homedirreq:{yes | no}   Sets whether a home directory is required.

/passwordchg:{yes | no}   Specifies whether users can change their own password. The default is yes.

/passwordreq:{yes | no}   Specifies whether a user account must have a password. The default is yes.

/profilepath:[path]   Sets a path for the user's logon profile. This path-name points to a registry profile.

/scriptpath:path   Sets a path for the user's logon script. Path cannot be an absolute path; path is relative to %systemroot

%\SYSTEM32\REPL\IMPORT\SCRIPTS./times:{times | all}   Specifies the times the user is allowed to use the computer. The times value is expressed as day[-day][,day[-day]] ,time[-time][,time[-time]], limited to 1-hour time increments. Days can be spelled out or abbreviated (M,T,W,Th,F,Sa,Su). Hours can be 12- or 24-hour notation. For 12-hour notation, use AM, PM, or A.M., P.M. The value all means a user can always log on. A null value (blank) means a user can never log on. Separate day and time with commas, and units of day and time with semicolons (for example, M,4AM−5PM;T,1PM−3PM). Do not use spaces when designating /times.

/usercomment:"text"   Enables an administrator to add or change the "User comment" for the account. Enclose the text in quotation marks.

/workstations:{computername[, . . .] | *}   Lists as many as eight workstations from which a user can log on to the network. Separate multiple entries in the list with commas. If /workstations has no list, or if the list is *, the user can log on from any computer.

Net View   Displays a list of domains, a list of computers, or the resources being shared by the specified computer.

net view [\\computername | /domain[:domainname]]

net view /network:nw [\\computername]

Parameters   none

Type net view without parameters to display a list of computers in your current domain.

\\computername   Specifies the computer whose shared resources you want to view.

/domain[:domainname]   Specifies the domain for which you want to view the available computers. If domainname is omitted, displays all domains in the network.

/network:nw   Displays all available servers on a NetWare network. If a computername is specified, the resources available on that computer in the NetWare network are displayed. Other networks that are added to the system may also be specified with this switch.

Finger   Displays information about a user on a specified system running the Finger service. Output varies based on the remote system. This command is available only if the TCP/IP protocol has been installed.

finger [-l] [user]@computer [. . .]

Parameters

-l   Displays information in long list format.

user   Specifies the user you want information about. Omit the user parameter to display information about all users on the specified computer.

@computer   Specifies the server on the remote system whose users you want information about.

Ipconfig   This diagnostic command displays all current TCP/IP network configuration values. This command is of particular use on systems running

DHCP, allowing users to determine which TCP/IP configuration values have been configured by DHCP.

ipconfig [/all | /renew [adapter] | /release [adapter]]

Parameters

all   Produces a full display. Without this switch, ipconfig displays only the IP address, subnet mask, and default gateway values for each network card.

renew [adapter]   Renews DHCP configuration parameters. This option is available only on systems running the DHCP Client service. To specify an adapter name, type the adapter name that appears when you use ipconfig without parameters.

release [adapter]   Releases the current DHCP configuration. This option disables TCP/IP on the local system and is available only on DHCP clients. To specify an adapter name, type the adapter name that appears when you use ipconfig without parameters.

With no parameters, the ipconfig utility presents all of the current TCP/IP configuration values to the user, including IP address and subnet mask. This utility is especially useful on systems running DHCP, allowing users to determine which values have been configured by DHCP.

Ipxroute   Displays and modifies information about the routing tables used by the IPX protocol. The command has different options for IPX routing and for source routing. Separate all options with spaces.

IPX Routing Options

ipxroute servers [/type=x]

ipxroute stats [/show] [/clear]

ipxroute table

Parameters

servers [/type=x]   Displays the SAP table for the specified server type. x is an integer. For example, /type=4 displays all file servers. If no /type is specified, then servers of all types are shown. The list is sorted by server name.

stats [/show] [/clear]   Displays or clears IPX router interface statistics. /show is the default. /clear clears the statistics.

table   Displays the IPX routing table, sorted by network number.

Source Routing Optionsipxroute board=n [clear] [def] [gbr] [mbr] [remove=**xxxxx**]

ipxroute config

Parameters

board=n   Specifies the network adapter card for which to query or set parameters.

clear   Clears the source routing table

def   Sends packets to the ALL ROUTES broadcast. If a packet is transmitted to a unique mac address that is not in the source routing table, the default is to send the packet to the SINGLE ROUTES broadcast.

gbr   Sends packets to the ALL ROUTES broadcast. If a packet is transmitted to the broadcast address (FFFFFFFFFFFF), the default is to send the packet to the SINGLE ROUTES broadcast.

mbr   Sends packets to the ALL ROUTES broadcast. If a packet is transmitted to a multicast address (C000xxxxxxxx), the default is to send the packet to the SINGLE ROUTES broadcast.

remove=xxxxx   Removes the given node address from the source routing table.

config   Displays information on all the bindings for which IPX is configured.

Nbtstat   This diagnostic command displays protocol statistics and current TCP/IP connections using NBT (NetBIOS over TCP/IP). This command is available only if the TCP/IP protocol has been installed.

nbtstat [-a remotename] [-A IP address] [-c] [-n] [-R] [-r] [-S] [-s] [interval]

Parameters

-a remotename   Lists the remote computer's name table using its name.

-A IP address   Lists the remote computer's name table using its IP address.

-c   Lists the contents of the NetBIOS name cache giving the IP address of each name.

-n   Lists local NetBIOS names. Registered indicates that the name is registered by broadcast (Bnode) or WINS (other node types).

-R   Reloads the LMHOSTS file after purging all names from the NetBIOS name cache.

-r   Lists name resolution statistics for Windows networking name resolution. On a Windows NT computer configured to use WINS, this option returns the number of names resolved and registered through broadcast or through WINS.

-S   Displays both client and server sessions, listing the remote computers by IP address only.

-s   Displays both client and server sessions. It attempts to convert the remote computer IP address to a name using the HOSTS file.

interval   Redisplays selected statistics, pausing interval seconds between each display. Press CTRL+C to stop redisplaying statistics. If this parameter is omitted, nbstat prints the current configuration information once.

Portuas   Merges a LAN Manager 2.x user accounts database into an existing Windows NT user accounts database.

```
portuas -f filename [-u username] [-v] [/codepage codepage] [/log
   filename]
```

Parameters

-f filename   Specifies the LAN Manager 2.x NET.ACC file.

-u username   Specifies a single user or group to restore.

-v   Displays all messages (verbose).

/codepage codepage   Specifies the OEM codepage the LAN Manager 2.x NET.ACC file is in.

/log filename   Specifies a file to log results.

Command Usage: Brief Networking Case Study

To provide you with some framework of understanding some of the commands, I issued some of them against some of the systems in the case study network that I work with. They constitute the remainder of this section.

IP Configuration on Renegade

Ipconfig
Host Name ....: RENEGADE
DNS Servers ....: 198.6.1.194
                              198.6.100.194
Node Type ....: Hybrid
NetBIOS Scope ID ....:
IP Routing Enabled ....: No
WINS Proxy Enabled ....: No
NetBIOS Resolution Uses DNS ....: Yes
0 Ethernet adapter :
Description ....: 3Com 3C90x Ethernet Adapter
Physical Address ....: 00–60–08–98–1D–33
DHCP Enabled ....: No
IP Address ....: 220.100.100.172
Subnet Mask ....: 255.255.255.0
Default Gateway ....: 127.0.0.2
Primary WINS Server ....: 220.100.100.137
Secondary WINS Server ....:

```
Lease Obtained  . . . . . . . . . . . . . . . :
Lease Expires   . . . . . . . . . . . . . . . : 1 Ethernet adapter :
Description  . . . . . . . . . . . . . . . . . .: AOL Adapter
Physical Address . . . . . . . . . . . . . . .: 44–45–53–54–61–6F
DHCP Enabled  . . . . . . . . . . . . . . . : Yes
IP Address . . . . . . . . . . . . . . . . . . .: 0.0.0.0
Subnet Mask . . . . . . . . . . . . . . . . . .: 0.0.0.0
Default Gateway . . . . . . . . . . . . . . .:
DHCP Server . . . . . . . . . . . . . . . . . : 255.255.255.255
Primary WINS Server . . . . . . . . . . . :
Secondary WINS Server . . . . . . . . . .:
Lease Obtained . . . . . . . . . . . . . . . .:
Lease Expires . . . . . . . . . . . . . . . . . :
2 Ethernet adapter  . . . . . . . . . . . . . :
Description  . . . . . . . . . . . . . . . . . .: PPP adapter.
Physical Address . . . . . . . . . . . . . . .: 44–45–53–54–00–00
DHCP enabled  . . . . . . . . . . . . . . . .: Yes
IP Address . . . . . . . . . . . . . . . . . . .: 208.252.2.187
Subnet Mask . . . . . . . . . . . . . . . . . .: 255.255.255.0
Default Gateway . . . . . . . . . . . . . . .: 208.252.2.187
DHCP Server  . . . . . . . . . . . . . . . . .: 255.255.255.255
Primary WINS Server  . . . . . . . . . . .:
Secondary WINS Server . . . . . . . . .:
Lease Obtained  . . . . . . . . . . . . . . . : 01 01 80 12:00:00 AM
Lease Expires  . . . . . . . . . . . . . . . .: 01 01 80 12:00:00 AM
```

IP Configuration on FATBOY

ipconfig
```
Host Name  . . . . . . . . . . . . . . . .: fatboy
DNS Servers . . . . . . . . . . . . . . . .:
Node Type . . . . . . . . . . . . . . . . .: Hybrid
NetBIOS Scope ID  . . . . . . . . . . .:
IP Routing Enabled  . . . . . . . . . .: Yes
WINS Proxy Enabled . . . . . . . . .: No
NetBIOS Resolution Uses DNS  : NoEthernet adapter
DC21×41:Description  . . . . . . . . : DEC DC21140 PCI Fast Ethernet Adapter
Physical Address . . . . . . . . . . . .: 00-C0-F0–30-D2–77
```

```
DHCP Enabled   . . . . . . . . . . . . .: No
IP Address  . . . . . . . . . . . . . . . . : 220.100.100.171
Subnet Mask  . . . . . . . . . . . . . . : 255.255.255.0
IP Address . . . . . . . . . . . . . . . .: 220.100.100.158
Subnet Mask . . . . . . . . . . . . . . .: 255.255.0.0
IP Address . . . . . . . . . . . . . . . .: 220.100.100.157
Subnet Mask  . . . . . . . . . . . . . . : 255.255.255.0
IP Address . . . . . . . . . . . . . . . .: 220.100.100.155
Subnet Mask . . . . . . . . . . . . . . .: 255.255.255.0
IP Address . . . . . . . . . . . . . . . .: 220.100.100.156
Subnet Mask  . . . . . . . . . . . . . . : 255.255.255.0
IP Address . . . . . . . . . . . . . . . .: 220.100.100.154
Subnet Mask . . . . . . . . . . . . . . .: 255.255.255.0
IP Address . . . . . . . . . . . . . . . .: 220.100.100.153
Subnet Mask . . . . . . . . . . . . . . .: 255.255.255.0
IP Address . . . . . . . . . . . . . . . .: 220.100.100.152
Subnet Mask . . . . . . . . . . . . . . .: 255.255.255.0
IP Address . . . . . . . . . . . . . . . .: 220.100.100.151
Subnet Mask . . . . . . . . . . . . . . .: 255.255.255.0
IP Address . . . . . . . . . . . . . . . .: 220.100.100.150
Subnet Mask . . . . . . . . . . . . . . .: 255.255.255.0
IP Address . . . . . . . . . . . . . . . .: 220.100.100.137
Subnet Mask . . . . . . . . . . . . . . .: 255.255.0.0
Default Gateway . . . . . . . . . . . . .: 127.0.0.2
Primary WINS Server . . . . . . . . : 220.100.100.132
Ethernet adapter NdisWan5 . . .:
Description  . . . . . . . . . . . . . . . .: NdisWan Adapter
Physical Address   . . . . . . . . . . . .: 00–00–00–00–00–00
DHCP Enabled   . . . . . . . . . . . . .: No
IP Address . . . . . . . . . . . . . . . .: 0.0.0.0
Subnet Mask . . . . . . . . . . . . . . .: 0.0.0.0
Default Gateway . . . . . . . . . . . . .: Ethernet adapter NdisWan4:
Description  . . . . . . . . . . . . . . . .: NdisWan Adapter
Physical Address . . . . . . . . . . . . .: 00–00–00–00–00–00
DHCP Enabled   . . . . . . . . . . . . .: No
IP Address . . . . . . . . . . . . . . . .: 0.0.0.0
Subnet Mask   . . . . . . . . . . . . . . .: 0.0.0.0
Default Gateway . . . . . . . . . . . . .:
```

Netstat command executed on FATBOY

Active Connections

Proto	Local Address	Foreign Address	State
TCP	0.0.0.0:21	0.0.0.0:0	LISTENING
TCP	0.0.0.0:70	0.0.0.0:0	LISTENING
TCP	0.0.0.0:80	0.0.0.0:0	LISTENING
TCP	0.0.0.0:135	0.0.0.0:0	LISTENING
TCP	0.0.0.0:135	0.0.0.0:0	LISTENING
TCP	0.0.0.0:1027	0.0.0.0:0	LISTENING
TCP	0.0.0.0:1028	0.0.0.0:0	LISTENING
TCP	127.0.0.1:1025	0.0.0.0:0	LISTENING
TCP	127.0.0.1:1025	127.0.0.1:1028	ESTABLISHED
TCP	127.0.0.1:1026	0.0.0.0:0	LISTENING
TCP	127.0.0.1:1028	127.0.0.1:1025	ESTABLISHED
TCP	220.100.100.137:137	0.0.0.0:0	LISTENING
TCP	220.100.100.137:138	0.0.0.0:0	LISTENING
TCP	220.100.100.137:139	0.0.0.0:0	LISTENING
UDP	0.0.0.0:135	*:*	
UDP	220.100.100.137:137	*:*	
UDP	220.100.100.137:138	*:*	

Netstat Command on The-HOSTAGE

Active Connections

Proto	Local Address	Foreign Address	State
TCP	THE-HOSTAGE:1040	220.100.100.178:10007	ESTABLISHED

Netstat –s Command on Renegade

IP Statistics

Packets Received	= 52005
Received Header Errors	= 0
Received Address Errors	= 11270
Datagrams Forwarded	= 0
Unknown Protocols Received	= 0
Received Packets Discarded	= 0
Received Packets Delivered	= 50335

Output Requests		= 39446
Routing Discards		= 0
Discarded Output Packets		= 0
Output Packet No Route		= 0
Reassembly Required		= 0
Reassembly Successful		= 0
Reassembly Failures		= 0
Datagrams Successfully Fragmented		= 0
Datagrams Failing Fragmentation		= 0
Fragments Created		= 0

ICMP Statistics

	Received	Sent
Messages	25	7
Errors	0	0
Destination Unreachable	18	0
Time Exceeded	0	0
Parameter Problems	0	0
Source Quenchs	0	0
Redirects	0	0
Echos	0	1
Echo Replies	1	0
Timestamps	0	0
Timestamp Replies	0	0
Address Masks	0	0
Address Mask Replies	0	0

TCP Statistics

Active Opens	= 464
Passive Opens	= 0
Failed Connection Attempts	= 7
Reset Connections	= 93
Current Connections	= 1
Segments Received	= 35358
Segments Sent	= 32561
Segments Retransmitted	= 51

UDP Statistics

Datagrams Received	= 13170
No Ports	= 933
Receive Errors	= 0
Datagrams Sent	= 5953

Additional administration information can be obtained about the case study network, but the purpose here is to provide an example to you the results of which can be obtained from some of the commands available. It is a good idea to obtain administrative information about the network as soon as the network is operational. Windows NT has built in commands that can be issued against a command and various information obtained.

Networking & Services in Windows

A strong aspect of Windows and previously, NT, is its networking ability and services built into the operating system. Fundamental to Windows and NT is the design intent for use in a networked environment. The following protocols and services are found in Windows and the Windows NT products. They are bundled as part of the operating systems and administrators select which ones they desire to use in any given instance.

- TCP/IP
- User Protocols and Applications
- Administrative Utilities
- Dynamic Host Configuration Protocol (DHCP)
- Windows Internet Naming Service (WINS)
- Domain Name System (DNS)
- NetBEUI
- IPX/SPX
- DLC
- STREAMS
- Remote Procedure Call (RPC)
- Service Advertising Protocol (SAP)
- Workstation
- NetBIOS
- Client Service for NetWare
- Server
- Remote Access Service (RAS)
- LMHosts

TCP/IP

TCP/IP is covered in much greater depth later in this book. If you desire more information now, refer to that chapter. However, it is appropriate to examine some TCP/IP aspects now as they relate to Windows NT. Consider Figure 15-7.

In Figure 15-7, NT and TCP/IP are illustrated together. Practically, all the layers of TCP/IP are represented in NT. However, not all functional aspects of TCP/IP are bundled into NT as a single unit, meaning all aspects have to be used or none can be used. For example, TCP and UDP are integral to NT. This is the case, because these transport layer protocols are required for protocols and applications to be used that reside above them. The same is true for the layer in TCP/IP wherein IP, ICMP, and the routing protocols reside. These components are required in order for TCP/IP to operate.

However, on the upper layers where applications reside, different choices can be made to use different components.

Figure 15-7
NT and TCP/IP

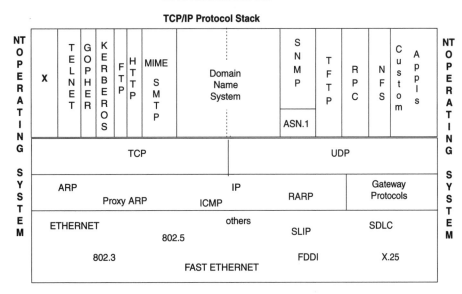

User Protocols & Applications

One example of a user protocol and application is File Transfer Protocol (FTP). Technically, FTP is a protocol and an application. FTP itself is an application divided into two parts; that is, the client and the server. However, from a user aspect, FTP is merely seen as an application that enables file transfers from one system to another.

TELNET is another protocol and application supported in NT. It, like FTP, consists of a client and server. The TELNET client is used to initiate a session between two hosts. It is a TELNET server that answers a TELNET clients request. Other TCP/IP protocols and applications are used as well with NT.

How Administrative Utilities are Used

This part of the chapter has a little redundancy and overlaps previous information, but it is nevertheless important. This part can help you see how I used the various commands and administrative tools against the network and some of my systems.

These utilities are actually commands that can be issued on the NT server or workstation command line. These commands are helpful tools in obtaining information used to manage the NT network. Some examples of these utilities include:

ARP (address resolution protocol) when entered on a command line of an NT workstation or server, it yields the following data:

```
Interface: 220.100.100.10 on Interface 2
Internet Address Physical Address Type
220.100.100.53 00-60-94-a5-cc-ee dynamic
```

Hostname When entered on a NT workstation or server command line, it yields the following:

```
Microsoft(R) Windows NT(TM)
(C) Copyright 1985-1996 Microsoft Corp.
C:\>hostname
BRAINS
```

```
C:\>hostname ?
```

sethostname: Use the Network Control Panel Applet to
  set hostname.

hostname -s is not supported.

```
C:\>
```

ipconfig When this command is entered on the command line of NT workstation or server, it yields the following information:

```
Windows NT IP Configuration
Ethernet adapter SMCISA1:
IP Address  . . . . . . . : 220.100.100.10
Subnet Mask   . . . . . . : 255.255.255.0
Default Gateway . . . . . :
Ethernet adapter NdisWan5 :
IP Address . . . . . . . : 0.0.0.0
Subnet Mask   . . . . . . : 0.0.0.0
Default Gateway . . . . . :
```

nbstat When this command is entered on a NT workstation or server command line, the following information is obtained depending on which argument is used with the command:

C:\>nbtstat Displays protocol statistics and current TCP/IP connections using NBT (NetBIOS over TCP/IP).
  NBTSTAT [-a RemoteName] [-A IP address] [-c] [-n]
  [-r] [-R] [-s] [-S] [interval]]

-a (adapter status) Lists the remote machine's name table given its name

-A (Adapter status) Lists the remote machine's name table given its IP address

-c (cache) Lists the remote name cache including the IP addresses

-n (names) Lists local NetBIOS names

-r (resolved) Lists names resolved by broadcast and through WINS

-R (Reload) Purges and reloads the remote cache name table

-S (Sessions) Lists sessions table with the destination IP addresses

-s (sessions) Lists sessions table converting destination IP addresses to host names through the hosts file

RemoteName- Remote host machine name

IP address- Dotted decimal representation of the IP address

interval- Redisplays selected statistics, pausing interval seconds between each display. Press Ctrl+C to stop redisplaying statistics

```
C:\>
------------------------------
Node IpAddress: [220.100.100.10] Scope Id: []
NetBIOS Local Name Table
Name Type Status
------------------------------
Registered Registered Registered Registered
MUSCLE <20> UNIQUE
MUSCLE <00> UNIQUE
INFO <00> GROUP
MUSCLE <06> UNIQUE
MUSCLE <03> UNIQUE
INFO <1E> GROUP
------------------------------
NetBIOS Names Resolution and Registration Statistics
Resolved By Broadcast = 1
Resolved By Name Server = 23
Registered By Broadcast = 7
Registered By Name Server = 2
------------------------------
NetBIOS Names Resolved By Broadcast
------------------------------- SILO
------------------------------
```

```
NetBIOS Connection Table
Local    State In/Out Remote Input  Output
Name                                Host
---------------------------- Connected
OutListening              Listening
MUSCLE <00>         CHEROKEE     ,20.        14KB   16KB
MUSCLE <03>
ADMINISTRATOR <03>
------------------------------
Node IpAddress: [220.100.100.10] Scope Id: []
NetBIOS Local Name Table
Name Type Status
-----------------------
Registered Registered Registered Registered Registered
MUSCLE <20> UNIQUE
MUSCLE <00> UNIQUE
INFO <00> GROUP
MUSCLE <06> UNIQUE
MUSCLE <03> UNIQUE
INFO <1E> GROUP
```

netstat   Depending on which argument is issued against this command, a variety of information can be obtained. Consider the following:

`C:\>netstat ? > n`   Displays protocol statistics and current TCP/IP network connections.

NETSTAT [-a] [-e] [-n] [-s] [-p proto] [-r] [interval]

-a Displays all connections and listening ports. (Server-side connections are normally not shown).

-e Displays Ethernet statistics. This may be combined with the -s option.

-n Displays addresses and port numbers in numerical form.

-p proto Shows connections for the protocol specified by proto; proto may be tcp or udp. If used with the -s option to display per-protocol statistics, proto may be tcp, udp, or ip.

-r Displays the contents of the routing table.

-s Displays per-protocol statistics. By default, statistics are shown for TCP, UDP and IP; the -p option may be used to specify a subset of the default.

interval Redisplays selected statistics, pausing interval seconds between each display. Press CTRL+C to stop redisplaying statistics. If omitted, netstat prints the current configuration information once.

```
C:\>type n
C:\>
Active Connections
Proto Local Address Foreign Address State
TCP CHEROKEE:1027 0.0.0.0:0 LISTENING
TCP CHEROKEE:135 0.0.0.0:0 LISTENING
TCP CHEROKEE:135 0.0.0.0:0 LISTENING
TCP CHEROKEE:13991 0.0.0.0:0 LISTENING
TCP CHEROKEE:1025 0.0.0.0:0 LISTENING
TCP CHEROKEE:1025 localhost:1027 ESTABLISHED
TCP CHEROKEE:1027 localhost:1025 ESTABLISHED
TCP CHEROKEE:137 0.0.0.0:0 LISTENING
TCP CHEROKEE:138 0.0.0.0:0 LISTENING
TCP CHEROKEE:nbsession 0.0.0.0:0 LISTENING
TCP CHEROKEE:nbsession 220.100.100.19:1035 SYN_RECEIVED
TCP CHEROKEE:nbsession 220.100.100.61:1042 SYN_RECEIVED
TCP CHEROKEE:nbsession 220.100.100.77:1038 SYN_RECEIVED
UDP CHEROKEE:135 *:*
UDP CHEROKEE:13991 *:*
UDP CHEROKEE:nbname *:*
UDP CHEROKEE:nbdatagram *:*
```

-ping When this command is entered on a command line of a NT workstation or server the following information can be obtained, depending on the arguments used against it.

Usage: ping [-t] [-a] [-n count] [-l size] [-f] [-i TTL] [-v TOS] [-r count] [-s count] [[-j host-list] | [-k host-list]] [-w timeout] destination-list

Options:

-t Ping the specifed host until interrupted.

-a Resolve addresses to hostnames.

-n count Number of echo requests to send.

-l size Send buffer size.

-f Set Don't Fragment flag in packet.

-i TTL Time To Live.

-v TOS Type Of Service.

-r count Record route for count hops.

-s count Timestamp for count hops.

-j host-list Loose source route along host-list.

-k host-list Strict source route along host-list.

-w timeout Timeout in milliseconds to wait for each reply.

Pinging cherokee [220.100.100.53] with 32 bytes of data:

Reply from 220.100.100.53: bytes=32 time=20ms TTL=128

Reply from 220.100.100.53: bytes=32 time<10ms TTL=128

Reply from 220.100.100.53: bytes=32 time<10ms TTL=128

Reply from 220.100.100.53: bytes=32 time<10ms TTL=128

————————————————————————————

Pinging brains [220.100.100.12] with 32 bytes of data:

Reply from 220.100.100.12: bytes=32 time=10ms TTL=128

Reply from 220.100.100.12: bytes=32 time<10ms TTL=128

Reply from 220.100.100.12: bytes=32 time<10ms TTL=128

Reply from 220.100.100.12: bytes=32 time<10ms TTL=128

- route

`C:\>route` Manipulates network routing tables.
   ROUTE [-f] [command [destination] [MASK netmask] [gateway] [MET-RIC metric]]

-f   Clears the routing tables of all gateway entries. If this is used in conjunction with one of the commands, the tables are cleared prior to running the command.

-p When used with the ADD command, makes a route persistent across boots of the system. By default, routes are not preserved when the system is restarted. When used with the PRINT command, displays the list of registered persistent routes. Ignored for all other commands, which always affect the appropriate persistent routes.

- command Specifies one of four commands

PRINT	Prints a route
ADD	Adds a route
DELETE	Deletes a route
CHANGE	Modifies an existing route

- destination Specifies the host.

- MASK If the MASK keyword is present, the next parameter is interpreted as the netmask parameter.

- netmask If provided, specifies a sub-net mask value to be associated with this route entry. If not specified, it defaults to 255.255.255.255.

- gateway Specifies gateway.

- METRIC specifies the metric/cost for the destination

All symbolic names used for destination are looked up in the network database file NETWORKS. The symbolic names for gateway are looked up in the host name database file HOSTS. If the command is print or delete, wildcards may be used for the destination and gateway, or the gateway argument may be omitted.

```
C:\>
Active Routes:
Network Address Netmask Gateway Address Interface
   Metric 127.0.0.0 255.0.0.0 127.0.0.1 127.0.0.1 1
220.100.100.0 255.255.255.0 220.100.100.8 220.100.100.8 1
   220.100.100.8 255.255.255.255 127.0.0.1 127.0.0.1 1
   220.100.100.255 255.255.255.255 220.100.100.8 220.100.100.8 1
224.0.0.0 224.0.0.0 220.100.100.8 220.100.100.8 1
255.255.255.255 255.255.255.255 220.100.100.8 220.100.100.8 1
```

- tracert   Depending on which argument is issued on the command line, the following information is obtained.

```
C:\>tracert
Usage: tracert [-d] [-h maximum_hops] [-j host-list] [-
w timeout] target_name
Options:
- d Do not resolve addresses to hostnames.
- h maximum_hops Maximum number of hops to search for target.
- j host-list Loose source route along host-list.
- w timeout Wait timeout milliseconds for each reply.
C:\>
```

Tracing route to renegade [220.100.100.79] over a maximum of 30 hops:
1 One of the IP options is invalid.
Trace complete.

————————————————————————————

Dynamic Host Configuration Protocol (DHCP)

DHCP has its roots in the Internet and RFCs that make the constituent parts what they are. In Windows NT, some variations exist with regard to DHCP concepts and terminology. So, for that reason, some native DHCP information is presented here and then information specific to Windows NT.

DHCP Considerations

DHCP was designed to supply DHCP clients with the configuration parameters defined in the Host Requirements RFCs. After obtaining parameters through DHCP, a DHCP client should be able to exchange packets with any other host in the Internet.

Not all of these parameters are required for a newly initialized client. A client and server may negotiate transmission of those parameters required by the client or specific to a particular subnet.

DHCP allows but does not require the configuration of client parameters not directly related to the IP protocol. DHCP also does not address registration of newly configured clients with the Domain Name System. DHCP original design intent is not intended to configure routers.

DHCP Terms

DHCP client   A DHCP client is an Internet host using DHCP to obtain configuration parameters such as a network address.

DHCP server   A DHCP server is an Internet or intranet host that returns configuration parameters to DHCP clients.

BOOTP relay agent   A BOOTP relay agent or relay agent is an Internet host or router that passes DHCP messages between DHCP clients and DHCP servers. DHCP is designed to use the same relay agent behavior as specified in the BOOTP protocol specification.

Binding   A binding is a collection of configuration parameters, including at least an IP address, associated with or bound to a DHCP client. Bindings are managed by DHCP servers.

DHCP Design Intent   The original design intent of DHCP includes:

- DHCP should be a mechanism rather than a policy. DHCP must allow local system administrators control over configuration parameters where desired; this means local system administrators should be able to enforce local policies concerning allocation and access to local resources, where desired.
- Clients should require no manual configuration. Each client should be able to discover appropriate local configuration parameters without user intervention and incorporate those parameters into its own configuration.
- Networks should require no manual configuration for individual clients. Under normal circumstances a network manager should not have to manually enter any per-client configuration parameters.
- DHCP should not require a server on each subnet. To allow for scale and economy, DHCP must work across routers or through the intervention of BOOTP relay agents.
- A DHCP client must be prepared to receive multiple responses to a request for configuration parameters. Some installations might include multiple, overlapping DHCP servers to enhance reliability and increase performance.
- DHCP must coexist with statically configured, non-participating hosts and with existing network protocol implementations.

- DHCP must work with the BOOTP relay agent behavior as described by RFC 951 and 1542.

- DHCP must provide service to existing BOOTP clients.

- DHCP requirements include the following, specific to the transmission of network layer parameters:

- Guarantee that any network address is not in use by more than one DHCP client at a time.

- Retain DHCP client configuration across DHCP client reboot. A DHCP client should, whenever possible, be assigned the same configuration parameters (for example, network address) in response to each request.

- Retain DHCP client configuration across server reboots.

- A DHCP client should be assigned the same configuration parameters despite restarts of the DHCP mechanism.

- Allow automated assignment of configuration parameters to new clients to avoid hand configuration for new clients.

- Support fixed or permanent allocation of configuration parameters to specific clients.

DHCP & NT

In Windows NT, DHCP is used the same way in the Internet and in intranets. It is designed around a client/server method of communication. A DHCP server and DHCP clients are required to be in the NT network for proper operation to be performed. The basic purpose for a DHCP server in a NT network is to provide IP addresses to NT clients who request them. In addition to allocation of DHCP addresses, a DHCP server is able to provide statistics about the network. The significance of DHCP servers cannot be overstated.

In an environment particularly with numerous hosts and hosts that are portable and moved frequently, a DHCP server is beneficial. In such an environment, the DHCP server administrates configuration information without having to have human intervention. Another feature DHCP provides is a security function. The security achieved is by the allocation of the IP addresses because these addresses can be revoked by a network administrator. Furthermore, the length of time wherein IP addresses are valid is controllable and therefore another angle of security is achieved.

DHCP assigns addresses to requesting clients because of an address range of addresses. This assignment of an IP address to a requesting client on behalf of a DHCP server is considered a *loan* from the DHCP server's perspective.

Windows Internet Naming Service (WINS)

The purpose of WINS is to map NetBIOS computer names to IP addresses in a TCP/IP network. WINS itself is based on RFCs 1001 and 1002. These RFCs define a NetBIOS name resolution over TCP/IP. NetBIOS is a session layer protocol and has in years past been the protocol used in Microsoft networks. However, now TCP/IP is built into Windows NT and is becoming the protocol of choice.

WINS provides a centralized management approach. With the WINS manager, WINS servers can be managed and replication partners set up. WINS also provides dynamic name registration, release, and renewal for clients using the service. Another advantage of WINS is the ability to browse resources in a computer network separated by a router without the need for a domain controller. Furthermore, broadcast traffic is reduced when a WINS server is used, because it supplies an IP address for each name query message received.

Domain Name System (DNS)

The organization of the domain system derives from some assumptions about the needs and usage patterns of its user community, and it is designed to avoid complicated problems found in general purpose databases.

The following assumptions concerning the DNS are:

1. The size of the total database initially is proportional to the number of hosts using the system, but eventually grows to be proportional to the number of users on those hosts, as mailboxes and other information are added to the domain system.

2. Most of the data in the system changes very slowly (for example, mailbox bindings, host addresses), but the system should be able to deal with subsets that change more rapidly (on the order of seconds or minutes).

3. The administrative boundaries used to distribute responsibility for the database usually correspond to organizations that have one or

more hosts. Each organization that has responsibility for a particular set of domains provides redundant name servers, either on the organization's own hosts or other hosts that the organization arranges to use.

4. Clients of the domain system should be able to identify a trusted name servers they prefer to use before accepting referrals to name servers outside of this "trusted" set.

5. Access to information is more critical than instantaneous updates or guarantees of consistency. Hence the update process enables updates to percolate out through the users of the domain system rather than guaranteeing that all copies are simultaneously updated. When updates are unavailable due to network or host failure, the usual course is to believe old information while continuing efforts to update it. The general model is that copies are distributed with timeouts for refreshing. The distributor sets the timeout value and the recipient of the distribution is responsible for performing the refresh. In special situations, very short intervals can be specified, or the owner can prohibit copies.

6. In any system that has a distributed database, a particular name server might be presented with a query that can only be answered by some other server. The two general approaches to dealing with this problem are "recursive," in which the first server pursues the query for the client at another server, and "iterative," in which the server refers the client to another server and enables the client to pursue the query. Both approaches have advantages and disadvantages, but the iterative approach is preferred for the datagram style of access. The domain system requires implementation of the iterative approach, but enables the recursive approach as an option.

7. The domain system assumes that all data originates in master files scattered through the hosts that use the domain system. These master files are updated by local system administrators. Master files are text files that are read by a local name server, and hence become available through the name servers to users of the domain system. The user programs access name servers through standard programs called resolvers.

8. The standard format of master files enables them to be exchanged between hosts (through FTP, mail, or some other mechanism); this facility is useful when an organization wants a domain, but doesn't

want to support a name server. The organization can maintain the master files locally using a text editor, transfer them to a foreign host which runs a name server, and then arrange with the system administrator of the name server to get the files loaded.

9. Each host's name servers and resolvers are configured by a local system administrator RFC−1033. For a name server, this configuration data includes the identity of local master files and instructions on which non-local master files are to be loaded from foreign servers. The name server uses the master files or copies to load its zones. For resolvers, the configuration data identifies the name servers, which should be the primary sources of information.

10. The domain system defines procedures for accessing the data and for referrals to other name servers. The domain system also defines procedures for caching retrieved data and for periodic refreshing of data defined by the system administrator.

A system administrators provides:

- The definition of zone boundaries.
- Master files of data.
- Updates to master files.
- Statements of the refresh policies desired.

The domain system provides:

- Standard formats for resource data.
- Standard methods for querying the database.
- Standard methods for name servers to refresh local data from foreign name servers.

Elements of DNS   The DNS has three major components: Domain Name Space and Resource Records, Name Servers, and Resolvers.

DOMAIN NAME SPACE and RESOURCE RECORDS   are specifications for a tree structured name space and data associated with the names. Conceptually, each node and leaf of the domain name space tree names a set of information, and query operations are attempts to extract specific types of information from a particular set. A query names the domain name of interest and describes the type of resource information that is desired.

For example, the Internet uses some of its domain names to identify hosts; queries for address resources return Internet host addresses.

NAME SERVERS are server programs that hold information about the domain tree's structure and set information. A name server may cache structure or set information about any part of the domain tree, but in general a particular name server has complete information about a subset of the domain space, and pointers to other name servers that can be used to lead to information from any part of the domain tree. Name servers know the parts of the domain tree for which they have complete information; a name server is said to be an AUTHORITY for these parts of the name space. Authoritative information is organized into units called zones, and these zones can be automatically distributed to the name servers, which provide redundant service for the data in a zone.

RESOLVERS are programs that extract information from the name servers in response to client requests. Resolvers must be able to access at least one name server and use that name server's information to answer a query directly, or pursue the query using referrals to other name servers. A resolver typically is a system routine that is directly accessible to user programs; hence no protocol is necessary between the resolver and the user program.

These three components roughly correspond to the three layers or views of the domain system. Consider a detailed explanation here that correlates this.

- From the user's point of view, the domain system is accessed through a simple procedure or OS call to a local resolver.

- The domain space consists of a single tree and the user can request information from any section of the tree.

- From the resolver's point of view, the domain system is composed of an unknown number of name servers. Each name server has one or more pieces of the whole domain tree's data, but the resolver views each database as essentially static.

- From a name server's point of view, the domain system consists of separate sets of local information called zones. The name server has local copies of some of the zones. The name server must periodically refresh its zones from master copies in local files or foreign name servers. The name server must concurrently process queries that arrive from resolvers.

In the interest of performance, implementations may couple these functions. For example, a resolver on the same machine as a name server might share a database consisting of the zones managed by the name server and the cache managed by the resolver.

Domain Name Space and Resource Records The domain name space is a tree structure. Each node and leaf on the tree corresponds to a resource set (which may be empty). The domain system makes no distinctions between the uses of the interior nodes and leaves, and this memo uses the term "node" to refer to both. Each node has a label, which is zero to 63 octets in length. Brother nodes may not have the same label, although the same label can be used for nodes that are not brothers. One label is reserved, and that is the null (that is, zero length) label used for the root.

The domain name of a node is the list of the labels on the path from the node to the root of the tree. By convention, the labels that compose a domain name are printed or read left to right, from the most specific (lowest, farthest from the root) to the least specific (highest, closest to the root).

Internally, programs that manipulate domain names should represent them as sequences of labels, where each label is a length octet followed by an octet string. Because all domain names end at the root, which has a null string for a label, these internal representations can use a length byte of zero to terminate a domain name.

By convention, domain names can be stored with arbitrary case, but domain name comparisons for all present domain functions are done in a case-insensitive manner, assuming an ASCII character set, and a high order zero bit. This means that you are free to create a node with label "A" or a node with label "a," but not both as brothers; you could refer to either using "a" or "A." When you receive a domain name or label, you should preserve its case. The rationale for this choice is that we might someday need to add full binary domain names for new services; existing services would not be changed.

When a user needs to type a domain name, the length of each label is omitted and the labels are separated by dots ("."). Because a complete domain name ends with the root label, this leads to a printed form, which ends in a dot. We use this property to distinguish between:

- A character string that represents a complete domain name (often called "absolute"). For example, "joejones.ISI.EDU."

- A character string that represents the starting labels of a domain name, which is incomplete, and should be completed by local software using knowledge of the local domain (often called "relative"). For example, "joejones" used in the ISI.EDU domain.

Relative names are either taken relative to a well known origin, or to a list of domains used as a search list. Relative names appear mostly at the user interface, where their interpretation varies from implementation to implementation, and in master files, where they are relative to a single origin domain name. The most common interpretation uses the root "." as either the single origin or as one of the members of the search list, so a multi-label relative name is often one where the trailing dot has been omitted to save typing.

To simplify implementations, the total number of octets that represent a domain name (that is, the sum of all label octets and label lengths) is limited to 255. A domain is identified by a domain name, and consists of that part of the domain name space that is at or below the domain name, which specifies the domain. A domain is a subdomain of another domain if it is contained within that domain. This relationship can be tested by seeing if the subdomain's name ends with the containing domain's name. For example, A.B.C.D is a subdomain of B.C.D, C.D, D, and " ".

DNS technical specifications do not mandate a particular tree structure or rules for selecting labels; its goal is to be as general as possible, so that it can be used to build arbitrary applications. In particular, the system was designed so that the name space did not have to be organized along the lines of network boundaries, name servers, and so on. The rationale for this is the choice of implied semantics should be left open to be used for the problem at hand, and different parts of the tree can have different implied semantics. For example, the IN-ADDR.ARPA domain is organized and distributed by network and host address, because its role is to translate from network or host numbers to names; NetBIOS domains RFC−1001, RFC−1002 are flat, because that is appropriate for that application.

However, some guidelines apply to the "normal" parts of the name space used for hosts, mailboxes, and so on. This makes the name space more uniform, provides for growth, and minimizes problems in conversion from host tables to DNS. The political decisions about the top levels of the tree originated in RFC−920.

Before the DNS can be used to hold naming information for some kind of object, two needs must be met:

- A convention for mapping between object names and domain names. This describes how information about an object is accessed.

- RR types and data formats for describing the object.

These rules can be quite simple or fairly complex. Very often, the designer must take into account existing formats and plan for upward compatibility for existing usage. Multiple mappings or levels of mapping might be required. For hosts, the mapping depends on the existing syntax for host names, which is a subset of the usual text representation for domain names, together with RR formats for describing host addresses, and so on. A reliable inverse mapping from address to host name requires a special mapping for addresses into the IN-ADDR.ARPA domain, and hence it is thus defined.

For mailboxes, the mapping is slightly more complex.

Mapping of mailbox info is performed in the following manner:

1. Mail address <local-part>@<mail-domain> is mapped into a domain name by converting <local-part> into a single label (regardless of dots it contains).

2. Conversion of <mail-domain> into a domain name using text format for domain names (dots denote label breaks), and then concatenation of the two to form a single domain name is performed.

3. Hence, the mailbox hostmaster@sri-nic.arpa is represented as a domain name by hostmaster.sri-nic.arpa. Reasons behind this design also must take into account the scheme for mail exchanges as explained in RFC−974 and those applicable since the issuance of that RFC.

A typical user is not concerned with defining these rules, but should understand that they usually are the result of numerous compromises between desires for upward compatibility with old usage, interactions between different object definitions, and the inevitable urge to add new features when defining the rules. The way the DNS is used to support some object is often more crucial than the restrictions inherent in the DNS.

The following figure shows a part of the current domain name space, and is used in many examples applicable in numerous RFCs. The actual tree is a very small subset of the actual name space.

In this example, the root domain has three immediate subdomains: MIL, EDU, and ARPA. The LCS.MIT.EDU domain has one immediate subdomain named XX.LCS.MIT.EDU.

Much more information about the DNS is available on the Internet. One of the best sources I have found is:

```
ftp://ftp.ncren.net
```

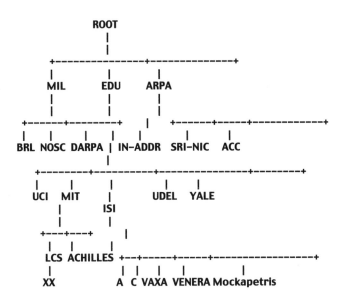

Some RFCs that provide helpful information for DNS include:

1031 MILNET name domain transition. W.D. Lazear. Nov−01−1987.
(Format:TXT=20137 bytes) (Status: UNKNOWN)

1032 Domain administrators guide. M.K. Stahl. Nov−01−1987.
(Format: TXT=29454 bytes) (Status: UNKNOWN)

1033 Domain administrators operations guide. M. Lottor. Nov−01−
1987. (Format: TXT=37263 bytes) (Status: UNKNOWN)

1034 Domain names—concepts and facilities. P.V. Mockapetris.
Nov−01−1987. (Format: TXT=129180 bytes) (Obsoletes RFC0973,
RFC0882, RFC0883) (Obsoleted by RFC1065, RFC2308) (Updated
by RFC1101, RFC1183, RFC1348, RFC1876, RFC1982, RFC2065,
RFC2181, RFC2308, RFC2535) (Also STD0013) (Status:
STANDARD)

1035 Domain names—implementation and specification. P.V.
Mockapetris. Nov−01−1987. (Format: TXT=125626 bytes) (Obsoletes
RFC0973, RFC0882, RFC0883) (Updated by RFC1101, RFC1183,
RFC1348, RFC1876, RFC1982, RFC1995, RFC1996, RFC2065,
RFC2181, RFC2136, RFC2137, RFC2308, RFC2535) (Also STD0013)
(Status: STANDARD)

1183 New DNS RR Definitions. C.F. Everhart, L.A. Mamakos, R. Ullmann, P.V. Mockapetris. Oct–01–1990. (Format: TXT=23788 bytes) (Updates RFC1034, RFC1035) (Status: EXPERIMENTAL)

1664 Using the Internet DNS to Distribute RFC1327 Mail Address Mapping Tables. C. Allocchio, A. Bonito, B. Cole, S. Giordano & R. Hagens. August 1994. (Format: TXT=50783 bytes) (Obsoleted by RFC2163) (Status: EXPERIMENTAL)

2535 Domain Name System Security Extensions. D. Eastlake. March 1999. (Format: TXT=110958 bytes) (Updates RFC2181, RFC1035, RFC1034) (Status: PROPOSED STANDARD)

2536 DSA KEYs and SIGs in the Domain Name System (DNS). D. Eastlake. March 1999. (Format: TXT=11121 bytes) (Status: PROPOSED STANDARD)

2537 RSA/MD5 KEYs and SIGs in the Domain Name System (DNS). D. Eastlake. March 1999. (Format: TXT=10810 bytes) (Status: PROPOSED STANDARD)

2538 Storing Certificates in the Domain Name System (DNS). D. Eastlake, O. Gudmundsson. March 1999. (Format: TXT=19857 bytes) (Status: PROPOSED STANDARD)

2539 Storage of Diffie-Hellman Keys in the Domain Name System (DNS). D. Eastlake. March 1999. (Format: TXT=21049 bytes) (Status: PROPOSED STANDARD)

2540 Detached Domain Name System (DNS) Information. D. Eastlake. March 1999. (Format: TXT=12546 bytes) (Status: EXPERIMENTAL)

2541 DNS Security Operational Considerations. D. Eastlake. March 1999. (Format: TXT=14498 bytes) (Status: INFORMATIONAL)

NetBEUI

NetBEUI is a protocol of evolution. NetBIOS, a session layer protocol, was developed in the early 1980s for IBM. One of its purposes was to make networking APIs available to user applications, so that they could obtain and provide network services. Inherent in NetBIOS was a transport layer protocol known as NetBIOS Frames Protocol (NBFP). This transport aspect of NetBIOS eventually became known as NetBIOS Extended User Interface (NetBEUI). NetBEUI became known as the protocol of choice to transport data traffic among small LANs.

As a result, NetBEUI became the transport protocol for Microsoft networks. A confusion still exist today between NetBIOS and NetBEUI. NetBIOS is a protocol, still widely used today, that can be intermixed and used with IPX/SPX and TCP/IP. Because NetBIOS is a session layer protocol, it can utilize the transport layer protocols found in IPX/SPX and TCP/IP. NetBEUI, on the other hand, is tied to NetBIOS. NetBEUI is a relatively small protocol (compared to the size of other protocols) and operationally it is quick. Because of the design of NetBEUI operations, it is not suited well for medium to large networks; its true forte is small networks.

IPX/SPX

IPX/SPX is a Novell network protocol. It is supported by Windows NT. Before examining the operating of IPX/SPX with NT, consider some IPX/SPX information.

NetWare can be evaluated by its layers based on the OSI model. Figure 15-8 best exemplifies this.

At the lowest layer, there is support for adapter cards. NetWare supports multiple adapter cards including:

- Ethernet
- Token ring
- 802.3
- FDDI

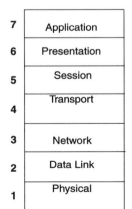

Figure 15-8
OSI layers and
Netware

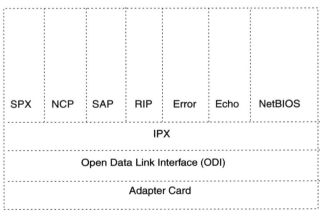

7	Application							
6	Presentation							
5	Session							
4	Transport	SPX	NCP	SAP	RIP	Error	Echo	NetBIOS
3	Network	IPX						
2	Data Link	Open Data Link Interface (ODI)						
1	Physical	Adapter Card						

- ATM
- others

The next layer is called the Open Data Link Interface (ODI). This is a specification for the data link layer providing hardware and thus media protocol independence. Some drawings of the NetWare protocol stack do not show this layer, but nevertheless it is there. The standard was the fruition of joint work among multiple corporations including Apple and Novell. Technically, the specification is more than just a data link specification, it defines four independent yet cohesive subcomponents. Before examining the details of ODI consider Figure 15-9 showing the sub-layers.

Figure 15-9 shows to sub-layers where ODI operates. ODI is shown compared to the OSI layers, particularly the data link layer as it is broken into the MAC and LLC sub-layers.

Internet Packet Exchange (IPX)   IPX operates at layer three based on the OSI model. It is a datagram protocol based on a best effort delivery system. As Figure 15-8 depicts, the correlation is directly with the network layer. It operates as a best effort delivery system where packet delivery is accomplished on a best effort delivery mechanism. In other words, packet

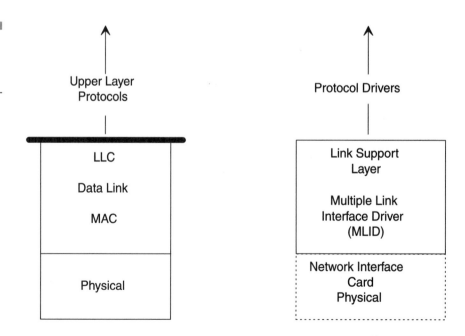

Figure 15-9
OSI layers 1 and 2 and Netware Integration

delivery has no relationship to other packets. This means no logical order of delivery.

IPX is connectionless oriented. This means that no acknowledgments are sent from the receiving hosts to the originating host to indicate receipt of packets. Because of this connectionless oriented nature, acknowledgment and related topics are left to higher level protocols or programs to perform. Hence, deduction is obvious that this protocol is faster than those above it, as shown in Figure 15-8.

Even though IPX operates at the network layer three based on the OSI model, it does perform transport layer functions. In this sense, a one-to-one correlation is not accurate between NetWare and the OSI model.

Sequenced Packet Exchange (SPX)   SPX operates above IPX. It is a connection-oriented protocol. Specialized applications can be built using this as the base protocol. Characteristics of SPX include insured packet delivery, and the capability of recovering from lost data and errors that might occur in the data being passed from origin to destination. Another characteristic that makes the protocol robust is that it does not acknowledge each and every packet but waits until the maximum number of outstanding packets is reached. In NetWare lingo, this is referred to as a *window*. Operationally, SPX performs some functions similar to the transport layer based on the OSI model, and after it is finished, makes a program call to IPX for packet delivery. In short, SPX and IPX operate together to some degree. Perspective of its relationship pictorially to the NetWare model is shown in Figure 15-8.

NetWare Core Protocol (NCP)   NetWare's NCP is a defined protocol that the procedure file servers' operating systems utilize to respond to requests and accept requests made to it. Functionally, NCP controls client and server operations by defining interactions between them. The NCP provides a similar service to SPX in that it performs some packet error checking. It also has built into it session control between entities. The NCP uses a number placed inside the request field of an NCP packet to request a given service. The reason for this is that NetWare services are given a number by a NetWare file server. Details of this protocol are Novell proprietary information. Hence, few details can be provided. It does seem however that general consensus agrees that NCP is the shell used on workstations.

Service Advertising Protocol (SAP)   Positionally, this protocol resides on top of IPX. It uses IPX to perform its function. SAP does as its name implies; it functions with nodes that provide services to *advertise* available services. Examples of available services include print and file servers. Gateway servers could be included in this as well. Those nodes that provide services broadcast SAP information periodically.

Router Information Protocol (RIP)   RIP is the routing information protocol used on NetWare networks. Functions performed by RIP include location of the best (fastest route) from a workstation to a network. RIP is used by routers to exchange information about routes, respond to request from routers and workstations, and perform periodic routing table broadcasts among routers.

Error Protocols   This protocol is operationally used among peer protocols. Programs that attempt to communicate with a host on a different network use NCP and IPX to attempt to reach that network. If, for some reason, that network is unreachable, an error packet is generated by a router and sent back to the requesting host regarding the state of the route to the target host. Interestingly, this function is portrayed in Figure 15-8 above the IPX layer, but functionally it seems that it operates at the IPX layer.

Echo   Understanding echo is similar to understanding PING in TCP/IP. This protocol is used to check the ability to check a path en route to a target destination. If the path is functional and the target node accessible, the echo protocol in the target node is designed such that it literally echos the packet back to the destination.

Review   NetWare is complex. It consist of multiple parts that perform different functions. Some are used in special situations whereas others are used in most installations. Many variations on the NetWare protocol stack exist. This is a solid representation of those constituent components of NetWare. This section did not address NetWare functionality in different environments, because those are discussed later.

Open Data Interface (ODI) Concepts   ODI is a concept for protocol independence. Its roots are in the philosophy of providing a consistent interface to multiple transport layer protocols. Hence, network hardware independence can be achieved. When this is achieved, greater implementation and flexibility is realized.

ODI actually consists of three parts. Consider Figure 15-10.

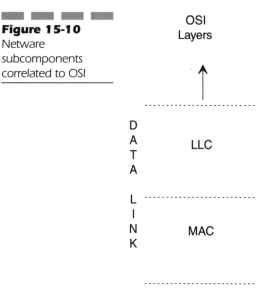

Figure 15-10
Netware
subcomponents
correlated to OSI

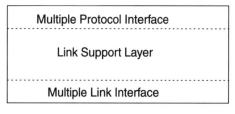

Figure 15-10 shows the subcomponents, they include:

- Multiple Protocol Interface
- Link support layer
- Multiple link interface driver

The protocol part of the specification calls for support for a diverse blend of protocols. In fact, if any protocol is coded against this OSI specification, then independence is achievable. These protocol drivers however, must operate at the network layer and above.

The next part of the specification is the link support layer. The primary purpose of this layer is routing. The routing referred to here is between protocol drivers and multiple link interface drivers. Figure 15-11 provides a closer view of the link support layer and its interaction with the layers above and below it.

Figure 15-11 shows two interfaces. One provides a connectivity point with the network layer, it is called the multiple protocol interface. As its name implies, the interface is designed to operate with multiple protocols at the network layer and above. This interface was designed for developers creating program code, so that they would have a standard interface to program into regardless the protocol.

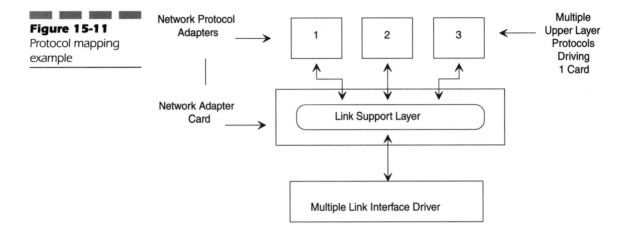

Figure 15-11
Protocol mapping
example

The multiple link interface has the same philosophy behind it as the multiple protocol interface. This interface was designed as a common ground for data link layer protocol developers to have a common standard to code against.

The link support layer includes performing a number of functions including: coordinate numbers assigned to multiple link interface drivers after these interface drivers have been identified with the link support layer, manage the protocol stack identification assigned to network protocol drivers, manage individual network protocol drivers through their identification number even though frames can be grouped according to MAC frame type, and be capable of manipulating media identification using specific frame formatting.

The fundamental purpose for having media identification and protocol identification is so the packets can be routed from a given upper layer protocol stack to the correct lower layer protocol interface. Basic to this idea is the notion that this be possible without re-booting the system.

The multiple link interface driver (MLID). The purpose of the multiple link interface driver is to pass data to and from the network media. The specification calls for these drivers to be protocol independent.

Implementing ODI   ODI is implemented differently according to operating system, device driver, network protocol, and NetWare version. The functionality behind it is a three-fold concept. Figure 15-12 is an example of the first concept behind the implementation.

Figure 15-12 shows multiple upper layer protocol drivers against one network interface card. This is possible because of the ODI concept. This example is one of the possible functions that can be performed.

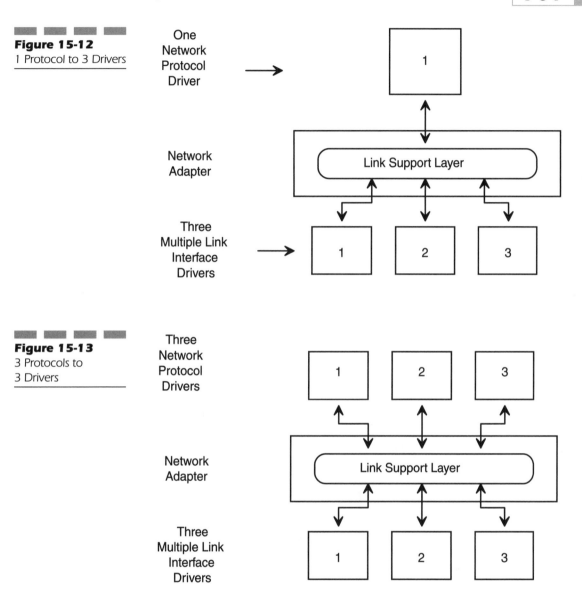

Figure 15-12
1 Protocol to 3 Drivers

One
Network
Protocol
Driver

Network
Adapter

Three
Multiple Link
Interface
Drivers

Figure 15-13
3 Protocols to
3 Drivers

Three
Network
Protocol
Drivers

Network
Adapter

Three
Multiple Link
Interface
Drivers

Figure 15-13 is a different example of how ODI functionality occurs.

Figure 15-13 is the converse of Figure 15-11. In Figure 15-12, one network protocol driver is used against the link support layer and three multiple link interface drivers are used. This is a ODI converse implementation.

Figure 15-14
Highlighted view of
ODI implementation

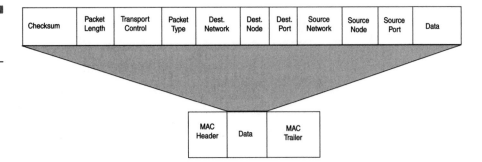

Checksum	Packet Length	Transport Control	Packet Type	Dest. Network	Dest. Node	Dest. Port	Source Network	Source Node	Source Port	Data

MAC Header	Data	MAC Trailer

Figure 15-14 is another example of how the ODI concept is implemented. In Figure 15-14, multiple network protocol drivers are hooked into the link support layer to drive three multiple link interface drivers. Three is not a magic number with this concept; it could be two or four just as easily.

How ODI is Managed   The functionality of an ODI implementation is managed through a configuration file. This file consists of basically three components:

- Protocol
- Link support
- Link driver

These components contain parameters that control the ODI operating environment. The protocol parameters are used in the logical *BIND*, which is created between the upper layer network protocol and the multiple link interface driver. Link support reflects storage used at this part of the layer. The link driver parameters reflect the characteristics of the interface board used. Other configuration parameters might be required by different environments and because of that variety the environment manuals need to be referenced.

IPX   IPX is used to define addressing schemes used in internetwork and intranetwork environments. NetWare network segments use numbers to identify them primarily for routing purposes. This section explores IPX packet structure and provides additional information concerning its function in a NetWare network.

IPX Packet Structure   IPX packets are carried in the data portion of a MAC frame. Details about MAC frames have been provided previously in this book and the focus here is on the IPX protocol; specifically its structure and contents. Figure 15.15 illustrates the IPX packet structure, components, and its relationship to a MAC frame.

Figure 15-15 shows the relationship between a MAC frame and an IPX packet. Inside the IPX packet are field names.

Sockets and Ports Novell refers to destination and source *sockets*. However, practically speaking these *sockets* are understood better by their function, and that function is a port. From henceforth, where Novell makes reference to a socket the term *port* is used, unless significant meaning is changed and then clarification of this is provided. The term socket actually refers to a network, host, and port number just as in TCP/IP protocols.

IPX Field Explanation Each field in the IPX packet has significant meaning. The following is a brief explanation of those meanings.

- Checksum. This field is responsible for performing packet level checking.
- Packet Length. This field contains the internetwork packet length. This includes the header and the data section.
- Transport Control. This field is used by routers between internetworks. Primarily this is used by NetWare based routers.
- Packet Type. This field indicates the service provided by the packet regardless of whether this service required or merely offered.

The packet type is indicated by a value. The value indicates the specific service provided. Some of the noted values and corresponding services include:

0   Unknown type of packet

1   Routing Information Packet (RIP)

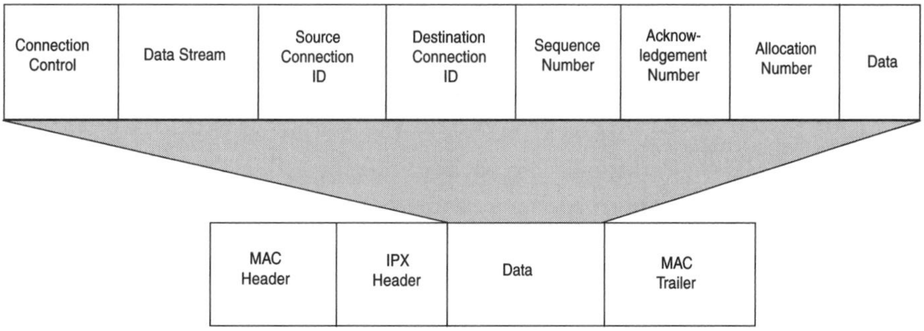

Figure 15-15
Highlighted view of MAC frame and IPX packet relationship

2   Echo Packet
3   Error Packet
4   Packet Exchange Packet
5   Sequenced Packet Protocol Packet
16–31   Designated experimental protocols
17   NetWare Core Protocol (NCP)

- Destination Network. This field identifies the target network. Each network in a NetWare networking environment requires unique network numbers.

- Destination Node. This address identifies nodes on a given network.

- Destination Port. This address indicates a *process or function* address.

- Source Network. This field identifies the network (by number) on which the source host is located.

- Source Node. This address indicates a given node address. In any given instance, a host may function as either a source or destination host.

- Source Port. This is the port number that originally submitted the packet onto the network.

- Data. This field includes user data and other information from higher layers.

IPX is the heart of NetWare. All protocols operating above it move down the protocol stack and are enveloped into this packet. Actually, it is similar to TCP/IP in this regard; for example, regardless if TCP or UDP protocols are used either are enclosed into an IP packet.

IPX Addressing   IPX uses an addressing scheme similar to TCP/IP. A network address is assigned to a NetWare network, Node addresses are assigned to each node on a given network, and the network protocol used by nodes on the network has identifiable ports or access points. In TCP/IP, the combination of a network, host, and port address create what is called a socket. In NetWare, the lingo uses sockets to refer to a parallel concept of a port.

In NetWare the network address is comprised by a 4 byte value. Host addresses use six bytes for an address. The socket address is a two byte address. The socket address reflects that address on which a server listens and receives a request. The following is an example of some identified sockets:

```
File Servers:
```

451h NetWAre Core Protocol

Routers:

452h   Service Advertising Protocol

453h   Routing Information Protocol

Workstations:

4000h—6000h Used for the interaction with file servers and other network communications

455h   NetBIOS

456   Diagnostics

Additional addressing is used in environments such as with the LAN-RES product, but these addresses affect that aspect of communications with NetWare that is located actually in a different network. The addressing affects NetWare indirectly.

Sequence Packet Exchange (SPX)   SPX is a connection-oriented protocol that applications requiring such services can use to operate in a NetWare network. By default, SPX uses IPX. However, SPX has a completely different set of functions.

SPX Packet Structure

SPX packet has its own fields that perform functions differently from IPX, but SPX utilizes IPX as it goes down the protocol stack. Consider Figure 15-16.

Figure 15-16 shows the SPX datagram behind an IPX header inside a MAC frame. This is how it appears at the data link layer.

Figure 15-16
SPX Packet Structure

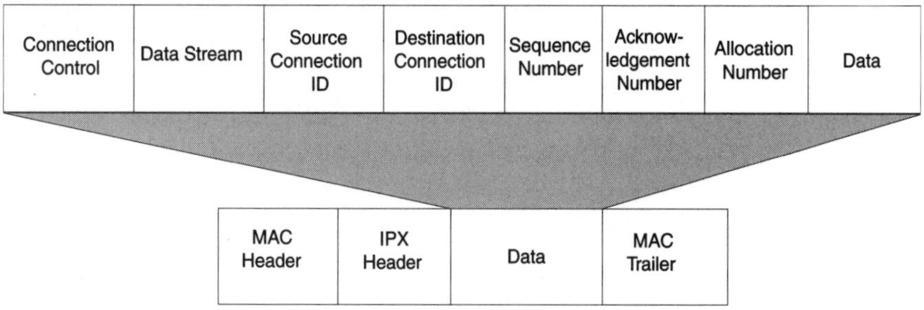

| Connection Control | Data Stream | Source Connection ID | Destination Connection ID | Sequence Number | Acknow-ledgement Number | Allocation Number | Data |

| MAC Header | IPX Header | Data | MAC Trailer |

SPX Field Contents   The following lists the fields and their purpose in an SPX packet.

- *Connection Control.*   This field controls bi-directional data flow between connections.

- *Datastream.*   This field indicates the type data found in the packet.

- *Source Connection ID.*   This field identifies the originating point of this packet. This field is also responsible for multiplexing packets of data as they leave the node, if this function is required.

- *Destination Connection ID.*   This field identifies the target point for the packet. The destination point may perform de-multiplexing if required.

- *Sequence Number.*   This field is responsible for maintaining a packet count on each side of the connection. The sending side maintains a count and the receiving side maintains a count.

- *Acknowledgment Number.*   This field performs packet orientation functions. It indicates sequence numbers of the expected SPX packets that should be received.

- *Allocation Number.*   This is a number that is used to indicate the number of outstanding receive buffers in a given direction at one time.

- *Data.*   This field contains data used by the application requiring the SPX protocol.

This packet, namely SPX itself, is considered a transport protocol that uses IPX as a delivery service from origin to destination. Packets exchanged between origin and destination SPX points have sequence numbers assigned to them. By these numbers a determination can be made to check for out-of-sequence, duplicate, or missing packets.

Not all applications require SPX, except specialized ones such as gateways and applications requiring session oriented services.

Even though this much detail is generally not presented with IPX/SPX operation in the same explanation with NT, the operational aspect of IPX/SPX is much the same as in native mode. In fact, the NWLink IPX/SPX compatible transport is Microsoft's "hook" if you will that supports IPX/SPX. Setup and operation of the NWLink is oriented to the native functions of IPX/SPX.

DLC

Data Link Control (DLC) is a protocol used to enable Windows NT connectivity to SNA networks. This protocol enables low levels of communication to be established, thus enabling upper layer applications in NT networks to communicate with SNA environments. It is a protocol that requires enabling for SNA interconnectivity and BackOffice application use.

STREAMS

This protocol option is probably not as widespread in use as some might think. Its purpose is to provide the support and utilities people might use to work with UNIX based, or styled, STREAMS drivers and protocols to a NT environment.

Remote Procedure Call (RPC)

RPC services is basically a set of dynamic load libraries that operate as runtime DLLs. They support distributed applications in a networked environment. The way RPC is implemented in a NT environment is utilization of a name service provider. This name service provider locates and registers servers on an NT network. Support for the Distributed Computing Environment (DCE) cell directory service and the Microsoft locator is provided.

Service Advertising Protocol (SAP)

The SAP support provided by NT is a service used to handle the NetWare compatible service advertisements, which would generally be native to NetWare.

Workstation

This service is part of NT that operates simply as a client. Its primary responsibility is directory sharing, file maintenance, and so forth.

NetBIOS

NetBIOS is the network basic input/output system. This is an interface that some programs require to interact with Windows 95, NT, OS/2 and some UNIX environments. Its operational nature is higher up in the layers of a network; it enables request for lower layer network services to be answered and achieved.

Client Service for NetWare

This service is provided to enable workstations and servers to interact with NetWare networks and workstations. This enables file and print sharing along with other NetWare services. This service must be enabled for inter-operation with NetWare.

Computer Browser

This service is what makes possible the viewing of other computers in the network. Without this service network, computers/systems are not visible.

Server

This is a service that enables the computer to operate as a server to clients on a network. It must be enabled for the network to function as a server.

Remote Access Service (RAS)

This is a feature that enables remote workstations to participate in the network as if they were physically attached to it. This service must be configured on the system operating as a server and on the systems operating as workstations for dial-up or switched connections to operate.

LMHosts

This is considered a service as well. Technically, it is a file that maps systems with IP addresses to NetBIOS computer names for those systems using NetBIOS in their network; this is particularly true for computers using NetBIOS outside the local subnet where the LMHosts file is located.

Windows 2000, Windows NT, and Servers

Selecting a network server is no trivial task. I believe you should spend a proportional amount of time and money to obtain the right server for your operations. In addition, take the necessary time to select the right operating system. At the time of this writing Windows 2000 is in server and Professional form. The information here is about a Netfinity server used in this case study.

If you intend to run only one server in your network, then you should know as much as possible about what its strengths and limitations are. You should also know what the current and future requirements are for your network and the server to be positioned in it. Consider Figure 15-17 as it illustrates a front view of a Netfinity 7000.

From the front, the Netfinity is very accessible. Disk drives can be easily removed and inserted (without any tools). The open bays are readily accessible, just behind a front panel that also can be removed without any tools. The LED display shows the status of the system during boot. Different LEDs immediately above it reveal any status information about devices such as power supplies, and so on.

Consider Figure 15-18.

This illustration shows a front and rear view of the Netfinnity. Notice the front view shows the system fans. They are easily accessible after the top cover is removed. The top cover can be removed without any tools, two strong thumb screws more than secure the top cover.

The rear of the Netfinity shows the power supplies, connection points, and vacant slots. The system's power supplies can be easily replaced. It is

Figure 15-17

View of lab server

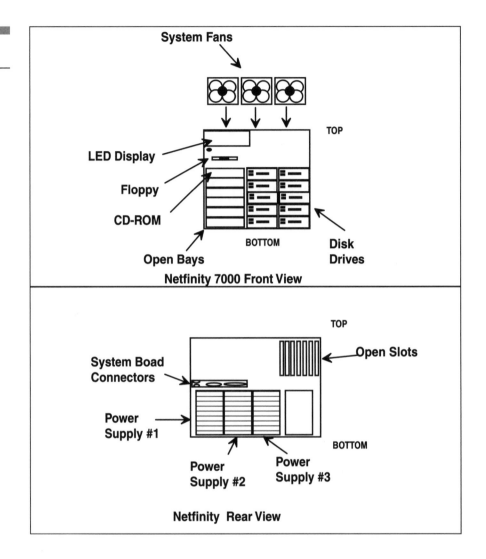

designed for three, however two are more than sufficient. Because the place exist for a third, I recommend having a third on-hand, just in case. The system is easily accessible with the open slots at the top and marked clearly.

Consider the inside view of Figure 15-19.

With the removal of a single panel, the Netfinity is very accessible. From the top, all memory is accessible. The memory card can be removed without any tools and upgrades made in literally minutes. The same is true for the processors. The processor card can be removed, upgraded, and re-inserted

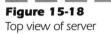
Figure 15-18
Top view of server

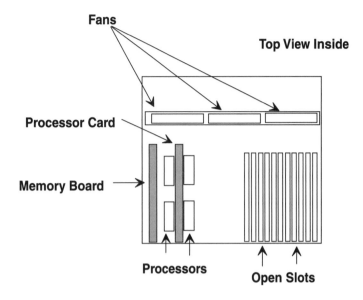

Netfinity Top View

in minutes. The open slots, which are numbered, are easy to work with when inserting interface boards. In short, the server used in this case study was able to utilize the power provided by Windows products (both 2000 in beta form and NT).

Windows 2000, Windows NT, and Servers

This case study used a NetFinity 7000 as mentioned previously. A unique aspect of the server is that it is typically offered as a *shell*, and then *dressed* to the degree deemed appropriate by the user. This server used RAID to accommodate the amount of storage used. This server also uses multiple interface cards due to its multihomed nature, SCSI storage adapter card for external silo storage, internal CD, multi-processors, and software to manage the system as a whole.

Many other servers exist in the marketplace and are well suited for Windows 2000 and Windows NT. For example, Compaq, Dell, Gateway, and Micron are companies that offer systems that are well suited for Windows 2000. I recommend you obtain additional information.

Figure 15-19
Typical peripherals
used with NT

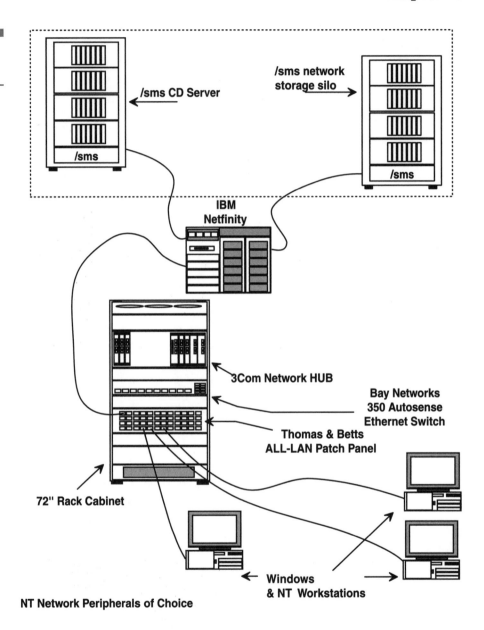

/sms CD Server

/sms network
storage silo

/sms

/sms

IBM
Netfinity

3Com Network HUB

Bay Networks
350 Autosense
Ethernet Switch

Thomas & Betts
ALL-LAN Patch Panel

72" Rack Cabinet

Windows
& NT Workstations

NT Network Peripherals of Choice

Windows Networking Peripherals

Another key part of any Windows based network is the network peripherals. Most networks today are increasingly intermixed with audio, video, data, and multimedia.

Network Storage Products

The demand for storage these various forms of information take puts heavy loads on systems as they were some five to eight years ago. Now, the norm is for ever increasing amounts of storage and that it be online. Consider Figure 15-20.

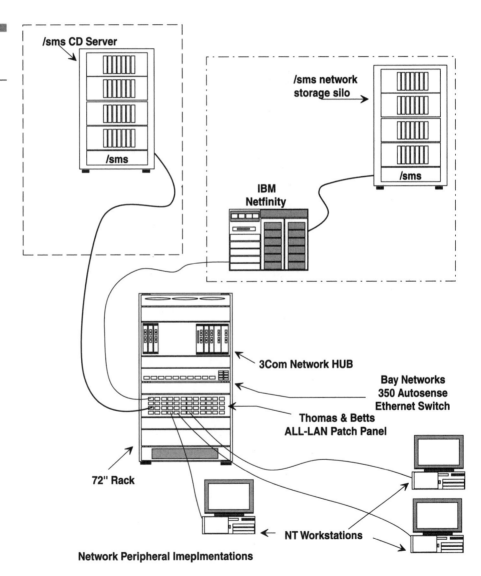

Figure 15-20
Network perifpheral implementations

Network Peripheral Imeplmentations

This illustration depicts one aspect of the network I designed. The /SMS storage products are probably the second most important components of the network after the Netfinity 7000. The /SMS products make large numbers of CDs, DVDs, and vast amounts of data, video, and multimedia available to the entire network. Figure 15-21 shows a different implementation of the same equipment.

Consider the /SMS servers as shown in Figure 15-21. One silo (as this author calls it) is connected to the IBM Netfinity. The other is directly connected to the network through the patch panel, where it is then connected to the BAY Network's Hub. The advantage of /SMS's multiple ways to connect their devices to a network enables load balancing from many different angles. For example, the Netfinity can accommodate the silo as shown in the illustration without any degradation. The other silo can be connected to the network, because it has a Fast Ethernet connectivity module than enables it to function as a stand-alone device. This level of modularity in regard to the /SMS device connectivity makes for an attractive network peripheral.

Two factors make /SMS products network peripherals of choice; those are flexibility and simplicity. The /SMS products ease of use is a refreshing experience. These devices are powerful network peripheral products and a main factor in their power is their ease of use. A point that could be overlooked about these products is their modularity. It is possible to break these systems down into bays of seven devices and implement them in an entirely different modular fashion.

Based on my experience with /SMS at all levels, their personnel are professionals from end to end. I had numerous conversations with a variety of individuals during the planning stages of this network design. I discovered one of the most talented individuals about SCSI technology I have spoke with in years. The /SMS products may be peripheral in regard to their place in the network, but the value they deliver is high. At the center of networks is information in some form or the other. The /SMS products make that information accessible. From that perspective, I think these products *are* the network, because they house the essence of the network.

Network Tape Drive

Most networks today require some form of backup ability. I determined early on in the design phase this network was no different, and in fact, it actually needed a superior method for backup. After exploring the options available, I selected a SONY AIT tape drive. Consider Figure 15-22.

This illustration shows the tape drive connected to a Windows workstation. This is exactly how I used it in this network. From that workstation alone, I can backup any device on the network. The beauty behind this design is that it offloads another function to a workstation that can be monitored and controlled like a stand-alone workstation or even managed remotely. Anyway the actual function of backup is performed, and the SONY AIT tape drive is a superior product. The media it uses has memory in the cassette; this makes for quick searches and location of stored data. The native amount of storage the device is designed to accommodate is 25

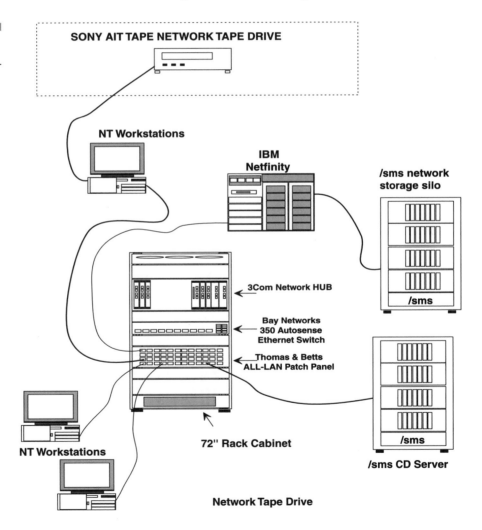

Figure 15-22
Network tape drive

GIG, and 50 GIG when compressed. It is an ideal device to backup any devices on the network whether they are workstations or servers.

Network Printing

Another critical aspect of network operation is network printing. Consider Figure 15-23.

Figure 15-23
Network printer

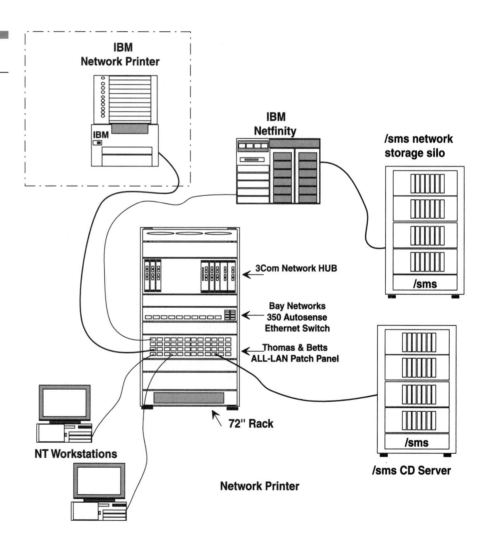

Windows Operating Systems support a variety of printers. In my network, I used a network printer. This illustration shows the IBM network printer used. I selected it for numerous reasons: dual network interface cards, the ability to accommodate large amounts of on-board memory, duplexing support, and multiple paper trays—including an envelope feeder that feeds and prints envelopes as simply as paper. The printer also has a secure mail-bin.

Windows Administration: Practical Examples

Windows 2000 and NT are both powerful operating systems. Different ways to obtain information about servers and workstations in a network exist, and all the methods provide valuable information. Technically, the best way to perform much administration is to do so prior to the implementation. I speak from experience, and this pre-supposes you have actual experience to do pre-administration planning. What I mean by pre-administration planning is to determine which protocol is used, security levels, domains to be named, workgroups to be identified, any remote access service to be used, and so forth. If you have this level of information in the early stages of network planning, you will be better off.

Network Administration Information

Knowing the state of the systems on your network is important. Microsoft has created and matured some excellent tools over the years to enable the users and administrators. Here, I am presented two different ways to obtain system information. First, is through Dr. Watson and the second is the system report method.

```
System snapshot taken on 4/21/99 5:21:17 PM.

*--> Summary/Overview <--*

Dr. Watson found nothing obviously unusual.

User's Remarks:

*--> System Information <--*

Microsoft Windows 98 4.10.1998
```

```
Upgrade using CD

/SrcDir5D:\WIN98 /IQ /U:xxxxxxxxxxxxxxxxx

IE 4.0 4.72.3110

Uptime: 0:08:29:09

Normal mode

On "THE-HOSTAGE" as "THE-HOSTAGE"

Microsoft

GenuineIntel Pentium(r) Processor

48MB RAM

58% system resources free

Windows-managed swap file on drive C (123MB free)

Temporary files on drive C (123MB free)

*--> Task list <--*

Program Type Path

------

1.  Kernel32.dll 4.10.1998 Microsoft Corporation

2.  MSGSRV32.EXE 4.10.1998 Microsoft Corporation

3.  Mprexe.exe 4.10.1998 Microsoft Corporation

4.  Mstask.exe 4.71.1769.1 Microsoft Corporation

5.  MMTASK.TSK 4.03.1998 Microsoft Corporation

6.  Explorer.exe 4.72.3110.1 Microsoft Corporation

7.  Systray.exe 4.10.1998 Microsoft Corporation

8.  Taskmon.exe 4.10.1998 Microsoft Corporation

9.  Dialotip.exe 1.2.3 Tactical Software

10. Realplay.exe 6.0.3.143 RealNetworks, Inc.

11. MS-DOS 4.10.1998 Microsoft Corporation

12. Msndc.exe 2.5.2.456 Microsoft Corporation

13. MS-DOS 4.10.1998 Microsoft Corporation

14. Aoltray.exe 4.00.000 America Online, Inc.

15. Cmmgr32.exe 6.0.612.0 Microsoft Corporation

16. Rnaapp.exe 4.10.1998 Microsoft Corporation

17. Tapisrv.exe 4.10.1998 Microsoft Corporation

18. Mcdetect.exe 2.5.2.455 Microsoft Corporation
```

19. Spool32.exe 4.10.1998 Microsoft Corporation

20. Drwatson.exe 4.03 Microsoft Corporation

――. Startup Items ,――

Name Loaded from Command

----

1. DOS21 Startup Group C:\WINDOWS\COMMAND.COM

2. MSN Quick View Startup Group "C:\Program Files\ONMSN\MSNDC.EXE"

3. DOS22 Startup Group C:\WINDOWS\COMMAND.COM

4. America Online Tray Icon Startup Group

C:\WINDOWS\aol\aoltray.exe -check

5. WebVCR Tidy Startup Group "C:\Program Files\NetResults\WebVCR\WebVcr.exe" /cleanup

6. SystemTray Registry (Machine Run) SysTray.Exe

7. ScanRegistry Registry (Machine Run) C:\WINDOWS\scanregw.exe /autorun

8. TaskMonitor Registry (Machine Run) C:\WINDOWS\taskmon.exe

9. bpcpost.exe Registry (Machine Run) C:\WINDOWS\SYSTEM\bpcpost.exe

10. LoadPowerProfile Registry (Machine Run)

Rundll32.exe powrprof.dll,LoadCurrentPwrScheme

11. _z_netmip Registry (Machine Run)

C:\Program Files\Tactical Software\DialOutIP\DIALOTIP.EXE

12. RealTray Registry (Machine Run)

C:\Program Files\Real\RealPlayer\RealPlay.exe SYSTEMBOOTHIDEPLAYER

13. SchedulingAgent Registry (Machine Service) mstask.exe

14. LoadPowerProfile Registry (Machine Service)

Rundll32.exe powrprof.dll,LoadCurrentPwrScheme

――. Kernel Drivers ,――

Driver Loaded from Type Likely path

----

1. VMM Microsoft Corporation Virtual Machine Manager

2. VCACHE Microsoft Corporation Cache manager

3. DFS 4.10.1998 Microsoft Corporation DFS Virtual Device (Version 4.0)

4. PERF Microsoft Corporation System Monitor data collection driver

5. VPOWERD4.10.1998 Microsoft Corporation VPOWERD Virtual Device (Version 4.0)

6. VPICD Microsoft Corporation Hardware interrupt manager

7. VrtwD 1.1.075.2 Intel Corporation Real-Time Clock VxD

8. VTD Microsoft Corporation Timer device driver

9. VWIN32 Microsoft Corporation Win32 subsystem driver

10. VXDLDR Microsoft Corporation Dynamic device driver loader

11. NTKERN Microsoft Corporation Windows Driver Model

12. CONFIGMG Microsoft Corporation Configuration manager

13. PCI 4.10.1998 Microsoft Corporation PCI Virtual Device (Version 4.0)

14. ISAPNP4.10.1998 Microsoft Corporation ISAPNP Virtual Device (Version 4.0)

15. BIOS 4.10.1998 Microsoft Corporation BIOS Virtual Device(Version 4.0)

16. VCDFSD Microsoft Corporation CD-ROM filesystem driver

17. IOS Microsoft Corporation I/O Supervisor

18. PAGEFILE Microsoft Corporation Swapfile driver

19. PAGESWAP Microsoft Corporation Swapfile manager

20. PARITY Microsoft Corporation Memory parity driver

21. REBOOT Microsoft Corporation Ctrl1Alt1Del manager

22. EBIOS Microsoft Corporation Extended BIOS driver

23. VDD Microsoft Corporation Display driver

24. S3MINI 4.10.1695 Microsoft Corporation S3 Virtual Device (Version 4.0)

25. VSD Microsoft Corporation Speaker driver

26. COMBUFF Microsoft Corporation Communications buffer driver

27. VCD Microsoft Corporation Communications port driver

28. VMOUSE Microsoft Corporation Mouse driver

29. MSMINI 4.10.1998 Microsoft Corporation MSMINI Virtual Device (Version 4.0)

30. VKD Microsoft Corporation Keyboard driver

31. VPD Microsoft Corporation Printer driver

32. INT13 Microsoft Corporation BIOS hard disk emulation driver

33. VMCPD Microsoft CorporationMath coprocessor driver

34. BIOSXLATMicrosoft Corporation BIOS emulation driver

35. VNETBIOS4.10.1998 Microsoft Corporation VNETBIOS Virtual Device (V. 4.0)

36. NDIS 4.10.1998 Microsoft Corporation NDIS Virtual Device (Version 4.0)

37. PPPMAC 4.10.1998 Microsoft Corporation Windows Virtual PPP Driver

38. NWLINK 4.10.1998 Microsoft Corporation Windows IPX/SPX-Compatible Protocol Driver

39. VTDI 4.10.1998 Microsoft Corporation Windows TDI Support Driver

40. NETBEUI 4.10.1998 Microsoft Corporation NETBEUI Virtual Device (Version 4.0)

41. WSOCK2 4.10.1998Microsoft Corporation Windows Sockets Driver 2 TCP/IP only.

42. WSOCK 4.10.1998 Microsoft Corporation Windows Sockets Driver

43. WSIP«TIM»4.10.1998 Microsoft Corporation Windows Sockets IPX/SPX Protocol Driver

44. NSCL 4.10.1998 Microsoft Corporation NSCL Virtual Device (Version 4.0)

45. VIP 4.10.1998 Microsoft Corporation Windows IP Driver

46. MSTCP 4.10.1998 Microsoft Corporation Windows TCP Driver

47. VDHCP 4.10.1726 Microsoft Corporation DHCP VxD Driver

48. VNBT 4.10.1719 Microsoft Corporation VNBT VxD Driver

49. AFVXD 4.10.1998 Microsoft Corporation Windows Sockets VTDI Driver

50. DOSMGR Microsoft Corporation MS-DOS emulation manager

51. VSHARE Microsoft Corporation File sharing driver

52. VMPOLL Microsoft Corporation System idle-time driver

53. VFIXD Version 1.00 Company Name VxD File Description

54. VCOMM Microsoft Corporation Communications port Plug and Play driver

55. VCOND Microsoft Corporation Console subsystem driver

56. VTDAPI Microsoft Corporation Multimedia timer driver

57. JAVASUP 4.79.2405 Microsoft Corporation
Microsoftw Virtual Machine Helper Device for Java

58. VFLATD Microsoft Corporation Linear aperture video driver

59. Display1

60. mmdevldr 4.10.1998 Microsoft Corporationmmdevldr Virtual Device(V4.0)

61. APIX _ Microsoft Corporation APIX Virtual Device (Version 4.0)

62. CDTSD 4.10.1998 Microsoft Corporation CDTSD Virtual Device (Version 4.0)

63. CDVSD 4.10.1998 Microsoft Corporation CDVSD Virtual Device (Version 4.0)

64. DiskTSD 4.10.1998 Microsoft Corporation DiskTSD Virtual Device (Version 4.0)

65. voltrack 4.10.1998 Microsoft Corporation
voltrack Virtual Device (Version 4.0)

scsi1hlp 4.10.1998 Microsoft Corporation scsi1hlp Virtual Device (Version 4.0)

67. BIGMEM4.10.1998 Microsoft Corporation BIGMEM Virtual Device (Version 4.0)

68. AOLMAC Version 1.27 America Online AOL Network Driver

69. SPAP 4.10.1998 Microsoft Corporation SPAP Virtual Device (Version 4.0)

70. HSFLOP 4.10.1998Microsoft Corporation HSFLOP
    Virtual Device (Version 4.0)

71. ESDI_5064.10.1998 Microsoft Corporation

ESDI_506 Virtual Device (Version 4.0)

72. LPTENUM 4.10.1998 Microsoft Corporation

LPTENUM Virtual Device (Version 4.0)

73. SERENUM4.10.1998Microsoft CorporationSERENUM
    Virtual Device (Version 4.0)

74. VSB16

75. DSOUND4.05.01.1998Microsoft CorporationDirectSound
    Virtual Device

76. vjoyd4.05.01.1998Microsoft CorporationJoystick
    Virtual Device

77. SBAWE4.37.00.1998Creative Technology Ltd.

Creative SB-AWE32 Synthesizer Virtual Device Driver

78. sage 4.71.1016Microsoft Corporation sage Virtual
    Device (Version 4.0)

79. TSPROXY

Version 1.00

Company Name

VxD File Description

80. WSHTCP 4.10.1998 Microsoft Corporation Windows
    Sockets TCP helper Driver

81. UNIMODEM4.10.1998Microsoft CorporationUNIMODEM
    Virtual Device(Version 4.0)

82. LOGGER4.10.1998Microsoft CorporationLOGGER Virtual
    Device (Version 4.0)

83. TSCOMMIP Version 1.00 Company Name VxD File
    Description

84. FIOLOG 4.10.1998 Microsoft Corporation File I/O
    Logging VxD for Application Defrag

85. DRVWCDB3.10.36aSeagate Software, Inc.Device Driver

86. DRVWPPQT3.10.36aSeagate Software, Inc.Device Driver

87. DRVWQ1173.10.36aSeagate Software, Inc.Device Driver

88. VDMADMicrosoft Corporation Direct Memory Access
    controller driver

89. V86MMGR Microsoft Corporation MS-DOS memory manager

90. SPOOLERMicrosoft Corporation Print spooler

91. VFAT Microsoft Corporation FAT filesystem driver

92. VDEF Microsoft Corporation Default filesystem driver

93. UDF Microsoft Corporation ?

94. CDFS 4.10.1998 Microsoft Corporation

CDFS Virtual Device (Version 4.0)

95. IFSMGR Microsoft Corporation File system manager

96. NWREDIR 4.10.1998 Microsoft Corporation

NWREDIR Virtual Device (Version 4.0)

97. VNETSUP 4.10.1998 Microsoft Corporation

VNETSUP Virtual Device (Version 4.0)

98. VREDIR 4.10.1998 Microsoft Corporation

VREDIR Virtual Device (Version 4.0)

99. VSERVER 4.10.1998 Microsoft Corporation

VSERVER Virtual Device (Version 4.0)

100. VFBACKUP Microsoft Corporation Floppy backup
     helper driver

101. SHELL Microsoft Corporation Shell device driver

102. DRWATSON 4.03 Microsoft Corporation Dr. Watson
     for Windows 98

103. el9032.05.00 3Com Corporation

3Com Fast EtherLink XL / EtherLink XL Network Miniport
  Driver

104. wmidrv

105. swenum

106. PCIMP

107. hidvkd

108. wdmfs

--> User-Mode Drivers <--*

Driver Type Path

------

1. mmsystem.dll 4.03.1998 Microsoft Corporation

2. power.drv 4.10.1998 Microsoft Corporation

3. sbfm.drv 4.00 Creative Technology Ltd.

4. sb16snd.drv 4.37.00.1998 Creative Technology Ltd.

5. msacm.drv 4.03.1998 Microsoft Corporation

6. midimap.drv 4.03.1998 Microsoft Corporation

7. msjstick.drv 4.05.01.1998 Microsoft Corporation

8. sbawe32.drv 4.37.00.1998 Creative Technology Ltd.

--> MS-DOS Drivers <--

Name Type

------

1. HIMEM Device driver

2. DBLBUFF Device driver

3. IFSHLP Device driver

4. DOSKEY TSR program

--> 16-bit Modules <--

Name Type Path

------

1. KERNEL 4.10.1998 Microsoft Corporation

2. SYSTEM 4.10.1998 Microsoft Corporation

3. KEYBOARD 4.10.1998 Microsoft Corporation

4. MOUSE 9.01.0.000 Microsoft Corporation

5. DISPLAY 4.10.1686 Microsoft Corporation

6. DIBENG 4.10.1998 Microsoft Corporation

7. SOUND 4.10.1998 Microsoft Corporation

8. COMM 4.10.1998 Microsoft Corporation

9. GDI 4.10.1998 Microsoft Corporation

10. USER 4.10.1998 Microsoft Corporation

11. DDEML 4.10.1998 Microsoft Corporation

12. MSPLUS 4.40.500 Microsoft Corporation

13. MSGSRV32 4.10.1998 Microsoft Corporation

14. MMSYSTEM 4.03.1998 Microsoft Corporation

15. POWER 4.10.1998 Microsoft Corporation

16. LZEXPAND 4.00.429 Microsoft Corporation

17. VER 4.10.1998 Microsoft Corporation

18. SHELL 4.10.1998 Microsoft Corporation

19. COMMCTRL 4.10.1998 Microsoft Corporation

```
20. NETWARE 4.10.1998 Microsoft Corporation
21. SBFM 4.00 Creative Technology Ltd.
22. SB16SND 4.37.00.1998 Creative Technology Ltd.
23. CSPMAN 4.12.1 Creative Technology Ltd.
24. MSACMMAP 4.03.1998 Microsoft Corporation
25. MSACM 4.03.1998 Microsoft Corporation
26. MMTASK 4.03.1998 Microsoft Corporation
27. MIDIMAP 4.03.1998 Microsoft Corporation
28. MSJSTICK 4.05.01.1998 Microsoft Corporation
29. SBAWE32 4.37.00.1998 Creative Technology Ltd.
30. SYSTHUNK 4.10.1998 Microsoft Corporation
31. OLECLI 1.20.000 Microsoft Corporation
32. OLESVR 1.10.000 Microsoft Corporation
33. COMMDLG 4.00.950 Microsoft Corporation
34. GRABBER 4.10.1998 Microsoft Corporation
35. WINOLDAP 4.10.1998 Microsoft Corporation
36. PIFMGR 4.10.1998 Microsoft Corporation
37. DCIMAN 4.03.1998 Intel(R) Corp., Microsoft Corp.
38. MSVIDEO 4.03.1998 Microsoft Corporation
39. TSP3216S 4.10.1998 Microsoft Corporation
40. UNIMDM 4.10.1998 Microsoft Corporation
41. UMDM16 4.10.1998 Microsoft Corporation
42. WAN 4.10.1998 Microsoft Corporation
43. NDSWAN16 4.10.1998 Microsoft Corporation
44. PSCRIPT 4.10.1998 Microsoft Corporation
45. TOOLHELP 4.10.1998 Microsoft Corporation
```

NT Diagnostic Report Information

The case study network used for obtaining information has numerous hosts located in it. I used multiple operating systems because of the number of systems required to perform an adequate case study. The following information is a diagnostic report I obtained to present to you for consideration.

This level of information is really helpful, particularly when you have different operating systems and multiple hosts in the same network. Notice some similarities exist between the server information listed previously and the workstation information that follows here for the workstation names *RICK*.

```
Diagnostics Report For \\RICK
-----------------------------------
OS Version Report
-----------------------------------
Microsoft (R) Windows NT (TM) Workstation
Version 4.0 (Build 1381: Service Pack 1)×86 Uniprocessor
Free
Registered Owner: Rick, The-Black-Hole
Product Number: 17597-OEM20023333-22375
-----------------------------------
System Report
-----------------------------------
System: AT/AT COMPATIBLE
Hardware Abstraction Layer: PC Compatible Eisa/Isa HAL
BIOS Date: 07/24 /97
BIOS Version: BIOS Version 0.11.01.DU0M- Beta
Processor list:
0:×86 Family 6 Model 3 Stepping 3 GenuineIntel ,265 Mhz
-----------------------------------
Video Display Report
-----------------------------------
BIOS Date: 07/21 /97
BIOS Version: S3 86C775/86  C785  Video  BIOS.  Version
1.01.11-C2.08.05
Adapter:
Setting: 640×480×256
60 Hz
Type: s3mini compatible display adapter
String: S3 Compatible Display Adapter
Memory: 2 MB
Chip Type: S3 Trio64V2
DAC Type: S3 SDAC
Driver:
Vendor: S3 Incorporated
File(s): s3mini.sys, s3disp.dll
Version: 1.03.10, 4.0.0
```

```
----------------------------------------
Drives Report
----------------------------------------
C:\ (Local-FAT) RICK Total: 1,023,824KB, Free: 783,664KB
D:\ (Local-FAT) RICK-D Total: 2,096,320KB, Free: 2,090,208KB
E:\ (Local-FAT) Total: 999,632KB, Free: 999,616KB
----------------------------------------
Memory Report
----------------------------------------
Handles: 1,300
Threads: 127
Processes: 19
Physical Memory (K)
Total: 32,180
Available: 5,752
File Cache: 6,844
----------------------------------------
Services Report
----------------------------------------
Computer Browser Running (Automatic)
IBM DMI Service Layer (DMI Service Layer) Running (Automatic)
EventLog (Event log) Running (Automatic)
Server Running (Automatic)
Workstation (NetworkProvider) Running (Automatic)
PC System Monitor Running (Automatic)
TCP/IP NetBIOS Helper Running (Automatic)
Messenger Running (Automatic)
Norton SpeedDisk Running (Automatic)
Plug and Play (PlugPlay) Running (Automatic)
Remote Access Autodial Manager Running (Automatic)
Remote Access Connection Manager (Network) Running (Manual)
Remote Procedure Call (RPC) Service Running (Automatic)
Spooler (SpoolerGroup) Running (Automatic)
Telephony Service Running (Manual)
----------------------------------------
Drivers Report
----------------------------------------
AFD Networking Support Environment (TDI) Running (Automatic)
Remote Access Mac (NDIS) Running (Automatic)
Beep (Base) Running (System)
Cdfs (File system) Running (Disabled)
```

```
Cdrom (SCSI CDROM Class) Running (System)
cs32ba11 (Base) Running (System)
Disk (SCSI Class) Running (Boot)
Intel 82557-based PRO Adapter Driver (NDIS) Running (Automatic)
Fastfat (Boot file system) Running (Disabled)
Floppy (Primary disk) Running (System)
i8042 Keyboard and PS/2 Mouse Port Driver (Keyboard Port)
Running (System)
Keyboard Class Driver (Keyboard Class) Running (System)
KSecDD (Base) Running (System)
LM78 Running (Automatic)
Mouse Class Driver (Pointer Class) Running (System)
Msfs (File system) Running (System)
Mup (Network) Running (Manual)
Microsoft NDIS System Driver (NDIS) Running (System)
Microsoft NDIS TAPI driver (NDIS) Running (System)
Remote Access WAN Wrapper (NDISWAN) Running (Automatic)
NetBIOS Interface (NetBIOSGroup) Running (Manual)
WINS Client(TCP/IP) (PNP_TDI) Running (Automatic)
Npfs (File system) Running (System)
Null (Base) Running (System)
Parallel (Extended base) Running (Automatic)
Parport (Parallel arbitrator) Running (Automatic)
ParVdm (Extended base) Running (Automatic)
PIIXIDE (SCSI miniport) Running (Boot)
Remote Access Auto Connection Driver (Streams Drivers)
Running (Automatic)
Remote Access ARP Service (PNP_TDI) Running (Automatic)
Rdr (Network) Running (Manual)
S3Inc (Video) Running (System)
Serial (Extended base) Running (Automatic)
Srv (Network) Running (Manual)
TCP/IP Service (PNP_TDI) Running (Automatic)
VgaSave (Video Save) Running (System)
------------------------------------
IRQ and Port Report
------------------------------------
Devices Vector Level Affinity
------------------------------------
i8042prt 1 1 0xffffffff
i8042prt 12 12 0xffffffff
```

```
Serial 4 4 0x00000000
cs32ball 55 7 0x00000001
E100B 10 10 0x00000000
Floppy 6 6 0x00000000
PIIXIDE 0 14 0x00000000
PIIXIDE 0 15 0x00000000
------------------------------------
Devices Physical Address Length
------------------------------------
i8042prt 0x00000060 0x0000000001
i8042prt 0x00000064 0x0000000001
Parport 0x000003bc 0x0000000003
Serial 0x000003f8 0x0000000007
cs32ball 0x00000530 0x0000000008
cs32ball 0x00000388 0x0000000004
E100B 0x0000ff40 0x0000000014
Floppy 0x000003f0 0x0000000006
Floppy 0x000003f7 0x0000000001
LM78 0x00000295 0x0000000002
PIIXIDE 0x000001f0 0x0000000008
PIIXIDE 0x0000ffa0 0x0000000008
PIIXIDE 0x00000170 0x0000000008
PIIXIDE 0x0000ffa8 0x0000000008
S3Inc 0x000003c0 0x0000000010
S3Inc 0x000003d4 0x0000000008
VgaSave 0x000003b0 0x000000000c
VgaSave 0x000003c0 0x0000000020
VgaSave 0x000001ce 0x0000000002
------------------------------------
DMA and Memory Report
------------------------------------
Devices Channel Port
------------------------------------
cs32ball 1 0
cs32ball 0 0
Floppy 2 0
------------------------------------
Devices Physical Address Length
------------------------------------
E100B 0xffbef000 0x00000014
E100B 0xffbef000 0x00000014
```

```
S3Inc 0×000a0000 0×00010000
S3Inc 0×000c0000 0×00008000
VgaSave 0×000a0000 0×00020000
-----------------------------------------
Environment Report
-----------------------------------
System Environment Variables
ComSpec=C:\WINNT40\system32\cmd.exe
Os2LibPath=C:\WINNT40\system32\os2\dll;
Path=C:\WINNT40\SYSTEM32;C:\WINNT40;C:\SVA\DMI\BIN
windir5C:\WINNT40
OS5Windows_NT
PROCESSOR_ARCHITECTURE=×86
PROCESSOR_LEVEL=6
PROCESSOR_IDENTIFIER=×86 Family 6 Model 3 Stepping 3, Gen-
uineIntel
PROCESSOR_REVISION=0303
NUMBER_OF_PROCESSORS=1
help=c:\ipfwin\help
ipf_path=c:\ipfwin
Environment Variables for Current User
TEMP=C:\TEMP
TMP=C:\TEMP
-----------------------------------
Network Report
-----------------------------------
Your Access Level: renegade
Workgroup or Domain: IWI
Network Version: 4.0
LanRoot: INFO
Logged On Users: 1
Current User (1): Administrator
Logon Domain: RICK
Logon Server: RICK
Transport: NetBT_E100B1, 00-60-94-45-43-F3, VC's: 2, Wan: Wan
Character Wait: 3,600
Collection Time: 250
Maximum Collection Count: 16
Keep Connection: 600
Maximum Commands: 5
Session Time Out: 45
Character Buffer Size: 512
```

```
Maximum Threads: 17
Lock Quota: 6,144
Lock Increment: 10
Maximum Locks: 500
Pipe Increment: 10
Maximum Pipes: 500
Cache Time Out: 40
Dormant File Limit: 45
Read Ahead Throughput: 4,294,967,295
Mailslot Buffers: 3
Server Announce Buffers: 20
Illegal Datagrams: 5
Datagram Reset Frequency: 60
Bytes Received: 16,527
SMB's Received: 58
```

As I mentioned previously, this level of detail is important for future planning, troubleshooting, and general record keeping. If you do not have a baseline and "know" what your systems are, then you should use the example here and some or all of the applicable following commands, and obtain one and keep it on file. The other aspect difficult to explain is how to make all this information work for your environment; diagnostic and troubleshooting are skills that are the result of years of commitment to understanding technology and applying that knowledge to problems that are potentially resolvable.

SUMMARY

In my opinion, Microsoft is the best place to get your information about their operating systems and other software. I have provided you with a cross-section of information here to help you become oriented into not only Windows 2000 but also Windows NT, because it is a product that will most likely stay around for some time. I say this because of practical experience; I have yet to see "the masses" upgrade anything in a single instance—it occurs over time.

The commands and administrative capabilities of Windows operating systems I presented here are commonplace in the day-to-day operation of servers or workstations. If you are using Windows 2000, take the time to access the information included with the product; I think you will find it well worth your time.

16

Transmission Control Protocol/ Internet Protocol

Introduction

I have worked with TCP/IP now some thirteen years. This chapter is one I have wanted to write for some time. I merge my experience, observations, and direct technical information from RFCs made available courtesy of The Internet Society. Information presented here excerpted from RFCs is not intended to replace them, but rather reveal the need for you to explore further information in the RFCs as they relate to each topic. The RFCs used in this chapter can be obtained at

```
ftp://ftp.ncren.net
```

Because of TCP/IP's popularity and widespread use around the world, I have selected topics and presented information I think to be of great value to you. This chapter is not exhaustive on the topic; in fact, numerous books have been written on this topic alone. However, I cover the following topics in this chapter:

- A Closer Look
- Growth in TCP/IP Technology
- Layer Analysis
- TCP/IP Network Requirements
- Internet Protocol Version 4
- Internet Protocol Version 6
- Internet Control Message Protocol
- Address Resolution Protocol
- Reverse Address Resolution Protocol
- Router Protocols
- Transmission Control Protocol
- User Datagram Protocol
- A Perspective on TCP/IP Addressing
- Popular TCP Applications
- Popular UDP Applications
- HyperText Transfer Protocol (HTTP)

At the end of this chapter, I include a list of RFCs that I consider to be significant and recommend you obtain them for additional details.

A Closer Look

In the late 1960s, an entity in the U.S. government called the *Advanced Research Projects Agency* (ARPA) was exploring technologies of all sorts. One of those technologies led to a need (desire) to create a network based on packet switching technology. It was also seen as a means whereby, then current, telephone lines could be used to connect scientists and personnel who were in physically different locations so they work together in this network.

By late in 1969, the necessary components had come together to create the ARPAnet. In short order, a few individuals had put together a network that was capable of exchanging data. Time passed, and additions and refinements were made to ARPAnet.

In the 1970s

In 1971 the *Defense Advanced Research Projects Agency* (DARPA) succeeded the *Advanced Research Project Agency* (ARPA). As a result, the ARPAnet came under the control of DARPA. DARPA's forte was satellite, radio, and packet switching technology.

During the same time, the ARPAnet was using what was called a *Network Control Program* (NCP). Because the NCP was so closely tied to the characteristics of ARPAnet, it had limitations for coping with the areas of research, capabilities, and other requirements. The protocols ARPAnet utilized (namely the NCP) were slow and had periods of network instability, because the technology of that day was primitive by today's standards. Because ARPAnet was now officially under DARPA's umbrella and the realization that a new approach to ARPAnet was needed, a different direction was taken.

In 1974 DARPA sponsored development for a new set of protocols to replace the ones in use at that time. This endeavor led to the development of protocols that were the basis for TCP/IP. The first TCP/IP began to appear in 1974. While these technical developments were in full force, another phenomenon was occurring.

In 1975 the U.S. *Department of Defense* (DoD) put ARPAnet under the control of the *Defense Communication Agency* (DCA). The DCA was responsible for operational aspects of the network. It was then that the ARPAnet became the foundation for the *Defense Data Network* (DDN).

Time passed and TCP/IP continued to be enhanced. Many networks emerged working with and connecting to the ARPAnet with TCP/IP protocols.

In 1978 TCP/IP was stable enough for a public demonstration from a mobile location connecting to a remote location through a satellite. It was a success.

In the 1980s

From 1978 until 1982, TCP/IP gained momentum and was continually refined. In 1982 multiple strides were made. First, DoD adopted TCP/IP protocols and became the overseeing entity for uniting distributed networks. The next year, 1983, DoD formally adopted TCP/IP as the standard protocol to use when connecting to the ARPAnet.

Early 1983, when DoD formally discontinued support for the *Network Control Program* (NCP) and adopted TCP/IP protocol, marks the birth of the Internet. The term Internet was an outgrowth of the term internetworking, which is a technical term used to refer to the interconnection of networks. The term Internet has remained the identifier for the multiple interconnected networks and individual hosts around the world today.

In the 1990s

During the 1990s, the Internet consisted of numerous interconnected networks and a growing number of *Internet Service Providers* (ISPs). The *National Research and Education Network* (NREN) is also a part of the Internet. It would be shortsighted of me if I did not mention America Online, which is a hybrid type ISP; regardless how AOL is categorized, it too is part of the Internet. A hybrid simply means that in the case of AOL, access to the Internet is provided and AOL offers "stuff" as well. In contrast to this are ISPs which offer what has historically been called "raw" Internet access, meaning that the ISP was in fact "invisible" and the user realized benefit of only what the Internet provided. Other networks that part of the Internet include: the *National Science Foundation* network (NSF), NASA, Department of Education, and many others, including educational institutions around the world.

Commercial, educational, and organizations of all types are connected to the Internet. An industry of service providers for the Internet has emerged at a dizzying pace in the 1990s. Many companies in the 1990s have been literally birthed as a result of the presence of Internet core technologies that were not necessarily commercial in their orientation.

The Internet in 21st Century

I think Internet growth is going to continue to rise for years to come for many reasons. I think the move to "everything possible" online is going to continue. There is an entire generation of individuals behind me (and I am not that old) who embrace technology with the same eagerness and openness that my generation did.

Further forces contributing to Internet growth in the next millennium are

- Increased support for Internet access from many different aspects of technology
- Decreased costs for consumers using the Internet
- Increased electronic commerce
- Greater advances in technology making current Internet technology even better
- Increased receptivity to the Internet for purchases on behalf of customers, as casual users today learn more practical ways to integrate the Internet into everyday life to increase productivity in work and communication
- I also believe the Internet, television, radio stations, telephone use, and faxes (as they are known today) are going to merge into one medium, which might well use the Internet as their common link.

Growth in TCP/IP Technology

The previous section gives insight to Internet history. Here, I am presenting some information to those who are beginners so to speak.

The Internet (big I) is based on TCP/IP as the U.S. Government made it the standard. The Internet is worldwide and all sorts of entities are connected to it. Knowing this, we can deduce these entities connected to it are using TCP/IP. This alone counts for a tremendous amount of TCP/IP in the marketplace. At the current rate, it is increasing rapidly.

The 1980s can be characterized as a decade of rapid technological growth. Many companies capitalized on the U.S. government's endorsement of TCP/IP being the standard for the Internet and began producing products to meet this need.

Rapid development of TCP/IP products and acceptance of it in the marketplace nursed the need for additional products. For example, in the 1980s two technologies dominated: PCs and LANs. With the proliferation of PCs and LANs, an entirely new industry began emerging. These technological forces seemed to propel TCP/IP forward, because TCP/IP and PCs made for a good match when implementing LANs. TCP/IP implemented on a single site/single company is referred to as an internet (little i).

Market Forces

A factor that contributed to the growth of TCP/IP in the market was corporate downsizing. This might seem strange, but during the 1980s, I witnessed many cases where TCP/IP based networks grew when others were shrinking. Granted this was not the only reason for TCP/IP's healthy marketshare, but it did contribute.

For example, I experienced downsizing. A corporation (which I will not name) had its corporate offices in the Northeastern United States. This corporation had many (over fifty) satellite offices around the nation. It needed these satellite offices to have independence for daily operations and at the same time be connected to the corporate data center through dedicated 56Kbps lines. They achieved this by implementing TCP/IP based LANs in their satellite offices, and then connecting them to the data center. This example is only one of many I have seen.

Availability

In the late 60's ARPA funded mainframe connectivity between UCLA, UC Santa Barbara, Stanford, and the University of Utah. At this time, a gentleman named Bob Taylor issued a request for proposal to some 140 or so companies to determine the architecture and costs in building the first digital computer network. Bolt, Beranek, and Newman (BBN) was a pivotal company in this endeavor. BBN's brain trust at the time was well known and their engineering prowess great. BBN won the RFP to build the network, and in the last years of the 60s a packet switched network design and implementation began. This is significant because the technology, ideas, and products began to spread. This continued on into the 1970's.

In the late 1970's TCP/IP was proven in a network environment and spread among the "technical intellectual" community- for lack of a better way to say it. In 1983 TCP/IP got an endorsement from the U.S. government with its declaration of compliance requiring entities to use it if they were to work with government agencies. UC Berkeley UNIX included TCP/IP, AT&T's UNIX System V began to incorporate its function, and even IBM had brought TCP/IP for MVS to market by 1990. These forces and growth in related technology seemed to push the availability of TCP/IP into the market.

Individual Knowledge

By the late 1970s and surely into the 1980s, TCP/IP was in most colleges and many educational institutions. Because by the mid 1980s it was shipping free with Berkeley UNIX and availability was there, it became dominant in learning institutions. The obvious occurred: Graduates of educational institutions with many backgrounds, including computer science, had been exposed to TCP/IP.

These individuals entered the workplace in the technical and managerial departments. When it came to a decision about a network protocol many decisions about a network protocol was based on experience. In the 1980s, the marketplace paid a premium for those who understood TCP/IP. Now the market has many individuals with TCP/IP knowledge.

All these factors weaved together to make TCP/IP as dominant as it is today. Surely other factors have contributed as well and as a result, TCP/IP has become a dominant upper layer protocol worldwide.

Layer Analysis

In the early days of the Internet, the term gateway became commonplace. It generally meant a connection from a specific location into the Internet. This was adequate at the time, however now confusion abounds with the use of this term.

According to the American Heritage Dictionary, the term gateway is defined as: "1. An opening, as in a wall or a fence, that may be closed by a gate. 2. A means of access." I believe the original intent of the term's meaning was "A means of access." You are probably wondering why it is even mentioned. Well, today an entire industry based around internetworking and integration has appeared, along with specialized devices. Once such device is a gateway.

A consensus among integrators and those who integrate heterogeneous networks is on the definition of the term *gateway*. It is a device that, at a minimum, converts upper layer protocols from one type to another. For example, TCP can convert to SNA. It can however, convert all seven layers of protocols.

The purpose of explaining this here is simple. Throughout this presentation on TCP/IP, the term gateway might appear. The term had such a foothold in the TCP/IP community that it is still used. Ironically, the term gateway is used in many instances with TCP/IP and the Internet when technically the term that should be used is *router*. Most people in the industry today in fact use the term router.

Overview and Correlation to the OSI Model

TCP/IP is an upper layer protocol. Upper layer protocols operate at layer three and above when analyzed in the context of the OSI model as a baseline. TCP/IP is implemented in software; however some specific implementations have abbreviated TCP/IP protocol stacks implemented in firmware. However, TCP/IP operates on many different hardware and software platforms and over many different data link layer protocols.

The OSI model is a representation of the layers that *should* exist in a network. Figure 16-1 shows TCP/IP with the OSI model layers to the left side.

Notice TCP/IP has three layers: network, transport, and the upper three layers combined together functioning as the application layer. TCP/IP is flexible when it comes to the lower two layers. It does not "see" them, therefore does not care. It can be implemented in a variety of ways. The data link and physical layer which can be used with TCP/IP vary widely and include all the popular data link protocols in use today, as well as use of many different physical interfaces.

TCP/IP can operate with a number of data link layer protocols. Some are listed in Figure 16-1. The remainder of this section highlights popular components at each layer.

Network Layer Components and Functions

OSI model layer three is the network layer. In TCP/IP it is the lowest layer in the TCP/IP protocol suite. TCP/IP network layer components include

Network
Layers

Figure 16-1
TCP/IP & OSI

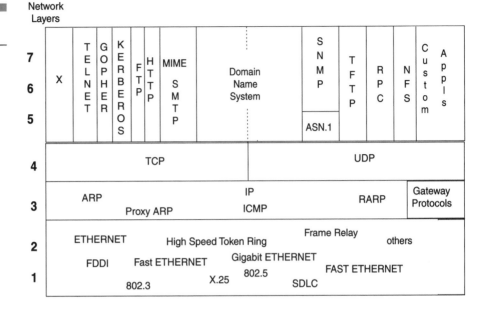

Internet Protocol (IP) IP has an addressing scheme used to identify the host in which it resides. IP is involved in routing functions.

Internet Control Message Protocol (ICMP) ICMP is a required component in each TCP/IP implementation.

Address Resolution Protocol (ARP) ARP dynamically translates IP addresses into physical (hardware interface card) addresses.

Reverse Address Resolution Protocol (RARP) RARP is used to obtain an IP address by broadcasting its hardware address. Typically a RARP server is designated and responds.

Routing Information Protocol (RIP) RIP is a routing protocol used at the network layer. If implemented, it performs routing of packets in the host on which it runs.

Open Shortest Path First (OSPF) This is a routing protocol implemented at the network layer as RIP, but it utilizes knowledge of the Internet topology (as opposed to DV metric) to route packets on the quickest route.

Transport Layer Components and Functions

Layer four at the OSI model is the transport layer, and in TCP/IP layer four is the transport layer. In TCP/IP, TCP and UDP operate.

TCP   This transport layer protocol is considered reliable and it performs retransmissions if necessary.

UDP   This transport layer protocol is considered unreliable, and it does not perform retransmissions; this is left up to the application using its services.

Popular Application Layer Offerings

Above the transport layer in TCP/IP, a number of popular applications exists. A list of these and brief explanations include

X   This is a windowing system that can be implemented in a multi-vendor environment.

TELNET   This application provides remote logon services.

File Transfer Protocol (FTP)   FTP provides file transfer capabilities among heterogeneous systems.

Simple Mail Transfer Protocol (SMTP)   SMTP provides electronic mail services for TCP/IP based users.

Domain Name Service (DNS)   DNS is designed to resolve destination addresses with a name in a TCP/IP network. This service is an automated method of distributing network addresses without having to update host tables manually.

Trivial File Transfer Protocol (TFTP)   This UDP application is often used in initialization of network devices where software must be downloaded. Because TFTP is a simple file transfer protocol, it meets this need well.

Simple Network Management Protocol (SNMP)   This is the way most TCP/IP networks are managed. SNMP is based on an agent and manager arrangement. The agent collects information about a host and the manager maintains status information about hosts by polling agents and accepting information from agents.

Network File System (NFS)   NFS is a protocol that enables remote file systems to appear to be part of the directory system of the client where the user is working.

Remote Procedure Call (RPC)   RPC is a protocol that enables a routine to be called and executed on a server.

Custom Applications   Custom applications can be written using UDP as a transport layer protocol. By doing so, peer-to-peer communications can be achieved between applications. For example, a program can be written to exchange data between a database on a TCP/IP based host and a database on a *Systems Network Architecture* (SNA) based host.

TCP/IP Network Requirements

Before exploring details of TCP/IP, we should discuss basic requirements for a TCP/IP network to function. For example, TCP/IP networks require all participating hosts have TCP/IP operating on each host, and they must be connected to an IP network.

Internet Protocol (IP) Version 4

IP resides at network layer three. IP routes packets (units of data) from the source to destination. Some individuals refer to a packet in the sense of IP as a datagram. An IP datagram is a basic unit moved through a TCP/IP network.

IP is connectionless. It implements two basic functions: fragmentation and addressing. Fragmentation (and reassembly) is accomplished by a field in the IP header. Fragmentation is required when large datagrams must be divided into multiple, smaller datagrams to pass through a network that only transports small datagrams.

IP Version 4 Header Format

The addressing function is also implemented in the IP header. The header includes the source and destination address. The IP header also includes additional information. Figure 16-2 is an example of an IP v.4 header.

The following is a list of the components in the IP header and their meaning.

Version   The version field is used to indicate the format of the IP header.

IHL   IHL stands for *Internet header length*. It is the length of the Internet header in 32 bit words and points to the beginning of data.

Type of Service   The type of service field specifies how the datagram is treated during its transmission through the network.

Total Length   This field indicates the total length of the datagram; this includes the IP header and data.

Flags   The flag field has three bits. They are used to indicate if fragmentation is supported, not to fragment, or indicates more and last fragments.

Figure 16-2
IP Version 4 header

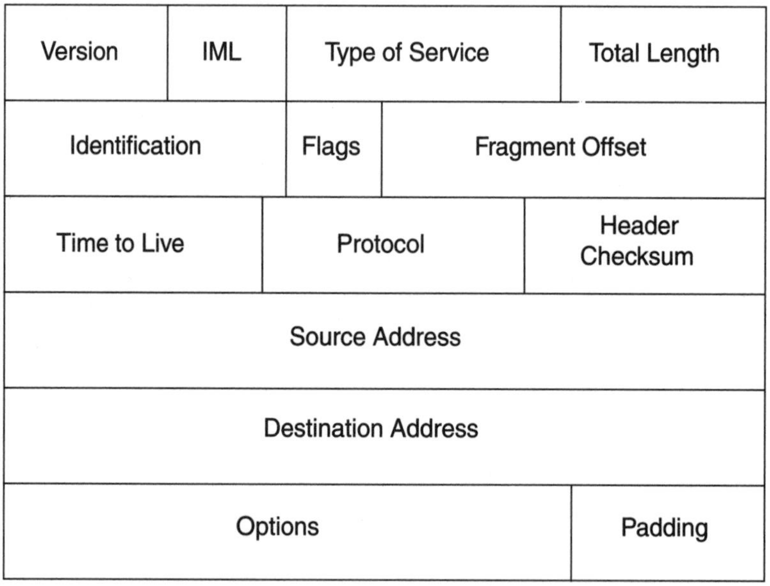

Version	IML	Type of Service	Total Length
Identification		Flags	Fragment Offset
Time to Live		Protocol	Header Checksum
Source Address			
Destination Address			
Options			Padding

Fragment Offset   It indicates where in the datagram the fragment belongs. (Assuming fragmentation has occurred.)

Time to Live   It indicates the maximum number of machines/routers through which the datagram may pass. When the value equals zero the datagram is destroyed. Originally time was measured in units per second, and each entity that processes the datagram must decrease the value by one even if the process time is measured in hops; for example, 16 hops.

Protocol   This field determines whether the data is TCP or UDP.

Header Checksum   This is a header checksum only. Some header fields change as the packet passes through routers and the header checksum is re-computed and verified at every place the header is processed to indicate the integrity of the data.

Source Address   It is the originator of the datagram. It consists of 32 bits.

Destination Address   This is target for the datagram. Be careful not to confuse MAC + IP destination addresses here.

Options   Options are optional. They may or may not appear in datagrams. Options must be implemented in IP modules; however they may not be used in any given transmission. A number of variables in the options field exists. The following is a list of those variables including a brief explanation.

No Option   This option can be used between options to correlate the beginning of a following option on a 32-bit boundary.

Security   Security is a mechanism used by DoD. It provides hosts a way to use security by means of compartmentalization, handling restrictions, and *transmission control codes* (TCC). Handling restrictions are defined by the Defense Intelligence Agency. TCC permits segregation of data traffic.

Loose Source and Record Route   This option provides a way for a source of a datagram to supply routing information for routers to aid in forwarding the datagram. It also serves to record the route information as well.

Strict Source and Record Route   This option permits the source of a datagram to supply information used by routers and record the route information.

Record Route   This option is simply a way to record the route of a datagram as it traverses the network.

Stream Identifier   This option provides a way for a data stream identifier to be carried through networks that do not support this stream concept.

Timestamp   This option includes a pointer, overflow, flag field, and an Internet address. Simply put, this provides the time and date when a router handles the datagram.

Padding   The padding is used to ensure the header ends on the 32 bit boundary.

Internet Protocol Version 6 (IPv6)

IP version 6 (IPv6) is a new version of the Internet Protocol, designed as a successor to *IP version 4* (IPv4) as RFC−791 indicates. The changes from IPv4 to IPv6 fall primarily into the following categories:

Expanded Addressing Capabilities

IPv6 increases the IP address size from 32 bits to 128 bits, to support more levels of addressing hierarchy, a much greater number of addressable nodes, and simpler auto-configuration of addresses. The scalability of multicast routing is improved by adding a scope field to multicast addresses. A new type of address called an "anycast address" is defined and used to send a packet to any one of a group of nodes.

Some IPv4 header fields have been dropped or made optional, to reduce the common-case processing cost of packet handling and to limit the bandwidth cost of the IPv6 header.

Improved Support for Extensions and Options

Changes in the way IP header options are encoded enables more efficient forwarding, less stringent limits on the length of options, and greater flexibility for introducing new options in the future.

Flow Labeling Capability

A new capability is added to enable the labeling of packets belonging to particular traffic flows for which the sender requests special handling. Some examples are non-default quality of service or "real-time" service.

Authentication and Privacy Capabilities

Extensions to support authentication, data integrity, and data confidentiality are specified for IPv6. This document supporting authentication specifies the basic IPv6 header and the initially defined IPv6 extension headers and options. It also discusses packet size issues, the semantics of flow labels and priority, and the effects of IPv6 on upper-layer protocols. The format and semantics of IPv6 addresses are specified separately in RFC−1884. The IPv6 version of ICMP, which all IPv6 implementations are required to include, is specified in RFC−1885.

IPv6 Terminology

Node   A node is a device that implements IPv6.

Router   A router is a node that forwards IPv6 packets not explicitly addressed to itself.

Host   A host is any node that is not a router.

Upper layer   The upper layer is a protocol layer immediately above IPv6. Examples are transport protocols such as TCP and UDP, control protocols such as ICMP, routing protocols such as OSPF, and Internet or lower-layer protocols being "tunneled" over (that is, encapsulated in) IPv6 such as IPX, AppleTalk, or IPv6 itself.

Link   A link is a communication facility or medium over which nodes can communicate at the link layer, that is, the layer immediately below IPv6. Examples are Ethernets (simple or bridged); PPP links; X.25, Frame Relay, or ATM networks; and Internet (or higher) layer tunnels, such as tunnels over IPv4 or IPv6 itself. Some examples are

Neighbors	Nodes attached to the same link
Interface	A node's attachment to a link
Address	An IPv6-layer identifier for an interface or a set of interfaces
Packet	An IPv6 header plus payload
Link MTU	The maximum transmission unit, that is, maximum packet size in octets, that can be conveyed in one piece over a link
Path MTU	The minimum link MTU of all the links in a path between a source node and a destination node

It is possible for a device with multiple interfaces to be configured to forward non-self-destined packets arriving from some set (fewer than all) of its interfaces, and to discard non-self-destined packets arriving from its other interfaces. Such a device must obey the protocol requirements for routers when receiving packets from, and interacting with neighbors over, the former (forwarding) interfaces. It must obey the protocol requirements for hosts when receiving packets from, and interacting with neighbors over, the latter (non-forwarding) interfaces.

IPv6 Header Format

Figure 16-3 presents an IP v.6 header format.

Version =	4-bit Internet Protocol version number = 6
Priority =	4-bit priority value
Flow Label =	24-bit flow label
Payload Length =	16-bit unsigned integer

16-bit unsigned integer   It is length of payload, that is, the rest of the packet following the IPv6 header, in octets. If zero, this indicates that the payload length is carried in a Jumbo Payload hop-by-hop option.

Next Header   It is an 8-bit selector and identifies the type of header immediately following the IPv6 header. It also uses the same values as the IP v.4 Protocol field.

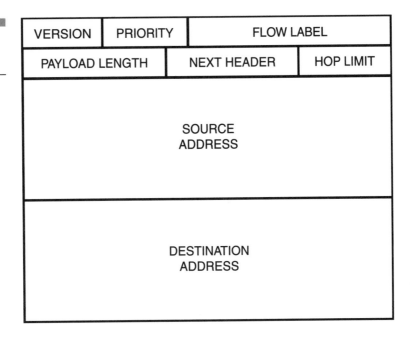

Figure 16-3
IP Version 6 Header format

Hop Limit   It is an 8-bit unsigned integer and is decremented by 1 by each node that forwards the packet. The packet is discarded if Hop Limit is decremented to zero.

Source Address   It is the 128-bit address of the originator of the packet.

Destination Address   It is the 128-bit address of the intended recipient of the packet (possibly not the ultimate recipient, if a Routing header is present).

IPv6 Extension Headers

In IP v.6, optional Internet-layer information is encoded in separate headers that may be placed between the IPv6 header and the upper-layer header in a packet. There are a small number of such extension headers, each identified by a distinct Next Header value. As illustrated in these examples, an IPv6 packet may carry zero, one, or more extension headers, each identified by the Next Header field of the preceding header:

```
+————————+——————————————
| IPv6 header | TCP header + data
| |
| Next Header = |
| TCP |
+————————+——————————————

+————————+——————————+——————————————
| IPv6 header | Routing header | TCP header + data
| | |
| Next Header = | Next Header = |
| Routing | TCP |
+————————+——————————+——————————————

+—————+——————————+——————————+——————————-
|IPv6 header | Routing header | Fragment header | fragment of TCP
| | | | header + data
| Next Header = | Next Header = | Next Header = |
| Routing | Fragment | TCP |
+————————+——————————+——————————-+—————
```

With one exception, extension headers are not examined or processed by any node along a packet's delivery path, until the packet reaches the node (or each of the set of nodes, in the case of multicast) identified in the Destination Address field. There, normal demultiplexing on the Next Header field invokes the module to process the first extension header, or the upper-layer header if no extension header is present. The contents and semantics of each extension header determine whether to proceed to the next header. Therefore, extension headers must be processed strictly in the order they appear in the packet. A receiver must not, for example, scan through a packet looking for a particular kind of extension header and process that header prior to processing all preceding ones.

The exception referred to in the preceding paragraph is the Hop-by-Hop Options header, which carries information that must be examined and processed by every node along a packet's delivery path, including the source and destination nodes. The Hop-by-Hop Options header, when present, must immediately follow the IPv6 header. Its presence is indicated by the value zero in the Next Header field of the IPv6 header.

When a node is processing a header and is required to proceed to the next header but the Next Header value in the header being process is unrecognized, the node should discard the entire packet. As a result of this discard, an ICMP parameter problem message is sent to the source of the packet's originating source. The ICMP value code is 2, meaning,

"Unrecognized Next Header Encountered" and the ICMP pointer field with the offset of the unrecognized header value in the original packet.

Each extension header is an integer multiple of 8 octets long, to retain 8-octet alignment for subsequent headers. Multi-octet fields within each extension header are aligned on their natural boundaries; that is, fields of width n octets are placed at an integer multiple of n octets from the start of the header, for $n = 1, 2, 4,$ or 8.

A full implementation of IPv6 includes implementation of the following extension headers:

Hop-by-Hop Options

Routing (Type 0)

Fragment

Destination Options

Authentication

Encapsulating Security Payload

IPv6 Address Architecture

IP v6 is more robust than its predecessor. The ability to accommodate more entities in the addressing scheme is only one of the abilities it has over IP v4.

This section defines the addressing architecture of the IPv6 protocol. It includes the IPv6 addressing model, text representations of IPv6 addresses, definition of IPv6 unicast addresses, anycast addresses, multicast addresses, and an IPv6 nodes required addresses. IPv6 addresses are 128-bit. There are three types of addresses:

- *Unicast* It is an identifier for a single interface. A packet sent to a unicast address is delivered to the interface identified by that address.

- *Anycast* Anycast is an identifier for a set of interfaces (typically belonging to different nodes). A packet sent to an anycast address is delivered to one of the interfaces identified by that address (the "nearest" one, according to the routing protocols' measure of distance).

- *Multicast* It is an identifier for a set of interfaces (typically belonging to different nodes). A packet sent to a multicast address is delivered to all interfaces identified by that address.

There are no broadcast addresses in IPv6. This type of address is superseded by a multicast addresses. Here address fields are given a specific name, for example subscriber. When this name is used with the *ID* for identifier after the name subscriber ID, it refers to the contents of that field. When it is used with the term prefix, it refers to all of the address up to including this field.

In IPv6, all zeros and ones are legal values for any field unless specifically excluded. Specifically, prefixes may contain zero-valued fields or end in zeros.

IPv6 Addressing

IPv6 addresses of all types are assigned to interfaces, *not nodes*. Because each interface belongs to a single node, any of that node's interfaces' unicast addresses may be used as an identifier for the node.

An IPv6 unicast address refers to a single interface. A single interface may be assigned multiple IPv6 addresses of any type (unicast, anycast, and multicast). There are two exceptions to this model.

1. A single address may be assigned to multiple physical interfaces if the implementation treats the multiple physical interfaces as one interface when presenting it to the Internet layer.

2. Routers may have unnumbered interfaces on point-to-point links to eliminate the necessity to manually configure and advertise addresses.

Addresses are not required for point-to-point interfaces on routers if those interfaces are not to be used as the origins or destinations of any IPv6 datagrams.

IPv6 continues the IPv4 subnet model that is associated with one link. Multiple subnets may be assigned to that link. There are three conventional forms for representing IPv6 addresses as text strings:

1. The preferred form is x:x:x:x:x:x:x:x, where the x's are the hexadecimal values of the eight 16-bit pieces of the address. Here are some examples:

   FEDC:BA98:7654:3210:FEDC:BA98:7654:3210

   1080:0:0:0:8:800:200C:417A

2. Due to the method of allocating certain styles of IPv6 addresses, it is common for addresses to contain long strings of zero bits. To make writing addresses containing zero bits easier a special syntax is available to compress the zeros. The use of (:) indicates multiple groups of 16-bits of zeros. The (:) can only appear once in an address. The (:) can also be used to compress the leading and/or trailing zeros in an address. Some examples are the following addresses:

```
1080:0:0:0:8:800:200C:417A      a unicast address
FF01:0:0:0:0:0:0:43         a multicast address
0:0:0:0:0:0:0:1    the loopback address
0:0:0:0:0:0:0:0    the unspecified addresses
```

These may be represented as

```
1080:8:800:200C:417A      a unicast address
FF01:43        a multicast address
:1      the loopback address
:       the unspecified addresses
```

3. An alternative form that is sometimes more convenient when dealing with a mixed environment of IPv4 and IPv6 nodes is x:x:x:x:x:x:d.d.d.d, where the x's are the hexadecimal values of the six high-order 16-bit pieces of the address, and the d's are the decimal values of the four low-order 8-bit pieces of the address (standard IPv4 representation). Here are some examples:

```
0:0:0:0:0:0:13.1.68.3
0:0:0:0:0:FFFF:129.144.52.38
```

In compressed form these appear like

```
:13.1.68.3
:FFFF:129.144.52.38
```

Address Type Representation

The specific type of an IPv6 address is indicated by the address's leading bits. The variable-length field comprising these leading bits is called the *Format Prefix* (FP). The initial allocation of these prefixes is shown in Table 16-1.

Table 16-1

Initial allocation of prefixes

Allocation Space	Prefix (binary)	Fraction of Address Space
Reserved	0000 0000	1/256
Unassigned	0000 0001	1/256
Reserved for NSAP Allocation	0000 001	1/128
Reserved for IPX Allocation	0000 010	1/128
Unassigned	0000 011	1/128
Unassigned	0000 1	1/32
Unassigned	0001	1/16
Unassigned	001	1/8
Provider-Based Unicast Address	010	1/8
Unassigned	011	1/8
Reserved for Geographically Based Unicast Addresses	100	1/8
Unassigned	101	1/8
Unassigned	110	1/8
Unassigned	1110	1/16
Unassigned	1111 0	1/32
Unassigned	1111 10	1/64
Unassigned	1111 110	1/128
Unassigned	1111 1110 0	1/512
Link Local Use Addresses	1111 1110 10	1/1024
Site Local Use Addresses	1111 1110 11	1/1024
Multicast Addresses	1111 1111	1/256

The unspecified address, the loopback address, and the IPv6 Addresses with embedded IPv4 Addresses are assigned out of the 0000 0000 format prefix space. This allocation supports the direct provider addresses allocation, local use addresses, and multicast addresses. Space is reserved for NSAP addresses, IPX addresses, and geographic addresses. The remainder of the address space is unassigned for future use. This can be used for expansion of existing use or new uses. Fifteen percent of the address space is initially allocated. The remaining 85 percent is reserved for future use.

Unicast addresses are distinguished from multicast addresses by the value of the high-order octet of the addresses: a value of FF (11111111) identifies an address as a multicast address; any other value identifies an address as a unicast address. Anycast addresses are taken from the unicast address space and are not syntactically distinguishable from unicast addresses.

Unicast Addresses

The IPv6 unicast address is contiguous bit-wise maskable, similar to IPv4 addresses under *Classless Interdomain Routing* (CIDR). There are several forms of unicast address assignment in IPv6, including the global provider based unicast address, the geographic based unicast address, the NSAP address, the IPX hierarchical address, the site-local-use address, the link-local-use address, and the IPv4-capable host address. Additional address types can be defined in the future.

IPv6 nodes may have considerable or little knowledge of the internal structure of the IPv6 address, depending on what the host does. Remember, a host is not necessarily a computer in the sense that a user does work on, it could be any valid network device. At a minimum, a node may consider that unicast addresses (including its own) have no internal structure:

```
|                    128 bits                    |
+————————————————————————————————————————————————+
|                  node address                  |
+————————————————————————————————————————————————+
```

A slightly sophisticated host may additionally be aware of subnet prefix(es) for the link(s) it is attached to and different addresses can have different n values:

```
|   n bits        |   128-n bits        |
+—————————————————+—————————————————————+
|  subnet prefix  |   interface ID      |
+—————————————————+—————————————————————+
```

More sophisticated hosts may be aware of other hierarchical boundaries in the unicast address. Though a very simple router may have no knowledge of the internal structure of IPv6 unicast addresses, routers more generally have knowledge of one or more of the hierarchical boundaries for the operation of routing protocols. The known boundaries differ from router to router, depending on what positions the router holds in the routing hierarchy.

An example of an Unicast address format likely to be common on LANs and other environments where IEEE 802 MAC addresses are available is

```
|    n bits                          | 80-n bits  | 48 bits     |
+———————————————————+————————+————————+
|    subscriber prefix               | subnet ID  | Interface ID |
+———————————————————+————————+————————+
```

In this example the 48-bit Interface ID is an IEEE−802 MAC address. The use of IEEE 802 MAC addresses as an interface ID is expected to be very common in environments where nodes have an IEEE 802 MAC address.

The inclusion of a unique global interface identifier, such as an IEEE MAC address, makes possible a very simple form of auto-configuration of addresses. A node may discover a subnet ID by listening to Router Advertisement messages sent by a router on its attached link(s), and then fabricate an IPv6 address for itself by using its IEEE MAC address as the interface ID on that subnet.

Another unicast address format example is where a site or organization requires additional layers of internal hierarchy. In this example, the subnet ID is divided into an area ID and a subnet ID. Its format is

```
|    s bits          |  n bits   |  m bits    | 128-s-n-m bits  |
+——————————+————  ——+———— ——+—————————+
|    subscriber prefix |  area ID  |  subnet ID |  interface ID   |
+——————————+————  ——+———— ——+—————————+
```

This technique can be continued to allow a site or organization to add additional layers of internal hierarchy. It might be desirable to use an interface ID smaller than a 48-bit IEEE 802 MAC address to allow more space for the additional layers of internal hierarchy. These could be interface IDs administratively created by the site or organization.

The address `0:0:0:0:0:0:0:0` is called the unspecified address. It must never be assigned to any node. It indicates the absence of an address. One example of its use is in the Source Address field of any IPv6 datagram sent by an initializing host before it has learned its own address.

The Unicast address `0:0:0:0:0:0:0:1` is called the loopback address. A node using the loopback address may use it to send an IPv6 datagram to itself. It may never be assigned to any interface. The loopback address must not be used as the source address in IPv6 datagrams that are sent outside of a single node. An IPv6 datagram with a destination address of loopback must never be sent outside of a single node.

IPv6 and IPv4 Addresses

The IPv6 transition mechanisms include a technique for hosts and routers to dynamically tunnel IPv6 packets over IPv4 routing infrastructure. IPv6 nodes that utilize this technique are assigned special IPv6 unicast addresses that carry an IPv4 address in the low-order 32-bits. This type of address is termed an IPv4-compatible IPv6 address and has the format

```
| 80 bits              | 16          | 32 bits        |
+————————————+———— ——-+————————+
| 0000 . . . . . 0000  | 00 . . . . .00 | IPv4 address  |
+————————————+———— ——-+————————+
```

A second type of IPv6 address, which holds an embedded IPv4 address, is also defined. This address is used to represent the addresses of IPv4-only nodes (those that do not support IPv6) as IPv6 addresses. This type of address is termed an IPv4-mapped IPv6 address and has the format

```
| 80 bits              | 16          | 32 bits        |
+————————————+———— ——-+————————+
| 0000 . . . . . 0000  | FFFF        | IPv4 address  |
+————————————+———— ——-+————————+
```

NSAP Addresses

This mapping of NSAP addresses into IPv6 addresses is as follows:

```
| 7         | 121 bits        |
+—————-+————————+
| 0000001   | to be defined   |
+—————-+————————+
```

IPX Addresses

This mapping of IPX addresses into IPv6 addresses is as follows:

```
| 7         | 121 bits        |
+—————-+————————+
| 0000010   | to be defined   |
+—————-+————————+
```

Global Unicast Addresses

This initial assignment plan for these unicast addresses is similar to assignment of IPv4 addresses under the CIDR scheme. The IPv6 global provider-based unicast address format is as follows:

```
| 3    | n bits    | m bits    | o bits      | 125-n-m-o bits  |
+——-+————+————+————-+——————-+
| 010  | registryID | provider ID | subscriber ID | intra-subscriber|
+——-+————+————+————-+——————-+
```

The high-order bit part of the address is assigned to registries, which assigns portions of the address space to providers, which assigns portions of the address space to subscribers, and so on. The registry ID identifies the registry that assigns the provider portion of the address. The term "registry prefix" refers to the high-order part of the address up to and including the registry ID.

The provider ID identifies a specific provider, which assigns the subscriber portion of the address. The term "provider prefix" refers to the high-order part of the address up to and including the provider ID. The subscriber ID distinguishes among multiple subscribers attached to the provider identified by the provider ID. The term "subscriber prefix" refers to the high-order part of the address up to and including the subscriber ID.

The intra-subscriber portion of the address is defined by an individual subscriber and is organized according to the subscriber's local Internet topology. It is likely that many subscribers will choose to divide the intra-subscriber portion of the address into a subnet ID and an interface ID. In this case, the subnet ID identifies a specific physical link and the interface ID identifies a single interface on that subnet.

IPv6 Unicast Addresses

There are two types of local-use unicast addresses defined. These are Link-Local and Site-Local. The Link-Local is for use on a single link and the Site-Local is for use in a single site. Link-Local addresses have the following format:

```
|10   | bits  | n bits   | 118-n bits    |
+——+————+—————+———————+
|1111111010 | 0        | interface ID   |
+——+————+—————+———————+
```

Link-Local addresses are designed to be used for addressing on a single link for purposes such as auto-address configuration, neighbor discovery, or when no routers are present. Routers are not permitted to forward any packets with a link-local source addresses.

Site-Local addresses have the following format:

```
| 10   | bits  | n bits   | m bits    | 118-n-m bits    |
+——+———+———-+————+—————+
| 1111111011 | 0        | subnet ID | interface ID    |
+——+———+———-+————+—————+
```

Site-Local addresses may be used for sites or organizations that are not (yet) connected to the global Internet. They do not need to request or "steal" an address prefix from the global Internet address space. IPv6 site-local addresses can be used instead. When the organization connects to the global Internet, it can then form global addresses by replacing the site-local prefix with a subscriber prefix. Routers MUST not forward any packets with site-local source addresses outside of the site.

Anycast Addresses

An IPv6 anycast address is an address that is assigned to more than one interface (typically belonging to different nodes) with the property that a packet sent to an anycast address is routed to the *nearest* interface having that address, according to the routing protocols' measure of distance.

Anycast addresses are allocated from the Unicast address space, using any of the defined Unicast address formats. Thus, Anycast addresses are syntactically indistinguishable from Unicast addresses. When a Unicast address is assigned to more than one interface, thus turning it into an Anycast address, the nodes to which the address is assigned must be explicitly configured to know that it is an anycast address.

For any assigned Anycast address, there is a longest address prefix P that identifies the topological region in which all interfaces belonging to that anycast address reside. Within the region identified by P, each member of the anycast set must be advertised as a separate entry in the routing system (referred to as a *host route*). Outside the region identified by P, the anycast address may be aggregated into the routing advertisement for prefix P.

Note that in the worst case, the prefix P of an anycast set may be the null prefix, that is, the members of the set may have no topological locality. In that case, the anycast address must be advertised as a separate routing entry throughout the entire Internet, which presents a severe scaling limit on how many such global anycast sets may be supported. Therefore, it is expected that support for global anycast sets may be unavailable or very restricted.

One expected use of anycast addresses is to identify the set of routers belonging to an Internet service provider. Such addresses could be used as intermediate addresses in an IPv6 Routing header to cause a packet to be delivered through a particular provider or sequence of providers. Some other possible uses are to identify the set of routers attached to a particular subnet, or the set of routers providing entry into a particular routing domain.

There is little experience with widespread, arbitrary use of Internet anycast addresses and some known complications and hazards when using them in their full generality. Until more experience has been gained and solutions agreed on for those problems, the following restrictions are imposed on IPv6 anycast addresses:

- An anycast address MUST NOT be used as the source address of an IPv6 packet.

- An anycast address MUST NOT be assigned to an IPv6 host, that is, it may be assigned to an IPv6 router only.

The Subnet-Router anycast address is predefined. Its format is

```
|  n bits         |  128-n bits          |
+————————+————————+
| subnet prefix   |  00000000000000      |
+————————+————————+
```

The subnet prefix in an anycast address is the prefix that identifies a specific link. This anycast address is syntactically the same as a unicast address for an interface on the link with the interface identifier set to zero.

Packets sent to the Subnet-Router anycast address are delivered to one router on the subnet. All routers are required to support the Subnet-Router anycast addresses for the subnets for which they have interfaces.

The subnet-router anycast address is intended to be used for applications where a node needs to communicate with one of a set of routers on a remote subnet. An example is when a mobile host needs to communicate with one of the mobile agents on its "home" subnet.

Multicast Addresses

An IPv6 multicast address is an identifier for a group of nodes. A node may belong to any number of multicast groups. Multicast addresses have the following format:

```
| 8        | 4    | 4    | 112 bits            |
+————————+————-+————-+————————————————————+
| 11111111 | flgs | scop | group ID            |
+————————+————-+————-+————————————————————+
```

11111111 at the start of the address identifies the address as being a multicast address.

flgs is a set of 4 flags: |0|0|0|T|

The high-order 3 flags are reserved and must be initialized to 0.

T = 0 Indicates a permanently-assigned ("well-known") multicast address, assigned by the global Internet numbering authority.

T = 1 Indicates a non-permanently-assigned multicast address. (It is also referred to as transient.)

Scope is a 4-bit multicast scope value used to limit the scope of the multicast group. The values are

0   reserved

1   node-local scope

2   link-local scope

3   (unassigned)

4   (unassigned)

5   site-local scope

6   (unassigned)

7   (unassigned)

8   organization-local scope

9   (unassigned)

A   (unassigned)

B   (unassigned)

C   (unassigned)

D (unassigned)

E global scope

F reserved

Group ID identifies the multicast group, as either permanent or transient, within the given scope. The meaning of a permanently assigned multicast address is independent of the scope value. For example, if the NTP servers group is assigned a permanent multicast address with a group ID of 43 (hex), then

- FF01:0:0:0:0:0:0:43 means all NTP servers on the same node as the sender.
- FF02:0:0:0:0:0:0:43 means all NTP servers on the same link as the sender.
- FF05:0:0:0:0:0:0:43 means all NTP servers at the same site as the sender.
- FF0E:0:0:0:0:0:0:43 means all NTP servers in the Internet.

Non-permanently-assigned multicast addresses are meaningful only within a given scope. For example, a group identified by the non-permanent, site-local multicast address FF15:0:0:0:0:0:0:43 at one site bears no relationship to a group using the same address at a different site, or to a non-permanent group using the same group ID with different scope, or to a permanent group with the same group ID.

Multicast addresses must not be used as source addresses in IPv6 datagrams or appear in any routing header.

Pre-Defined Multicast Addresses

The following well-known multicast addresses are pre-defined:

Reserved Multicast Addresses:

```
FF00:0:0:0:0:0:0:0
FF01:0:0:0:0:0:0:0
FF02:0:0:0:0:0:0:0
FF03:0:0:0:0:0:0:0
FF04:0:0:0:0:0:0:0
FF05:0:0:0:0:0:0:0
```

```
FF06:0:0:0:0:0:0:0
FF07:0:0:0:0:0:0:0
FF08:0:0:0:0:0:0:0
FF09:0:0:0:0:0:0:0
FF0A:0:0:0:0:0:0:0
FF0B:0:0:0:0:0:0:0
FF0C:0:0:0:0:0:0:0
FF0D:0:0:0:0:0:0:0
FF0E:0:0:0:0:0:0:0
FF0F:0:0:0:0:0:0:0
```

The previous multicast addresses are reserved and shall never be assigned to any multicast group.

All Nodes Addresses:

```
FF01:0:0:0:0:0:0:1
FF02:0:0:0:0:0:0:1
```

The previous multicast addresses identify the group of all IPv6 nodes, within scope 1 (node-local) or 2 (link-local).

All Routers Addresses:

```
FF01:0:0:0:0:0:0:2
FF02:0:0:0:0:0:0:2
```

The previous multicast addresses identify the group of all IPv6 routers, within scope 1 (node-local) or 2 (link-local).

DHCP Server/Relay-Agent: `FF02:0:0:0:0:0:0:C` The previous multicast address identifies the group of all IPv6 DHCP Servers and Relay Agents within scope 2 (link-local).

Solicited-Node Address: `FF02:0:0:0:0:1:XXXX:XXXX` The previous multicast address is computed as a function of a node's unicast and anycast addresses. The solicited-node multicast address is formed by taking the low-order 32 bits of the address (unicast or anycast) and appending those bits to the 96-bit prefix FF02:0:0:0:0:1 resulting in a multicast address in the range:

FF02:0:0:0:0:1:0000:0000 to FF02:0:0:0:0:1:FFFF:FFFF

For example, the solicited-node multicast address corresponding to the IPv6 address `4037:01:800:200E:8C6C` is `FF02:1:200E:8C6C`. IPv6 addresses that differ only in the high-order bits, for example, due to multiple high-order prefixes associated with different providers, map to the same solicited-node address, thereby reducing the number of multicast addresses a node must join.

A node is required to compute and support a solicited-node multicast addresses for every unicast and anycast address it is assigned.

IP v6 Node Address Requirement

A host is required to recognize the following addresses as identifying itself:

- Its Link-Local Address for each interface
- Assigned Unicast Addresses
- Loopback Address
- All-Nodes Multicast Address
- Solicited-Node Multicast Address for each of its assigned unicast and anycast addresses
- Multicast Addresses of all other groups which the host belongs.

A router is required to recognize the following addresses as identifying itself:

- Its Link-Local Address for each interface
- Assigned Unicast Addresses
- Loopback Address
- The Subnet-Router anycast addresses for the links for which it has interfaces.
- All other Anycast addresses with which the router has been configured.
- All-Nodes Multicast Address
- All-Router Multicast Address
- Solicited-Node Multicast Address for each of its assigned unicast and anycast addresses
- Multicast Addresses of all other groups which the router belongs.

The only address prefixes that should be predefined are

- Unspecified Address
- Loopback Address
- Multicast Prefix (FF)
- Local-Use Prefixes (Link-Local and Site-Local)
- Pre-Defined Multicast Addresses
- IPv4-Compatible Prefixes

Implementations should assume all other addresses are unicast unless specifically configured (for example, anycast addresses).

Internet Control Message Protocol (ICMP)

ICMP works with IP and is also located at layer three with IP. Because IP is connectionless, it has no way to relay messages or errors to the originating host. ICMP performs these functions on behalf of IP. ICMP sends status messages and error messages to the sending host.

ICMP Message Structure

ICMP utilizes IP to carry the ICMP data within it through a network. Just because ICMP uses IP as a vehicle does not make IP reliable, it means that IP carries the ICMP message.

The structure of an ICMP message is shown in Figure 16-4.

The first part of the ICMP message is the TYPE field. This field has a numeric value reflecting its meaning and identifies its format as well. The numeric values and their meanings that can appear in the type field as shown in Figure 16-5.

The next field in the ICMP message is the CODE field. It too has a numeric value assigned to it. These numeric values have an associated meaning as shown in Figure 16-6.

The CHECKSUM is computed from the ICMP message starting with the ICMP type.

The NOT USED field means that; RFC 792.

The next field is the IP HEADER AND DATA DATAGRAM.

Type
Code
Checksum
Not used or Parameters
IP Header and Original Data Datagram

Type	Meaning of Message
0	Echo reply
3	Destination unreachable
4	Source quench
5	Redirect
8	Echo request
11	Time exceeded for a Datagram
12	Parameter problem on a Datagram
13	Timestamp request
14	Timestamp reply
17	Address mask request
18	Address mask reply

ICMP is the source for many messages a user sees on their display. For example, if a user attempts a remote logon and the host is not reachable, then the user sees the message *host unreachable* on their screen. This message comes from ICMP.

ICMP reports problems; meaning it responds to errors. IP requires ICMP to be implemented.

Figure 16-6
ICMP codes and
meanings

0	Network unreachable
1	Host unreachable
2	Protocol unreachable
3	Port unreachable
4	Fragmentation needed
5	Source route failed
6	Destination Network unknown
7	Destination Host unknown
8	Source Host isolated
9	Administrative restrictions to destination Network. Communication prohibited
10	Communication with destination Host prohibited by Administration
11	Network unreachable for service type
12	Host unreachable for service type

Address Resolution Protocol (ARP)

ARP is located at layer three along with IP and ICMP. ARP determines the MAC address corresponding to the IP address. Because TCP/IP works at layer three and four, it must have a mechanism communicate with interface boards. When TCP/IP is implemented, it is done so in software. This is the case whether or not TCP/IP is running as a protocol stack running on a host or a partial compliment of the protocol operating from a PROM (or similar chip) within some specific type network device.

Because any data link protocol could be used, IP requires a way to map the IP address and the data link address. Data link addresses are generally considered hardware addresses. For example, if TCP/IP is implemented with Ethernet a 48-bit Ethernet address is mapped to the 32-bit IP address. Or, if Token Ring is used, a 12-digit hexadecimal address (this is 48 bits) is used as the hardware address. Neither of these data link protocol addresses are used to form the 32-bit IP address of TCP/IP. This is the reason for ARP.

ARP Theory of Operation

Using Ethernet for a data link, ARP can be explained this way. Assume five hosts reside on an Ethernet network. Assume a user on host *A* wants to connect to host *E*. Host *A* broadcasts an ARP packet that includes *A's* IP Ethernet address and host *E's* IP address.

All five hosts on the network "hear" the ARP broadcast for host *E*. However, only host *E* recognizes its IP address inside the ARP request. Figure 16-7 depicts this.

When host *E* recognizes its hardware address, it replies to host *A* with its IP address. Figure 16-8 is an example of this process.

All hosts shown in Figure 16-7 must examine the ARP request because it's a broadcast. This is expensive in regards to Ethernet interrupts and utilization on each node, both in terms of the node and the medium. To avoid queries, an ARP cache is maintained. This is a list of network hosts' physical and IP address. As a result, this curbs the number of ARP packets on the network.

When a host receives an ARP reply, the host keeps the IP address of the other host in its ARP table. Then, when a host wants to communicate with another host on the network it first examines its ARP cache for the IP address. If the desired IP address is found in the cache, there is no need to perform an ARP broadcast. The communication occurs through hardware; for example, Ethernet boards communicating with one another. Remember, a reply to a broadcast only occurs if an IP stack is loaded.

Figure 16-7
ARP request

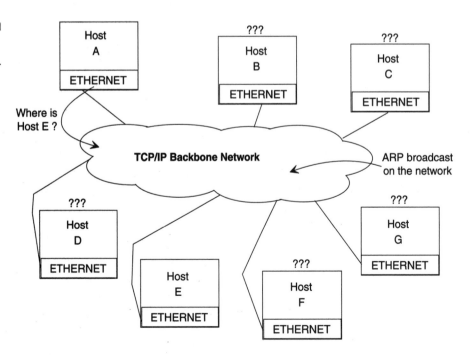

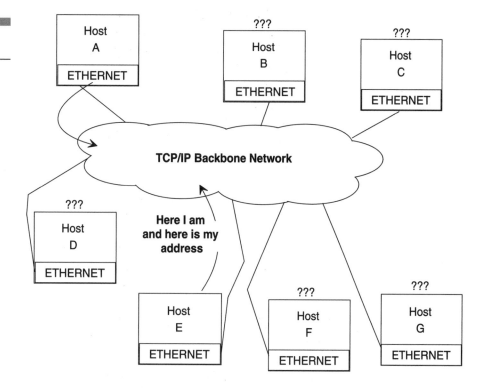

Figure 16-8
ARP response

ARP Message Format

Figure 16-9 is an example of ARP message format.

The following lists the fields in an ARP packet and briefly explains their meaning.

Hardware Type. It indicates the hardware interface type.

Protocol Type. It specifies the upper level protocol address the originator sent.

Hardware Address Length. It specifies the length of the bytes in the packet.

Protocol Address Length. It specifies the length in bytes of the high level protocol.

Operation Code. It specifies one of the following: ARP request, ARP response, RARP request, or RARP response.

Sender Hardware Address. If this address known it is supplied by the sender.

Figure 16-9
ARP message format

Physical Layer Header
Hardware Type
Protocol Type
Hardware Address Length
Protocol Address Length
Operation Code
Sender Hardware Address
Sender Protocol Address
Target Hardware Address
Target Protocol Address

Sender Protocol Address.　This address is like the hardware address; it is sent if known.

Target Hardware Address.　This address is the destination address.

Target Protocol Address.　It contains the IP address of the destination host.

Conceptually, the frame carrying the ARP message and the frame appears like Figure 16-10.

ARP's dynamic address translation provides a method for obtaining an unknown IP address from a MAC address. The efficiency of ARP is in the utilization of the caching mechanism.

Reverse Address Resolution Protocol (RARP)

RARP is the compliment of ARP. It is used commonly where diskless workstations are implemented. When a diskless workstation boots, it knows its hardware address because it is in the interface card connecting it to the network. However, it does not know its IP address.

Figure 16-10
ARP frame and ARP
message

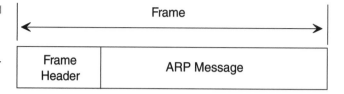

RARP Request & Server Operation

Devices using RARP require a RARP server be present on the network to answer RARP request. The question RARP requests ask is: "what is my IP address?" This is broadcast on the network and a RARP server, if available, replies by examining the physical address received in the RARP packet, comparing it against its tables of IP addresses, and sending a response back to the requesting host. Figure 16-11 is an example of a RARP broadcast.

Figure 16-11 shows the RARP request going to all hosts on the network. It also shows a RARP server. Notice in Figure 16-12 the RARP server answers the RARP request.

For RARP to be used in a network, a RARP server must exist. In most implementations when RARP is used, multiple RARP servers are used.

Router Protocols

This section focuses on Interior Gateway Protocols. This is defined as routing within an autonomous system. An autonomous system is a collection of routers controlled by one administrative authority and that use a common interior gateway protocol. Four popular routing protocols exist in this category. They are: *Interior Gateway Router Protocol* (IGRP), *Exterior Gateway Router Protocol* (EGRP), *Router Information Protocol* (RIP), and *Open Shortest Path First* (OSPF).

These protocols are used by network devices such as routers, hosts, and other devices. These protocols can be implemented by firmware. This section explains RIP and OSPF.

Figure 16-11
RARP broadcast

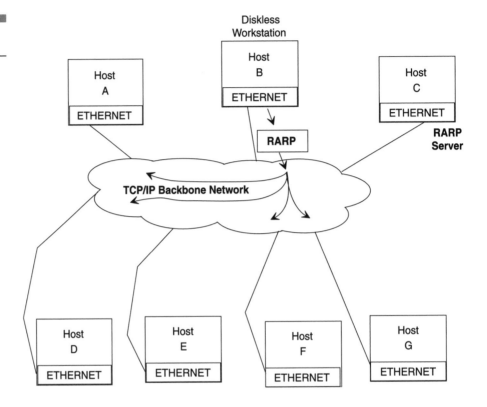

RIP

RIP has its origins in Xerox's network systems protocol. It has been included in the software distribution of TCP/IP with Berkley UNIX.

RIP is an example of a de facto protocol. It was implemented before a standard RFC existed. It was provided with TCP/IP, it worked, and it was needed; all the ingredients to make a product popular!

For further information about RIP, obtain RFC 1058.

RIP Header Analysis

Consider Figure 16-13, which is an example of the RIP message format.
The following is a brief description of each field in the RIP message format.

Command   This specifies an operation that could be a request or response.

Version   It identifies the protocol version.

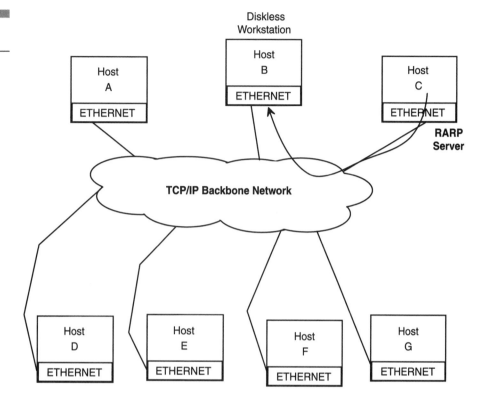

Figure 16-12
RARP response

Zero   Zero means a blank field.

Address Family Indentifier   This is used to identify the protocol family under which the message should be interpreted.

IP Address   The IP address usually has a default route attached to it.

Distance to Net n   It is a value indicating the distance to the target network.

RIP messages are either conveying routing information or requesting routing information. RIP is based on broadcast technology. In addition to broadcasts and updates from that process, RIP also gets updates due to changes in the network configuration. These updates are referred to as triggered updates.

Another characteristic of RIP is that it relies on other devices (adjacent nodes) for routing information for targets that are more than one "hop" away. RIP also calculates its distances by hop. The metric is the number of hops. The maximum hops RIP can make along one path is fifteen.

Command
Version
Zero
Address Family Identfier
Zero
IP Address
Zero
Zero
Distance to Net A

RIP maintains routing tables. RIP sends the full routing table on every update. Information contained in each entry in this table includes

■ The destination IP address

■ The number of hops required to reach the destination

■ The IP address for the next router in the path

■ Any indication if the route has recently changed

RIP is used today mainly on UNIX based hosts. Many vendors support it. In certain environments, it might be a good router protocol to use. For example, on a LAN it might be a good protocol to use. However, many vendors support *Open Shortest Path First* (OSPF).

Open Shortest Path First (OSPF)

The philosophy of OSPF differs from RIP. It was recommended as a standard in 1990 and by mid to late 1991, version 2 OSPF was available. Some OSPF features include

■ Type of service routing

■ Offers route distribution

■ Minimized broadcasts

■ Supports a method for trusted routers

Other features are supported by OSPF and depending on the vendor, a variety of them might be implemented.

OSPF Advertisements

OSPF uses what is called *advertisements*. These advertisements are ways that routers can inform other routers about paths. Four distinct types of advertisements include

- *Autonomous* It has information of routes in other autonomous systems.
- *Network* It contains a list of routers connected to the network.
- *Router* It contains information about given router interfaces in certain areas.
- *Summary* It maintains route information outside a given area.

Besides the advertisements, OSPF uses a number of messages for communication. Some of these messages include

- Hello
- Database Description
- Link State Request
- Link State Update
- Link State Acknowledgment

Additional insight on the operation of OSPF can be obtained through RFCs: 1245, 1246, and 1247.

OSPF Header Analysis

The OSPF packet header appears like Figure 16-14.
The following OSPF header fields are listed and briefly explained:

VERSION Indicates the protocol version.

TYPE This field indicates messages as one of the following:

1. Hello
2. Database Description
3. Link Status
4. Link Status Update
5. Link Status Acknowledgment

Figure 16-14
OSPF packet header

Version
Type
Packet Length
Router ID
Area ID
Checksum
Authentication type
Authentication

Message Length   It indicates the length of the field including the OSPF header.

Source Gateway IP Address   It provides the sender's address.

Area ID   It identifies the area from which the packet was transmitted.

Checksum   The checksum is performed on the entire packet.

Authentication Type   it identifies the authentication type that is used.

Authentication   This field includes a value from the authentication type.

The HELLO packet includes messages that are periodically send on each link to establish if a destination can be reached. The HELLO packet appears like Figure 16-15.

The following includes a list of fields in the HELLO packet and a brief explanation of each.

- *OSPF Header*   It is required.
- *Network Mask*   It contains the network mask for the network from where the message originated.
- *Dead Timer*   It is a value (in seconds) that indicates a neighbor is dead if no response is received.
- *Hello Interval*   This field has a value, in seconds.
- *Router Priority*   This field is used if a designated router is used as a backup.
- *Designated* or *Backup Router*   This field identifies the backup router.
- *Neighbor Router ID*   This field, and subsequent ones, indicate the IDs of routers which have recently received HELLO packets within the network.

The Database Description packet message includes an OSPF header and fields of information. These fields include information about messages

Figure 16-15
Hello packet format

OSPF Header
Network Mask
Dead Timer
Hello Interval
Router Priority
Designated or Backup Router
Neighbor 1 IP Address
Neighbor 2 IP Address
Neighbor 3 IPAddress
etc
.
.
.

Figure 16-15
Hello packet format

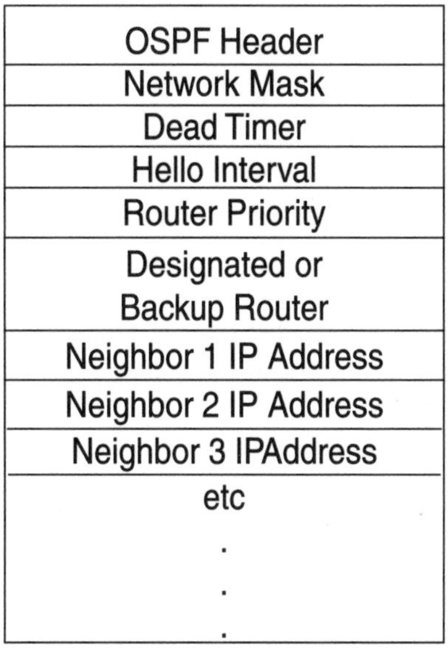

received and can be broken into smaller units. The packet also includes information about the type link and its ID. A checksum is provided to ensure that corruption has not occurred.

The Link State packet header includes an OSPF header and fields that provide information such as: router, network, link station type, and other information.

OSPF reduces traffic overhead (relative to RIP) in the network, because it performs individual updates rather than broadcasts (broadcast do not go through routers). OSPF also provides an ability for authentication. Another strength of OSPF is that it can exchange subnet masks, as well as subnet addresses.

Transmission Control Protocol (TCP)

TCP is a connection-oriented, end-to-end reliable protocol designed to fit into a layered hierarchy of protocols that support multi-network applications. The TCP protocol provides for reliable inter-process communication between pairs of processes on host computers. TCP assumes it can obtain a simple, potentially unreliable datagram service from the lower level protocols. TCP is able to operate over communication systems ranging from hard-wired connections to packet-switched and circuit-switched networks.

TCP interfaces, on one side, to user or application processes and, on the other side, to a lower level protocol such as Internet Protocol. The interface between an application process and TCP consists of a set of calls much like the calls an operating system provides to an application process for manipulating files. For example, there are calls to open and close connections and to send and receive data on established connections. It is also expected that TCP can asynchronously communicate with application programs. Although considerable freedom is permitted to TCP implementers to design interfaces that are appropriate to a particular operating system environment, a minimal functionality is required at the TCP/user interface for any valid implementation.

The interface between TCP and lower level protocol is essentially unspecified except that it is assumed there is a mechanism whereby the two levels can asynchronously pass information to each other. TCP is designed to work in a very general environment of interconnected networks.

TCP Operation

As noted previously, the primary purpose of TCP is to provide reliable, connection oriented service between pairs of processes. To provide this service on top of an unreliable Internet communication system requires facilities in the following areas:

- Basic Data Transfer
- Reliability
- Flow Control
- Multiplexing
- Connections
- Precedence and Security

Basic Data Transfer

TCP is able to transfer a continuous stream of octets in each direction between its users by packaging octets into segments for transmission through the network.

Sometimes users need to be sure that all the data they have submitted to TCP has been transmitted. For this purpose, a push function is defined.

To assure that data submitted to TCP is actually transmitted, the sending user indicates that it should be pushed through to the receiving user. A push causes the TCPs to promptly forward and deliver data to the receiver.

The exact push point might not be visible to the receiving user and the push function does not supply a record boundary marker.

Reliability

TCP must recover from data that is damaged, lost, duplicated, or delivered out of order by the network. This is achieved by counting packets transmitted, and requiring a positive *acknowledgment* (ACK) from the receiving TCP stack. If the ACK is not received within a timeout interval, the data is retransmitted. At the receiver, the sequence numbers are used to reorder any segments that were received out of order and to eliminate duplicates. Damage is handled by adding a checksum to each segment transmitted, checking it at the receiver, and discarding damaged segments.

Flow Control

TCP provides a means for the receiver to govern the amount of data sent by the sender. This is achieved by returning a "window" with every ACK indicating a range of acceptable sequence numbers beyond the last segment successfully received. The window indicates an allowed number of octets that the sender may transmit before receiving further permission.

Multiplexing

To allow for many processes within a single host to use TCP communication facilities simultaneously, TCP provides a set of addresses or ports within each host. In addition to the network and host addresses from the Internet communication layer, the port number specifies a socket. A pair of sockets uniquely identifies each connection. That is, a socket may be simultaneously used in multiple connections. The binding of ports to processes is handled independently by each Host. However, it proves useful to maintain frequently used processes. These services can then be accessed through the well known addresses. Establishing and learning the port addresses of other processes might involve more dynamic mechanisms.

Connections

The reliability and flow control mechanisms described previously require that TCP initialize and maintain certain status information for each data stream. The combination of this information, including sockets, sequence numbers, and window sizes, is called a *connection*.

Each connection is uniquely specified by a pair of sockets identifying its two sides. When two processes want to communicate, TCP must first establish a connection (initialize the status information on each side). When communication is complete, the connection is terminated or closed to free the resources for other uses. Because connections must be established between unreliable hosts and over the unreliable Internet, a three-stage handshake mechanism is used in startup.

Precedence and Security

The users of TCP may indicate the security and precedence of their communication. Provision is made for default values to be used when these features are not needed. However in reality, most sites do not use them.

TCP & the Host Environment

TCP is typically a module in an operating system; a part of the protocol suite running on a given host. Users transparently access TCP, as they would access the file system. TCP may call on other operating system functions, for example, to manage data structures. The actual interface to the network is generally controlled by a device driver module. TCP does not call on the network device driver directly, but rather calls on the Internet datagram protocol module, which may in turn call on the device driver.

The mechanisms of TCP do not preclude implementation of the TCP in a front-end processor. For those of you unfamiliar with SNA, a front-end processor is a processor that primarily handles communications issues in an SNA network. However, in such an implementation, a host-to-front-end protocol must provide the functionality to support the type of TCP-user interface described in this document.

Interfaces & TCP

The TCP user interface provides for calls made by the user on the TCP stack to OPEN or CLOSE a connection, to SEND or RECEIVE data, or to obtain STATUS about a connection. These calls are like other calls from user programs on the operating system, for example, the calls to open, read from, and close a file.

TCP/Internet interface provides calls to send and receive datagrams addressed to TCP modules in hosts anywhere in the Internet system. These calls have parameters for passing the address, type of service, precedence, security, and other control information.

TCP Reliability

A stream of data sent on a TCP connection is delivered reliably and in order, at the destination. Transmission is made reliable through the use of sequence numbers and acknowledgments. Conceptually, each octet of data is assigned a sequence number. The sequence number of the first octet of data in a segment is transmitted with that segment and is called the segment sequence number. Segments also carry an acknowledgment number, which is the sequence number of the next expected data octet of transmissions in the reverse direction. When the TCP transmits a segment containing data, it puts a copy on a retransmission queue and starts a timer; when the acknowledgment for that data is received, the segment is deleted from the queue. If the acknowledgment is not received before the timer runs out, the segment is retransmitted.

An acknowledgment by TCP does not guarantee that the data has been delivered to the end user; it does mean that the receiving TCP has taken the responsibility to do so. To govern the flow of data between TCP, a flow control mechanism is employed. The receiving TCP reports a "window" to the sending TCP. This window specifies the number of octets, starting with the acknowledgment number, that the receiving TCP is currently prepared to receive.

TCP Connection Establishment/Clearing

To identify the separate data streams that a TCP stack may handle, a TCP stack provides port identifiers. To provide for unique addresses within each TCP, we concatenate an Internet address identifying the TCP with a port identifier to create a *socket,* which is unique throughout all networks connected together.

A connection is fully specified by the pair of sockets at the ends. A *local socket* may participate in many connections to different foreign sockets. A connection can be used to carry data in both directions; it is full duplex.

TCP is free to associate ports with processes however it chooses. However, several basic concepts are necessary in any implementation. There must be well-known sockets that the TCP associates by some means only with the appropriate processes.

A connection is specified in the OPEN call by the local port and foreign socket arguments. In return, TCP supplies a (short) local connection name by which the user refers to the connection in subsequent calls. To store this information, there is typically a data structure called a *Transmission Control Block* (TCB). One implementation strategy would have the local connection name be a pointer to the TCB for this connection. The OPEN call also specifies whether the connection establishment is to be active.

A passive OPEN request means that a process accepts incoming connection requests rather than attempting to initiate a connection. Often a process requesting a passive OPEN accepts a connection request from a caller. In this case, a foreign socket of all zeros is used to denote an unspecified socket. Unspecified foreign sockets are allowed only on passive OPENs. A service process that wants to provide services for unknown other processes issues a passive OPEN request with an unspecified foreign socket. Then a connection can be made with any process that requests a connection to this local socket.

Well-known ports are a convenient mechanism for a priori associating a socket address with a standard service. For instance, the Telnet-Server process is permanently assigned to port 23, and other ports are reserved for File Transfer, Remote Job Entry, Text Generator (chargen), Echoer, and Sink processes. A socket address might be reserved for access to a Look-Up service that would return the specific socket at which a newly created service would be provided.

Processes can issue passive OPENs, wait for matching active OPENs from other processes, and be informed when connections have been established. This flexibility is critical for the support of distributed computing in which components act asynchronously with respect to each other.

There are two principal cases for matching the sockets in the local passive OPENs and any foreign active OPENs. In the first case, the local passive OPENs has fully specified the foreign socket. In this case, the match must be exact. In the second case, the local passive OPENs has left the foreign socket unspecified. In this case, any foreign socket is acceptable as long as the local sockets match.

If there are several pending passive OPENs (recorded in TCBs) with the same local socket, a foreign active OPEN is matched to a TCB with the specific foreign socket in the foreign active OPEN, if such a TCB exists, before selecting a TCB with an unspecified foreign socket.

A connection is initiated by the rendezvous of an arriving segment (containing a SYN) and a waiting TCB entry, each created by a user OPEN command. The matching of local and foreign sockets determines when a connection has been initiated. The connection becomes *established* when sequence numbers have been exchanged in both directions. The clearing of a connection also involves the exchange of segments, in this case, carrying the FIN control flag.

TCP & Data Communication

The data that flows on a connection may be thought of as a stream of bytes. The sending user indicates in each SEND call whether the data in that call (and any preceding calls) should be immediately pushed through to the receiving user by the setting of the PUSH flag.

A sender is allowed to collect data from the sending user and to send that data in segments when convenient, until the push function is signaled, then it must send all unsent data. When a destination TCP sees the PUSH flag, it must not wait for more data from the sender before passing the data to the receiving process.

There is no necessary relationship between push functions and segment boundaries. The data in any particular segment may be the result of a single SEND call, in whole or part, or of multiple SEND calls.

The purpose of the push function and the PUSH flag is to push data through from the sending user to the receiving user. It does not provide a record oriented service.

There is a coupling between the push function and the use of buffers of data that cross the TCP/user interface. Each time a PUSH flag is associated with data placed into the receiving user's buffer, the buffer is returned to the user for processing even if the buffer is not filled. If data arrives that fills the user's buffer before a PUSH is seen, the data is passed to the user in buffer size units.

TCP also provides a means to communicate to the receiver that, at some point further along in the data stream than the receiver is currently reading there, is urgent data. TCP does not define the user action on being notified of ending urgent data, but the general notion is that the receiving process acts to process the urgent data quickly.

TCP Precedence & Security

TCP uses a type of service field and security option to provide precedence and security on a per connection basis. Few TCP modules function in a multilevel secure environment; some are limited to unclassified use only, and others may operate at only one security level and compartment. Consequently, almost all TCP implementations and services to users are limited to a subset of the multilevel secure case.

TCP modules, which operate in a multilevel secure environment, must properly mark outgoing segments with the security, compartment, and precedence. Such TCP modules must also provide to their users or higher level protocols, such as Telnet or FTP, an interface to allow them to specify the desired security level, compartment, and precedence of connections.

TCP Segment (Header) Format

TCP segments are sent as IP format datagrams. The Internet Protocol header carries several information fields, including the source and destination host addresses. A TCP header follows the IP header, supplying information specific to the TCP protocol. This division allows protocols other than TCP. TCP Segment Format is shown in Figure 16-16.

Source Port   It is 16 bits and the source port number.

Destination Port   It is 16 bits and the destination port number.

Sequence Number   It is 32 bits and the sequence number of the first data octet in this segment (except when SYN is present). If SYN is present, the sequence number is the *initial sequence number* (ISN) and the first data octet is ISN+1.

Acknowledgment Number   It is 32 bits. If the ACK control bit is set, this field contains the value of the next sequence number the sender is expecting to receive. After a connection is established, this is always sent.

Figure 16-16
TCP segment

Source Port
Destination Port
Sequence Number
Acknowledgement Number
Data Offset
Reserved
Urgent
Acknowledgement
Push
Reset
Synchronizer
Finished
Window
Checksum
Urgent Pointer
Options
Padding
Data

Data Offset It is 4 bits and the number of 32 bit words in the TCP Header. This indicates where the data begins. The TCP header (even one including options) is an integral number of 32 bits long.

Reserved It is 6 bits and means reserved for future use. It must be zero.

Control Bits Control bits are 6 bits (from left to right):

    URG   Urgent Pointer field significant

    ACK   Acknowledgment field significant

    PSH   Push Function

    RST   Reset the connection

    SYN   Synchronize sequence numbers

    FIN   No more data from sender

Window It is 16 bits and is the number of data octets, beginning with the one indicated in the acknowledgment field, that the sender of this segment is willing to accept.

Checksum   It is 16 bits. The checksum field is the 16-bit one's complement of the one's complement sum of all 16-bit words in the header and text. If a segment contains an odd number of header and text octets to be check-summed, the last octet is padded on the right with zeros to form a 16-bit word for checksum purposes. The pad is not transmitted as part of the seg-ment. While computing the checksum, the checksum field itself is replaced with zeros.

The checksum also covers a 96-bit pseudo-header conceptually prefixed to the TCP header. This pseudo header contains the Source Address, the Destination Address, the Protocol, and TCP length. This gives TCP protec-tion against misrouted segments. This information is carried in the Inter-net Protocol and is transferred across the TCP/Network interface in the arguments (or results) of calls by TCP on IP.

```
+————+————+————+————+
| Source Address                |
+————+————+————+————+
| Destination Address           |
+————+————+————+————+
| zero      | PTCL   | TCP Length  |
+————+————+————+————+
```

The TCP Length is the TCP header length plus the data length in octets (this is not an explicitly transmitted quantity, but is computed), and it does not count the 12 octets of the pseudo header.

Urgent Pointer   It is 16 bits. This field communicates the current value of the urgent pointer as a positive offset from the sequence number in this segment. The urgent pointer points to the sequence number of the octet fol-lowing the urgent data. This field is only to be interpreted in segments with the URG control bit set.

Options   It means variable. Options may occupy space at the end of the TCP header and are a multiple of 8 bits in length. All options are included in the checksum. An option may begin on any octet boundary. There are two cases for the format of an option:

- Case 1: A single octet of option-kind.
- Case 2: An octet of option-kind, an octet of option-length, and the actual option-data octets.

The option-length counts the two octets of option-kind and option-length as well as the option-data octets.

The list of options may be shorter than the data offset field might imply. The content of the header beyond the End-of-Option option must be header padding (that is, zero). A TCP must implement all options.

Defined options include (kind indicated in octal):
Kind Length Meaning

—— ———— ————-

0—End of option list.
1—No-Operation.
2 4 Maximum Segment Size.

Specific Option Definitions:
End of Option List
```
+————+
|00000000|
+————+
```
Kind=0

This option code indicates the end of the option list. This might not coincide with the end of the TCP header according to the Data Offset field. This is used at the end of all options, not the end of each option, and need only be used if the end of the options would not otherwise coincide with the end of the TCP header.

No-Operation
```
+————+
|00000001|
+————+
```
Kind=1

This option code may be used between options, for example, to align the beginning of a subsequent option on a word boundary. There is no guarantee that senders will use this option, so receivers must be prepared to process options even if they do not begin on a word boundary.

Maximum Segment Size
```
+————+————+————-+————+
|00000010|00000100| max seg size |
+————+————+————-+————+
```
Kind=2 Length=4

Maximum Segment Size Option Data   It is 16 bits. If this option is present, then it communicates the maximum receive segment size at the TCP that sends this segment. This field must only be sent in the initial connection request (that is, in segments with the SYN control bit set). If this option is not used, any segment size is allowed.

Padding It is variable. The TCP header padding is used to ensure that the TCP header ends and data begins on a 32-bit boundary. The padding is composed of zeros.

TCP Terminology

It is important to understand some detailed terminology of TCP. Consider the following information. The maintenance of a TCP connection requires the remembering of several variables. We conceive of these variables being stored in a connection record called a *Transmission Control Block* (TCB). Among the variables stored in the TCB are the local and remote socket numbers, the security and precedence of the connection, pointers to the user's send and receive buffers, and pointers to the retransmit queue and to the current segment. In addition several variables relating to the send and receive sequence numbers are stored in the TCB.

Knowing When to Keep Quiet

To be sure that a TCP does not create a segment that carries a sequence number which may be duplicated by an old segment remaining in the network, the TCP stack must keep quiet for a *maximum segment lifetime* (MSL) before assigning any sequence numbers on starting up or recovering from a crash in which memory of sequence numbers in use was lost. For this specification, the MSL is taken to be 2 minutes. This is an engineering choice, and might be changed if experience indicates it is desirable to do so. If TCP is reinitialized in some sense, yet retains its memory of sequence numbers in use, it need not wait; it must only be sure to use sequence numbers larger than those recently used.

TCP Quiet Time Concept

This specification provides that hosts which "crash" without retaining any knowledge of the last sequence numbers transmitted on each active (that is, not closed) connection shall delay emitting any TCP segments for at least the agreed *Maximum Segment Lifetime* (MSL) in the Internet system of which the host is a part. In the following paragraphs, an explanation for this specification is given.

TCP consumes a sequence number each time a segment is formed and entered into the network output queue at a source host. The duplicate detection and sequencing algorithm in the TCP protocol relies on the unique binding of segment data to sequence space. This is done under the assumption that sequence numbers do not cycle through all 2**32 values before the segment data bound to those sequence numbers has been delivered and acknowledged by the receiver and all duplicate copies of the segments have "drained" from the Internet.

Two distinct TCP segments could otherwise be assigned to the same or overlapping sequence numbers and cause confusion at the receiver as to which data is new and which is old. Remember that each segment is bound to as many consecutive sequence numbers as there are octets of data in the segment.

Under normal conditions, TCP keeps track of the next sequence number to emit the oldest awaiting acknowledgment to avoid mistakenly using a sequence number over before its first use has been acknowledged. This does not guarantee that old duplicate data is drained from the net, so the sequence space has been made very large to reduce the probability that a delayed duplicate causes trouble on arrival. At 2 megabits/sec it takes 4.5 hours to use up 2**32 octets of sequence space. Because the maximum segment lifetime in the net is not likely to exceed a few tenths of seconds, this is deemed ample protection. At 100 megabits/sec, the cycle time is 5.4 minutes.

The basic duplicate detection and sequencing algorithm in TCP can be problematic, however, if a source TCP stack does not have any memory of the sequence numbers it last used on a given connection. For example, if TCP were to start all connections with the sequence number 0, then on crashing and restarting, a TCP might re-form an earlier connection (possibly after half-open connection resolution) and emit packets with sequence numbers identical to or overlapping with packets still in the network, which were emitted on an earlier incarnation of the same connection. In the absence of knowledge about the sequence numbers used on a particular connection, the TCP specification recommends that the source delays for MSL seconds before emitting segments on the connection. This allows time for segments from the earlier connection incarnation to drain from the system.

Even hosts that can remember the time of day and used it to select initial sequence number values are not immune from this problem that is, even if time of day is used to select an initial sequence number for each new connection incarnation).

Suppose a connection is opened starting with sequence number S. Suppose that this connection is not used much, and that eventually the *initial sequence number function* (ISN(t)) takes on a value equal to the sequence number, say $S1$, of the last segment sent by this TCP on a particular connection. Now suppose, at this instant, the host crashes, recovers, and establishes a new incarnation of the connection. The initial sequence number chosen is $S1 = $ ISN(t)—last used sequence number on old incarnation of connection! If the recovery occurs quickly enough, any old duplicates in the net bearing sequence numbers in the neighborhood of $S1$ may arrive and be treated as new packets by the receiver of the new incarnation of the connection.

The problem is that the recovering host may not know for how long it crashed, nor does it know whether there are still old duplicates in the system from earlier connection incarnations.

One way to deal with this problem is to deliberately delay emitting segments for one MSL after recovery from a crash—this is the *quiet time* specification. Hosts, which prefer to avoid waiting, are willing to risk possible confusion of old and new packets at a given destination may choose not to wait for the *quiet time*. Implementers may provide TCP users with the ability to select on a connection-by-connection basis whether to wait after a crash, or may informally implement the quiet time for all connections.

Obviously, even where a user selects to "wait," this is not necessary after the host has been "up" for at least MSL seconds. To summarize: Every segment emitted occupies one or more sequence numbers in the sequence space. The numbers occupied by a segment are *busy* or *in use* until MSL seconds have passed. On crashing, a block of space-time is occupied by the octets of the last emitted segment. If a new connection is started too soon and uses any of the sequence numbers in the footprint of the last segment of the previous connection incarnation, there is a potential sequence number overlap area, which could cause confusion at the receiver.

Establishing a TCP Connection

The *three-way handshake* is the procedure used to establish a connection. This procedure normally is initiated by one TCP stack and responded to by another. The procedure also works if two TCP stacks simultaneously initiate the procedure. When simultaneous attempts occur, each TCP stack receives a "SYN" segment that carries no acknowledgment after it has sent a "SYN." Of course, the arrival of an old duplicate "SYN" segment can potentially make it appear, to the recipient, that a simultaneous connection initiation is in progress. Proper use of "reset" segments can disambiguate these cases. Although examples do not show connection synchronization using data-carrying segments, this is perfectly legitimate, so long as the receiving TCP stack doesn't deliver the data to the user until it is clear the data is valid. This means the data must be buffered at the receiver until the connection reaches the ESTABLISHED state. The three-way handshake reduces the possibility of false connections. It is the implementation of a trade-off between memory and messages to provide information for this checking.

The simplest three-way handshake is shown in the illustration that follows this text. This should be interpreted in the following way.

Each line is numbered for reference purposes. Right arrows (—>) indicate departure of a TCP segment from TCP A to TCP B, or arrival of a segment at B from A. Left arrows (<—) indicate the reverse. Ellipsis (. . .) indicates a segment that is still in the network (delayed). An "XXX" indicates a segment that is lost or rejected. Comments appear in parentheses. TCP states represent the state AFTER the departure or arrival of the segment (whose contents are shown in the center of each line). Segment contents are shown in abbreviated form with sequence number, control flags, and ACK field. Other fields such as window, addresses, lengths, and text have been left out in the interest of clarity.

```
  TCP STACK -A                                  TCP STACK-B

1 CLOSED                                        LISTEN

2 SYN-SENT-> <SEQ=100><CTL=SYN> ->              SYN-RECEIVED

3 ESTABLISHED <-<SEQ=300><ACK=101>
    <CTL=SYN,ACK>                               <- SYN-RECEIVED

4 ESTABLISHED -><SEQ=101><ACK=301>              ESTABLISHED
    <CTL=ACK>->

5 ESTABLISHED-><SEQ=101><ACK=301>               >ESTABLISHED
    <CTL=ACK><DATA>->
```

In line 2 TCP stack A begins by sending a SYN segment indicating that it uses sequence numbers starting with sequence number 100. In line 3, B sends a SYN and acknowledges the SYN it received from A. Note that the acknowledgment field indicates B is now expecting to hear sequence 101, acknowledging the SYN that occupied sequence 100. At line 4, A responds with an empty segment containing an ACK for B's SYN; and in line 5, A sends some data. Note that the sequence number of the segment in line 5 is the same as in line 4, because the ACK does not occupy sequence number space (if it did, we would wind up ACKing ACKs!).

Simultaneous initiation is only slightly more complex. Each TCP cycles from CLOSED to SYN-SENT to SYN-RECEIVED to ESTABLISHED.

```
TCP STACK- A                              TCP STACK-B
1 CLOSED                                  CLOSED
2 SYN-SENT-> <SEQ=100><CTL=SYN>  . . .
3 SYN-RECEIVED <-<SEQ=300>
  <CTL=SYN><- SYN-SENT
4  . . . <SEQ=100><CTL=SYN>->    SYN-RECEIVED
5 SYN-RECEIVED -><SEQ=100>                . . .
  <ACK=301><CTL=SYN,ACK>
6 ESTABLISHED <-<SEQ=300>        <-SYN-RECEIVED
  <ACK=101><CTL=SYN,ACK>
7  . . . <SEQ=101><ACK=301>
  <CTL=ACK>-> ESTABLISHED
```

The reason for the three-way handshake is to prevent old duplicate connection initiations from causing confusion. To deal with this, a special control message, reset, has been devised. If the receiving TCP stack is in a non-synchronized state (that is, SYN-SENT, SYN-RECEIVED), it returns to LISTEN on receiving an acceptable reset. If the TCP stack is in one of the synchronized states (ESTABLISHED, FIN-WAIT-1, FIN-WAIT-2, CLOSE-WAIT, CLOSING, LAST-ACK, TIME-WAIT), it aborts the connection and informs its user.

Consider half-open connections shown as follows.

```
TCP STACK- A                              TCP STACK-B
1 CLOSED                                  LISTEN
2 SYN-SENT-><SEQ=100>                     . . .
  <CTL=SYN>
3 (duplicate) . . .  <SEQ=90>    SYN-RECEIVED
  <CTL=SYN>->
4 SYN-SENT <-<SEQ=300>           SYN-RECEIVED
  <ACK=91><CTL=SYN,ACK><-
5 SYN-SENT-><SEQ=91>             LISTEN
  <CTL=RST>->
6  . . .  <SEQ=100><CTL=SYN>->   SYN-RECEIVED
7 SYN-SENT<-<SEQ=400>            SYN-RECEIVED
  <ACK=101><CTL=SYN,ACK><-
8 ESTABLISHED-><SEQ=101>         ESTABLISHED
  <ACK=401><CTL=ACK>->
```

At line 3, an old duplicate SYN arrives at B. B cannot tell that this is an old duplicate, so it responds normally (line 4). A detects that the ACK field is incorrect and returns a RST (reset) with its SEQ field selected to make the segment believable. B, on receiving the RST, returns to the LISTEN state.

When the original SYN (pun intended) finally arrives at line 6, the synchronization proceeds normally. If the SYN at line 6 had arrived before the RST, a more complex exchange might have occurred with RSTs sent in both directions.

Half-Open Connections and Other Anomalies

An established connection is said to be *half-open* if one of the TCP stacks has closed or aborted the connection at its end without the knowledge of the other, or if the two ends of the connection have become desynchronized owing to a crash that resulted in loss of state. Such connections automatically reset if an attempt is made to send data in either direction. However, *half-open* connections are expected to be unusual, and the recovery procedure is involved.

If at site A, the connection no longer exists, then an attempt by a user at site B to send any data using the connection results in the site B TCP receiving a reset control message. Such a message indicates to site B TCP stack that something is wrong, and it is expected to abort the connection.

Assume that two user processors, A and B, are communicating with one another when a crash occurs causing loss of memory contents to A's TCP stack. Depending on the operating system supporting A's TCP stack, it is likely that some error recovery mechanism exists. When TCP is up again, A is likely to start again from the beginning or from a recovery point. As a result, A probably tries to OPEN the connection again or tries to SEND on the connection it believes is open. In the latter case, it receives the error message "connection not open" from the local (A's) TCP. In an attempt to establish the connection, A's TCP sends a segment containing SYN.

After TCP A crashes, the user attempts to re-open the connection. TCP B, in the meantime, thinks the connection is open. Consider the following.

```
TCP A                                TCP B
1 (CRASH)                            (send 300,receive 100)
2 CLOSED                             ESTABLISHED
3 SYN-SENT-><SEQ=400>                (??)
  <CTL=SYN>->
```

```
4 (!!)<-<SEQ=300><ACK=100>
  <CTL=ACK><-ESTABLISHED
5 SYN-SENT-><SEQ=100>            (Abort!!)
  <CTL=RST>->
6 SYN-SENT                       CLOSED
7 SYN-SENT-><SEQ=400><CTL=SYN>   ->
```

When the SYN arrives at line 3, TCP B, being in a synchronized state and the incoming segment outside the window, responds with an acknowledgment indicating what sequence it next expects to hear (ACK 100). TCP A sees that this segment does not acknowledge anything it sent and, being unsynchronized, sends a *reset* (RST) because it has detected a half-open connection. TCP B aborts at line 5. TCP A continues to try to establish the connection; the problem is now reduced to the basic three-way handshake.

An interesting alternative case occurs when TCP A crashes and TCP B tries to send data on what it thinks is a synchronized connection. This is illustrated in the example after this text. In the following case, the data arriving at TCP A from TCP B (line 2) is unacceptable because no such connection exists, so TCP A sends a RST. The RST is acceptable, so TCP B processes it and aborts the connection.

```
TCP A                           TCP B
1 (CRASH)                       (end 300,receive 100)
2 (??) <-<SEQ=300><ACK=100>     <-ESTABLISHED
  <DATA=10><CTL=ACK>
3 -><SEQ=100><CTL=RST>->        (ABORT!!)
```

In the following illustration, two TCPs, A and B, with passive connections are waiting for SYN. An old duplicate arriving at TCP B (line 2) stirs B into action. A SYN-ACK is returned (line 3) and causes TCP A to generate a RST (the ACK in line 3 is not acceptable). TCP B accepts the reset and returns to its passive LISTEN state.

```
TCP A                           TCP B
1 LISTEN                        LISTEN
2  . . . <SEQ=Z><CTL=SYN>->     SYN-RECEIVED
3 (??)<-<SEQ=X><ACK=Z11>        SYN-RECEIVED
  <CTL=SYN,ACK><-
4 -><SEQ=Z11><CTL=RST>->        (return to LISTEN!)
5 LISTEN                        LISTEN
```

Old Duplicate SYN initiates a Reset on two Passive Sockets by the following rules for RST generation and processing.

Reset Generation

As a general rule, *reset* (RST) must be sent whenever a segment arrives which apparently is not intended for the current connection. A reset must not be sent if it is not clear that this is the case. There are three groups of states:

1. If the connection does not exist (CLOSED), then a reset is sent in response to any incoming segment, except another reset. In particular, SYNs addressed to a non-existent connection are rejected by this means. If the incoming segment has an ACK field, the reset takes its sequence number from the ACK field of the segment. Otherwise the reset has sequence number zero and the ACK field is set to the sum of the sequence number and segment length of the incoming segment. The connection remains in the CLOSED state.

2. If the connection is in any non-synchronized state (LISTEN, SYN-SENT, SYN-RECEIVED), and the incoming segment acknowledges something not yet sent (the segment carries an unacceptable ACK), or if an incoming segment has a security level or compartment, which does not exactly match the level and compartment requested for the connection, a reset is sent.

   If our SYN has not been acknowledged and the precedence level of the incoming segment is higher than the precedence level requested, then either raise the local precedence level (if allowed by the user and the system) or send a reset. Or if the precedence level of the incoming segment is lower than the precedence level requested, then continue as if the precedence matched exactly. (If the remote TCP cannot raise the precedence level to match ours, this is detected in the next segment it sends, and the connection is then terminated.) If our SYN has been acknowledged (perhaps in this incoming segment), the precedence level of the incoming segment must match the local precedence level exactly, if it does not a reset must be sent.

   If the incoming segment has an ACK field, the reset takes its sequence number from the ACK field of the segment. Otherwise the reset has sequence number zero and the ACK field is set to the sum of the sequence number and segment length of the incoming segment. The connection remains in the same state.

3. If the connection is in a synchronized state
   (ESTABLISHED, FIN-WAIT-1, FIN-WAIT-2, CLOSE-WAIT,

CLOSING, LAST-ACK, TIME-WAIT), any unacceptable segment (out of window sequence number or unacceptable acknowledgment number) must elicit only an empty acknowledgment segment containing the current send-sequence number and an acknowledgment indicating the next sequence number expected to be received, and the connection remains in the same state.

4. If an incoming segment has a security level, compartment, or precedence which does not exactly match the level, compartment, and precedence requested for the connection, a reset is sent and connection goes to the CLOSED state. The reset takes its sequence number from the ACK field of the incoming segment.

TCP Reset Processing

In all states except SYN-SENT, all *reset* (RST) segments are validated by checking their SEQ-fields. A reset is valid if its sequence number is in the window. In the SYN-SENT state (a RST received in response to an initial SYN), the RST is acceptable if the ACK field acknowledges the SYN.

The receiver of a RST first validates it, and then changes state. If the receiver was in the LISTEN state, it ignores it. If the receiver was in SYN-RECEIVED state and had previously been in the LISTEN state, then the receiver returns to the LISTEN state, otherwise the receiver aborts the connection and goes to the CLOSED state. If the receiver was in any other state, it aborts the connection, advises the user, and goes to the CLOSED state.

Closing a TCP Connection

CLOSE is an operation meaning "I have no more data to send." The notion of closing a full-duplex connection is subject to ambiguous interpretation, of course, because it might not be obvious how to treat the receiving side of the connection. We have chosen to treat CLOSE in a simplex fashion. The user who CLOSEs might continue to RECEIVE until he is told that the other side has CLOSED also. Thus, a program could initiate several SENDs followed by a CLOSE, and then continue to RECEIVE until signaled that a RECEIVE failed because the other side has CLOSED. We assume that the TCP signals a user, even if no RECEIVEs are outstanding, that the other side has closed, so the user can terminate his side gracefully. A TCP reliably delivers all buffers SENT before the connection is CLOSED. This ensures a user who expects no data in return need only wait to hear the connection was CLOSED successfully to know that all his data was received at the destination TCP. Users must keep reading connections they close for sending until the TCP says no more data.

Essentially three cases exist:

1. The user initiates by telling the TCP to CLOSE the connection.
2. The remote TCP initiates by sending a FIN control signal.
3. Both users CLOSE simultaneously.

Case 1 Local User Initiates the Close In this case, a FIN segment can be constructed and placed on the outgoing segment queue. No further SENDs from the user are accepted by the TCP, and it enters the FIN-WAIT-1 state. RECEIVEs are allowed in this state. All segments preceding and including FIN are retransmitted until acknowledged. When the other TCP has both acknowledged the FIN and sent a FIN of its own, the first TCP can ACK this FIN. Note that a TCP receiving a FIN ACKs but does not send its own FIN until its user has CLOSED the connection also.

Case 2 TCP Receives a FIN from the Network If an unsolicited FIN arrives from the network, the receiving TCP can ACK it and tell the user that the connection is closing. The user responds with a CLOSE, on which the TCP can send a FIN to the other TCP after sending any remaining data. The TCP then waits until its own FIN is acknowledged before it deletes the connection. If an ACK is not forthcoming, after the user timeout the connection is aborted and the user is told.

Case 3 Both Users Close Simultaneously A simultaneous CLOSE by users at both ends of a connection causes FIN segments to be exchanged. When all segments preceding the FINs have been processed and acknowledged, each TCP can ACK the FIN it has received. On receiving these ACKs, both delete the connection.

```
  TCP A                                 TCP B
1 ESTABLISHED                           ESTABLISHED
2 Close FIN-WAIT-1-><SEQ=100>           CLOSE-WAIT
  <ACK=300><CTL=FIN,ACK>->
3 FIN-WAIT-2<-<SEQ=300>                 CLOSE-WAIT
  <ACK=101><CTL=ACK><-
4 Close TIME-WAIT<-<SEQ=300>            <-LAST-ACK
  <ACK=101><CTL=FIN,ACK>
```

```
5 TIME-WAIT-><SEQ=101>                CLOSED
  <ACK=301><CTL=ACK>->
6 2 MSL                               CLOSED

TCP A                                 TCP B
1 ESTABLISHED                         ESTABLISHED
2 Close                               Close
FIN-WAIT-1-><SEQ=100><ACK=300>
<CTL=FIN,ACK>                         . . . FIN-WAIT-1
<-<SEQ=300><ACK=100><CTL=FIN,
ACK><- . . .
<SEQ=100><ACK=300><CTL=FIN,
ACK>->
3 CLOSING-><SEQ=101><ACK=301>        <-
  <CTL=ACK> . . . CLOSING
<- <SEQ=301><ACK=101><CTL=ACK>
  . . . <SEQ=101><ACK=301>
  <CTL=ACK>                           ->
4 TIME-WAIT                           TIME-WAIT
2 MSL                                 2 MSL
CLOSED                                CLOSED
```

Precedence and Security

The intent is that connections be allowed only between ports operating with exactly the same security and compartment values, and at the higher of the two precedence levels requested by the two ports. The precedence and security parameters used in TCP are exactly those defined in the *Internet Protocol* (IP). Throughout this TCP specification the term *security/compartment* is intended to indicate the security parameters used in IP including security, compartment, user group, and handling restriction. A connection attempt with mismatched security/compartment values or a lower precedence value must be rejected by sending a reset. Rejecting a connection due to too low a precedence only occurs after an acknowledgment of the SYN has been received. TCP modules, which operate only at the default value of precedence, still have to check the precedence of incoming segments and possibly raise the precedence level they use on the connection.

The security parameters may be used even in a non-secure environment (the values would indicate unclassified data), thus hosts in non-secure environments must be prepared to receive the security parameters, though they need not send them.

TCP & Data Communication

After the connection is established, data is communicated by the exchange of segments. Because segments might be lost due to errors (checksum test failure) or network congestion, TCP uses retransmission (after a timeout) to ensure delivery of every segment. Duplicate segments might arrive due to network or TCP retransmission. As discussed in the section on sequence numbers, the TCP performs certain tests on the sequence and acknowledgment numbers in the segments to verify their acceptability.

The sender of data keeps track of the next sequence number to use in the variable SND.NXT. The receiver of data keeps track of the next sequence number to expect in the variable RCV.NXT. The sender of data keeps track of the oldest unacknowledged sequence number in the variable SND.UNA. If the data flow is momentarily idle and all data sent has been acknowledged, then the three variables are equal. When the sender creates a segment and transmits it, the sender advances SND.NXT. When the receiver accepts a segment, it advances RCV.NXT and sends an acknowledgment. When the data sender receives an acknowledgment, it advances SND.UNA. The extent to which the values of these variables differ is a measure of the delay in the communication.

The amount by which the variables are advanced is the length of the data in the segment. Note that once in the ESTABLISHED state, all segments must carry current acknowledgment information. The CLOSE user call implies a push function, as does the FIN control flag in an incoming segment.

TCP Retransmission Timeout

Because of the variability of the networks that compose an internetwork system and the wide range of uses of TCP connections, the retransmission timeout must be dynamically determined. One procedure for determining a retransmission time out is given here as an illustration.

An example Retransmission Timeout Procedure is to measure the elapsed time between sending a data octet with a particular sequence number and receiving an acknowledgment that covers that sequence number (segments sent do not have to match segments received).

TCP Communication of Urgent Information

The objective of the TCP urgent mechanism is to allow the sending user to stimulate the receiving user to accept some urgent data and to permit the receiving TCP to indicate to the receiving user when all the currently known urgent data has been received by the user. This mechanism permits a point in the data stream to be designated as the end of urgent information. Whenever this point is in advance of the receive sequence number (RCV.NXT) at the receiving TCP, that TCP must tell the user to go into "urgent mode." When the receive sequence number catches up to the urgent pointer, the TCP must tell user to go into "normal mode." If the urgent pointer is updated while the user is in "urgent mode," the update is invisible to the user.

This method employs an urgent field, which is carried in all segments transmitted. The URG control flag indicates that the urgent field is meaningful and must be added to the segment sequence number to yield the urgent pointer. The absence of this flag indicates that there is no urgent data outstanding.

To send an urgent indication the user must also send at least one data octet. If the sending user also indicates a push, timely delivery of the urgent information to the destination process is enhanced.

Managing the Window

The window sent in each segment indicates the range of sequence numbers the sender of the window (the data receiver) is currently prepared to accept. There is an assumption that this is related to the currently available data buffer space available for this connection.

Indicating a large window encourages transmissions. If more data arrives than can be accepted, it might be discarded. This might result in excessive retransmissions, adding unnecessarily to the load on the network and the TCP stacks. Indicating a small window might restrict the transmission of data to the point of introducing a round trip delay between each new segment transmitted; that is, it has become synchronized, send/receive.

The mechanisms provided allow a TCP stack to advertise a large window and to subsequently advertise a much smaller window. This, so called *shrinking the window*, is strongly discouraged. According to RFC 793, the robustness principle dictates that TCP not shrink the window itself, but be prepared for such behavior on the part of other TCP stacks.

The sending TCP stack must be prepared to accept data/packets from the user and send at least one octet of new data even if the send window is zero. The sending TCP stack must regularly retransmit to the receiving TCP stack even when the window is zero. Two minutes is recommended for the retransmission interval when the window is zero. This retransmission is essential to guarantee that when either TCP has a zero window, the re— opening, that is, size increases of the window, is reliably reported to the other stack.

When the receiving TCP stack has a zero window and a segment arrives, it must still send an acknowledgment showing its next expected sequence number and current window (zero).

The sending TCP packages the data to be transmitted into segments that fit the current window, and may repackage segments on the retransmission queue. Such repackaging is not required, but might be helpful.

In a connection with a one-way data flow, the window information is carried in acknowledgment segments that all have the same sequence number: There is no way to reorder the segments if they arrive out of order. This is not a serious problem, but it allows the window information to be, on occasion, temporarily based on old reports from the data receiver. A refinement to avoid this problem is to act on the window information from segments that carry the highest acknowledgment number (that is segments with an acknowledgment number equal or greater than the highest previously received).

Window management procedure has significant influence on the communication performance. Consideration the following

- Allocating a small window causes data to be transmitted in many small segments when better performance is achieved using fewer large segments

- Another suggestion for avoiding small windows is for the receiver to defer updating a window until the additional allocation is at least X percent of the maximum receive allocation possible for the connection (where X might be 20 to 40).

- Another suggestion is for the sender to avoid sending small segments by waiting until the window is large enough before sending data. However, if the user signals a push function, then the data must be sent even if it is a small segment.

Acknowledgments should not be delayed or unnecessary retransmissions result. One strategy would be to send an acknowledgment when a small segment arrives (without updating the window information), and then to send another acknowledgment with new window information when the window is larger. The segment sent to probe a zero window may also begin a break up of transmitted data into smaller and smaller segments. If a segment containing a single data octet sent to probe a zero window is accepted, it consumes one octet of the window now available. If the sending TCP stack simply sends as much as it can whenever the window is non zero, the transmitted data is broken into alternating big and small segments.

TCP implementations need to actively attempt to defragment small window allocations into larger windows, because the mechanisms for managing the window tend to lead to many small windows in the simplest minded implementations.

Two TCP interfaces are of concern: the user/TCP interface and the TCP/lower-level interface.

User/TCP Interface

The following functional description of user commands to the TCP stack is, at best hypothetical, because every operating system has different facilities. Consequently, I must warn readers that different TCP stack implementations might have different user interfaces. However, all TCP must provide a certain minimum set of services to guarantee that all TCP implementations can interoperate.

TCP User Commands

The following sections functionally characterize a USER/TCP interface. The notation used is similar to most procedure or function calls in high level languages, but this usage is not meant to rule out trap-type service calls.

User commands described as follows specify the basic functions the TCP must perform to support interprocess communication. Individual implementations must define their own exact format, and may provide combinations or subsets of the basic functions in single calls. In particular, some implementations might want to automatically OPEN a connection on the first SEND or RECEIVE issued by the user for a given connection.

In providing interprocess communication facilities, the TCP stack must not only accept commands, but must also return information to the processes it serves. The information consists of

1. General information about a connection (for example, interrupts, remote close, binding of unspecified foreign socket

2. Replies to specific user commands indicating success or various types of failure

Open

Format: OPEN (local port, foreign socket, active/passive [, timeout] [, precedence] [, security/compartment] [, options]) -> local connection name

We assume that the local TCP stack is aware of the identity of the processes it serves and checks the authority of the process to use the connection specified. Depending on the implementation of the TCP, the local network and TCP identifiers for the source address are supplied either by the TCP or by the lower level protocol (for example, IP). These considerations are the result of concern about security, to the extent that no TCP be able to masquerade as another one, and so on.

If the active/passive flag is set to passive, then this is a call to LISTEN for an incoming connection. A passive open may have either a fully specified foreign socket to wait for a particular connection or an unspecified foreign socket to wait for any call. A fully specified passive call can be made active by the subsequent execution of a SEND.

A *transmission control block* (TCB) is created and partially filled in with data from the OPEN command parameters. On an active OPEN command, the TCP begins the procedure to synchronize (that is, establish) the connection at once. The timeout, if present, permits the caller to set up a timeout for all data submitted to TCP. If data is not successfully delivered to the destination within the timeout period, the TCP aborts the connection. The present global default is five minutes.

The TCP or some component of the operating system verifies the user's authority to open a connection with the specified precedence or security/compartment. The absence of precedence or security/compartment specification in the OPEN call indicates the default values must be used.

TCP accepts incoming requests as matching only if the security/compartment information is exactly the same and only if the precedence is equal to or higher than the precedence requested in the OPEN call.

The precedence for the connection is the higher of the values requested in the OPEN call and received from the incoming request, and fixed at that value for the life of the connection. Implementers may want to give the user control of this precedence negotiation. For example, the user might be allowed to specify that the precedence must be exactly matched, or that any attempt to raise the precedence be confirmed by the user.

A local connection name is returned to the user by the TCP. The local connection name can then be used as a short hand term for the connection defined by the <local socket, foreign socket> pair.

Send

Format: SEND (local connection name, buffer address, byte count, PUSH flag, URGENT flag [,timeout])

This call causes the data contained in the indicated user buffer to be sent on the indicated connection. If the connection has not been opened, the SEND is considered an error. Some implementations may allow users to SEND first; in which case, an automatic OPEN would be done. If the calling process is not authorized to use this connection, an error is returned.

If the PUSH flag is set, the data must be transmitted promptly to the receiver, and the PUSH bit is set in the last TCP segment created from the buffer. If the PUSH flag is not set, the data may be combined with data from subsequent SENDs for transmission efficiency.

If the URGENT flag is set, segments sent to the destination TCP have the urgent pointer set. The receiving TCP signals the urgent condition to the receiving process if the urgent pointer indicates that data preceding the urgent pointer has not been consumed by the receiving process. The purpose of urgent is to stimulate the receiver to process the urgent data and to indicate to the receiver when all the currently known urgent data has been received. The number of times the sending user's TCP signals urgent is not necessarily equal to the number of times the receiving user is notified of the presence of urgent data.

If no foreign socket was specified in the OPEN, but the connection is established (for example, because a LISTENing connection has become specific due to a foreign segment arriving for the local socket), then the designated buffer is sent to the implied foreign socket. Users who make use of OPEN with an unspecified foreign socket can make use of SEND without knowing explicitly the foreign socket address.

However, if a SEND is attempted before the foreign socket becomes specified, an error is returned. Users can use the STATUS call to determine the status of the connection. In some implementations, the TCP might notify the user when an unspecified socket is bound.

If a timeout is specified, the current user timeout for this connection is changed to the new one. In the simplest implementation, SEND would not return control to the sending process until either the transmission was complete or the timeout had been exceeded. However, this simple method is both subject to deadlocks (for example, both sides of the connection might try to do SENDs before doing any RECEIVEs) and offers poor performance, so it is not recommended. A more sophisticated implementation would return immediately to allow the process to run concurrently with network I/O, and, furthermore, to allow multiple SENDs to be in progress.

Multiple SENDs are served in first come, first served order, so the TCP queues those it cannot service immediately.

We have implicitly assumed an asynchronous user interface in which a SEND later elicits some kind of SIGNAL or pseudo-interrupt from the serving TCP. An alternative is to return a response immediately. For instance, SENDs might return

- Immediate local acknowledgment, even if the segment sent had not been acknowledged by the distant TCP. We could optimistically assume eventual success. If we are wrong, the connection closes anyway due to the timeout. In implementations of this kind (synchronous), there are still some asynchronous
- Signals, but these deal with the connection itself, and not with specific segments or buffers.

In order for the process to distinguish among error or success indications for different SENDs, it might be appropriate for the buffer address to be returned along with the coded response to the SEND request. TCP-to-user signals are discussed as follows, indicating the information that should be returned to the calling process.

Receive

Format: RECEIVE (local connection name, buffer address, byte count) -> byte count, urgent flag, push flag

This command allocates a receiving buffer associated with the specified connection. If no OPEN precedes this command or the calling process is not authorized to use this connection, an error is returned. In the simplest implementation, control would not return to the calling program until either the buffer was filled, or some error occurred, but this scheme is highly subject to deadlocks. A more sophisticated implementation would permit several RECEIVEs to be outstanding at once. These would be filled as segments arrive. This strategy permits increased throughput at the cost of a more elaborate scheme (possibly asynchronous) to notify the calling program that a PUSH has been seen or a buffer filled.

If enough data arrive to fill the buffer before a PUSH is seen, the PUSH flag is not set in the response to the RECEIVE. The buffer is filled with as much data as it can hold. If a PUSH is seen before the buffer is filled, the buffer is returned partially filled and PUSH indicated. If there is urgent data the user is informed as soon as it arrives through a TCP-to-user signal. The receiving user should thus be in "urgent mode." If the URGENT flag is on, additional urgent data remains. If the URGENT flag is off, this call to RECEIVE has returned all the urgent data, and the user may now leave "urgent mode." Note that data following the urgent pointer (non-urgent data) cannot be delivered to the user in the same buffer with preceding urgent data unless the boundary is clearly marked for the user.

To distinguish among several outstanding RECEIVEs and to take care of the case that a buffer is not completely filled, the return code is accompanied by both a buffer pointer and a byte count indicating the actual length of the data received.

Alternative implementations of RECEIVE might have the TCP allocate buffer storage, or the TCP might share a ring buffer with the user.

Close

Format: CLOSE (local connection name)

This command causes the connection specified to be closed. If the connection is not open or the calling process is not authorized to use this connection, an error is returned. Closing connections is intended to be a graceful operation in the sense that outstanding SENDs are transmitted (and retransmitted), as flow control permits, until all have been serviced. Thus, it should be acceptable to make several SEND calls, followed by a CLOSE, and expect all the data to be sent to the destination. It should also be clear that users should continue to RECEIVE on CLOSING connections, because the other side might be trying to transmit the last of its data. Thus, CLOSE means "I have no more to send" but does not mean "I will not." receive any more." It might happen (if the user level protocol is not well thought out) that the closing side is unable to get rid of all its data before timing out. In this event, CLOSE turns into ABORT, and the closing TCP gives up.

The user may CLOSE the connection at any time on his own initiative, or in response to various prompts from the TCP (for example, remote close executed, transmission timeout exceeded, destination inaccessible). Because closing a connection requires communication with the foreign TCP, connections may remain in the closing state for a short time. Attempts to reopen the connection before the TCP replies to the CLOSE command result in error responses. Close also implies push function.

Status

Format: STATUS (local connection name) -> status data

This is an implementation-dependent user command and could be excluded without adverse effect. Information returned would typically come from the TCB associated with the connection.

This command returns a data block containing the following information:

Local socket

Foreign socket

Local connection name

Receive window

Send window

Connection state

Number of buffers awaiting acknowledgment

Number of buffers pending receipt

Urgent state

Precedence

Security/compartment

Transmission timeout

Depending on the state of the connection, or on the implementation itself, some of this information may not be available or meaningful. If the calling process is not authorized to use this connection, an error is returned. This prevents unauthorized processes from gaining information about a connection.

Abort

Format: ABORT (local connection name)

This command causes all pending SENDs and RECEIVES to be aborted, the TCB to be removed, and a special RESET message to be sent to the TCP on the other side of the connection. Depending on the implementation, users may receive abort indications for each outstanding SEND or RECEIVE, or may simply receive an ABORT-acknowledgment.

TCP-to-User Messages

It is assumed that the operating system environment provides a means for the TCP to asynchronously signal the user program. When the TCP does signal a user program, certain information is passed to the user. Often in the specification, the information is an error message. In other cases there is information relating to the completion of processing a SEND or RECEIVE or other user call. The following information is provided:

Local Connection Name Always

Response String Always

Buffer Address Send & Receive

Byte count (counts bytes received) Receive

Push flag Receive

Urgent flag Receive

TCP/Lower-Level Interface

TCP calls a lower-level protocol module to actually send and receive information over a network. One case is that of the ARPA Internet where the lower level module is the *Internet Protocol* (IP). The lower level protocol is IP and it provides arguments for a type of service and for a time to live. TCP uses the following settings for these parameters:

- Type of Service = Precedence: routine, Delay: normal,   Throughput: normal, Reliability: normal; or 00000000.

- Time to Live = one minute, or 60 seconds

The assumed maximum segment lifetime is one minute.

Here we explicitly ask that a segment be destroyed if it cannot be delivered by the Internet system within one minute. If the lower level is IP (or other protocol that provides this feature) and source routing is used, the interface must allow the route information to be communicated. This is especially important so that the source and destination addresses used in the TCP checksum be the originating source and ultimate destination. It is also important to preserve the return route to answer connection requests.

Any lower level protocol has to provide the source address, destination address, and protocol fields, and some way to determine the TCP length, both to provide the functional equivalent service of IP and to be used in the TCP checksum.

The Internet Society's RFC 793 has exhaustive details about TCP. The information here is presented courtesy of The Internet Society. I recommend you obtain additional information from

```
ftp://ftp.ncren.net
```

User Datagram Protocol (UDP)

User datagram protocol (UCP) resides at transport layer four. In many ways, it is the opposite of TCP. UDP is connectionless-oriented and unreliable with regard to the transmission of data. It does little more than provide a transport layer protocol for applications that reside above it.

UDP Header Analysis

The extent of information about UDP is brief compared to TCP. An example of the UDP datagram is shown in Figure 16-17.

The following lists the components of a UDP datagram and provides a brief description as well.

Source Port   The value in this field identifies the origin port. (Ports are used in addressing and are discussed in detail in the section on addressing.)

Destination Port   This identifies the recipient port for the data.

Length   The value in this field indicates the length of the data sent, including the header.

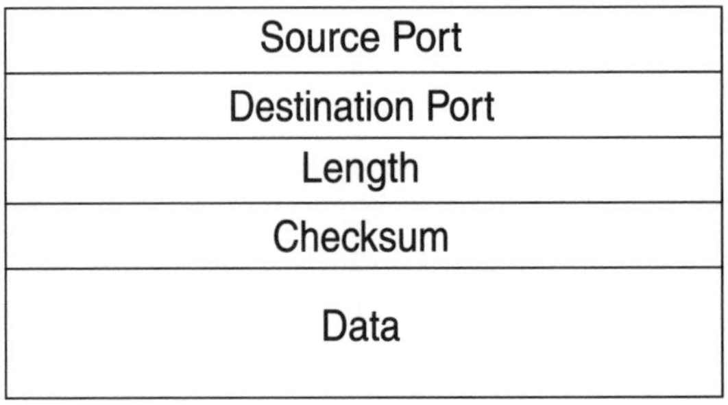

Figure 16-17
UDP datagram

Source Port
Destination Port
Length
Checksum
Data

Checksum   This field contains the pseudo-IP header, UDP header, and data value.

Data   The data field is the data passed from applications using UDP.

UDP Applications

UDP is a useful protocol. UDP is a good transport protocol to accomplish this task. Because UCP is unreliable, does not perform re-transmissions, and other services that TCP offers, applications must perform these functions if they require them (not all do). Because of UDP's nature, this leaves work for application programmers. These necessary operations can be achieved through the application.

Messages sent to UDP from applications are forwarded to IP for transmission. Some applications that use UDP protocol also pass messages directly to IP and ICMP for transmission.

A Perspective on TCP/IP Addressing

Addressing in TCP/IP involves of a variety of factors that work together to make TCP/IP a functioning upper layer network protocol. Some of these factors include

IP v4 Addressing

■ Address Classifications

■ Ports

- Well-Known-Ports
- Port manipulation
- Sockets
- Hardware addresses

Each are presented and synthesized to aid in understanding how they relate.

IP V.4 Addressing

The marketplace is still predominantly IP V.4 and consequently information on the topic is presented here. Internet Protocol V.4 uses a 32-bit addressing scheme. This addressing is implemented in software; however in some network devices it is implemented in firmware and/or non-volatile ram.

Each host participating in a TCP/IP network is identified through a 32-bit IP address. This is significant because it is different from the host's hardware address.

The IP addressing scheme structure appears like Figure 16-18.

In Figure 16-18 shows five classes of IP addresses. The IP addressing scheme is most easily expressed using dotted decimal notation. The classes of address indicate how many bits are used for a network address and how many for a host address. Before examining these in detail, a word about how these addresses are assigned is beneficial.

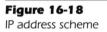

Figure 16-18
IP address scheme

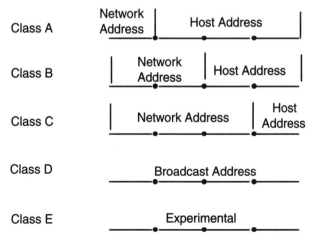

As Figure 16-18 shows, multiple classes of addresses exists. A reasonable question is, "why?" Two implementations of TCP/IP networks are possible: the Internet (big I) and internets (little i).

The Internet is a worldwide network that has thousands of entities connecting to it. An agency responsible for maintaining Internet addresses assigns IP addresses to entities connecting to the Internet. If a TCP/IP network is implemented in a corporation for example, then the IP addressing scheme is determined by the implementers responsible for that corporate network. In other words, it is locally administrated.

When the latter applies, the implementers must understand the ramifications of selecting a particular IP addressing scheme. Multiple factors apply when selecting an IP addressing scheme.

Address Classifications

In Figure 16-18, five classes of addresses were shown. Table 16-2 explains the meaning of each and how this effects hosts implemented with IP addresses.

Class A addresses have the least bits allocated to the network portion (one byte) and more bits (three bytes) allocated to host addressing. In other words, more hosts can be implemented than networks, according to the addressing scheme.

Class B addressing allocates an equal amount of bits for network addressing (two bytes) and host addressing (two bytes).

Class C addressing allocates more bits (three bytes) to the network portion and fewer bits (one byte) to the hosts portion.

Class D is used as a multicast address.

Class E networks are for experimental purposes. This author knows of no class E networks implemented.

Table 16-2

Effects on IP addresses

Address Class	Assigned Numbers
A	0—127
B	128—191
C	192—223
D	224—239
E	240—255

Implementing an internet uses these addresses in conjunction with machine names. For example, an address assigned to a host would usually have a name associated with it. A host with a class B address such as `137.1.0.99`, might have an alias name of FATBOY. This name and the internet address reside in a file (on UNIX systems) called `/etc/hosts`. This same file is named hosts under the Windows 2000 and NT operating system; located in `c:\windows` and `c:\winnt\system32\drivers\etc`, respectively. Another file related to this is the `/etc/networks file`. These two files, in a UNIX environment are normal in the configuration.

Ports

Ports are the addressable end point at TCP and UDP. This is partially how applications atop TCP and UDP are addressed.

Well-Known-Ports

TCP and UDP have popular applications that use them for a transport protocol. Without some standard mapping of ports and relationships to applications, chaos could exist. As a result, TCP and UDP have applications that are assigned to a Well-Known-Port.

Port Manipulation (Changing Port Numbers)

Port numbers can be changed, but usually they are not. However, there is reason for this capability to exist. For example, some network devices in the Internet community have little known abilities built into them for swapping say the telnet port from 23 to a different number. Another example could be changing the FTP port from 21 to something else. Why do this? Well, many reasons exist; typically, it is for administrative purposes.

Nevertheless, TCP and UDP applications can have their port changed. Some port numbers are available for development of custom applications. During the explanation of UDP, the concept of custom applications was presented. This is an example where being able to use a "free" port number would be required.

The downside of changing a port number is that it could cause problems in the network from a user perspective; the user's application would not find the new port number if it still used the old one.

Sockets

A socket is the combination of an IP address and port number. Sockets are used in programming and are not normally visible to general users. However, in some instances (such as programming, debugging, and so on) it is important to understand the socket concept.

Hardware Address

TCP/IP operates at layers three and above in a network, therefore it stands to reason an interface of some type is needed for a TCP/IP host to participate in a network. The question then becomes, "what is the lower layer protocol used?" If it is Ethernet, a 48 bit addressing scheme is used. If token ring, a 12 digit hexadecimal address, is used with other lower layer protocols—each have their own addressing scheme.

Understanding this addressing scheme is vital for those who troubleshoot networks. It is also important for those designing networks and implementers who have to make it work.

Synthesis

Understanding the previous information in this section is important for planning a TCP/IP network. The network size, purpose, and other site-specific parameters should be considered for selecting IP address classes and other issues presented here. Careful planning, with the technical implications understood in the beginning, can save time, money, and headaches in the long run.

Popular TCP Applications

In this section, some popular applications, which use TCP as a transport layer protocol, are explained. A list of those presented in this section include

- The X Window System
- TELNET
- File Transfer Protocol (FTP)

- Simple Mail Transfer Protocol (SMTP)
- Domain Name System (DNS)

X Window System

X is a distributed windowing system. At MIT in the early 1980s developers were looking for a way to develop applications in a distributed computed environment. They found that a distributed windowing system would meet their needs very well.

After the MIT guys met Stanford guys who had performed similar work, Stanford University gave MIT considerable help. The group at Stanford working on a distributed windowing system dubbed it *W*, for windowing. The individuals at MIT renamed it *X* based on the reason that it was the next letter in the alphabet. The name stuck.

By the late 1980s, X commanded a lot of attention in the market because it was free in UNIX based environments. One of the factors for its growth is its hardware and software independent. X is a dominant user interface in the UNIX environment; and it has spread into PC and Mini environments as well.

X is asynchronous and based on a client/server model. It can manipulate two- and three-dimensional graphics on a bitmapped display. Before examining some of the operational aspects of X, consider the layer of X and its relationship to the TCP/IP protocol suite in Figure 16-19.

Figure 16-19 shows the TCP/IP protocol suite, but the focus is on X. The protocol suite is there to understand the relationship of X with TCP/IP. X is not a transport layer protocol, however it uses TCP for a transport protocol.

X can be evaluated two ways. From a TCP/IP perspective, it comprises layers 5, 6, and 7. However, X itself has five layers. X's layer names and functions include

- *Protocol*   This is the lowest layer in X. It hooks into TCP (meaning it passes data directly to TCP.) This layer is actually one of the X protocol components.
- *Library*   The X library consist of a collection of C language routines which implements the X protocol. X library routines perform functions such as responding to the pressing a mouse button.
- *Toolkit*   The X toolkit is a higher level of programming tools. Examples of support provided from this layer is functions in programming related to scroll bar and menu functions.

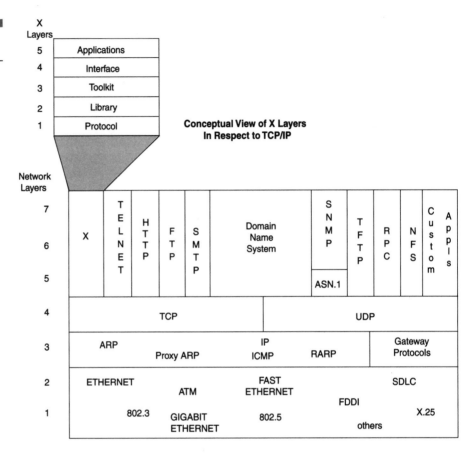

Figure 16-19
TCP/IP protocol suite

- *Interface*   The interface is what a user sees. Examples of an interface include CDE, SUN's OpenLook, HP's OpenView, and OSF's interfaces to name a few.
- *Applications*   X applications can be defined as client applications that use X and conform to X programming standards that interact with the X server.

X Theory of Operation

X clients and X servers function differently than other clients and servers do in the TCP/IP environment. What is considered normal operation of a client is it *initiates* something and servers *serve or answer* the request of clients. In X, the concept is reversed. For example, an X Server initiates and a Client answers the Server request.

A X display manager exists in the X environment. The X display manager itself can be started manually or automatically. In respect to X, the display manager (often referred to as Xdm) is a client application.

A X display server (usually the application/program called "X" interfaces between hardware components (displays, keyboard, mouse) and X client applications. The *X Display Server* (Xds) operates by catching data entered and directs it to the appropriate X client application.

The correlation of the X Display Manager and the X Display Server can be understood by considering the following scenario. Consider two windows are active on a physical display. Each window functions as a client application. This is required to maintain order because multiple windows may be on the display (say four or five).

In summary the X display manager and X server control the appearance of the display, which is what a user sees. However, most entities in an X environment function as X client applications. An example of clients are: Xclock, Xterm (which is a terminal emulator), and TN3270 (an emulation software package used to access a 3270 data stream in a SNA environment).

TELNET

TELNET is a TCP application. It provides the ability to perform remote logons to remote hosts. TELNET operates using a client and server. The majority of TCP/IP software implementations have TELNET, simply because it is part of the protocol suite. An exception to this is that TELNET is not a requirement in the TCP/IP suite; it is merely popular. Furthermore, TELNET can be a stand-alone application in the sense of how it is packaged and sold. As previously stated, *clients* initiate something (in this case, a remote logon) and *servers* serve requests of clients. Figure 16-20 shows the TCP/IP protocol suite with TELNET highlighted, showing its client and server.

In Figure 16-20, TELNET's client and server are shown. This example of TELNET is the same on practically all TCP/IP host implementations if the protocol suite has been developed according to the RFCs. Most host implementations such as UNIX, VMS, MVS, VM, VSE, NT, and some other operating systems the TELNET client and server are available.

Figure 16-21 is an example of TELNET client and server interaction between hosts. It shows a RS/6000 user invoking TELNET client. The RISC/6000 user wants to logon to the SUN host. The SUN host is running

Figure 16-20
Highlighted view
of TELNET

TELNET

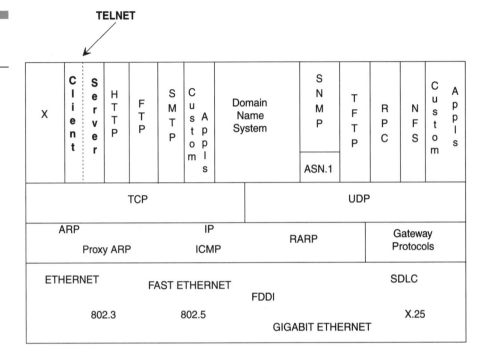

Figure 16-21
TELNET client/server
operation

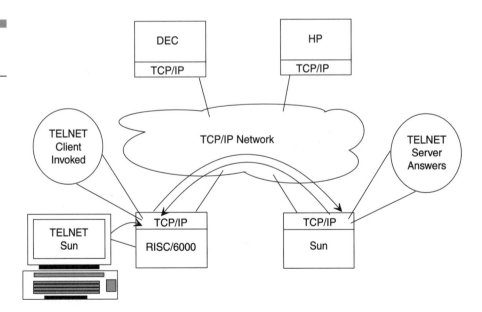

a TELNET server, the TELNET server answers the client's request and a logical connection is established between the RS/6000 and the SUN host. The RS/6000 user appear to be physically connected to the SUN.

TELNET works with the majority of major vendors in the marketplace today. The key to understanding the client/server concept is to remember clients *initiate* and servers *serve* clients request. The exception to this as of this writing is Microsoft. As of this writing, Microsoft has not included a TELNET server in their operating system software. One exception I am aware of is that the TELNET server is available in the services for UNIX and in the Options pack as well. However, companies such as Seattle Labs do offer a TELNET server that operates with Microsoft operating systems.

File Transfer Protocol (FTP)

FTP is a file transfer application that uses TCP for a transport protocol. FTP has a client and server like TELNET; they work in a similar manner. What differs between TELNET and FTP is TELNET enables remote logon whereas FTP permits file transfers.

FTP does not actually transfer a file from one host to another—it copies it. Hence, the original file exists and a copy of it has been put on a different machine. Figure 16-22 depicts this scenario.

Figure 16-22 shows a user on a SUN host performing two steps. First the SUN user executes FTP HP and a logon is established. Second, the SUN user issues the FTP command GET and designates the filename as FILEABC. The dotted line shows the file is copied from the HP disk to the SUN's disk.

Figure also shows a SUN, HP, and MVS host. The same operation can be performed either of these as well. The MVS host can perform any of the TCP/IP functions just as the SUN or MVS.

An interesting twist this scenario shown in Figure 16-22 is that a HP user could TELNET to the HP, then from the HP execute a FTP against the IBM and move a file *to* or *from* the IBM. That is, one can interact with multiple machines as part of a single session if desired.

Another twist is with the MVS host in Figure 16-22. In this scenario a HP user could execute a FTP against the MVS host and *PUT* the FILEABC into the MVS JES2 subsystem and have it print on the printer attached to the MVS printer.

These examples are practically as many as one could imagine. These are only a few examples to convey some simple operations.

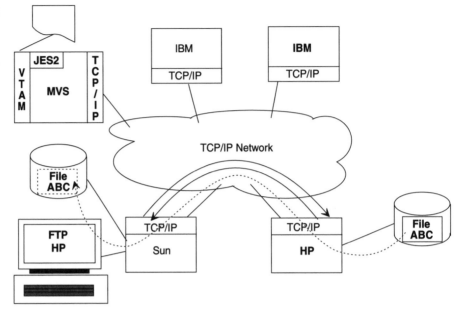

Figure 16-22
FTP client/server
operation

Step 1: Logon
Step2: Get file ABC

Simple Mail Transfer Protocol (SMTP)

SMTP is another TCP Application. It uses a client and server, on port number 25. SMTP utilizes what is called a user agent and a message transfer agent. Figure 16-23 is a simple example of how SMTP operates.

Sending mail is accomplished by invoking a user agent typically causes an editor to appear on the user's display. After the mail message is created and sent from the user agent, it is passed to the message transfer agent. The message transfer agent is responsible for establishing communication with a corresponding message transfer agent on the destination host. After this is accomplished, the sending message transfer agent sends the message to the receiving message transfer agent, then stores it in the appropriate queue for the user. The recipient of the mail only needs to invoke the user agent locally to read the mail.

Domain Name System (DNS)

The Internet originally used *hosts.txt* files to keep track of hosts on the Internet. This meant that when new hosts were added to the Internet all

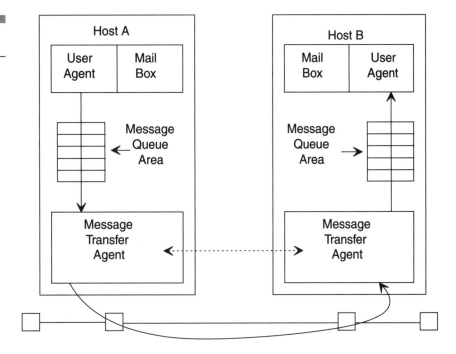

Figure 16-23
SMTP components

participating hosts had to have their *hosts.txt* file updated. As the Internet grew, this task became impossible in a timely manner. The *Domain Name System* (DNS) was designed to obviate updating host's files.

The philosophy of DNS was to replace the need to FTP updated *hosts* files throughout the entire network. DNS uses a distributed database architecture.

DNS Structure DNS is a hierarchical structure that conceptually appears as an inverted tree. The root is at the top and branches are below. Figure 16-24 is an example of how DNS is implemented in the Internet.

The legend for the DNS structure in Figure 16-24 is ROOT which is just a (.).

The root server contains information about itself and the top level domains immediately beneath it.

- *GOV*   Refers to government entities
- *EDU*   Refers to any educational institutions
- *ARPA*   Refers to any ARPANET (Internet) host
- *COM*   Refers to any commercial organizations

Figure 16-24
DNS structure

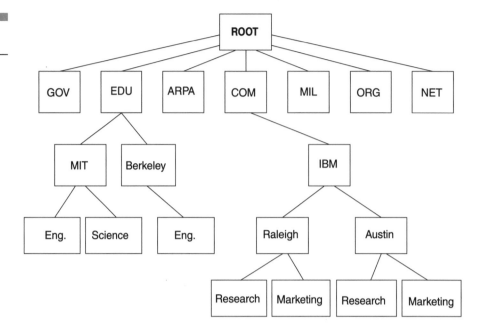

- *MIL*   Refers to military organizations
- *NET*   Refers to networks
- *ORG*   Serves as a miscellaneous category for those not formally covered

Figure 16-24 shows the Internet implementation of DNS. Notice IBM is under COM (which is commercial), beneath IBM is Raleigh and Austin, and beneath each of them are research and marketing. The other examples are MIT and Berkeley. The example with MIT shows beneath it two *zones*, engineering and science. (A zone is complete information about some part of a domain name space.) The Berkeley example has one layer beneath it entitled engineering.

DNS Components   To better understand DNS knowing its components that make it functional is helpful. These components include

- *Domain*   The last part in a domain name is considered the domain. For example, eng.mit.edu; here edu is the domain. The entire name is the *Fully Qualified Domain Name* (FQDN).
- *Domain Name*   Defined by the DNS as being the sequence of names and domain. For example, a domain name could be eng.mit.edu.

- *Name Server* A program (operating on a host) that maps names to addresses; it does this by mapping domain names to IP addresses. *In addition*, name server may be used to refer to a dedicated machine running name server software to permit client DNS lookups.

- *Name Resolver* This is software that functions as a client interacting with a name server. Sometimes it is referred to simply as the DNS client.

- *Name Cache* This is storage used by the name resolver to store information frequently used.

- *Zone* This is a contiguous part of a domain.

Theory of Operation Figure 16-25 shows a TCP/IP network with five hosts.

Of these five hosts, host B has been designated as the name server. It has a database with a list of NAMES and IP addresses of participating hosts in the network. When the user on host A wants to communicate with host C, the name resolver checks its local cache, and if no match is found then the name resolver client sends a request (also known as a query) to the name server.

Figure 16-25
Conceptual view
of DNS

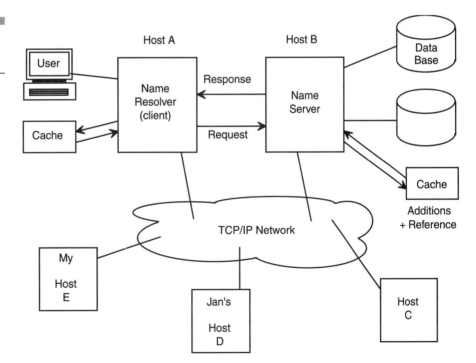

The name server in turn checks its cache for a match. If no match is found then the name server checks its database. Though not shown in this figure, if the name server were unable to locate the name in its cache or database, it would generally be confined to forward the request to another name server closer to the DNS root servers and then return the response back to host A.

In an Internet environment that implements DNS, some assumptions exist. For example, a name resolver is required, a name server, and usually a foreign name server is part of the network.

Implementation with UDP   The DNS provides service using TCP and UDP, this is why the figures have shown DNS above both TCP and UDP. It servers TCP zone transfers and UDP lookups.

Obtaining Additional Information   Additional information should be consulted on this issue if DNS is implemented. The following RFCs are a good beginning point.

RFC	882
RFC	883
RFC	920
RFC	973
RFC	974
RFC	1034
RFC	1123
RFC	1032
RFC	1033
RFC	1034
RFC	1035

Popular UDP Applications

This section presents popular UDP applications. A list of those covered include

- Simple Network Management Protocol (SNMP)
- Trivial File Transfer Protocol (TFTP)

- Network File System (NFS)
- Remote Procedure Call (RPC)
- Custom Applications
- PING

Simple Network Management Protocol (SNMP)

SNMP is the de facto standard for managing TCP/IP networks. SNMP uses agents and application managers (or simply managers). An agent can reside on any node that supports SNMP, and each agent maintains status information about the node on which it operates. These nodes, which may be a host, gateway, router, or other type network device, are called *network elements* in SNMP lingo. The term *element* is merely a generic reference to a node.

Normally, multiple *elements* exit in a TCP/IP network and each has their agent. Typically, one node is a network management node, the "network manager." The network manager node runs an application that communicates with all network elements to obtain the status of all element. The network management node and the element communicate through different message types. Some of these messages are

- *GET REQUEST* This type of request is used by the network manager to communicate with an element to request a variable from the particular network element.
- *GET RESPONSE* This is a reply to a GET REQUEST, SET REQUEST, and GET NEXT REQUEST.
- *GET NEXT REQUEST* This request is used to sequentially read information about an element.
- *SET REQUEST* This request enables variable values to be set in an element.
- *TRAP* This type message is designed to report information such as
- Link status
- Whether or not a neighbor responds
- Whether or not a message is received
- Status of the element

Information stored on elements is maintained in a *Management Information Base* (MIB). This MIB is a database containing information about a particular element; each element has a MIB. Examples of MIB information includes

- Statistical information regarding segments transferred to and from the manager application
- A community name
- Interface type
- And, other element specific information

MIB information structure is defined using *Structure of Management Information* (SMI) language. SMI is a language used to define a data structure and methods for identifying an element for the manager application. This information identifies object variables in the MIB. A minimum of object descriptions defined by SMI include

- ACCESS   Object access control is maintained through this description.
- DEFINITION   This provides a textual description of an object.
- NAMES   This is also synonymous with object identifiers.
- OBJECT DESCRIPTOR   This is a text name ascribed to the object.
- OBJECT IDENTIFIER   This is a numeric ID used to identify the object.
- STATUS   This describes the level of object support for status.

SNMP implementations use ASN.1 for defining data structures in network elements. Because this language is based on a data type definition, it can be used to define practically any element on a network.

SNMP itself is event oriented. An event is generated when a change occurs to an object. An example of a SNMP operation is typically that every ten minutes the manager application communicates with each network element regarding and reads MIB data from each.

Additional information can be obtained from the following RFCs.

RFC 1155

RFC 1156

RFC 1157

Trivial File Transfer Protocol (TFTP)

TFTP is an application that uses UDP as a transport mechanism. The program itself is simpler than its counterpart FTP, which uses TCP as a transport mechanism. TFTP is small enough in size that it can be burned into ROM on diskless workstations.

TFTP maximum packet size is 512 bytes. Because of this and the nature of operation, TFTP is popular with network devices such as routers and bridges. If implemented it is normally used on initial device boot.

TFTP utilizes no security provision or authentication; however, it does have some basic timing and re-transmission capabilities. TFTP uses five basic types of *protocol data units* (PDUs):

- Acknowledgment
- Data
- Error
- Read Request
- Write Request

These PDUs are used by UDP during file transfer. The first TFTP packet establishes a session with the target TFTP program. It then requests a file transfer between the two. Next it identifies a filename and whether or not a file is read or written.

These five PDUs comprise the operational ability of TFTP. It is much less complex than FTP.

Additional information can be obtained from the following RFCs.

RFC 783

RFC 1068

Remote Procedure Call (RPC)

RPC is a protocol. It can operate over TCP or UDP as a transport mechanism. Applications use RPC to call a routine; a client makes a call against a server on possibly a remote host. This type application programming is a high level, peer relationship between an application and a RPC server. These applications are portable to the extent that RPC is implemented.

RPC uses the *eXternal Data Representation* (XDR) protocol. XDR data description language can be used to define data types, allowing heterogeneous hosts to be integrated. XDR permits requests to be made against files on machines of different architecture/OS. In short, XDR permits data type definition in the form of parameters and transmission of these encoded parameters.

XDR provides data transparency by transforming data at the application layer; lower layers do not have to perform any conversion. A powerful aspect of XDR is automatic data conversion performed through declaration statements and the XDR compiler. The XDR compiler generates required XDR calls, thus making code generation less manual in nature. Figure 16-26 is an example of this type of implementation.

RPC implements a port mapper; it starts when the RPC server initializes. When RPC services start, the operating system assigns a port number to each service.

Client applications issue a service request to a port mapper. The port mapper in turn identifies the requested service and returns the output to the requesting client application. In other words, the port mapper is similar in function to a manager knowing what services are available and the address of each.

The port mapper can be used in a broadcast scenario. For example, a requesting RPC call can broadcast a call to all hosts on a network. Applicable port mappers report back with the information sought after by the client. Additional information on RPC and related components can be found in the following RFCs.

RFC   1057

RFC   1014

Figure 16-26
Conceptual view of
RPC and XDR

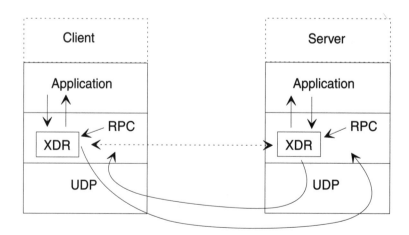

Network File System (NFS)

NFS is a product of Sun Microsystems. It permits users to access these files: they may be local or remote in respect to the user. Users might create, read, or remove a directory. Files themselves might be written to or deleted. NFS provides a distributed file system that permits users to access servers not just their local file system.

NFS uses *Remote Procedure Call* (RPC). NFS uses RPC to make an execution of a routine on a remote server possible. Conceptually, NFS, RPC, and UDP (which it typically uses) appear as Figure 16-27.

NFS enables you to have a single copy of each application on a server that all users on a network can access. The consequence is that software (and updates) can be installed on one server and not on multiple hosts in a networked environment. NFS is based on a client/server model. However, with NFS a single NFS server can function to serve the request of many client requests.

NFS's origins are in UNIX, where the file system is implemented in a hierarchical (tree) structure. NFS uses a *mount* protocol. This protocol maps a file system and remote host to a local user's file system. NFS's mount is registered with the port mapper, and thus is accessible by requesting client applications.

Figure 16-27
Conceptual view of NFS, RPC, and UDP

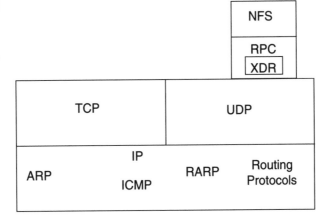

NFS also uses the UDP protocol. NFS uses port number 2049 in many cases, however this is not published as a well-known-port number. Consequently, you should determine the NFS port number using the port mapper.

From a user perspective, NFS is transparent. Typical user commands are entered, and then passed to the NFS server, and in most cases, a user does not know the physical location of a file in a networked environment.

Additional information about the Network File System and related components can be obtained through the following RFCs.

RFC   1094

RFC   1014

RFC   1057

Custom Applications

Custom applications can be written to use UDP as a transport mechanism. One scenario could be where two hosts need peer program communication through a network. Writing a custom application using UDP can achieve this task as Figure 16-28 shows.

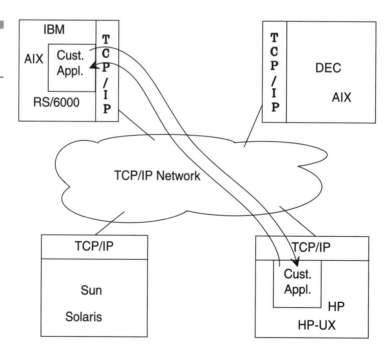

Figure 16-28
Custom applications using UDP

PING & Finger

Packet Internet Groper (PING) is actually an application. It is used to send a message to a host and wait for that host to respond to the message (if the target host is *alive*). PING uses ICMP echo messages and echo reply messages on NT, UDP & ICMP on UNIX/Cisco.

PING is a helpful tool on the TCP/IP networks that is used to determine if a device is running and accessible. A PING can also be issued against a remote host *name*. PING is generally used to troubleshoot TCP/IP networks.

FINGER is a command issued against a host that causes the target host to return information about users logged onto that host. An example of some information retrievable through FINGER includes user name, user interface, and that the user is running.

Additional information can be obtained about FINGER at The Internet Society's RFC 1288. A good location on the Internet to access RFCs is

```
ftp://ftp.ncren.net
```

HyperText Transfer Protocol (HTTP)

Hypertext Transfer Protocol (HTTP) is an application-level protocol for distributed, collaborative, hypermedia information systems. The first version (publicly available) of HTTP, referred to as HTTP/0.9, was a simple protocol for raw data transfer across the Internet. HTTP/1.0 improved the protocol by allowing messages to be in MIME-like message meta-information about the data to be transferred and modifiers on the request/response semantics. However, HTTP/1.0 does not take into consideration some of the effects of hierarchical proxies, caching, the need for persistent connections or virtual hosts. In addition, the proliferation of incompletely implemented applications calling themselves "HTTP 1.0" has necessitated a protocol version change in order for two communicating applications to determine each other's true capabilities.

Presented here is the HTTP protocol *HTTP 1.1*. This protocol is more stringent than HTTP/1.0 to ensure reliable implementation of its features. Practical information systems require more functionality than simple retrieval, including search, front-end update, and annotation. HTTP allows an open-ended set of methods that indicate the purpose of a request. It builds on the *Uniform Resource Identifier* (URI), as a *location* (URL) or *name* (URN), for indicating the resource to which a method is to be applied.

Terminology

This specification uses a number of terms to refer to the roles played by participants in, and objects of, the HTTP communication.

- *Connection*   A transport layer virtual circuit established between two programs for the purpose of communication

- *Message*   The basic unit of HTTP communication, consisting of a structured sequence of octets matching the syntax defined in section 4 and transmitted through the connection

- *Request*   An HTTP request message

- *Response*   An HTTP response message

- *Resource*   A network data object or service that can be identified by a URI. Resources may be available in multiple representations (for example multiple languages, data formats, size, resolutions) or vary in other ways.

- *Entity*   The information transferred as the payload of a request or response. An entity consists of meta-information in the form of entity-header fields and content in the form of an entity-body.

- *Representation*   An entity included with a response that is subject to content negotiation. There may exist multiple representations associated with a particular response status.

- *Content negotiation*   The mechanism for selecting the appropriate representation when servicing a request. The representation of entities in any response can be negotiated (including error responses).

- *Variant*   A resource may have one, or more than one, representation(s) associated with it at any given instant. Each representation is termed a *variant*. Use of the term *variant* does not necessarily imply that the resource is subject to content negotiation.

- *Client*   A program that establishes connections for the purpose of sending requests

- *User Agent*   The client which initiates a request. These are often browsers, editors, spiders (web-traversing robots), or other end user tools.

- *Server*   An application program that accepts connections to service requests by sending back responses. Any given program may be capable of being both a client and a server. My use of these terms refers only to the role being performed by the program for a particular connection, rather than to the program's capabilities in general. Likewise, any server may act as an origin server, proxy, gateway, or tunnel, switching behavior based on the nature of each request.

- *Origin Server* The server on which a given resource resides or is to be created

- *Proxy* An intermediary program which acts as both a server and a client making requests on behalf of other clients. Requests are serviced internally or by passing them on, with possible translation, to other servers. A proxy must implement both a client and server.

- *Tunnel* An intermediary program that is acting as a blind relay between two connections. After active, a tunnel is considered invisible to the HTTP communication, though the tunnel may have been initiated by an HTTP request. The tunnel ceases to exist when both ends of the relayed connections are closed.

- *Cache* A program's local store of data files and the subsystem that controls message storage, retrieval, and deletion. A cache stores cacheable responses to reduce the response time and network bandwidth consumption on future, equivalent requests.

- *Cacheable* A response is cacheable if a cache is allowed to store a copy of the response message for use in answering subsequent requests. Even if a resource is cacheable, there may be additional constraints on whether a cache can use the cached copy for a particular request.

- *First-hand* A response is first-hand if it comes directly from the origin server, perhaps through one or more proxies. A response is also first hand if its validity has just been checked directly with the origin server; that is authenticated.

- *Explicit Expiration Time* The time at which the origin server intends that an entity should no longer be returned by a cache, but should be revalidated

- *Heuristic Expiration Time* An expiration time assigned by a cache when no explicit expiration time is available.

- *Age* The age of a response is the time since it was sent by, or successfully validated with, the origin server.

- *Freshness Lifetime* The length of time between the generation of a response and its expiration time

- *Fresh* A response is fresh if its age has not yet exceeded its freshness lifetime.

- *Stale*   A response is stale if its age has passed its freshness lifetime.
- *Semantically*   **Author – missing text???**
- *Transparent*   A cache behaves in a "semantically transparent" manner, with respect to a particular response, when its use affects neither the requesting client nor the origin server, except to improve performance. When a cache is semantically transparent, the client receives exactly the same response (except for hop-by-hop headers) that it would have received had its request been handled directly by the origin server.
- *Validator*   A protocol element (for example, an entity tag or a Last-Modified time) that is used to find out whether a cache entry is an equivalent copy of an entity

Overall Operation

The HTTP protocol is a request/response protocol. A client sends a request to the server in the form of a request method, URI, and protocol version, followed by a MIME-like message containing request modifiers, client information, and possible body content over a connection with a server. The server responds with a status line, including the message's protocol version and a success or error code, followed by a MIME-like message containing server information, entity meta-information, and possible entity-body content.

Most HTTP communication is initiated by a user agent and consists of a request to be applied to a resource on some origin server. In the simplest case, this may be accomplished through a single connection (v) between the *user agent* (UA) and the *origin server* (O).

```
request chain ————————————————>
UA ——————————————-v——————————— O
<————————————————— response chain
```

A more complicated situation occurs when one or more intermediaries are present in the request/response chain. There are three common forms of intermediary: proxy, gateway, and tunnel. A proxy is a forwarding agent, receiving requests for a URI in its absolute form, rewriting all or part of the message, and forwarding the reformatted request toward the server identified by the URI. A gateway is a receiving agent, acting as a layer above some other server(s) and, if necessary, translating the requests to the underlying server's protocol. A tunnel acts as a relay point between two connections without changing the messages. Tunnels are used when the communication needs to pass through an intermediary (such as a firewall) even when the intermediary cannot understand the contents of the messages.

```
request chain —————————————————————>
UA ——-v——- A ——-v——- B ——-v——- C ——-v——- O
<——————————————————- response chain
```

The previous figure shows three intermediaries (A, B, and C) between the user agent and origin server. A request or response message that travels the whole chain passes through four separate connections. This distinction is important because some HTTP communication options may apply only to the connection with the nearest, non-tunnel neighbor, only to the end-points of the chain, or to all connections along the chain. Although the diagram is linear, each participant may be engaged in multiple, simultaneous communications. For example, B may be receiving requests from many clients other than A, and/or forwarding requests to servers other than C, at the same time that it is handling A's request.

Any party to the communication, which is not acting as a tunnel, may employ an internal cache for handling requests. The effect of a cache is that the request/response chain is shortened if one of the participants along the chain has a cached response applicable to that request. The following illustrates the resulting chain if B has a cached copy of an earlier response from O (through C) for a request that has not been cached by UA or A.

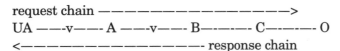

```
request chain ——————————————>
UA ——-v——- A ——-v——- B—————- C————- O
<————————————- response chain
```

Not all responses are usefully cacheable, and some requests may contain modifiers that place special requirements on cache behavior. In fact, there are a wide variety of architectures and configurations of caches and proxies currently being experimented with or deployed across the World Wide Web. These systems include national hierarchies of proxy caches to save transoceanic bandwidth, systems that broadcast or multicast cache entries, organizations that distribute subsets of cached data through CD-ROM, and so on. HTTP systems are used in corporate intranets over high-bandwidth links, and for access through PDAs with low-power radio links and intermittent connectivity. The goal of HTTP 1.1 is to support the wide diversity of configurations already deployed, while introducing protocol constructs that meet the needs of those who build Web applications that require high reliability and, failing that, at least reliable indications of failure.

HTTP communication usually takes place over TCP/IP connections. The default port is TCP 80, but other ports can be used. This does not preclude

HTTP from being implemented on top of any other protocol on the Internet, or on other networks. HTTP only presumes a reliable transport, and any protocol that provides such guarantees can be used. The mapping of the HTTP 1.1 request and response structures onto the transport data units of the protocol in question is outside the scope of this specification.

In HTTP 1.0, most implementations used a new connection for each request/response exchange. In HTTP 1.1, a connection may be used for one or more request/response exchanges, although connections may be closed for a variety of reasons.

Protocol Parameters

HTTP uses a <major>.<minor> numbering scheme to indicate versions of the protocol. The protocol versioning policy is intended to allow the sender to indicate the format of a message and its capacity for understanding further HTTP communication, rather than the features obtained through that communication. No change is made to the version number for the addition of message components which do not affect communication behavior or which only add to extensible field values.

The <minor> number is incremented when the changes made to the protocol add features which do not change the general message parsing algorithm, but which may add to the message semantics and imply additional capabilities of the sender. The <major> number is incremented when the format of a message within the protocol is changed.

The version of an HTTP message is indicated by an HTTP-Version field in the first line of the message.

HTTP-Version   =   "HTTP"   "/"   1*DIGIT   "."   1*DIGIT

Major and minor numbers MUST be treated as separate integers and that each may be incremented higher than a single digit. Thus, HTTP 2.4 is a lower version than HTTP 2.13, which in turn is lower than HTTP 12.3. Leading zeros must be ignored by recipients and must not be sent.

Applications sending Request or Response messages, as defined by this specification, must include an HTTP-Version of HTTP 1.1. Use of this version number indicates that the sending application is at least conditionally compliant with this specification.

The HTTP version of an application is the highest HTTP version for which the application is at least conditionally compliant.

Proxy and gateway applications must be careful when forwarding messages in protocol versions different from that of the application. Because the protocol version indicates the protocol capability of the sender, a proxy/gateway MUST never send a message with a version indicator that is greater than its actual version. If a higher version request is received, the proxy/gateway MUST either downgrade the request version, respond with an error, or switch to tunnel behavior. Requests with a version lower than that of the proxy/gateway's version MAY be upgraded before being forwarded; the proxy/gateway's response to that request MUST be in the same major version as the request.

Uniform Resource Identifiers (URIs)

URIs have been known by many names: WWW addresses, Universal Document Identifiers, Universal Resource Identifiers , and finally the combination of *Uniform Resource Locators* (URL) and *Names* (URN). As far as HTTP is concerned, Uniform Resource Identifiers are simply formatted strings which identify—through name, location, or any other characteristic —a General Syntax.

URIs in HTTP can be represented in absolute form or relative to some known base URI, depending on the context of their use. The two forms are differentiated by the fact that absolute URIs always begin with a scheme name followed by a colon.

URI = (absoluteURI | relativeURI) ["#" fragment]

absoluteURI = scheme ":" *(uchar | reserved)

relativeURI = net_path | abs_path | rel_path

net_path = "//" net_loc [abs_path]

abs_path = "/" rel_path

rel_path = [path] [";" params] ["?" query]

path = fsegment *("/" segment)

fsegment = 1*pchar

segment = *pchar

params = param *(";" param)

param = *(pchar | "/")

scheme = 1*(ALPHA | DIGIT | "+" | "-" | ".")

net_loc = *(pchar | ";" | "?")

query = *(uchar | reserved)

fragment = *(uchar | reserved)

pchar = uchar | ":" | "@" | "&" | "=" | "+"

uchar = unreserved | escape

unreserved = ALPHA | DIGIT | safe | extra | national

escape = "%" HEX HEX

reserved = ";" | "/" | "?" | ":" | "@" | "&" | "=" | "+"

extra = "!" | "*" | "'" | "(" | ")" | ","

safe = "$" | "-" | "_" | "."

unsafe = CTL | SP | <"> | "#" | "%" | "<" | ">"

national = <any OCTET excluding ALPHA, DIGIT, reserved, extra, safe, and unsafe>

The HTTP protocol does not place a priori limit on the length of a URI. Servers MUST be able to handle the URI of any resource they serve, and SHOULD be able to handle URIs of unbounded length if they provide GET-based forms that could generate such URIs. A server SHOULD return 414 (Request-URI Too Long) status if a URI is longer than the server can handle. Servers should be cautious about depending on URI lengths above 255 bytes, because some older client or proxy implementations may not properly support these lengths.

HTTP URL

The http scheme is used to locate network resources through the HTTP protocol. This section defines the scheme-specific syntax and semantics for http URLs.

http_URL	=	"http:" "//" host [":" port] [abs_path]
Host	=	A legal Internet host domain name or IP address (in dotted-decimal form)
Port	=	*DIGIT

If the port is empty or not given, port 80 is assumed. The semantics are that the identified resource is located at the server listening for TCP connections on that port of that host, and the Request-URI for the resource is abs_path. The use of IP addresses in URLs SHOULD be avoided whenever possible (see RFC 1900 [24]). If the abs_path is not present in the URL, it MUST be given as "/" when used as a Request-URI for a resource.

URI Comparison   When comparing two URIs to decide if they match or not, a client SHOULD use a case-sensitive octet-by-octet comparison of the entire URIs, with these exceptions:

- A port that is empty or not given is equivalent to the default port for that URI
- Comparisons of host names MUST be case-insensitive
- Comparisons of scheme names MUST be case-insensitive
- An empty abs_path is equivalent to an abs_path of "/"

Characters other than those in the reserved and unsafe sets are equivalent to their % HEX HEX encodings.

For example, the following three URIs are equivalent:

```
http://abc.com:80/,smith/home.html
http://ABC.com/%7Esmith/home.html
http://ABC.com:/%7esmith/home.html
```

Status Code Definitions

Each Status-Code is described as follows, including a description of which method(s) it can follow and any meta-information required in the response.

Informational 1xx   This class of status code indicates a provisional response, consisting only of the Status-Line and optional headers, and is terminated by an empty line. Because HTTP 1.0 did not define any 1xx status codes, servers MUST NOT send a 1xx response to an HTTP 1.0 client except under experimental conditions.

100 Continue   The client may continue with its request. This interim response is used to inform the client that the initial part of the request has been received and has not yet been rejected by the server. The client SHOULD continue by sending the remainder of the request or, if the request has already been completed, ignore this response. The server MUST send a final response after the request has been completed.

101 Switching Protocols   The server understands and is willing to comply with the client's request, through the Upgrade message header field, for a change in the application protocol being used on this connection. The server switches protocols to those defined by the response's Upgrade header field immediately after the empty line that terminates the 101 response.

The protocol should only be switched when it is advantageous to do so. For example, switching to a newer version of HTTP is advantageous over older versions.

Successful 2xx

This class of status code indicates that the client's request was successfully received, understood, and accepted.

200 OK   The request has succeeded. The information returned with the response is dependent on the method used in the request, for example:

- GET an entity corresponding to the requested resource is sent in the response
- HEAD the entity-header fields corresponding to the requested resource are sent in the response without any message-body
- POST an entity describing or containing the result of the action
- TRACE an entity containing the request message as received by the end server

201 Created   The request has been fulfilled and resulted in a new resource being created. The newly created resource can be referenced by the URI(s) returned in the entity of the response, with the most specific URL for the resource given by a Location header field. The origin server MUST create the resource before returning the 201 status code. If the action cannot be carried out immediately, the server should respond with 202 (Accepted) response instead.

202 Accepted   The request has been accepted for processing, but the processing has not been completed. The request MAY or MAY NOT eventually be acted on, as it MAY be disallowed when processing actually takes place. There is no facility for re-sending a status code from an asynchronous operation such as this.

The 202 response is intentionally non-committal. Its purpose is to allow a server to accept a request for some other process (perhaps a batch-oriented process that is only run once per day) without requiring that the user agent's connection to the server persist until the process is completed. The entity returned with this response SHOULD include an indication of the request's current status, and either a pointer to a status monitor or some estimate of when the user can expect the request to be fulfilled.

203 Non-Authoritative Information   The returned meta-information in the entity-header is not the definitive set as available from the origin server, but is gathered from a local or a third-party copy. The set presented MAY be a subset or superset of the original version. For example, including local annotation information about the resource MAY result in a superset of the meta-information known by the origin server. Use of this response code is not required and is only appropriate when the response would otherwise be 200 (OK).

204 No Content   The server has fulfilled the request but there is no new information to send back. If the client is a user agent, it SHOULD NOT change its document view from that which caused the request to be sent. This response is primarily intended to allow input for actions to take place without causing a change to the user agent's active document view. The response MAY include new meta-information in the form of entity-headers, which SHOULD apply to the document currently in the user agent's active view.

The 204 response MUST NOT include a message-body, and thus is always terminated by the first empty line after the header fields.

205 Reset Content   The server has fulfilled the request and the user agent SHOULD reset the document view that caused the request to be sent. This response is primarily intended to allow input for actions to take place through user input, followed by a clearing of the form in which the input is given so that the user can easily initiate another input action. The response MUST NOT include an entity.

206 Partial Content   The server has fulfilled the partial GET request for the resource. The request must have included a Range header field indicating the desired range. The response MUST include either a Content-Range header field indicating the range included with this response, or a multipart/byteranges Content-Type including Content-Range fields for each part. If multipart/byteranges is not used, the Content-Length header field in the response MUST match the actual number of OCTETs transmitted in the message-body.

A cache that does not support the Range and Content-Range headers MUST NOT cache 206 (Partial) responses.

Redirection 3xx

This class of status code indicates that further action needs to be taken by the user agent to fulfill the request. The action required MAY be carried out by the user agent without interaction with the user if and only if the method used in the second request is GET or HEAD. A user agent SHOULD NOT automatically redirect a request more than 5 times, because such redirections usually indicate an infinite loop.

300 Multiple Choices   The requested resource corresponds to any one of a set of representations, each with its own specific location, and agent-driven negotiation information (section 12) is being provided so that the user (or user agent) can select a preferred representation and redirect its request to that location.

   Unless it was a HEAD request, the response SHOULD include an entity containing a list of resource characteristics and location(s) from which the user or user agent can choose the one most appropriate. The entity format is specified by the media type given in the Content-Type header field. Depending on the format and the capabilities of the user agent, selection of the most appropriate choice may be performed automatically. However, this specification does not define any standard for such automatic selection.

   If the server has a preferred choice of representation, it SHOULD include the specific URL for that representation in the Location field; user agents MAY use the Location field value for automatic redirection. This response is cacheable unless indicated otherwise.

301 Moved Permanently   The requested resource has been assigned a new permanent URI and any future references to this resource SHOULD be done using one of the returned URIs. Clients with link editing capabilities SHOULD automatically re-link references to the Request-URI to one or more of the new references returned by the server, where possible. This response is cacheable unless indicated otherwise. If the new URI is a location, its URL SHOULD be given by the location field in the response. Unless the request method was HEAD, the entity of the response SHOULD contain a short hypertext note with a hyperlink to the new URI(s).

   If the 301 status code is received in response to a request other than GET or HEAD, the user agent MUST NOT automatically redirect the request unless it can be confirmed by the user, because this might change the conditions under which the request was issued.

When automatically redirecting a POST request after receiving a 301 status code, some existing HTTP/1.0 user agents erroneously change it into a GET request.

302 Moved Temporarily   The requested resource resides temporarily under a different URI. Because the redirection may be altered on occasion, the client SHOULD continue to use the Request-URI for future requests. This response is only cacheable if indicated by a Cache-Control or Expires header field.

If the new URI is a location, its URL SHOULD be given by the Location field in the response. Unless the request method was HEAD, the entity of the response SHOULD contain a short hypertext note with a hyperlink to the new URI(s).

If the 302 status code is received in response to a request other than GET or HEAD, the user agent MUST NOT automatically redirect the request unless it can be confirmed by the user, because this might change the conditions under which the request was issued.

When automatically redirecting a POST request after receiving a 302 status code, some existing HTTP/1.0 user agents erroneously change it into a GET request.

303 See Other   The response to the request can be found under a different URI and SHOULD be retrieved using a GET method on that resource. This method exists primarily to allow the output of a POST-activated script to redirect the user agent to a selected resource. The new URI is not a substitute reference for the originally requested resource. The 303 response is not cacheable, but the response to the second (redirected) request MAY be cacheable.

If the new URI is a location, its URL SHOULD be given by the Location field in the response. Unless the request method was HEAD, the entity of the response SHOULD contain a short hypertext note with a hyperlink to the new URI(s).

304 Not Modified   If the client has performed a conditional GET request and access is allowed, but the document has not been modified, the server SHOULD respond with this status code. The response MUST NOT contain a message-body. The response MUST include the following header fields:

- Date

- ETag and/or Content-Location   If the header would have been sent in a 200 response to the same request

- Expires, Cache-Control, and/or Vary   If the field-value might differ from that sent in any previous response for the same variant

If the conditional GET used a strong cache validator, the response SHOULD NOT include other entity-headers. Otherwise (that is, the conditional GET used a weak validator), the response MUST NOT include other entity-headers; this prevents inconsistencies between cached entity-bodies and updated headers.

If a 304 response indicates an entity not currently cached, then the cache MUST disregard the response and repeat the request without the conditional.

If a cache uses a received 304 response to update a cache entry, the cache MUST update the entry to reflect any new field values given in the response.

The 304 response MUST NOT include a message-body, and thus is always terminated by the first empty line after the header fields.

305 Use Proxy   The requested resource MUST be accessed through the proxy given by the Location field. The Location field gives the URL of the proxy. The recipient is expected to repeat the request through the proxy.

Client Error 4xx

The 4xx class of status code is intended for cases in which the client seems to have erred. Except when responding to a HEAD request, the server SHOULD include an entity containing an explanation of the error situation and whether it is a temporary or permanent condition. These status codes are applicable to any request method. User agents SHOULD display any included entity to the user.

If the client is sending data, a server implementation using TCP should be careful to ensure that the client acknowledges receipt of the packet(s) containing the response, before the server closes the input connection. If the client continues sending data to the server after the close, the server's TCP stack sends a reset packet to the client, which may erase the client's unacknowledged input buffers before they can be read and interpreted by the HTTP application.

400 Bad Request   The request could not be understood by the server due to malformed syntax. The client SHOULD NOT repeat the request without modifications.

401 Unauthorized   The request requires user authentication. The response MUST include a WWW-Authenticate header field containing a challenge applicable to the requested resource. The client MAY repeat the request with a suitable Authorization header field. If the request already included Authorization credentials, then the 401 response indicates that authorization has been refused for those credentials. If the 401 response contains the same challenge as the prior response, and the user agent has already attempted authentication at least once, then the user SHOULD be presented with the entity that was given in the response, because that entity MAY include relevant diagnostic information.

402 Payment Required   This code is reserved for future use.

403 Forbidden   The server understood the request, but is refusing to fulfill it. Authorization does not help and the request SHOULD NOT be repeated. If the request method was not HEAD and the server wants to make public why the request has not been fulfilled, it SHOULD describe the reason for the refusal in the entity. This status code is commonly used when the server does not want to reveal exactly why the request has been refused, or when no other response is applicable.

404 Not Found   The server has not found anything matching the Request-URI. No indication is given of whether the condition is temporary or permanent. If the server does not want to make this information available to the client, the status code 403 (Forbidden) can be used instead. The 410 (Gone) status code SHOULD be used if the server knows, through some internally configurable mechanism, that an old resource is permanently unavailable and has no forwarding address.

405 Method Not Allowed   The method specified in the Request-Line is not allowed for the resource identified by the Request-URI. The response MUST include an Allow header containing a list of valid methods for the requested resource.

406 Not Acceptable   The resource identified by the request is only capable of generating response entities which have content characteristics not acceptable according to the accept headers sent in the request. Unless it was a HEAD request, the response SHOULD include an entity containing a list of available entity characteristics and location(s) from which the user or user agent can choose the one most appropriate. The entity format is specified by the media type given in the Content-Type header field. Depending on the format and the capabilities of the user agent, selection of the most appropriate choice may be performed automatically. However, this specification does not define any standard for such automatic selection.

HTTP 1.1 servers are allowed to return responses which are not acceptable according to the accept headers sent in the request. In some cases, this may even be preferable to sending a 406 response. User agents are encouraged to inspect the headers of an incoming response to determine if it is acceptable. If the response could be unacceptable, a user agent SHOULD temporarily stop receipt of more data and query the user for a decision on further actions.

407 Proxy Authentication Required   This code is similar to 401 (Unauthorized), but indicates that the client MUST first authenticate itself with the proxy. The proxy MUST return a Proxy-Authenticate header field containing a challenge applicable to the proxy for the requested resource. The client MAY repeat the request with a suitable Proxy-Authorization header field.

408 Request Timeout   The client did not produce a request within the time that the server was prepared to wait. The client MAY repeat the request without modifications at any later time.

409 Conflict   The request could not be completed due to a conflict with the current state of the resource. This code is only allowed in situations where it is expected that the user might be able to resolve the conflict and resubmit the request. The response body SHOULD include enough information for the user to recognize the source of the conflict. Ideally, the response entity would include enough information for the user or user agent to fix the problem; however, that may not be possible and is not required.

Conflicts are most likely to occur in response to a PUT request. If versioning is being used and the entity being PUT includes changes to a resource which conflict with those made by an earlier (third-party) request, the server MAY use the 409 response to indicate that it can't complete the request. In this case, the response entity SHOULD contain a list of the differences between the two versions in a format defined by the response Content-Type.

410 Gone   The requested resource is no longer available at the server and no forwarding address is known. This condition SHOULD be considered permanent. Clients with link editing capabilities SHOULD delete references to the Request-URI after user approval. If the server does not know, or has no facility to determine, whether or not the condition is permanent, the status code 404 (Not Found) SHOULD be used instead. This response is cacheable unless indicated otherwise.

The 410 response is primarily intended to assist the task of web maintenance by notifying the recipient that the resource is intentionally unavailable and that the server owners desire that remote links to that resource be removed. Such an event is common for limited-time, promotional services and for resources belonging to individuals no longer working at the server's site. It is not necessary to mark all permanently unavailable resources as gone or to keep the mark for any length of time—that is left to the discretion of the server owner.

411 Length Required   The server refuses to accept the request without a defined Content-Length. The client MAY repeat the request if it adds a valid Content-Length header field containing the length of the message-body in the request message.

412 Precondition Failed   The precondition given in one or more of the request-header fields evaluated to false when it was tested on the server. This response code allows the client to place preconditions on the current resource meta-information (header field data) and thus prevent the requested method from being applied to a resource other than the one intended.

413 Request Entity Too Large   The server is refusing to process a request because the request entity is larger than the server is willing or able to process. The server may close the connection to prevent the client from continuing the request.

If the condition is temporary, the server SHOULD include a Retry-After header field to indicate that it is temporary and after what time the client may try again.

414 Request-URI Too Long   The server is refusing to service the request because the Request-URI is longer than the server is willing to interpret. This rare condition is only likely to occur when a client has improperly converted a POST request to a GET request with long query information, when the client has descended into a URL "black hole" of redirection (for example, a redirected URL prefix that points to a suffix of itself), or when the server is under attack by a client attempting to exploit security holes present in some servers using fixed-length buffers for reading or manipulating the Request-URI.

415 Unsupported Media Type   The server is refusing to service the request because the entity of the request is in a format not supported by the requested resource for the requested method.

Server Error 5xx

Response status codes beginning with the digit "5" indicate cases in which the server is aware that it has erred or is incapable of performing the request. Except when responding to a HEAD request, the server SHOULD include an entity containing an explanation of the error situation, and whether it is a temporary or permanent condition. User agents SHOULD display any included entity to the user. These response codes are applicable to any request method.

500 Internal Server Error   It means the server encountered an unexpected condition that prevented it from fulfilling the request.

501 Not Implemented   The server does not support the functionality required to fulfill the request. This is the appropriate response when the server does not recognize the request method and is not capable of supporting it for any resource.

502 Bad Gateway   The server, while acting as a gateway or proxy, received an invalid response from the upstream server it accessed in attempting to fulfill the request.

503 Service Unavailable   The server is currently unable to handle the request due to a temporary overloading or maintenance of the server. The implication is that this is a temporary condition that is alleviated after some delay. If known, the length of the delay may be indicated in a Retry-After header. If no Retry-After is given, the client SHOULD handle the response as it would for a 500 response.

The existence of the 503 status code does not imply that a server must use it when becoming overloaded. Some servers may want to simply refuse the connection.

504 Gateway Timeout   The server, while acting as a gateway or proxy, did not receive a timely response from the upstream server it accessed in attempting to complete the request.

505 HTTP Version Not Supported   The server does not support, or refuses to support, the HTTP protocol version that was used in the request message. The server is indicating that it is unable or unwilling to complete the request using the same major version as the client other than with this error message. The response SHOULD contain an entity describing why that version is not supported and what other protocols are supported by that server.

Additional Information

The Internet Society is the source to turn to for reliable information about the Internet. I am including a list of some RFCs that I have found important. You can obtain a complete list of RFCs at

```
ftp://ftp.ncren.net
```

Internet Official Protocol Standards 2400
Assigned Numbers 1700
Host Requirements—Communications 1122
Host Requirements—Applications 1123
IP Internet Protocol 791
IP Subnet Extension 950
IP Broadcast Datagrams 919
IP Broadcast Datagrams with Subnets 922
ICMP Internet Control Message Protocol 792
IGMP Internet Group Multicast Protocol 1112
UDP User Datagram Protocol 768
TCP Transmission Control Protocol 793
TELNET Telnet Protocol 854,855
FTP File Transfer Protocol 959
SMTP Simple Mail Transfer Protocol 821
SMTP-SIZE SMTP Service Ext for Message Size 1870
SMTP-EXT SMTP Service Extensions 1869
MAIL Format of Electronic Mail Messages 822
CONTENT Content Type Header Field 1049
NTPV2 Network Time Protocol (Version 2) 1119
DOMAIN Domain Name System 1034,1035
DNS-MX Mail Routing and the Domain System 974
SNMP Simple Network Management Protocol 1157

SUMMARY

TCP/IP is a complex topic. I have presented information in this chapter that has been helpful to me. So much of the chapter is based on years of experience intertwined with excerpts from RFCs for accuracy. Many good books have been written on this topic. However, I recommend that you refer to The Internet Society for further information. They can be reached at

```
ftp://ftp.ncren.net
```

BIBLIOGRAPHY

Abbatiello, Judy and Sarch, Ray edited by, 1987, *Tele Communications & Data Communications Factbook*, New York, NY: Data Communications; Ramsey, NJ: CCMI/McGraw-Hill, Inc.

Apple Computer, Inc., 1992, *Technical Introduction to the Macintosh Family Second Edition*, Menlo Park, CA: Addison-Wesley Publishing Company.Apple Computer, Inc., 1991, *Planning and Managing AppleTalk Networks*, Menlo Park, CA: Addison-Wesley Publishing Company.

Ashley, Ruth, Fernandez, Judi N., 1984, *Job Control Language*, New York, NY: John Wiley & Sons, Inc.

Aspray, William, 1990, *John Von Neumann and The Origins of Modern Computing*, Cambridge, MA: MIT Press.

Bach, Maurice J., 1986, *The Design of The UNIX Operating System*, Englewood Cliffs, New Jersey: Prentice Hall, Inc.

Baggott, Jim, 1992, *The Meaning of Quantum Theory*, New York, NY: Oxford University Press Inc.

Bashe, Charles J., Johnson, Lyle R., Palmer, John H., and Pugh, Emerson W., 1986, *IBM's Early Computers*, Cambridge, MA: MIT Press.

Berson, Alex, 1990, APPC Introduction to LU6.2, New York, NY: McGraw-Hill, Inc.

Black, Uyless, 1992, *TCP/IP and Related Protocols*, New York, NY: McGraw-Hill, Inc.

Black, Uyless, 1991, *The X Series Recommendations Protocols for Data Communications Networks*, New York, NY: McGraw-Hill, Inc.

Black, Uyless,1991, *The V Series Recommendations Protocols for Data Communications Over the Telephone Network*, New York, NY: McGraw-Hill, Inc.Black, Uyless, 1989, *Data Networks Concepts, Theory, and Practice*, Englewood Cliffs, New Jersey: Prentice Hall, Inc.

Blyth, W. John, Blyth, Mary M., 1990, *Telecommunications: Concepts, Development, and Management*, Mission Hills, CA: Glencoe/McGraw-Hill, Inc.

Bohl, Marilyn, 1971, *Information Processing*, Third Edition, Chicago, NY: Science Research Associates, Inc.

Bradbeer, Robin, De Bono, Peter, and Laurie, Peter, 1982, *The Beginner's Guide to Computers*: Addison-Wesley Publishing Company.

Brookshear, J. Glenn, 1988, *Computer Science: An Overview*, Menlo Park, CA: The Benjamin/Cummings Publishing Company, Inc.

Bryant, David, 1971, *Physics*, Great Britain: Hodder and Stoughton Ltd.

Campbell, Joe, 1984, *The RS-232 Solution*, Alameda, CA: SYBEX.

Campbell, Joe, 1987, *C Programmer's Guide to Serial Communications*, Carmel, IN: Howard W. Sams & Company.

Chorafas, Dimitris N., 1989, *Local Area Network Reference*, New York, NY: McGraw-Hill, Inc.

Comer, Douglas, 1988, *Internetworking With TCP/IP Principles, Protocols, and Architecture*, Englewood Cliffs, New Jersey: Prentice Hall.

Comer, Douglas E., 1991, *Internetworking With TCP/IP Vol I: Principles, Protocols, and Architecture*, Englewood Cliffs, NJ: Prentice Hall.

Comer, Douglas E., and Stevens, David L., 1991, *Internetworking With TCP/IP Vol II: Design, Implementation, and Internals*, Englewood Cliffs, New Jersey: Prentice Hall.

Dayton, Robert L., 1991, *Telecommunications: The Transmission of Information*, New York, NY: McGraw-Hill, Inc.

Dern, Daniel P., 1994, *The Internet Guide for New Users*, New York, NY: McGraw-Hill, Inc.

Edmunds, John J., 1992, *SAA/LU 6.2 Distributed Networks and Applications*, New York, NY: McGraw-Hill, Inc.

Feit, Sidnie, 1993, *TCP/IP Architecture, Protocols, and Implementation*, New York, NY: McGraw-Hill, Inc.

Fortier, Paul J., 1989, *Handbook of LAN Technology*, New York, NY: Intertext Publications/Multiscience Press, Inc.

Forney, James S., 1992, *DOS Beyond 640K 2nd Edition*: Windcrest/McGraw-Hill, Inc.

Forney, James S., 1989, *MS-DOS Beyond 640K Working with Extended and Expanded Memory*, Blue Ridge Summit, PA: Windcrest Books.

Gasman, Lawrence, 1994, *Broadband Networking*, New York, NY: Van Nostrand Reinhold.

Graubart-Cervone, H. Frank, 1994, *VSE/ESA JCL Utilities, Power, and VSAM*, New York, NY: McGraw-Hill, Inc.

Groff, James R., and Weinbert, Paul N., 1983, *Understanding UNIX A Conceptual Guide*, Carmel, IN: Que Corporation.

Hecht, Jeff, 1990, *Understanding Fiber Optics*, Carmel, IN, Howard W. Sams & Company.

Hewlett Packard Company, 1992, *Using HP-UX: Hp 9000 Workstations*, B2910-90001, Ft. Collins, CO: Hewlett Packard Company.

Hewlett Packard Company, 1991, *Using the X Window System*, B1171-90037,Ft. Collins, CO: Hewlett Packard Company.

Hewlett Packard Company, 1992, *HP OpenView SNMP Agent Administrator's Reference*, J2322-90002, Ft.Collins, CO: Hewlett Packard Company.

Hewlett Packard Company, 1992, *HP OpenView Windows User's Guide*, J2316-90000, Ft. Collins, CO: Hewlett Packard Company.

IBM Corp., 1994, *LAN Resource Extension and Services/MVS: General Information*, GC24-5625-03, Endicott, NY: IBM Corp.

IBM Corp., 1994, *LAN Resource Extension and Services/MVS: Guide and Reference*, SC24-5623-02, Endicott, NY: IBM Corp.

IBM Corp., 1994, *Lan Resource Extension and Services/VM: General Information*, GC24-5618-03, Endicott, NY: IBM Corp.

IBM Corp., 1993, *IBM Network Products Implementation Guide*, GG24-3649-01, Raleigh NC: IBM Corp.

IBM Corp., 1993, *IBM VSE/Interactive Computing and Control Facility: Primer*, SC33-6561-01, Charlotte, NC: IBM Corp.

IBM Corp., 1993, *LAN File Services/ESA: VM Guide and Reference*, SH24-5264-00, Endicott, NY: IBM Corp.

IBM Corp., 1993, *LAN Resource Extension and Services/VM: Guide and Reference*, SC24-5622-01, Endicott, NY: IBM Corp.

IBM Corp., 1993, *MVS/ESA JES2 Commands*, GC23-0084-04, Poughkeepsie, NY: IBM Corp.

IBM Corp., 1993, *MVS/ESA: JES2 Command Reference Summary*, GX22-0017-03, Poughkeepsie, NY: IBM Corp.

IBM Corp., 1993, *MVS/ESA: System Commands*, GC28-1626-05, Poughkeepsie, NY: IBM Corp.

IBM Corp., 1993, *NetView: Command Quick Reference*, SX75-0090-00, Research Triangle Park, NC: IBM Corp.

IBM Corp., 1993, *NetView: Installation and Administration*, SC31-7084-00, Research Triangle Park, NC: IBM Corp.

IBM Corp., 1993, *System Information Architecture: Formats*, GA27-3136, Research Triangle Park, NC: IBM Corp.

IBM Corp., 1993, *System Network Architecture: Architecture Reference, Version 2*, SC30-3422-03, Research Triangle Park, NC: IBM Corp.

IBM Corp., 1993, *The Host as a Data Server Using LANRES and Novell NetWare*, GG24-4069-00, Poughkeepsie, NY: IBM Corp.

IBM Corp., 1993, *Virtual Machine / Enterprise Systems Architecture*, SC24-5460-03, Endicott, NY: IBM Corp.

IBM Corp., 1993, *VTAM: Operation*, SC31-6420-00, Research Triangle Park, NC: IBM Corp.

IBM Corp., 1993, *VTAM: Resource Definition Reference Version 4 Release 1 for MVS / ESA*, SC31-6427-00, Research Triangle Park, NC: IBM Corp.

IBM Corp., 1992, *APPN Architecture and Product Implementations Tutorial*, GG24-3669-01, Research Triangle Park, NC: IBM Corp.

IBM Corp., 1992, *ES / 9000 Multi-Image Processing Volume1: Presentation and Solutions Guidelines*, GG24-3920-00, Poughkeepsie, NY: IBM Corp.

IBM Corp., 1992, *High Speed Networking Technology: An Introductory Survey*, GG24-3816-00, Raleigh, NC: IBM Corp.

IBM Corp., 1992, *IBM Networking Systems: Planning and Reference*, SC31-6191-00, Research Triangle Park, NC: IBM Corp.

IBM Corp., 1992, *MVS / ESA: General Information for MVS / ESA System Product Version 4*, GC28-1600-04, Poughkeepsie, NY: IBM Corp.

IBM Corp., 1992, *Synchronous Data Link Control: Concepts,* GA27-3093-04, Research Triangle Park, NC: IBM Corp.

IBM Corp., 1992, *TCP / IP Version2 Release 2.1 for MVS: Offload of TCP / IP Processing*, SA31-7033-00, Research Triangle Park, NC: IBM Corp.

IBM Corp., 1992, *TCP / IP Version 2 Release 2.1 for MVS: Planning and Customization*, SC31-6085-02, Research Triangle Park, NC: IBM Corp.

IBM Corp., 1992, *The IBM 6611 Network Processor*, GG24-3870-00, Raleigh, NC: IBM Corp.

IBM Corp., 1992, *VM / ESA: CMS Primer*, SC24-5458-02, Endicott, NY: IBM Corp.

IBM Corp., 1992, *VM / ESA Release 2 Overview*, GG24-3860-00, Poughkeepsie, NY: IBM Corp.

IBM Corp., 1992, *VSE / ESA Version 1.3: An Introduction Presentation Foil Master*, GG24-4008-00, Raleigh, NC: IBM Corp.

IBM Corp., 1992, *3172 Interconnect Controller: Planning Guide*, GA27-3867-05, Research Triangle Park, NC: IBM Corp.

IBM Corp., 1992, *3172 Interconnect Controller: Operator's Guide*, GA27-3970-00, Research Triangle Park, NC: IBM Corp.

IBM Corp., 1992, *3270 Information Display System: Data Stream Programmer's Reference*, GA23-0059-07, Research Triangle Park, NC: IBM Corp.

IBM Corp., 1991, *Dictionary of Computing*, SC20-1699-8, Poughkeepsie, NY: IBM Corp.

IBM Corp., 1991, *Enterprise Systems Architecture / 390 ESCON I / O Interface: Physical Layer*, SA23-0394-00, Kingston, NY: IBM Corp.

IBM Corp., 1991, *Enterprise Systems Connection: ESCON I / O Interface*, SA22-7202-01, Poughkeepsie, NY: IBM Corp.

IBM Corp., 1991, *Enterprise Systems Connection*, GA23-0383-01, Kingston, NY: IBM Corp.

IBM Corp., 1991, *Enterprise Systems Connection Manager*, GC23-0422-01, Kingston, NY: IBM Corp.

IBM Corp., 1991, *Installation Guidelines for the IBM Token-Ring Network Products*, GG24-3291-02, Research Triangle Park, NC: IBM Corp.

IBM Corp., 1991, *Systems Network Architecture: Concepts and Products*, GC30-3072-4, Research Triangle Park, NC: IBM Corp.

IBM Corp., 1991, *Systems Network Architecture: Technical Overview*, GC30-3073-3, Research Triangle Park, NC: IBM Corp.

IBM Corp., 1991, *Systems Network Architecture: Type 2.1 Node Reference*, Version 1, SC20-3422-2, Research Triangle Park, NC: IBM Corp.

IBM Corp., 1991, *Virtual Machine / Enterprise System Architecture: General Information*, GC24-5550-02, Endicott, NY: IBM Corp.

IBM Corp., 1990, *Enterprise Systems Architecture / 390: Principles of Operation*, SA22-7201-00, Poughkeepsie, NY: IBM Corp.

IBM Corp., 1990, *IBM VSE / ESA: System Control Statements*, SC33-6513-00, Mechanicsburg, PA: IBM Corp.

IBM Corp., 1990, *IBM 3172 Interconnect Controller: Presentation Guide*, White Plains, NY: IBM Corp.

IBM Corp., 1990, *MVS / ESA SP Version 4 Technical Presentation Guide*, GG24-3594-00, Poughkeepsie, NY: IBM Corp.

IBM Corp., 1990, *Virtual Machine/Enterprise Systems Architecture*, GC24-5441, Endicott, NY: IBM Corp.

IBM Corp., 1989, *MVS/ESA Operatons: System Commands Reference Summary*, GX22-0013-1, Poughkeepsie, NY: IBM Corp

IBM Corp., 1988, *IBM Enterprise Systems Architecture/370: Principles of Operation*, SA22-7200-0, Poughkeepsie, NY: IBM Corp.

IBM Corp., 1988, *3270 Information Display System: Introduction*, GA27-2739-22, Research Triangle Park, NC: IBM Corp.

IBM Corp., 1987, *IBM System/370: Principles of Operation*, GA22-7000-10, Poughkeepsie, NY: IBM Corp.

IBM Corp., 1985, *IBM 3270 Information Display System: 3274 Control Unit Description and Programmer's Guide*, GA23-0061-2, Research Triangle Park, NC: IBM Corp.

IBM Corp., 1983, *IBM System/370 Extended Architecture: Principles of Operation*, SA22-7085-0, Research Triangle Park, NC: IBM Corp.

IBM Corp., 1980, *IBM Virtual Machine Facility: Terminal User's Guide*, GC20-1810-9, Poughkeepsie, NY: IBM Corp.

Jain, Bijendra N., and Agrawala, Ashok K., 1993, *Open Systems Interconnection*, New York, NY: McGraw-Hill, Inc.

Kessler, Gary C., and Train, David A., 1992, *Metropolitan Area Networks Concepts, Standards, and Services*, New York, NY: McGraw-Hill, Inc.

Kessler, Gary C., 1990, *ISDN*, New York, NY: McGraw-Hill, Inc.

Kochan, Stephen G, Wood, Patrick H., 1984, *Exploring the UNIX System*, Indianapolis, IN: Hayden Books.

Killen, Michael, 1992, *SAA and UNIX IBM's Open Systems Strategy*, New York, NY: McGraw-Hill, Inc.

Killen, Michael, 1992, *SAA Managing Distributed Data*, New York, NY: McGraw-Hill, Inc.

Madron, Thomas W., 1988, *Local Area Networks The Next Generation*, New York, NY: John Wiley & Sons, Inc.

McClain, Gary R., 1991, *Open Systems Interconnection Handbook*, New York, NY: Intertext Publications/Multiscience Press.

Meijer, Anton, 1987, *Systems Network Architecture: A Tutorial*, London, England: Pitman; New York, NY: John Wiley & Sons, Inc.

Merrow, Bill, 1994, *VSE/ESA Concepts and Facilities*, New York, NY: McGraw-Hill, Inc.

Martin, James, 1989, *Local Area Networks Architectures and Implementa-tions*, Englewood Cliffs, New Jersey: Prentice Hall, Inc.

Nash, Stephen G., Editor, 1990, *A History of Scientific Computing*, New York, NY: ACM Press.

Naugle, Matthew, 1994, *Network Protocol Handbook*, New York, NY: McGraw-Hill, Inc.

Naugle, Matthew G., 1991, *Local Area Networking*, New York, NY: McGraw-Hill, Inc.

Nemzow, Martin A. W., 1992, *The Ethernet Management Guide Keeping the Link, Second Edition*, New York, NY: McGraw-Hill, Inc.

O'Dell, Peter, 1989, *The Computer Networking Book*, Chapel Hill, NC: Ventana Press, Inc.

Parker, Sybil P., 1984, *McGraw-Hill Dictionary of Science and Engineering*, New York, NY: McGraw-Hill, Inc.

Pugh, Emerson W., Johnson, Lyle R., and Palmer, John H., *IBM's 360 and Early 370 Systems*, Cambridge, MA: MIT Press.

Pugh, Emerson W., 1984, *Memories That Shaped an Industry*, Cambridge, MA: MIT Press.

Ranade, Jay, Sackett, George C., 1989, *Introduction to SNA Networking Using VTAM / NCP*, New York, NY: McGraw-Hill, Inc.

Rose, Marshall T., 1991, *The Simple Book An Introduction to Management of TCP/IP-Based Internets*, Englewood Cliffs, New Jersey: Prentice Hall.

Rose Marshall T., 1990, *The Open Book A Practical Perspective on OSI*, Englewood Cliffs, New Jersey: Prentice Hall, Inc.

Savit, Jeffrey, 1993, *VM / CMS Concepts and Facilities*, New York, NY: McGraw-Hill, Inc.

Samson, Stephen L., 1990, *MVS Performance Management*, New York, NY: McGraw-Hill, Inc.

Schatt, Stan, 1990, *Understnding Local Area Networks*, Second Edition, Carmel, IN: Howard W. Sams & Company.

Schlar, Serman K., 1990, *Inside X.25: A Manager's Guide*, New York, NY: McGraw-Hill, Inc.

Seyer, Martin D., 1991, *RS-232 Made Easy: connecting Computers, Printers, Terminals, and Modems*, Englewood Cliffs, New Jersey: Prentice Hall, Inc.

Spohn, Darren L., 1993, *Data Network Design*, New York, NY: McGraw-Hill, Inc.

Stallings, William, 1989, *ISDN: an Introduction*, New York, NY: Macmillan Publishing Company.

Stallings, William, 1988, *Handbook of Computer-Communications Standards Volume 3*, New York, NY: Macmillan Publishing Company.

Stallings, William, 1987, *Handbook of Computer-Communications Standards Volume 2*, New York, NY: Macmillan Publishing Company.

Stallings, William, 1987, *Handbook of Computer Communications Standards Volume 1*, New York, NY: Macmillan Publishing Company.

Stamper, David A., 1986, *Business Data Communications*, Menlo Park, CA: The Benjamin/Cummings Publishing Company, Inc.

Sidhu, Gursharan S., Andrews, Richard F. Oppenheimer, Alan B., 1990, *Inside AppleTalk, Second Edition*, Menlo Park, CA: Addison-Wesley Publishing Company.

Tang, Adrian, and Scoggins, Sophia, 1992, *Open Networking with OSI*, Englewood Cliffs, New Jersey: Prentice Hall, Inc.

The ATM Forum, 1993, *ATM User-Network Interface Specification*, Englewood Cliffs, New Jersey: Prentice Hall, Inc.

Umar, Amjad, 1993, *Distributed Computing: A Practical Synthesis*, Englewood Cliffs, New Jersey: Prentice-Hall, Inc.

White, Gene, 1992, *Internetworking and Addressing*, New York, NY: McGraw-Hill, Inc.

ZWass, Vladimir, 1981, *Introduction to Computer Science*, New York, NY: Barnes & Noble Books.

TRADEMARKS

Microsoft C is a registered trademark of the Microsoft Corporation.

NFS is a registered trademark of Sun Microsystems, Incorporated.

PC-NFS is a registered trademark of Sun Microsystems, Incorporated.

Portmapper is a registered trademark of Sun Microsystems, Incorporated.

Sun is a registered trademark of Sun Microsystems, Incorporated.

SunOS is a registered trademark of Sun Microsystems, Incorporated.

UNIX is a registered trademark of UNIX System Laboratories, Inc.

Apollo is a registered trademark of Apollo Computer, Inc.

HYPERchannel is a registered trademark of Network Systems Corporation.

NCS is a registered trademark of Apollo Computer, Inc.

Network Computing System is a registered trademark of Apollo Computer, Inc.

Network File System is a registered trademark of Sun Microsystems, Inc.

NFS is a registered trademark of Sun Microsystems, Inc.

Portmapper is a registered trademark of Sun Microsystems, Inc.

PostScript is a registered trademark of Adobe Systems, Inc.

Sun is a registered trademark of Sun Microsystems, Inc.

DEC is a registered trademark of Digital Equipment Corporation.

DECNET is a registered trademark of Digital Equipment Corporation.

LattisNet is a registered trademark of SynOptics Communications, Inc.

NAP is a registered trademark of Automated Network Management, Inc.

NETMAP is a registered trademark of SynOptics Communications, Inc.

UNIX is a registered trademark of UNIX System Laboratories, Inc.

OSF is a registered trademark of the Open Software Foundation, Inc.

OSF/Motif is a registered trademark of the Open Software Foundation.

AppleShare is a trademark of Apple Computer, Inc.

AppleTalk is a trademark of Apple Computer, Inc.

EtherCard PLUS is a trademark of Western Digital Corporation.

Etherlink is a trademark of 3Com Corporation.

LaserWriter is a trademark of Apple Computer, Inc.

Macintosh is a trademark of Apple Computer, Inc.

Madge is a trademark of Madge Networks Ltd.

Microsoft is a trademark of Microsoft Corporation.

NetWare is a trademark of Novell, Inc.

Novell is a trademark of Novell, Inc.

PostScript is a trademark of Adobe Systems, Inc.

Windows is a trademark of Microsoft Corporation.

Word for Windows is a trademark of Microsoft Corporation.

80386, 80486, 80386SX 80486SX are trademarks of Intel Corporation.

AppleTalk is a registered trademark of Apple Computer, Inc.

Internetwork Packet eXchange is a registered trademark of Novell, Inc.

IPX is a registered trademark of Novell, Inc.

MS-DOS is a registered trademark of Microsoft Corporation.

NetWare is a registered trademark of Novell, Inc.

Novell is a registered trademark of Novell, Inc.

AppleTalk is a trademark of Apple Computer, Inc.

DEC is a trademark of Digital Equipment Corporation.

DECnet is a trademark of Digital Equipment Corporation.

Ethernet is a trademark of Xerox Corporation.

IPX is a trademark of Novell, Inc.

NetWare is a trademark of Novell, Inc.

NFS is a trademark of Sun Microsystems, Inc.

Novell is a trademark of Novell, Inc.

Sun is a trademark of Sun Microsystems, Inc.

UNIX is a trademark of Unix System Laboratories, Inc.

Windows is a trademark of Microsoft, Inc.

X-Windows is a trademark of Massachusetts Institute of Technology.

Xerox is a trademark of Xerox Corporation.

Cisco is a registered trademark of Cisco Systems, Inc.

Intel is a registered trademark of Intel Corporation.

Internetwork Packet Exchange (Novell Corporation).

IPX is a registered trademark of Novell Corporation.

Microsoft Windows is a registered trademark of Microsoft Corporation.

XNS is a trademark of the Xerox Corporation.

AIX is a trademark of International Business Machines Corporation.

AIXwindows is a trademark of International Business Machines Corporation.

DEC is a trademark of Digital Equipment Corporation.

VT100, VT220, and VT330 are trademarks of Digital Equipment Corporation.

HP is a trademark of Hewlett-Packard Company.

IBM is a registered trademark of International Business Machines Corporation.

PC-AT are trademarks of International Business Machines Corporation.

PS/2 are trademarks of International Business Machines Corporation.

POSIX is a trademark of the Institute of Electrical and Electronic Engineers.

PostScript is a trademark of Adobe Systems Incorporated.

Proprinter is a trademark of International Business Machines Corporation.

RISC System/6000 is a trademark of International Business Machines Corporation.

RT is a trademark of International Business Machines Corporation.

SUN is a trademark of Sun Microsystems.

UNIX is licensed by and is a registered trademark of UNIX System Laboratories, Inc.

UNIX is a registered trademark of AT&T Information Systems.

AS/400 is a registered trademark of IBM Corporation.

DB2 is a registered trademark of IBM Corporation.

DECnet is a registered trademark of Digital Equipment Corporation.

Ethernet is a registered trademark of Xerox Corporation.

HP is a registered trademark of Hewlett-Packard Company.

IMS, DB2, CICS is a registered trademark of International Business Corporation.

Information Warehouse is a registered trademark of IBM Corporation.

Kerberos is a registered trademark of the Massachusetts Institute of Technology.

Macintosh is a registered trademark of Apple Computers, Inc.

MVS, MVS/ESA, MVS/XA are registered trademarks of International Business Corporation.

Netview is a registered trademark of IBM Corporation.

Network File System is a registered trademark of Sun Microsystems, Inc.

NFS is a registered trademark of Sun Microsystems Inc.

OS/2 is a registered trademark of IBM Corporation.

RS6000 is a registered trademark of IBM Corporation.

SNA, VTAM, NCP, SDLC are registered trademarks of International Business Corporation.

VAX is a registered trademark of Digital Equipment Corporation.

X/Open is a registered trademark of X.Open Company Ltd.

XWindow is a registered trademark of the Massachusetts Institute of Technology.

The following are registered trademarks of the IBM Corporation:

ACF/VTAM	Hiperbatch
CICS	IBM
CICS/ESA	IBMLink
CICS/MVS	IMS/ESA
DATABASE 2	MVS/DFP
DB2	MVS/ESA
DFSMS	MVS/SP
DFSMS.MVS	MVS/XA
Enterprise System/3090	NetView
Enterprise System/4381	OS/2
Enterprise System/9000	OpenEdition
Enterprise Systems Architecture/370	PR/SM
Enterprise Systems Architecture/390	Presentation Manager
Enterprise Systems connection Architecture	Processor Resource/Systems Manager
ESCON	PSF
ESCON XDF	PS/2
ES/3090	RACF
ES/4381	Sysplex Timer
ES/9000	SystemView
ESA/370	System/370
ESA/390	VM/ESA
GDDM	VM/XA
Hardware Configuration Definition	VTAM
Hiperspace	3090

INDEX

SOFTWARE AND INFORMATION LICENSE

The software and information on this diskette (collectively referred to as the "Product") are the property of The McGraw-Hill Companies, Inc. ("McGraw-Hill") and are protected by both United States copyright law and international copyright treaty provision. You must treat this Product just like a book, except that you may copy it into a computer to be used and you may make archival copies of the Products for the sole purpose of backing up our software and protecting your investment from loss.

By saying "just like a book," McGraw-Hill means, for example, that the Product may be used by any number of people and may be freely moved from one computer location to another, so long as there is no possibility of the Product (or any part of the Product) being used at one location or on one computer while it is being used at another. Just as a book cannot be read by two different people in two different places at the same time, neither can the Product be used by two different people in two different places at the same time (unless, of course, McGraw-Hill's rights are being violated).

McGraw-Hill reserves the right to alter or modify the contents of the Product at any time.

This agreement is effective until terminated. The Agreement will terminate automatically without notice if you fail to comply with any provisions of this Agreement. In the event of termination by reason of your breach, you will destroy or erase all copies of the Product installed on any computer system or made for backup purposes and shall expunge the Product from your data storage facilities.

LIMITED WARRANTY

McGraw-Hill warrants the physical diskette(s) enclosed herein to be free of defects in materials and workmanship for a period of sixty days from the purchase date. If McGraw-Hill receives written notification within the warranty period of defects in materials or workmanship, and such notification is determined by McGraw-Hill to be correct, McGraw-Hill will replace the defective diskette(s). Send request to:

Customer Service
McGraw-Hill
Gahanna Industrial Park
860 Taylor Station Road
Blacklick, OH 43004-9615

The entire and exclusive liability and remedy for breach of this Limited Warranty shall be limited to replacement of defective diskette(s) and shall not include or extend any claim for or right to cover any other damages, including but not limited to, loss of profit, data, or use of the software, or special, incidental, or consequential damages or other similar claims, even if McGraw-Hill has been specifically advised as to the possibility of such damages. In no event will McGraw-Hill's liability for any damages to you or any other person ever exceed the lower of suggested list price or actual price paid for the license to use the Product, regardless of any form of the claim.

THE McGRAW-HILL COMPANIES, INC. SPECIFICALLY DISCLAIMS ALL OTHER WARRANTIES, EXPRESS OR IMPLIED, INCLUDING BUT NOT LIMITED TO, ANY IMPLIED WARRANTY OF MERCHANTABILITY OR FITNESS FOR A PARTICULAR PURPOSE. Specifically, McGraw-Hill makes no representation or warranty that the Product is fit for any particular purpose and any implied warranty of merchantability is limited to the sixty day duration of the Limited Warranty covering the physical diskette(s) only (and not the software or information) and is otherwise expressly and specifically disclaimed.

This Limited Warranty gives you specific legal rights; you may have others which may vary from state to state. Some states do not allow the exclusion of incidental or consequential damages, or the limitation on how long an implied warranty lasts, so some of the above may not apply to you.

This Agreement constitutes the entire agreement between the parties relating to use of the Product. The terms of any purchase order shall have no effect on the terms of this Agreement. Failure of McGraw-Hill to insist at any time on strict compliance with this Agreement shall not constitute a waiver of any rights under this Agreement. This Agreement shall be construed and governed in accordance with the laws of New York. If any provision of this Agreement is held to be contrary to law, that provision will be enforced to the maximum extent permissible and the remaining provisions will remain in force and effect.